TOWER HAMLETS

91 000 004 651 78 4

D0346147

WORLD ATLAS

COMPACT

idea

Library Learning Information

To renew this item call:

0115 929 3388

or visit

www.ideastore.co.uk

TOWER HAMLETS

Created and managed by Tower Hamlets Council

WITHDRAWN

DK | Penguin Random House

FOR THE SIXTH EDITION

SENIOR CARTOGRAPHIC EDITOR
Simon Mumford

PRODUCTION CONTROLLER
Rita Sinha

SENIOR PRODUCER
Luca Frassinetti

PUBLISHER
Andrew Macintyre

PUBLISHING DIRECTOR
Jonathan Metcalf

ASSOCIATE PUBLISHING DIRECTOR
Liz Wheeler

ART DIRECTOR
Philip Ormerod

TOWER HAMLETS LIBRARIES	
91000004631784	
Bertrams	07/05/2015
912	£9.99
THISWM	TH15000082

First published in Great Britain in 2001
by Dorling Kindersley Limited
80 Strand, London WC2R 0RL

Reprinted with revisions 2002. Second edition 2003. Reprinted with revisions 2004.
Third edition 2005. Fourth edition 2009. Fifth edition 2012. Sixth edition 2015.

Copyright © 2001, 2002, 2003, 2004, 2005, 2009, 2012, 2015
Dorling Kindersley Limited
A Penguin Random House Company

10 9 8 7 6 5 4 3 2 1
001–265178–May/2015

All rights reserved. No part of this publication may be reproduced, stored in or introduced into a retrieval system,
or transmitted in any form or by any other means, electronic, mechanical, photocopying, recording
or otherwise, without the prior written permission of the copyright owner.

A CIP catalogue record for this book is available from the British Library
ISBN 978-0-2411-8963-4

Printed and bound in Hong Kong

A WORLD OF IDEAS:
SEE ALL THERE IS TO KNOW

www.dk.com

Key to map symbols

Physical features

Elevation

6000m/19,686ft
4000m/13,124ft
3000m/9843ft
2000m/6562ft
1,000m/3281ft
500m/1640ft
250m/820ft
0
Below sea level

△ Mountain

▽ Depression

△ Volcano

)(Pass/tunnel

Sandy desert

Drainage features

Major perennial river

Minor perennial river

- - - Seasonal river

Canal

| Waterfall

Perennial lake

Seasonal lake

Wetland

Ice features

Permanent ice cap/ice shelf

Winter limit of pack ice

Summer limit of pack ice

Borders

Full international border

- - - - - Disputed de facto border

· · · · · Territorial claim border

×—×—× Cease-fire line

- - - Undefined boundary

Internal administrative boundary

Communications

Major road

Minor road

Railway

✈ International airport

Settlements

⊙ Above 500,000

◉ 100,000 to 500,000

○ 50,000 to 100,000

○ Below 50,000

● National capital

● Internal administrative capital

Miscellaneous features

+ Site of interest

⊓⊔⊓⊔⊓ Ancient wall

Graticule features

Line of latitude/longitude/ Equator

- - - Tropic/Polar circle

25° Degrees of latitude/ longitude

Names

Physical features

Andes	
Sahara	Landscape features
Ardennes	
Land's End	Headland
Mont Blanc 4,807m	Elevation/volcano/pass
Blue Nile	River/canal/waterfall
Ross Ice Shelf	Ice feature
PACIFIC OCEAN	
Sulu Sea	Sea features
Palk Strait	
Chile Rise	Undersea feature

Regions

FRANCE	Country
BERMUDA (to UK)	Dependent territory
KANSAS	Administrative region
Dordogne	Cultural region

Settlements

PARIS	Capital city
SAN JUAN	Dependent territory capital city
Chicago	
Kettering	Other settlements
Burke	

Inset map symbols

Urban area

City

Park

▪ Place of interest

□ Suburb/district

WORLD ATLAS

COMPACT

Contents

The World's Regions

North & Central America

South America

Africa

Europe

North & West Asia

South & East Asia

Australasia & Oceania

Index – Gazetteer

The Political World

Global features

Total number of countries: 196

Largest country: Russian Federation 6,592,735 sq miles (17,075,200 sq km)

Smallest country: Vatican City 0.17 sq miles (0.44 sq km)

Country with most international borders: China 14 / Russ. Fed. 14

Continental Key

North & Central America

South America

Africa

Europe

Asia

Australasia & Oceania

POLITICAL STATUS:
Eg. MEXICO: independent state
Eg. FAEROE ISLANDS (to Denmark): self-governing territory, with parent state indicated
Eg. *Andaman Islands (to India):* non self-governing territory, with parent stated indicated

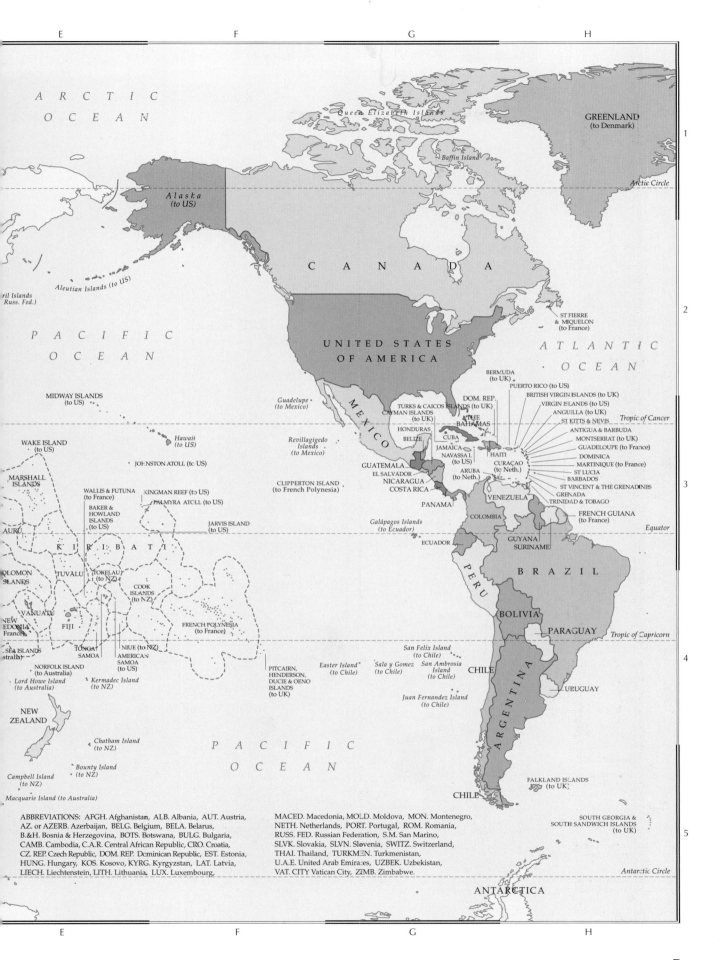

A R C T I C
O C E A N

Queen Elizabeth Islands

GREENLAND
(to Denmark)

1

Baffin Island

Arctic Circle

Alaska
(to US)

ril Islands
Russ. Fed.)

Aleutian Islands (to US)

C A N A D A

2

P A C I F I C
O C E A N

UNITED STATES
OF AMERICA

A T L A N T I C

O C E A N

ST PIERRE
& MIQUELON
(to France)

MIDWAY ISLANDS
(to US)

Guadelupe
(to Mexico)

BERMUDA
(to UK)

PUERTO RICO (to US)

BRITISH VIRGIN ISLANDS (to UK)

VIRGIN ISLANDS (to US)

ANGUILLA (to UK)

Tropic of Cancer

DOM. REP.

TURKS & CAICOS ISLANDS
(to UK)

CAYMAN ISLANDS
(to UK)

THE
BAHAMAS

ST KITTS & NEVIS

ANTIGUA & BARBUDA

WAKE ISLAND
(to US)

Hawaii
(to US)

Revillagigedo
Islands
(to Mexico)

HONDURAS

BELIZE

CUBA

MONTSERRAT (to UK)

GUADELOUPE (to France)

JAMAICA

DOMINICA

M
E
X
I
C
O

JOHNSTON ATOLL (to US)

NAVASSA I.
(to US)

HAITI

MARTINIQUE (to France)

MARSHALL
ISLANDS

GUATEMALA

EL SALVADOR

CURAÇAO
(to Neth.)

ST LUCIA

BARBADOS

3

WALLIS & FUTUNA
(to France)

KINGMAN REEF (to US)

NICARAGUA

ARUBA
(to Neth.)

ST VINCENT & THE GRENADINES

GRENADA

AURU

PALMYRA ATOLL (to US)

COSTA RICA

CLIPPERTON ISLAND
(to French Polynesia)

PANAMA

VENEZUELA

TRINIDAD & TOBAGO

JARVIS ISLAND
(to US)

BAKER &
HOWLAND
ISLANDS
(to US)

COLOMBIA

Galápagos Islands
(to Ecuador)

FRENCH GUIANA
(to France)

Equator

K I R I B A T I

ECUADOR

GUYANA

SURINAME

OLOMON
SLANDS

TUVALU

TOKELAU
(to NZ)

COOK
ISLANDS
(to NZ)

P E R U

B R A Z I L

VANUATU

NEW
EDONIA
France)

FIJI

FRENCH POLYNESIA
(to France)

BOLIVIA

PARAGUAY

Tropic of Capricorn

SEA ISLANDS
ustralia)

TONGA

SAMOA

NIUE (to NZ)

AMERICAN
SAMOA
(to US)

San Felix Island
(to Chile)

4

NORFOLK ISLAND
(to Australia)

PITCAIRN,
HENDERSON,
DUCIE & OENO
ISLANDS
(to UK)

Easter Island
(to Chile)

Sala y Gomez
(to Chile)

San Ambrosia
Island
(to Chile)

CHILE

A
R
G
E
N
T
I
N
A

Lord Howe Island
(to Australia)

Kermadec Island
(to NZ)

Juan Fernandez Island
(to Chile)

URUGUAY

NEW
ZEALAND

Chatham Island
(to NZ)

P A C I F I C

Bounty Island
(to NZ)

O C E A N

Campbell Island
(to NZ)

FALKLAND ISLANDS
(to UK)

Macquarie Island (to Australia)

CHILE

ABBREVIATIONS: AFGH. Afghanistan, ALB. Albania, AUT. Austria,
AZ. or AZERB. Azerbaijan, BELG. Belgium, BELA. Belarus,
B.&H. Bosnia & Herzegovina, BOTS. Botswana, BULG. Bulgaria,
CAMB. Cambodia, C.A.R. Central African Republic, CRO. Croatia,
CZ. REP. Czech Republic, DOM. REP. Dominican Republic, EST. Estonia,
HUNG. Hungary, KOS. Kosovo, KYRG. Kyrgyzstan, LAT. Latvia,
LIECH. Liechtenstein, LITH. Lithuania. LUX. Luxembourg,

MACED. Macedonia, MOLD. Moldova, MON. Montenegro,
NETH. Netherlands, PORT. Portugal, ROM. Romania,
RUSS. FED. Russian Federation, S.M. San Marino,
SLVK. Slovakia, SLVN. Slovenia, SWITZ. Switzerland,
THAI. Thailand, TURKMEN. Turkmenistan,
U.A.E. United Arab Emirates, UZBEK. Uzbekistan,
VAT. CITY Vatican City, ZIMB. Zimbabwe.

SOUTH GEORGIA &
SOUTH SANDWICH ISLANDS
(to UK)

5

Antarctic Circle

ANTARCTICA

The Physical World

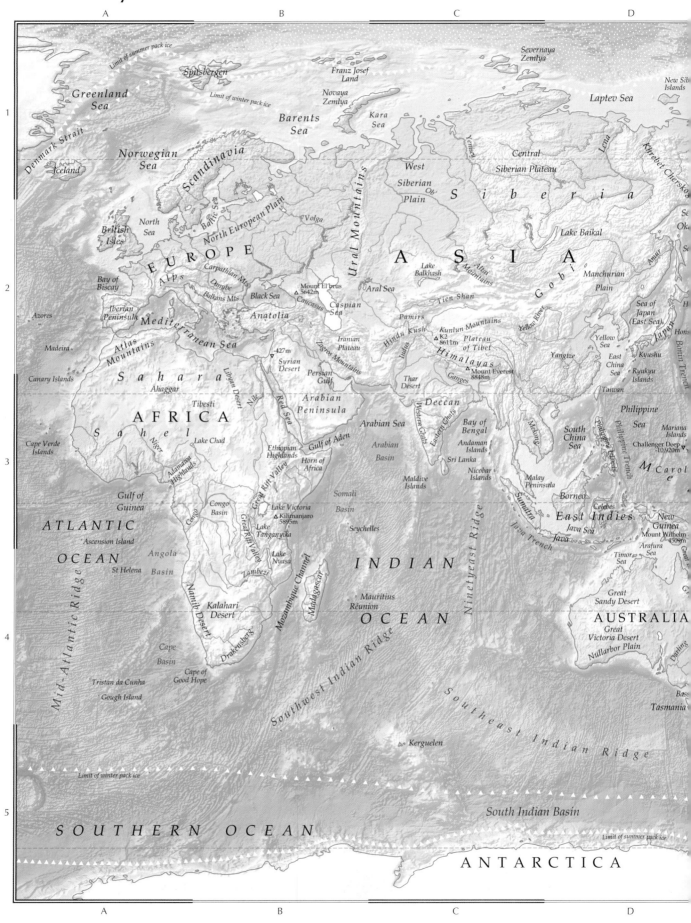

A   **B**   **C**   **D**

Limit of summer pack ice

Greenland Sea

Spitsbergen

Franz Josef Land

Severnaya Zemlya

Limit of winter pack ice

Novaya Zemlya

Barents Sea

Kara Sea

Laptev Sea

New Sib Islands

1

Norwegian Sea

Denmark Strait

Iceland

Scandinavia

West Siberian Plain

Yenisei

Ob

Central Siberian Plateau

Lena

S i b e r i a

Khrebet Cherskoe

Se Ok

British Isles

North Sea

Baltic Sea

Volga

Ural Mountains

A S I A

Lake Baikal

EUROPE

North European Plain

Lake Balkhash

Altai Mountains

G o b i

Manchurian Plain

Amur

Se

2

Bay of Biscay

Alps

Carpathian Mts

Danube

Balkans Mts

Black Sea

Mount El'brus
5642m △

Caucasus

Aral Sea

Tien Shan

Sea of Japan (East Sea)

Hons

Iberian Peninsula

Mediterranean Sea

Anatolia

Caspian Sea

Pamirs

Kunlun Mountains

Yellow River

Japan

Bonin Trench

Azores

Iranian Plateau

Hindu Kush

K2
8611m △

Plateau of Tibet

Yangtze

Yellow Sea

Kyushu

Madeira

Atlas Mountains

Zagros Mountains

-427m

Syrian Desert

Himalayas

East China Sea

Ryukyu Islands

Canary Islands

S a h a r a

Ahaggar

Libyan Desert

Nile

Red Sea

Persian Gulf

Arabian Peninsula

Thar Desert

Ganges

Mount Everest
8848m △

Taiwan

Tibesti

Deccan

Philippine Sea

AFRICA

S a h e l

Lake Chad

Niger

Ethiopian Highlands

Gulf of Aden

Arabian Sea

Arabian Basin

Bay of Bengal

Western Ghats

Eastern Ghats

South China Sea

Mariana Islands

Philippine Trench

Cape Verde Islands

Adamawa Highlands

Horn of Africa

Andaman Islands

Sri Lanka

Mekong

M Carol

Challenger Deep
-10,920m

3

Gulf of Guinea

Congo Basin

Congo

Great Rift Valley

Lake Victoria

Kilimanjaro
5895m △

Somali Basin

Maldive Islands

Nicobar Islands

Malay Peninsula

Sumatra

Java Trench

Borneo

East Indies

Celebes

New Guinea

ATLANTIC OCEAN

Ascension Island

St Helena

Angola Basin

Great Rift Valley

Lake Tanganyika

Lake Nyasa

Zambezi

Seychelles

I N D I A N

Java Sea

Java

Mount Wilhelm
4509m △

Timor Sea

Arafura Sea

Great

Mid-Atlantic Ridge

Namib Desert

Kalahari Desert

Mozambique Channel

Madagascar

Mauritius

Réunion

O C E A N

Ninetyeast Ridge

Southeast Indian Ridge

Great Sandy Desert

AUSTRALIA

G

4

Cape Basin

Tristan da Cunha

Gough Island

Drakensberg

Cape of Good Hope

Southwest Indian Ridge

Great Victoria Desert

Nullarbor Plain

Darling

Bass

Tasmania

Kerguelen △

Limit of winter pack ice

South Indian Basin

5

S O U T H E R N   **O C E A N**

Limit of summer pack ice

A N T A R C T I C A

A   **B**   **C**   **D**

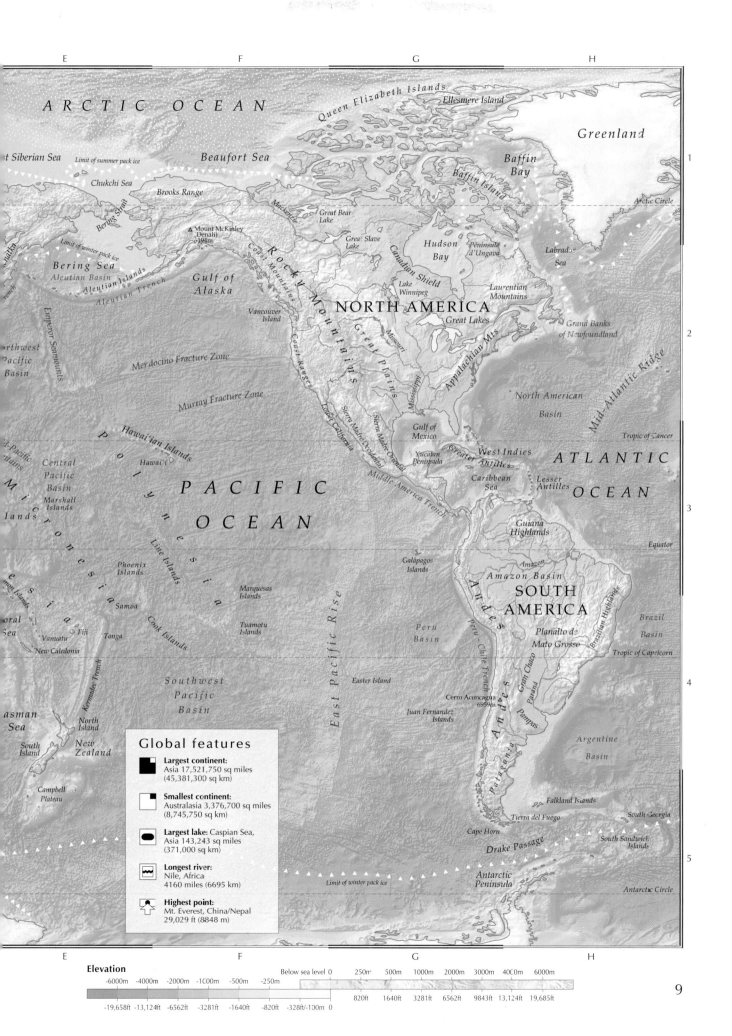

ARCTIC OCEAN

Queen Elizabeth Islands

Ellesmere Island

Greenland

t Siberian Sea Limit of summer pack ice *Beaufort Sea* *Baffin Bay*

1

Chukchi Sea *Brooks Range* *Arctic Circle*

Mackenzie Great Bear Lake *Baffin Island*

Bering Strait

Limit of winter pack ice △ Mount McKinley (Denali) 6194m Grea Slave Lake Hudson Bay Péninsule d'Ungava *Labrado Sea*

Bering Sea *Aleutian Basin* *Gulf of Alaska* Lake Winnipeg Canadian Shield *Laurentian Mountains*

Aleutian Islands Aleutian Trench

Emperor Seamounts Vancouver Island **NORTH AMERICA** Great Lakes Grand Banks of Newfoundland

rthwest Pacific Basin Mer docino Fracture Zone Coast Ranges Great Plains Missouri *North American Basin* *Mid-Atlantic Ridge*

2

Murray Fracture Zone Mississippi Appalachian Mts

Hawaiian Islands Sierra Madre Occidental Gulf of Mexico *Tropic of Cancer*

Central Pacific Basin Hawai'i Sierra Madre Oriental Yucatan Peninsula Greater Antilles West Indies **ATLANTIC**

PACIFIC Lower California Middle America Trench Caribbean Sea Lesser Antilles **OCEAN**

Marshall Islands **OCEAN**

lands 3

Guiana Highlands

Line Islands Galápagos Islands *Equator*

Phoenix Islands Amazon

Marquesas Islands *Amazon Basin* **SOUTH AMERICA**

Samoa Tuamotu Islands Peru Basin Planalto de Mato Grosse *Brazil Basin*

oral Sea Vanuatu Fiji Tonga Cook Islands *East Pacific Rise* Gran Chaco Brazilian Highlands

New Caledonia Easter Island Paraná *Tropic of Capricorn*

4

Southwest Pacific Basin Cerro Aconcagua 6959m Pampas

Juan Fernandez Islands *Argentine Basin*

asman Sea North Island Patagonia

South Island New Zealand

Campbell Plateau Falkland Islands South Georgia

Tierra del Fuego South Sandwich Islands

Cape Horn

Drake Passage

5

Limit of winter pack ice *Antarctic Peninsula* *Antarctic Circle*

Global features

Largest continent:
Asia 17,521,750 sq miles
(45,381,300 sq km)

Smallest continent:
Australasia 3,376,700 sq miles
(8,745,750 sq km)

Largest lake: Caspian Sea,
Asia 143,243 sq miles
(371,000 sq km)

Longest river:
Nile, Africa
4160 miles (6695 km)

Highest point:
Mt. Everest, China/Nepal
29,029 ft (8848 m)

Elevation

-6000m -4000m -2000m -1000m -500m -250m Below sea level 0 250m 500m 1000m 2000m 3000m 4000m 6000m

-19,658ft -13,124ft -6562ft -3281ft -1640ft -820ft -328ft/-100m 0 820ft 1640ft 3281ft 6562ft 9843ft 13,124ft 19,685ft

Standard Time Zones

The numbers at the top of the map indicate how many hours each time zone is ahead or behind Coordinated Universal Time (UTC). The row of clocks indicate the time in each zone when it is 12:00 noon UTC.

TIME ZONES

Because Earth is a rotating sphere, the Sun shines on only half of its surface at any one time. Thus, it is simultaneously morning, evening, and night time in different parts of the world. Because of these disparities, each country or part of a country adheres to a local time. A region of the Earth's surface within which a single local time is used is called a time zone.

COORDINATED UNIVERSAL TIME (UTC)

Coordinated Universal Time (UTC) is a reference by which the local time in each time zone is set. UTC is a successor to, and closely approximates, Greenwich Mean Time (GMT). However, UTC is based on an atomic clock, whereas GMT is determined by the Sun's position in the sky relative to the 0° longitudinal meridian, which runs through Greenwich, UK.

THE INTERNATIONAL DATELINE

The International Dateline is an imaginary line from pole to pole that roughly corresponds to the 180° longitudinal meridian. It is an arbitrary marker between calendar days. The dateline is needed because of the use of local times around the world rather than a single universal time.

The —
WORLD
ATLAS

THE MAPS IN THIS ATLAS ARE ARRANGED CONTINENT BY CONTINENT, STARTING FROM THE INTERNATIONAL DATE LINE, AND MOVING EASTWARD. THE MAPS PROVIDE A UNIQUE VIEW OF TODAY'S WORLD, COMBINING TRADITIONAL CARTOGRAPHIC TECHNIQUES WITH THE LATEST REMOTE-SENSED AND DIGITAL TECHNOLOGY.

Western Canada & Alaska

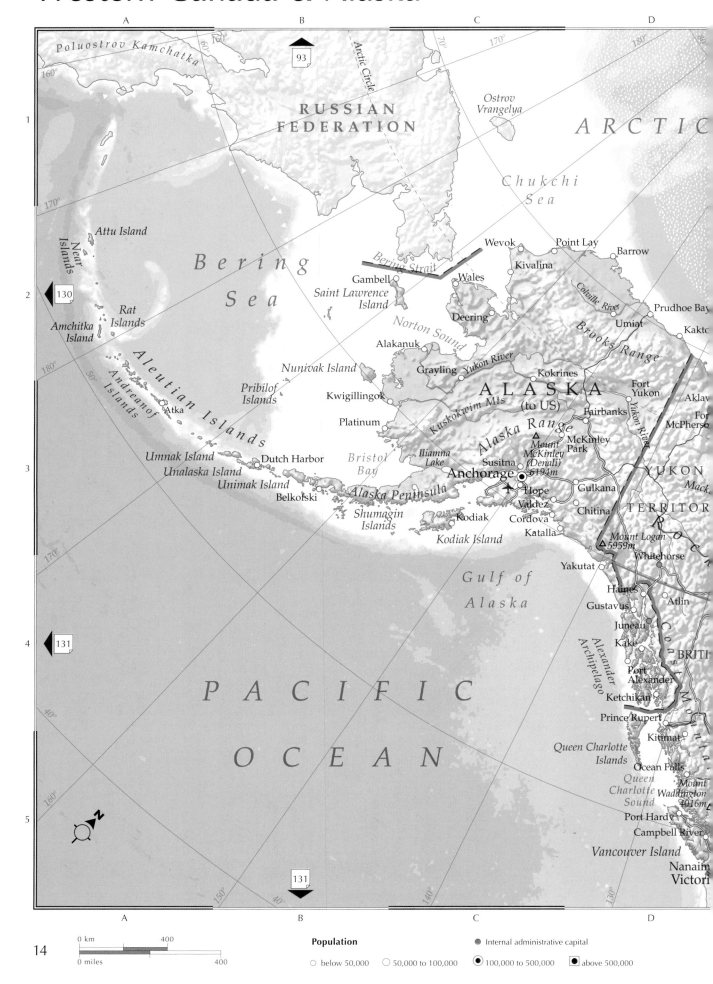

Poluostrov Kamchatka

Arctic Circle

RUSSIAN
FEDERATION

Ostrov
Vrangelya

ARCTIC

Chukchi
Sea

Attu Island

Near
Islands

Bering
Sea

Bering Strait

Wevok
Point Lay
Barrow

Gambell
Wales
Kivalina

Saint Lawrence
Island

Deering
Prudhoe Bay

Coleville River
Umiat
Kaktc

Rat
Islands

Norton Sound

Brooks Range

Amchitka
Island

Alakanuk

Andreanof
Islands

Nunivak Island

Grayling
Yukon River

Kokrines

ALASKA
(to US)

Fort
Yukon

Aklav

Aleutian Islands

Pribilof
Islands

Kwigillingok

Kuskokwim Mts

Fairbanks

Yukon River

For
McPherso

Atka

Platinum

Alaska Range

Mount
McKinley

McKinley
Park

Umnak Island

Dutch Harbor

Bristol
Bay

Iliamna
Lake

Mount
McKinley
(Denali)
6194m

YUKON

Unalaska Island

Susitna

Unimak Island

Belkofski

Alaska Peninsula

Anchorage

Hope
Valdez

Gulkana

TERRITOR

Chitina

Mack.

Shumagin
Islands

Kodiak

Cordova

Mount Logan
5959m

Whitehorse

Kodiak Island

Katalla

R

Yakutat

Gulf of
Alaska

Haines

Atlin

Gustavus

Juneau

PACIFIC

Kake

BRITI

Alexander
Archipelago

Port
Alexander

Ketchikan

Prince Rupert

OCEAN

Kitimat

Queen Charlotte
Islands

Ocean Falls

Queen
Charlotte
Sound

Mount
Waddington
4016m

Port Hardy

Campbell River

Vancouver Island

Nanaim
Victori

0 km   400

0 miles   400

Population

Internal administrative capital

○ below 50,000   ○ 50,000 to 100,000   ◉ 100,000 to 500,000   ◉ above 500,000

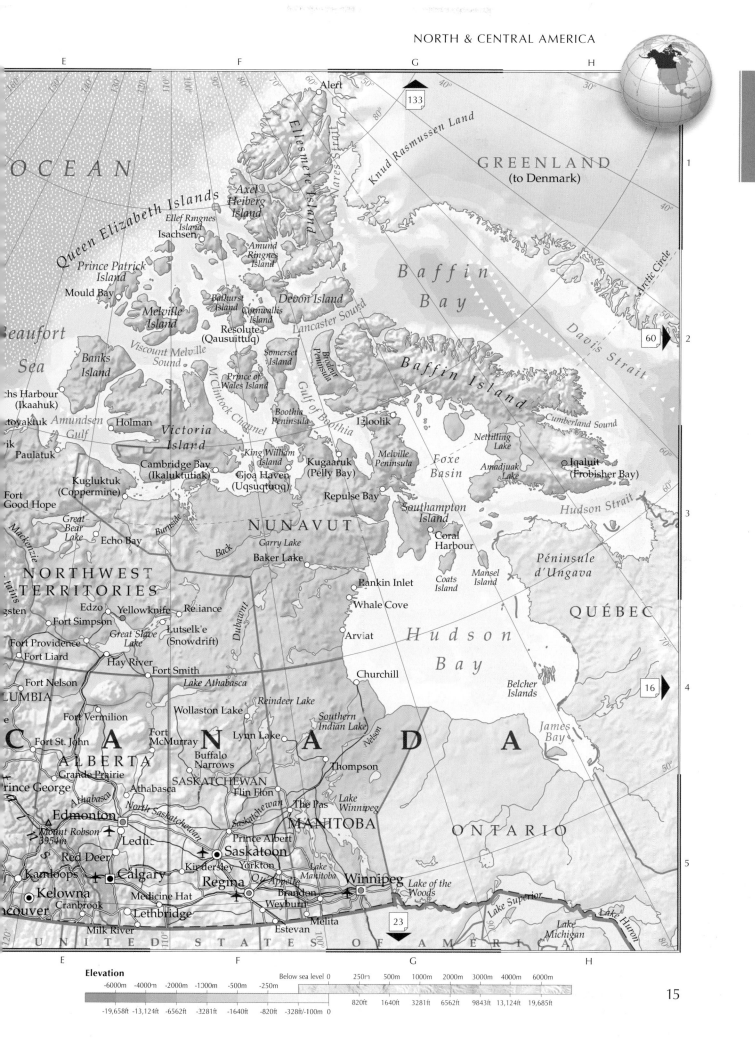

GREENLAND
(to Denmark)

Knud Rasmussen Land

O C E A N

Queen Elizabeth Islands

Axel
Heiberg
Island

Ellef Ringnes
Island
Isachsen

Amund
Ringnes
Island

Ellesmere Island

Nares Strait

Alert

133

60

Prince Patrick
Island

Mould Bay

Melville
Island

Bathurst
Island

Cornwallis
Island

Devon Island

Lancaster Sound

Baffin
Bay

Arctic Circle

Davis Strait

Beaufort
Sea

Banks
Island

Viscount Melville
Sound

Resolute
(Qausuittuq)

Somerset
Island

Prince of
Wales Island

Brodeur
Peninsula

Baffin Island

Cumberland Sound

chs Harbour
(Ikaahuk)

Holman

Amundsen
Gulf

Victoria
Island

M Clintock Channel

Boothia
Peninsula

Gulf of Boothia

Igloolik

Nettilling
Lake

ik

Paulatuk

Cambridge Bay
(Ikaluktutiak)

King William
Island

Gjoa Haven
(Uqsuqtuuq)

Kugaaruk
(Pelly Bay)

Melville
Peninsula

Foxe
Basin

Amadjuak
Lake

Iqaluit
(Frobisher Bay)

Fort
Good Hope

Kugluktuk
(Coppermine)

Repulse Bay

60

Mackenzie

Great
Bear
Lake

Echo Bay

Burnside

NUNAVUT

Garry Lake

Southampton
Island

Hudson Strait

Back

Baker Lake

Coral
Harbour

Péninsule
d'Ungava

NORTHWEST
TERRITORIES

sten

Edzo

Yellowknife

Reliance

Rankin Inlet

Mansel
Island

QUÉBEC

Fort Simpson

Great Slave
Lake

Lutselk'e
(Snowdrift)

Dubawnt

Whale Cove

Coats
Island

Fort Providence

Fort Liard

Hay River

Fort Smith

Arviat

Hudson

Bay

70

Fort Nelson

Lake Athabasca

Churchill

LUMBIA

Fort Vermilion

Reindeer Lake

Belcher
Islands

James
Bay

C A N A D A

Fort St. John

Fort
McMurray

Lynn Lake

Southern
Indian Lake

Nelson

50

ALBERTA

Grande Prairie

Buffalo
Narrows

Thompson

rince George

Athabasca

Athabasca

SASKATCHEWAN

Flin Flon

ONTARIO

Edmonton

North Saskatchewan

Saskatchewan

The Pas

Lake
Winnipeg

MANITOBA

Mount Robson
3954m

Leduc

Prince Albert

Red Deer

Saskatoon

Kindersley

Yorkton

Lake
Manitoba

Kamloops

Calgary

Regina

Qu'Appelle

Winnipeg

Lake of the
Woods

Lake Superior

Kelowna

Medicine Hat

Brandon

Lake Huron

ncouver

Cranbrook

Lethbridge

Weyburn

Lake Superior

Milk River

Estevan

Melita

23

Lake
Michigan

U N I T E D   S T A T E S   O F   A M E R I C A

E   F   G   H

Elevation

| | | | | | | Below sea level 0 | 250m | 500m | 1000m | 2000m | 3000m | 4000m | 6000m |

-6000m -4000m -2000m -1000m -500m -250m

-19,658ft -13,124ft -6562ft -3281ft -1640ft -820ft -328ft/-100m 0

820ft 1640ft 3281ft 6562ft 9843ft 13,124ft 19,685ft

Eastern Canada

NORTHWEST TERRITORIES

NUNAVUT

SASKATCHEWAN

MANITOBA

Churchill

Southern
Indian Lake

Nelson

Hayes

Cedar
Lake

Lake
Winnipeg

Lake
Winnipegosis

Sandy Lake

Lake
Manitoba

C A N

O N T A R I O

Hudson
Bay

Coats
Island

Ivujivik

Charles
Island

Mansel
Island

Péninsule
d' Ungava

Ottawa Islands

Inukjuak
(Port Harrison)

Riviēre
Feui

Lac
Minto

Fort Severn

Severn

Peawanuk

Winisk

Attawapiskat

Attawapiskat

Belcher
Islands

James
Bay

Akimiski
Island

Fort
Albany

Albany

Moosonee

Bien

Eastmain

Q U A

Rivière de Rupert

Lac
Mistassini

Chibougamau

Réservoir
Gouin

Lac Seul

Kenora

Dryden

Armstrong

Lake
Nipigon

Longlac

Hearst

Kapuskasing

Cochrane

Amos

Rouyn-Noranda

Lake of
the Woods

Fort Frances

Atikokan

Nipigon

Marathon

Tip Top Mountain
△ 640m

Timmins

Foleyet

Val-d'Or

NORTH
DAKOTA

Rainy
Lake

Red River

Thunder Bay

Lake Superior

Wawa

Kirkland
Lake

MINNESOTA

MICHIGAN

Sault Ste.Marie

Sudbury

North
Bay

Pembroke

Gatineau

Hull

La

OTTAWA

SOUTH
DAKOTA

U N I T E D   S T A T E S

WISCONSIN

Lake Michigan

Manitoulin
Island

Georgian
Bay

Lake
Huron

Midland

Peterborough

Kingsto

O F   A M E R I C A

NEBRASKA

IOWA

Mississippi River

ILLINOIS

INDIANA

Brampton

Kitchener

Sarnia

Hamilton

London

Windsor

Leamington

Oshawa

Toronto

St.Catharines

Niagara
Falls

Lake
Ontar

NEW YORK

Lake Erie

OHIO

PENNSYLVANIA

Population

○ below 50,000   ○ 50,000 to 100,000   ◉ 100,000 to 500,000   ■ above 500,000

● National capital   ● Internal administrative capital

16

0 km   300

0 miles   300

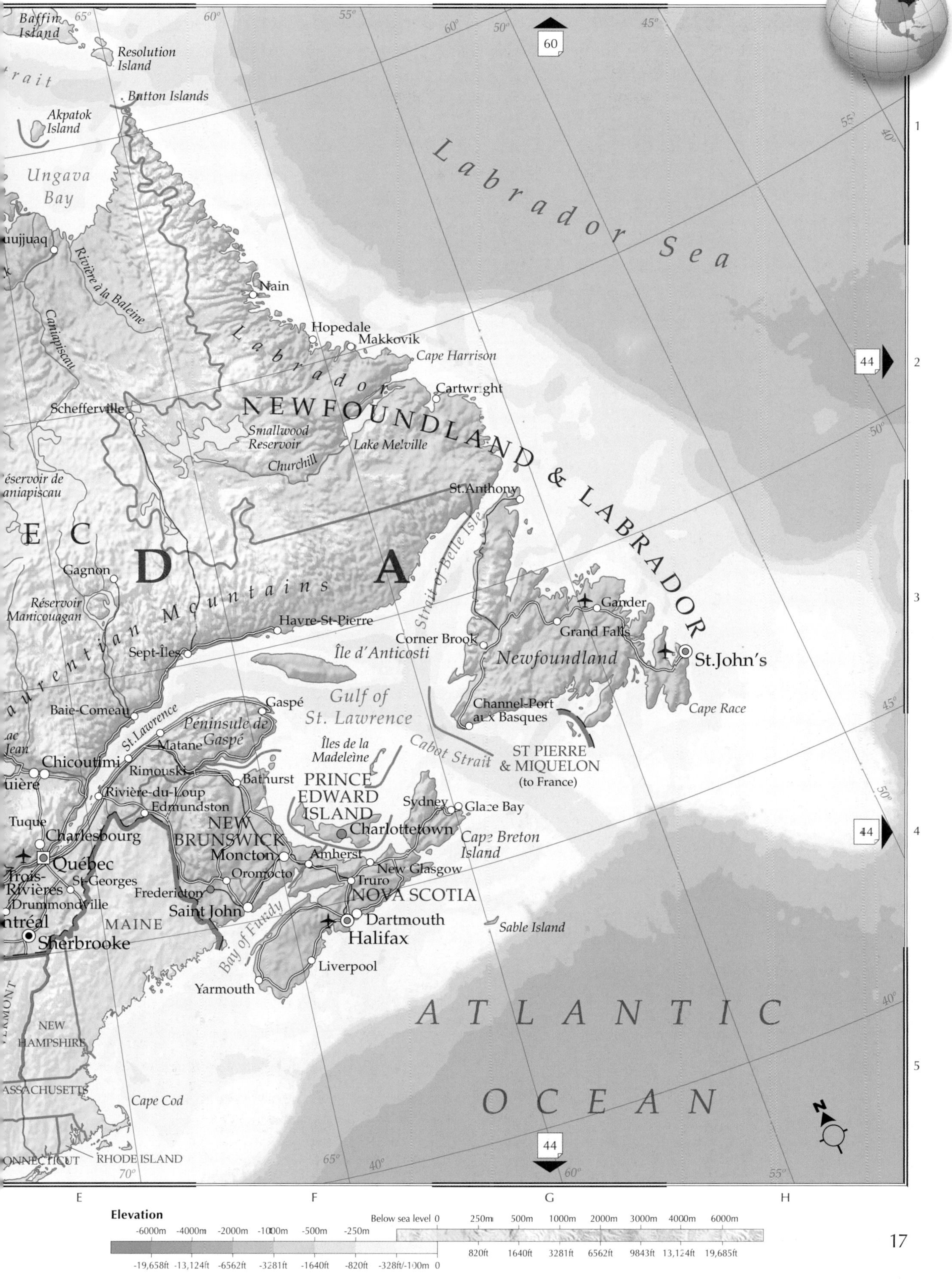

E   F   G   H

60

44

Baffin Island

Resolution Island

Button Islands

Akpatok Island

Ungava Bay

uujjuaq

Rivière à la Baleine

Caniapiscau

Nain

Hopedale

Makkovik

Cape Harrison

L a b r a d o r   S e a

Schefferville

N E W F O U N D L A N D

Cartwright

Smallwood Reservoir

Lake Melville

Churchill

&   L A B R A D O R

éservoir de aniapiscau

E   C

D

A

Gagnon

St.Anthony

Réservoir Manicouagan

Strait of Belle Isle

Havre-St-Pierre

Gander

L a u r e n t i a n   M o u n t a i n s

Corner Brook

Grand Falls

St.John's

Sept-Îles

Île d'Anticosti

Newfoundland

Baie-Comeau

Gaspé

Gulf of St. Lawrence

Cape Race

Lac Jean

St.Lawrence

Péninsule de Gaspé

Matane

Îles de la Madeleine

Channel-Port aux Basques

Chicoutimi

Rimouski

Cabot Strait

ST PIERRE & MIQUELON
(to France)

uière

Rivière-du-Loup

Bathurst

PRINCE EDWARD ISLAND

Sydney

Glace Bay

Tuque

Edmundston

NEW

Charlottetown

Cape Breton Island

Charlesbourg

BRUNSWICK

Moncton

Amherst

New Glasgow

Québec

St-Georges

Oromocto

Truro

Trois-Rivières

Fredericton

NOVA SCOTIA

Drummondville

Saint John

Sable Island

ntréal

MAINE

Dartmouth

Sherbrooke

Bay of Fundy

Halifax

Liverpool

A T L A N T I C

Yarmouth

NEW HAMPSHIRE

Cape Cod

O C E A N

ASSACHUSETTS

ONNECTICUT   RHODE ISLAND

44

E   F   G   H

Elevation

Below sea level 0   250m   500m   1000m   2000m   3000m   4000m   6000m

-6000m   -4000m   -2000m   -1000m   -500m   -250m

-19,658ft   -13,124ft   -6562ft   -3281ft   -1640ft   -820ft   -328ft/-100m   0

820ft   1640ft   3281ft   6562ft   9843ft   13,124ft   19,685ft

USA: The Northeast

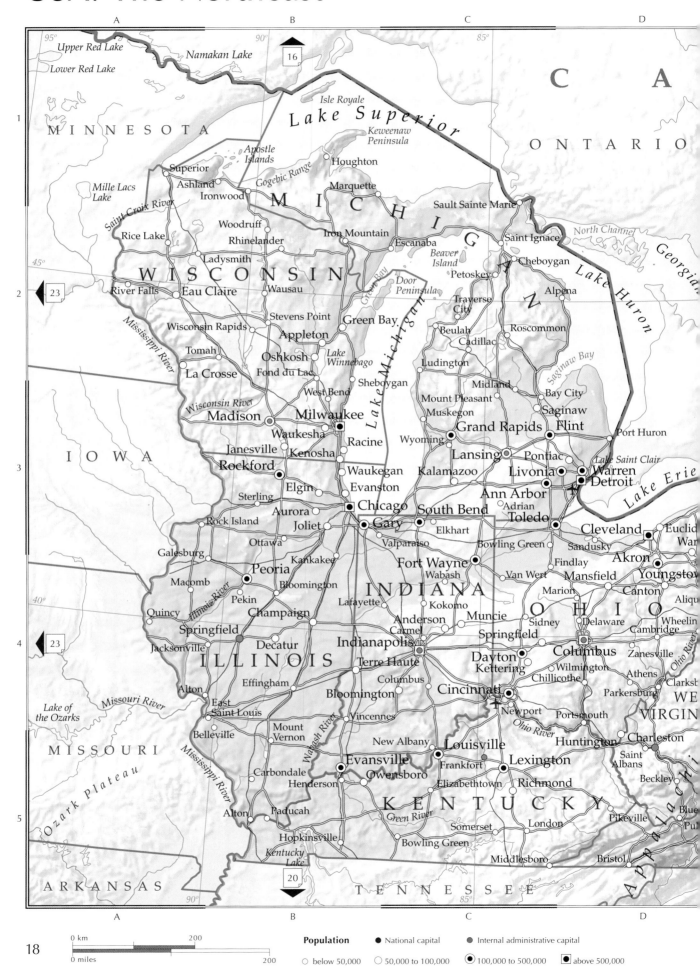

Population

	National capital		Internal administrative capital
○ below 50,000	○ 50,000 to 100,000	◉ 100,000 to 500,000	■ above 500,000

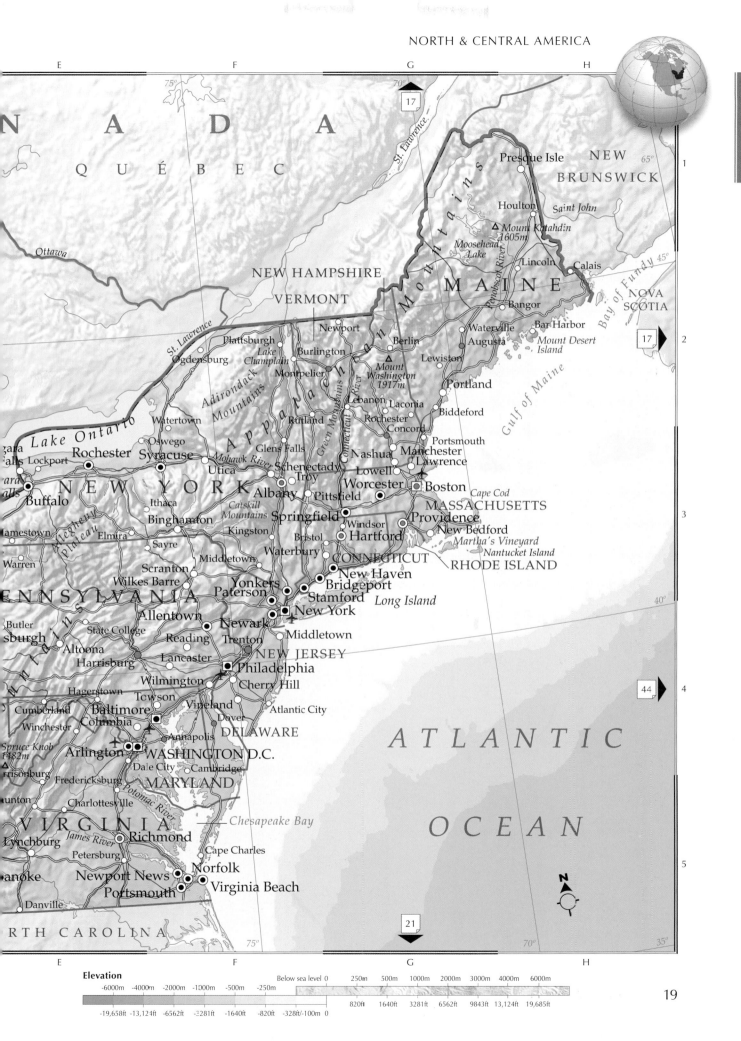

C A N A D A

Q U É B E C

Ottawa

NEW BRUNSWICK

St. Lawrence

Presque Isle

Houlton   *Saint John*

△ *Mount Katahdin*
1605m

Moosehead Lake

Lincoln   Calais

NEW HAMPSHIRE

VERMONT

M A I N E

Bangor

NOVA SCOTIA

Bay of Fundy

Plattsburgh
Lake Champlain
Burlington   Berlin
Ogdensburg
Montpelier   Waterville
St. Lawrence   Augusta
                    Mount Washington 1917m   Lewiston   Bar Harbor
Adirondack Mountains   *Mount Desert Island*

Gulf of Maine

Lebanon   Laconia   Portland

Watertown   Lebanon   Rochester   Biddeford

Lake Ontario   Oswego   Glens Falls   Concord
Rochester   Syracuse   Portsmouth
Niagara Falls   Lockport   *Mohawk River*   Schenectady   Nashua   Manchester
Buffalo   Utica   Troy   Lowell   Lawrence
N E W   Y O R K   Albany   Worcester   Boston
Ithaca   Pittsfield   *Cape Cod*
Jamestown   Binghamton   *Catskill Mountains*   Springfield   MASSACHUSETTS
Warren   Elmira   Springfield   Windsor   Providence
     Sayre   Kingston   Bristol   Hartford   New Bedford
Allegheny Plateau   Waterbury   *Martha's Vineyard*
P E N N S Y L V A N I A   Middletown   CONNECTICUT   *Nantucket Island*
Scranton   New Haven   RHODE ISLAND
Wilkes Barre   Yonkers   Bridgeport
Butler   Paterson   Stamford   *Long Island*
Pittsburgh   Allentown   Newark   New York
State College   Reading   Trenton
Altoona   Lancaster   Middletown
Harrisburg   NEW JERSEY
Cumberland   Philadelphia
Hagerstown   Wilmington   Cherry Hill
Spruce Knob 1482m △   Towson   Vineland
Winchester   Columbia   Atlantic City
Harrisonburg   Baltimore   Dover
Arlington   Annapolis   DELAWARE
WASHINGTON D.C.
Dale City   Cambridge
Fredericksburg   MARYLAND
Staunton   Charlottesville   *Chesapeake Bay*
Potomac River
V I R G I N I A
Lynchburg   *James River*   Richmond
Petersburg   Cape Charles
Roanoke   Newport News   Norfolk
Danville   Portsmouth   Virginia Beach

NORTH CAROLINA

A T L A N T I C

O C E A N

N

Elevation

						Below sea level 0	250m	500m	1000m	2000m	3000m	4000m	6000m
-6000m	-4000m	-2000m	-1000m	-500m	-250m								
-19,658ft	-13,124ft	-6562ft	-3281ft	-1640ft	-820ft	-328ft/-100m 0		820ft	1640ft	3281ft	6562ft	9843ft	13,124ft	19,685ft

USA: The Southeast

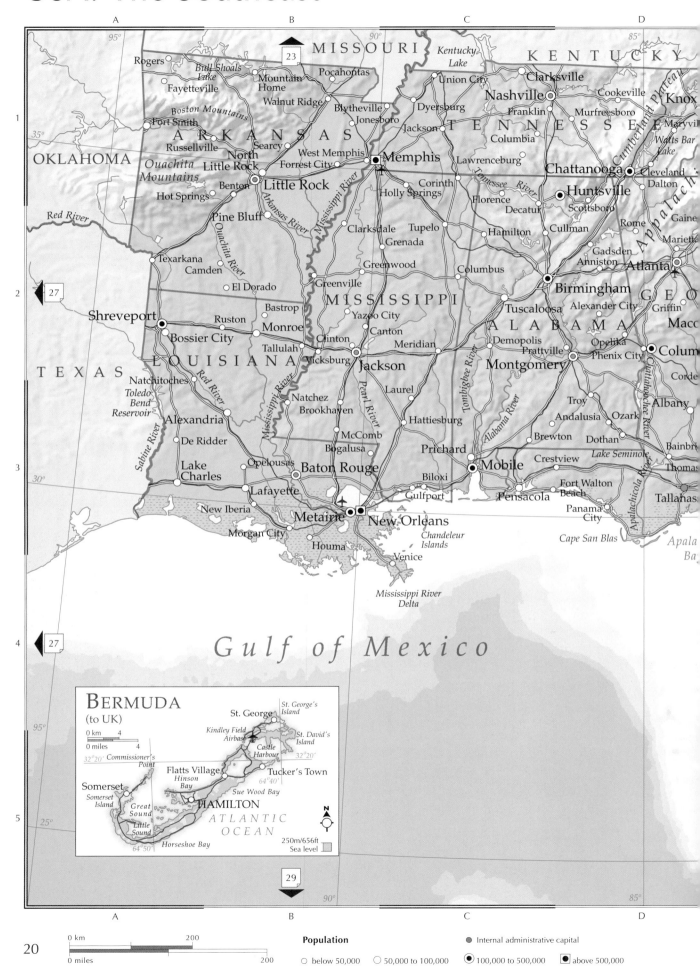

MISSOURI

Kentucky Lake

KENTUCKY

Rogers
Bull Shoals Lake
Mountain Home
Pocahontas
Union City
Clarksville
Cookeville
Knox

Fayetteville
Walnut Ridge
Nashville
Franklin
Murfreesboro
Maryvi

Fort Smith
Boston Mountains
Blytheville
Jonesboro
Dyersburg
Columbia
Watts Bar Lake

ARKANSAS
Searcy
West Memphis
Jackson
Lawrenceburg
Chattanooga
Cleveland

Russellville
North Little Rock
Forrest City
Memphis
Corinth
Dalton

OKLAHOMA
Ouachita Mountains
Little Rock
Holly Springs
Florence
Huntsville
Scottsboro
Rome
Gaine

Benton
Hot Springs
Clarksdale
Tupelo
Decatur
Cullman
Gadsden
Anniston
Mariett

Red River
Pine Bluff
Grenada
Hamilton
Columbus
Atlanta

Texarkana
Camden
Greenwood
MISSISSIPPI
Birmingham
GEO

El Dorado
Greenville
Tuscaloosa
Alexander City
Griffin
Macc

Shreveport
Bastrop
Yazoo City
ALABAMA
Opelika
Colum

Bossier City
Ruston
Monroe
Canton
Demopolis
Prattville
Phenix City
Corde

TEXAS
Tallulah
Clinton
Meridian
Montgomery
Albany

LOUISIANA
Vicksburg
Jackson
Laurel
Troy

Natchitoches
Red River
Natchez
Pearl River
Hattiesburg
Andalusia
Ozark

Toledo Bend Reservoir
Alexandria
Brookhaven
Brewton
Dothan
Bainbri

De Ridder
McComb
Prichard
Crestview
Lake Seminole
Thomas

Lake Charles
Opelousas
Bogalusa
Mobile
Fort Walton Beach
Tallahas

Lafayette
Baton Rouge
Biloxi
Pensacola
Panama City

New Iberia
Metairie
Gulfport
Cape San Blas
Apala Ba

Morgan City
New Orleans
Chandeleur Islands

Houma
Venice

Mississippi River Delta

Gulf of Mexico

BERMUDA
(to UK)

0 km 4
0 miles 4

St. George's Island
St. George
Kindley Field Airbase
St. David's Island

Commissioner's Point
Castle Harbour
Tucker's Town

Flatts Village
Hinson Bay
Sue Wood Bay

Somerset
Somerset Island

HAMILTON
Great Sound
Little Sound
ATLANTIC OCEAN

Horseshoe Bay

250m/656ft
Sea level

0 km 200
0 miles 200

Population

Internal administrative capital

○ below 50,000   ○ 50,000 to 100,000   ◉ 100,000 to 500,000   ■ above 500,000

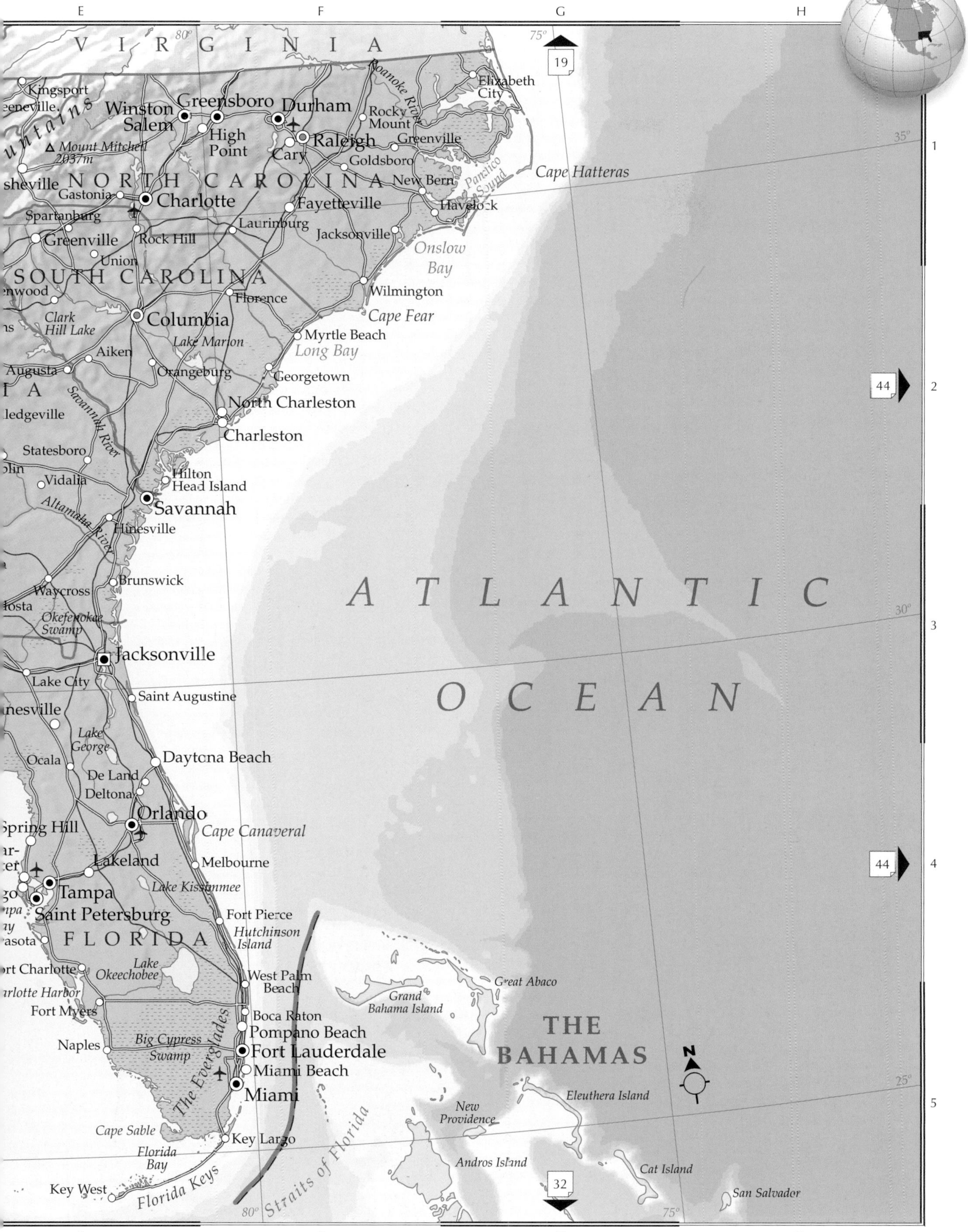

VIRGINIA

Kingsport
Greenville
Mountains
Mount Mitchell
2037m
△

Winston
Salem
Greensboro
High
Point
Durham
Cary
Raleigh

Asheville
NORTH CAROLINA
Gastonia
Charlotte
Fayetteville
Goldsboro
New Bern

Spartanburg
Laurinburg
Jacksonville

Greenville
Rock Hill
Florence

SOUTH CAROLINA
Union

Greenwood

Clark
Hill Lake
Columbia
Lake Marion
Myrtle Beach

Aiken
Orangeburg
Georgetown

Augusta
North Charleston
Long Bay

Milledgeville
Charleston

Statesboro

Dublin
Vidalia
Hilton
Head Island

Altamaha R.
Savannah

Hinesville

Brunswick

Waycross

Valdosta
Okefenokee
Swamp

Jacksonville

Lake City

Gainesville
Saint Augustine

Lake
George

Ocala
Daytona Beach

De Land
Deltona

Spring Hill
Orlando
Cape Canaveral

Clearwater
Lakeland
Melbourne

Tampa
Lake Kissimmee

Saint Petersburg
Fort Pierce

Tampa
Bay
Hutchinson
Island

Sarasota
FLORIDA

Port Charlotte
Lake
Okeechobee
West Palm
Beach

Charlotte Harbor
Boca Raton

Fort Myers
Pompano Beach

Naples
Big Cypress
Swamp
Fort Lauderdale

The Everglades
Miami Beach

Cape Sable
Miami

Florida
Bay
Key Largo

Key West
Florida Keys
Straits of Florida

Roanoke River
Elizabeth
City

Rocky
Mount
Greenville

Cape Hatteras
Havelock

Pamlico Sound

Onslow
Bay

Wilmington
Cape Fear

ATLANTIC

OCEAN

THE

BAHAMAS

Grand
Bahama Island
Great Abaco

New
Providence
Eleuthera Island

Andros Island
Cat Island

San Salvador

N

19

44

44

32

75°
80°
35°
30°
25°

E
F
G
H

1
2
3
4
5

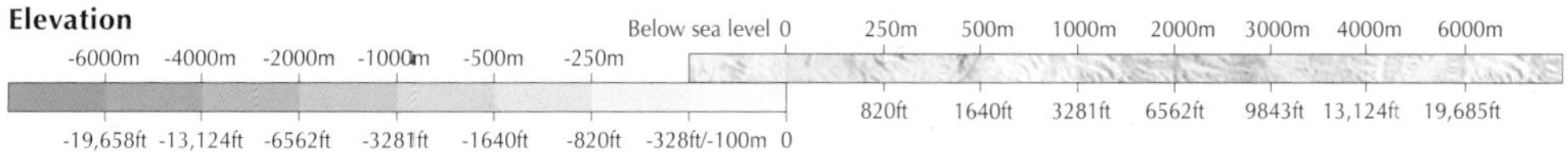

21

Elevation

						Below sea level 0	250m	500m	1000m	2000m	3000m	4000m	6000m
-6000m	-4000m	-2000m	-1000m	-500m	-250m								
-19,658ft	-13,124ft	-6562ft	-3281ft	-1640ft	-820ft	-328ft/-100m 0	820ft	1640ft	3281ft	6562ft	9843ft	13,124ft	19,685ft

USA: Central States

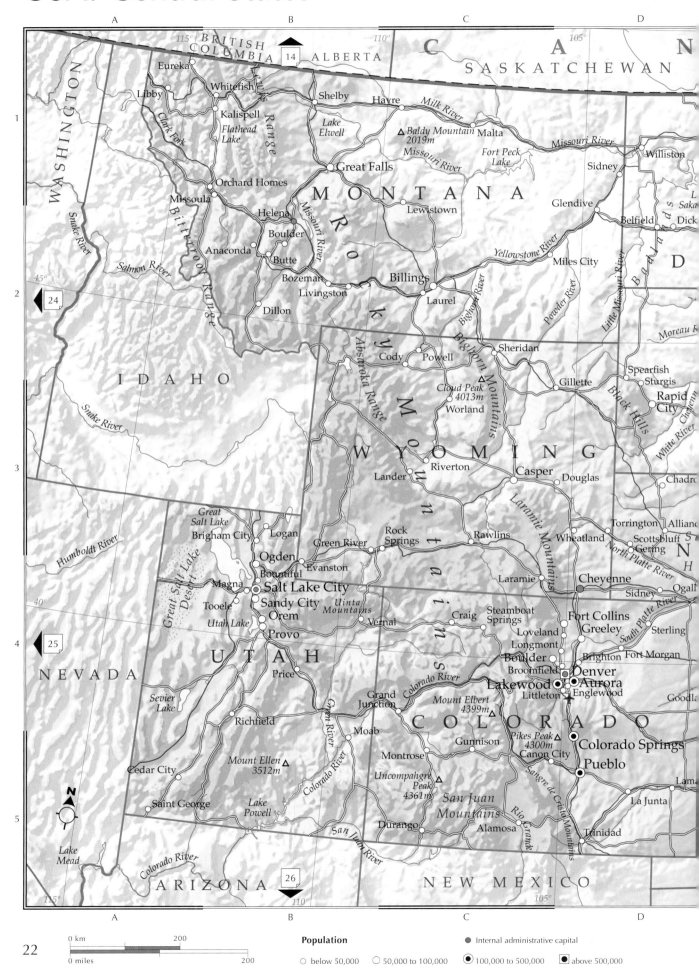

Population

○ below 50,000 ○ 50,000 to 100,000 ◉ 100,000 to 500,000 ■ above 500,000

● Internal administrative capital

0 km   200
0 miles   200

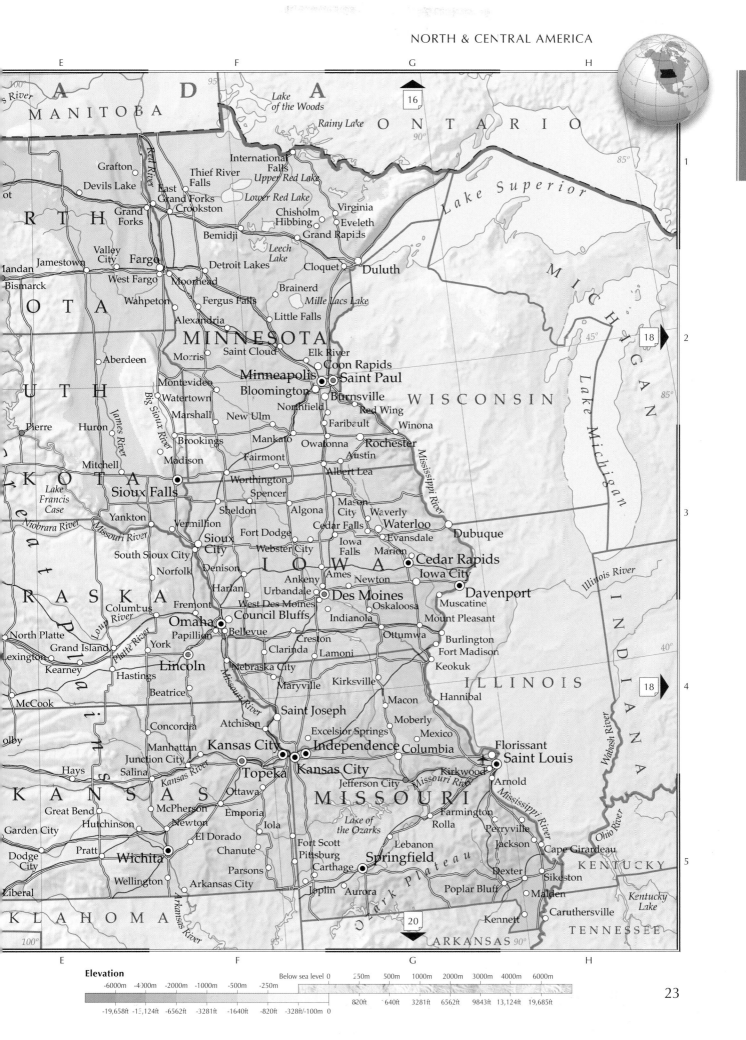

Elevation

-6000m	-4000m	-2000m	-1000m	-500m	-250m	Below sea level 0	250m	500m	1000m	2000m	3000m	4000m	6000m
-19,658ft	-13,124ft	-6562ft	-3281ft	-1640ft	-820ft	-328ft/-100m 0	820ft	640ft	3281ft	6562ft	9843ft	13,124ft	19,685ft

USA: The West

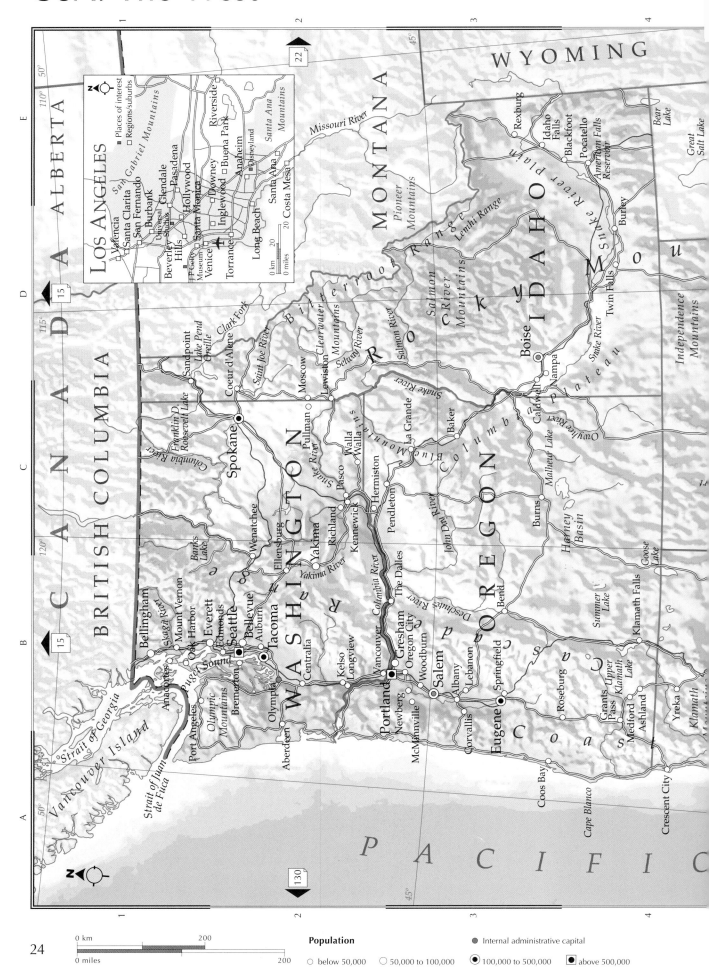

Population

- ○ below 50,000
- ○ 50,000 to 100,000
- ◉ 100,000 to 500,000
- ◼ above 500,000

- ● Internal administrative capital

0 km   200
0 miles   200

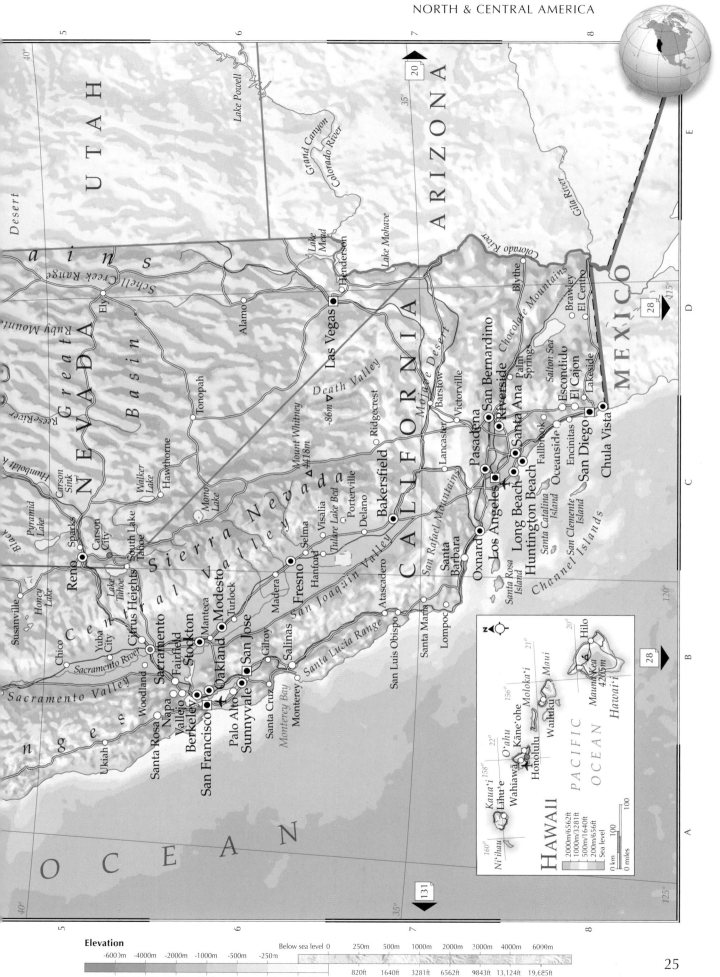

UTAH

Desert

Great Basin

NEVADA

Ruby Mounta

Schell Creek Range

Reese River

Ely

Alamo

Tonopah

Hawthorne

Walker Lake

Mono Lake

Pyramid Lake

Honey Lake

Carson Sink

Black

Sparks

Reno

Carson City

Lake Tahoe

South Lake Tahoe

Citrus Heights

Sierra Nevada

Susanville

Chico

Yuba City

Sacramento River

Woodland

Sacramento

Napa

Santa Rosa

Vallejo

Fairfield

Stockton

Berkeley

Oakland

Palo Alto

Sunnyvale

San Francisco

San Jose

Manteca

Modesto

Turlock

Madera

Merced

Central Valley

Santa Cruz

Monterey Bay

Monterey

Gilroy

Salinas

Santa Lucia Range

San Luis Obispo

Fresno

Hanford

Selma

Visalia

Tulare Lake Bed

Porterville

Delano

Atascadero

San Joaquin Valley

Santa Maria

Lompoc

Santa Barbara

CALIFORNIA

Bakersfield

Ridgecrest

Mount Whitney ▲4418m

Death Valley

−86m ▽

Lancaster

San Rafael Mountains

Oxnard

Pasadena

Los Angeles

Long Beach

Huntington Beach

Santa Catalina Island

Santa Rosa Island

Channel Islands

San Clemente Island

Mojave Desert

Barstow

Victorville

San Bernardino

Riverside

Santa Ana

Palm Springs

Salton Sea

Escondido

El Cajon

Lakeside

Oceanside

Encinitas

Fallbrook

San Diego

Chula Vista

Brawley

El Centro

Chocolate Mountains

Colorado River

Gila River

MEXICO

ARIZONA

Lake Mead

Henderson

Las Vegas

Lake Mohave

Blythe

Grand Canyon

Colorado River

Lake Powell

PACIFIC OCEAN

Ukiah

Sacramento Valley

R a n g e s

Hawaii inset

20
28
131
28

HAWAII

Ni'ihau

Kaua'i

Lihu'e

Wahiawā

O'ahu

Kāne'ohe

Honolulu

Waihuku

Moloka'i

Maui

Mauna Kea 4205m

Hilo

Hawai'i

PACIFIC OCEAN

2000m/6562ft
1000m/3281ft
500m/1640ft
200m/656ft
Sea level

0 km   100
0 miles   100

Elevation

| -6000m | -4000m | -2000m | -1000m | -500m | -250m | Below sea level 0 | 250m | 500m | 1000m | 2000m | 3000m | 4000m | 6000m |

-19,658ft -13,124ft -6562ft -3281ft -1640ft -820ft -328ft/-100m 0 820ft 1640ft 3281ft 6562ft 9843ft 13,124ft 19,685ft

USA: The Southwest

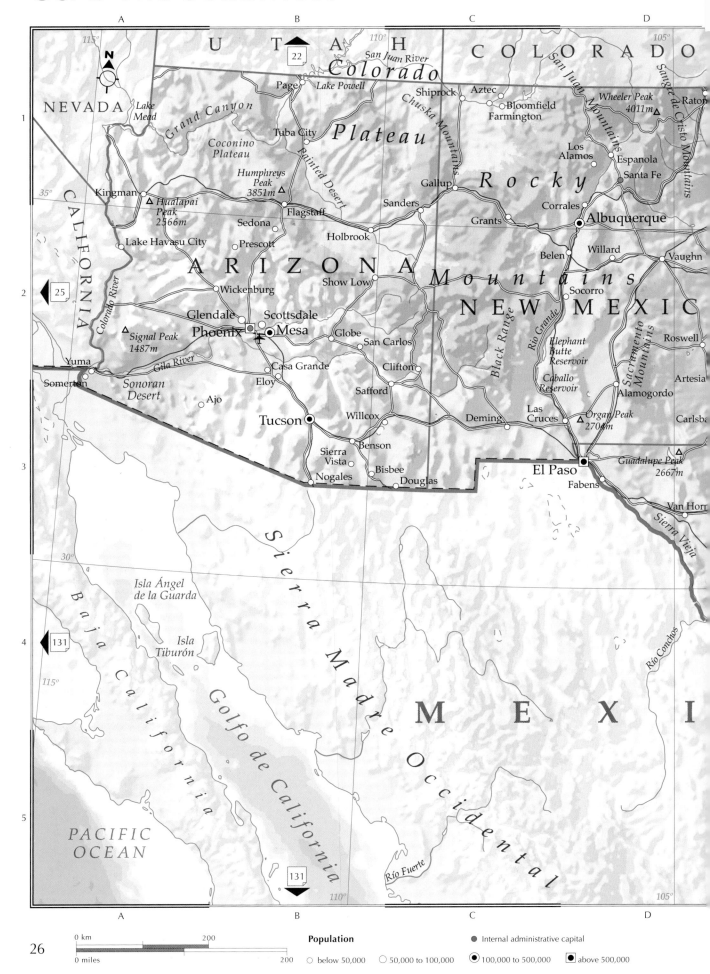

A

B

C

D

NEVADA

115°

UTAH

22

COLORADO

San Juan River

Colorado

Page

Lake Powell

Shiprock

Aztec

San Juan Mountains

Wheeler Peak 4011m △

Raton

Sangre de Cristo Mountains

105°

1

Lake Mead

Grand Canyon

Coconino Plateau

Tuba City

Plateau

Chuska Mountains

Bloomfield

Farmington

Los Alamos

Espanola

Santa Fe

Rocky

35°

Kingman

△ *Hualapai Peak 2566m*

Humphreys Peak 3851m △

Painted Desert

Flagstaff

Sedona

Gallup

Sanders

Grants

Corrales

Albuquerque

Lake Havasu City

Prescott

Holbrook

A R I Z O N A

Mountains

Belen

Willard

Vaughn

2

25

California

Colorado River

Wickenburg

Show Low

N E W   M E X I C

Socorro

Glendale

Phoenix

△ *Signal Peak 1487m*

Scottsdale

Mesa

Globe

San Carlos

Clifton

Black Range

Rio Grande

Elephant Butte Reservoir

Caballo Reservoir

Roswell

Sacramento Mountains

Yuma

Gila River

Casa Grande

Eloy

Safford

Artesia

Somerton

Sonoran Desert

Ajo

Tucson

Willcox

Deming

Las Cruces

Organ Peak 2704m △

Alamogordo

Carlsba

3

Sierra Vista

Benson

Bisbee

Nogales

Douglas

El Paso

Fabens

Guadalupe Peak 2667m △

30°

Van Horn

Sierra Madre Occidental

Sierra Vieja

Isla Ángel de la Guarda

4

131

115°

Isla Tiburón

M   E   X   I

Baja California

Río Conchos

5

PACIFIC OCEAN

Golfo de California

131

110°

Río Fuerte

105°

A

B

C

D

26

0 km   200

0 miles   200

Population

○ below 50,000

○ 50,000 to 100,000

◉ 100,000 to 500,000

◼ above 500,000

● Internal administrative capital

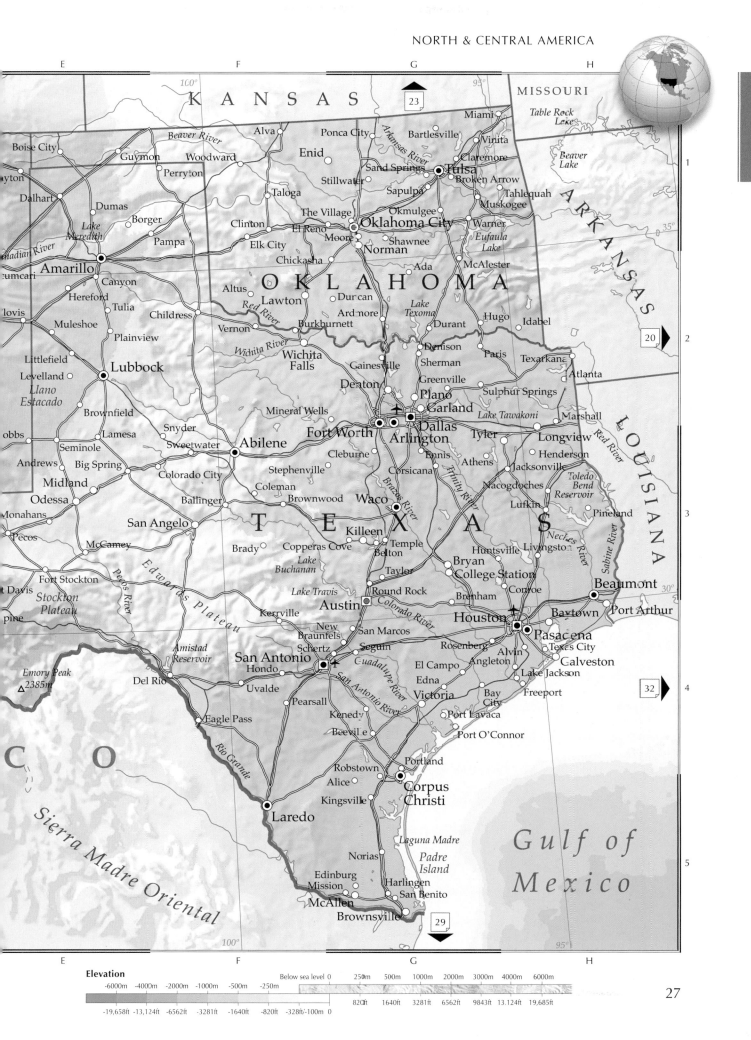

KANSAS

MISSOURI

Boise City
Guymon
Woodward
Perryton
dayton
Dalhart
Dumas
Borger
Pampa
adian River
Amarillo
Canyon
umcari
Hereford
Tulia
lovis
Muleshoe
Plainview
Littlefield
Levelland
Lubbock
Llano
Estacado
Brownfield
obbs
Lamesa
Snyder
Seminole
Sweetwater
Andrews
Big Spring
Midland
Colorado City
Odessa
Ballinger
Monahans
San Angelo
Pecos
McCamey
t Davis
Fort Stockton
Stockton
Plateau
pine
Emory Peak
△ 2385m

Alva
Ponca City
Bartlesville
Miami
Vinita
Enid
Sand Springs
Claremore
Stillwater
Tulsa
Broken Arrow
Taloga
Sapulpa
Tahlequah
The Village
Okmulgee
Muskogee
Clinton
Oklahoma City
Warner
El Reno
Moore
Shawnee
Eufaula
Lake
Elk City
Norman
Chickasha
Ada
McAlester
Altus
Lawton
Durcan
Hugo
Idabel
Red River
Ardmore
Lake
Texoma
Durant
Vernon
Burkburnett
Denison
Paris
Texarkana
Atlanta
Wichita River
Wichita
Falls
Gainesville
Sherman
Greenville
Denton
Sulphur Springs
Marshall
Mineral Wells
Plano
Garland
Lake Tawakoni
Fort Worth
Dallas
Arlington
Tyler
Longview
Cleburne
Ennis
Athens
Henderson
Stephenville
Corsicana
Jacksonville
Coleman
Nacogdoches
Brownwood
Waco
Lufkin
Pineland
Killeen
Huntsville
Livingston
Brady
Copperas Cove
Temple
Bryan
Beaumont
Lake
Buchanan
Belton
College Station
Conroe
Baytown
Port Arthur
Tayler
Brenham
Lake Travis
Round Rock
Houston
Kerrville
Austin
Pasadena
New
Braunfels
San Marcos
Rosenberg
Texas City
Schertz
Seguin
Alvin
Galveston
San Antonio
El Campo
Angleton
Lake Jackson
Hondo
Edna
Freeport
Uvalde
Victoria
Bay
City
Pearsall
Port Lavaca
Del Rio
Kenedy
Port O'Connor
Eagle Pass
Beeville
Robstown
Portland
Alice
Corpus
Christi
Kingsville
Laredo
Norias
Padre
Island
Edinburg
Mission
Harlingen
San Benito
McAllen
Brownsville

ARKANSAS
LOUISIANA
OKLAHOMA
TEXAS
Brazos River
Trinity River
Neches River
Sabine River
Toledo
Bend
Reservoir
Edwards Plateau
Pecos River
Amistad
Reservoir
Colorado River
Guadalupe River
San Antonio River
Rio Grande
Sierra Madre Oriental
Laguna Madre
Gulf of
Mexico
Beaver River
Arkansas River
Beaver
Lake
Table Rock
Lake
Lake
Meredith

CO
MEXICO

100°
95°
35°
30°
100°
95°

23
20
32
29

E   F   G   H
1
2
3
4
5

Elevation   Below sea level 0   250m   500m   1000m   2000m   3000m   4000m   6000m
-6000m -4000m -2000m -1000m -500m -250m

-19,658ft -13,124ft -6562ft -3281ft -1640ft -820ft -328ft/-100m 0   820ft   1640ft   3281ft   6562ft   9843ft   13,124ft   19,685ft

Mexico

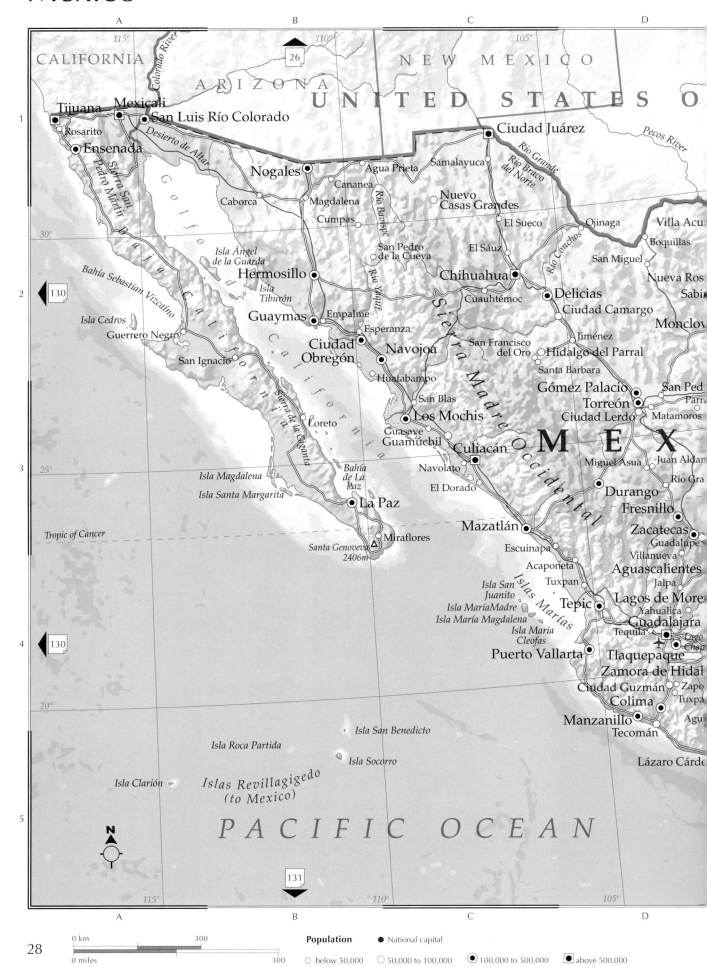

CALIFORNIA

ARIZONA

NEW MEXICO

UNITED STATES O

Colorado River

Pecos River

Tijuana
Mexicali
San Luis Río Colorado
Rosarito
Ensenada

Desierto de Altar

Ciudad Juárez

Rio Grande

Nogales
Agua Prieta
Samalayuca

Río Bravo
del Norte

Cananea
Caborca
Magdalena
Cumpas

Nuevo
Casas Grandes

El Sueco
Ojinaga
Villa Acu

Sierra San Pedro Mártir

Golfo

Isla Ángel
de la Guarda

San Pedro
de la Cueva

El Sáuz

Río Conchos

Boquillas

San Miguel

Bahía Sebastián Vizcaíno

Hermosillo

Isla
Tiburón

Río Yaqui

Chihuahua

Cuauhtémoc

Delicias
Ciudad Camargo

Nueva Ros

Sabi

Isla Cedros
Guerrero Negro

Guaymas
Empalme
Esperanza

San Francisco
del Oro

Jiménez
Hidalgo del Parral

Monclov

San Ignacio

Baja California

Ciudad
Obregón
Navojoa

Santa Barbara

Huatabampo

San Blas

Gómez Palacio
Torreón
Ciudad Lerdo

San Ped
Parr

Loreto

Los Mochis
Guasave
Guamúchil

Matamoros

M E X

Sierra de la Giganta

Culiacán

Sierra Madre Occidental

Miguel Asua
Juan Aldar

Isla Magdalena

Bahía
de La
Paz

Navolato

Río Gra

Isla Santa Margarita

El Dorado

Durango
Fresnillo

Tropic of Cancer

La Paz

Mazatlán

Zacatecas
Guadalupe

Santa Genoveva
2406m

Miraflores

Escuinapa

Villanueva

Acaponeta

Aguascalientes
Jalpa

Isla San
Juanito
Isla MaríaMadre
Isla María Magdalena

Tuxpan

Islas Marías

Tepic

Lagos de More
Xahualica

Isla María
Cleofas

Guadalajara
Tequila

Lago
Chap

Isla San Benedicto

Puerto Vallarta

Tlaquepaque
Zamora de Hidal

Isla Roca Partida

Ciudad Guzmán
Colima

Zapo
Tuxpa

Isla Socorro

Manzanillo
Tecomán

Agu

Isla Clarión

Islas Revillagigedo
(to Mexico)

Lázaro Cárde

PACIFIC OCEAN

N

28

0 km		300
0 miles		300

Population ● National capital

○ below 50,000   ◉ 50,000 to 100,000   ◉ 100,000 to 500,000   ▪ above 500,000

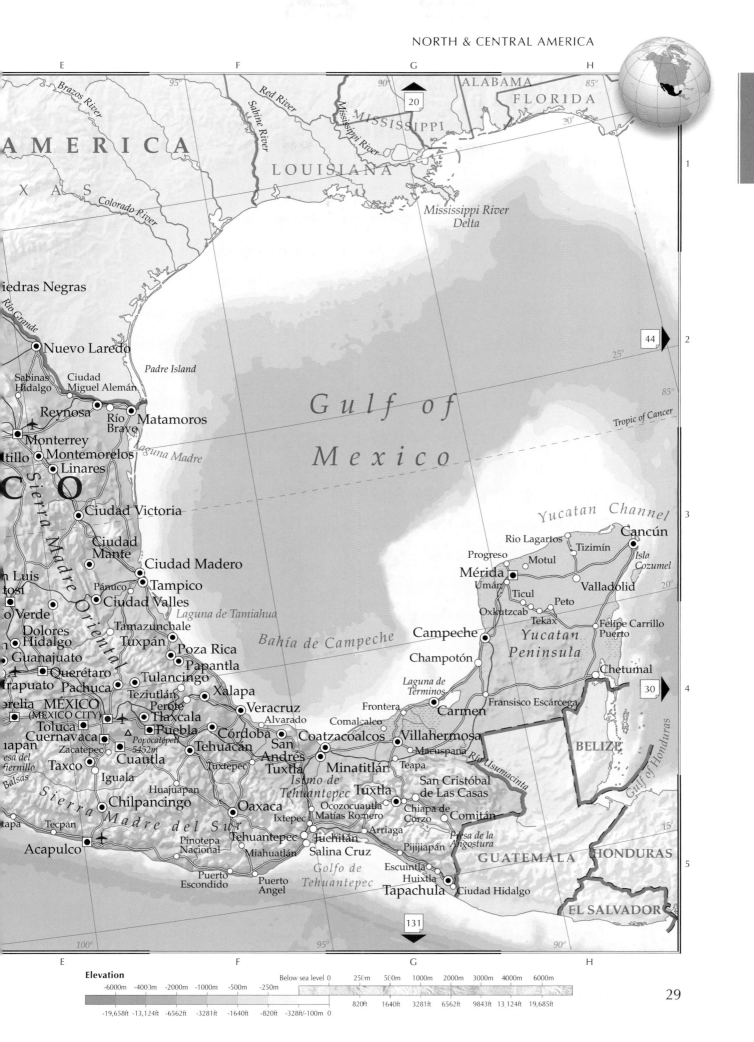

E   F   G   H

95°   90°   85°

ALABAMA

20

FLORIDA

MISSISSIPPI

1

Red River

Sabine River

LOUISIANA

Mississippi River

A M E R I C A

Brazos River

Colorado River

T E X A S

Mississippi River
Delta

iedras Negras

Rio Grande

44

2

25°

Nuevo Laredo

85°

Sabinas   Ciudad
Hidalgo   Miguel Alemán

Padre Island

Tropic of Cancer

G u l f   o f

Reynosa   Río
Bravo   Matamoros

M e x i c o

Monterrey

Laguna Madre

tillo   Montemorelos

Linares

C O

Yucatan Channel

3

Ciudad Victoria

Rio Lagartos   Tizimín   Cancún

Ciudad
Mante

Progreso   Motul   *Isla
Cozumel*

n Luis   Ciudad Madero

Mérida

tosí   Pánuco   Tampico

Umán   Ticul   Valladolid   20°

o Verde   Ciudad Valles

Laguna de Tamiahua

Peto

Dolores   Tamazunchale

Oxkutzcab   Tekax

Felipe Carrillo
Puerto

Hidalgo   Tuxpán

Bahía de Campeche   Campeche   *Yucatan*

Guanajuato   Poza Rica

Champotón   *Peninsula*

rapuato   Querétaro   Papantla

Chetumal

Pachuca   Tulancingo

*Laguna de
Términos*

30

4

relia   MÉXICO   Teziutlán   Xalapa

Fransisco Escárcega

Toluca   (MEXICO CITY)   Perote   Veracruz

Frontera   Carmen

Tlaxcala

Cuernavaca   Puebla   Alvarado   Comal-calco

Villahermosa

uapan   Zacatepec   Córdoba   Coatzacoalcos

BELIZE

esa del   △Popocatépetl   San   Macuspana

iernillo   Taxco   5452m   Tehuacán   Andrés   *Río Usumacinta*

Balsas   Iuxtepec   Tuxtla   Minatitlán   Teapa

Cuautla

Iguala   *Sierra*

Huajuapan   *Istmo de*   Tuxtla

Chilpancingo   *Tehuantepec*   San Cristóbal   *Gulf of Honduras*

M a d e r   d e l   S u r   Ocozocuautla   de Las Casas

Oaxaca   Matías Romero   Chiapa de   Comitán   15°

tapa   Tecpan   Ixtepec   Corzo

Arriaga   *Presa de la*   HONDURAS

Acapulco   Tehuantepec   Juchitán   Pijijiapán   *Angostura*   5

Pinotepa   Miahuatlán   Salina Cruz   Escuintla   GUATEMALA

Nacional   *Golfo de*   Huixtla

Puerto   Puerto   *Tehuantepec*   Tapachula   Ciudad Hidalgo

Escondido   Angel   EL SALVADOR

131

E   F   G   H

100°   95°   90°

Elevation

-6000m -4000m -2000m -1000m -500m -250m   Below sea level 0   250m   500m   1000m   2000m   3000m   4000m   6000m

-19,658ft -13,124ft -6562ft -3281ft -1640ft -820ft -328ft/-100m 0   820ft   1640ft   3281ft   6562ft   9843ft 13,124ft 19,685ft

Central America

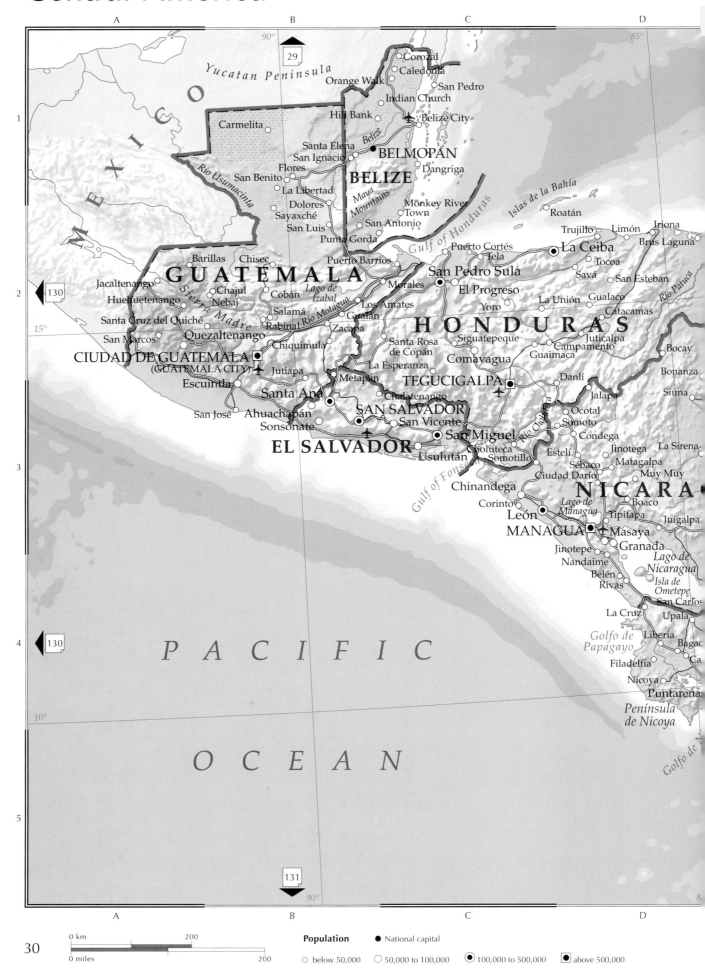

MEXICO

Yucatan Peninsula

Carmelita

Corozal
Caledonia
Orange Walk
San Pedro
Indian Church
Hill Bank
Belize City

Santa Elena
San Ignacio
Flores
BELMOPAN
Río Usumacinta
San Benito
BELIZE
Dangriga
La Libertad
Dolores
Maya Mountains
Monkey River Town
Sayaxché
San Antonio
San Luis
Punta Gorda
Roatán
Islas de la Bahía

Barillas   Chisec
Puerto Barrios
Gulf of Honduras
Trujillo   Limón   Iriona
Brus Laguna

GUATEMALA
Jacaltenango
Chajul
Cobán
Lago de Izabal
Puerto Cortés
Tela
La Ceiba
Tocoa
Sierra Madre
Nebaj
Salamá
Morales
San Pedro Sula
El Progreso
Savá
San Esteban
Huehuetenango
Río Motagua
Los Amates
Yoro
La Unión   Gualaco
Catacamas
Río Patuca
Santa Cruz del Quiché
Rabinal
Gualán
Zacapa
San Marcos
Quezaltenango
Chiquimula
HONDURAS
Siguatepeque   Campamento
Juticalpa
Bocay
Santa Rosa de Copán
Guaimaca
CIUDAD DE GUATEMALA
La Esperanza
Comayagua
Bonanza
(GUATEMALA CITY)   Jutiapa
Metapán
TEGUCIGALPA
Danlí
Siuna
Escuintla
Santa Ana
Chalatenango
Jalapa
San José
Ahuachapán
SAN SALVADOR
San Vicente
Ocotal
Sonsonate
San Miguel
Somoto
Condega
Río Choluteca
EL SALVADOR
Usulután
Choluteca
Estelí
Jinotega   La Sirena
Somotillo
Ciudad Darío
Sébaco   Matagalpa
Gulf of Fonseca
Chinandega
NICARA
Corinto
Lago de Managua
Boaco
Muy Muy
León
Tipitapa
Juigalpa
MANAGUA
Masaya
Jinotepe
Granada
Nandaime
Lago de Nicaragua
Belén
Rivas
Isla de Ometepe
La Cruz
San Carlos
Upala
Golfo de Papagayo
Liberia
Bagac
Filadelfia
Nicoya
Puntarena
Península de Nicoya

PACIFIC

OCEAN

0 km   200

0 miles   200

Population   ● National capital

○ below 50,000   ○ 50,000 to 100,000   ◉ 100,000 to 500,000   ◼ above 500,000

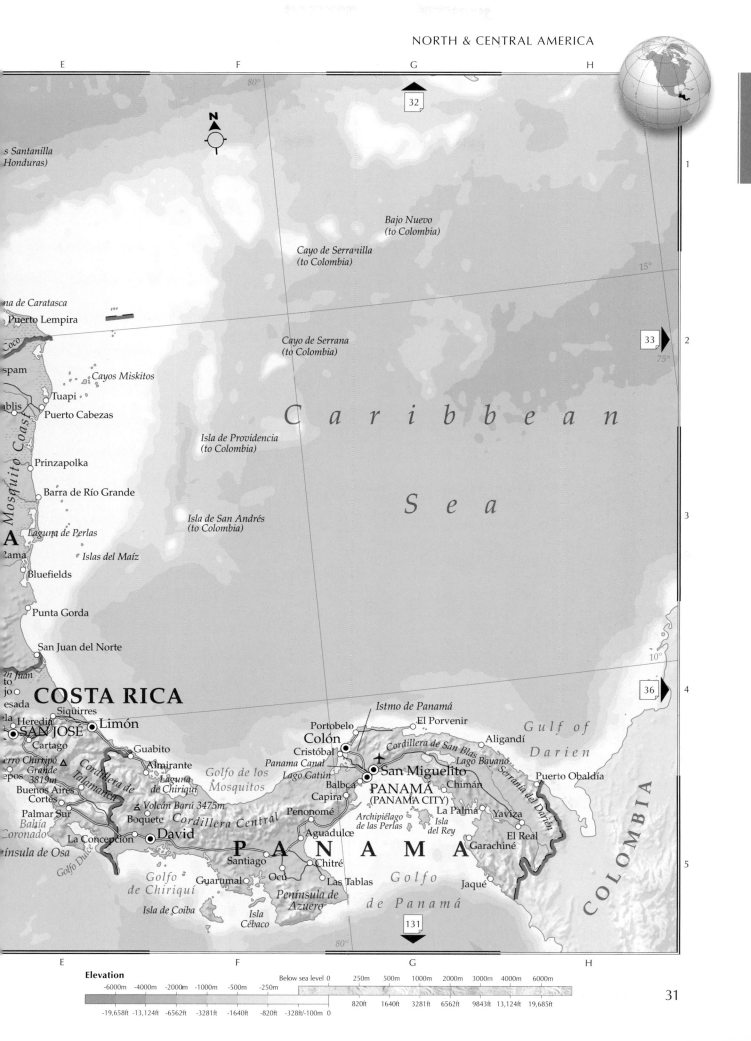

E   F   G   H

80°

32

N

s Santanilla
Honduras)

1

Bajo Nuevo
(to Colombia)

Cayo de Serranilla
(to Colombia)

15°

na de Caratasca

Puerto Lempira

33

2

Cayo de Serrana
(to Colombia)

75°

spam

Coco

Cayos Miskitos

Tuapi

ablis

Puerto Cabezas

C a r i b b e a n

Prinzapolka

Isla de Providencia
(to Colombia)

Barra de Río Grande

S e a

3

Laguna de Perlas

ama

Islas del Maíz

Bluefields

Isla de San Andrés
(to Colombia)

Punta Gorda

San Juan del Norte

10°

n Juan
to
jo

36

4

esada

COSTA RICA

Istmo de Panamá

Gulf of

la

Siquirres

El Porvenir

Heredia

Limón

Portobelo

Aligandí

Darien

SAN JOSÉ

Colón

Cordillera de San Blas

Cartago

Cristóbal

Puerto Obaldía

erro Chirripó

Guabito

Panama Canal

Lago Bayano

Grande

Almirante

Golfo de los

Capira

San Miguelito

Chimán

Serranía del Darién

3819m

pos

Laguna

Mosquitos

Lago Gatún

PANAMÁ

de Chiriquí

Balboa

(PANAMA CITY)

La Palma

Yaviza

Buenos Aires

Capira

Penonomé

Archipiélago

Cortés

Volcán Barú 3475m

de las Perlas

Isla

El Real

Palmar Sur

Boquete

Cordillera Central

Aguadulce

del Rey

Garachiné

Bahía

La Concepción

David

P A N A M A

Coronado

nsula de Osa

Santiago

Chitré

5

Golfo Dulce

Guarumal

Ocú

Jaqué

Golfo

Las Tablas

Golfo

de Chiriquí

Península de

de P a n a m á

Azuero

Isla de Coiba

Isla

Cébaco

131

C O L O M B I A

80°

E   F   G   H

Elevation

| | | | | | | Below sea level 0 | 250m | 500m | 1000m | 2000m | 3000m | 4000m | 6000m |

-6000m -4000m -2000m -1000m -500m -250m

-19,658ft -13,124ft -6562ft -3281ft -1640ft -820ft -328ft/-100m 0

820ft 1640ft 3281ft 6562ft 9843ft 13,124ft 19,685ft

The Caribbean

A   B   C   D

21

85° 80° 75°

Grand Bahama Island

Marsh Harbour

Freeport *Great Abaco*

UNITED STATES OF AMERICA

Bimini Islands

Northeast Providence Channel

1 25°

Gulf of Mexico

Berry Islands

Nicholls Town

NASSAU *Eleuthera Island*

New Providence Rock Sound

Florida Keys Andros Town *Cat Island*

Straits of Florida *Andros Island* *Exuma Cays* *Exuma Sound*

Tropic of Cancer *Cay Sal* *San Salvador*

THE BAHAMAS

LA HABANA (HAVANA) *Anguilla Cays* George Town *Rum Cay*

Guanabacoa *Great Exuma Island* *Long Island*

Artemisa Cárdenas *Archipiélago de Camagüey* Clarence Town *Crooked Island Passage* *Crooked Island*

Pinar del Río Matanzas Sagua la Grande *Crooked Island Passage* Mayagu

La Fé Consolación del Sur Santa Clara *Ragged Island Range* Acklins Island *Mayaguana Passage* *Caicos Passag*

2 Cienfuegos Placetas

Nueva Gerona *Cayo Largo* Morón *Little Inagua*

Isla de la Juventud Sancti Spíritus Ciego de Ávila Nuevitas *Lake Rosa*

Archipiélago de los Canarreos **CUBA** *Great Inag*

20° Camagüey Holguín Matthew Town

Archipiélago de los Jardines de la Reina Las Tunas Bayamo Guantánamo Cap Haïtie

Manzanillo Palma Soriano Santiago de Cuba Guantánamo Bay (to US) Gonaïves

Little Cayman *Cayman Brac* Jérémie PORT-AU-PRINCE HAÏ

GEORGE TOWN *Grand Cayman* **NAVASSA ISLAND** (to US) Cayes Jacm

CAYMAN ISLANDS (to UK)

3 Montego Bay

Spanish Town *Jamaica Channel*

Portmore KINGSTON

JAMAICA

Pedro Cays

30

Caribbean

HONDURAS

15°

30

JAMAICA

77°

Caribbean Sea

78°

Montego Bay Falmouth Discovery Bay St Ann's Bay

Lucea *The Cockpit Country* Ocho Rios

Cambridge Annotto Bay Buff Bay

Christiana Ewarton Port Antonio

Savanna-La-Mar Spanish Town *Blue Mountain Peak △ 2258m*

Mandeville Town KINGSTON

18° Black River May Pen Portmore

Old Harbour Morant Bay

Portland Bight

18°

N

Caribbean Sea

77°

0 km 20
0 miles 20

2000m/6562ft	
1000m/3281ft	
500m/1640ft	
200m/656ft	
Sea level	

4

NICARAGUA

5

COSTA RICA

85° 10°

31

80° 75°

COLOMBI

A   B   C   D

0 km 200
0 miles 200

Population ● National capital

○ below 50,000 ◎ 50,000 to 100,000 ◉ 100,000 to 500,000 ▣ above 500,000

St Lucia

Gros Islet
CASTRIES
Caribbean Sea
Anse La Raye
Dennery
Soufrière
△ Mount Gimie 950m
Micoud
Vieux Fort

14°00'
61°00'

500m/1640ft
200m/656ft
Sea level

0 km 10
0 miles 10

Barbados

ATLANTIC OCEAN

Speightstown
Mt Hillaby 340m △
Bathsheba
Holetown
Welchman Hall
BRIDGETOWN
The Crane
Oistins

200m/656ft
Sea level

13°10'
59°30'

0 km 10
0 miles 10

Tropic of Cancer

TKS
AICOS
NDS
CKBURN TOWN

ATLANTIC

OCEAN

Leeward Islands

DOMINICAN REPUBLIC
Puerto Plata
Santiago
San Francisco de Macorís
La Vega
La Romana
SANTO DMINGO
Isla Saona
Mona Passage
Isla Mona

SAN JUAN
Caguas
Ponce
Mayagüez
PUERTO RICO
(to US)

VIRGIN ISLANDS
(to US)
ROAD TOWN
CHARLOTTE AMALIE
St Croix

BRITISH VIRGIN ISLANDS
(to UK)

ANGUILLA
(to UK)
THE VALLEY
Sint Maarten
(to Netherlands)

Barbuda
ANTIGUA & BARBUDA
ST JOHN'S
Antigua

BASSETERRE
SAINT KITTS & NEVIS
BRADES
MONTSERRAT
(to UK)
Grande Terre
Pointe-à-Pitre
GUADELOUPE
(to France)
BASSE-TERRE
Basse-Terre
Marie-Galante

DOMINICA
ROSEAU
Martinique Passage

MARTINIQUE
(to France)
FORT-DE-FRANCE
St Lucia Channel

ST LUCIA
CASTRIES
Vieux Fort
Saint Vincent Passage

Saint Vincent
SAINT VINCENT & THE GRENADINES
KINGSTOWN
The Grenadines

GRENADA
ST GEORGE'S

BARBADOS
BRIDGETOWN

Windward Islands

tilles
Lesser Antilles
Sea
Lesser Antilles

ARUBA
(to Netherlands)
ORANJESTAD
CURAÇAO
(to Neth.)
BONAIRE
(to Neth.)
KRALENDIJK
WILLEMSTAD
Islas Los Roques
Isla La Orchila

Isla Blanquilla
Islas Los Testigos

Isla de Margarita
Isla La Tortuga

Tobago
TRINIDAD & TOBAGO
PORT-OF-SPAIN
Trinidad
San Fernando
Gulf of Paria

de Venezuela
VENEZUELA

70° 65° 10° 60° 10°

Elevation

					Below sea level 0	250 m	500m	1000m	2000m	3000m	4000m	6000m
-6000m	-4000m	-2000m	-1000m	-500m	-250m							
-19,658ft	-13,124ft	-6562ft	-3281ft	-1640ft	-820ft	-328ft/-100m 0	820f	1640ft	3281ft	6562ft	9843ft	13,124ft	19,685ft

South America

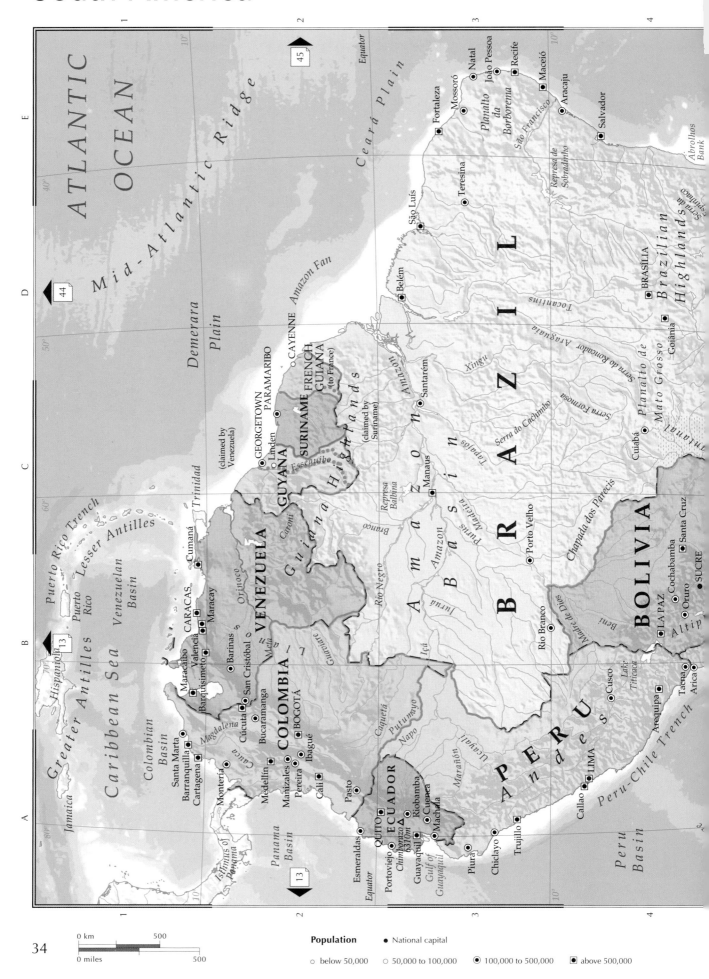

ATLANTIC OCEAN

Mid-Atlantic Ridge

Equator

Ceará Plain

Mossoró · Natal
João Pessoa
Recife
Maceió
Aracaju
Salvador

Fortaleza

Planalto da Borborena

São Francisco

Represa de Sobradinho

Abrolhos Bank

Teresina

São Luís

Belém

BRASÍLIA

Brazilian Highlands

Serra da Espinhaço

Demerara Plain

Amazon Fan

Tocantins

B R A Z I L

GEORGETOWN
PARAMARIBO
CAYENNE

SURINAME FRENCH GUIANA (to France)

(claimed by Venezuela)

Santarém

Amazon

Xingu

Serra do Cachimbo

Cuiabá

Planalto de Mato Grosso

Goiânia

Serra Formosa

Serra do Roncador

Araguaia

(claimed by Suriname)

Linden
GUYANA

Essequibo

G u i a n a   H i g h l a n d s

Manaus

Represa Balbina

Tapajós

Pantanal

Trinidad

Cumaná

Caroni

Orinoco

Rio Negro

Branco

A m a z o n   B a s i n

Madeira

Purus

Juruá

Iça

Porto Velho

Chapada dos Parecis

Rio Branco

BOLIVIA

Santa Cruz

Cochabamba

SUCRE

Oruro

Lesser Antilles

Puerto Rico Trench

Puerto Rico
Hispaniola

Venezuelan Basin

CARACAS
Maracay
Valencia

Barinas

San Cristóbal

VENEZUELA

Meta

Guaviare

Jamaica

Caribbean Sea

Colombian Basin

Santa Marta
Barranquilla
Cartagena

Maracaibo
Barquisimeto

Cúcuta
Bucaramanga

Magdalena

Cauca

Montería

Medellín
Manizales
Pereira
Cali

COLOMBIA
BOGOTÁ
Ibagué

Pasto

Caquetá

Putumayo

Napo

Marañón

LA PAZ

Lake Titicaca

Altiplano

Cusco

Arequipa

Tacna
Arica

P E R U

A n d e s

Beni

Madre de Dios

Ucayali

Iriavi

LIMA
Callao

Trujillo
Chiclayo

Piura

ECUADOR
QUITO
Chimborazo △ 6310m

Portoviejo
Riobamba
Cuenca
Machala
Guayaquil
Gulf of Guayaquil

Esmeraldas

Equator

Panama Basin

Isthmus of Panama

Peru-Chile Trench

Peru Basin

0 km   500
0 miles   500

Population   · National capital

○ below 50,000   ○ 50,000 to 100,000   ◉ 100,000 to 500,000   ■ above 500,000

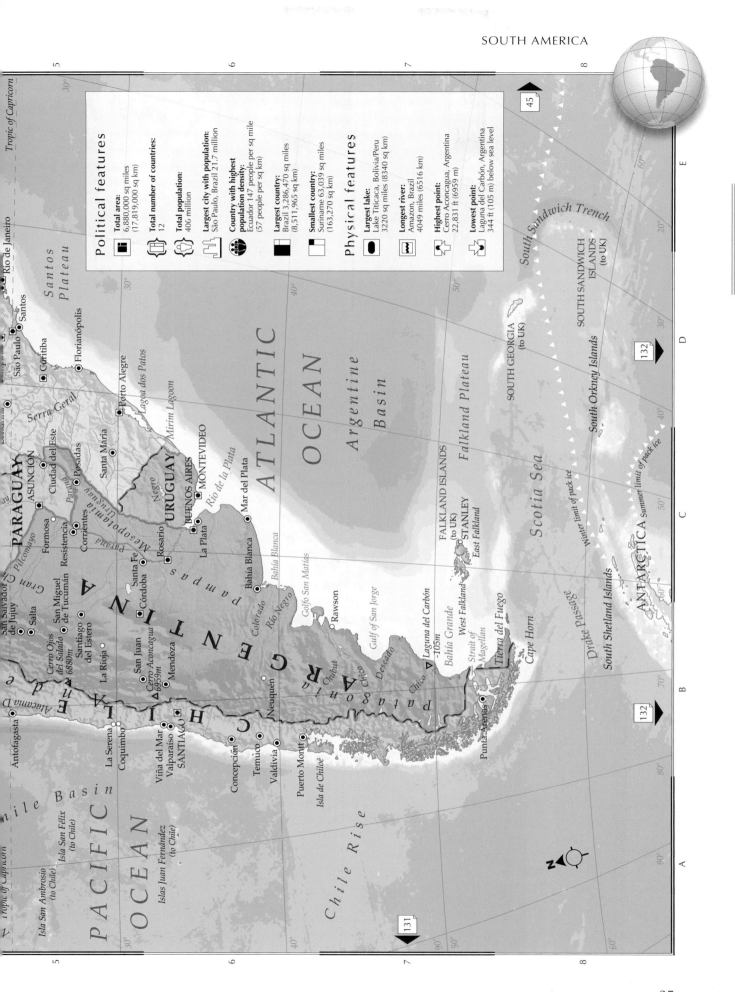

Political features

Total area:
6,680,000 sq miles
(17,819,000 sq km)

Total number of countries:
12

Total population:
406 million

Largest city with population:
São Paulo, Brazil 21.7 million

Country with highest population density:
Ecuador 147 people per sq mile
(57 people per sq km)

Largest country:
Brazil 3,286,470 sq miles
(8,511,965 sq km)

Smallest country:
Suriname 63,039 sq miles
(163,270 sq km)

Physical features

Largest lake:
Lake Titicaca, Bolivia/Peru
3220 sq miles (8340 sq km)

Longest river:
Amazon, Brazil
4049 miles (6516 km)

Highest point:
Cerro Aconcagua, Argentina
22,831 ft (6959 m)

Lowest point:
Laguna del Carbón, Argentina
344 ft (105 m) below sea level

Rio de Janeiro

Santos Plateau

Santos

São Paulo · Curitiba

Florianópolis

Serra Geral

Porto Alegre

Lagoa dos Patos

PARAGUAY

ASUNCIÓN

Ciudad del Este

Posadas

Santa Maria

Formosa

Resistencia · Corrientes

Paraná

Pilcomayo

Gran Chaco

San Salvador de Jujuy

Salta

Cerro Ojos del Salado 6880m

Santiago del Estero

Mesopotamia · Uruguay

Negro

URUGUAY

Mirim Lagoon

MONTEVIDEO

BUENOS AIRES

Río de la Plata

La Plata

Mar del Plata

Bahía Blanca

Bahía Blanca

Golfo San Matías

A T L A N T I C

O C E A N

Argentine Basin

San Salvador

Santa Fe

Córdoba

San Juan

Cerro Aconcagua 6959m

Mendoza

La Rioja

San Miguel de Tucumán

A R G E N T I N A

Pampas

Colorado

Río Negro

Neuquén

Rawson

Chubut

Chico

Chico

Desado

Gulf of San Jorge

Laguna del Carbón -105m

Bahía Grande

West Falkland

Strait of Magellan

Tierra del Fuego

Punta Arenas

Cape Horn

Drake Passage

South Shetland Islands

FALKLAND ISLANDS (to UK)

STANLEY

East Falkland

Falkland Plateau

SOUTH GEORGIA (to UK)

Scotia Sea

South Orkney Islands

SOUTH SANDWICH ISLANDS (to UK)

South Sandwich Trench

Winter limit of pack ice

Summer limit of pack ice

ANTARCTICA

Antofagasta

La Serena

Coquimbo

Viña del Mar

Valparaíso

SANTIAGO

Concepción

Temuco

Valdivia

Puerto Montt

Isla de Chiloé

C H I L E

A n d e s

Atacama

Chile Basin

Isla San Ambrosio (to Chile)

Isla San Félix (to Chile)

Islas Juan Fernández (to Chile)

P A C I F I C

O C E A N

Chile Rise

Tropic of Capricorn

131

132

132

45

35

Northern South America

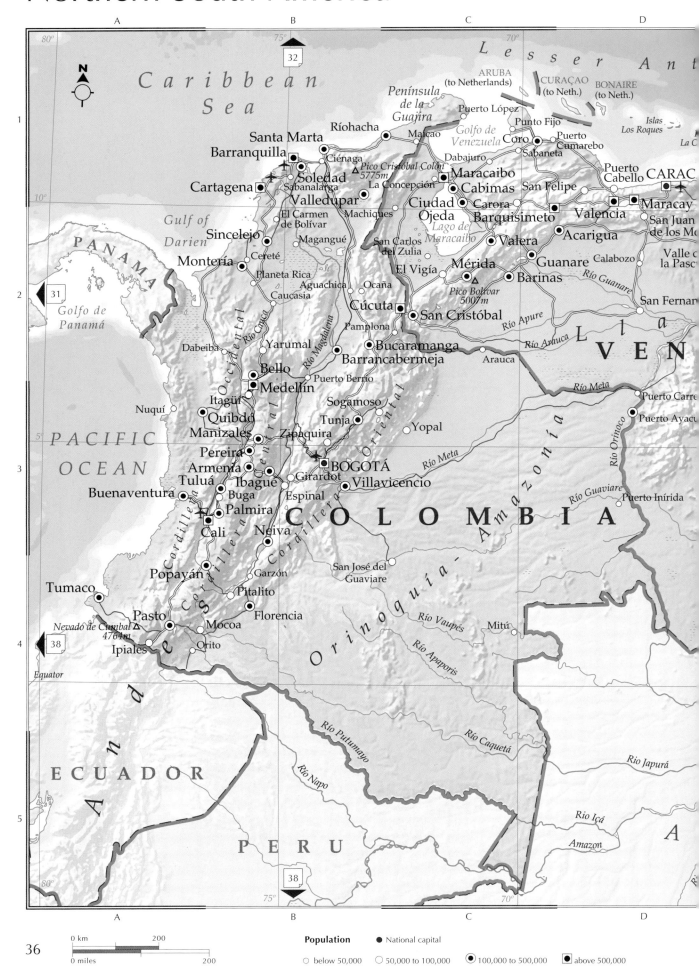

Caribbean Sea

PANAMA

Golfo de Panamá

PACIFIC OCEAN

ECUADOR

PERU

Lesser Ant

ARUBA (to Netherlands)
CURAÇAO (to Neth.)
BONAIRE (to Neth.)
Islas Los Roques

Península de la Guajira

Golfo de Venezuela

Lago de Maracaibo

Gulf of Darien

Cities and places:

Puerto López
Ríohacha
Santa Marta
Barranquilla
Ciénaga
Maicao
Coro
Puerto Cumarebo
Sabaneta
Puerto Cabello
CARAC
Punto Fijo
Dabajuro
Soledad
Cartagena
Sabanalarga
La Concepción
Maracaibo
Cabimas
San Felipe
Maracay
Valledupar
El Carmen de Bolívar
Machiques
Ciudad Ojeda
Carora
Barquisimeto
Valencia
San Juan de los Mo
Sincelejo
Magangué
San Carlos del Zulia
Valera
Acarigua
Monteria
Cereté
El Vigía
Mérida
Guanare
Calabozo
Valle de la Pasc
Planeta Rica
Aguachica
Ocaña
Pico Bolívar 5007m
Barinas
Caucasia
Dabeiba
Yarumal
Cúcuta
Pamplona
San Cristóbal
Río Apure
San Fernan
Bello
Bucaramanga
Arauca
Puerto Carre
Medellín
Puerto Berrío
Barrancabermeja
Río Meta
Puerto Ayacu
Itagüí
Sogamoso
Nuquí
Quibdó
Tunja
Manizales
Zipaquira
Yopal
Pereira
Armenia
BOGOTÁ
Villavicencio
Río Meta
Tuluá
Ibagué
Girardot
Puerto Inírida
Buenaventura
Buga
Espinal
Río Guaviare
Palmira
Cali
Neiva
COLOMBIA
Popayán
Garzón
San José del Guaviare
Tumaco
Pitalito
Río Vaupés
Mitú
Pasto
Mocoa
Florencia
Nevado de Cumbal 4764m
Orito
Río Apaporis
Ipiales
Río Putumayo
Río Caquetá

Pico Cristóbal Colón 5775m

Cordillera Occidental
Cordillera Central
Cordillera Oriental
Río Cauca
Río Magdalena

Orinoquía-Amazonía

L l a
V E N

Río Guanare
Río Arauca
Río Orinoco

A n d e s
Cordillera de

Equator

Río Napo
Río Putumayo

Orinoquía-

Río Japurá
Río Içá
Amazon

0 km 200
0 miles 200

Population ● National capital
○ below 50,000   ○ 50,000 to 100,000   ◉ 100,000 to 500,000   ■ above 500,000

A   B   C   D

E   F   G   H

60°   55°

33

SAINT VINCENT &
THE GRENADINES

BARBADOS

GRENADA

Isla Blanquilla

*Isla de
Margarita*

Islas Los Testigos

Tobago

1

tuga
La Asunción
rlamar
ná
Carúpano
Cariaco
Güiria
*Gulf of
Paria*
TRINIDAD &
TOBAGO

Trinidad

A T L A N T I C

10°

Puerto La Cruz
Barcelona
San Mateo
Maturín
The Serpent's Mouth
Anaco
Cantaura
za
El Tigre
Tucupita

O C E A N

Río Orinoco
Ciudad Guayana
Upata

S
Ciudad
Bolívar

Embalse de Guri

45

2

U E L A
El Callao

Matthews
Ridge
Charity

El Dorado

Spring Garden
Parika
Aurora
GEORGETOWN
New
Amsterdam

Río Paragua

Peters Mine
Bartica

PARAMARIBO
Nieuw Amsterdam

Totness

Chyuni River
Rockstone

Kamarang
Linden
Nieuw
Nickerie
St-Laurent-du-Maroni
Sinnamary
Kourou

Río Caroní

*Salto
Angel*

Orealla
Apoera
Kaaimanston
5°

Mount Roraima
2810m
GUYANA
Kurupukari
*W. J. van
Blommesteinmeer*

CAYENNE

3

Pakaraima Mountains

Essequibo River
SURINAME

*Juliana Top
1230m*
Grand-
Santi
*Montagnes
de la Trinité*
*Montagne
Tortue*
Ouanary

a
Orinoco

(Venezuela claims all
of Guyana west of
Essequibo River)

Lethem

Courantyne River

FRENCH
GUIANA
(to France)

St-Georges

Camop

Highlands

Tumuc-Humac Mountains

(claimed by
Suriname)

Acarai Mountains

Amazon

(claimed by
Suriname)

4

Orinoco

Rio Negro

Equator

Amazon

B   R   A   Z   I   L

zon   *Basin*

5

Amazon

Amazon

Rio Purus
Rio Tapajós

40

60°   55°

E   F   G   H

Elevation

Below sea level 0   250m   500m   1000m   2000m   3000m   4000m   6000m

-6000m   -4000m   -2000m   -1000m   -500m   -250m

-19,658ft -13,124ft -6562ft -3281ft -1640ft -820ft -328ft -100m 0   820ft   1640ft   3281ft   6562ft   9843ft   13,124ft   19,685ft

Western South America

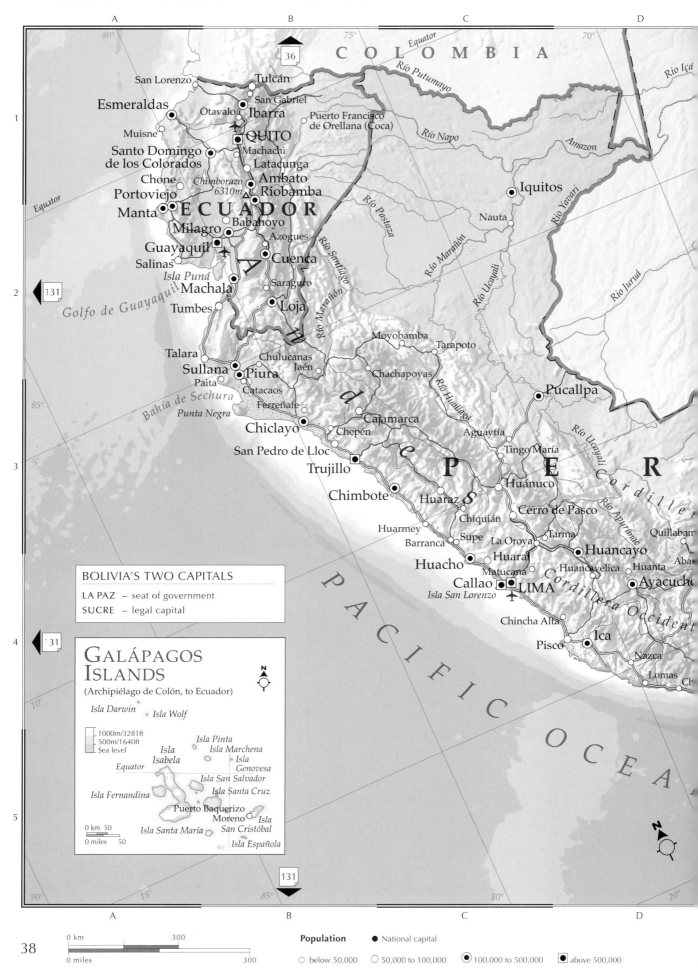

COLOMBIA

Equator

San Lorenzo
Tulcán
Esmeraldas
San Gabriel
Otavalo
Ibarra
Muisne
QUITO
Machachi
Santo Domingo
de los Colorados
Latacunga
Chone
Chimborazo
6310m
Ambato
Riobamba
Portoviejo
Manta
ECUADOR
Babahoyo
Milagro
Azogues
Guayaquil
Cuenca
Salinas
Isla Puná
Saraguro
Machala
Tumbes
Loja

Río Putumayo

Puerto Francisco
de Orellana (Coca)
Río Napo

Amazon
Iquitos
Nauta
Río Pastaza

Río Santiago
Río Marañón

Río Ulcayali

Río Yavari

Río Juruá

Moyobamba
Tarapoto

Talara
Sullana
Chulucanas
Jaén
Paita
Piura
Catacaos
Chachapoyas
Pucallpa
Río Huallaga

Ferreñafe
Punta Negra
Bahía de Sechura
Cajamarca
Aguaytía
Río Ucayali
Chiclayo
Chepén
San Pedro de Lloc
Tingo María
Trujillo
Huánuco
PER
Chimbote
Huaraz
Chiquián
Cerro de Pasco
Quillaban
Huarmey
Tarma
Huancayo
Aba
Barranca
Supe
La Oroya
Huaral
Huancavelica
Huanta
Matucana
Ayacucho
Huacho
Callao
LIMA
Isla San Lorenzo
Cordillera Occident

Chincha Alta
Pisco
Ica
Nazca
Lomas

Golfo de Guayaquil

PACIFIC OCEAN

BOLIVIA'S TWO CAPITALS

LA PAZ — seat of government
SUCRE — legal capital

GALÁPAGOS ISLANDS

(Archipiélago de Colón, to Ecuador)

N

Isla Darwin
Isla Wolf

1000m/3281ft
500m/1640ft
Sea level

Isla Pinta
Isla Marchena
Isla
Isabela
Isla
Genovesa
Equator
Isla San Salvador
Isla Fernandina
Isla Santa Cruz
Puerto Baquerizo
Moreno
Isla
San Cristóbal
Isla Santa María
Isla Española

0 km 50
0 miles 50

N

38

0 km 300
0 miles 300

Population   ● National capital

○ below 50,000   ○ 50,000 to 100,000   ◉ 100,000 to 500,000   ◼ above 500,000

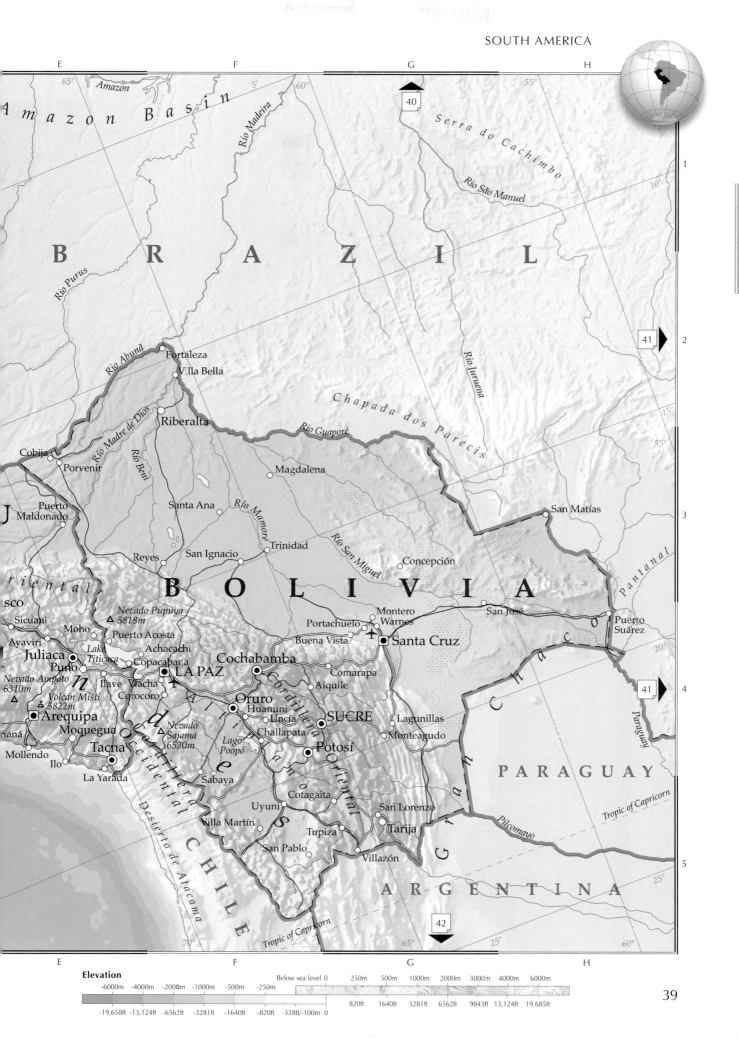

E   F   G   H

65°   5°   60°   55°

Amazon

A m a z o n   B a s i n

Rio Madeira

Serra do Cachimbo

40

Rio São Manuel

10°

1

B   R   A   Z   I   L

Rio Purus

Rio Juruena

41   2

15°

Chapada dos Parecis

Rio Abunã

Fortaleza
Villa Bella

Rio Madre de Dios

Riberalta

Rio Guaporé

55°

Cobija
Porvenir

Magdalena

Rio Beni

San Matías

J

Puerto
Maldonado

Santa Ana

Rio Mamoré

Pantanal   3

Reyes

San Ignacio

Trinidad

Rio San Miguel

Concepción

Oriental

sco

B   O   L   I   V   I   A

Sicuani

Nevado Pupuya
△ 5818m

Montero
Warnes

San José

Puerto
Suárez

Moho

Puerto Acosta

Portachuelo

Ayaviri

Achacachi

Buena Vista

Santa Cruz

20°

Juliaca

Lake
Titicaca

Copacabana

Cochabamba

Puno

LA PAZ

Comarapa

Nevado Ampato
6310m
△

Ilave   Viacha

Corocoro

Aiquile

Volcán Misti
△ 5822m

Oruro

Huanuni

SUCRE

Lagunillas

C h a c o

41   4

Arequipa

Uncía

Challapata

Monteagudo

Paraguay

Moquegua

Nevado
Sajama
6520m

Lago
Poopó

Potosí

Mollendo

Ilo

Tacna

Sabaya

G r a n

P   A   R   A   G   U   A   Y

La Yarada

Cotagaita

Villa Martín

Uyuni

San Lorenzo

Pilcomayo

Tropic of Capricorn

San Pablo

Tupiza

Tarija

25°

Occidental

Desierto de Atacama

C   H   I   L   E

Villazón

5

A   R   G   E   N   T   I   N   A

25°

60°

Tropic of Capricorn

42

70°   65°   60°

E   F   G   H

Elevation

Below sea level 0   250m   500m   1000m   2000m   3000m   6000m

-6000m   -4000m   -2000m   -1000m   -500m   -250m

-19,658ft   -13,124ft   -6562ft   -3281ft   -1640ft   -820ft   -328ft/-100m 0

820ft   1640ft   3281ft   6562ft   9843ft   13,124ft   19,685ft

39

Brazil

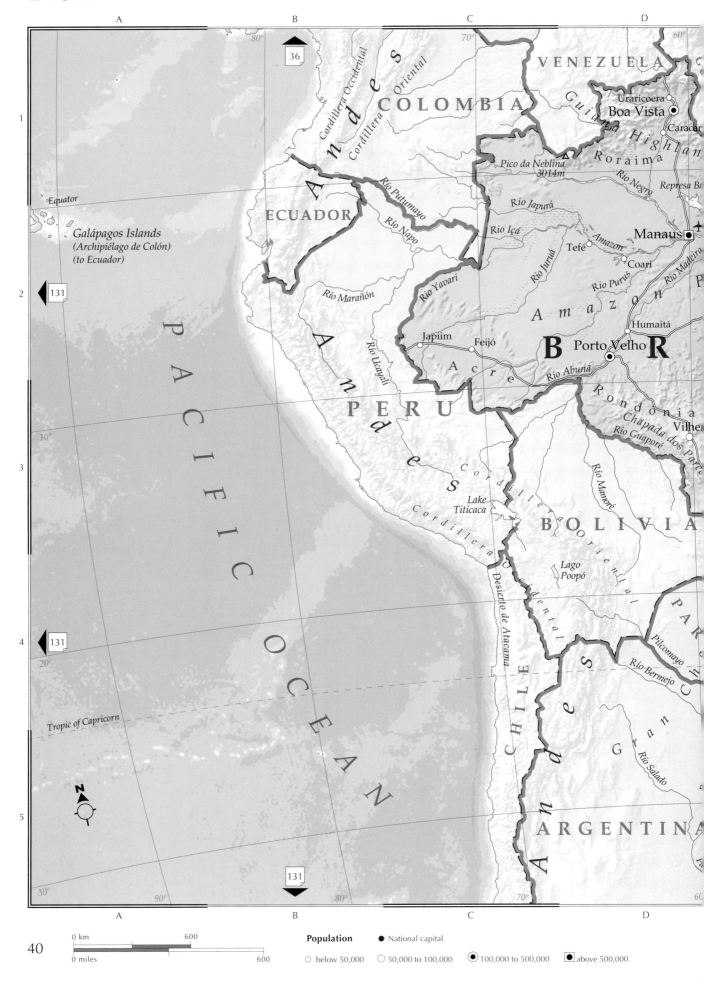

80° 70° 60°

36

VENEZUELA

COLOMBIA

Uraricoera
Boa Vista
Caracar

Cordillera Occidental

Cordillera Oriental

Guiana Highlan

Roraima

Pico da Neblina
3014m

ECUADOR

Río Putumayo

Río Napo

Río Negro

Represa B

Rio Japurá

Rio Içá

Manaus

Galápagos Islands
(Archipiélago de Colón)
(to Ecuador)

Tefé

Amazon

Coari

Río Madeira

Río Marañón

Río Yavari

Rio Iuruá

Río Purus

131

Humaitá

A   n   d   e   s

Japiim

Feijó

Porto Velho

B

R

Acre

Rio Abuná

Rondônia

P

A N D E S

Río Ucayali

10°

Chapada dos Pare

Río Guaporé

Vilhe

PERU

Cordillera

Río Mamoré

Cordillera

Lake
Titicaca

BOLIVIA

Cordillera Occidental

Lago
Poopó

P A C I F I C   O C E A N

Desierto de Atacama

131

20°

Pilcomayo

Río Bermejo

PAR

Tropic of Capricorn

A N D E S

Río Salado

G

N

Rio Salado

N

ARGENTINA

131

30° 90° 80° 70° 60°

0 km   600
0 miles   600

Population   ● National capital

○ below 50,000   ○ 50,000 to 100,000   ◉ 100,000 to 500,000   ◼ above 500,000

ATLANTIC OCEAN

SURINAME

FRENCH GUIANA (to France)

Tumuc-Humac Mountains

Mouths of the Amazon

Amapá
Macapá
Ilha Caviana de Fora
Ilha de Marajó
Baía de Marajó
Belém
Baía de São Marcos

Alenquer
Amazon
Santarém
Altamira
Itaituba
Rio Xingu
Marabá
Pará
Maranhão
Imperatriz

São Luís
Parnaíba
Camocim
Bacabal
Piripiri
Teresina
Floriano
Carolina
Balsas
Picos

Fortaleza
Ceará
Mossoró
Assu
Atol das Rocas
San Fernando de Noronha (to Brazil)
Cabo de São Roque
Natal
Rio Grande do Norte
Juazeiro do Norte
João Pessoa
Campina Grande
Paraíba
Pernambuco
Alagoas
Recife
Maceió

BRAZIL

Serra do Cachimbo

Serra Formosa

Mato Grosso

Rio Araguaia

Rio Tocantins

Palmas do Tocantins
Tocantins
Taguatinga
Goiás

Represa de Tucuruí

Represa de Sobradinho

Rio São Francisco

Chapada Diamantina

Juazeiro
Aracaju
Estância
Feira de Santana
Salvador
Baía de Todos os Santos

Cuiabá
Anápolis
BRASÍLIA
Central
Goiânia
Jataí
Planalto
Minas Gerais
Araguari

Jananba
Montes Claros
Araçuai
Vitória da Conquista
Canavieiras
Itabuna

ndonópolis

Mato Grosso do Sul

Campo Grande
Aquidauana

Uberlândia
Uberaba

Governador Valadares
Espírito Santo

Ribeirão Preto
esidente Prudente
Marília
São Paulo
Juiz de Fora
Belo Horizonte
Divinópolis
Vitória
Campos dos Goytacazes

Londrina
Maringá
São Paulo
Campinas
Nova Iguaçu
Rio de Janeiro
Santos

Paraná
Represa de Itaipú
Saltos do Rio Iguaçu
Iguaçu
Ponta Grossa
Curitiba
Joinville
Blumenau
Florianópolis
Santa Catarina

Rio Grande
Passo Fundo
nta Maria
do Sul
Canoas
Porto Alegre
Bagé
Lagoa dos Patos
Rio Negro
Rio Grande
Mirim Lagoon

URUGUAY

ATLANTIC OCEAN

Equator
Tropic of Capricorn

50° 40° 30°

Elevation

						Below sea level 0	250m	500m	1000m	2000m	3000m	4000m	6000m
-6000m	-4000m	-2000m	-1000m	-500m	-250m								
-19,658ft	-13,124ft	-6562ft	-3281ft	-1640ft	-820ft	-328ft/-100m 0	820ft	1640ft	3281ft	6562ft	983ft	13,124ft	19,685ft

Southern South America

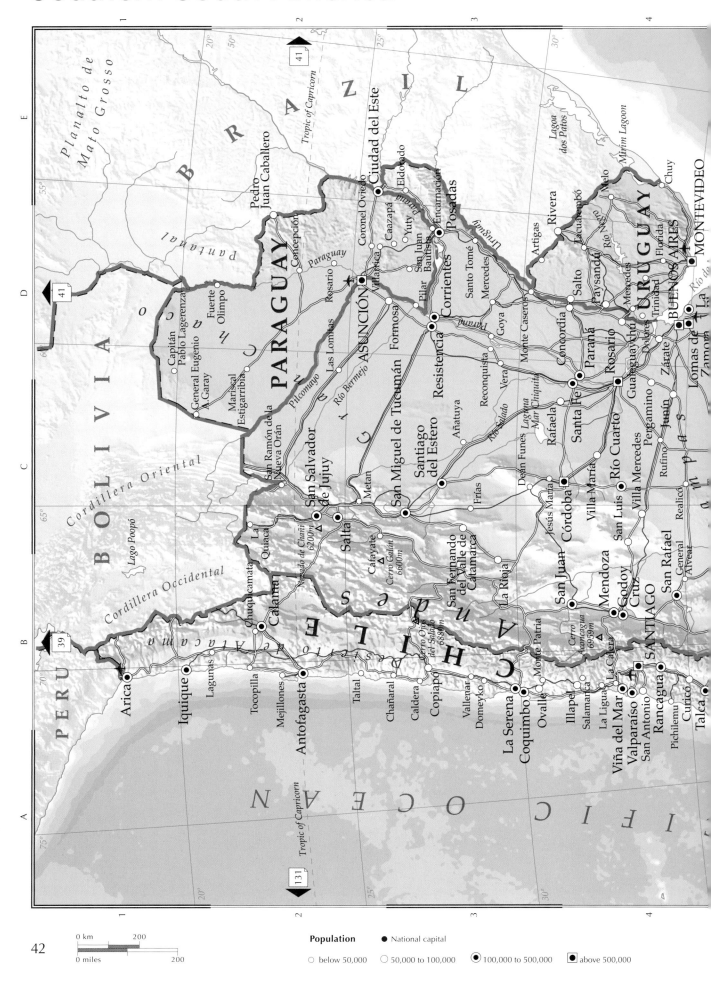

Planalto de Mato Grosso

B R A Z I L

Tropic of Capricorn

BOLIVIA

PARAGUAY

Pedro Juan Caballero
Concepción
Capitán Pablo Lagerenza
Fuerte Olimpo
General Eugenio A.Garay
Mariscal Estigarribia
San Ramón de la Nueva Orán

Cordillera Oriental
Lago Poopó
Cordillera Occidental

PERU

Arica
Iquique
Lagunas
Tocopilla
Mejillones
Antofagasta
Taltal
Chañaral
Caldera
Copiapó
Vallenar
Domeyko
La Serena
Coquimbo
Ovalle
Illapel
Salamanca
La Ligua
Viña del Mar
Valparaíso
San Antonio
Rancagua
Pichilemu
Curicó
Talca

Chuquicamata
Calama

San Salvador de Jujuy
La Quiaca
Nevado de Chañi 6200m
Salta
Cafayate
Cerro Galán 6600m
Metan

San Miguel de Tucumán
Santiago del Estero
Añatuya
Frías

CHILE
Desierto de Atacama
Cerro Ojos del Salado 6886m
Cerro Aconcagua 6959m
Monte Patria
SANTIAGO

San Fernando del Valle de Catamarca
La Rioja
Deán Funes
Jesús María
Córdoba
Villa María
Río Cuarto
Villa Mercedes
Pergamino
Rufino
Realicó
General Alvear
San Rafael
Mendoza
Godoy Cruz
San Juan
San Luis
Junín

A N D E S

Laguna Mar Chiquita
Rafaela
Santa Fe
Paraná
Rosario
Zárate
Lomas de Zamora
BUENOS AIRES
La

Ciudad del Este
Eldorado
Coronel Oviedo
Caazapá
Yuty
San Juan Bautista
Villarrica
Pilar
ASUNCIÓN
Formosa
Resistencia
Corrientes
Goya
Reconquista
Vera
Río Salado

Encarnación
Posadas
Santo Tomé
Mercedes
Monte Caseros
Concordia
Paysandú
Dolores
Gualeguaychú

Artigas
Rivera
Salto
Mercedes
Trinidad
Florida

URUGUAY
Melo
Tacuarembó
Chuy
MONTEVIDEO

Lagoa dos Patos
Mirim Lagoon

Río Uruguay
Paraguay
Pilcomayo
Río Bermejo
Paraná
Río de la Plata

Tropic of Capricorn

P A C I F I C   O C E A N

41
131
39

Population   ● National capital

0 km 200   0 miles 200

○ below 50,000   ◎ 50,000 to 100,000   ◉ 100,000 to 500,000   ■ above 500,000

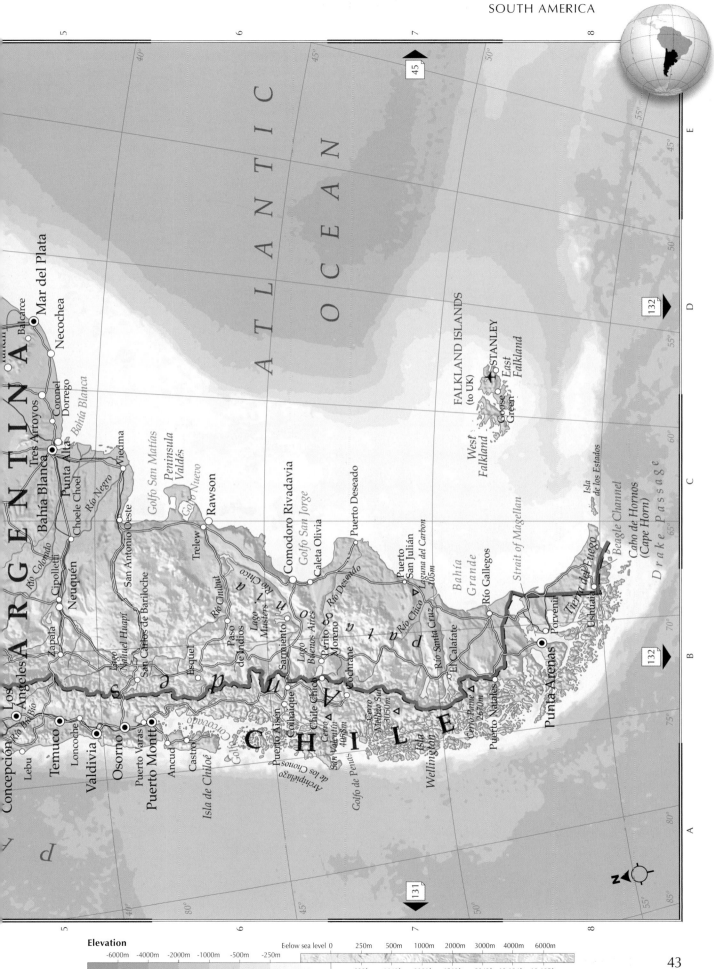

132

132

131

A T L A N T I C

O C E A N

ARGENTINA

Mar del Plata
Balcarce
Necochea
Coronel
Dorrego
Tres Arroyos
Punta Alta
Bahía Blanca
Viedma
Choele Choel
Río Negro
Bahía Blanca
San Antonio Oeste
Golfo San Matías
Península
Valdés
Golfo Nuevo
Rawson
Río Colorado
Cipolletti
Neuquén
Zapala
Trelew
Río Chubut
San Carlos de Bariloche
Lago
Nahuel Huapí
Paso
de Indios
Lago
Musters
Comodoro Rivadavia
Golfo San Jorge
Caleta Olivia
Puerto Deseado
Río Deseado
Río Chico
Sarmiento
Lago
Buenos Aires
Perito
Moreno
Río Chico
Puerto
San Julián
Laguna del Carbón
-105m
Bahía
Grande
Río Santa Cruz
Río Gallegos
El Calafate
Puerto Natales
Strait of Magellan
Punta Arenas
Porvenir
Tierra del Fuego
Ushuaia
Beagle Channel
Cabo de Hornos
(Cape Horn)
Isla
de los Estados
Drake Passage

FALKLAND ISLANDS
(to UK)
STANLEY
East
Falkland
Goose
Green
West
Falkland

Concepción
Los
Angeles
Río Bío Bío
Lebu
Temuco
Loncoche
Valdivia
Osorno
Puerto Varas
Puerto Montt
Ancud
Castro
Isla de Chiloé
Golfo
Corcovado
Archipiélago
de los Chonos
Golfo de Penas
Isla
Wellington
Isla
Wellington
Puerto Aisén
Coihaique
Chile Chico
Cerro
San Valentín
4058m
Cochrane
Cerro Melimoyu Sur
3050m
CHILE
Cerro Payne
1670m
Esquel

CHILE

Elevation

| -6000m | -4000m | -2000m | -1000m | -500m | -250m | | Below sea level 0 | 250m | 500m | 1000m | 2000m | 3000m | 4000m | 6000m |

-19,658ft -13,124ft -6552ft -3281ft -1640ft -820ft -328ft/-100m 0   820ft 1640ft 3281ft 6562ft 9843ft 13,124ft 19,685 t

The Atlantic Ocean

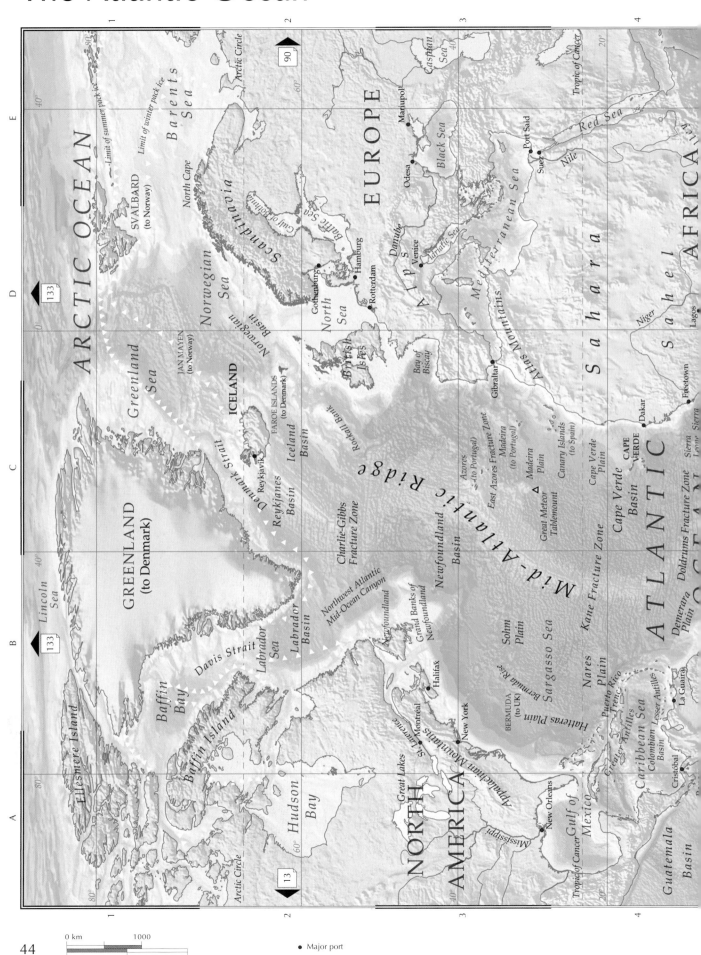

ARCTIC OCEAN

Limit of summer pack ice
Limit of winter pack ice

Barents Sea

SVALBARD (to Norway)

North Cape

Scandinavia

Gulf of Bothnia

Baltic Sea

EUROPE

Mariupol
Black Sea
Caspian Sea
Odesa
Red Sea
Port Said
Suez
Nile

AFRICA

Danube
Venice
Adriatic Sea
Alps
Mediterranean Sea
Atlas Mountains
Gibraltar

Hamburg
Rotterdam
Gothenburg
North Sea
British Isles

Bay of Biscay

Rockall Bank

Norwegian Sea
Norwegian Basin

JAN MAYEN (to Norway)
ICELAND
FAROE ISLANDS (to Denmark)

Greenland Sea
Denmark Strait
Reykjanes Basin
Reykjavik
Iceland Basin

Sahara
Sahel

Niger
Lagos

Azores (to Portugal)
East Azores Fracture Zone
Madeira (to Portugal)
Madeira Plain
Canary Islands (to Spain)
Great Meteor Tablemount

Dakar
Freetown
Sierra Leone
Sierra

Cape Verde Plain
Cape Verde Basin
CAPE VERDE

GREENLAND (to Denmark)

Charlie-Gibbs Fracture Zone

Mid-Atlantic Ridge

Northwest Atlantic Mid-Ocean Canyon

Newfoundland
Grand Banks of Newfoundland
Newfoundland Basin

Labrador Sea
Labrador Basin

Davis Strait

Baffin Bay

Baffin Island

Lincoln Sea

Ellesmere Island

Hudson Bay

Great Lakes

St. Lawrence
Appalachian Mountains
Montreal
New York

Halifax

Sohm Plain

Sargasso Sea

Bermuda Rise
BERMUDA (to UK)
Hatteras Plain

Nares Plain

Kane Fracture Zone

Doldrums Fracture Zone

ATLANTIC OCEAN

Demerara Plain

Puerto Rico Trench
Greater Antilles
Lesser Antilles
Caribbean Sea
Colombian Basin
La Guaira
Cristobal

NORTH AMERICA

Mississippi
New Orleans
Gulf of Mexico
Tropic of Cancer

Guatemala Basin

Arctic Circle

Major port

0 km   1000
0 miles   1000

44

90
133
133
13

Arctic Circle
Tropic of Cancer

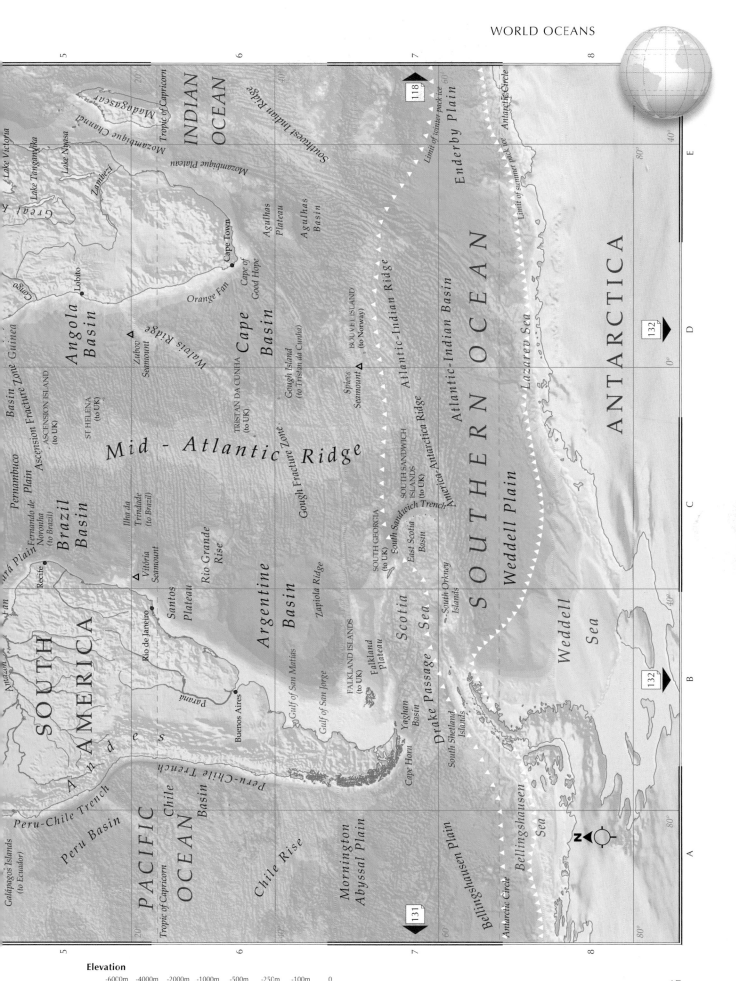

INDIAN OCEAN

Madagascar

Tropic of Capricorn

Mozambique Channel

Lake Victoria

Lake Tanganyika

Lake Nyasa

Zambezi

Great

Mozambique Plateau

Southwest Indian Ridge

Congo

Lobito

Angola Basin

Basin Fracture Zone Guinea

Ascension Fracture Zone

ASCENSION ISLAND
(to UK)

ST HELENA
(to UK)

Orange Fan

Cape Town

Cape of Good Hope

Zubov Seamount

Walvis Ridge

Cape Basin

Agulhas Plateau

Agulhas Basin

TRISTAN DA CUNHA
(to UK)

Gough Island
(to Tristan da Cunha)

BOUVET ISLAND
(to Norway)

Spiess Seamount

Atlantic-Indian Ridge

Enderby Plain

Limit of winter pack ice

Antarctic Circle

Limit of summer pack ice

Lazarev Sea

Atlantic-Indian Basin

SOUTHERN OCEAN

ANTARCTICA

Mid - Atlantic Ridge

Pernambuco

Fernando de Noronha
(to Brazil)

Brazil Basin

Ilha da Trindade
(to Brazil)

Vitória Seamount

Rio Grande Rise

Santos Plateau

Rio de Janeiro

Argentine Basin

Zapiola Ridge

Gulf of San Matias

Gulf of San Jorge

Gough Fracture Zone

SOUTH GEORGIA
(to UK)

South Sandwich Trench

SOUTH SANDWICH ISLANDS
(to UK)

America-Antarctica Ridge

East Scotia Basin

Scotia Sea

South Orkney Islands

Weddell Plain

Weddell Sea

SOUTH AMERICA

Andes

Recife

Amazon

Paraná

Buenos Aires

FALKLAND ISLANDS
(to UK)

Falkland Plateau

Yaghan Basin

Cape Horn

Drake Passage

South Shetland Islands

Bellingshausen Plain

Bellingshausen Sea

Antarctic Circle

PACIFIC OCEAN

Tropic of Capricorn

Galápagos Islands
(to Ecuador)

Peru-Chile Trench

Peru Basin

Chile Basin

Chile Rise

Mornington Abyssal Plain

Peru-Chile Trench

131

118

132

132

20°

40°

40°

80°

60°

80°

0°

40°

80°

5

6

7

8

20°

60°

80°

Elevation

-6000m	-4000m	-2000m	-1000m	-500m	-250m	-100m	0
-19,658ft	-13,124ft	-6562ft	-3281ft	-1640ft	-820ft	-328ft/-100m	0

Africa

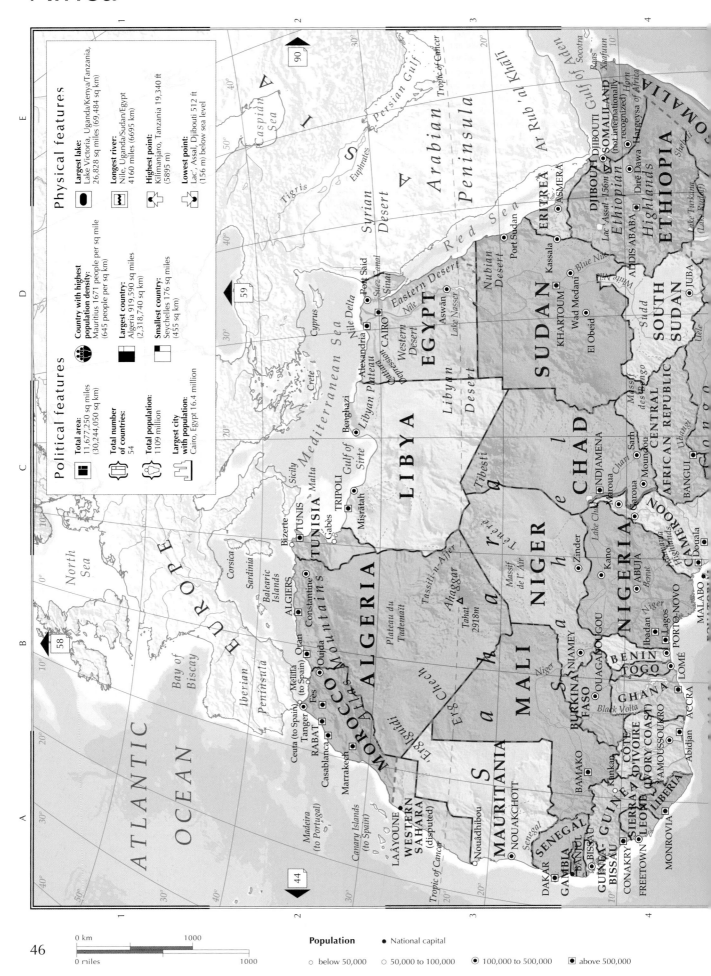

Political features

Total area:
11,677,250 sq miles
(30,244,050 sq km)

**Total number
of countries:**
54

Total population:
1109 million

**Largest city
with population:**
Cairo, Egypt 16.4 million

**Country with highest
population density:**
Mauritius 1671 people per sq mile
(645 people per sq km)

Largest country:
Algeria 919,590 sq miles
(2,318,740 sq km)

Smallest country:
Seychelles 176 sq miles
(455 sq km)

Physical features

Largest lake:
Lake Victoria, Uganda/Kenya/Tanzania,
26,828 sq miles (69,484 sq km)

Longest river:
Nile, Uganda/Sudan/Egypt
4160 miles (6695 km)

Highest point:
Kilimanjaro, Tanzania 19,340 ft
(5895 m)

Lowest point:
Lac' Assal, Djibouti 512 ft
(156 m below sea level

Population   • National capital

○ below 50,000   ◎ 50,000 to 100,000   ◉ 100,000 to 500,000   ■ above 500,000

0 km   1000

0 miles   1000

Northwest Africa

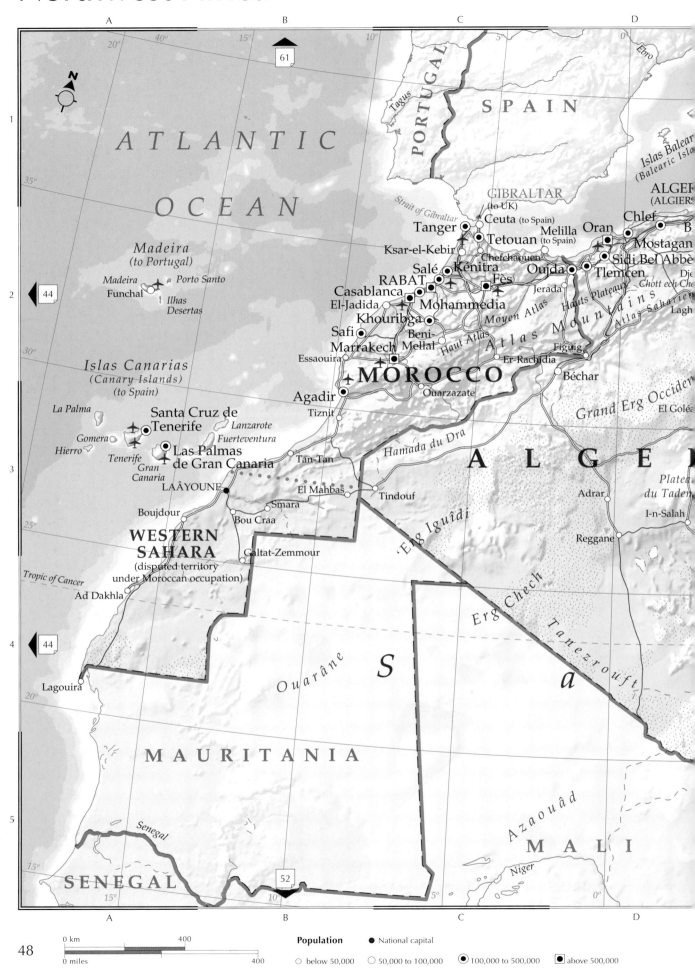

ATLANTIC

OCEAN

SPAIN

PORTUGAL

Tagus

Ebro

Islas Baleare
(Balearic Isla

GIBRALTAR
(to UK)

ALGER
(ALGIERS

Strait of Gibraltar

Ceuta (to Spain)

Chlef

Tanger

Oran

B

Tetouan

Melilla
(to Spain)

Mostagan

Ksar-el-Kebir

Chefchaouen

Sidi Bel Abbè

Madeira
(to Portugal)

Salé

Kenitra

Oujda

Tlemcen

Dje

Madeira

Porto Santo

RABAT

Fès

Funchal

Ilhas
Desertas

Casablanca

Jerada

Hauts Plateaux

Chott ech Che

El-Jadida

Mohammedia

Moyen Atlas

Atlas Saharie

Lagh

Khouribga

Beni-

Safi

Mellal

Figuig

Islas Canarias
(Canary Islands)
(to Spain)

Marrakech

Haut Atlas

Atlas Mountains

Essaouira

Er-Rachidia

Béchar

La Palma

MOROCCO

Ouarzazate

Grand Erg Occider

El Golé

Agadir

Santa Cruz de
Tenerife

Lanzarote

Tiznit

Gomera

Fuerteventura

A L G E R

Hierro

Las Palmas
de Gran Canaria

Tenerife

Gran
Canaria

Tan-Tan

Hamada du Dra

Platea
du Tade

LAÂYOUNE

El Mahbas

Tindouf

Adrar

Boujdour

Smara

I-n-Salah

Bou Craa

Erg Iguîdi

WESTERN
SAHARA
(disputed territory
under Moroccan occupation)

Galtat-Zemmour

Reggane

Tropic of Cancer

Ad Dakhla

Erg Chech

Tanezrouft

Lagouira

S

Ouarâne

a

M A U R I T A N I A

Azaouâd

M A L I

Senegal

Niger

S E N E G A L

Population
● National capital
○ below 50,000
◉ 50,000 to 100,000
⦿ 100,000 to 500,000
▪ above 500,000

0 km   400
0 miles   400

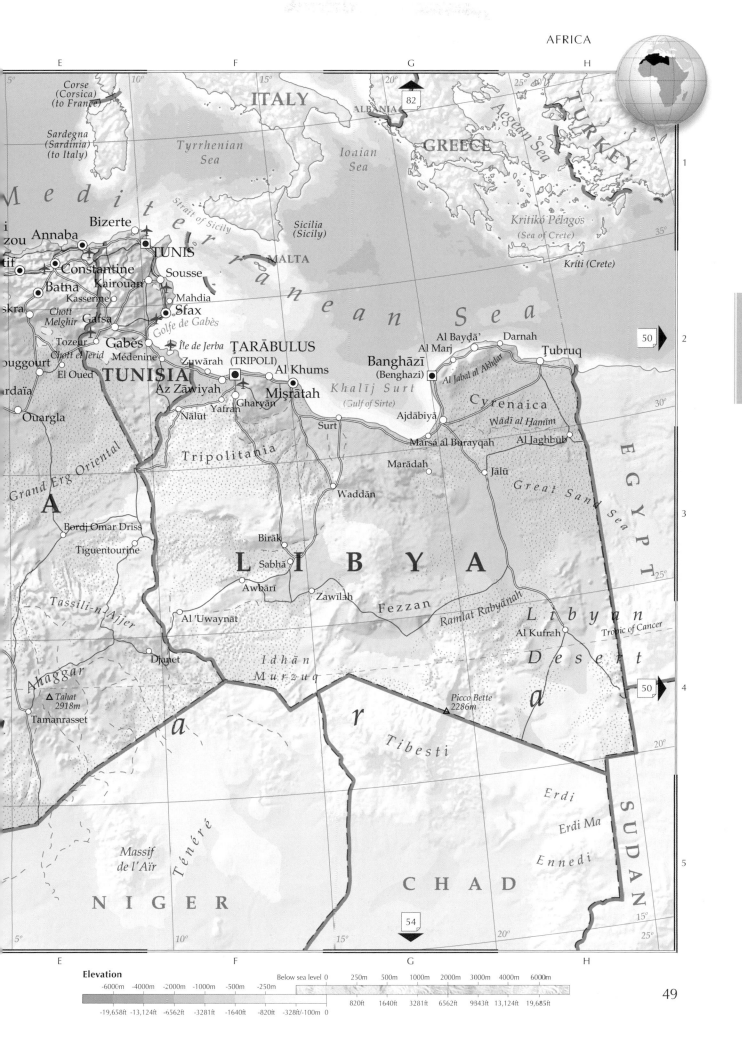

Elevation

-6000m	-4000m	-2000m	-1000m	-500m	-250m	Below sea level 0	250m	500m	1000m	2000m	3000m	4000m	6000m

-19,658ft -13,124ft -6562ft -3281ft -1640ft -820ft -328ft/-100m 0

820ft 1640ft 3281ft 6562ft 9843ft 13,124ft 19,685ft

Northeast Africa

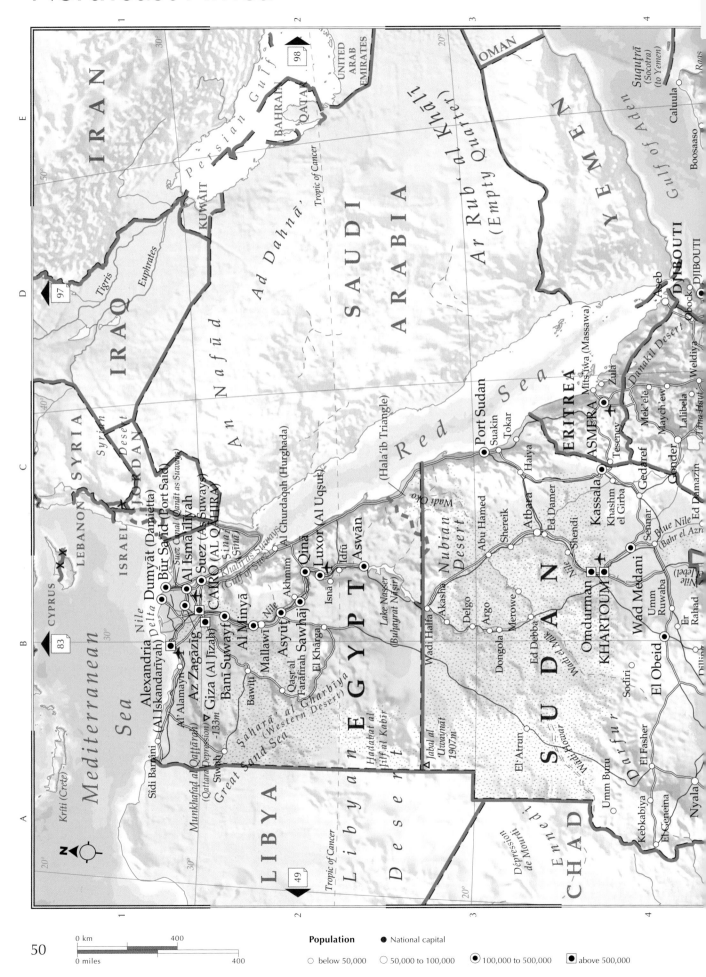

0 km   400

0 miles   400

Population   ● National capital

○ below 50,000   ○ 50,000 to 100,000   ◉ 100,000 to 500,000   ◼ above 500,000

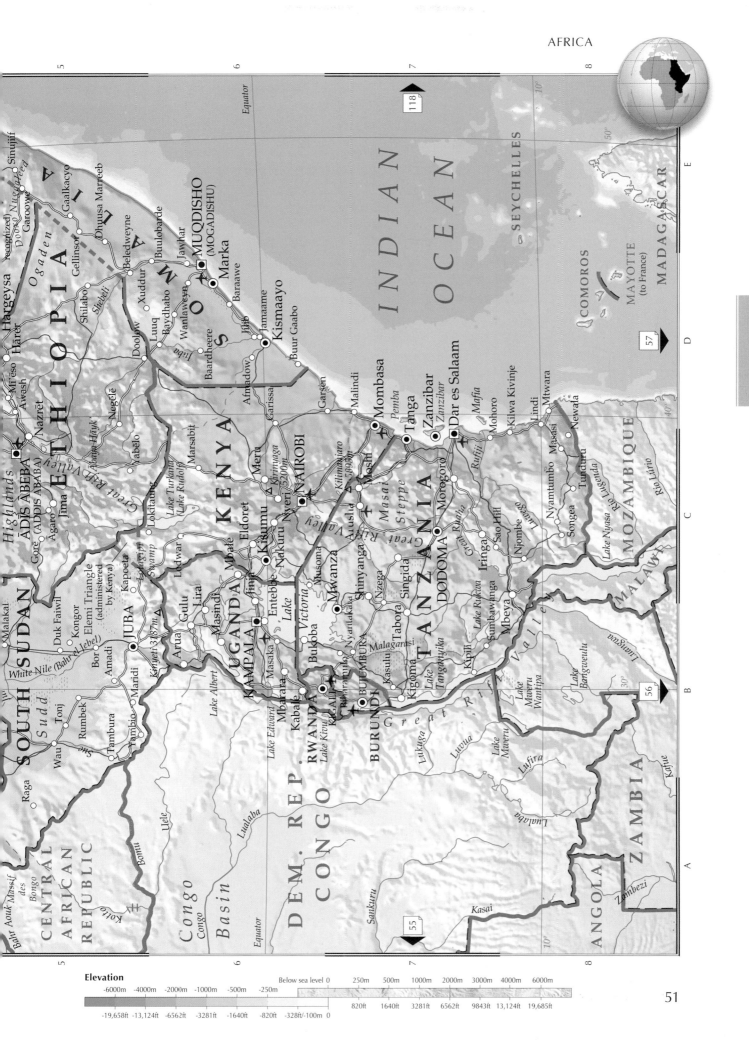

INDIAN

OCEAN

SEYCHELLES

COMOROS

MAYOTTE
(to France)

MADAGASCAR

Sinujiif

Doxo Nugaaleed

Garoowe

Gaalkacyo

Ogaden

Dhuusa Marreeb

SOMALIA

(not fully recognized)

Hargeysa

Harēr

Mi'ēso

Awash

Nazrēt

ĀDĪS ĀBEBA
(ADDIS ABABA)

ETHIOPIA

Highlands

Gorē

Agaro

Jīma

Negēlē

Yabelo

Abaya Hāyk'

Shilabo

Shebeli

Beledweyne

Buulobarde

Jawhar

MUQDISHO
(MOGADISHU)

Marka

Baraawe

Gellinsor

Xuddur

Baydhabo

Wanlaweyn

Doolow

Luuq

Baardheere

Jubba

Afmadow

Jilib

Jamaame

Kismaayo

Buur Gaabo

Garissa

Garsen

Malindi

Mombasa

Pemba

Tanga

Zanzibar
Zanzibar

Dar es Salaam

Mafia

Mohoro

Kilwa Kivinje

Lindi

Mtwara

Newala

Masasi

Tundura

Songea

Nyamtumbo

Njombe

Sao Hill

MOZAMBIQUE

MALAWI

Lake Nyasa

Rio Lúrio

Rio Lugenda

KENYA

Meru

Marsabit

Lake Turkana
(Lake Rudolf)

Lokitaung

Lodwar

Sagan

Sudd Swamp

Kapoeta

JUBA

Kenyetti 31870m △

Elemi Triangle
(administered
by Kenya)

Eldoret

Kisumu

Nakuru

Nyeri

NAIROBI

*Kirinyaga
5200m*

Kilimanjaro
5895m

Moshi

Arusha

*Masai
Steppe*

Mbale

Jinja

Entebbe

KAMPALA

UGANDA

Masaka

Lake
Victoria

Bukoba

Mwanza

Shinyanga

Nzega

Musoma

Nyahururu

Tabora

Singida

DODOMA

Morogoro

Rufiji

Ruaha

Iringa

Mbeya

Lake Rukwa

Sumbawanga

Kipili

TANZANIA

Kigoma

Kasulu

*Lake
Tanganyika*

Mpanda

Malagarasi

BUJUMBURA

BURUNDI

KIGALI

RWANDA

Kabale

Lake Kivu

Lukuga

Luvua

Great Rift Valley

Great Rift Valley

Lake Mweru

*Lake Mweru
Wantipa*

*Lake
Bangweulu*

Luapula

Lufira

ZAMBIA

ANGOLA

Zambezi

Kafue

Kasai

Sankuru

DEM. REP.
CONGO

Congo Basin

Lualaba

Lualaba

Congo

Equator

SOUTH
SUDAN

Malakal

Sudd

White Nile (Bahr el Jebel)

Bor

Duk Faiwil

Kongor

Amadi

Maridi

Tambura

Yambio

Ezo

Raga

Wau

Tonj

Rumbek

Sobat

CENTRAL
AFRICAN
REPUBLIC

Bahr Aouk

*Massif
des
Bongo*

Uele

Bomu

Kotto

Gulu

Lira

Arua

Masindi

Mbarara

Kabale

Lake Edward

Lake Albert

Mbale

Maralal

Nyahururu

Elevation

Below sea level 0   250m   500m   1000m   2000m   3000m   4000m   6000m

-6000m -4000m -2000m -1000m -500m -250m

-19,658ft -13,124ft -6562ft -3281ft -1640ft -820ft -328ft/-100m 0

820ft   1640ft   3281ft   6562ft   9843ft   13,124ft   19,685ft

118

57

56

55

Equator

West Africa

25°   20°   15°   10°

44

N

44

Tropic of Cancer

25°

20°

ATLANTIC

WESTERN SAHARA
(disputed territory
under Moroccan occupation)

'Aïn Ben Tili
Bîr Mogreïn

'Erg Iguîdi

Kâghet
El Hamk

Fdérik   Zouérat
Touâjîl

Ouarâne

S

Nouâdhibou

Choûm

Akchâr

Atâr   Chinguetti

El Mreyyé

**CAPE
VERDE**

Ilhas de Barlavento

Santo Antão
Mindelo
São
Vicente
São
Nicolau
Pedra Lume
Sal
Boa Vista

Santiago
Fogo
PRAIA
Maio

Ilhas de Sotavento

Akjoujt

MAURITANIA

Tîchît

Idîni
NOUAKCHOTT
Boutilimit
Tidjikja
Boûmdeïd
Oualâta

Rkîz
Magta'
Lahjar
Aoukâr

Rosso
Aleg
Tâmchekket
'Ayoûn el 'Atroûs
Néma
Amourj
Richard Toll
Dagana
Senegal
Kaédi
Kiffa

Saint Louis
Timbedgha
Bassikou

Louga
Matam
Sélibabi
Kobenni

Mékhé
Thiès   Mbaké
SENEGAL
Nioro
Ténenko

DAKAR
Mbour
Diourbel
Kayes
S
Kolokani

Sokone
Kaolack
Koulikoro
Ségou

BANJUL **GAMBIA**
Tambacounda
Toukoto
Kita

Bignona
Kolda
Gambia
Bafing
BAMAKO
Kouti
Ziguinchor
Sédhiou
Bafata

BISSAU
Gaoual

**GUINEA-
BISSAU**
Boké
Labé
Dinguiraye
Tikinsso
Siguiri
Bougouni
Sik

G U I N E A
Pita
Mamou
Kankan
Odienné
Ferkessédo

Kindia
Faranah
Tengréla

CONAKRY
Tokounou
Boundiali
Kor
Makeni
Kissidougou
**CÔTE
D'IVOIRE**
Beyla

**SIERRA
LEONE**
Katiola
FREETOWN
Bo
Nzérékoré
IVORY COAST
Kenema
Gbanga
Danané
YAMOUSSOUKRO
Gagnoa
Tubmanburg
MONROVIA
Harbel
Zwedru
Divo
Buchanan
LIBERIA
Sassan
Harper
San-Pédro

A T L A N T I C

O C E A N

0 km	400
0 miles	400

Population   ● National capital

○ below 50,000   ○ 50,000 to 100,000   ◉ 100,000 to 500,000   ◼ above 500,000

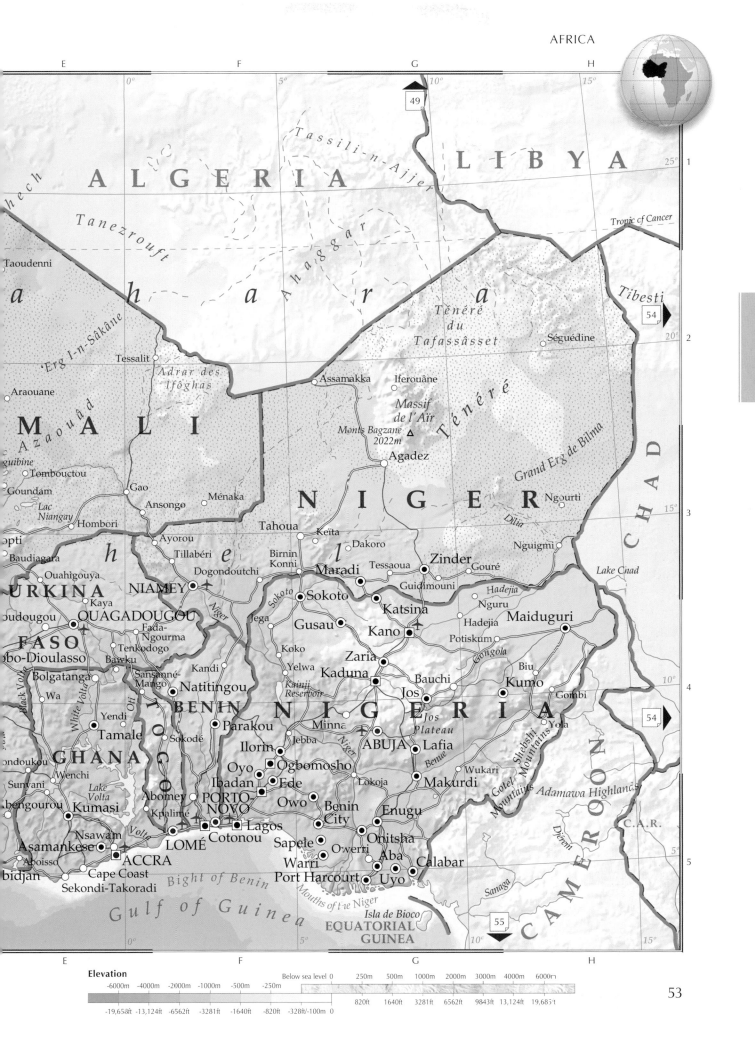

E   F   G   H

ALGERIA   LIBYA

Tassili-n-Ajjer

25°   1

Tanezrouft

Tropic of Cancer

Taoudenni

a   h   a   r   a

Ahaggar

Tibesti

*Ténéré
du
Tafassâsset*

54

20°   2

Erg I-n-Sâkâne

Tessalit

Séguédine

Araouane

*Adrar des
Ifôghas*

Assamakka   Iferouâne

*Massif
de l'Aïr*

Ténéré

MALI

Azaouâd

guibine

Tombouctou

Monts Bagzane
△
2022m

Gao   Agadez

Goundam

Ansongo   Ménaka

Grand Erg de Bilma

NIGER   Ngourti

C H A D

15°   3

*Lac
Niangay*

Hombori

Tahoua   Keïta

Dilia

opti

Ayorou   Dakoro

Nguigmi

Baudiagara

h   Tillabéri   *e*   Birnin
Konni   *l*   Tessaoua   Zinder

Ouahigouya   Dogondoutchi   Maradi   Gouré

Lake Chad

URKINA   NIAMEY   *Hadejia*

Kaya   *Sokoto*   Sokoto   Guidimouni

oudougou   OUAGADOUGOU   Nguru

FASO   Fada-   Jega   Gusau   Katsina   Hadejia   Maiduguri

Ngourma   Koko   Kano   Potiskum

bo-Dioulasso   Tenkodogo   *Gongola*

Bawku   Yelwa   Zaria   Biu

Bolgatanga   Kandi   Kaduna   Bauchi   Kumo

Wa   Sansanné-   Jos   Gombi

Mango   Natitingou   Jos   Yola

BENIN   N I G E R I A   *Jos
Plateau*   54

Yendi

Tamale   Parakou   *Kainji
Reservoir*   Minna   ABUJA   Lafia   *Shebshi
Mountains*

Sokodé   Jebba   *Niger*   *Benue*

GHANA   Ilorin   Wukari   *Adamawa Highland*

Wenchi   Oyo   Ogbomosho   Lokoja   Makurdi   *Gotel
Mountains*

bengourou   Ibadan   Ede   C.A.R.

Abomey   Owo   Benin   Enugu   *Djérem*

Kumasi   PORTO-   City

Kpalimé   NOVO   Onitsha

Nsawam   Lagos   Sapele   Owerri   Aba

Asamankese   Cotonou   Warri   Calabar

Aboisso   LOMÉ   Port Harcourt   Uyo

bidjan   ACCRA

Cape Coast   *Bight of Benin*   *Mouths of the Niger*   *Sanaga*

Sekondi-Takoradi   *Isla de Bioco*   C A M E R O O N

Gulf of Guinea   EQUATORIAL
GUINEA   55

5°

E   F   G   H

Elevation

						Below sea level 0	250m	500m	1000m	2000m	3000m	4000m	6000m
-6000m	-4000m	-2000m	-1000m	-500m	-250m								
-19,658ft	-13,124ft	-6562ft	-3281ft	-1640ft	-820ft	-328ft/-100m 0		820ft	1640ft	3281ft	6562ft	9843ft	13,124ft	19,685ft

Central Africa

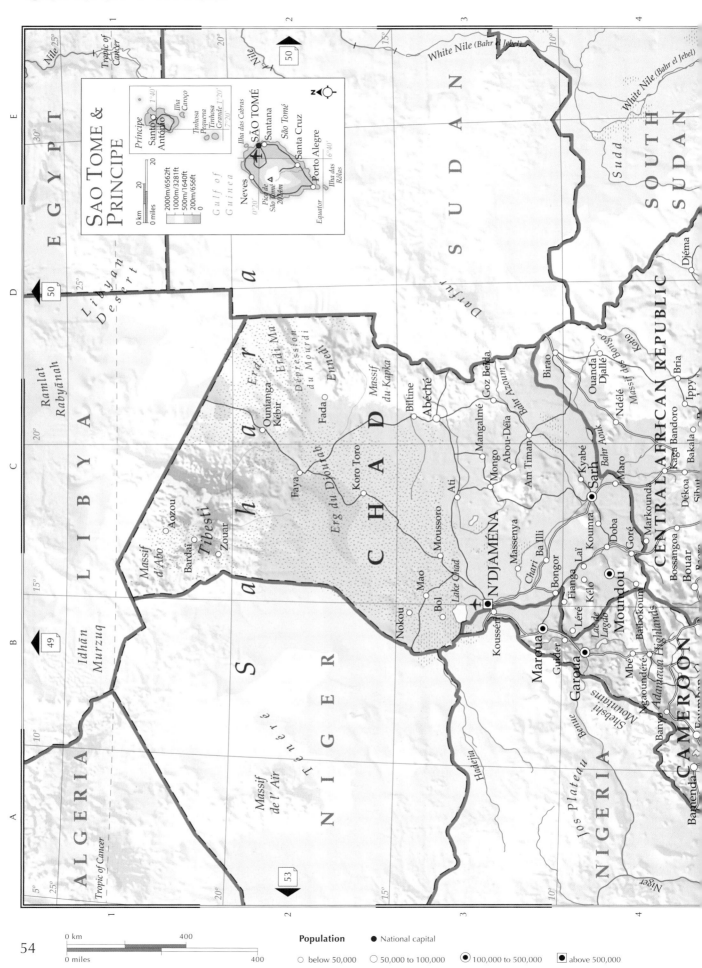

SÃO TOMÉ & PRINCIPE

Príncipe
Santo António
Tinhosa Pequena
Tinhosa Grande
Ilha Caroço
Ilha das Cabras
SÃO TOMÉ
Santana
Santa Cruz
São Tomé
Porto Alegre
Neves
Pico de São Tomé 2024m
Ilha das Rôlas
Equator
Gulf of Guinea

2000m/6562ft
1000m/3281ft
500m/1640ft
200m/656ft

0 km   20
0 miles   20

EGYPT

Nile
Tropic of Cancer

ALGERIA

LIBYA

Libyan Desert

Ramlat Rabyānah

Idhān Murzuq

SAHARA

NIGER

Ténéré

Massif de l'Aïr

Hadejia

Niger

NIGERIA

Jos Plateau

CAMEROON

Benue
Bamenda
Foumban
Banyo
Ngaoundéré
Adamaua Highlands
Mbé
Shebshi Mountains
Maroua
Garoua
Guider
Mora

CHAD

Tibesti
Massif d'Abo
Aozou
Bardaï
Zouar
Emi Koussi

Erg du Djourab
Faya
Koro Toro
Ati
Moussoro
Mao
Bol
Nokou
Lake Chad
Kousséri
N'DJAMÉNA
Massenya
Bongor
Chari
Ba Illi
Fianga
Léré
Lac de Léré
Lac de Léré
Kélo
Laï
Doba
Goré
Moundou
Baïbokoum
Bossangoa

Erdi
Ounianga Kébir
Fada
Erdi Ma
Dépression du Mourdi
Ennedi
Massif du Kapka
Biltine
Abéché
Mangalmé
Mongo
Abou-Déïa
Am Timan
Goz Beïda
Bahr Azoum

Birao
Ndélé
Ouanda Djallé
Massif des Bongo
Koko
Bria
Bandoro
Kaga Bandoro
Bakala
Dékoa
Sibut
Markounda
Bouar
Koumra
Kyabé
Sarh
Maro
Bahr Aouk

CENTRAL AFRICAN REPUBLIC

Ippy
Djéma

SUDAN

Darfur

Sudd

SOUTH SUDAN

White Nile (Bahr el Jebel)
White Nile (Bahr el Jebel)

Population

● National capital

○ below 50,000
◐ 50,000 to 100,000
◉ 100,000 to 500,000
◼ above 500,000

0 km   400
0 miles   400

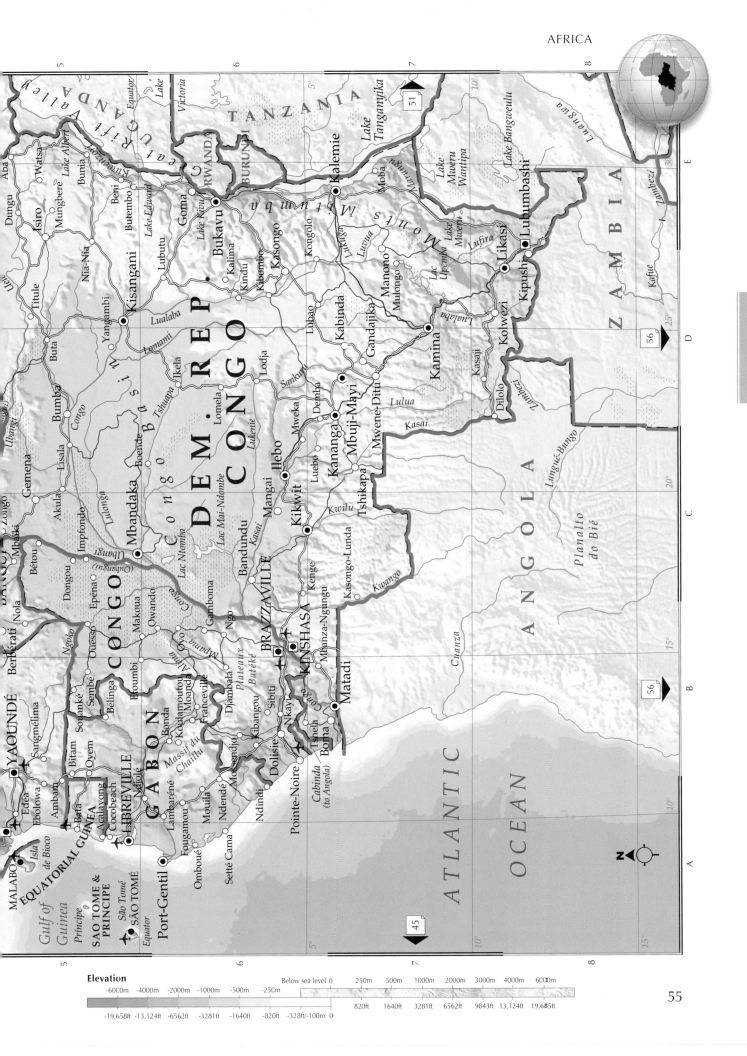

TANZANIA

BURUNDI

RWANDA

DEM. REP.

CONGO

CONGO

GABON

EQUATORIAL GUINEA

SAO TOME & PRINCIPE

ZAMBIA

ANGOLA

ATLANTIC OCEAN

Gulf of Guinea

Equator

Lake Victoria

Lake Kivu

Lake Edward

Lake Albert

Lake Tanganyika

Lake Mweru Wantipa

Lake Bangweulu

Lake Mweru

Great Rift Valley

Plateaux Batéké

Massif du Chaillu

Planalto do Bié

Congo Basin

Monts Mitumba

Elevation

| Below sea level 0 | 250m | 500m | 1000m | 2000m | 3000m | 4000m | 6000m |

-6000m -4000m -2000m -1000m -500m -250m

-19,658ft -13,124ft -6562ft -3281ft -1640ft -820ft -328ft/-100m 0

820ft 1640ft 3281ft 6562ft 9843ft 13,124ft 19,685ft

YAOUNDÉ

MALABO

Isla de Bioco

Principe

São Tomé

SÃO TOMÉ

Port-Gentil

Omboué

Settè Cama

Fougamou

Mouila

Ndendé

Lambaréné

Ndjolé

LIBREVILLE

Oyem

Bitam

Sangmélima

Ebolowa

Edéa

Ambam

Bata

Acalayong

Cocobeach

Souanké

Sembé

Bélinga

Bonda

Mékambo

Makokou

Booué

Koulamoutou

Moanda

Franceville

Djambala

Sibiti

Dolisie

Mossendjo

Kibangou

Nkayi

Pointe-Noire

Cabinda (to Angola)

Tshela

Boma

Matadi

Mbanza-Ngungu

KINSHASA

BRAZZAVILLE

Ngo

Gamboma

Owando

Makoua

Epéna

Dongou

Bétou

Nola

Berbérati

Ngoto

Ouesso

Impfondo

Mbaïki

Bangui

Gemena

Akula

Lisala

Bumba

Buta

Titule

Aba

Dungu

Watsa

Asiro

Mungbere

Beni

Butembo

Bunia

Nia-Nia

Kisangani

Yangambi

Mbandaka

Boende

Ikela

Bandundu

Mangai

Ilebo

Kikwit

Kenge

Kasongo-Lunda

Lodja

Lusambo

Mweka

Demba

Kananga

Mbuji-Mayi

Mwene-Ditu

Tshikapa

Kabinda

Gandajika

Kasaji

Dilolo

Kolwezi

Kamina

Manono

Mulongo

Kongolo

Kasongo

Kindu

Kalima

Kabambare

Goma

Bukavu

Kalemie

Moba

Likasi

Lubumbashi

Kipushi

Lake Nyasa

Ubangi

Lualaba

Lomami

Tshuapa

Lulonga

Congo

Lukenie

Kasai

Kwilu

Kwango

Lukuga

Luvua

Lufira

Lualaba

Lulua

Sankuru

Lomela

Luebo

Kafue

Zambezi

Cuanza

Lungué-Bungo

Lac Mai-Ndombe

Lac Ntomba

Lac Upemba

Luanginga

N

51

56

56

45

55

Europe

133

44

44

46

Political features

Total area:
4,809,200 sq miles
(12,456,000 sq km)

Total number of countries:
44

Total population:
721 million

Largest city with population:
Moscow, European Russia 16.7 million

Country with highest population density:
Monaco 48,181 people per sq mile
(18,531 people per sq km)

Largest country:
European Russia 1,527,341 sq miles
(3,955,818 sq km)

Smallest country:
Vatican City, Italy 0.17 sq miles
(0.44 sq km)

Physical features

Largest lake:
Lake Lagoda, European Russia
7,100 sq miles (18,390 sq km)

Longest river:
Volga, European Russia
2,290 miles (3,688 km)

Highest point:
El'brus, Caucasus, European Russia
18,510ft (5,642 m)

Lowest point:
Volga Delta, Caspian Sea, European
Russia 92 ft (28m) below sea level

Population   ● National capital

○ below 50,000   ◎ 50,000 to 100,000   ◉ 100,000 to 500,000   ■ above 500,000

0 km   500
0 miles   500

E 20° 30° 40° 50° 60° 70° F 80° G H

Barents Sea

133

70°

North Cape

Ostrov Kolguyev

80°

1

Murmansk

Kola Peninsula

Ob'

Irtysh

White Sea

Archangel

FINLAND

Gulf of Bothnia

Tampere

Lake Onega

Northern Dvina

R U S S I A N

Perm'

90

2

Turku HELSINKI

Lake Ladoga

F E D E R A T I O N

70°

Uppsala TALLINN

Saint Petersburg

Vologda

Ufa

50°

STOCKHOLM

ESTONIA

Yaroslavl'

Kazan'

Baltic Sea

LATVIA

MOSCOW

Nizhniy Novgorod

Ul'yanovsk

Orenburg

Aral Sea

3

RIGA

European Plain

Samara

Ural

LITHUANIA

Syr Darya

Kaliningrad Vitsyebsk

Volga Uplands

VILNIUS

Central Russian Upland

MINSK

Volga

KALININGRAD (to Russ Fed)

Babruysk

BELARUS

Homyel'

Voronezh

Ural

60°

Amu Darya

WARSAW

Brest

Pripet Marshes

Dnieper Lowlands

Don

POLAND

Bug

KIEV

Kharkiv

Volgograd

Kraków

L'viv

Dnieper

Astrakhan'

Volga Delta -28m

40°

SLOVAKIA

UKRAINE

Dnipropetrovs'k

Chernivtsi

Donets'k

BUDAPEST

MOLDOVA

Rostov-na-Donu

Dniester

HUNGARY

CHIŞINĂU

Stavropol'

Caspian Sea

Cluj-Napoca

Odesa

Crimea

ROMANIA

Braşov

Simferopol

Caucasus

90

4

BELGRADE

(the Ukrainian territory of Crimea was annexed by Russia in 2014)

El'brus 5642m

BUCHAREST

Constanţa

Black Sea

SERBIA

Danube

KOSOVO (disputed)

BULGARIA

Varna

30°

PRISTINA

Balkan Mountains

Burgas

ORTH

SOFIA

MACED

SKOPJE

TURKEY

TIRANA

ALBANIA

Aegean Sea

Anatolia

5

GREECE

Pindus Mountains

ATHENS

Piraeus

Zagros Mountains

Peloponnese

50°

Sea

Irákleio

Cyprus

96

Tigris

Euphrates

Crete

40°

30°

E F G H

59

The North Atlantic

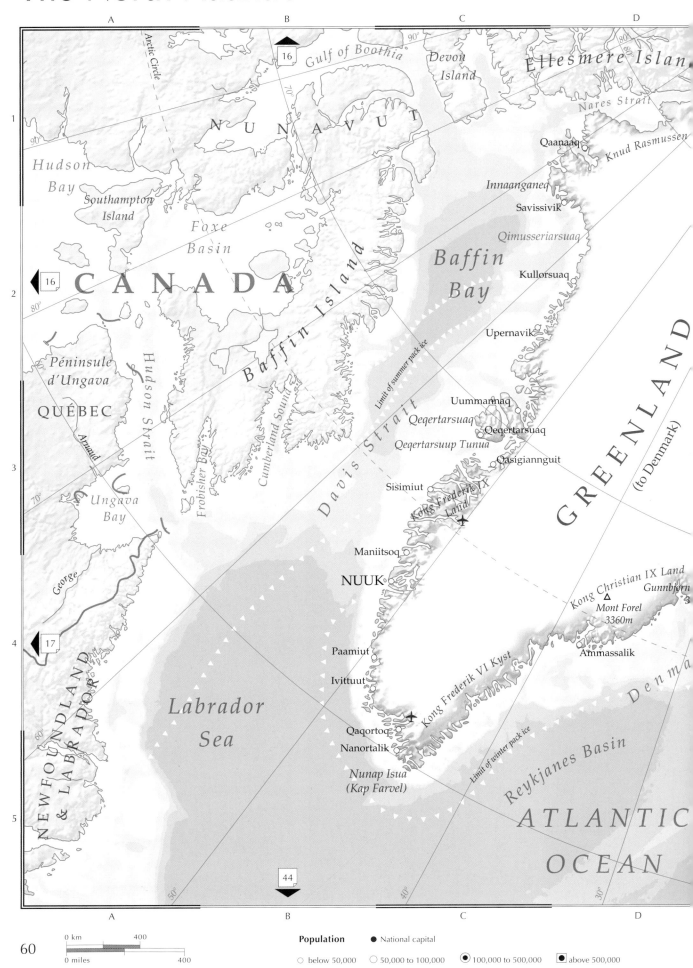

A B C D

16 Gulf of Boothia   Devon Island   Ellesmere Islan

Arctic Circle

90°   90°   80°

N U N A V U T   Nares Strait

1

Qaanaaq   Knud Rasmussen

Hudson Bay   70°

Southampton Island   Innaanganeq

Savissivik

Foxe Basin   Qimusseriarsuaq

Baffin Bay   Kullorsuaq

16   C A N A D A   80°

2

Baffin Island   Upernavik

Limit of summer pack ice

Péninsule d'Ungava   Uummannaq

Hudson Strait   Qeqertarsuaq

QUÉBEC   Davis Strait   Qeqertarsuaq

Arnaud   Qeqertarsuup Tunua   Qasigianguit

Frobisher Bay   Sisimiut   Qasigianguit

3   Cumberland Sound   Kong Frederik IX Land   G R E E N L A N D

70°   Ungava Bay   (to Denmark)

George   Maniitsoq

Kong Christian IX Land   Gunnbjørn

NUUK   3

Mont Forel 3360m

4   17   Paamiut   Kong Frederik VI Kyst   Ammassalik

Ivittuut   Denma

60°   Labrador Sea   Qaqortoq

N E W F O U N D L A N D & L A B R A D O R   Nanortalik

Limit of winter pack ice   Reykjanes Basin

Nunap Isua (Kap Farvel)   ATLANTIC

5   40°

50°   44   40°   OCEAN   30°

A B C D

60

0 km   400
0 miles   400

Population   ● National capital
○ below 50,000   ○ 50,000 to 100,000   ◉ 100,000 to 500,000   ■ above 500,000

Lincoln
Sea

Kap Morris Jesup

Wandel
Sea

Independence Fjord

Nord

SVALBARD
(to Norway)

ARCTIC

OCEAN

133

Zemlya
Frantsa-Iosifa

Novaya
Zemlya

1

Kvitøya

Nordaustlandet

Kong Karls Land

Barentsøya

Spitsbergen

Edgeøya

LONGYEARBYEN

Barentsburg

Storfjorden

Barents
Sea

88

2

Kong Frederik VIII Land

Greenland
Sea

Limit of winter pack ice

Christian X
Land

Bjørnøya
(to Norway)

70°

Petermann Bjerg
2940m

Daneborg

Nordkapp
(North Cape)

FINLAND

3

Limit of summer pack ice

Kong Oscar Fjord

Mohns Ridge

30°

Ittoqqortoormiit

Kangertittivaq

Kangikajik

JAN MAYEN
(to Norway)

Norwegian
Sea

Vestfjorden

Arctic Circle

62

4

rait

ICELAND

olungarvík

Siglufjörður

Raufarhöfn

jörður

Húsavík

Akureyri

Stykkishólmur

Seyðisfjörður

REYKJAVÍK

Neskaupstaður

Selfoss

Vatnajökull

Djúpivogur

orlákshöfn

urtsey

Hvannadalshnúkur
2119m

Vestmannaeyjar

Norwegian Basin

S W E D E N

Gulf
of
Bothnia

FAROE ISLANDS
(to Denmark)

TÓRSHAVN

N O R W A Y

5

N

Shetland
Islands

63

Elevation

| | | | | | | | Below sea level 0 | 250m | 500m | 1000m | 2000m | 3000m | 4000m | 6000m |

-6000m -4000m -2000m -1000m -500m -250m

-19,658ft -13,124ft -6562ft -3281ft -1640ft -820ft -328ft/-100m 0

820ft 1640ft 3281ft 6562ft 9843ft 13,124ft 19,685ft

Scandinavia & Finland

RUSSIAN FEDERATION

FINLAND

ARCTIC OCEAN

Barents Sea

Norwegian Sea

Lapland

Kiruna

Nordkapp (North Cape)

Mageroya

Soroya

Ringvassoya

Kvaloya

Senja

Andoya

Vesteralen

Lofoten

Vestfjorden

Namsos

Steinkjer

Mosjoen

Vega

Mo i Rana

Bodo

Fauske

Arvidsjaur

Storuman

Vilhelmina

Dorotea

Lycksele

Angerman

Skelleftealven

Storjord

Kvikkjokk

Jokkmokk

Skalka

Gallivare

Malmberget

Boden

Luleälven

Lulea

Pitea

Skelleftea

Boden

Kalix

Haparanda

Tornio

Kemi

Kokkola (Karleby)

Raahe

Kempele

Oulu

Hailuoto

Oulujoki

Kajaani

Oulujärvi

Sotkamo

Kuhmo

Suomussalmi

Kuusamo

Pudasjärvi

Kemijärvi

Rovaniemi

Kuusamo

Sattanen

Sodankylä

Kittilä

Kolari

Muonio

Muonionjoki

Ounasjoki

Tornionjoki

Visttasjohka

Kaaresuvanto

Karesuando

Torneträsk

Kebnekaise 2117m

Sarek

Kiruna

Kirkenes

Varangerfjorden

Varangerhalvoya

Tana Bru

Deatnu

Valljohka

Karigasniemi

Inarijoki

Kaamanen

Ivalo

Saariselkä

Inari

Kilpisjärvi

Finnmarksvidda

Porsangerfjorden

Nordkapp

Alta

Talvik

Lakselv

Tromso

Harstad

Narvik

Rombak

Kemijoki

Kemi

Lieksa

Liminka

Barents Sea

Arctic Circle

ARCTIC OCEAN

Arctic Circle

0 km	200
0 miles	200

Population   ● National capital

○ below 50,000   ○ 50,000 to 100,000   ◉ 100,000 to 500,000   ◼ above 500,000

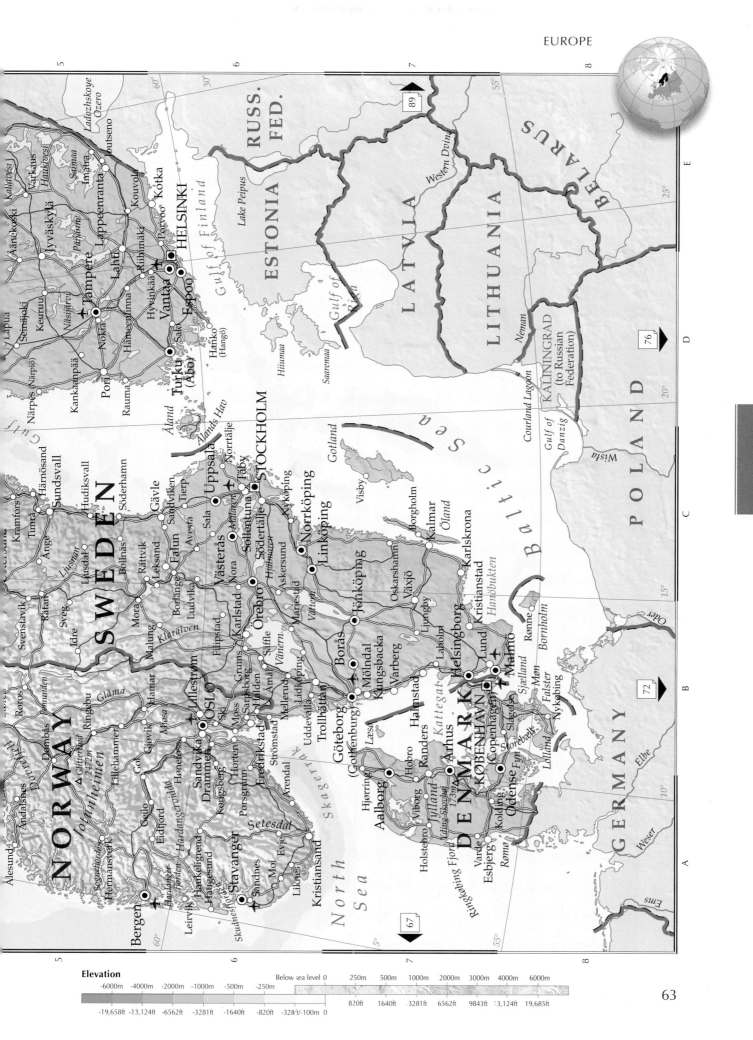

RUSS. FED.

BELARUS

ESTONIA

LATVIA

LITHUANIA

KALININGRAD
(to Russian
Federation)

POLAND

GERMANY

NORWAY

SWEDEN

DENMARK

FINLAND

HELSINKI

STOCKHOLM

OSLO

KØBENHAVN
(Copenhagen)

Baltic Sea

North Sea

Gulf of Finland

Gulf of Riga

Gulf of Bothnia

Skagerrak

Kattegat

Ladozhskoye Ozero

Saimaa

Lake Peipus

Western Dvina

Neman

Courland Lagoon

Gulf of Danzig

Wisła

Oder

Elbe

Weser

Ems

Hiiumaa

Saaremaa

Gotland

Öland

Bornholm

Sjælland

Fyn

Lolland

Falster

Møn

Åland

Ålands Hav

Glittertind 2472m

Galdhøpiggen 2469m

Yttygran 173m

Tampere
Espoo
Vantaa
Turku (Åbo)
Kotka
Porvoo
Lappeenranta
Lahti
Kouvola
Hyvinkää
Hämeenlinna
Kirkkonummi
Salo
Hanko (Hangö)
Pori
Rauma
Kankaanpää
Kristiinankaupunki
Närpes
Lapua
Seinäjoki
Keuruu
Jyväskylä
Äänekoski
Varkaus
Kalajoki
Haukivesi
Imatra
Outseno
Näsijärvi
Päijänne
Nokia

Luleälven
Klarälven
Glåma
Mosa

HELSINKI

STOCKHOLM
Uppsala
Norrtälje
Täby
Sollentuna
Södertälje
Enköping
Västerås
Nyköping
Norrköping
Linköping
Jönköping
Borås
Göteborg (Gothenburg)
Mölndal
Kungsbacka
Varberg
Halmstad
Helsingborg
Lund
Malmö
Landskrona
Ljungby
Växjö
Oskarshamn
Kalmar
Borgholm
Karlskrona
Kristianstad
Visby
Ronne

Gävle
Sandviken
Söderhamn
Hudiksvall
Sundsvall
Härnösand
Kramfors
Timrå
Ange
Svenstavik
Rätan
Sveg
Idre
Mora
Malung
Borlänge
Falun
Leksand
Rättvik
Bollnäs
Ludvika
Avesta
Sala
Tierp
Nora
Örebro
Karlstad
Filipstad
Arvika
Säffle
Åmål
Lidköping
Vänersborg
Trollhättan
Uddevalla
Strömstad
Fredrikstad
Halden
Moss
Sarpsborg
Mellerud
Grums
Ski
Lillestrøm
Drammen
Sandvika
Kongsberg
Horten
Porsgrunn
Skien
Arendal
Kristiansand
Mandal
Lyngdal
Flekkefjord
Egersund
Sandnes
Stavanger
Haugesund
Leirvik
Bergen

Hamar
Gjøvik
Lillehammer
Elverum
Rena
Røros
Oppdal
Dombås
Otta
Vinstra
Ringebu
Fagernes
Gol
Geilo
Eidfjord
Voss
Odda
Haukeligrend

OSLO
Tønsberg

Roskilde
Slagelse
Næstved
Nykøbing
Odense
Svendborg
Nyborg
Kolding
Vejle
Fredericia
Middelfart
Esbjerg
Varde
Rømø
Holstebro
Herning
Viborg
Hobro
Randers
Århus
Silkeborg
Skanderborg
Horsens
Grenå
Hjørring
Aalborg
Frederikshavn

Storebælt
Øresund
Hanöbukten
Ringkøbing Fjord

Vättern
Vänern
Mälaren
Hjälmaren

Setesdal

Elevation

Below sea level	0							
-6000m	-4000m	-2000m	-1000m	-500m	-250m			
-19,658ft	-13,124ft	-6562ft	-3281ft	-1640ft	-820ft	-328ft/-100m	0	

250m	500m	1000m	2000m	3000m	4000m	6000m
820ft	1640ft	3281ft	6562ft	9843ft	13,124ft	19,685ft

63

The Low Countries

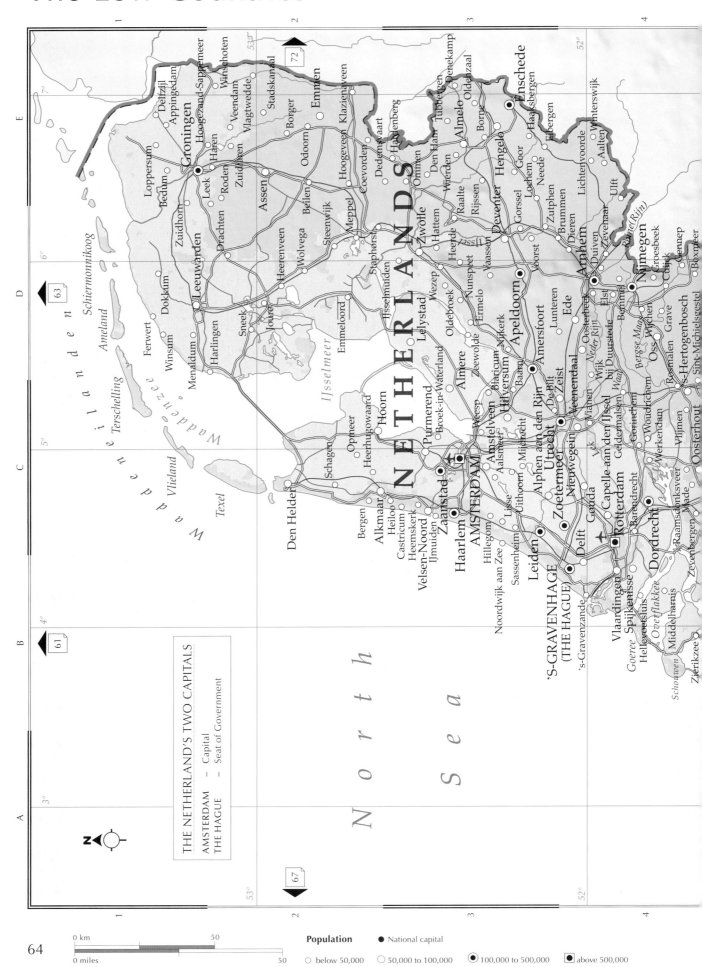

THE NETHERLAND'S TWO CAPITALS

AMSTERDAM – Capital
THE HAGUE – Seat of Government

North Sea

NETHERLANDS

Population

- ● National capital
- ○ below 50,000
- ○ 50,000 to 100,000
- ◉ 100,000 to 500,000
- ■ above 500,000

0 km   50

0 miles   50

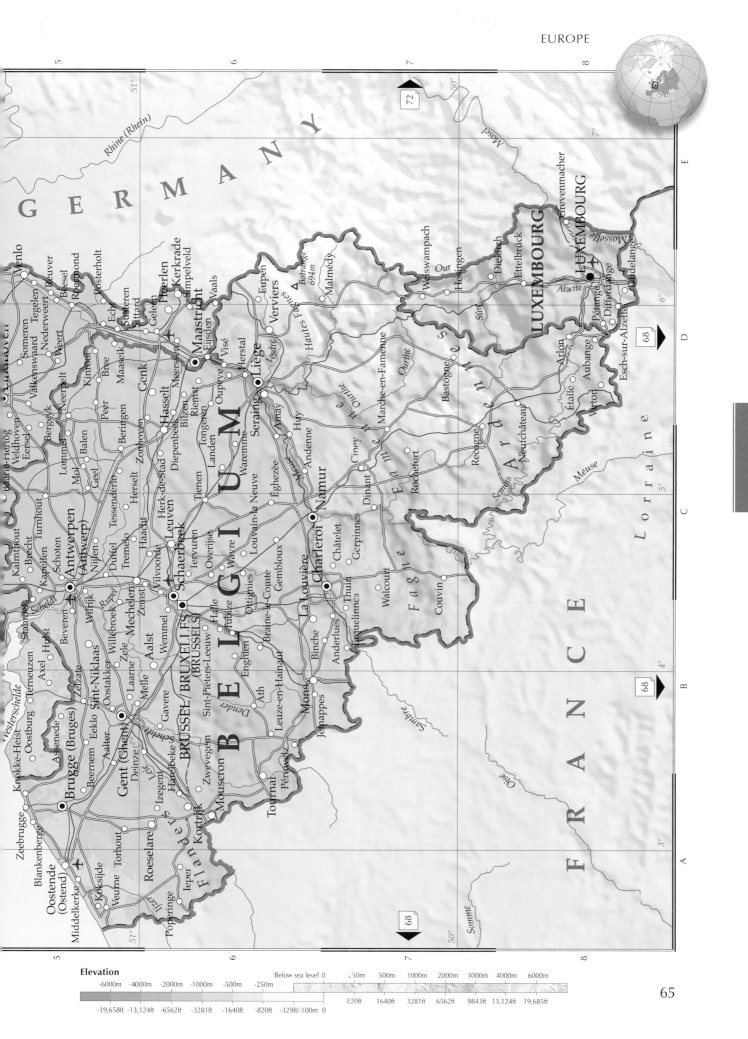

Elevation

Below sea level 0	250m	500m	1000m	2000m	3000m	4000m	6000m

-6000m	-4000m	-2000m	-1000m	-500m	-250m

-19,658ft	-13,124ft	-6562ft	-3281ft	-1640ft	-820ft	-328ft/-100m	0

820ft	1640ft	3281ft	6562ft	9843ft	13,124ft	19,685ft

The British Isles

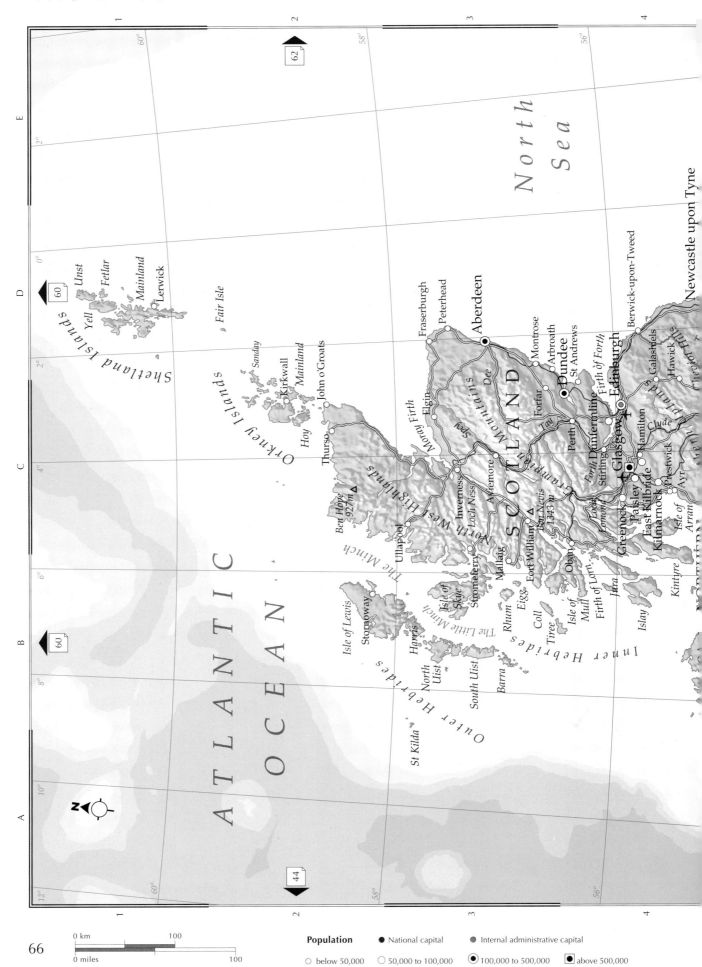

North Sea

ATLANTIC OCEAN

Shetland Islands

Unst
Fetlar
Yell
Mainland
Lerwick

Fair Isle

Sanday
Orkney Islands
Kirkwall
Mainland
Hoy
John o'Groats

Thurso

Ben Hope
927m

North West Highlands
The Minch

Ullapool

Isle of Lewis
Stornoway

Harris

North Uist
South Uist
Barra
Outer Hebrides

St Kilda

The Little Minch
Isle of Skye
Stromeferry
Rhum
Eigg
Coll
Tiree
Isle of Mull
Firth of Lorn
Inner Hebrides
Islay
Jura
Kintyre
Isle of Arran

Mallaig
Fort William
Ben Nevis
1343 m
Oban

Fraserburgh
Peterhead
Aberdeen

Montrose
Arbroath
Dundee
St Andrews
Firth of Forth

Elgin
Moray Firth
Spey
Dee
Grampian Mountains
Tay
Forfar
Perth

SCOTLAND

Aviemore
Inverness
Loch Ness
Grampian Mountains
Loch Lomond
Stirling
Forth
Dunfermline
Edinburgh
Glasgow
Greenock
Paisley
Hamilton
Clyde
East Kilbride
Kilmarnock
Prestwick
Ayr

Galashiels
Hawick
Cheviot Hills
Southern Uplands

Berwick-upon-Tweed

Newcastle upon Tyne

0 km   100
0 miles   100

Population   ● National capital   ● Internal administrative capital

○ below 50,000   ○ 50,000 to 100,000   ◉ 100,000 to 500,000   ◼ above 500,000

5   6   7   8

54°

Middlesbrough

Whitby
Scarborough
Northallerton
Darlington
Whitehaven
Workington

Kingston upon Hull

Great
Yarmouth
Lowestoft
Norwich
Ipswich
Felixstowe
Harwich
Colchester
Southend-
on-Sea
Margate
Canterbury
Dover
Folkestone
Hastings
Eastbourne

Bridlington
Beverley
Grimsby
Skegness
Louth
Lincoln

The
Wash

King's Lynn
Fens
Peterborough
Newmarket
Cambridge
Bedford
Milton Keynes
Stevenage
Luton
Harlow
Watford
LONDON
Croydon
Crawley
Brighton
Hove

UNITED KINGDOM

Harrogate
York
Leeds
Bradford
Huddersfield
Sheffield
Doncaster
Castleford
Nottingham
Derby
Leicester
Nuneaton
Coventry
Northampton
Cheltenham
Oxford
Swindon
Reading
Woking
Guildford
Winchester
Havant
Portsmouth
Newport

Manchester
Bolton
Preston
Blackpool
Liverpool
Birkenhead
Chester
Crewe
Stoke-on-Trent
Stafford
Shrewsbury
Wolverhampton
Birmingham
Kidderminster
Worcester
Gloucester
Bristol
Bath
Weston-super-
Mare
Yeovil
Eastleigh
Southampton
Poole
Bournemouth

Barrow-in-
Furness
Lancaster
Kendal

ENGLAND

WALES

Cardiff
Swansea
Port Talbot
Llanelli
Carmarthen
Barmouth
Tywyn
Aberystwyth
Bangor
Holyhead
Anglesey

Cambrian
Mountains

Brecon
Beacons

Snowdonia

ISLE OF MAN
(British Crown
Dependency)
DOUGLAS

Irish Sea

Belfast
Downpatrick
Newry
Armagh
Omagh
Enniskillen

Lough
Neagh

Lower Lough Erne
Upper
Lough Erne

Donegal Bay

Castlebar

Connaught

Sligo
Longford

IRELAND

Munster

Leinster

DUBLIN
Dún Laoghaire
Drogheda
Dundalk
Lucan
Newbridge
Athlone
Port Laoise
Carlow
Kilkenny
Clonmel
Wexford
Waterford
Wicklow
Mts
Wicklow

Limerick
Ennis
Galway
Galway Bay
Lough Corrib
Lough
Derg

Cork
Killarney
Tralee
Dingle
Bay
Bantry Bay

Celtic Sea

St George's Channel

Cardigan Bay

Haverfordwest
Milford Haven
Fishguard

Ilfracombe
Barnstaple
Bideford
Taunton
Tiverton
Exeter
Exmouth
Bridport
Lyme
Weymouth
Torquay
Plymouth
Saltash
Tamar
Dartmoor
Bodmin
Newquay
St Austell
Truro
Falmouth
Penzance
Land's End
Isles of Scilly

Exmoor

Bristol Channel

England FRANCE

English Channel

Seine

Channel
Tunnel

GUERNSEY
(British Crown
Dependency)
ST PETER PORT
Alderney
Sark
ST HELIER
JERSEY
(British Crown
Dependency)
Channel
Islands

Isle of Wight
Newport

52°

50°

Elevation

-6000m -4000m -2000m -1000m -500m -250m
-19,658ft -13,124ft -6562ft -3281ft -1640ft -820ft -328ft/-100m 0

Below sea level 0 250m 500m 1000m 2000m 4000m 6000m
820ft 1640ft 3281ft 6562ft 9843ft 13,124ft 19,685ft

LONDON

Watford
Enfield
Barnet
Edgware
Wembley
Dagenham
Walthamstow
Finchley
Hampstead
Trafalgar Square
Buckingham Palace
Houses
of Parliament
Richmond
Wimbledon
Kingston
upon Thames
Epsom
Croydon
Bromley
Orpington
Bexley
Dartford
Greenwich
St Paul's
Cathedral
The City
Wandsworth
Heathrow

Thames

Places of interest
Regions/suburbs

0 km 10
0 miles 10

64
68
68
44

France, Andorra & Monaco

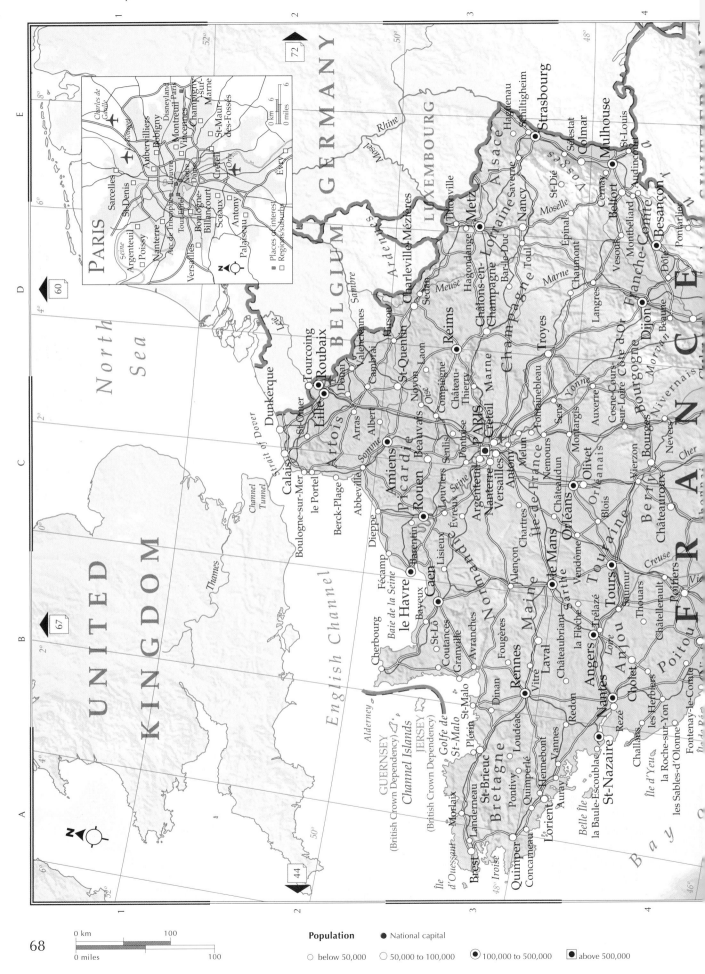

Population   ● National capital

○ below 50,000   ○ 50,000 to 100,000   ◉ 100,000 to 500,000   ■ above 500,000

0 km   100
0 miles   100

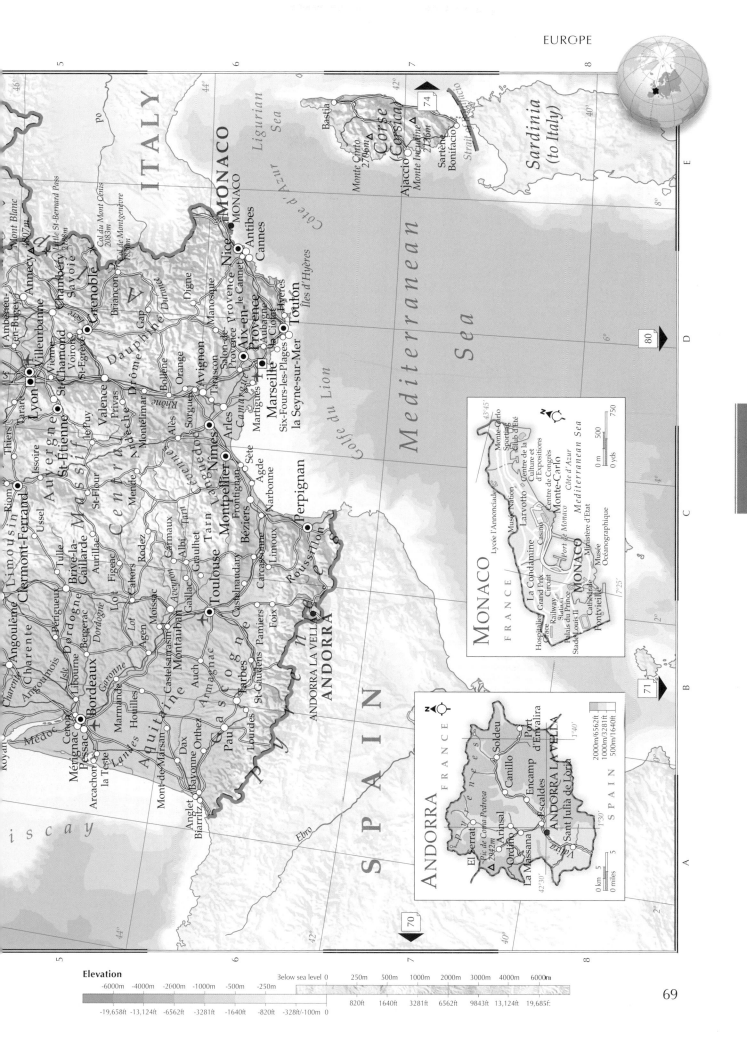

ITALY

SPAIN

Mont Blanc
4807m △

Col du Mont Cenis 2083m
Little St-Bernard Pass
Col de Montgenèvre 1855m

Ambérieu-en-Bugey
Annecy
Chambéry
Savoie
Voiron
Vienne
Grenoble
Villeurbanne
Lyon
Tarare
St-Chamond
St-Égrève
Briançon
St-Étienne
Thiers
Roanne
Issoire
Riom
Clermont-Ferrand
Ussel
Brive-la-Gaillarde
Tulle
Aurillac
St-Flour
Mende
Millau
Rodez
Figeac
Cahors
Carmaux
Albi
Gaillac
Castres
Montauban
Toulouse
Castelsarrasin
Moissac
Agen
Villeneuve
Marmande
Bergerac
Libourne
Périgueux
Angoulême
Angoulnois
Royan
Médoc
Cenon
Bordeaux
Pessac
Mérignac
Arcachon
la Teste
Landes
Mont-de-Marsan
Dax
Orthez
Pau
Lourdes
St-Gaudens
Tarbes
Auch
Condom
Castelnaudary
Limoux
Foix
Pamiers
Carcassonne
Narbonne
Béziers
Agde
Sète
Montpellier
Nîmes
Arles
Avignon
Tarascon
Salon-de-Provence
Aix-en-Provence
Marseille
Martigues
Six-Fours-les-Plages
la Seyne-sur-Mer
Toulon
Hyères
Îles d'Hyères
le Cannet
Antibes
Cannes
Nice
MONACO
MONACO

Gap
Digne
Manosque
Orange
Bollène
Montélimar
Privas
Valence
le Puy
Aubenas

Durance
Drôme
Rhône
Isère
Drac

Dauphiné
Savoie
Auvergne
Limousin
Central
Massif
Tarn
Languedoc
Roussillon
Gascogne
Aquitaine
Lande

ANDORRA LA VELLA
ANDORRA

Perpignan

Po

Corse
Corsica

Monte Cinto 2706m △
Monte Incudine 2136m △

Bastia
Ajaccio
Sartène
Bonifacio
Strait of Bonifacio

Sardinia
(to Italy)

Ligurian
Sea

Côte d'Azur

Mediterranean
Sea

Golfe du Lion

Gulf of Biscay

Charente
Dordogne
Lot
Garonne
Isle
Gironde
Ebro

74

80

71

70

MONACO

FRANCE

Monte-Carlo
Sporting Club d'Été
Centre de la Culture et d'Expositions
Larvotto
Musée National
Centre de Congrès
Casino
Port de Monaco
Monte-Carlo
La Condamine
Grand Prix Circuit
Stadium
Railway
Palais du Prince
Stade Louis II
Fontvieille
Cathédrale
Ministère d'Etat
Musée Océanographique
Lycée l'Annonciade
Hôpital
MONACO
Côte d'Azur
Mediterranean Sea

43°45'
7°25'

0 m   500   750
0 yds

ANDORRA

FRANCE

SPAIN

Soldeu
Port d'Envalira
Canillo
Encamp
Escaldes
ANDORRA LA VELLA
Sant Julià de Lòria
La Massana
Arinsal
Ordino
El Serrat
Pic de Coma Pedrosa 2942m △

Pyrenees
Valira

2000m/6562ft
1000m/3281ft
500m/1640ft

1°40'
1°30'
42°30'

0 km   5
0 miles   5

Elevation

| -6000m | -4000m | -2000m | -1000m | -500m | -250m | Below sea level 0 | 250m | 500m | 1000m | 2000m | 3000m | 4000m | 6000m |

-19,658ft -13,124ft -6562ft -3281ft -1640ft -820ft -328ft/-100m 0 820ft 1640ft 3281ft 6562ft 9843ft 13,124ft 19,685ft

Spain & Portugal

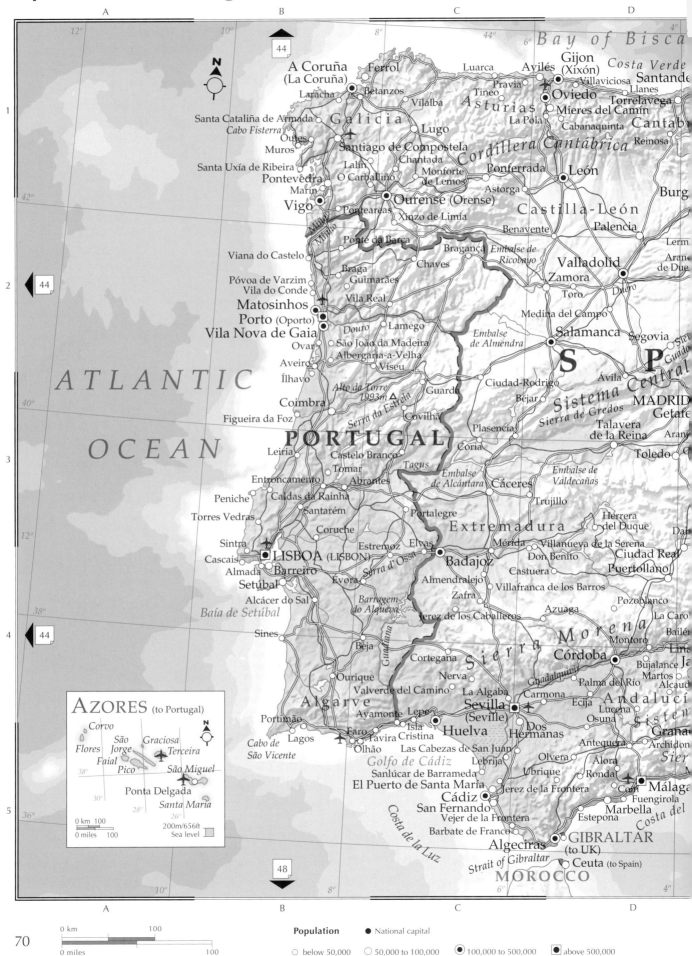

Bay of Bisca
Costa Verde

A Coruña
(La Coruña)
Ferrol
Luarca
Avilés
Gijón
(Xixón)
Villaviciosa
Santander
Betanzos
Pravia
Tineo
Oviedo
Llanes
Larracha
Vilalba
Asturias
Mieres del Camín
Torrelavega
Santa Catalíña de Armada
Cabo Fisterra
Lugo
La Pola
Cabanaquinta
Cantábr
Outes
Muros
Santiago de Compostela
Chantada
Cordillera Cantábrica
Reinosa
Santa Uxía de Ribeira
Lalín
O Carballiño
Monforte de Lemos
Ponferrada
León
Pontevedra
Marín
Ourense (Orense)
Astorga
Castilla-León
Burg
Vigo
Ponteareas
Xinzo de Limia
Benavente
Palencia
Lerm
Ponte da Barca
Zamora
Valladolid
Arán de Due
Viana do Castelo
Bragança
Embalse de Ricobayo
Toro
Braga
Chaves
Medina del Campo
Guimarães
Vila Real
Duero
Póvoa de Varzim
Vila do Conde
Embalse de Almendra
Salamanca
Segovia
Matosinhos
Porto (Oporto)
Lamego
Viseu
S
P
Vila Nova de Gaia
São João da Madeira
Ciudad-Rodrigo
Ávila
Central
Ovar
Albergaria-a-Velha
Béjar
MADRID
Aveiro
Alto da Torre 1993m
Guarda
Sistema
Getafe
Ílhavo
Serra da Estrela
Covilhã
Sierra de Gredos
Talavera de la Reina
Coimbra
Plasencia
Figueira da Foz
PORTUGAL
Coria
Toledo
Leiria
Castelo Branco
Embalse de Valdecañas
Tomar
Tagus
Cáceres
Entroncamento
Abrantes
Embalse de Alcántara
Trujillo
Peniche
Caldas da Rainha
Portalegre
Herrera del Duque
Torres Vedras
Santarém
Extremadura
Sintra
Coruche
Estremoz
Elvas
Mérida
Villanueva de la Serena
Ciudad Real
Cascais
Almada
LISBOA (LISBON)
Évora
Serra d' Ossa
Badajoz
Castuera
Puertollano
Barreiro
Almendralejo
Setúbal
Don Benito
Villafranca de los Barros
Alcácer do Sal
Barragem do Alqueva
Zafra
Pozoblanco
La Caro
Baía de Setúbal
Jerez de los Caballeros
Azuaga
Sines
Guadiana
Morena
Beja
Cortegana
Córdoba
Montoro
Ourique
Nerva
Sierra
Guadalquivir
Bujalance
Ja
Valverde del Camino
La Algaba
Palma del Río
Martos
Alcaud
Algarve
Carmona
Ecija
Andalucí
Portimão
Ayamonte
Lepe
Sevilla
(Seville)
Osuna
Sistem
Faro
Isla Cristina
Huelva
Dos Hermanas
Antequera
Archidon
Grana
Cabo de São Vicente
Lagos
Olhão
Tavira
Las Cabezas de San Juan
Lucena
Sier
Golfo de Cádiz
Lebrija
Olvera
Álora
Costa del
Sanlúcar de Barrameda
Ubrique
Ronda
Málaga
El Puerto de Santa María
Jerez de la Frontera
Fuengirola
Costa de la Luz
Cádiz
Com
Marbella
San Fernando
Vejer de la Frontera
Estepona
Costa del
Barbate de Franco
Algeciras
GIBRALTAR
(to UK)
Strait of Gibraltar
Ceuta (to Spain)
MOROCCO

ATLANTIC

OCEAN

AZORES (to Portugal)

Corvo
Flores
São Jorge
Graciosa
Terceira
Faial
Pico
São Miguel
Ponta Delgada
Santa Maria

0 km 100
0 miles 100

200m/656ft
Sea level

0 km 100
0 miles 100

Population   ● National capital

○ below 50,000   ○ 50,000 to 100,000   ◉ 100,000 to 500,000   ■ above 500,000

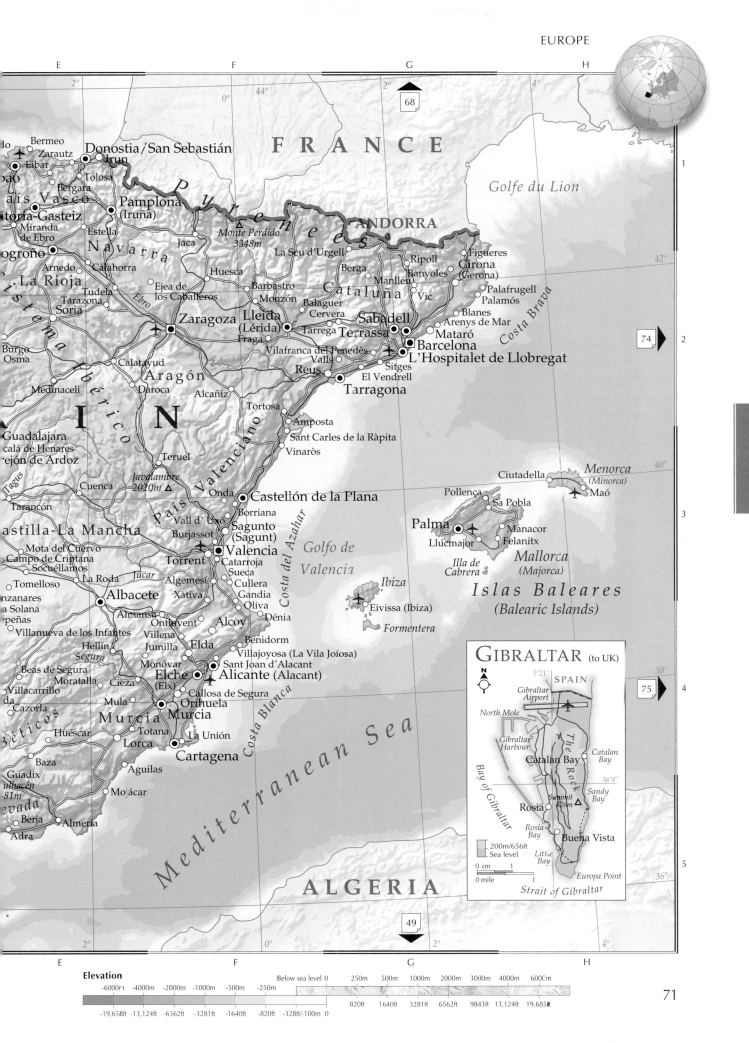

E · F · G · H

68

F R A N C E

Golfe du Lion

Bermeo
Zarautz
Donostia / San Sebastián
Eibar · Irun
Tolosa
Bergara
aís Vasco
Pamplona
(Iruña)
toria-Gasteiz
Miranda
de Ebro
Estella
Navarra
ogroño
Arnedo
Calahorra
La Rioja
Tudela
Tarazona
Soria
Pyrenees
Jaca
Monte Perdido
3348m
La Seu d'Urgell
ANDORRA
Ripoll
Berga
Banyoles
Manlleu
Figueres
Girona
(Gerona)
Palafrugell
Palamós
Cataluña
Vic
Blanes
Arenys de Mar
Costa Brava
Burgo
Osma
Huesca
Ejea de
los Caballeros
Barbastro
Monzón
Balaguer
Cervera
Sabadell
Mataró
stema Ibérico
Zaragoza
Lleida
(Lérida)
Tàrrega
Terrassa
Barcelona
L'Hospitalet de Llobregat
Fraga
Aragón
Calatayud
Daroca
Alcañiz
Vilafranca del Penedès
Valls
Reus
Sitges
El Vendrell
Tarragona
Medinaceli
I N
Tortosa
Amposta
Sant Carles de la Ràpita
Guadalajara
calá de Henares
ejón de Ardoz
Teruel
Vinaròs
Tagus
Cuenca
Javalambre
2020m
Onda
Castellón de la Plana
Ciutadella
Menorca
(Minorca)
Maó
Tarancón
Borriana
Pollença
Sa Pobla
astilla-La Mancha
Vall d' Uxó
Sagunto
(Sagunt)
Burjassot
Costa del Azahar
Golfo de
Valencia
Palma
Llucmajor
Manacor
Felanitx
Mota del Cuervo
Campo de Criptana
Socuéllamos
Torrent
Valencia
Catarroja
Sueca
Júcar
Jucar
Algemesí
Cullera
Gandia
Oliva
Illa de
Cabrera
Mallorca
(Majorca)
Tomelloso
La Roda
Xàtiva
Ibiza
Islas Baleares
(Balearic Islands)
nzanares
a Solana
peñas
Albacete
Almansa
Ontinyent
Villena
Alcoy
Dénia
Eivissa (Ibiza)
Formentera
Villanueva de los Infantes
Hellín
Jumilla
Elda
Benidorm
Villajoyosa (La Vila Joíosa)
Segura
Beas de Segura
Moratalla
Monóvar
Cieza
Elche
(Elx)
Sant Joan d'Alacant
Alicante (Alacant)
Villacarrillo
da
Cazorla
Mula
Orihuela
Callosa de Segura
Murcia
Murcia
Costa Blanca
éticos
Huéscar
Totana
La Unión
Baza
Lorca
Cartagena
Guadix
alhacén
81m
Aguilas
Mojácar
vada
Berja
Almería
Adra

M e d i t e r r a n e a n   S e a

A L G E R I A

49

GIBRALTAR (to UK)

N
5°21′
SPAIN
Gibraltar
Airport
North Mole
Gibraltar
Harbour
Bay of Gibraltar
Catalan Bay
The Rock
Catalan
Bay
36°8′
Rosia
Summit
426m
Sandy
Bay
Rosia
Bay
Buena Vista
Little
Bay
Europa Point
Strait of Gibraltar

200m/656ft
Sea level
0 km   1
0 mile   1

74

75

Elevation

-6000m -4000m -2000m -1000m -500m -250m

-19,658ft -13,124ft -6562ft -3281ft -1640ft -820ft -328ft/-100m 0

Below sea level 0   250m   500m   1000m 2000m 3000m 4000m 600Cm

820ft 1640ft 3281ft 6562ft 9843ft 13,124ft 19,685ft

Germany & The Alpine States

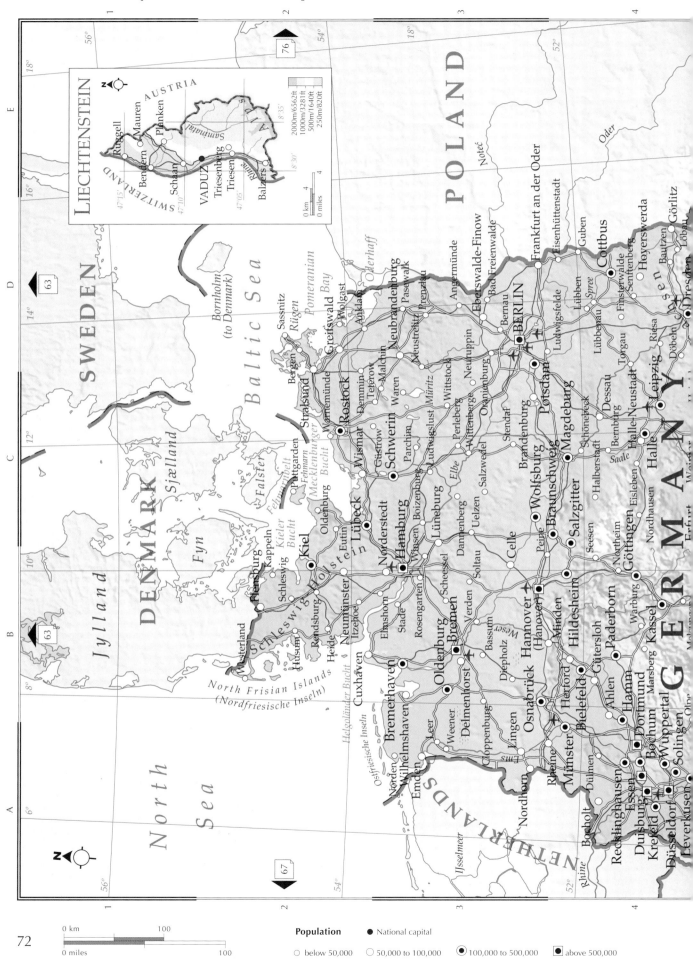

Population

○ below 50,000 ○ 50,000 to 100,000 ◉ 100,000 to 500,000 ◼ above 500,000

● National capital

LIECHTENSTEIN

AUSTRIA

SWITZERLAND

Ruggell
Mauren
Bendern
Planken
Schaan
VADUZ
Triesenberg
Triesen
Balzers

2000m/6562ft
1000m/3281ft
500m/1640ft
250m/820ft

0 km
0 miles

POLAND

SWEDEN

DENMARK

NETHERLANDS

Baltic Sea

North Sea

Jylland

Sjælland

Fyn

Falster

Bornholm
(to Denmark)

Sassnitz
Rügen
Bergen
Stralsund
Pomeranian
Greifswald Bay
Wolgast
Anklam
Oderhaff
Pasewalk
Prenzlau
Frankfurt an der Oder
Eisenhüttenstadt
Guben
Cottbus
Hoyerswerda
Görlitz
Bautzen
Dresden

Warnemünde
Rostock
Demmin
Neubrandenburg
Angermünde
Eberswalde-Finow
Bad Freienwalde
Bernau
BERLIN
Potsdam
Ludwigsfelde
Lübben
Senftenberg
Spree
Lübbenau
Finsterwalde
Torgau
Riesa
Döbeln

Wismar
Schwerin
Güstrow
Waren
Malchin
Teterow
Neustrelitz
Wittstock
Neuruppin
Oranienburg
Brandenburg
Magdeburg
Dessau
Halle-Neustadt
Leipzig
Halle

Mecklenburger
Bucht
Fehmarn
Lübeck
Parchim
Ludwigslust
Müritz
Perleberg
Wittenberge
Stendal
Salzwedel
Schönebeck
Bernburg
Halberstadt
Eisleben
Erfurt

Fehmarn
Puttgarden
Oldenburg
Eutin
Hamburg
Norderstedt
Boizenburg
Dannenberg
Wolfsburg
Braunschweig
Salzgitter
Seesen
Nordhausen
Weimar

Kiel
Kieler
Bucht
Fehmarnbelt
Schleswig-Holstein
Neumünster
Itzehoe
Wittenberge
Uelzen
Celle
Peine
Hildesheim
Göttingen
Northeim
Kassel

Flensburg
Kappeln
Schleswig
Husum
Rendsburg
Heide
Stade
Scheessel
Soltau
Verden
Minden
Hannover
(Hanover)
Warburg
Marburg

Westerland
Cuxhaven
Elmshorn
Rosengarten
Wissen
Lüneburg
Diepholz
Herford
Bielefeld
Paderborn
Ahlen
Hamm

North Frisian Islands
(Nordfriesische Inseln)
Helgoländer Bucht
Bremerhaven
Wilhelmshaven
Bremen
Oldenburg
Bassum
Osnabrück
Gütersloh
Hertford

Ostfriesische Inseln
Norden
Emden
Leer
Weener
Delmenhorst
Cloppenburg
Lingen
Rheine
Münster
Bocholt
Recklinghausen
Duisburg
Krefeld
Düsseldorf
Leverkusen

IJsselmeer
Nordhorn
Dülmen
Bochum
Dortmund
Essen
Wuppertal
Solingen
Olpe

Rhine
Ems
Weser
Elbe
Saale
Oder
Noteć
Samfnatal
Falkentwill

G E R M A N Y

Elevation

-6000m	-4000m	-2000m	-1000m	-500m	-250m

Below sea level 0   250m   500m   1000m   2000m   3000m   4000m   6000m

-19,658ft -13,124ft -6562ft -3281ft -1640ft -820ft -328ft/-100m 0

820ft   1640ft   3281ft   6562ft   9843ft   13,124ft   19,685ft

Italy

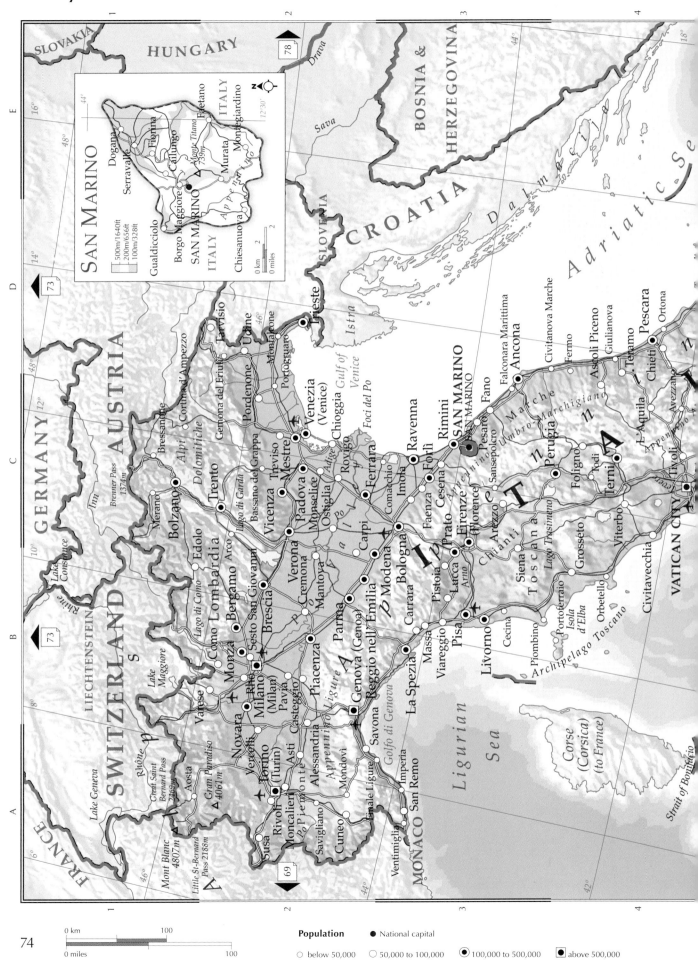

SAN MARINO

Dogana
Serravalle
Fiorina
Calungo
Faetano
Monte Titano 739m
Murata
Montegiardino

Gualdicciolo
Borgo Maggiore
SAN MARINO
ITALY
Chiesanuova

500m/1640ft
200m/656ft
100m/328ft

2 km
2 miles

ITALY

BOSNIA &
HERZEGOVINA

CROATIA

Drava
Sava

Dalmatia

Adriatic Sea

SLOVENIA

73

73

69

AUSTRIA
GERMANY
SWITZERLAND
LIECHTENSTEIN
FRANCE
MONACO

Tarvisio
Udine
Monfalcone
Trieste
Istra
Pordenone
Gemona del Friuli
Portogruaro
Genova del Friuli

Venezia (Venice)
Gulf of Venice
Chioggia
Foci del Po
Rovigo
Adige

Bassano del Grappa
Treviso
Mestre
Vicenza
Padova
Monselice
Ostiglia
Po

Cortina d'Ampezzo
Alpi
Dolomitiche
Bressanone
Merano
Bolzano
Trento
Lago di Garda
Arco
Edolo
Lombardia
Brenner Pass 1374m
Inn

Lago di Como
Lago Maggiore
Como
Bergamo
Sesto San Giovanni
Brescia
Cremona
Mantova
Verona
Carpi
Modena
Bologna
Ferrara
Comacchio
Imola
Faenza
Cesena
Forlì
Ravenna
Rimini
San Marino
Fano
Pesaro
Falconara Marittima
Ancona
Civitanova Marche
Fermo
Ascoli Piceno
Giulianova
Teramo
Pescara
Ortona
Chieti
Avezzano
L'Aquila

Rho
Milano (Milan)
Monza
Pavia
Castegio
Piacenza
Parma
Reggio nell'Emilia
Carrara
Massa
Viareggio
Lucca
Pistoia
Prato
Firenze (Florence)
Arezzo
Sansepolcro
Todi
Foligno
Perugia
Terni
Tivoli

Novara
Vercelli
Torino (Turin)
Asti
Alessandria
Mondovì
Savona
Finale Ligure
Imperia
San Remo
Ventimiglia

Lake Geneva
Lake Constance
Rhône
Rhine
Great Saint Bernard Pass 2469m
Mont Blanc 4807m
Little St-Bernard Pass 2188m
Gran Paradiso 4061m
Aosta
Susa
Rivoli
Moncalieri
Savigliano
Cuneo
Piemonte
Po
Appennino Ligure
Golfo di Genova
Genova (Genoa)
La Spezia
Livorno
Cecina
Piombino
Portoferraio
Isola d'Elba
Archipelago Toscano
Toscana
Siena
Lago Trasimeno
Grosseto
Orbetello
Chianti
Viterbo
Civitavecchia

Ligurian Sea

Corse (Corsica) (to France)

Strait of Bonifacio

Umbro-Marchigiano
Marche
Appennino
Appennino Umbro-Marchigiano

VATICAN CITY

Po
Valle

0 km 100

0 miles 100

Population   ● National capital

○ below 50,000   ○ 50,000 to 100,000   ◉ 100,000 to 500,000   ◼ above 500,000

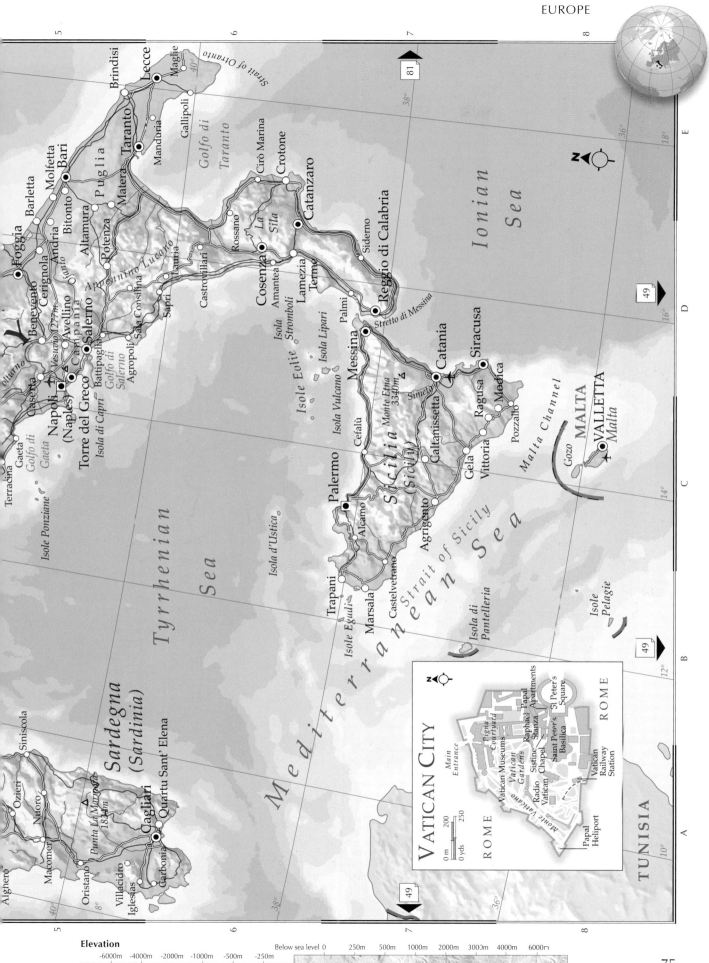

81

38°

40°

36°

E

49

D

16°

49

C

14°

B

12°

A

10°

5

6

7

8

Brindisi
Lecce
Maglie
Gallipoli
Strait of Otranto
Golfo di Taranto
40°

Taranto
Manduria
Matera
Puglia
Bari
Molfetta
Bitonto
Andria
Altamura
Barletta
Cerignola
Foggia
Benevento
Campania
Avellino
Potenza
Salerno
Sala Consilina
Appennino Lucano
Vesuvio 1277m
Caserta
Napoli (Naples)
Torre del Greco
Battipaglia
Golfo di Salerno
Agropoli
Isola di Capri
Gaeta
Golfo di Gaeta
Terracina
Isole Ponziane
Gioia Tauro

Volturno

Ciò Marina
Crotone
Catanzaro
La Sila
Rossano
Cosenza
Amantea
Lamezia Terme
Palmi
Siderno
Reggio di Calabria
Stretto di Messina
Sapri
Castrovillari

Ionian Sea

Isola Stromboli
Isole Eolie
Isola Lipari
Isola Vulcano
Messina
Cefalù
Monte Etna 3340m
Simeto
Catania
Siracusa
Medica
Ragusa
Pozzallo

Palermo
Alcamo
Sicilia (Sicily)
Caltanissetta
Gela
Vittoria
Agrigento
Castelvetrano

Trapani
Isole Egadi
Marsala
Isola d'Ustica

Tyrrhenian Sea

Strait of Sicily
Mediterranean Sea
Isola di Pantelleria

Malta Channel
Gozo
MALTA
VALLETTA
Malta
Isole Pelagie

Sardegna (Sardinia)
Siniscola
Ozieri
Nuoro
Macomer
Oristano
Alghero
Punta La Marmora 1834m
Cagliari
Quartu Sant'Elena
Carbonia
Iglesias
Villacidro

TUNISIA

36°

8°

40°

5

6

7

8

Vatican City

Main Entrance
Vigna Courtyard
Papal Apartments
Raphael Stanza
St Peter's Square
Vatican Museums
Vatican Gardens
Radio Vatican
Sistine Chapel
Saint Peter's Basilica
Monte Vaticano
Vatican Railway Station
Papal Heliport

ROME
R O M E

0 m   200
0 yds   250

Elevation

-6000m	-4000m	-2000m	-1000m	-500m	-250m	Below sea level 0	250m	500m	1000m	2000m	3000m	4000m	6000m

-19,658ft -13,124ft -6562ft -3281ft -1640ft -820ft -328ft/-100m 0

820ft 1640ft 3281ft 6562ft 9843ft 13,124ft 19,685ft

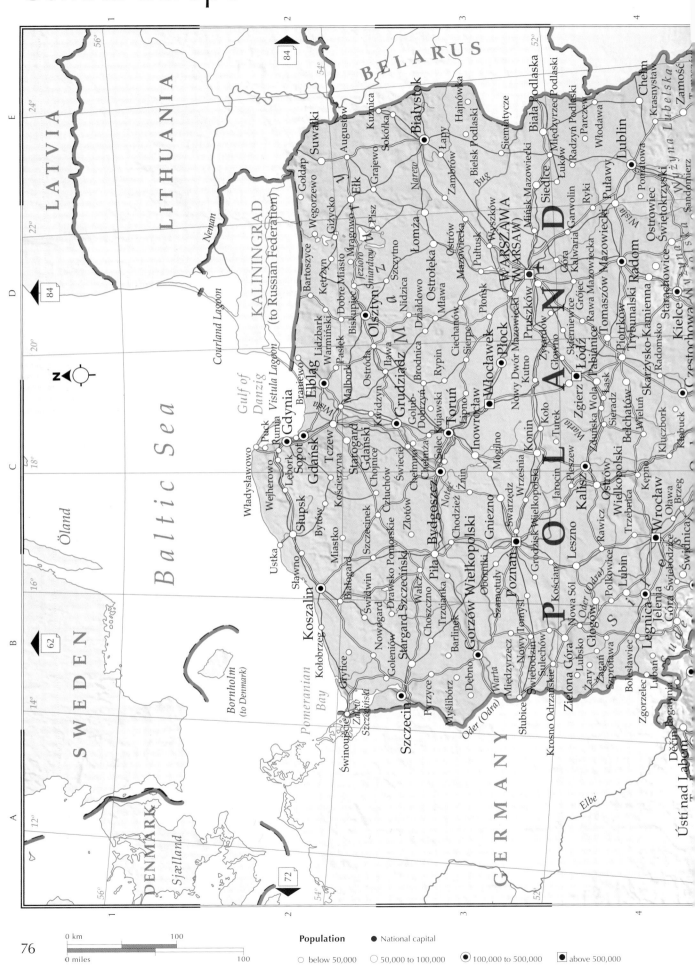

Baltic Sea

Öland

SWEDEN

DENMARK

S:ælland

Bornholm
(to Denmark)

LATVIA

LITHUANIA

Neman

KALININGRAD
(to Russian Federation)

Courland Lagoon

Gulf of
Danzig

Vistula Lagoon

Pomeranian
Bay

Szczeciński

BELARUS

POLAND

WARSZAWA
(WARSAW)

GERMANY

Elbe

Oder (Odra)

Warta

Odra

Ústí nad Labem

Population

● National capital

○ below 50,000 ◎ 50,000 to 100,000 ◉ 100,000 to 500,000 ■ above 500,000

0 km   100

0 miles   100

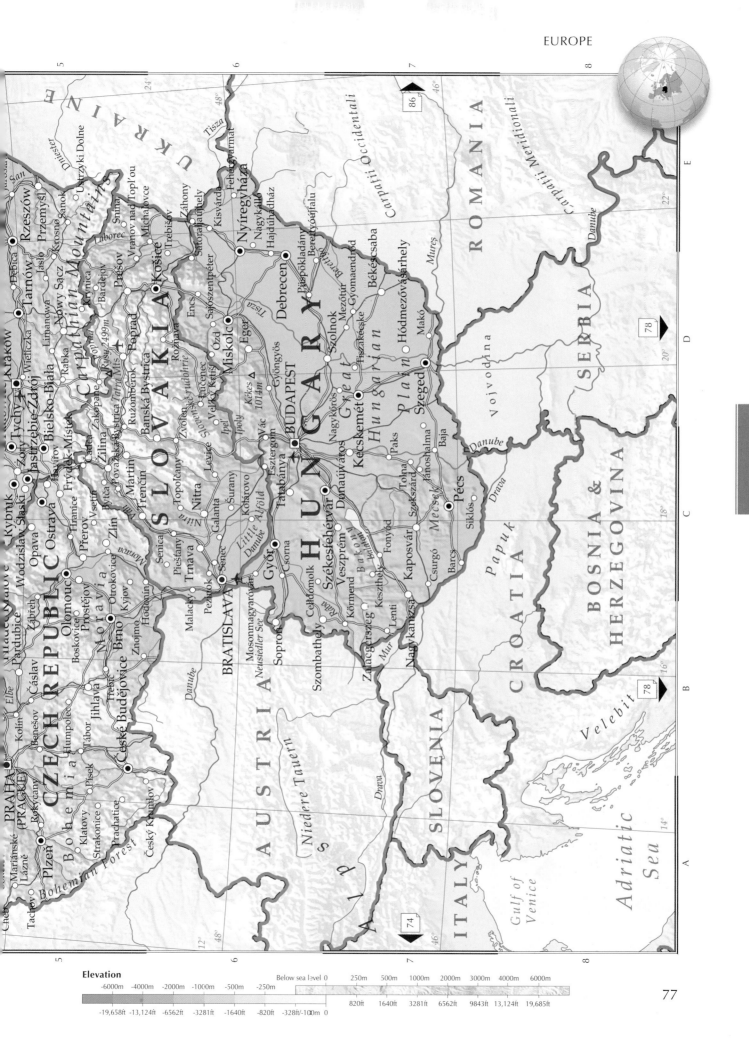

78

78

74

Elevation

						Below sea level 0	250m	500m	1000m	2000m	3000m	4000m	6000m
-6000m	-4000m	-2000m	-1000m	-500m	-250m								

| -19,658ft | -13,124ft | -6562ft | -3281ft | -1640ft | -820ft | -328ft/-100m 0 | | 820ft | 1640ft | 3281ft | 6562ft | 9843ft | 13,124ft | 19,685ft |

Southeast Europe

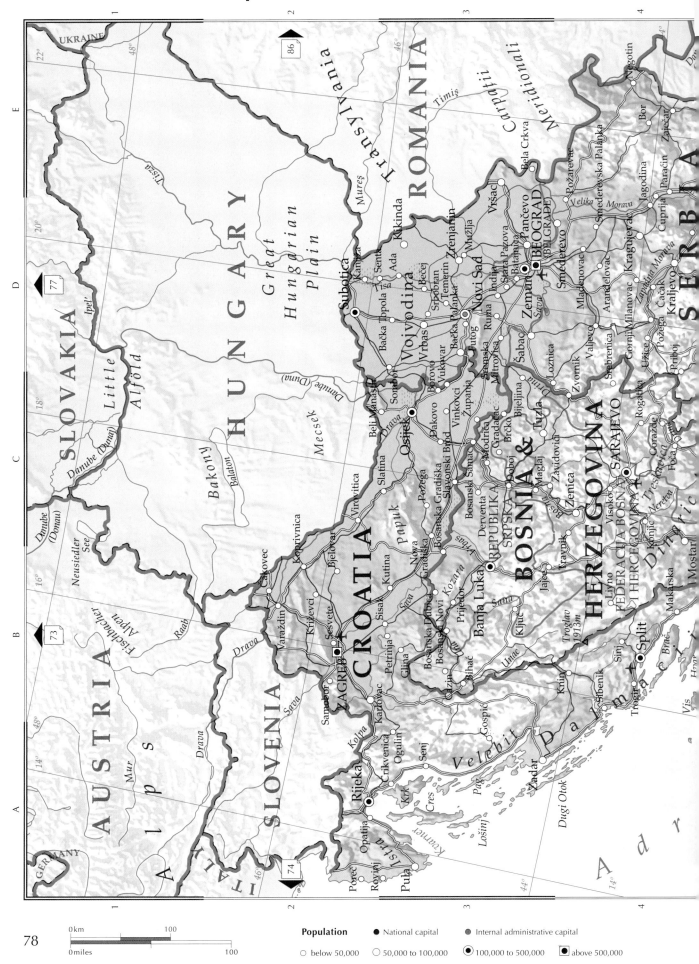

UKRAINE

SLOVAKIA

AUSTRIA

Alps

Fischbacher Alpen

GERMANY

ITALY

SLOVENIA

HUNGARY

Great Hungarian Plain

Little Alföld

Bakony

Mecsek

Balaton

Neusiedler See

ROMANIA

Transylvania

Carpaţii Meridionali

SERBIA

CROATIA

BOSNIA & HERZEGOVINA

REPUBLIKA SRPSKA

FEDERACIJA BOSNA I HERCEGOVINA

Dinaric

Velebit

Parnati

Voivodina

Danube (Donau)
Danube (Dunaj)
Danube (Duna)

Ipel'
Tisza
Raab
Mur
Drava
Drava
Sava
Sava
Kolpa
Korana
Una
Sana
Vrbas
Bosna
Drina
Sava
Tara
Neretva
Zapadna Morava
Velika Morava
Južna Morava
Timiş
Mureş
Tisa
Sio

ZAGREB
BEOGRAD
BELGRADE
SARAJEVO
RIJEKA

Subotica
Kanjiža
Senta
Ada
Kikinda
Bačka Topola
Bečej
Srbobran
Temerin
Zrenjanin
Vršac
Pančevo
Zemun
Novi Sad
Vrbas
Bačka Palanka
Ruma
Indija
Stara Pazova
Batajnica
Smederevo
Mladenovac
Aranđelovac
Kragujevac
Čačak
Kraljevo
Cuprija
Jagodina
Paraćin
Smederevska Palanka
Požarevac
Bela Crkva
Bor
Zaječar
Negotin
Velika
Požega
Pribojё

Beli Manastir
Osijek
Đakovo
Vinkovci
Županja
Sombor
Borovo
Vukovar
Srpska Mitrovica
Šabac
Loznica
Bijeljina
Tuzla
Zvornik
Valjevo
Srebrenica
Gornji Milanovac
Užice
Rogatica
Goražde
Foča
Tjentište
Bosanski Šamac
Brčko
Modriča
Derventa
Gradačac
Doboj
Bosanska Gradiška
Bosanski Brod
Slavonski Brod
Nova Gradiška
Požega
Slatina
Virovitica
Koprivnica
Čakovec
Varaždin
Bjelovar
Sesvete
Samobor
Karlovac
Jastrebarsko
Petrinja
Sisak
Kutina
Glina
Bosanska Dubica
Bosanski Novi
Prijedor
Banja Luka
Zenica
Zavidovići
Maglaj
Visoko
Konjic
Mostar
Makarska
Split
Trogir
Šibenik
Knin
Sinj
Livno
Ključ
Unac
Bihać
Cazin
Ogulin
Crikvenica
Senj
Gospić
Zadar
Vis
Hvar
Brač
Pag
Cres
Lošinj
Krk
Dugi Otok
Rijeka
Opatija
Poreč
Rovinj
Pula
Istra
Kvarner
Kozara
Papuk
Troglav 1913m

Adriatic

Population ● National capital ● Internal administrative capital

○ below 50,000 ○ 50,000 to 100,000 ◉ 100,000 to 500,000 ◼ above 500,000

0 km — 100
0 miles — 100

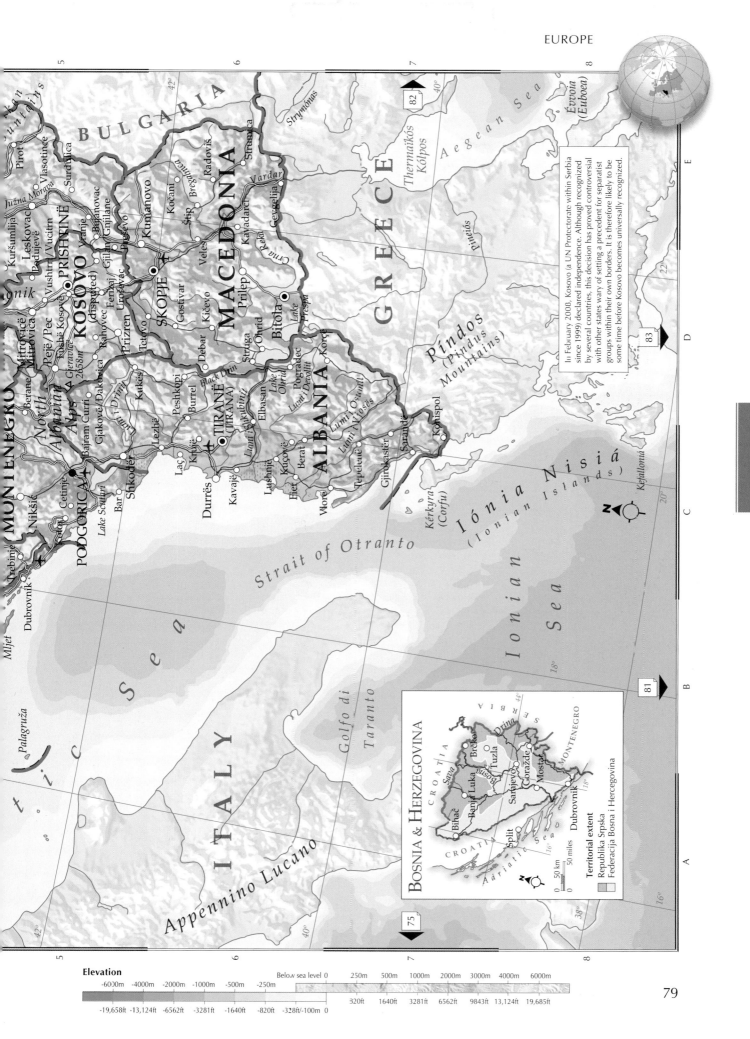

The Mediterranean

ATLANTIC OCEAN

Bay of Biscay

FRANCE

GERMANY
München (Munich)

Quimper
St-Nazaire
Île d'Yeu
Nantes
Île de Ré
Île d'Oléron

Tours
Loire

Dijon
Zürich
BERN
SWITZ.
LIECH.
VADUZ
Innsbr

Limoges
Clermont-Ferrand
Lyon
Lake Geneva
Mont Blanc
4807m

Milano
(Milan)
Venezi
(Venice

Bordeaux
Garonne
Dordogne
Toulouse
Montpellier
Nîmes
MONACO
Marseille
Nice
Côte d'Azur

Torino
(Turin)
Po

Genova
(Genoa)
Golfo di
Genova
Bologna
Pisa
SAN
MAR
ROMA
(ROME)

A Coruña
Santander
Bilbao
Pyrenees
ANDORRA
Perpignan
Golfe du Lion

Ligurian
Sea
Corse
(Corsica)
Isola
d'Elba
VATICAN
CITY

Vigo
Cordillera Cantábrica
Sistema Ibérico
Ebro
Zaragoza
Barcelona
Tarragona
Costa Braca
Ajaccio
Isola Asinara

Porto
Duero
Valladolid
Sardegna
(Sardinia)
Sassari

MADRID
Castellón
de la Plana
Mallorca
(Majorca)
Menorca
(Minorca)

PORTUGAL
SPAIN
Sistema Central
Tagus
Golfo de
Valencia
Palma
Tyrrhen
Sea

LISBOA
(LISBON)
Valencia
Ibiza
Islas Baleares
(Balearic Islands)

Sierra Morena
Guadalquivir
Alicante
Formentera
Mediter

Sevilla
(Seville)
Sistemas Béticos
Murcia
Costa Blanca
Sicilia
(Sicily)
Pale

Golfo de
Cádiz
Cádiz
Málaga
Almería
Cartagena
Cap
Bougaroun
Annaba
Golfe de
Tunis
Cap Bon

ALGER
(ALGIERS)
Tizi Ouzou
TUNIS
Isola
Pante

GIBRALTAR (to UK)
Costa del Sol
Ceuta (to Spain)
Oran
Mostaganem
Atlas Tellien
Constantine
Sétif
Golfe
de
Hammamet
Is
P

Strait of Gibraltar
Tanger
Tétouan
Melilla
(to Spain)
Tlemcen
Massif de l'Aurès
Sousse

Fès
Oujda
Chott ech
Chergui
Chott el
Hodna
Sfax
Île de
Kerkenah

RABAT
MOROCCO
Hauts Plateaux
Chott Melghir
Chott
el Jerid
Gabès
Golfe de
Gabès
Île de Jerba

Casablanca
Moyen Atlas
Haut Atlas
Atlas Mountains
TUNISIA
TARABULU
(TRIPO

Safi
ALGERIA
Gharyâ

MALTA

Mediterranean Sea
14°30'
36°

Victoria
Nadur
Kemmuna
(Comino)

Gozo
Mġarr

Mellieħa
San Ġiljan
Sliema

Mosta
VALLETTA

Hamrun
Paola

Malta
Rabat
Birżebbuġa

250m/820ft
100m/328ft
Sea Level

0 km   10
0 miles   10

CYPRUS

TURKISH REPUBLIC OF
NORTHERN CYPRUS
(recognized only
by Turkey)

Mediterranean Sea
Lapta
(Lápithos)
Girne
(Kerýneia)
Yenierenköy
(Agialoúsa)

Güzelyurt Körfezi
(Kólpos Mórfou)
Değirmenlik
(Kythréa)
Gazimağusa Körfezi
(Kólpos Ammóchostos)

Pólis
NICOSIA
Gazimağusa
(Ammóchostos,
Famagusta)

Tróödos
Dhekelia
Lárnaka

Páfos
Sovereign
Base Area
(to UK)
Sovereign
Base Area
(to UK)

Akrotirion
Lemesós
(Limassol)

1000m/3281ft
500m/1640ft
250m/820ft
Sea Level

0 km   25
0 miles   25

Sahara

0 km   400
0 miles   400

Population   ● National capital

○ below 50,000   ○ 50,000 to 100,000   ◉ 100,000 to 500,000   ■ above 500,000

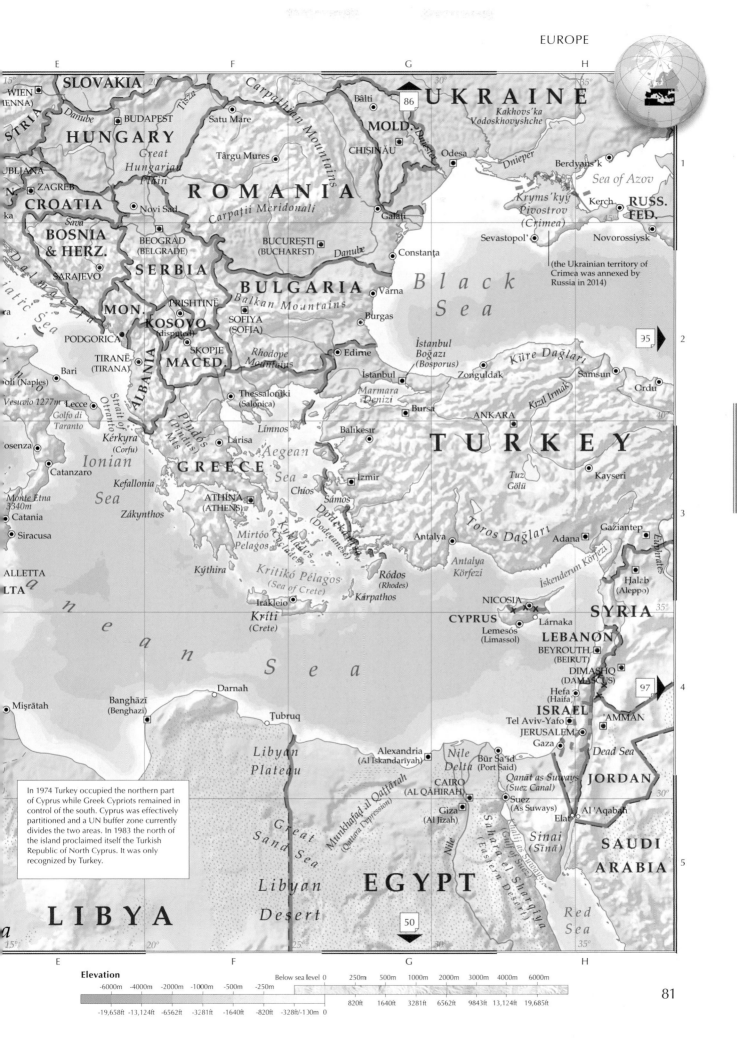

SLOVAKIA
MENNA
WIEN
HUNGARY
BUDAPEST
Danube
Great
Hungarian
Plain
Tisza
Satu Mare
Târgu Mures
Carpathian Mountains
Bălți
86
UKRAINE
MOLD.
CHIȘINĂU
Dniester
Odesa
Kakhovs'ka
Vodoskhovyshche
Dnieper
Berdyans'k
Sea of Azov
1
ZAGREB
CROATIA
Novi Sad
ROMANIA
Carpații Meridonali
Gălați
Krym's'kyy
Pivostrov
(Crimea)
Sevastopol'
Kerch
RUSS.
FED.
Novorossiysk
Sava
BOSNIA
& HERZ.
SARAJEVO
BEOGRAD
(BELGRADE)
SERBIA
BUCUREȘTI
(BUCHAREST)
Danube
Constanța
Black
Sea
(the Ukrainian territory of
Crimea was annexed by
Russia in 2014)
MON.
PODGORICA
PRISHTINË
KOSOVO
(disputed)
BULGARIA
Balkan Mountains
Varna
Burgas
35
2
TIRANË
(TIRANA)
SKOPJE
MACED.
SOFIYA
(SOFIA)
Rhodope
Mountains
Edirne
İstanbul
Boğazı
(Bosporus)
Zonguldak
Küre Dağları
Samsun
Ordu
Bari
ALBANIA
Pindos
(Pindus)
Mts
Thessaloníki
(Salónica)
İstanbul
Marmara
Denizi
Bursa
ANKARA
Kızıl Irmak
40
Vesuvio 1277m
Lecce
Strait of Otranto
Límnos
Lárisa
Aegean
Sea
Balıkesir
TURKEY
Kırşehir
Kayseri
Golfo di
Taranto
Kérkyra
(Corfu)
GREECE
İzmir
Tuz
Gölü
Gažiantep
Ionian
Kefallonia
Chíos
Sámos
Adana
Euphrates
osenza
Monte Etna
3340m
Catania
Sea
Zákynthos
ATHÍNA
(ATHENS)
Kykládes
(Cyclades)
Dodecanese
(Dodecanese)
Toros Dağları
İskenderun Körfezi
Ḥalab
(Aleppo)
3
Siracusa
Kýthira
Mirtóo
Pelagos
Kritikó Pélagos
(Sea of Crete)
Ródos
(Rhodes)
Antalya
Antalya
Körfezi
NICOSIA
SYRIA
35
ALLETTA
LTA
Irákleio
Kríti
(Crete)
Kárpathos
CYPRUS
Lemesós
(Limassol)
Lárnaka
LEBANON
BEYROUTH
(BEIRUT)
DIMASHQ
(DAMASCUS)
97
4
Mişrātah
Banghāzī
(Benghazi)
Darnah
Ṭubruq
Hefa
(Haifa)
ISRAEL
Tel Aviv-Yafo
JERUSALEM
Gaza
'AMMĀN
Dead Sea
JORDAN
30
n
Sea
Libyan
Plateau
Alexandria
(Al Iskandarīyah)
Nile
Delta
Būr Sa'īd
(Port Said)
Qanāt as Suways
(Suez Canal)
Suez
(As Suways)
Al 'Aqabah
Elat
In 1974 Turkey occupied the northern part
of Cyprus while Greek Cypriots remained in
control of the south. Cyprus was effectively
partitioned and a UN buffer zone currently
divides the two areas. In 1983 the north of
the island proclaimed itself the Turkish
Republic of North Cyprus. It was only
recognized by Turkey.
Munkhafad al Qațțārah
(Qattara Depression)
CAIRO
(AL QĀHIRAH)
Giza
(Al Jīzah)
Khalīj as Suways
(Gulf of Suez)
Sinai
(Sīnā)
Sahara el Sharqīya
(Eastern Desert)
SAUDI
5
LIBYA
Great
Sand
Sea
Libyan
Desert
EGYPT
50
Nile
Red
Sea
ARABIA

Elevation

					Below sea level 0	250m	500m	1000m	2000m	3000m	4000m	6000m

-6000m -4000m -2000m -1000m -500m -250m

-19,658ft -13,124ft -6562ft -3281ft -1640ft -820ft -328ft/-100m 0   820ft 1640ft 3281ft 6562ft 9843ft 13,124ft 19,685ft

Bulgaria & Greece

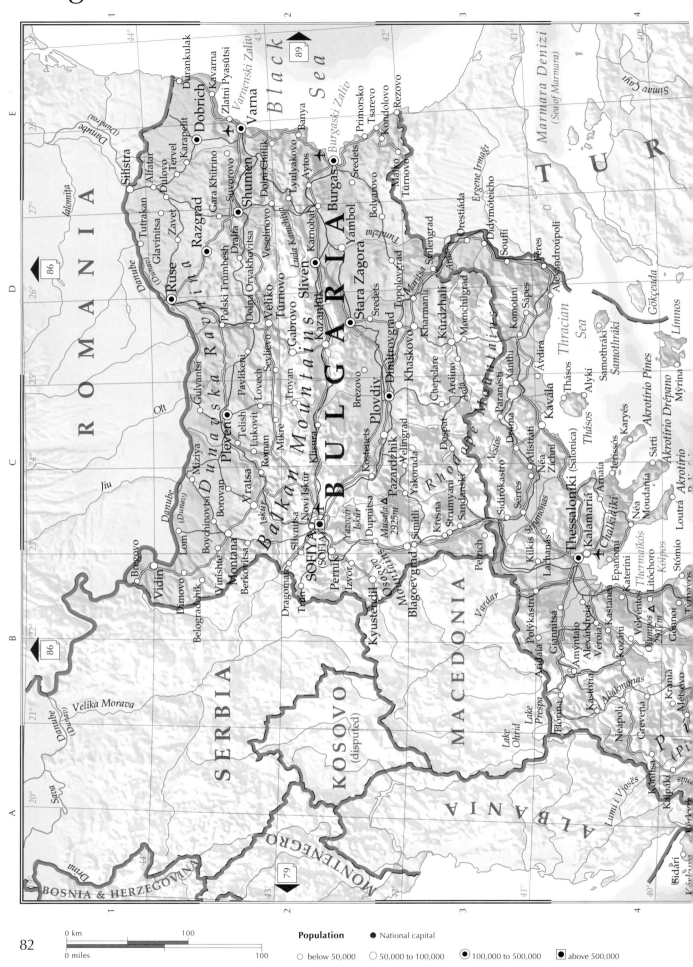

Population   ● National capital

○ below 50,000   ○ 50,000 to 100,000   ◉ 100,000 to 500,000   ⬤ above 500,000

Y

Gediz Nehri

Büyükmenderes Nehri

94

Ródos
(Rhodes)
Lindos

Chalki

Ródos
(Rhodes)

Kattaviá

Kárpathos
Kárpathos

Sária

Kásos

81

Mytilíni

Lésvos
(Lesbos)

Plomári

Chíos
Chíos

Psará

Antípsara

Ikaría

Sámos
Sámos

Agathonísi

Pátmos
Léros
Leipsoí
Arkoí

Agía
Marína
Kálymnos

Kos
Kos

Nísyros
Tílos

Astypálaia

Dodekánisa (Dodecanese)

Amorgós
Amorgós
Akrotírio Floúda

Anáfi

Síteía
Neápoli
Ágios Nikólaos
Ierápetra

Mýkonos

Naxos
Náxos

Íos

Thíra

Santoríni

Kritikó Pélagos
(Sea of Crete)

Kríti (Crete)
Irákleio
Díkti
Zarós
Mýrtos

Kríti (Crete)

Pánormos
Spíli
Tympáki
Gávdos

Lefká Óri
Chóra Stakíon

aegean Sea

Gean Sea

Skýros

Évvoia
(Euboea)

Kými

Skýros

Spórades

Skáthos
Skópelos
Vóreï
Strofyliá

Andros
Andros

Tínos
Tínos

Sýros

Ermoúpoli
Kýthnos

Kýklades (Cyclades)

Páros
Paroikiá
Náxos

Chóra
Kástro

Sífnos

Sérifos

Folégandros

Pláka

Mílos

Kéa
Tzía
Íoulís

Kárystos

Marathónas
Keratéa

ATHÍNA
(ATHENS)
Lávrio
Palaiá Epídavros
Póros

Peiraías
(Piraeus)
Mégara

Ýdra

Ermióni

Leonídio

Geráki

Neápoli
Daimoniá

Karavás
Kýthira

Mirtóo Pelagos

Mirtóo Pélagos

Kýthira
Kýthira

Antikýthira
Potamós

Chaniá
Kíssamos
Kántanos

Mediterranean Sea

GREECE

Lamía

Domokós
Sotírpi
Agrovótiano
Mólos
Livanátes
Malesína
Chalkída
Alivéri
Ýlia

Kappenísi
Lidoríki
Náfpaktos

Amfilochía
Thérmo
Neochóri
Katoúna

Lamía

Domokós

Aliartos

Aígio
Korinthíakos
Kólpos
Kiáto
Kórinthos
(Corinth)
Neméa

Xylokastro

Pelopónnisos
(Peloponnese)

Kláto Achaía

Páos

Lechainá
Gastoúni
Kerí

Pátra

Lámpeia
Pýrgos
Zacháro
Kyparissía

Alfeiós

Trípoli

Argos
Náfplio

Spárti

Messíni
Kalámata

Koróni

Aréopoli

Gýtheio

Lakonikós Kólpos

Gerolímenas

Préveza
Lefkáda
Vasilikí
Lixoúri
Argostóli

Lefkáda

Kefalloniá

Zákynthos

Ióni Nisiá
(Ionian Islands)

Páxoi
Antípaxoi

Ionian Sea

N

81

81

81

Elevation

-6000m -4000m -2000m -100cm -500m -250m

Below sea level 0 250m 500m 1000m 2000m 3000m 4000m 6000m

-19,658ft -13,124ft -6562ft -328ft -1640ft -820ft -328ft/-100m 0

820ft 1640ft 3281ft 6562ft 9843ft 13,124ft 19,685ft

The Baltic States & Belarus

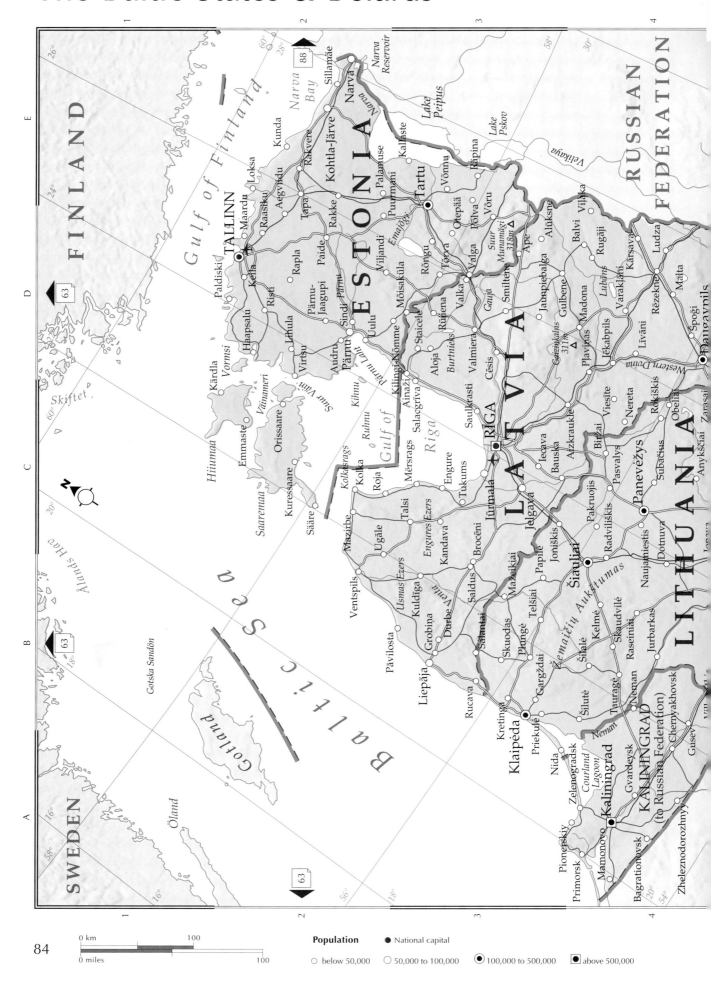

SWEDEN

FINLAND

Öland

Gotska Sandön

Skiftet

Ålands Hav

Gulf of Finland

Narva Bay

ESTONIA

TALLINN

Paldiski
Maardu
Loksa
Raasiku
Aegviidu
Kunda
Rakvere
Tapa
Rakke
Kohtla-Järve
Sillamäe
Narva

Narva Reservoir

Lake Peipus

Lake Pskov

RUSSIAN FEDERATION

Velikaya

Kärdla
Vormsi
Haapsalu
Keila
Risti
Lihula
Virtsu
Paide
Rapla
Pärnu-Jaagupi
Sindi
Pärnu
Audru
Kilingi-Nõmme
Tõstamaa
Kõmme
Viljandi
Mõisaküla
Rongu
Torva
Tartu
Võnnu
Otepää
Põlva
Võru
Palamuse
Puurmani
Kallaste
Rapina

Suur Munamägi 318m

Ape
Alūksne
Balvi
Rugāji
Kārsava
Vilaka

Väinameri

Hiiumaa

Saaremaa

Emmaste
Orissaare
Kuressaare
Sääre

Suur Väin

Pärnu Laht

Kihnu

Ruhnu

Ainaži
Salacgrīva
Staicele
Aloja
Mazsalaca
Rūjiena
Valka
Valga
Smiltene
Strenči
Cēsis
Valmiera
Burtnieks

Gauja

Jaunpiebalga
Gulbene
Madona
Varakļāni
Lubāns
Rēzekne
Malta
Ludza
Zilupe
Spoģi
Dagavpils

LATVIA

RĪGA
Jūrmala
Saulkrasti
Tukums
Engure
Kandava
Talsi
Ugāle

Gulf of Riga

Mērsrags
Roja
Kolka

Kolkasrags

Mazirbe
Ventspils
Pāvilosta
Liepāja
Grobiņa
Rucava

Usmas Ezers
Engures Ezers

Kuldīga
Saldus
Brocēni
Dobele
Jelgava
Iecava
Bauska
Aizkraukle
Pļaviņas
Jēkabpils
Līvāni
Viesīte
Nereta
Rokiškis

Gaiziņkalns 311m

Western Dvina

Skrunda
Mažeikiai
Papilė
Joniškis
Pakruojis
Radviliškis
Pasvalys
Subačius
Biržai

Skuodas
Plungė
Telšiai
Kelmė
Šiauliai

Žemaičių Aukštumas

Gargždai
Kretinga
Priekulė
Klaipėda
Nida

Courland Lagoon

KALININGRAD
(to Russia Federation)

Zelenogradsk
Pionerskiy
Primorsk
Mamonovo
Kaliningrad
Gvardeysk
Bagrationovsk
Zheleznodorozhnyy
Gusev
Chernyakhovsk

LITHUANIA

Panevėžys
Naujamiestis
Dotnuva
Anykščiai
Zarasai
Obeliai

Neman

Šilutė
Šilalė
Tauragė
Jurbarkas
Raseiniai
Skaudvilė
Šakiai
Neman

Baltic Sea

Gotland

Population
- ○ below 50,000
- ◎ 50,000 to 100,000
- ◉ 100,000 to 500,000
- ▣ above 500,000

● National capital

0 km   100
0 miles   100

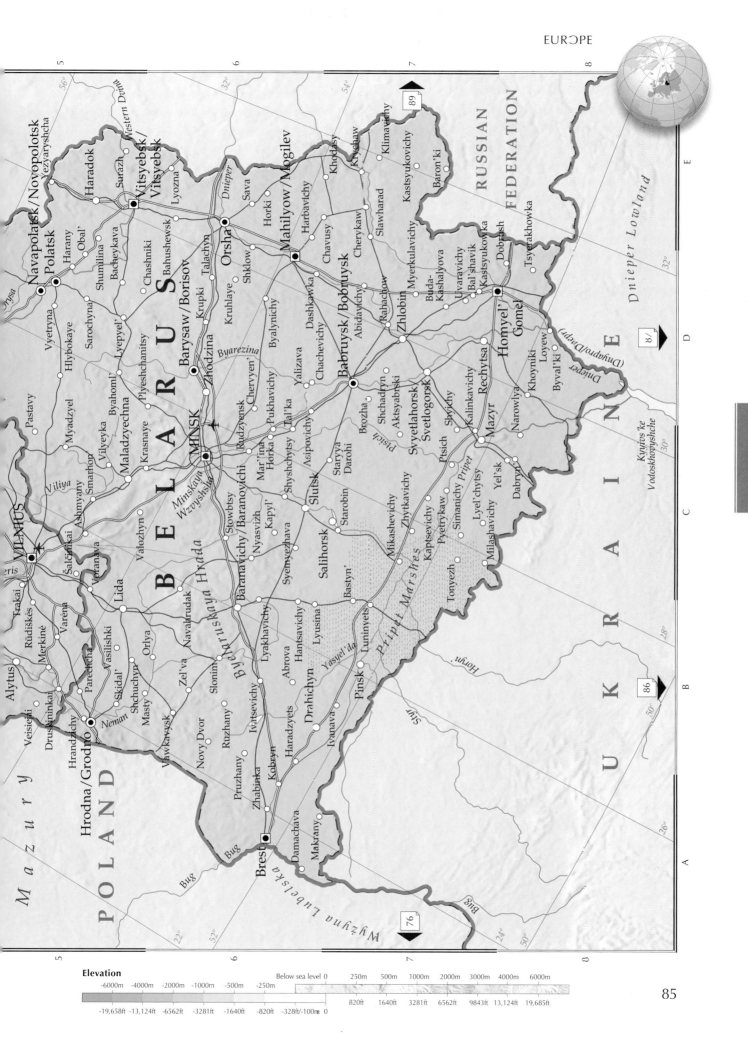

Elevation

| -6000m | -4000m | -2000m | -1000m | -500m | -250m | | Below sea level 0 | 250m | 500m | 1000m | 2000m | 3000m | 4000m | 6000m |

| -19,658ft | -13,124ft | -6562ft | -3281ft | -1640ft | -820ft | -328ft/-100m | 0 | 820ft | 1640ft | 3281ft | 6562ft | 9843ft | 13,124ft | 19,685ft |

Ukraine, Moldova & Romania

Population   ● National capital

○ below 50,000   ○ 50,000 to 100,000   ⊙ 100,000 to 500,000   ▣ above 500,000

E   32°   F   34°   G   36°   38°   H

88

52°

40°

1

Dnieper
(Dnyapro)

Horodnya
Shostka
Shchors
Hlukhiv
Chernihiv
Krolevets'
Konotop
Bakhmach
Nizhyn
Sumy
Nosivka
Romny
Pryluky
Lebedyn
Yahotyn
Pyryatyn
Okhtyrka
Zolochiv
Hrebinka
Lubny
Myrhorod
Derhachi
Lyubotyn
Kharkiv
Merefa
Kup''yans'k
Poltava

Desna

Desna

Psel

Donets

Oskol

Don

R U S S I A N
F E D E R A T I O N

Srednerusskaya
Vozvyshennost'

50°

88

2

KIV
IV
arka
Vasyl'kiv
stiv
Bila Tserkva
Bohuslav
Horodyshche
venyhorodka
Tal'ne
Holovanivs'k
Ulyanivka
Brovary
Kaniv
Zolotonosha
Cherkasy
Smila
Chyhyryn
Shpola
Oleksandrivka
Mala Vyska
Znam''yanka
Svitlovods'k
Kremenchuk
Izyum
Starobil's'k
Kremenchuts'ke
Vodoskhovyshche
Slov''yans'k   Kreminna
Rubizhne
Kramators'k   **Syeverodonets'k**
Lysychans'k
Zolote
Kostyantynivka
Luhans'k
Novomoskovs'k
Pavlohrad
Horlivka
Stakhanov
Krasnodon
Yenakiyeve
Krasnyy Luch
Makiyivka
Torez
Donets'k
Amvrosiyivka
Dokuchayevs'k

Kaniv'ke
Vodoskhovyshche

Dniprodzerzhyns'ke
Vodoskhovyshche

48°

3

Kirovohrad
Zhovti Vody
Dniprodzerzhyns'k
P''yatykhatky
Dnipropetrovs'k
Synel'nykove
Pervomays'k
Bobrynets'
Dolyns'ka
Pokrovs'ke
Kryvyy Rih
Kryve Ozero
Arbuzynka
Inhulets'
Novyy Buh
Voznesens'k
Ordzhonikidze
Nikopol
Marhanets'
Orikhiv
Volnovakha
Kam''yanka-Dniprovs'ka
Zaporizhzhya
Dniprorudne
Polohy
Tokmak
Mariupol'
Novoazovs'k
Molochans'k
Don

Inhulets'

Pivdennyy Buh

Dnieper
(Dnipro)

4

B l a c k   S e a
Mykolayiv
Zhovtneve
Kakhovka
Melitopol'
Kakhovs'ka
Vodoskhovyshche
L o w l a n d
Ochakiv
Kherson
Yakymivka
Prymors'k
Berdyans'k
Gulf of Taganrog
Yeya
Illichivs'k
Odesa
Hola Prystan'
Tsyurupyns'k
Chaplynka
Novotroyits'ke
Kalanchak
Heniches'k
Armyans'k
46°

S e a   o f   A z o v

Karkinits'ka Zatoka
Krasnoperekops'k
Rozdol'ne
Dzhankoy
Nyzhn'ohirs'kyy
R U S S I A N
Krasnohvardiys'ke
Zatoka
Syvash
Kerch Strait
Chornomors'ke
Kerch
F E D E R A T I O N
Kryms'kyy Pivostriv
Lenine
Kuban'
Yevpatoriya
(Crimea)
Saky
Simferopol'
Feodosiya
Bakhchysaray
Kryms'ki Hory
(the Ukrainian territory of
Crimea was annexed by
Russia in 2014)
Sevastopol'
Alushta
Yalta
Alupka

44°

5

B l a c k   S e a

94

E   32°   F   34°   G   36°   38°   H

Elevation

-6000m	-4000m	-2000m	-1000m	-500m	-250m	Below sea level 0	250m	500m	1000m	2000m	3000m	4000m	6000m
-19,658ft	-13,124ft	-6562ft	-3281ft	-1640ft	-820ft	-328ft/-100m	0	820ft	1640ft	3281ft	6562ft	9843ft	13,124ft	19,685ft

European Russia

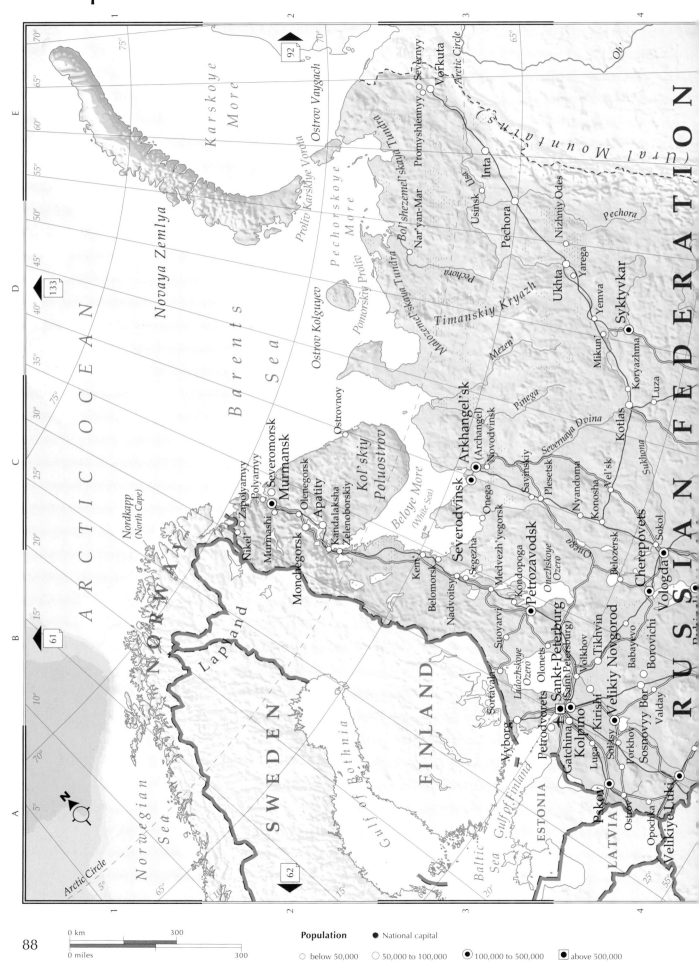

Population   ● National capital

○ below 50,000   ◎ 50,000 to 100,000   ◉ 100,000 to 500,000   ■ above 500,000

0 km   300
0 miles   300

Elevation

Below sea level	0	250m	500m	1000m	2000m	3000m	4000m	6000m

-6000m   -4000m   -2000m   -1000m   -500m   -250m

-19,658ft   -13,124ft   -6562ft   -3281ft   -1640ft   -820ft   -328ft/-100m   0

820ft   1640ft   3281ft   6562ft   9843ft   13,124ft   19,685ft

North & West Asia

ARCTIC

Franz Josef Land

Ostrov Komsomolets

Ostrov Oktyabr'skoy Revolyutsii
Ostrov Bol'shevik

Severnaya Zer

Poluostrov Taymyr
O:
Ta

North Siber

Kheta

Summer limit of pack ice

Winter limit of pack ice

Norwegian
Sea   North Cape

Barents
Sea

Ostrov
Kolguyev

Novaya Zemlya

East Novaya Zemlya Trench

Kara Sea

Poluostrov
Yamal

Noril'sk

Central
Siberian
Plateau

Kureyka

Arctic Circle

White Sea

Murmansk
Kola
Peninsula

RUSSIAN F
S i

Archangel

West Siberian
Plain

Lower Tunguska

Ob'

Ob'

Yenisey

Stony Tunguska

Angara

Gulf of Bothnia

Lake
Onega

Northern
Divina

Ural Mountains

Irtysh

Irtysh

Saint Petersburg

Lake Ladoga

Vologda

Perm'

Yekaterinburg

Ishim

Ob'

Chulym

Tomsk

Krasnoyarsk

Yaroslavl'

Nizhniy
Novgorod

MOSCOW

Central
Russian
Upland

Kazan'
Ufa

Ul'yanovsk

Samara

Chelyabinsk

Omsk

Novosibirsk

Novokuznetsk

Baltic Sea

Kaliningrad

KALININGRAD
(to Russ. Fed.)

Voronezh

Saratov

Orenburg

Ural'sk

ASTANA

Karagandy

Semipalatinsk

Sayanskiy Khrebet

Irkut

A

S

Volga

Volga

Ural

Kirghiz
Steppe

Kazakh Uplands

Altai Mountains

Volgograd

Don

(the Ukrainian territory of
Crimea was annexed by
Russia in 2014)

EUROPE

Rostov-na-Donu

Astrakhan'

Aral'sk

Syr Darya

KAZAKHSTAN

Ozero
Zaysan

Danube

Stavropol'

Aral
Sea

Ustyurt
Plateau

Kyzyl
Kum

Lake
Balkhash

Kyzylorda

Taraz

Ili

Almaty

Black Sea

El'brus
5642m

Caucasus

Caspian
Sea

Aktau

Dasoguz

UZBEKISTAN

Amu Darya

BISHKEK

Tien Shan

Jengish Chokusu/Tömür Feng 7443m

Istanbul

Kire Daglari

GEORGIA

ARMENIA

TBILISI

BAKU

TURKMENISTAN

Garagum

TASHKENT

KYRGYZSTAN

G

ANKARA

YEREVAN

AZERB.

Lake
Van

Garagum

DUSHANBE

TAJIKISTAN

TURKEY

Gaziantep

Tabriz

ASHGABAT

Hindu Kush

Kunlun Mountains

Adana

Aleppo

Mosul

Qom

TEHRAN

KABUL

Jalalabad

CYPRUS

SYRIA

IRAQ

Isfahan

IRAN

Herat

Khyber Pass

H i m a l a y a s

Mediterranean Sea

BEIRUT

LEBANON

DAMASCUS

BAGHDAD

Syrian
Desert

Tigris

Euphrates

Zagros Mountains

Iranian
Plateau

AFGHANISTAN

ISRAEL

AMMAN

Basra

JERUSALEM

JORDAN

Dead Sea
-427m

KUWAIT

An Nafud

KUWAIT

Shiraz

Zahedan

Thar Desert

Indus Fan

Ganges

SAUDI
ARABIA

MANAMA

Persian Gulf

Bandar-e 'Abbas

Dubai

Murray Ridge

Ganges Fan

BAHRAIN

RIYADH

QATAR

DOHA

U.A.E.

ABU
DHABI

MUSCAT

Sur

Bay of
Bengal

Tropic of Cancer

Jedda

Arabian
Peninsula

Gulf of Oman

OMAN

At Ta'if

Nile

Red Sea

Ar Rub' al Khali

AFRICA

N

SANA

YEMEN

Ta'izz

Aden

Gulf of Aden

Socotra
(to Yemen)

Arabian
Sea

133

59

81

47

0 km   800

0 miles   800

Population   ● National capital

○ below 50,000   ◎ 50,000 to 100,000   ◉ 100,000 to 500,000   ▣ above 500,000

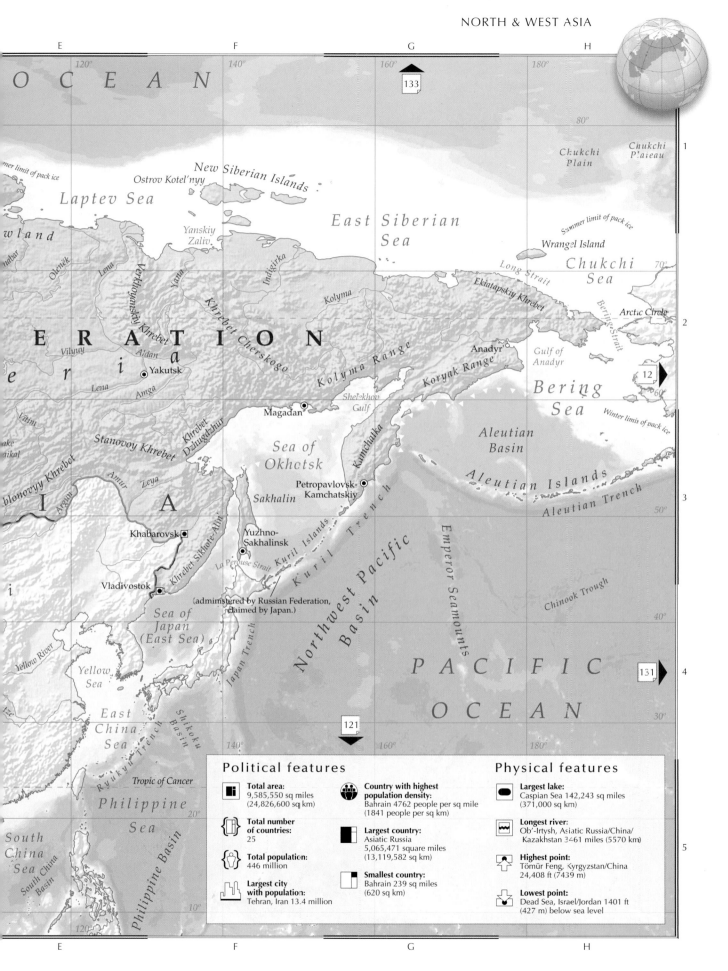

O C E A N

E 120° F 140° G 160° H 180° 80°

133

Summer limit of pack ice

Chukchi
Plain

Chukchi
Plateau

1

New Siberian Islands

Ostrov Kotel'nyy

Laptev Sea

Yanskiy
Zaliv

East Siberian
Sea

Summer limit of pack ice

Wrangel Island

Chukchi
Sea

70°

Long Strait

E R A T I O N

Olenëk Lena Verkhoyanskiy Khrebet Yana Indigirka Kolyma

Khrebet Cherskogo

Ekiatapskiy Khrebet

Bering Strait

Arctic Circle

2

Vilyuy Aldan

● Yakutsk

Kolyma Range

Anadyr' ●

Gulf of
Anadyr

12

e r i a

Lena Amga

Koryak Range

Bering

160°

Magadan ●

Shelekhov
Gulf

Sea

Winter limit of pack ice

Stanovoy Khrebet Khrebet Dzhugdzhur

Sea of
Okhotsk

Kamchatka

Aleutian
Basin

3

I A

Amur Zeya

Petropavlovsk-●
Kamchatskiy

Aleutian Islands

50°

Sakhalin

Aleutian Trench

Khabarovsk ■

Yuzhno-
Sakhalinsk ●

Kuril Islands

Kuril Trench

Northwest Pacific Basin

Emperor Seamounts

Chinook Trough

40°

La Perouse Strait

Vladivostok ■

(administered by Russian Federation,
claimed by Japan.)

Sea of
Japan
(East Sea)

Japan Trench

P A C I F I C

131

4

Yellow River

Yellow
Sea

O C E A N

30°

East
China
Sea

Shikoku
Basin

140° 160° 180°

121

Ryukyu Trench

Tropic of Cancer

Philippine

20°

Sea

South
China
Sea

Philippine Basin

South China Basin

10°

120°

E F G H

Political features

Total area:
9,585,550 sq miles
(24,826,600 sq km)

**Total number
of countries:**
25

Total population:
446 million

**Largest city
with population:**
Tehran, Iran 13.4 million

**Country with highest
population density:**
Bahrain 4762 people per sq mile
(1841 people per sq km)

Largest country:
Asiatic Russia
5,065,471 square miles
(13,119,582 sq km)

Smallest country:
Bahrain 239 sq miles
(620 sq km)

Physical features

Largest lake:
Caspian Sea 142,243 sq miles
(371,000 sq km)

Longest river:
Ob'-Irtysh, Asiatic Russia/China/
Kazakhstan 3461 miles (5570 km)

Highest point:
Tömür Feng, Kyrgyzstan/China
24,408 ft (7439 m)

Lowest point:
Dead Sea, Israel/Jordan 1401 ft
(427 m) below sea level

5

Turkey & The Caucasus

ROMANIA

Danube

Iacul Sinoie

BULGARIA

Varnenski Zaliv

Burgaski Zaliv

Maritsa

UKRAINE

Kryms'kyy Pivostriv (Crimea)

(the Ukrainian territory of Crimea was annexed by Russia in 2014)

Black Sea

82

Kırklareli
Edirne
Çorlu
Tekirdağ
Ergene Çayi

İstanbul
İzmit
Adapazarı
Marmara Denizi (Sea of Marmara)
Yalova
İznik Gölü
Bandırma
Bursa
Bilecik
Çanakkale
Çanakkale Boğazı (Dardanelles)

Sinav Çayi

Zonguldak
Bartın
Devrek
Çerkeş
Gerede
Bolu
Çankırı

Cide
İnebolu
Küre Dağları
Karabük
Kastamonu
Kargı
Merzifon

Sinop
Gerze
Bafra
Samsun
Ün
Orc
Canik Dağları

Kızıl Irmak
Kalecik
Çorum
Alaca
Tokat
Yıldızeli

Balıkesir
Edremit
Ayvalık
Lésvos
Chíos
Akhisar
Manisa
Gediz Nehri
İzmir
Ödemiş
Alaşehir

Bozüyük
Eskişehir
Kütahya
Simav
Gediz
Uşak
Afyon

ANKARA
Polatlı
Kırıkkale
Kulu
Hirfanlı Baraji

T U R K

Şarkışla
Boğazlıyan
Siv
Bünyan
Gürün

Sámos
Söke
Aydın
Nazilli
Büyükmenderes Nehri
Denizli
Burdur
Tavas
Milas
Muğla
Bodrum

Dinar
Beyşehir Gölü
Akşehir
Cihanbeyli
Aksaray
Tuz Gölü
Nevşehir
İncesu

Anatolia

Kayseri
Göksun
Gü

Dodekánisa (Dodecánese)
Marmaris
Dalaman
Fethiye
Kaş
Ródos (Rhodes)
Kárpathos

İsparta
Burdur Gölü
Antalya
Manavgat
Alanya
Mut
Finike
Antalya Körfezi
Anamur

Toros Dağları
Suğla Gölü
Konya
Karaman
Ereğli
Niğde
Silifke

Kahramanma
Gazi
Ceyhan
Tarsus
Adana
Osmaniye
Mersin (İçel)
İskenderun
Kilis
Antakya
Kırıkhan

Mediterranean Sea

CYPRUS

TURKISH REPUBLIC OF NORTHERN CYPRUS
(recognized only by Turkey)

Orantes

LEBANON

GREECE

50

83

86

0 km   200
0 miles   200

Population   ● National capital

○ below 50,000   ○ 50,000 to 100,000   ◉ 100,000 to 500,000   ◼ above 500,000

RUSSIAN

FEDERATION

Caucasus

Gagra
Gudauta
Sokhumi
Ochamchire
Ap'khazet'i
Enguri
Mestia
Kazbek
5047m
South
Ossetia
Kutaisi
Samtredia
Poti
Gori
Tsalka
GEORGIA
TBILISI
Kustavi
Akhaltsikhe
Kobuleti
Batumi
Achara
Hopa
Lesser Caucasus
Zaqatala
Greater Caucasus
Xaçmaz
Quba
Siyäzän
Şäki
Pazar
Rize
Of
Artvin
Gyumri
Vanadzor
Gäncä
Mingäçevir
Yevlax
Märäzä
Sumqayıt
BAKI
(BAKU)
Trabzon
Giresun
Doğu Karadeniz Dağları
Çoruh Nehri
Kars
Artik
Sevan
ARMENIA
YEREVAN
Sevana Lich
AZERBAIJAN
Nagorno-
Karabakh
Imişli
Qazımämmäd
Äli-Bayramı
İspir
Sarıkamış
Aras
Artashat
Xankändi
Büläsuvar
Kura
ümüşhane
Aşkale
Pasinler
Horasan
*Büyükağrı Dağı
(Mount Ararat)*
5137m
Goris
Aras
Länkäran
ahiye
Erzincan
Tercan
Erzurum
Ağrı
Doğubayazıt
AZERBAIJAN
Nax̦ıvan
Kemah
*Keban
Barajı*
Bingöl
Muş
Patnos
Erciş
Muradiye
Van
*Van
Gölü*
*Daryācheh-ye
Orūmīyeh*
*Reshteh-ye Kūhhā-ye Alborz
(Elburz Mountains)*
ohan
Elazığ
Tatvan
Bitlis
Gevaş
Toroslar
E
Y
alatya
D
o
ğ
u
Silvan
Siirt
ṭiyaman
Diyarbakır
Batman
Şırnak
K
u
r
d
i
s
t
a
n
IRAN
Silverek
*Atatürk
Barajı*
Viranşehir
Mardin
Nusaybin
Şanlıurfa
Ceylanpınar
Tigris
Al Jazīrah
Euphrates
IRAQ
ḥayrat
Asad
Jabal Bishrī
RIA
*Buḩayrat
ath
Tharthār*
*Kūhhā-ye Zagros
(Zagros Mountains)*

Caspian

Sea

Elevation

-6000m	-4000m	-2000m	-1000m	-500m	-250m	Below sea level 0	250m	500m	1000m 2000m 3000m 4000m 6000m

-19,658ft -13,124ft -6562ft -3281ft -1640ft -820ft -328ft/-100m 0

820ft 1640ft 3281ft 6562ft 9843ft 13,124ft 19,685ft

The Near East

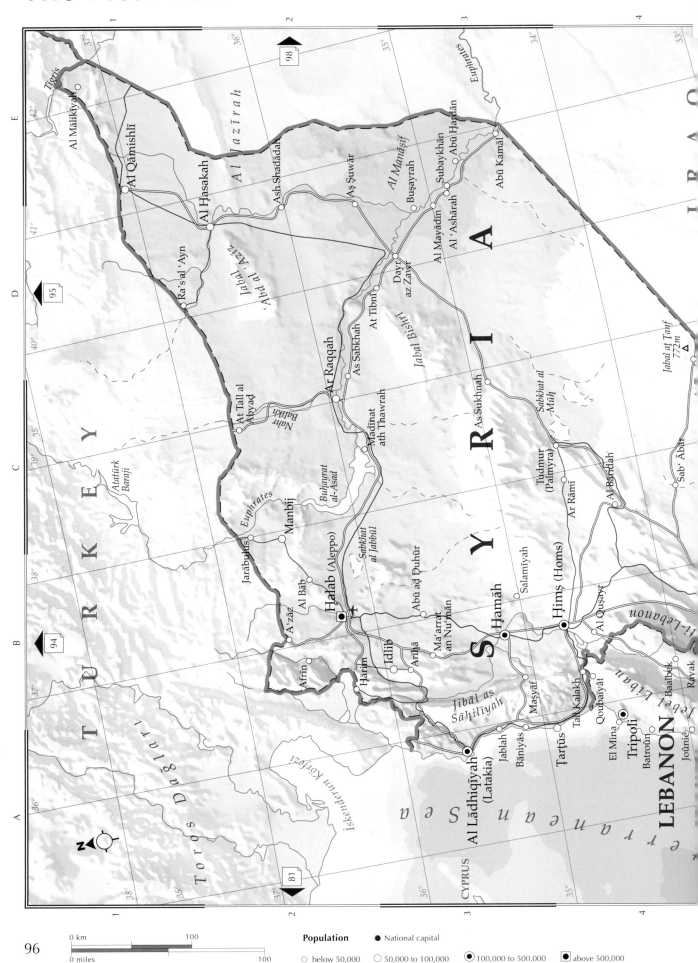

CYPRUS

LEBANON

SYRIA

TURKEY

IRAQ

Mediterranean Sea

İskenderun Körfezi

Toros Dağları

Tigris

Euphrates

Nahr Balikh

Buhayrat al-Asad

Al Jazīrah

Jabal 'Abd al 'Azīz

Jabal Bishrī

Jibāl as Sāhilīyah

Jabal Lubnān

Anti-Lebanon

Sabkhat al Mūḥ

Sabkhat al Jabbūl

Jabal aţ Ţanf 772m

Al Mālikīyah
Al Qāmishlī
Al Ḩasakah
Ra's al 'Ayn
Ash Shadādah
Aş Şuwār
Al Manāşif
Buşayrah
Subaykhān
Abū Ḩardān
Abū Kamāl
Al Mayādīn
Al 'Asharah
Dayr az Zawr
At Tibnī
At Sabkhah
As Sabkhah
Ar Raqqah
Madīnat ath Thawrah
Al Tall al Abyaḑ
Manbij
Jarābulus
Al Bāb
Ḩalab (Aleppo)
A'zāz
Afrīn
Ḩārim
Idlib
Arīḩā
Abū aḑ Ḑuhūr
Ma'arrat an Nu'mān
Ḩamāh
Salamīyah
Ḩimş (Homs)
As Sukhnah
Tudmur (Palmyra)
Ar Rāmī
Al Baddah
Al Quşayr
'Sab' Ābār
Al Lādhiqīyah (Latakia)
Jablah
Bāniyās
Maşyāf
Ţarţūs
Tall Kalakh
Qoubaïyât
El Mīna
Tripoli
Batroûn
Baalbek
Ra'yak
Jounié

Atatürk Baraji

0 km   100
0 miles   100

Population   ● National capital

○ below 50,000   ○ 50,000 to 100,000   ◉ 100,000 to 500,000   ■ above 500,000

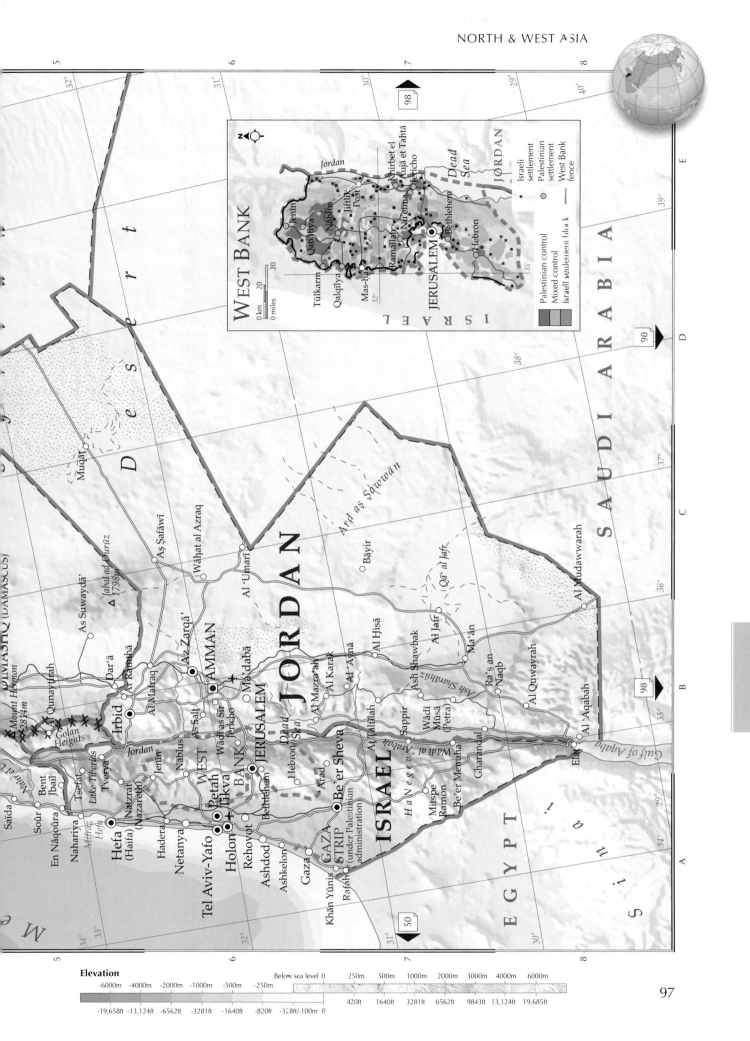

WEST BANK

Jordan

Khirbet el   Auja et Tahtã

Jenin
Qabãtiya
Nãblus
Jiftlik
Post
Nu'eima   Jericho

Tülkarm
Qalqïlya
Mas-ha
Ramallah

JERUSALEM   Bethlehem

Hebron

Dead Sea

JORDAN

ISRAEL

Israeli settlement
Palestinian settlement
West Bank fence

Palestinian control
Mixed control
Israeli settlement block

0 km   20
0 miles   20

Desert

Muḍat

As Safãwi
Wãhat al Azraq

Ard aṣ Ṣawwãn

Bãyir
Qã' al Jafr

JORDAN

Al 'Umari

Al Hisã
Al Jafr
Ma'ãn

Al Mudawwarah

SAUDI ARABIA

RIYADH (DAMASCUS)

△Jabal ad Durüz
1798m

As Suwaydã'

Az Zarqã'
AMMAN
Mãdabã

As Salt
Wãdïas Sir
Jericho

Al Mazra'ah
Al Karak
At Tafïlah
Ash Shawbak
Wãdï Müsã (Petra)
Sappir
Ra's an
Naqb
Al Quwayrah

Ash Sharãhiz

Be'er Menuha
Gharandal

Al 'Aqabah
Elat

Gulf of Aqaba

Mount Hermon
△2814m
Al Qunaytirah
Golan Heights

Saïda
Soûr
En Nâqoûra
Nahariya
Tsefat
Tverya
Lake Tiberias
Bent Jbaïl
Nahr el Litãni

Hefa (Haifa)
Mitspe Hefa

Netanya
Hadera

Tel Aviv-Yafo
Holon
Rehovot
Ashdod
Ashkelon

Gaza
GAZA STRIP
(under Palestinian administration)
Khãn Yûnis
Rafah

As Suwaydã'
Dar'ã
At Ramthã
Al Mafraq
Irbid

Natzrat (Nazareth)
Petah Tikva

Jenin
Nãblus
WEST BANK
JERUSALEM
Bethlehem
Hebron

Arad

Be'er Sheva

HaNegev
Mitspe Ramon

Jordan

Dead Sea

Wãdï al 'Arabãh

ISRAEL

EGYPT

Sinai

Me[...]

Elevation

-6000m	-4000m	-2000m	-1000m	-500m	-250m	Below sea level 0	250m	500m	1000m	2000m	3000m	4000m	6000m
-19,658ft	-13,124ft	-6562ft	-3281ft	-1640ft	-820ft	-328ft/-100m 0		820ft	1640ft	3281ft	6562ft	9843ft	13,124ft	19,685ft

The Middle East

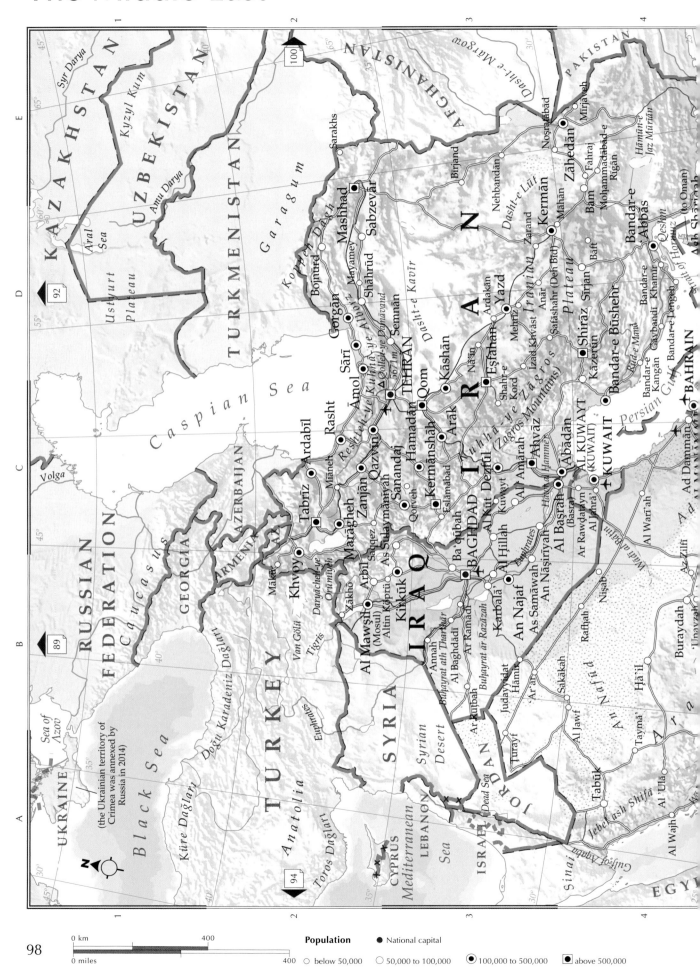

0 km 400

0 miles 400

Population

● National capital

○ below 50,000 ○ 50,000 to 100,000 ◉ 100,000 to 500,000 ■ above 500,000

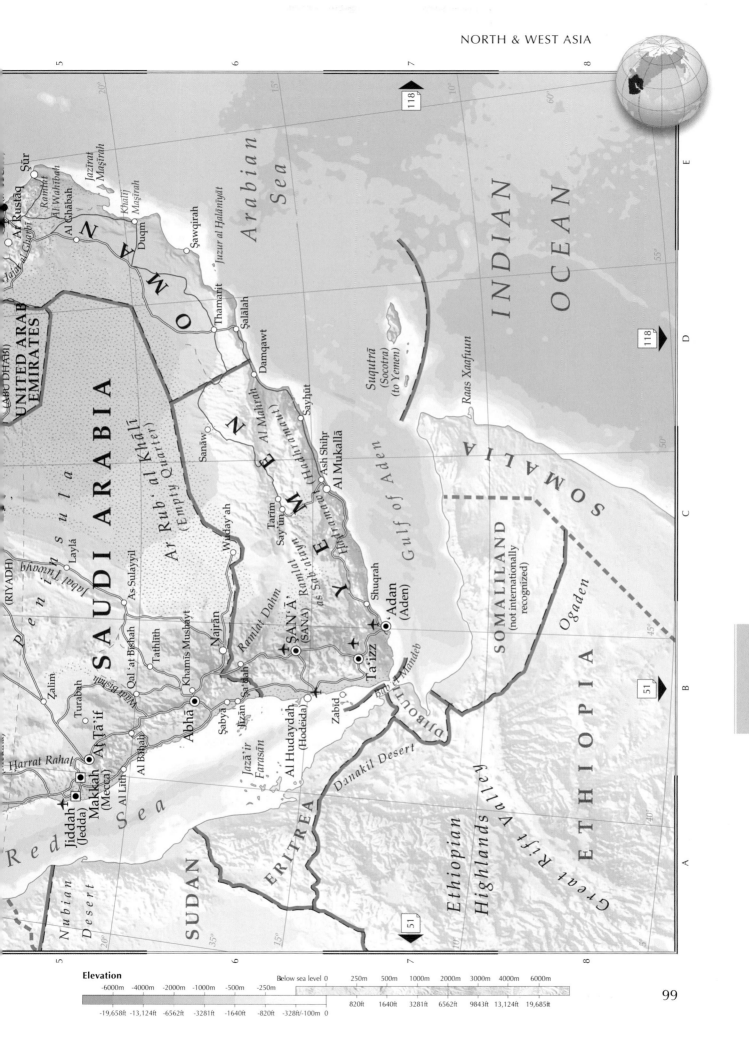

Central Asia

RUSSIAN
FEDERATION

GEORGIA

Caspian
Sea

AZERBAIJAN

Ustyurt
Plateau

Aral
Sea

Mo'ynoq

Chimboy

Taxtako'pir

Köneürgenç
Taxiatosh
Gurbansoltan Eje
Daşoguz

Nukus
Gubadag

Urganch

UZBEK

Uchqudu

K y z y

Garabogaz
Aylagy

Türkmenbaşy

Türkmenbaşy
Aylagy
Hazar

Türkmen
Aylagy

Balkanabat

Bereket

Gaplaňgyr Platosy
Uçhagan Gumy

Xiva
Gazojak
Lebap
Zarafsho

To'rtko'l

Üngüz
Derweze
Angyrsyndaky *Garagum*

TURKMENISTAN

Köpetdag Gershi

Serdar
Magtymguly
Baharly

Esenguly

Gökdepe
Abadan
Gora Chapan
2889m

AŞGABAT
(ASHGABAT)

Kaka

Tejen

Garagum

Murgap

Mary
Baýramaly

Uzb

Garagum K

Galkynyş
Seýdi
Türkmenabat

G'ijdu
Buxoro

Gazl

Kc

Saýat

Ke

Andkl

Mùrgab

Sarahs

Garabil
Belentligi

Maimana

Bālā Murghāb

Daryā-ye Morg

Serhetabat
Towraghoudī

Selseleh-ye Safid Kūh

Ghōrian
Herāt

IRAN

Reshteh-ye Kūhhā-ye Alborz

AFGHA

Shīndand

Kūhhā-ye Zāgros

Farāh Rūd

Dasht-e Khāsh

Farāh
Dilārām

Geres

Iranian

Plateau

Hāmūn-e
Şāberī

Lashkar Gāh

Chakhānsūr
Zaranj

Dasht-e Mārgow

Dīshū

Kūchna
Darwēs

Daryā-ye Helmand

Rēges

Chāgai Hills

100

0 km   200

0 miles   200

Population   ● National capital

○ below 50,000   ◎ 50,000 to 100,000   ◉ 100,000 to 500,000   ◼ above 500,000

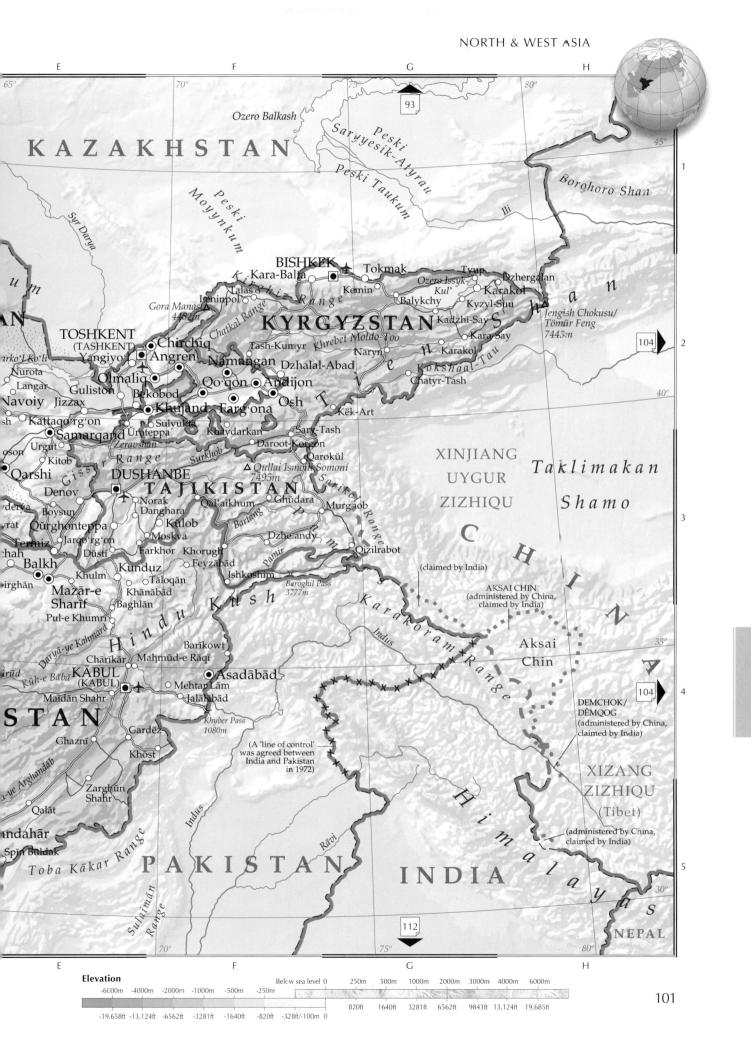

KAZAKHSTAN

Ozero Balkash

Peski Sarьyesik-Atьrau

Peski Taukum

Peski Moyynkum

Syr Darya

Ili

Borohoro Shan

BISHKEK
Kara-Balta •   • Tokmak
Kirghiz Range   • Tyup
Talas • • Kemin   *Ozero Issyk-*   • Dzhergalan
Ieninpol •   • Balykchy   *Kul'*   • Karakol
Gora Manas   Kadzhi-Say •   • Kyzyl-Suu
4482m   *Chatkal Range*   KYRGYZSTAN   • Kara-Say   *Jengish Chokusu/*
                                                    Tömür Feng
TOSHKENT   Tash-Kumyr •   *Khrebet Moldo-Too*   • Karakol   7443m
(TASHKENT) • Chirchiq   Naryn •
Yangiyo'l • • Angren   Dzhalal-Abad   *Kokshaal-Tau*
Nurota   • Olmaliq   Namangan   • Chatyr-Tash
Langar   Guliston   Qo'qon   Andijon   *T*
Navoiy • Jizzax • Bekobod   Farg'ona   • Osh
Kattaqo'rg'on   • Khujand   • Kёk-Art
Samarqand   Ŭroteppa   *Zeravshan*   Khaydarkan   • Sary-Tash
Urgut   Kitob   *Range*   Daroot-Korgon   XINJIANG   *Taklimakan*
Qarshi   *Gissar*   *Surkhob*   • Qarokŭl   UYGUR   *Shamo*
Denov   DUSHANBE   △ *Qullai Ismoili Somoni*   ZIZHIQU
                      7495m   *Sarikol Range*
        Norak   • Ghŭdara   *C*
Boysun   Danghara   Qal'aikhum   • Murg'ob   *H*
Qŭrghonteppa   Kŭlob   *Bartang*   *I*
Termiz   Jarqo'rg'on   Moskva   Dzhe andy   Qizilrabot   *N*
         Dŭsti   Farkhor   Khorugh   *Pamir*
Balkh   Khulm   Kunduz   Feyzābād   Ishkoshim   *(claimed by India)*   *A*
        Tāloqān   *Baroghil Pass*
Mazâr-e   Khānābād   3777m   AKSAI CHIN
Sharif   Baghlān   *Hindu Kush*   *Indus*   (administered by China,
Pul-e Khumri   claimed by India)
                                        Aksai
Barīkowt •   *Karakoram Range*   Chin
Chārīkār • Mahmūd-e Rāqī   DEMCHOK/
KABUL   DÊMQOG
(KABUL) • Mehtar Lām   (administered by China,
Maīdān Shahr • Jalālābād   claimed by India)
                                                  XIZANG
Khyber Pass   *Indus*   ZIZHIQU
Ghaznī   1080m   (Tibet)
Gardēz   (A 'line of control'
          was agreed between   *Himalayas*   (administered by China,
Khōst   India and Pakistan   claimed by India)
          in 1972)
Zarghūn
Shahr
Qalāt
Spīn Buldak
Toba Kākar Range   PAKISTAN   INDIA
Kandahār   *Ravi*
                                              NEPAL
Sulaimān Range   *Indus*

Elevation

					Below sea level 0	250m	500m	1000m	2000m	3000m	4000m	6000m
-6000m	-4000m	-2000m	-1000m	-500m	-250m							

820ft 1640ft 3281ft 6562ft 9843ft 13,124ft 19,685ft

-19,658ft -13,124ft -6562ft -3281ft -1640ft -820ft -328ft/-100m 0

South & East Asia

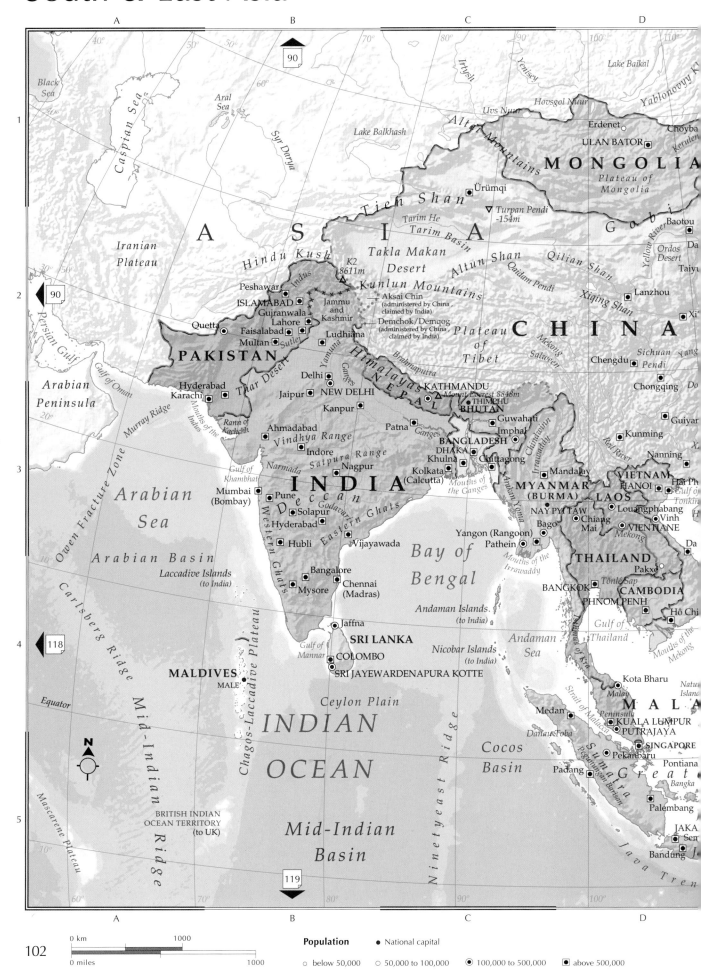

Black Sea

Caspian Sea

Aral Sea

Iranian Plateau

Syr Darya

Lake Balkhash

Irtysh

Yenisey

Lake Baikal

Yablonovyy K

Uvs Nuur

Hovsgol Nuur

Erdenet

Choyba

ULAN BATOR

Kerulen

MONGOLIA

Plateau of Mongolia

Altai Mountains

Ürümqi

Turpan Pendi -154m

Gobi

Baotou

Ordos Desert

Da

Tien Shan

Tarim He

Tarim Basin

Takla Makan Desert

Altun Shan

Qilian Shan

Taiyu

A S I A

Hindu Kush

K2 8611m

Kunlun Mountains

Quidam Pendi

Xiqing Shan

Lanzhou

Persian Gulf

Peshawar

Indus

Aksai Chin (administered by China, claimed by India)

C H I N A

Xi

ISLAMABAD

Jammu and Kashmir

Demchok/Demqog (administered by China, claimed by India)

Plateau of Tibet

Chengdu

Sichuan Pendi

Yang

Gujranwala

Lahore

Quetta

Mekong

Salween

Chongqing

Do

Faisalabad

Multan

Sutlej

Ludhiana

Arabian Peninsula

Gulf of Oman

PAKISTAN

Thar Desert

Yamuna

Delhi

Ganges

Himalayas

Brahmaputra

NEPAL

Mount Everest 8848m

KATHMANDU

THIMPHU

BHUTAN

Guwahati

Guiyar

Arabian

Hyderabad

Karachi

Jaipur

NEW DELHI

Kanpur

Kunming

Murray Ridge

Mouths of the Indus

Rann of Kachchh

Ahmadabad

Vindhya Range

Patna

Ganges

Imphal

BANGLADESH

DHAKA

Chindwin

Nanning

Mouths of the Indus

Indore

Satpura Range

Nagpur

Khulna

Chittagong

Mandalay

Red River

X

Narmada

Kolkata (Calcutta)

Mouths of the Ganges

Arakan Yoma

VIETNAM

HANOI

Hai Ph

Owen Fracture Zone

Gulf of Khambhat

INDIA

Mumbai (Bombay)

Pune

Godavari

Deccan

Solapur

MYANMAR (BURMA)

LAOS

Gulf of Tonkin

Arabian Sea

Hyderabad

Eastern Ghats

NAY PYI TAW

Louangphabang

Vinh

Arabian Basin

Laccadive Islands (to India)

Western Ghats

Hubli

Vijayawada

Bay of Bengal

Mouths of the Irrawaddy

Bago

Chiang Mai

VIENTIANE

Da

Bangalore

Chennai (Madras)

Yangon (Rangoon)

Pathein

THAILAND

Mekong

Mysore

Carlsberg Ridge

Andaman Islands (to India)

BANGKOK

Tônlé Sap

Pakxe

Jaffna

Gulf of Mannar

SRI LANKA

Nicobar Islands (to India)

Andaman Sea

CAMBODIA

PHNOM PENH

Hô Chi

COLOMBO

Gulf of Thailand

SRI JAYEWARDENAPURA KOTTE

Mouths of the Mekong

Chagos-Laccadive Plateau

MALDIVES

MALE

Ceylon Plain

Kota Bharu

Natu Island

Strait of Kra

Malay Peninsula

MALA

Equator

INDIAN

Medan

Strait of Malacca

OCEAN

Danau Toba

Cocos Basin

KUALA LUMPUR

PUTRAJAYA

SINGAPORE

N

Mascarene Plateau

Mid-Indian Ridge

Pekanbaru

Pontiana

Padang

Sumatra

Gre a t

BRITISH INDIAN OCEAN TERRITORY (to UK)

Palembang

Bangka

Mid-Indian Basin

Ninetyeast Ridge

Pegunungan Barisan

JAKA

Sen

Bandung

Java Tren

0 km 1000

0 miles 1000

Population ● National capital

○ below 50,000 ◦ 50,000 to 100,000 ◉ 100,000 to 500,000 ◼ above 500,000

Political features

Total area:
7,936,200 sq miles
(20,554,700 sq km)

Total number of countries:
24

Total population:
3775 million

Largest city with population:
Tokyo, Japan 39.4 million

Country with highest population density:
Singapore 22,881 people per sq mile
(8852 peop e per sq km)

Largest country:
China 3,705,386 sq miles
(9,596,960 sq km)

Smallest country:
Maldives 116 sq miles
(300 sq km)

Physical features

Largest lake,
Tônlé Sap, Cambodia
1000 sq miles (2850 sq km)

Longest river:
Chang Jiang (Yangtze), China
3965 miles (6380 km)

Highest point:
Mount Everest, China/Nepal
29,029 ft (8848 m)

Lowest point:
Turpan Pendi (Turfan Basin), China
505 ft (154 m) below sea leve

Western China & Mongolia

R U S S I A N   F E

KAZAKHSTAN

Kazakhskiy
Melkosopochnik

Ozero
Balkhash

Kulunda
Steppe

Zapadnyy Sayan

Yenisey

Hövsgöl
Nuur

Uvs Nuur

Ulaangom

Ölgiy

Ozero
Zaysan

Altay

Har Us Nuur

Hovd

Hyargas
Nuur

Har Nuur

Hangayn Nuruu

Tsetserle

Altay

Bayanhongor

M O N

Ulungur
Hu

Karamay

Gurbantünggüt
Shamo

Kuytun

Shihezi

Fukang

Jimsar

Qitai

△ *Aj Bogd Uul*
3802m

Mör

Ozero Issyk-Kul'

KYRGYZSTAN

Yining

Ürümqi

Turpan

Hami

Atas Bogd
△ 2695m

G

T i e n   S h a n

Borohoro Shan

Turpan
Pendi

Dalain Ho

△ *Jengish Chokusu/Tomür Feng*
7443m

Bosten Hu

Korla

Kuruktag

Xingxingxia

Kashi

Yengisar

Shache

Tarim He

Tarim   Basin

XINJIANG UYGUR

ZIZHIQU

Lop Nur

GANSU

Qilian Shan

TAJIKISTAN

AFGH.

Yecheng
(claimed
by India)

Pishan

Moyu

Taklimakan
Shamo

Ruoqiang

Altun   Shan

Danghe Nanshan

Qaidam Pendi

Qinghai H

Karakoram Range

K2
△ 8611m

Hotan

Qira

K u n l u n   S h a n

Golmud

Burhan Budai Shan

Dulan

Animaqen

Qinghai

PAKISTAN

Kashmir

AKSAI
CHIN

AKSAI CHIN
(administered by
China, claimed
by India)

C

QINGHAI

Bayan Har Sh

JAMMU
AND
KASHMIR

Qingzang Gaoyuan

Tongtian He

112

Rutog

(Plateau of Tibet)

DEMCHOK/DÊMQOG
(administered by China,
claimed by India)

Gar Xincun

X I Z A N G

Tanggula Shan

Amdo

Yushu

Mekong

Qamdo

Zanda

Gozhê

Siling Co

Nagqu

Salween

ZIZHIQU

Tangra
Yumco

Gyaring
Co

Ngangzê
Co

Nam Co

Damxung

Jinsha Jiang

Yamuna

Ganges

NEPAL

Brahmaputra

(Tibet)

Nyainqêntanglha Shan

Maizhokunggar

ARUNACHAL
PRADESH
(claimed by China)

Lhazê

Xigazê

Lhasa

Heilonglon Shan

I N D I A

Gonggar

Gyangzê

△ *Mount Everest*
8848m

BHUTAN

I N D I A

MYANMAR
(BURMA)

0 km   400

0 miles   400

Population   ● National capital   ● Interna administrative capital

○ below 50,000   ○ 50,000 to 100,000   ◉ 100,000 to 500,000   ◼ above 500,000

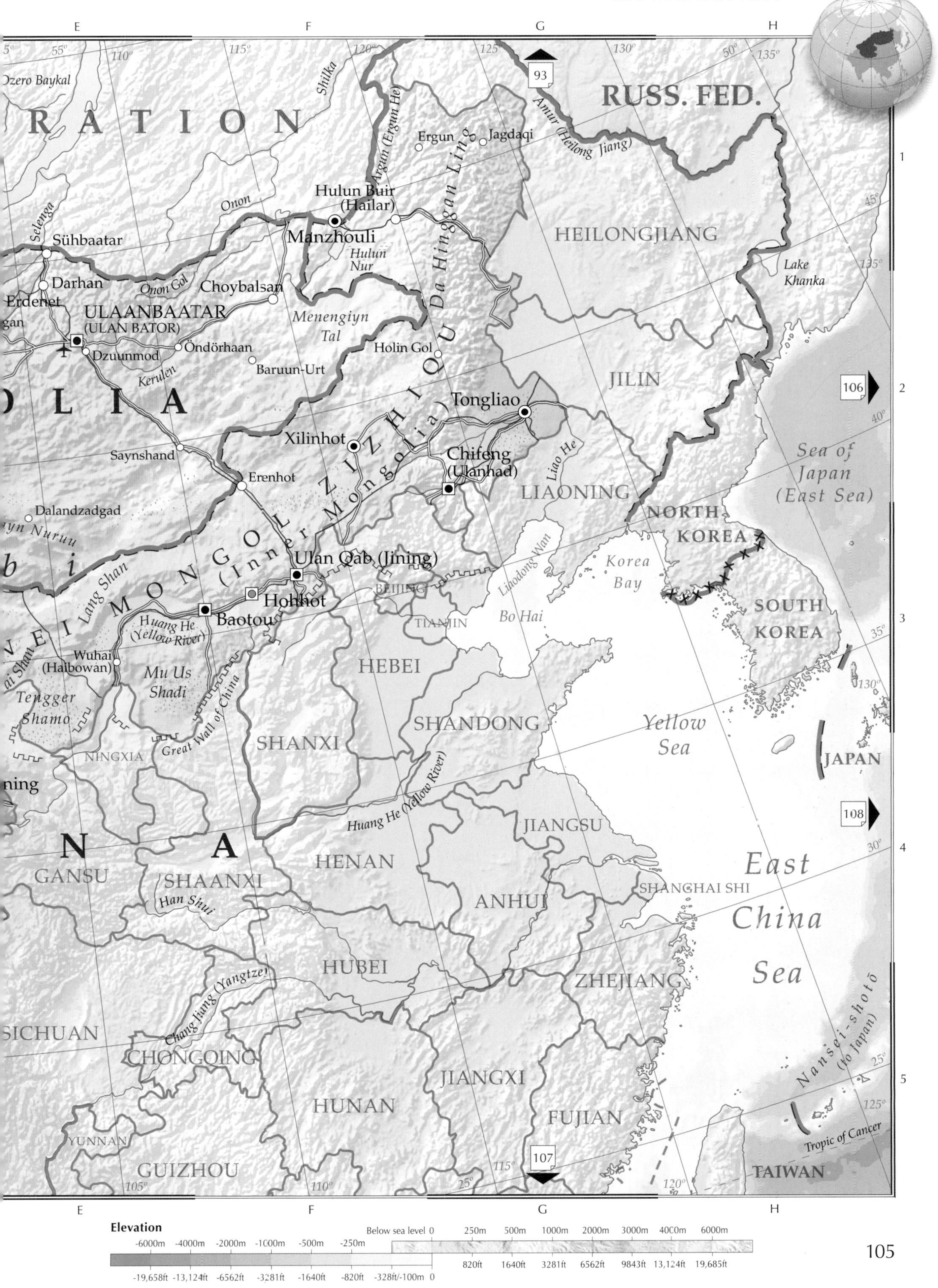

RATION

Ozero Baykal

RUSS. FED.

93

Amur (Heilong Jiang)

Ergun

Jagdaqi

HEILONGJIANG

Lake Khanka

Shilka

Argun (Ergun He)

Hulun Buir (Hailar)

Manzhouli

Onon

Sühbaatar

Darhan

Choybalsan

Erdenet

ULAANBAATAR
(ULAN BATOR)

Dzuunmod

Öndörhaan

Hulun Nur

Menengiyn Tal

Holin Gol

JILIN

Selenga

Onon Gol

Da Hinggan Ling

106

Baruun-Urt

Kerulen

OLIA

Tongliao

Saynshand

Xilinhot

Chifeng
(Ulanhad)

Liao He

Sea of Japan
(East Sea)

Erenhot

LIAONING

Dalandzadgad

NORTH
KOREA

Korea
Bay

Lixiadong Wan

SOUTH
KOREA

iyn Nuruu

b i

Ulan Qab (Jining)

Bo Hai

130

JAPAN

ning

Hohhot

Baotou

Huang He
(Yellow River)

BEIJING

TIANJIN

Yellow
Sea

108

Wuhai
(Haibowan)

Mu Us
Shadi

HEBEI

Tengger
Shamo

NINGXIA

Great Wall of China

SHANDONG

SHANXI

Huang He (Yellow River)

JIANGSU

East

N

A

HENAN

SHANGHAI SHI

China

GANSU

SHAANXI

ANHUI

Han Shui

Sea

SICHUAN

HUBEI

ZHEJIANG

Chang Jiang (Yangtze)

CHONGQING

JIANGXI

Nansei-shotō (to Japan)

HUNAN

FUJIAN

107

YUNNAN

GUIZHOU

Tropic of Cancer

TAIWAN

Elevation

-6000m -4000m -2000m -1000m -500m -250m   Below sea level 0   250m   500m   1000m   2000m   3000m   4000m   6000m

-19,658ft -13,124ft -6562ft -3281ft -1640ft -820ft -328ft/-100m 0   820ft   1640ft   3281ft   6562ft   9843ft   13,124ft   19,685ft

105

Eastern China & Korea

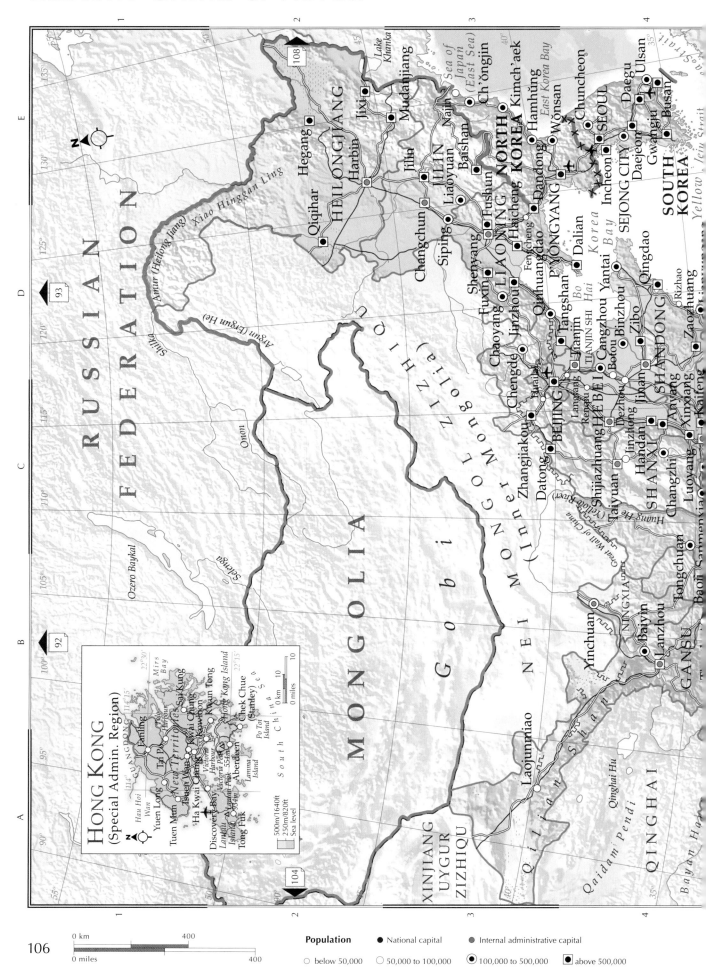

Population

○ below 50,000

○ 50,000 to 100,000

◉ 100,000 to 500,000

■ above 500,000

● National capital

● Internal administrative capital

0 km   400

0 miles   400

Map labels

RUSSIAN FEDERATION

MONGOLIA

NEI MONGOL (Inner Mongolia)

HEILONGJIANG

JILIN

LIAONING

HEBEI

SHANXI

SHANDONG

NINGXIA

GANSU

QINGHAI

XINJIANG UYGUR ZIZHIQU

NORTH KOREA

SOUTH KOREA

Sea of Japan (East Sea)

Yellow Sea

Korea Bay

East Korea Bay

Bo Hai

West Korea Bay

Lake Khanka

Ozero Baykal

South China Sea

Gobi

Qilian Shan

Xiao Hinggan Ling

Amur (Heilong Jiang)

Argun (Ergun He)

Shilka

Onon

Selenga

Huang He

Yellow River (Yellow River)

Great Wall of China

Qinghai Hu

Qaidam Pendi

Bayan Har

Hegang
Jixi
Mudanjiang
Harbin
Qiqihar
Jilin
Changchun
Siping
Liaoyuan
Baishan
Naijin
Ch'ŏngjin
Kimch'aek
Hamhŭng
Wonsan
Chuncheon
SEOUL
Daegu
Ulsan
Busan
Gwangju
Daejeon
SEJONG CITY
Incheon
PYONGYANG
Dandong
Haicheng
Fengcheng
Fushun
Shenyang
Fuxin
Chaoyang
Jinzhou
Fujin
Qinhuangdao
Chengde
Dalian
Yantai
Cangzhou
Binzhou
Zibo
Qingdao
Rizhao
Zaozhuang
Tangshan
Tianjin
TIANJIN SHI
Langfang
Renqiu
Botou
Dezhou
Jinan
Jining
BEIJING
Zhangjiakou
Datong
Shijiazhuang
Handan
Anyang
Xinxiang
Kaifeng
Changzhi
Taiyuan
Jinzhong
Luoyang
Tongchuan
Baoji
Sanmenxia
Baiyin
Lanzhou
Yinchuan
Laojunmiao
Laojunmiao

Hong Kong inset

HONG KONG
(Special Admin. Region)

Mirs Bay

GUANGDONG

Hau Hoi Wan

Yuen Long
Fanling
Tai Po
Sheung Shui
Sai Kung
New Territories
Tsuen Wan
Kwai Chung
Ha Kwai Chung
Tuen Mun
Kowloon
Kwun Tong
Hong Kong Island
Victoria Harbour
Victoria Peak 554ft
Aberdeen
Chek Chue (Stanley)
Discovery Bay
Lantau Island
Lantau Peak 934ft
Tong Fuk
Lamma Island
Po Toi Island

China

500m/1640ft
250m/820ft
Sea level

0 km   10
0 miles   10

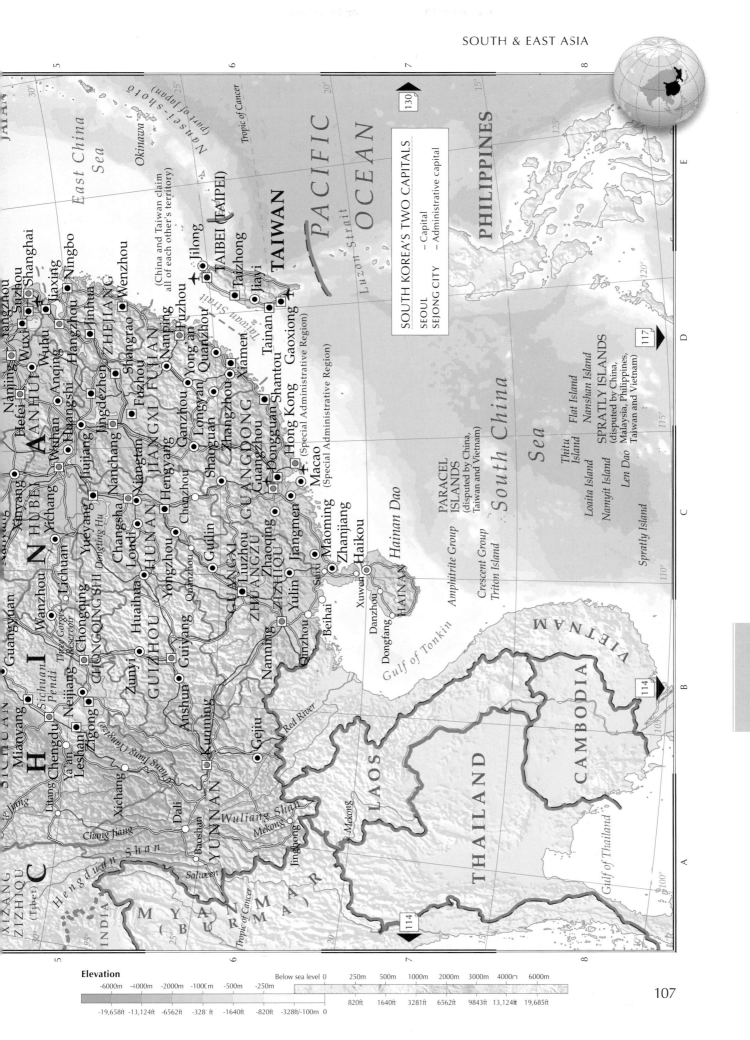

JAPAN

East China Sea

N a n s e i - s h o t ō (*Sea of Japan*)

Okinawa

Tropic of Cancer

(China and Taiwan claim all of each other's territory)

PACIFIC OCEAN

Shanghai
Suzhou
Wuxi
Jiaxing
Ningbo
Wuhu
Hangzhou
Jinhua
Wenzhou
Shangrao
ZHEJIANG
Fuzhou
Nanping
Yong'an
Quanzhou
FUJIAN
Xiamen

TAIBEI (TAIPEI)
Jilong
Taizhong
Jiayi
Tainan
Gaoxiong
TAIWAN

Luzon Strait

PHILIPPINES

Nanjing
Hefei
ANHUI
Wuhan
HUBEI
Jingdezhen
JIANGXI
Nanchang
Xinyang
Yichang
Huangshi
Jiujiang
Ganzhou
Shaoguan
GUANGDONG
Longyan
Zhangzhou
Shantou
Chaozhou
Hong Kong
(Special Administrative Region)
Macao
(Special Administrative Region)

HUNAN
Changsha
Xiangtan
Loudi
Hengyang
Yongzhou
Chenzhou
Guangzhou
Foshan
Dongguan

South China Sea

SOUTH KOREA'S TWO CAPITALS
SEOUL – Capital
SEJONG CITY – Administrative capital

Guangyuan
Wanzhou
Lichuan
CHONGQING SHI
Chongqing
Yueyang
HUBEI
Dongting Hu
Huaihua
GUIZHOU
Guilin
GUANGXI
ZHUANGZU
Liuzhou
Guiyang
Anshun
Zunyi
Quanzhou
Yulin
Jinzhou
Beihai
Zhanjiang
Maoming
Haikou
HAINAN
Hainan Dao
Danzhou
Dongfang

Gulf of Tonkin

PARACEL ISLANDS
(disputed by China, Taiwan and Vietnam)
Amphitrite Group
Crescent Group
Triton Island

SPRATLY ISLANDS
(disputed by China, Malaysia, Philippines, Taiwan and Vietnam)
Thitu Island
Flat Island
Nanshan Island
Loaita Island
Namyit Island
Len Dao
Spratly Island

SICHUAN
Mianyang
Chengdu
Sichuan Pendi
Neijiang
Zigong
Leshan
Ya'an
Litang
Xichang
Dali
Baoshan
YUNNAN
Kunming
Gejiu
Zunyi
Anshun
GUIZHOU

Hengduan Shan
Chang Jiang
Salween
Jinsha Jiang (Yangtze)
Wuliang Shan
Mekong
Jinghong

XIZANG ZIZHIQU (Tibet)

INDIA
MYANMAR (BURMA)
Tropic of Cancer

LAOS
VIETNAM
THAILAND
CAMBODIA
Red River
Mekong
Gulf of Thailand

Elevation

| -6000m | -4000m | -2000m | -100Cm | -500m | -250m | Below sea level 0 | 250m | 500m | 1000m | 2000m | 3000m | 4000m | 6000m |

| -19,658ft | -13,124ft | -6562ft | -328 ft | -1640ft | -820ft | -328ft/-100m 0 | 820ft | 1640ft | 3281ft | 6562ft | 9843ft | 13,124ft | 19,685ft |

107

Japan

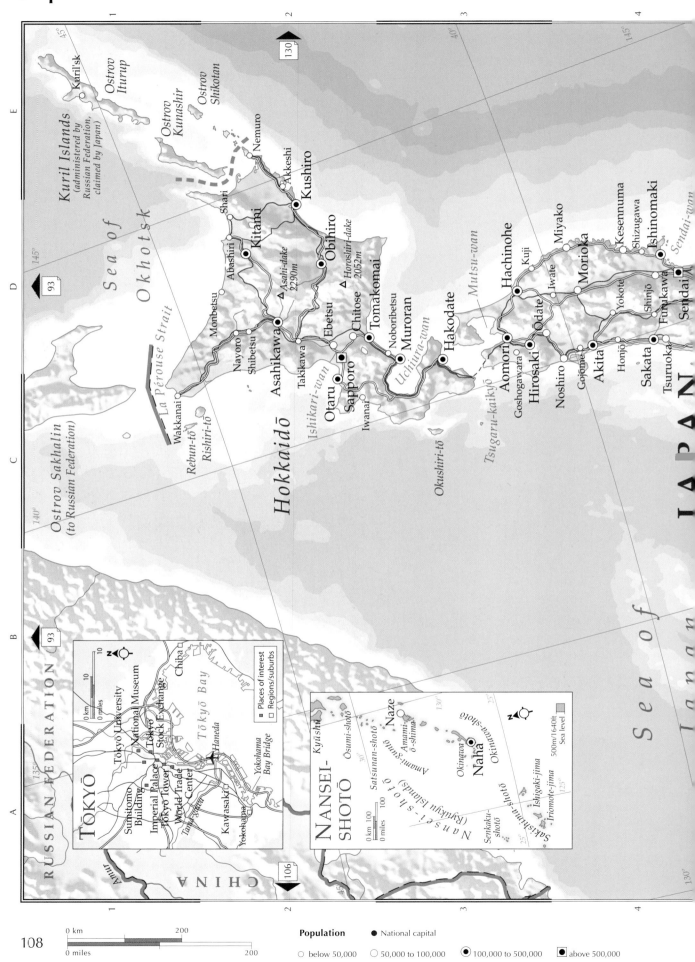

Kuril Islands
(administered by
Russian Federation,
claimed by Japan)

Sea of Okhotsk

Ostrov Iturup

Kuril'sk

Ostrov Shikotan

Ostrov Kunashir

Nemuro

Akkeshi

Kushiro

Shari

Kitami

Abashiri

Monbetsu

△ Asahi-dake
2290m

Obihiro

△ Horoshiri-dake
2052m

Asahikawa

Nayoro

Shibetsu

Takikawa

Ebetsu

Chitose

Tomakomai

Noboribetsu

Muroran

Hakodate

Mutsu-wan

Hachinohe

Kuji

Miyako

Kesennuma

Shizugawa

Ishinomaki

Sendai-wan

Iwate

Morioka

Yokote

Sendai

Aomori

Odate

Shinjō

Funakawa

Goshogawara

Hirosaki

Honjō

Sakata

Noshiro

Gojome

Tsuruoka

Akita

Tsugaru-kaikyō

Ishikari-wan

Otaru

Sapporo

Iwanai

Takikawa

Uchiura-wan

Okushiri-tō

Wakkanai

Rishiri-tō

Rebun-tō

La Pérouse Strait

Ostrov Sakhalin
(to Russian Federation)

Sea of Okhotsk

Hokkaidō

JAPAN

Sea of Japan

RUSSIAN FEDERATION

CHINA

Amur

TŌKYŌ

Chiba

Tōkyō University

National Museum

Tōkyō
Stock Exchange

Tōkyō Bay

Sumitomo
Building

Imperial Palace

Tōkyō Tower

World Trade
Center

Tama-gawa

Haneda

Yokohama
Bay Bridge

Kawasaki

Yokohama

Places of interest

Regions/suburbs

0 km 10

0 miles 10

NANSEI-SHOTŌ

Kyūshū

Ōsumi-shotō

Naze

Amami-guntō

Amami-
ō-shima

Satsunan-shotō

Nansei-shotō
(Ryukyu Islands)

Okinawa-shotō

Okinawa

Naha

Ishigaki-jima

Iriomote-jima

Sakishima-shotō

Senkaku-shotō

500m/1640ft

Sea level

0 km 100

0 miles 100

108

0 km 200

0 miles 200

Population

● National capital

○ below 50,000 ○ 50,000 to 100,000 ◉ 100,000 to 500,000 ■ above 500,000

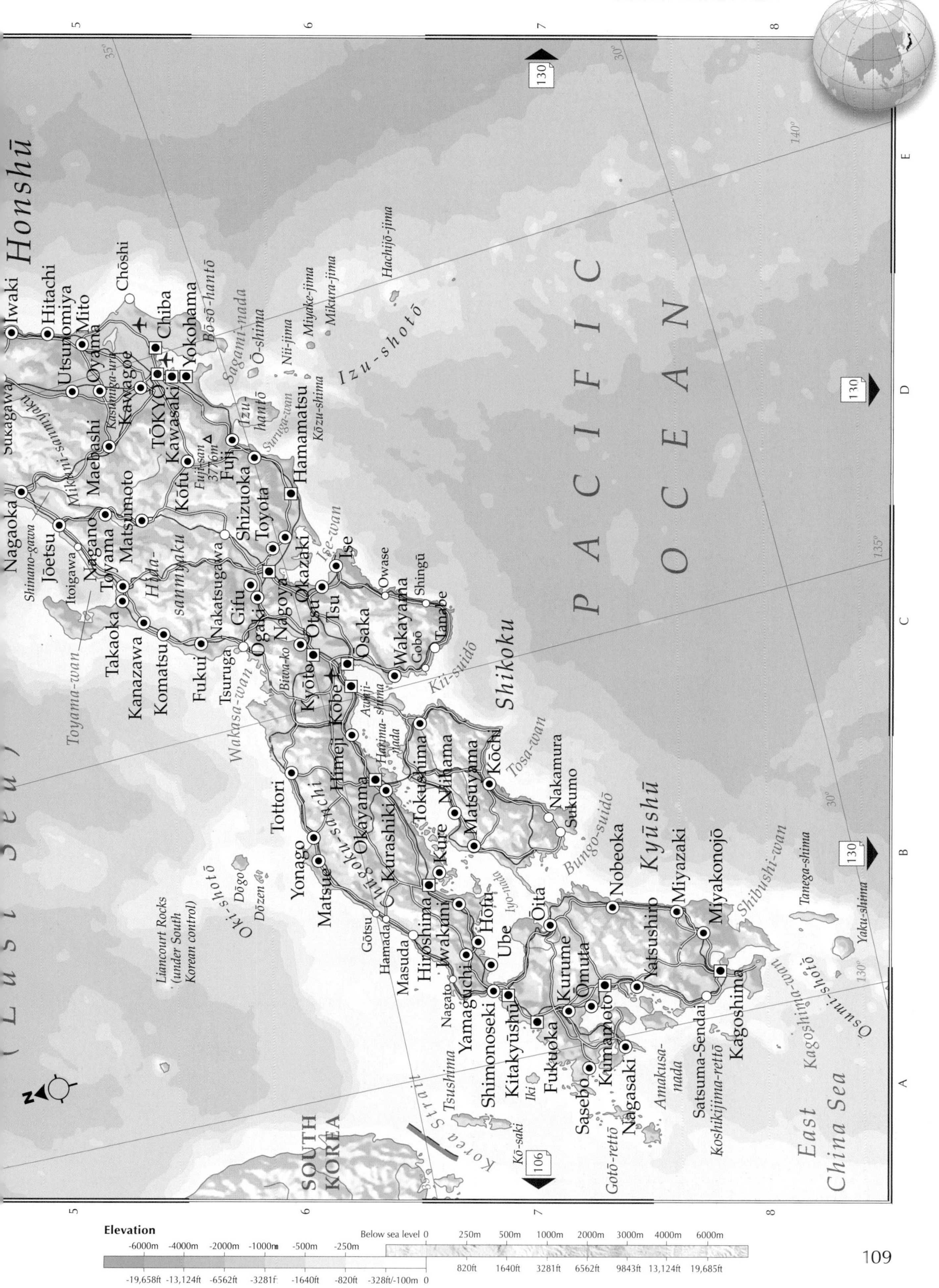

PACIFIC OCEAN

Honshū

Shikoku

Kyūshū

(East Sea)

East China Sea

SOUTH KOREA

Korea Strait

Iwaki
Hitachi
Utsunomiya
Mito
Ōyama
Sukagawa
Kashima-nada
Kawagoe
Chiba
Yokohama
Chōshi
Bōsō-hantō
Kawasaki
TOKYO
Maebashi
Nagaoka
Nagano
Toyama
Matsumoto
Kōfu
Fujisan △ 3776m
Fuji
Shizuoka
Toyota
Hamamatsu
Sagami-nada
Izu-hantō
Suruga-wan
Ō-shima
Nii-jima
Kōzu-shima
Miyake-jima
Mikura-jima
Hachijō-jima
Izu-shotō
Jōetsu
Itoigawa
Shinano-gawa
Takaoka
Kanazawa
Komatsu
Fukui
Tsuruga
Hida-sanmyaku
Mikuni-sanmyaku
Gifu
Nakatsugawa
Ōgaki
Nagoya
Okazaki
Ōtsu
Tsu
Ise
Ise-wan
Owase
Shingū
Tanabe
Gobō
Wakayama
Osaka
Kōbe
Kyōto
Biwa-ko
Wakasa-wan
Awaji-shima
Kii-suidō
Himeji
Okayama
Kurashiki
Takamatsu
Tokushima
Kōchi
Matsuyama
Niihama
Kure
Iwakuni
Harima-nada
Chūgoku-sanchi
Tottori
Yonago
Matsue
Oki-shotō
Dōgo
Dōzen
Liancourt Rocks
(under South
Korean control)
Toyama-wan
Gōtsu
Hamada
Masuda
Hiroshima
Hōfu
Ube
Yamaguchi
Nagato
Shimonoseki
Kitakyūshū
Fukuoka
Iki
Kō-saki
Tsushima
Saseho
Nagasaki
Goto-rettō
Kumamoto
Ōmuta
Kurume
Yatsushiro
Amakusa-nada
Koshikijima-rettō
Satsuma-Sendai
Kagoshima
Kagoshima-wan
Ōsumi-shotō
Ōsumi-wan
Tanega-shima
Yaku-shima
Shibushi-wan
Miyakonojō
Miyazaki
Nobeoka
Ōita
Bungo-suidō
Iyo-nada
Suō-nada
Tosa-wan
Nakamura
Sukumo
Muroto
Shibushi-shotō
Yonago
Mikkabi-san

130
106

Elevation

| -6000m | -4000m | -2000m | -1000m | -500m | -250m | Below sea level 0 | 250m | 500m | 1000m | 2000m | 3000m | 4000m | 6000m |

| -19,658ft | -13,124ft | -6562ft | -3281f | -1640ft | -820ft | -328ft/-100m 0 | 820ft | 1640ft | 3281ft | 6562ft | 9843ft | 13,124ft | 19,685ft |

South India & Sri Lanka

Arabian Sea

Lakshadweep
(Laccadive Islands)
(to India)

Amīndivi Islands

Kavaratti Island

Nine Degree Channel

Kalpeni Island

Minicoy Island

Eight Degree Channel

Ihavandhippolhu Atoll

MALDIVES

Faadhippolhu Atoll

Horsburgh Atoll

Ari Atoll

Male' Atoll
MALE'

Felidhu Atoll

Mulakatholhu

Kolhumadulu

Hadhdhunmathi Atoll

North Huvadhu Atoll

Equator

South Huvadhu Atoll

Gan

Addu Atoll

INDIA

Mumbai (Bombay)

Kalyān
Pune
Ahmadnagar
Bārāmati
Nizāmābād
Nānded
Karimnagar
Jagdalp
Telangana
Godāvari

Solāpur
Sangli
Kolhāpur
Gulbarga
Hyderābād
Secunderābād
Vizianagaram
Visākhapati
Rājahmur
Kākin

Belgaum
Karnātaka
Deccan
Rāichūr
Krishna
Vijayawāda
Machilīpatnam

Gadag
Panaji
Hubli
Kurnool
Nandyāl
Andhra
Pradesh
Chirāla
Ongole
Kāvali

Dāvangere
Tungabhadra Reservoir
Tādpatri
Anantapur
Nellore

Shimoga
Bhadrāvati
Cuddapah

Udupi
Tumkūr
Vellore
Chennai (Mad ras)

Mangalore
Bangalore
Kānchīpuram
Coromandel Coast

Kāsaragod
Mandya
Krishnagiri
Tiruppattur

Kannur (Cannanore)
Mysore
Salem
Pondicherry

Kozhikode (Calicut)
Erode
Neyveli

Coimbatore
Tamil Nādu

Thrissur (Trichūr)
Tiruchchirāppalli

Ernākulam
Dindigul
Madurai
Jaffna
Palk Strait

Kochi (Cochin)
SRI LANK

Alappuzha (Alleppey)
Rājapālaiyam
Mannar
Vavuniya
Trincomalee

Kollam (Quilon)
Tuticorin
Puttalam
Anuradhapura
Batticaloa

Thiruvananthapuram (Trivandrum)
Gulf of Mannar

Nāgercoil
Matale
Negombo
Kandy

SRI JAYEWARDENAPURA KOTTE
COLOMBO
Kalutara
Ratnapura

Galle
Matara

INDIAN

SRI LANKA'S TWO CAPITALS

| COLOMBO | – Capital |
| SRI JAYEWARDENAPURA KOTTE | – Administrative capital |

Western Ghats
Eastern Ghats
Kerala

0 km   300
0 miles   300

Population   ● National capital

○ below 50,000   ◐ 50,000 to 100,000   ● 100,000 to 500,000   ■ above 500,000

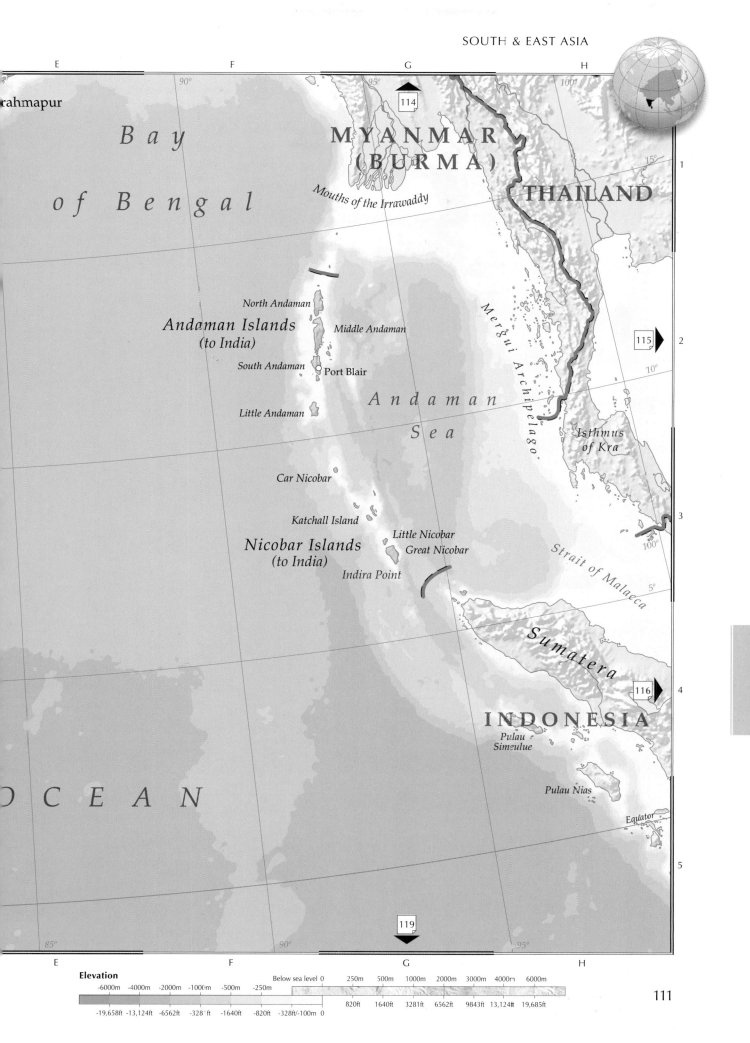

E 90° F G 95° H

Brahmapur

Bay

114

MYANMAR

of Bengal

(BURMA)

1

THAILAND

Mouths of the Irrawaddy

15°

North Andaman

Andaman Islands

Middle Andaman

(to India)

115

2

South Andaman ○ Port Blair

10°

A n d a m a n

Little Andaman

S e a

*Isthmus
of Kra*

Car Nicobar

Katchall Island

Nicobar Islands

Little Nicobar

3

(to India)

Great Nicobar

100°

Indira Point

Strait of Malacca

5°

S u m a t e r a

116

4

INDONESIA

*Pulau
Simeulue*

O C E A N

Pulau Nias

Equator

5

119

E 90° F G 95° H

Elevation

| Below sea level 0 | 250m | 500m | 1000m | 2000m | 3000m | 4000m | 6000m |

-6000m -4000m -2000m -1000m -500m -250m

-19,658ft -13,124ft -6562ft -328ft -1640ft -820ft -328ft/-100m 0

820ft 1640ft 3281ft 6562ft 9843ft 13,124ft 19,685ft

Mergui Archipelago

Northern India, Pakistan & Bangladesh

A B C D

35° 60° 65° 70° 75°

(claimed by India)
(A "line of con
was agreed bet
India and Pak
in 1972)

Selseleh-ye Safid Kūh

Hindū Kush

Karakoram Range

K2
8611m

Dasht-e Lūt

AFGHANISTAN

Khyber Pass
1080m

Mingāora

Mardān

Peshāwar

ISLĀMĀBĀD

Wāh

Rāwalpindi

Jamm
and
Kashm

IRAN

Jhelum

Jammu

Himacha

Potwar Plateau

Sargodha

Gujrāt

Gujrānwāla

Chaman

Toba Kākar Range

Faisalābād

Lahore

Pradesh

Amritsar

Jalandhar

Daryā-ye Helmand

Indus

Chenāb

Rāvi

Ludhiāna

Quetta

Dera Ghāzi Khan

Okara

Chandīgarh

Chāgai Hills

Sibi

Multān

Sāhīwāl

Bathinda

Karna

Kālat

Haryāna

PAKISTAN

Sutlej

Delhi

Baluchistan

Jacobābād

Bahāwalpur

Bīkāner

NEW DELHI

Me

Shikārpur

Rahīmyār Khān

Farīdābād

Central Makrān Range

Lārkāna

Sukkur

Alwar

Kirthār Range

Khairpur

Thar Desert

Jaipur

Jaisalmer

Etav

Turbat

Nawābshāh

Jodhpur

Ajmer

Gwalior

Gwādar

Pasni

Mīrpur Khās

Pāli

Beāwar

Jha

Karāchi

Hyderābād

R a j a s t h ā n

Kota

Shivpuri

Sind

Udaipur

Madh

Tropic of Cancer

Sujāwal

Mouths of the Indus

Rann of Kachchh

Pālanpur

I N

Gujarāt

Ahmadābād

Ratlām

Sāga

Gāndhīdhām

Godhra

Bhop

Gulf of
Kachchh

Surendranagar

Vindhya Range

Indore

Jāmnagar

Rājkot

Vadodara

Khandwa

Porbandar

Bhāvnagar

Bharūch

Sātpura Range

Nāg

Gulf of
Khambhāt

Sūrat

Bhusāwal

Amrāva

Damān

Manmād

Nāshik

Aurangābād

A r a b i a n

Maharashtra

D e

Kalyān

Nānd

S e a

Mumbai
(Bombay)

Ahmadnagar

Pune

Nizāmābād

Bārāmati

Karimn

Western Ghāts

Secunderabā

Solāpur

Hyderābād

Sangli

Telangān

Kolhāpur

Mahbūbnagar

15°

20°

25°

30°

N

65° 70° 75°

A B C D

0 km   300
0 miles   300

Population ● National capital

○ below 50,000   ○ 50,000 to 100,000   ● 100,000 to 500,000   ■ above 500,000

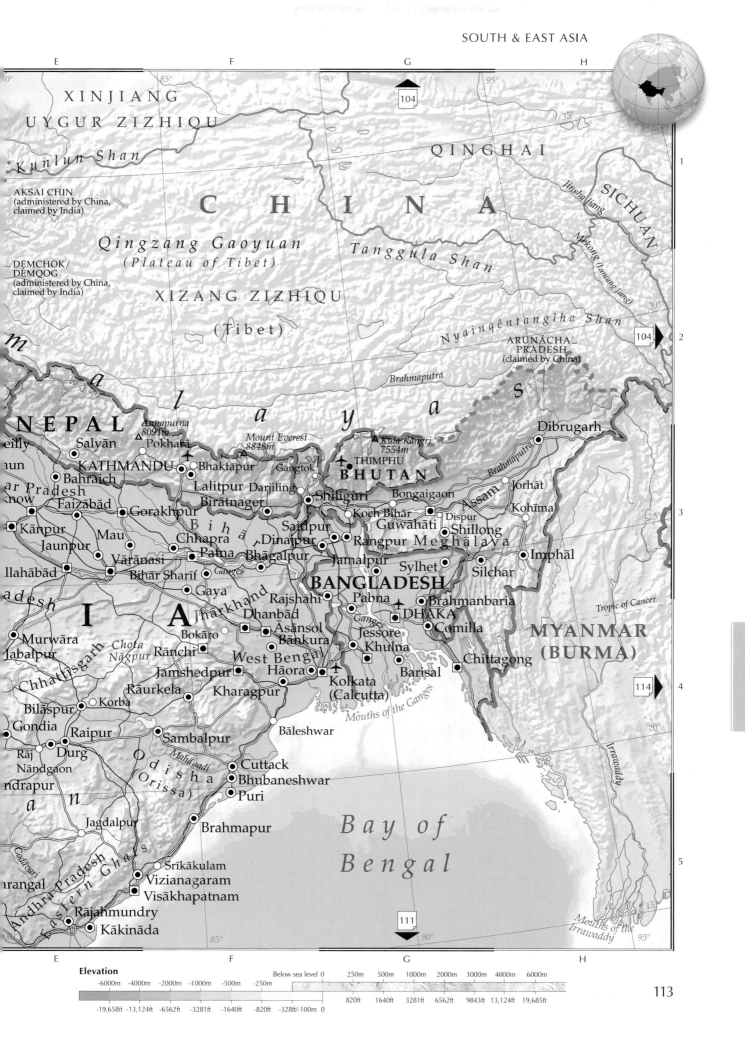

XINJIANG
UYGUR ZIZHIQU
Kunlun Shan
QINGHAI

AKSAI CHIN
(administered by China,
claimed by India)

C H I N A

Qingzang Gaoyuan
(Plateau of Tibet)

Tanggula Shan

DEMCHOK/
DÉMQOG
(administered by China,
claimed by India)

XIZANG ZIZHIQU
(Tibet)

Nyainqêntanglha Shan

ARUNACHAL
PRADESH
(claimed by China)

Brahmaputra

SICHUAN

Jinsha Jiang

Mekong (Lancang Jiang)

H i m a l a y a s

NEPAL
△ *Annapurna*
8091m
Salyān Pokharā
Mount Everest
8848m
△ *Kula Kangri*
7554m
Dibrugarh

KATHMANDU Bhaktapur
Gangtok
THIMPHU
BHUTAN

Bahraich
Lalitpur Darjiling
Shiligūri
Bongaigaon
Assam
Jorhat

ar Pradesh
Faizābād
Gorakhpur
Biratnager
Koch Bihar
Dispur
Kohīma

now

Kānpur
Mau
Chhapra
Dinajpur
Rangpur Meghālaya
Shillong

Jaunpur
B i h a r
Patna
Bhāgalpur
Jamalpur
Guwahati

Vārānasi
Ganges
Silchar
Imphāl

llahābād
Bihar Sharif
Sylhet

adesh
Gaya
BANGLADESH

I A
J h a r k h a n d
Rajshahi
Pabna
Brahmanbaria
Tropic of Cancer

Murwāra
Dhanbād
DHAKA

Jabalpur
Bokāro
Āsānsol
Bānkura
Jessore
Comilla
MYANMAR
(BURMA)

C h o t a
Nāgpur Rānchi
West Bengal
Khulna

Chhattīsgarh
Jamshedpur
Hāora
Barisal

Bilāspur
Korba
Rāurkela
Kharagpur
Kolkata
(Calcutta)
Chittagong

Gondia
Raipur
Mouths of the Ganges

Rāj
Durg
Sambalpur
Bāleshwar

Nāndgaon
Mahānadi
O d i s h a
(Orissa)
Cuttack

ndrapur
a n
Bhubaneshwar
Puri

Jagdalpur
Brahmapur

Bay of
Bengal

arangal
Srīkākulam
Vizianagaram

Andhra Pradesh
Eastern Ghats
Visākhapatnam
Irrawaddy

Rājahmundry
Kākināda
Mouths of the
Irrawaddy

Elevation

| Below sea level 0 | 250m | 500m | 1000m | 2000m | 3000m | 4000m | 6000m |

-6000m -4000m -2000m -1000m -500m -250m

-19,658ft -13,124ft -6562ft -3281ft -1640ft -820ft -328ft/-100m 0

820ft 1640ft 3281ft 6562ft 9843ft 13,124ft 19,685ft

Mainland Southeast Asia

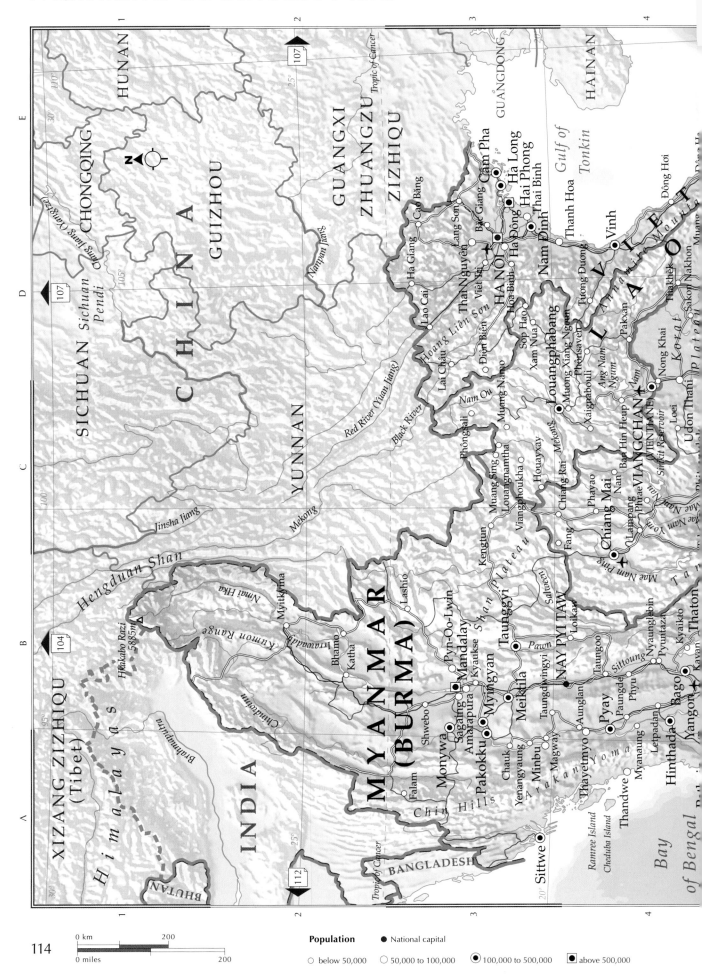

0 km   200

0 miles   200

Population   ● National capital

○ below 50,000   ○ 50,000 to 100,000   ◉ 100,000 to 500,000   ◼ above 500,000

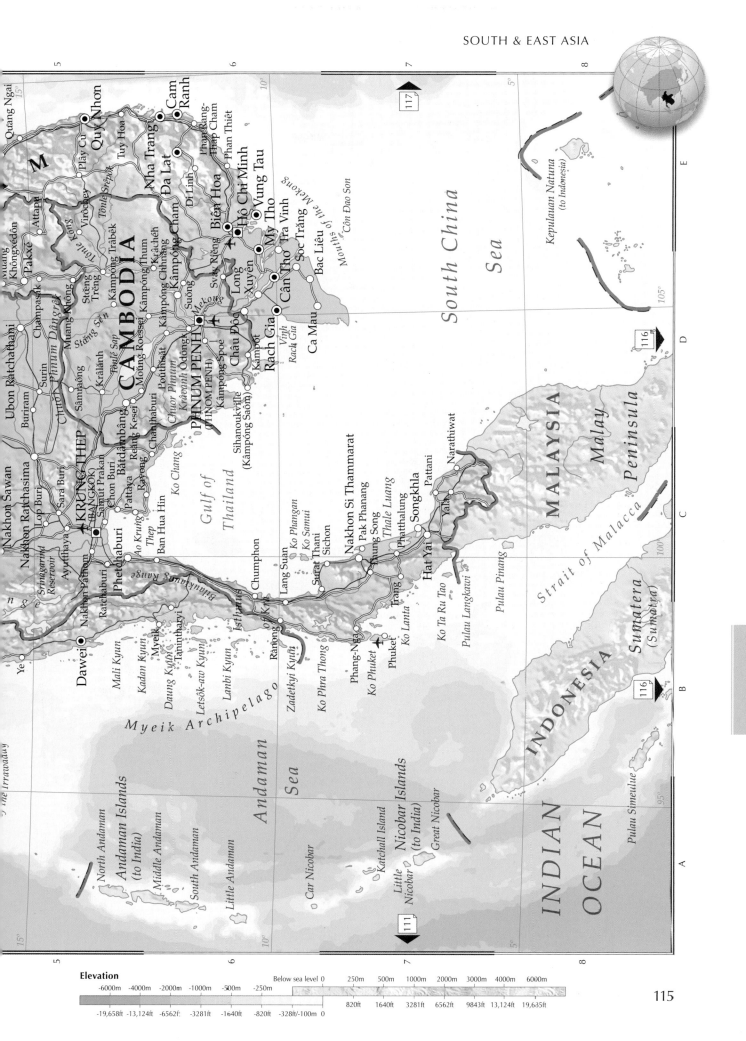

Elevation

						Below sea level 0	250m	500m	1000m	2000m	3000m	4000m	6000m

-6000m -4000m -2000m -1000m -500m -250m

-19,658ft -13,124ft -6562f: -3281ft -1640ft -820ft -328ft/-100m 0

820ft 1640ft 3281ft 6562ft 9843ft 13,124ft 19,635ft

Maritime Southeast Asia

SINGAPORE

0 km   10
0 miles   10

MALAYSIA

Causeway
Johore Strait
Pulau Tekong
Pulau Ubin

Lim Chu Kang
Hougang
Bukit Panjang
New Town
Choa Chu Kang
Changi
Bukit Timah 176m
Queenstown
Bedok New Town
Jurong Industrial Estate
City
Telok Blangah
Sentosa
Selat Pandan
Pulau Sudong
Pulau Pawai
Strait of Singapore

103°50'
104°
1°20'
103°40'
10°

Urban areas
Open areas
Nature reserves

MYANMAR (BURMA)

LAOS

Gulf of Tonkin

Hainan Dao (to China)

THAILAND

VIETNAM

CAMBODIA

Mekong

Mouths of the Mekong

PARACEL ISLANDS
(disputed by China, Taiwan and Vietnam)

South China Sea

SPRATLY ISLANDS
(disputed by China, Malaysia, Philippines, Taiwan and Vietnam)

Andaman Sea

Gulf of Thailand

Nicobar Islands (to India)

Isthmus of Kra

Strait of Malacca

Banda Aceh
Sigli
George Town
Kota Bharu
Butterworth
Pulau Pinang
Taiping
Kuala Terengganu
Langsa
Ipoh
Dungun
Meulaboh
Cukai
Kuantan
Pulau Simeulue
Medan
Tebingtinggi
Klang
KUALA LUMPUR
Kepulauan Natuna
Pematangsiantar
PUTRAJAYA
Melaka
Keluang
Danau Toba
Muar
Johor Bahru
Kepulauan Banyak
Sibolga
Batu Pahat
SINGAPORE
Pulau Nias
Pekanbaru
Singkawang
Sidas
Kepulauan Lingga
Solok
Rengat
Pontianak
Equator
Padang
Batang Hari
Kualatungkal
Pulau Siberut
Jambi
Bangka
Sungaipenuh
Pangkalpinang
Kepulauan Mentawai
Palembang
Bengkulu
Lahat
Pulau Belitung

Kepulauan Natuna

BRUNEI
Kota Kinabalu
BANDAR SERI BEGAWAN
Miri
Bintulu
Sibu
Sarawak
Sri Aman
Kuching
Batang Rajang
Selat Serasan
Sungai Kapuas
Pegunungan Müller
Borneo
Kalimantan
Samarinda
Balikpapan
Sampit
Banjarmasin
Pulau Laut
Sungai Barito

Sumatera (Sumatra)

Kotabumi
Bandar Lampung
Cirebon
Tegal
Java Sea
Serang
JAKARTA
Pekalongan
Semarang
Bogor
Kudus
Pulau Madura
Sukabumi
Bandung
Surabaya
Tasikmalaya
Probolinggo
Jawa (Java)
Cilacap
Jember
Magelang
Kediri
Malang
Bali
Denpasar
Yogyakarta
Madiun
Surakarta
Pulau Lombok

INDIAN OCEAN

10°

MALAYSIA'S TWO CAPITALS

KUALA LUMPUR — Capital
PUTRAJAYA — Administrative capital

0 km   200
0 miles   200

Population   ● National capital

○ below 50,000   ○ 50,000 to 100,000   ◉ 100,000 to 500,000   ■ above 500,000

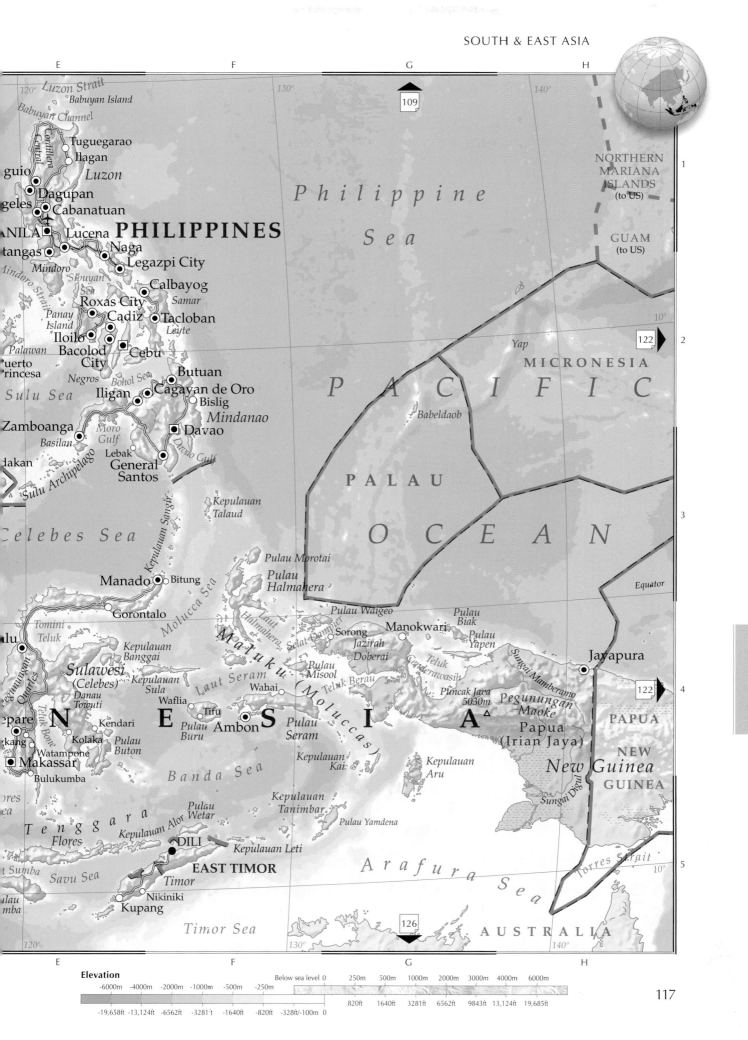

Luzon Strait
120°
Babuyan Island
Babuyan Channel
Cordillera Central
Tuguegarao
Ilagan
guio
Luzon
Dagupan
geles
Cabanatuan
NILA
Lucena **PHILIPPINES**
tangas
Naga
Mindoro
Legazpi City
Sibuyan
Mindoro Strait
Sea
Calbayog
Roxas City
Samar
Palawan
Cadiz
Tacloban
Panay
Island
Iloilo
Leyte
Bacolod
Cebu
City
uerto
rincesa
Negros
Butuan
Sulu Sea
Bohol Sea
Iligan
Cagayan de Oro
Zamboanga
Bislig
akan
Basilan
Moro
Gulf
Mindanao
Davao
Sulu Archipelago
Lebak
Davao Gulf
General
Santos
Kepulauan
Talaud

Philippine
Sea

130°
109

140°

NORTHERN
MARIANA
ISLANDS
(to US)

GUAM
(to US)

10°

122

Yap

MICRONESIA

PACIFIC

Babeldaob

PALAU

OCEAN

3

Celebes Sea
Kepulauan Sangir
Pulau Morotai
Pulau
Halmahera
Manado
Bitung
Gorontalo
Tomini
Teluk
lu
Kepulauan
Banggai
Sulawesi
(Celebes)
Kepulauan
Sula
Quarles
Danau
Towuti
pare
N
Kendari
E
kang
Kolaka
Pulau
Buton
Watampone
Teluk
Bone
Makassar
Bulukumba
Banda Sea

Laut
Halmahera
Selat Dampier
Pulau Waigeo
Sorong
Jazirah
Doberai
Pulau
Misool
Laut Seram
Wahai
Waflia
Tifu
Pulau
Buru
Ambon
S
Pulau
Seram
Pulau
Maluku (Moluccas)
Kepulauan
Kai
Banda Sea

Pulau Biak
Manokwari
Pulau
Yapen
Teluk
Cenderawasih
Puncak Jaya
5030m
Pegunungan
Maoke
I
Papua
(Irian Jaya)
A
Kepulauan
Aru

Sungai Mamberamo
Jayapura

122
4

PAPUA

NEW
GUINEA

New Guinea

Equator

res
ea
Tenggara
Flores
Sumba
Savu Sea
lau
mba
Kupang
Timor Sea

Pulau
Wetar
Kepulauan Alor
DILI
EAST TIMOR
Timor
Nikiniki
130°

Pulau
Kepulauan Leti
Kepulauan
Tanimbar
Pulau Yamdena

Arafura
Sea

Sungai Digul

Torres Strait
10°

AUSTRALIA
140°

126

5

Elevation

Below sea level 0   250m   500m   1000m   2000m   3000m   4000m   6000m

-6000m -4000m -2000m -1000m -500m -250m

-19,658ft -13,124ft -6562ft -3281ft -1640ft -820ft -328ft/-100m 0

820ft   1640ft   3281ft   6562ft   9843ft 13,124ft 19,685ft

117

The Indian Ocean

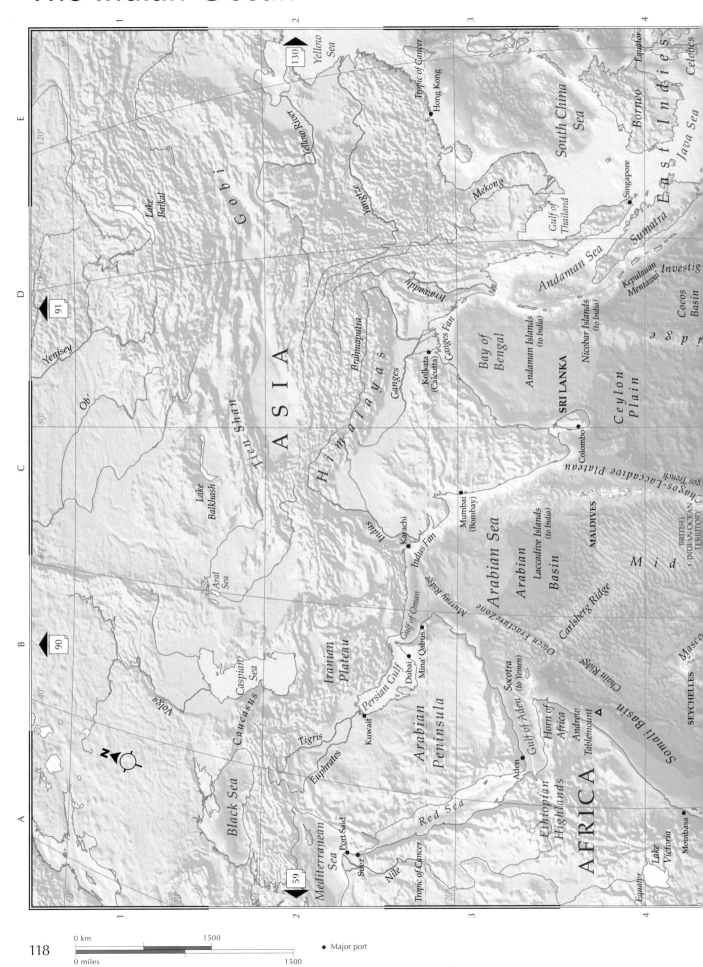

130

91

90

59

Yellow Sea

Yellow River

Lake Baikal

G o b i

Yangtze

Tropic of Cancer

Hong Kong

South China Sea

Borneo

E a s t   I n d i e s

Java Sea

Celebes

Equator

Singapore

Sumatra

Mekong

Gulf of Thailand

Andaman Sea

Kepulauan Mentawai

Investig

A S I A

Irrawaddy

Brahmaputra

Ganges Fan

Bay of Bengal

Andaman Islands (to India)

Nicobar Islands (to India)

Cocos Basin

i d g e

Yenisey

Ob'

Tien Shan

H i m a l a y a s

Ganges

Kolkata (Calcutta)

SRI LANKA

Ceylon Plain

Colombo

Lake Balkhash

Indus

Karachi

Indus Fan

Mumbai (Bombay)

Arabian Sea

Laccadive Islands (to India)

MALDIVES

Arabian Basin

Chagos-Laccadive Plateau

gos Trench

BRITISH INDIAN OCEAN TERRITORY (

M i d

Aral Sea

Iranian Plateau

Gulf of Oman

Murray Ridge

Owen Fracture Zone

Carlsberg Ridge

Caspian Sea

Volga

Caucasus

Persian Gulf

Dubai

Mina' Qabus

Socotra (to Yemen)

Chain Ridge

Mascas

SEYCHELLES

Black Sea

Tigris

Kuwait

Arabian Peninsula

Gulf of Aden

Horn of Africa

Andrew

Tablemount

Somali Basin

Euphrates

Aden

Ethiopian Highlands

A F R I C A

Mediterranean Sea

Port Said

Suez

Red Sea

Nile

Tropic of Cancer

Equator

Lake Victoria

Mombasa

N

0 km   1500

0 miles   1500

● Major port

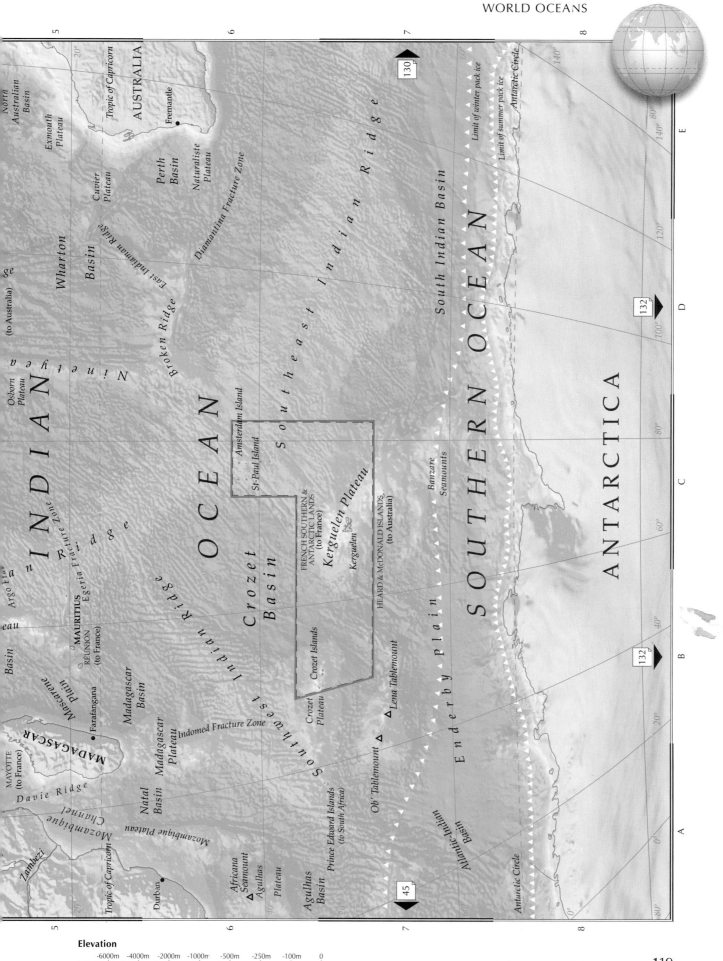

AUSTRALIA

Fremantle

North Australian Basin

Exmouth Plateau

Cuvier Plateau

Perth Basin

Naturaliste Plateau

(to Australia)

Wharton Basin

East Indian Ridge

Diamantina Fracture Zone

Broken Ridge

Ninetyeast

Osborn Plateau

INDIAN

OCEAN

Ridge

Southeast Indian Ridge

South Indian Basin

SOUTHERN OCEAN

Amsterdam Island

St-Paul Island

Southwest Indian Ridge

FRENCH SOUTHERN & ANTARCTIC LANDS (to France)

Kerguelen Plateau

Kerguelen

HEARD & McDONALD ISLANDS (to Australia)

Banzare Seamounts

Crozet Basin

Egeria Fracture Zone

MAURITIUS

RÉUNION (to France)

Mascarene Plain

Madagascar Basin

Farafangana

Central Indian Ridge

Crozet Islands

Crozet Plateau

Lena Tablemount

Ob' Tablemount

Enderby Plain

ANTARCTICA

Indomed Fracture Zone

Madagascar Plateau

MADAGASCAR

MAYOTTE (to France)

Natal Basin

Davie Ridge

Mozambique Channel

Mozambique Plateau

Zambezi

Durban

Tropic of Capricorn

Africana Seamount

Agulhas Plateau

Agulhas Basin

Prince Edward Islands (to South Africa)

Atlantic-Indian Basin

Antarctic Circle

Limit of winter pack ice

Limit of summer pack ice

Antarctic Circle

Elevation

| -6000m | -4000m | -2000m | -1000m | -500m | -250m | -100m | 0 |

| -19,658ft | -13,124ft | -6562ft | -3281ft | -1640ft | -820ft | -328ft/-100m | 0 |

Australasia & Oceania

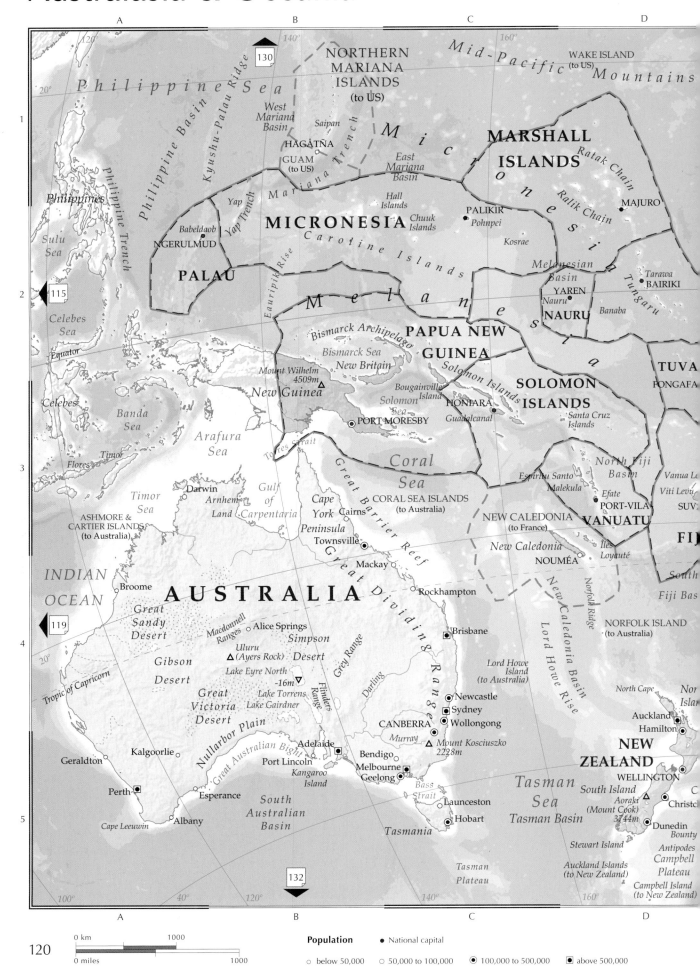

Philippine Sea

Mid-Pacific Mountains

WAKE ISLAND (to US)

NORTHERN MARIANA ISLANDS (to US)

130

West Mariana Basin

Saipan

HAGÅTÑA
GUAM (to US)

Philippines

Philippine Basin

Kyushu-Palau Ridge

Philippine Trench

Yap Trench

Mariana Trench

MARSHALL ISLANDS

Ratak Chain

Ralik Chain

MAJURO

East Mariana Basin

Hall Islands

PALIKIR

Pohnpei

Yap

Chuuk Islands

MICRONESIA

Caroline Islands

Kosrae

Babeldaob

NGERULMUD

115

Celebes Sea

Sulu Sea

Eauripik Rise

PALAU

Melanesian Basin

Tarawa
BAIRIKI

YAREN
Nauru

Banaba

Tungaru

NAURU

TUVA
FONGAFA

Equator

Celebes

Bismarck Archipelago

PAPUA NEW GUINEA

Banda Sea

Bismarck Sea

New Britain

Mount Wilhelm 4509m

New Guinea

Bougainville Island

Solomon Islands

SOLOMON ISLANDS

North Fiji Basin

Vanua L

Timor

Flores

Arafura Sea

Solomon Sea

HONIARA

Guadalcanal

Santa Cruz Islands

Espiritu Santo

Malekula

Viti Levu

PORT-VILA

SUV

PORT MORESBY

Coral Sea

Torres Strait

Efate

VANUATU

FI

Timor Sea

Darwin

Arnhem Land

Gulf of Carpentaria

Cape York Peninsula

Cairns

Great Barrier Reef

CORAL SEA ISLANDS (to Australia)

NEW CALEDONIA (to France)

Îles Loyauté

ASHMORE & CARTIER ISLANDS (to Australia)

Townsville

New Caledonia

NOUMÉA

South Fiji Bas

INDIAN OCEAN

Broome

AUSTRALIA

Mackay

Rockhampton

New Caledonia Basin

Norfolk Ridge

Lord Howe Rise

NORFOLK ISLAND (to Australia)

North Cape

Nor Islar

119

Great Sandy Desert

Macdonnell Ranges

Alice Springs

Simpson Desert

Grey Range

Brisbane

Lord Howe Island (to Australia)

Gibson Desert

Uluru (Ayers Rock)

Lake Eyre North -16m

Darling

Auckland

Hamilton

Great Victoria Desert

Lake Torrens

Lake Gairdner

Flinders Range

Newcastle

Sydney

Wollongong

Tropic of Capricorn

Nullarbor Plain

CANBERRA

Murray

Mount Kosciuszko 2228m

NEW ZEALAND

Kalgoorlie

Adelaide

Bendigo

WELLINGTON

Geraldton

Port Lincoln

Melbourne

Geelong

Bass Strait

Tasman Sea

South Island

Aoraki (Mount Cook) 3744m

Christ

Perth

Esperance

Kangaroo Island

South Australian Basin

Launceston

Tasman Basin

Dunedin

Bounty

Cape Leeuwin

Albany

Hobart

Stewart Island

Antipodes

Campbell Plateau

Tasmania

Tasman Plateau

Auckland Islands (to New Zealand)

Campbell Island (to New Zealand)

Great Australian Bight

Great Dividing Range

Eauripik Rise

0 km   1000
0 miles   1000

Population ● National capital

○ below 50,000   ○ 50,000 to 100,000   ◉ 100,000 to 500,000   ▣ above 500,000

E | F | G | H

160° 140°

131

160° 120° 20°

Hawai'ian Islands (to US)

JOHNSTON ATOLL (to US)

Clarion Fracture Zone

1

PACIFIC

Central Pacific Basin

KINGMAN REEF (to US)

Christmas Ridge

OCEAN

Clipperton Fracture Zone

PALMYRA ATOLL (to US)

Teraina *Tabuaeran*

BAKER & HOWLAND ISLANDS (to US)

Kiritimati

131

JARVIS ISLAND (to US)

Line Islands

a

i

2

R I B A T I

Galapagos Fracture Zone *Equator*

Phoenix Islands

Malden Island *Starbuck Island*

Marquesas Islands

TOKELAU (to NZ)

Northern Cook Islands *Penrhyn*

Marquesas Fracture Zone

bie Ridge

Manihiki *Manihiki Plateau*

Millennium Island *Flint Island*

Tiki Basin

3

WALLIS UTUNA (to France)

SAMOA *Savai'i*

Samoa Basin

Penrhyn Basin

TĀ'UTU *Upolu* **ĀPIA** *Tutuila*

Tuamotu Islands

Tuamotu Fracture Zone

PAGO PAGO

TONGA

AMERICAN SAMOA (to US)

COOK ISLANDS (to NZ)

Society Islands

PAPEETE *Tahiti*

Vava'u Group

Southern Cook Islands

n

e

NIUE (to NZ)

JKU'ALOFA

AVARUA *Rarotonga*

y

FRENCH POLYNESIA (to France)

Tonga Trench

Îles Australes

Austral Fracture Zone

Îles Gambier

PITCAIRN, HENDERSON, DUCIE & OENO ISLANDS (to UK)

20°

131

4

madec Islands *New Zealand)*

l

Marotiri

Pitcairn Island

Tropic of Capricorn

kmadec Trench

Louisville Ridge

o

Southwest

132

Pacific Basin

140° 120°

P

Rise

Chatham Islands (to New Zealand)

N

160°

40°

160°

Political features

🗺 **Total area:**
3,376,700 sq miles (8,745,750 sq km)

🏛 **Total number of countries:**
14

👤 **Total population:**
37.5 million

🏙 **Largest city with population:**
Sydney, Australia 4.8 million

👥 **Country with highest population density:**
Nauru 1165 people per sq mile (449 people per sq km)

⬛ **Largest country:**
Australia 2,967,892 sq miles (7,686,850 sq km)

◻ **Smallest country:**
Nauru 8 sq miles (21 sq km)

Physical features

⬛ **Largest lake:**
Lake Eyre, Australia 3700 sq miles (9583 sq km)

〰 **Longest river:**
Murray-Darling, Australia 2330 miles (3750 km)

🔺 **Highest point:**
Mt. Wilhelm Papua New Guinea 14,794 ft (4509 m)

🔻 **Lowest point:**
Lake Eyre, Australia 52 ft (16 m) below sea level

E | F | G | H

The Southwest Pacific

Population

● National capital

○ below 50,000
○ 50,000 to 100,000
◉ 100,000 to 500,000
◼ above 500,000

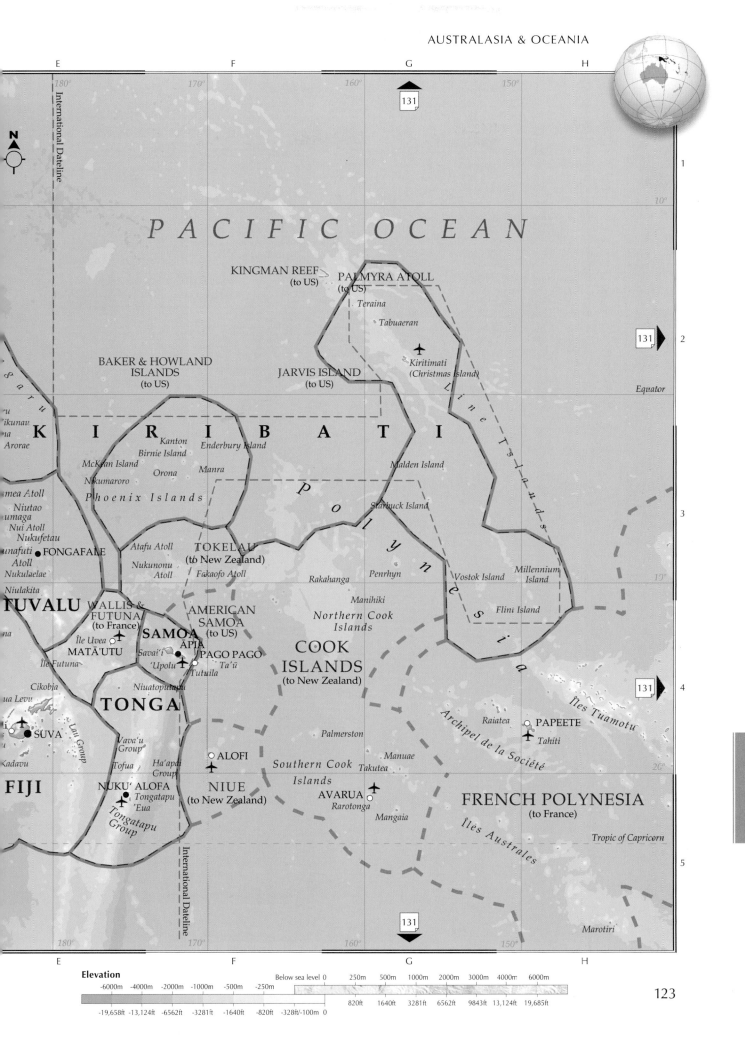

E   F   G   H

1

180°   170°   160°   150°

10°

International Dateline

N

P A C I F I C   O C E A N

KINGMAN REEF
(to US)

PALMYRA ATOLL
(to US)

Teraina

Tabuaeran

131

2

BAKER & HOWLAND
ISLANDS
(to US)

JARVIS ISLAND
(to US)

*Kiritimati
(Christmas Island)*

Equator

K I R I B A T I

Line Islands

Kanton
Birnie Island   *Enderbury Island*

McKean Island

Malden Island

Orona   *Manra*

Nikumaroro

P h o e n i x   I s l a n d s

P

Starbuck Island

3

Atafu Atoll

TOKELAU
(to New Zealand)

o

*Nukunonu
Atoll*

Fakaofo Atoll

Rakahanga

Penrhyn

Vostok Island

*Millennium
Island*

15°

Niulakita

TUVALU

WALLIS &
FUTUNA
(to France)

AMERICAN
SAMOA
(to US)

Manihiki

*Northern Cook
Islands*

l

y

n

Flint Island

Île Uvea

SAMOA

Savai'i   ĀPIA

MATĀ'UTU

Île Futuna

'*Upolu*

PAGO PAGO

Ta'ū
Tutuila

COOK
ISLANDS
(to New Zealand)

e

s

Cikobia

Niuatoputapu

TONGA

i

a

SUVA

*Vava'u
Group*

Lau Group

Palmerston

Raiatea

Archipel de la Société

PAPEETE

Tahiti

4

131

Kadavu

Tofua

*Ha'apai
Group*

ALOFI

*Southern Cook
Islands*

Manuae

Takutea

Îles Tuamotu

FIJI

NUKU'ALOFA

Tongatapu
'*Eua*

NIUE
(to New Zealand)

AVARUA

Rarotonga

FRENCH POLYNESIA
(to France)

26°

*Tongatapu
Group*

Mangaia

Îles Australes

Tropic of Capricorn

International Dateline

Marotiri

5

131

180°   170°   160°   150°

E   F   G   H

Elevation

| -6000m | -4000m | -2000m | -1000m | -500m | -250m | Below sea level 0 | 250m | 500m | 1000m | 2000m | 3000m | 4000m | 6000m |

-19,658ft   -13,124ft   -6562ft   -3281ft   -1640ft   -820ft   -328ft/-100m   0

820ft   1640ft   3281ft   6562ft   9843ft   13,124ft   19,685ft

Western Australia

Population

● Internal administrative capital

○ below 50,000   ○ 50,000 to 100,000   ◉ 100,000 to 500,000   ◼ above 500,000

0 km ———— 300
0 miles ———— 300

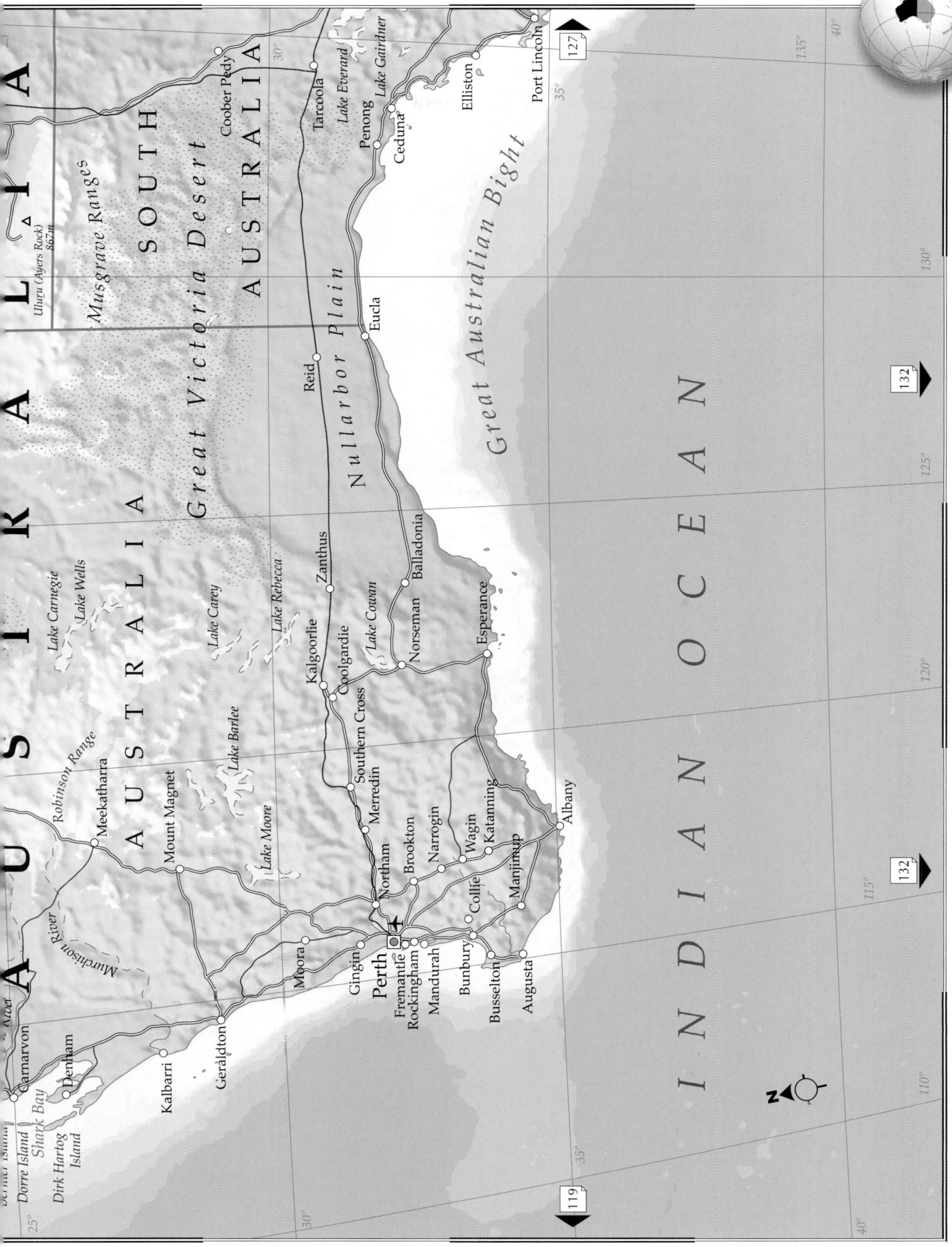

AUSTRALIA

SOUTH

Musgrave Ranges

Uluru (Ayers Rock)
867m

Great Victoria Desert

AUSTRALIA

SOUTH AUSTRALIA

Coober Pedy

Tarcoola

Lake Everard

Penong

Lake Gairdner

Ceduna

Elliston

Port Lincoln

127

Nullarbor Plain

Eucla

Reid

Great Australian Bight

132

AUSTRALIA

Lake Carnegie

Lake Wells

Lake Carey

Lake Rebecca

Zanthus

Balladonia

Lake Cowan

Kalgoorlie

Coolgardie

Norseman

Esperance

AUSTRALIA

Robinson Range

Meekatharra

Mount Magnet

Lake Barlee

Lake Moore

Southern Cross

Merredin

Northam

Brookton

Narrogin

Wagin

Katanning

Manjimup

Albany

I N D I A N   O C E A N

Mingenew

Gingin

Perth

Fremantle

Rockingham

Mandurah

Bunbury

Collie

Busselton

Augusta

132

Murchison River

Carnarvon

Denham

Shark Bay

Dorre Island

Dirk Hartog
Island

Kalbarri

Geraldton

119

N

35°

30°

35°

40°

Elevation

| -6000m | -4000m | -2000m | -1000m | -500m | -250m |
| | | | | | |

Below sea level 0   250m   500m   1000m   2000m   3000m   4000m   6000m

-19,658ft   -13,124ft   -6562ft   -3281ft   -1640ft   -820ft   -328ft/-100m   0

820ft   1640ft   3281ft   6562ft   9843ft   13,124ft   19,685ft

125

Eastern Australia

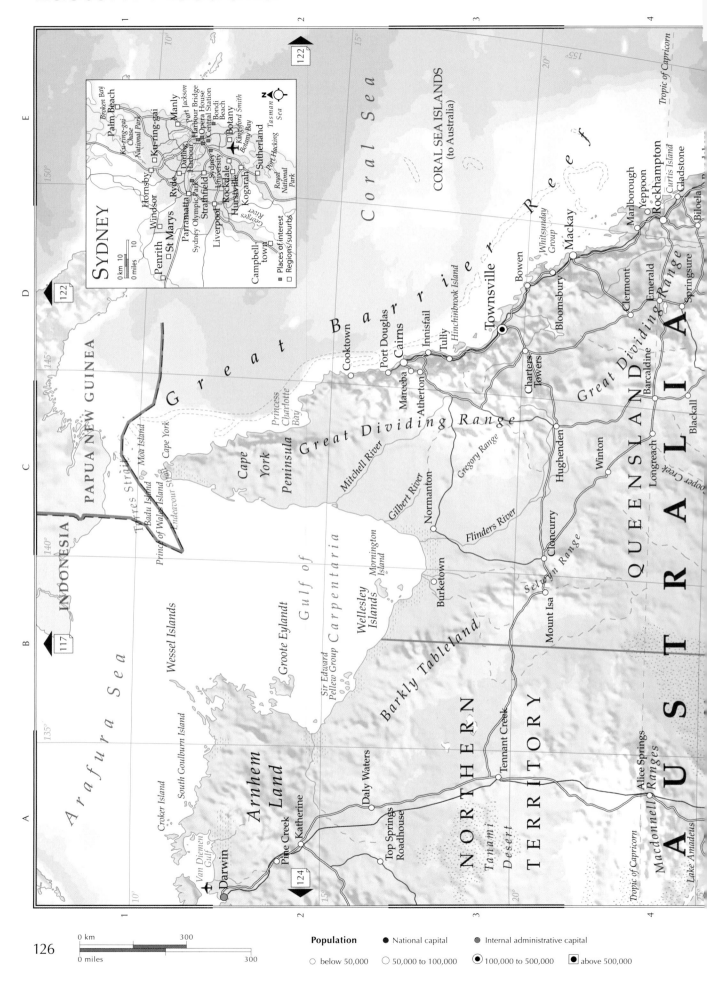

SYDNEY

Broken Bay
Palm Beach
Ku-ring-gai Chase National Park
Manly
Ku-ring-gai
Port Jackson
Harbour Bridge
Opera House
Central Station
Bondi Beach
Botany
Kingsford Smith
Botany Bay
Hornsby
Windsor
Ryde
Darling Harbour
Parramatta
St Marys
Sydney Olympic Park
Strathfield
Sydney University
Rockdale
Liverpool
Hurstville
Kogarah
Sutherland
Port Hacking
Royal National Park
Campbelltown

Penrith

0 km   10
0 miles   10

■ Places of interest
□ Regions/suburbs

CORAL SEA ISLANDS
(to Australia)

Coral Sea

Tasman Sea

Great Barrier Reef

PAPUA NEW GUINEA

INDONESIA

Arafura Sea

Torres Strait

Cape York

Cape York Peninsula

Great Dividing Range

Princess Charlotte Bay

Cooktown
Port Douglas
Cairns
Innisfail
Tully
Hinchinbrook Island
Townsville
Bowen
Whitsunday Group
Mackay
Bloomsbury
Marlborough
Yeppoon
Rockhampton
Curtis Island
Gladstone
Biloela
Springsure
Emerald
Clermont
Barcaldine
Blackall

Mareeba
Atherton
Charters Towers
Hughenden
Winton
Longreach
Cooper Creek

Mitchell River
Gilbert River
Gregory Range
Flinders River
Normanton
Cloncurry
Selwyn Range
Mount Isa

Gulf of Carpentaria

Wellesley Islands
Mornington Island
Burketown

Sir Edward Pellew Group

Groote Eylandt

Wessel Islands

South Goulburn Island

Croker Island

Van Diemen Gulf

Darwin
Pine Creek
Katherine

Arnhem Land

Barkly Tableland

Tennant Creek

Top Springs Roadhouse

Daly Waters

NORTHERN TERRITORY

Tanami Desert

Alice Springs
Macdonnell Ranges
Lake Amadeus

Tropic of Capricorn

QUEENSLAND

AUSTRALIA

Great Dividing Range

Moa Island
Badu Island
Prince of Wales Island
Endeavour Strait

0 km   300
0 miles   300

Population   ● National capital   ● Internal administrative capital

○ below 50,000   ○ 50,000 to 100,000   ◉ 100,000 to 500,000   ◼ above 500,000

117

122

124

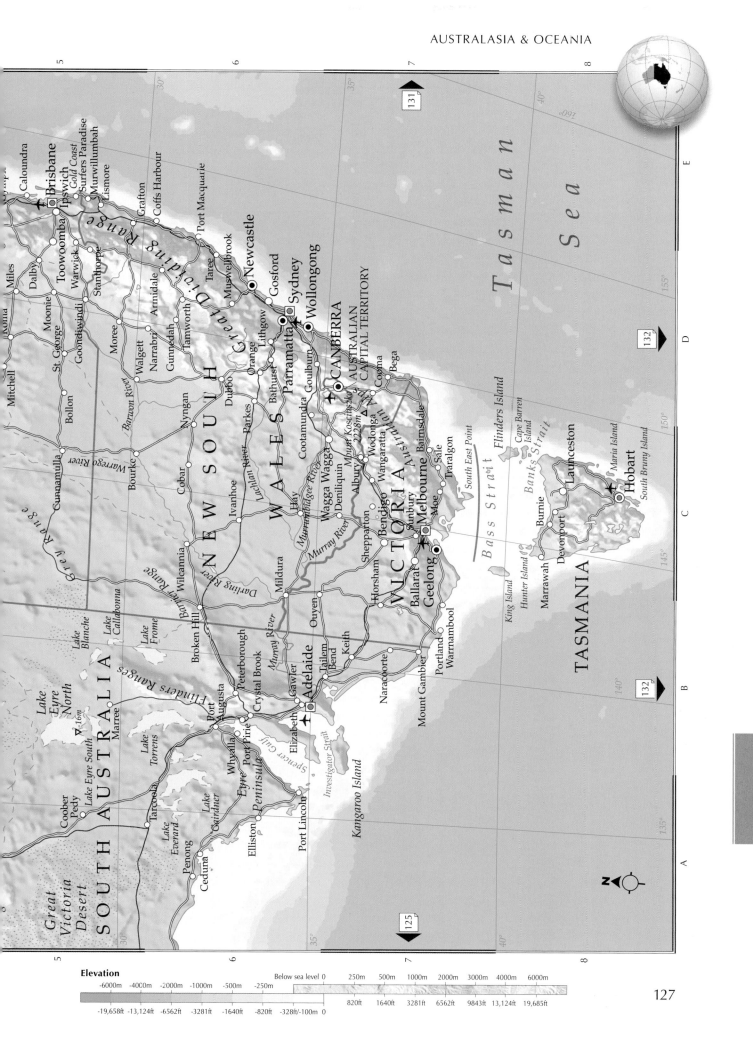

131

132

132

125

Tasman Sea

SOUTH AUSTRALIA

NEW SOUTH WALES

VICTORIA

TASMANIA

AUSTRALIAN CAPITAL TERRITORY

Great Dividing Range

Great Victoria Desert

Caloundra
Brisbane
Ipswich
Gold Coast
Surfers Paradise
Murwillumbah
Lismore
Grafton
Coffs Harbour
Port Macquarie
Toowoomba
Warwick
Stanthorpe
Miles
Dalby
Moonie
St. George
Goondiwindi
Bollon
Mitchell
Moree
Walgett
Narrabri
Gunnedah
Armidale
Tamworth
Taree
Muswellbrook
Gosford
Newcastle
Sydney
Parramatta
Wollongong
Lithgow
Orange
Bathurst
Dubbo
Parkes
Nyngan
Cobar
Bourke
Cunnamulla
Warrego River
Barwon River
Wilcannia
Ivanhoe
Lachlan River
Hay
Murrumbidgee River
Wagga Wagga
Deniliquin
Griffith
Narrandera
Goulburn
CANBERRA
Cooma
Bega
Cootamundra
Mount Kosciuszko
2228m
Albury
Wodonga
Wangaratta
Bairnsdale
Sale
Traralgon
Moe
Melbourne
Bendigo
Shepparton
Sunbury
Ballarat
Geelong
Horsham
Mildura
Ouyen
Murray River
Darling River
Broken Hill
Barrier Range
Peterborough
Crystal Brook
Port Pirie
Whyalla
Port Augusta
Adelaide
Elizabeth
Gawler
Tailem Bend
Keith
Naracoorte
Warrnambool
Portland
Mount Gambier
Kangaroo Island
Investigator Strait
Spencer Gulf
Eyre Peninsula
Port Lincoln
Elliston
Ceduna
Penong
Tarcoola
Marree
Lake Eyre North
-16m
Lake Eyre South
Lake Torrens
Lake Gairdner
Lake Everard
Lake Frome
Lake Callabonna
Lake Blanche
Coober Pedy
Flinders Ranges
Grey Range
South East Point
Bass Strait
Banks Strait
Flinders Island
Cape Barren Island
King Island
Hunter Island
Marrawah
Burnie
Devonport
Launceston
Maria Island
Hobart
South Bruny Island

127

Elevation

| -6000m | -4000m | -2000m | -1000m | -500m | -250m | Below sea level 0 | 250m | 500m | 1000m | 2000m | 3000m | 4000m | 6000m |

-19,658ft | -13,124ft | -6562ft | -3281ft | -1640ft | -820ft | -328ft/-100m | 0 | 820ft | 1640ft | 3281ft | 6562ft | 9843ft | 13,124ft | 19,685ft

127

New Zealand

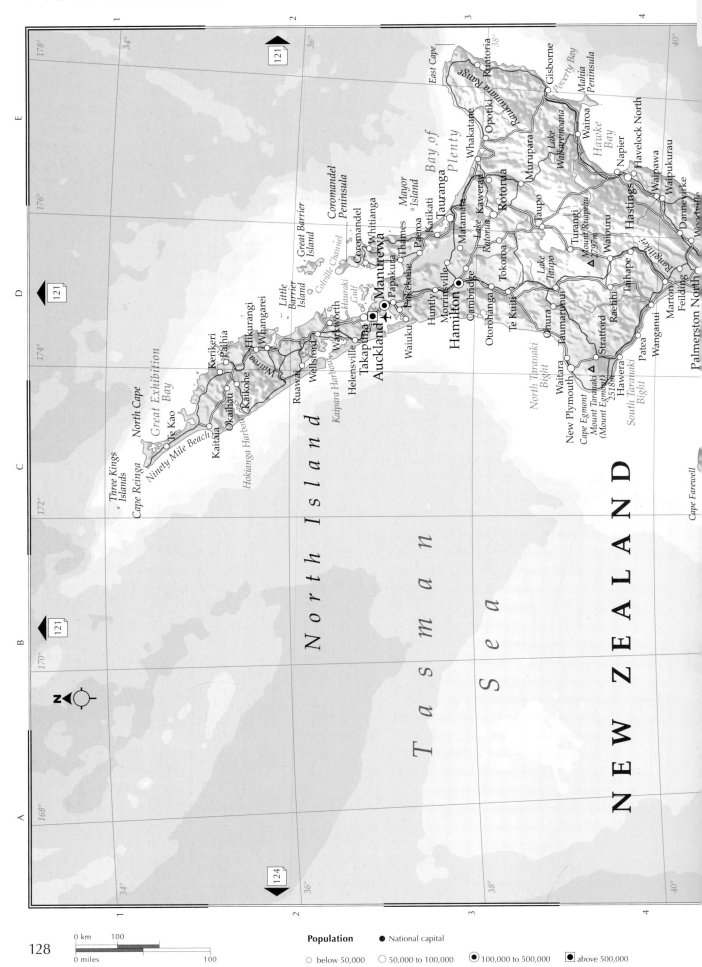

178° 176° 174° 172° 170° 168°

34°

36°

38°

40°

E

D

C

B

A

121

121

121

124

N

Three Kings Islands
Cape Reinga
North Cape
Great Exhibition Bay
Te Kao
Ninety Mile Beach
Kaitaia
Okaihau
Kaikohe
Hokianga Harbour
Kerikeri
Pahia
Hikurangi
Whangarei
Ruawai
Wairoa
Wellsford
Kaipara Harbour
Helensville
Warkworth
Takapuna
Auckland
Waiuku
Manurewa
Papakura
Pukekohe
Thames
Paeroa
Katikati
Huntly
Morrinsville
Cambridge
Hamilton
Te Kuiti
Otorohanga
Tokoroa
Waitomo
Taumarunui
Ohura

Little Barrier Island
Great Barrier Island
Coromandel Peninsula
Coromandel
Whitianga
Colville Channel
Hauraki Gulf
Mayor Island
Whakatane
Opotiki
Tauranga
Matamata
Lake Kawerau
Rotorua
Lake Rotorua
Bay of Plenty

East Cape
Raukumara Range
Ruatoria
Gisborne
Poverty Bay
Mahia
Mahia Peninsula
Wairoa
Hawke Bay
Murupara
Lake Waikaremoana
Taupo
Lake Taupo
Turangi
Mount Ruapehu
2797m △
Waiouru
Taihape
Raetihi
Patea
Wanganui
Marton
Feilding
Palmerston North
Waipawa
Napier
Hastings
Havelock North
Waipukurau
Dannevirke
Woodville
Ruahine

New Plymouth
Waitara
Stratford
Hawera
North Taranaki Bight
Cape Egmont
Mount Taranaki
(Mount Egmont)
2518m △
South Taranaki Bight

N o r t h   I s l a n d

T a s m a n   S e a

N E W   Z E A L A N D

Cape Farewell

0 km 100
0 miles 100

Population   ● National capital

○ below 50,000   ○ 50,000 to 100,000   ◉ 100,000 to 500,000   ◼ above 500,000

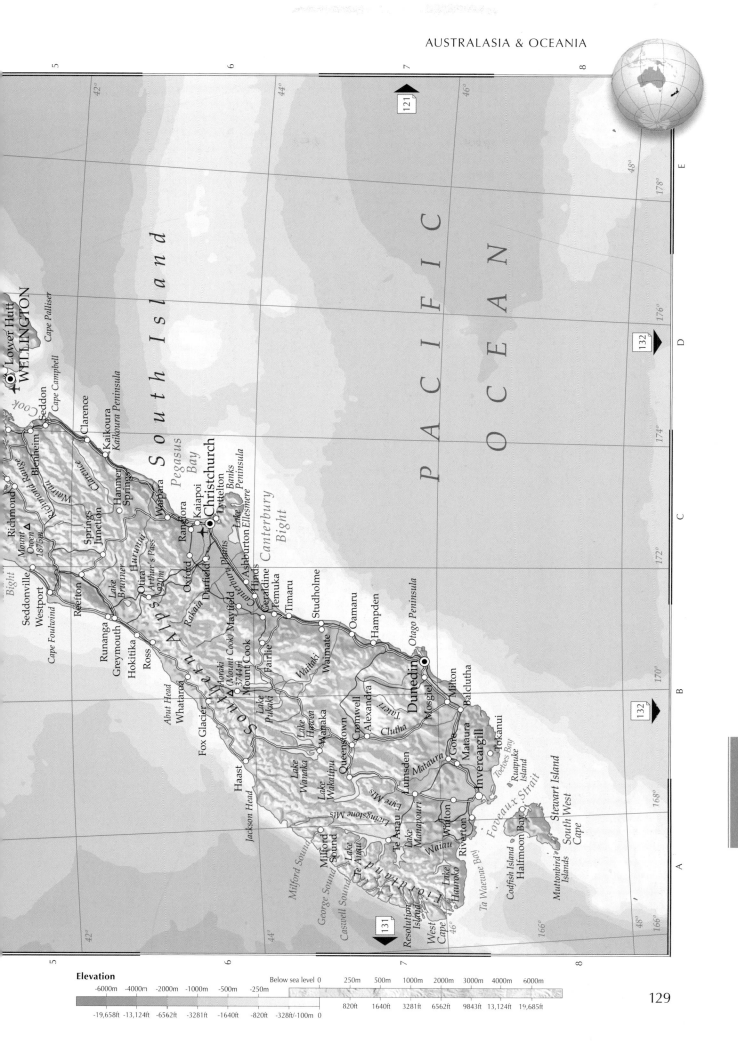

121
132
132
131

Elevation

-6000m	-4000m	-2000m	-1000m	-500m	-250m	Below sea level 0	250m	500m	1000m	2000m	3000m	4000m	6000m

-19,658ft -13,124ft -6562ft -3281ft -1640ft -820ft -328ft/-100m 0   820ft 1640ft 3281ft 6562ft 9843ft 13,124ft 19,685ft

The Pacific Ocean

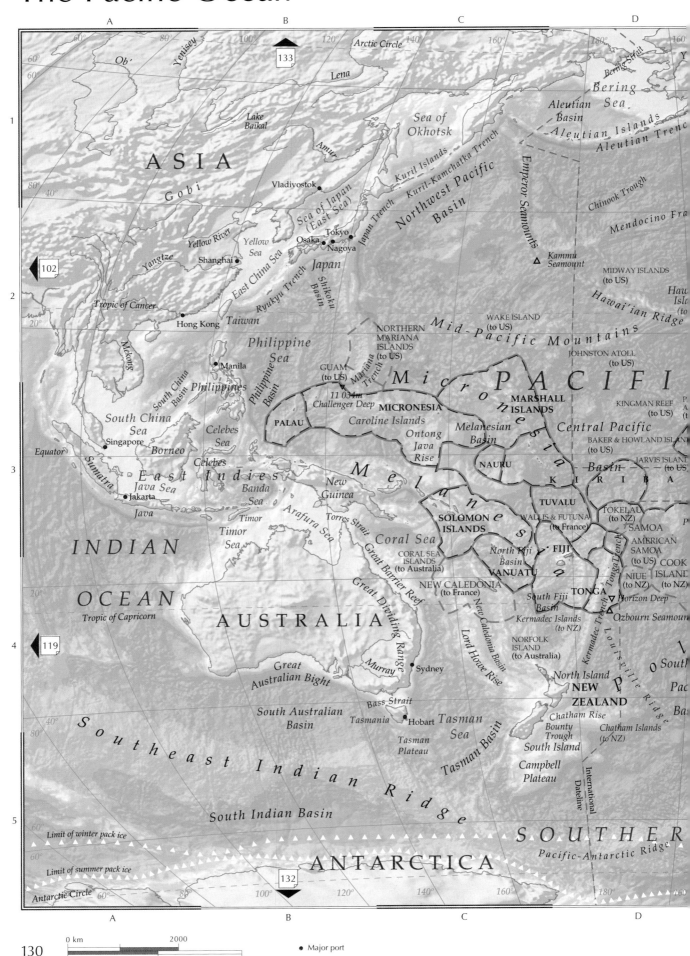

133

102

119

A · B · C · D

ASIA

Ob'
Yenisey
Lena
Arctic Circle
Lake Baikal
Amur
Gobi
Vladivostok
Sea of Okhotsk
Kuril Islands
Kuril-Kamchatka Trench
Northwest Pacific Basin
Bering Sea
Aleutian Basin
Aleutian Islands
Aleutian Trench
Bering Strait
Chinook Trough
Mendocino Fra
Emperor Seamounts
Kammu Seamount
MIDWAY ISLANDS (to US)
Yellow River
Yellow Sea
Tokyo
Osaka
Nagoya
Japan
Japan Trench
Shikoku Basin
Shanghai
Tropic of Cancer
Hong Kong
Taiwan
East China Sea
Ryukyu Trench
Hawaiian Ridge (to
Hau Isla
Mid-Pacific Mountains
WAKE ISLAND (to US)
Philippine Sea
NORTHERN MARIANA ISLANDS (to US)
Micro
PACIFI
JOHNSTON ATOLL (to US)
Mekong
Manila
Philippine Basin
GUAM (to US)
Mariana Trench
11 034m
Challenger Deep
MICRONESIA
Caroline Islands
MARSHALL ISLANDS
n
e
s
i
a
KINGMAN REEF (to US)
South China Basin
Philippines
PALAU
Melanesian Basin
Central Pacific
BAKER & HOWLAND ISLAN (to US)
South China Sea
Celebes Sea
Ontong Java Rise
NAURU
Basin
JARVIS ISLAN (to US
Singapore
Borneo
Celebes
East Indies
M
e
l
a
K
I
R
I
B
A
Equator
Sumatra
Java Sea
Banda Sea
New Guinea
n
e
TUVALU
WALLIS & FUTUNA (to France)
TOKELAU (to NZ)
Jakarta
Java
Timor
Timor Sea
Arafura Sea
Torres Strait
s
SOLOMON ISLANDS
SAMOA
AMERICAN SAMOA (to US)
INDIAN
Great Barrier Reef
Coral Sea
i
a
North Fiji Basin
FIJI
COOK ISLAND (to NZ)
NIUE (to NZ)
CORAL SEA ISLANDS (to Australia)
VANUATU
OCEAN
Tropic of Capricorn
NEW CALEDONIA (to France)
New Caledonia Basin
TONGA
Horizon Deep
Ozbourn Seamoun
Tonga Trench
South Fiji Basin
AUSTRALIA
Great Dividing Range
Lord Howe Rise
Kermadec Islands (to NZ)
NORFOLK ISLAND (to Australia)
Kermadec Trench
Louisville Ridge
P
O
Souti
Pac
Ba
Great Australian Bight
Murray
Sydney
North Island
NEW ZEALAND
South Australian Basin
Bass Strait
Tasmania
Hobart
Tasman Sea
Tasman Basin
Chatham Rise
Bounty Trough
Chatham Islands (to NZ)
Tasman Plateau
South Island
Campbell Plateau
International Dateline
Southeast Indian Ridge
South Indian Basin
S O U T H E R
Pacific-Antarctic Ridge
Limit of winter pack ice
Limit of summer pack ice
Antarctic Circle
ANTARCTICA
132

0 km   2000
0 miles   2000

● Major port

130

E   F   G   H

120°   100°   80°   60°   40°   20°   0°

Arctic Circle

NORTH AMERICA

Rocky Mountains

Vancouver

Cascadia Basin

San Francisco

Colorado

Long Beach

ray Fracture Zone

okai Fracture Zone

Clarion Fracture Zone

OCEAN

Clipperton Fracture Zone

CLIPPERTON ISLAND
(to France)

Galapagos Fracture Zone

Gallego Rise

Marquesas Islands

Marquesas Fracture Zone

Tiki Basin

FRENCH POLYNESIA
(to France)

Îles Gambier

PITCAIRN, HENDERSON, DUCIE & OENO ISLANDS
(to UK)

Austral Fracture Zone

Australes

Agassiz Fracture Zone

Eltanin Fracture Zone

OCEAN

Southeast Pacific Basin

Amundsen Plain

PETER LØY
(to Norway)

Hudson Bay

Great Lakes

Appalachian Mountains

Mississippi

Gulf of California

Gulf of Mexico

Greater Antilles

Middle America Trench

Guatemala Basin

Cocos Ridge

Panama City

Galápagos Islands
(to Ecuador)

Bauer Basin

Galapagos Rise

Mendaña Fracture Zone

Peru Basin

East Pacific Rise

Sala y Gomez
(to Chile)

Sala y Gomez Ridge

Easter Fracture Zone

Easter Island
(to Chile)

Isla San Félix
(to Chile)

Isla San Ambrosio
(to Chile)

Islas Juan Fernández
(to Chile)

Valparaiso

Challenger Fracture Zone

Chile Rise

Mornington Abyssal Plain

Cape Horn

Bellingshausen Plain

Drake Passage

Antarctic Circle

Labrador Sea

ATLANTIC

OCEAN

Tropic of Cancer

Caribbean Sea

Lesser Antilles

Peru-Chile Trench

Nazca Ridge

Chile Basin

Amazon

Callao

SOUTH AMERICA

Andes

Paraná

Tropic of Capricorn

ATLANTIC

OCEAN

N

Equator

60°   40°   20°   0°

20°   40°   20°   0°   20°   60°

1   2   3   4   5

133   44   45   132

E   F   G   H

Elevation

| -6000m | -4000m | -2000m | -1000m | -500m | -250m | -100m | 0 |

| -19,658ft | -13,124ft | -6562ft | -3281ft | -1640ft | -820ft | -328ft/-100m | 0 |

Antarctica

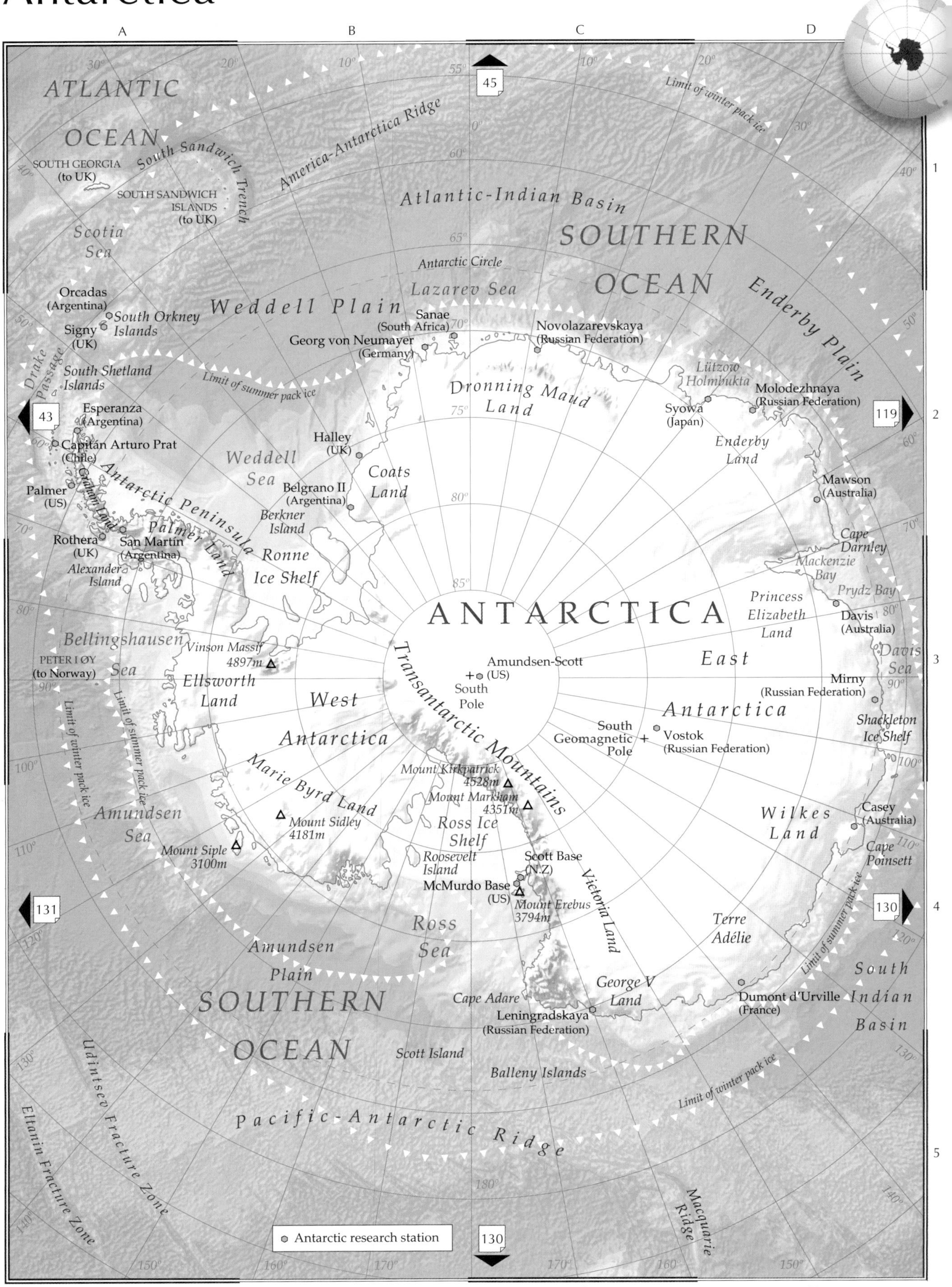

45

ATLANTIC

OCEAN

SOUTH GEORGIA
(to UK)

South Sandwich Trench

SOUTH SANDWICH
ISLANDS
(to UK)

*Scotia
Sea*

America-Antarctica Ridge

Atlantic-Indian Basin

SOUTHERN

OCEAN

Enderby Plain

Antarctic Circle

Lazarev Sea

Orcadas
(Argentina)

South Orkney
Islands

Weddell Plain

Sanae
(South Africa)

Novolazarevskaya
(Russian Federation)

Signy
(UK)

Georg von Neumayer
(Germany)

*Lützow
Holmbukta*

Molodezhnaya
(Russian Federation)

*South Shetland
Islands*

Limit of summer pack ice

*Dronning Maud
Land*

Syowa
(Japan)

43

Esperanza
(Argentina)

Halley
(UK)

*Enderby
Land*

119

Capitán Arturo Prat
(Chile)

*Weddell
Sea*

*Coats
Land*

Mawson
(Australia)

Palmer
(US)

Belgrano II
(Argentina)

*Cape
Darnley*

Rothera
(UK)

San Martín
(Argentina)

*Berkner
Island*

*Mackenzie
Bay*

*Palmer
Land*

Prydz Bay

*Alexander
Island*

*Ronne
Ice Shelf*

*Princess
Elizabeth
Land*

Davis
(Australia)

Bellingshausen

Vinson Massif
4897m

East

*Davis
Sea*

PETER I ØY
(to Norway)

Sea

*Ellsworth
Land*

Amundsen-Scott
(US)

South
Pole

Antarctica

Mirny
(Russian Federation)

*West
Antarctica*

Transantarctic Mountains

South
Geomagnetic
Pole

Vostok
(Russian Federation)

*Shackleton
Ice Shelf*

Marie Byrd Land

Mount Kirkpatrick
4528m

Mount Markham
4351m

*Wilkes
Land*

Casey
(Australia)

Mount Sidley
4181m

*Ross Ice
Shelf*

*Cape
Poinsett*

*Amundsen
Sea*

Mount Siple
3100m

*Roosevelt
Island*

Scott Base
(N.Z.)

McMurdo Base
(US)

Mount Erebus
3794m

Victoria Land

*Terre
Adélie*

130

131

*Amundsen
Plain*

*Ross
Sea*

*George V
Land*

Dumont d'Urville
(France)

*South
Indian
Basin*

SOUTHERN

OCEAN

Cape Adare

Leningradskaya
(Russian Federation)

Udintsev Fracture Zone

Scott Island

Balleny Islands

*Macquarie
Ridge*

Eltanin Fracture Zone

Pacific-Antarctic Ridge

Antarctic research station

130

0 km 500

0 miles 500

Elevation

Below sea level 0   250m   500m   1000m   2000m   3000m   4000m   6000m

-6000m -4000m -2000m -1000m -500m -250m

820ft 1640ft 3281ft 6562ft 9843ft 13,124ft 19,685ft

-19,658ft -13,124ft -6562ft -3281ft -1640ft -820ft -328ft/-100m 0

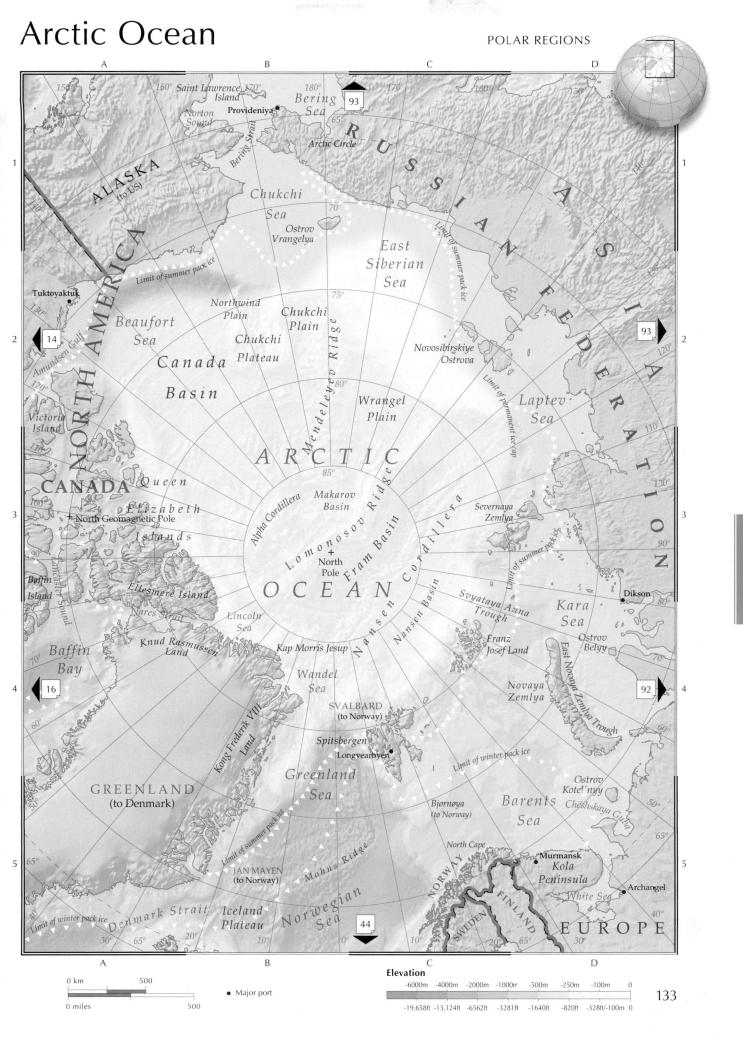

Major labels and place names:

ALASKA (to US)

NORTH AMERICA

CANADA

Tuktoyaktuk

Victoria Island

Baffin Island

Queen Elizabeth Islands

North Geomagnetic Pole

Ellesmere Island

Knud Rasmussen Land

Nares Strait

Lancaster Sound

Amundsen Gulf

Beaufort Sea

Canada Basin

Northwind Plain

Chukchi Plain

Chukchi Plateau

Chukchi Sea

Ostrov Vrangelya

Saint Lawrence Island

Norton Sound

Provideniya

Bering Sea

Bering Strait

Arctic Circle

RUSSIAN FEDERATION

ASIA

East Siberian Sea

Novosibirskiye Ostrova

Wrangel Plain

Laptev Sea

Severnaya Zemlya

Mendeleyev Ridge

Alpha Cordillera

Makarov Basin

Lomonosov Ridge

North Pole

Fram Basin

Nansen Cordillera

Nansen Basin

Svyataya Anna Trough

Franz Josef Land

Kara Sea

Ostrov Belyy

Dikson

East Novaya Zemlya Trough

Novaya Zemlya

ARCTIC OCEAN

Lincoln Sea

Kap Morris Jesup

Wandel Sea

Baffin Bay

Kong Frederik VIII Land

SVALBARD (to Norway)

Spitsbergen

Longyearbyen

Bjørnøya (to Norway)

GREENLAND (to Denmark)

Greenland Sea

JAN MAYEN (to Norway)

Mohns Ridge

Iceland Plateau

Denmark Strait

Norwegian Sea

North Cape

NORWAY

SWEDEN

FINLAND

Murmansk

Kola Peninsula

White Sea

Archangel

Chëshskaya Guba

Ostrov Kotel'nyy

Barents Sea

EUROPE

Limit of summer pack ice

Limit of winter pack ice

Limit of permanent ice cap

Marginal reference boxes: 93, 14, 93, 16, 92, 44

Elevation

-6000m	-4000m	-2000m	-1000m	-500m	-250m	-100m	0
-19,658ft	-13,124ft	-6562ft	-3281ft	-1640ft	-820ft	-328ft/-100m	0

0 km — 500

0 miles — 500

• Major port

Country Profiles

This Factfile is intended as a guide to a world that is continually changing as political fashions and personalities come and go. Nevertheless, all the material in these factfiles has been researched from the most up-to-date and authoritative sources to give an incisive portrait of the geographical, political, and social characteristics that make each country so unique.

There are currently 196 independent countries in the world - more than at any previous time - and over 50 dependencies. Antarctica is the only land area on Earth that is not officially part of, and does not belong to, any single country.

Country profile key

Formation Date of formation denotes the date of political origin or independence of a state, i.e. its emergence as a recognizable entity in the modern political world / date current borders were established

Population Total population / population density – based on total *land* area

Languages An asterisk (*) denotes the official language(s)

Calorie consumption Average number of kilocalories consumed daily per person

AFGHANISTAN
Central Asia

Page 100 D4

Landlocked in Central Asia, Afghanistan has suffered decades of conflict. The Islamist taliban, ousted by a US-led offensive in 2001, continue to resist subsequent elected governments.

Official name Islamic Republic of Afghanistan
Formation 1919 / 1919
Capital Kabul
Population 30.6 million / 122 people per sq mile (47 people per sq km)
Total area 250,000 sq miles (647,500 sq km)
Languages Pashtu*, Tajik, Dari*, Farsi, Uzbek, Turkmen
Religions Sunni Muslim 80%, Shi'a Muslim 19%, Other 1%
Ethnic mix Pashtun 38%, Tajik 25%, Hazara 19%, Uzbek anc Turkmen 15%, Other 3%
Government Nonparty system
Currency Afghani = 100 puls
Literacy rate 32%
Calorie consumption 2107 kilocalories

ALBANIA
Southeast Europe

Page 79 C6

Lying at the southeastern end of the Adriatic Sea, Albania – or the "land of the eagles" – underwent upheavals after 1991 to emerge from its communist-period isolation.

Official name Republic of Albania
Formation 1912 / 1921
Capital Tirana
Population 3.2 million / 302 people per sq mile (117 people per sq km)
Total area 11,100 sq miles (28,748 sq km)
Languages Albanian*, Greek
Religions Sunni Muslim 70%, Albanian Orthodox 20%, Roman Catholic 10%
Ethnic mix Albanian 98%, Greek 1%, Other 1%
Government Parliamentary system
Currency Lek = 100 qindarka (qintars)
Literacy rate 97%
Calorie consumption 3023 kilocalories

ALGERIA
North Africa

Page 48 C3

Lying mostly in the Sahara, this former French colony was riven by civil war after Islamists were denied electoral victory in 1992. Fighting has subsided but Islamic extremists remain a threat.

Official name People's Democratic Republic of Algeria
Formation 1962 / 1962
Capital Algiers
Population 39.2 million / 43 people per sq mile (16 people per sq km)
Total area 919,590 sq miles (2,381,740 sq km)
Languages Arabic*, Tamazight (Kabyle, Shawia, Tamashek), French
Religions Sunni Muslim 99%, Christian & Jewish 1%
Ethnic mix Arab 75%, Berber 24%, European & Jewish 1%
Government Presidential system
Currency Algerian dinar = 100 centimes
Literacy rate 73%
Calorie consumption 3220 kilocalories

ANDORRA
Southwest Europe

Page 69 B6

A tiny landlocked principality, Andorra lies between France and Spain, high in the eastern Pyrenees. Its economy, based on tourism, also features low tax and duty-free shopping.

Official name Principality of Andorra
Formation 1278 / 1278
Capital Andorra la Vella
Population 85,293 / 474 people per sq mile (183 people per sq km)
Total area 181 sq miles (468 sq km)
Languages Spanish, Catalan*, French, Portuguese
Religions Roman Catholic 94%, Other 6%
Ethnic mix Spanish 46%, Andorran 28%, Other 18%, French 8%
Government Parliamentary system
Currency Euro = 100 cents
Literacy rate 99%
Calorie consumption Not available

ANGOLA
Southern Africa

Page 56 B2

An oil- and diamond-rich former Portuguese colony in Southwest Africa, Angola is badly scarred by decades of civil war, though fighting formally ended in 2002.

Official name Republic of Angola
Formation 1975 / 1975
Capital Luanda
Population 21.5 million / 45 people per sq mile (17 people per sq km)
Total area 481,351 sq miles (1,246,700 sq km)
Languages Portuguese*, Umbundu, Kimbundu, Kikongo
Religions Roman Catholic 68%, Protestant 20%, Indigenous beliefs 12%
Ethnic mix Ovimbundu 37%, Kimbundu 25%, Other 25%, Bakongo 13%
Government Presidential system
Currency Readjusted kwanza = 100 lwei
Literacy rate 71%
Calorie consumption 2400 kilocalories

ANTIGUA & BARBUDA
West Indies

Page 33 H3

Lying on the Atlantic edge of the Leeward Islands, Antigua was in turn a Spanish, French, and British colony. Tourism is the economic mainstay, with the best beaches on Barbuda.

Official name Antigua and Barbuda
Formation 1981 / 1981
Capital St. John's
Population 90,156 / 530 people per sq mile (205 people per sq km)
Total area 170 sq miles (442 sq km)
Languages English*, English patois
Religions Anglican 45%, Other Protestant 42%, Roman Catholic 10%, Other 2%, Rastafarian 1%
Ethnic mix Black African 95%, Other 5%
Government Parliamentary system
Currency East Caribbean dollar = 100 cents
Literacy rate 99%
Calorie consumption 2396 kilocalories

ARGENTINA
South America

Page 43 B5

From semiarid lowlands, through fertile grasslands, to the glacial southern tip of South America, Argentina has enjoyed democratic rule since 1983 but struggled with high foreign debts.

Official name Republic of Argentina
Formation 1816 / 1816
Capital Buenos Aires
Population 41.4 million / 39 people per sq mile (15 people per sq km)
Total area 1,068,296 sq miles (2,766,890 sq km)
Languages Spanish*, Italian, Amerindian languages
Religions Roman Catholic 70%, Other 18%, Protestant 9%, Muslim 2%, Jewish 1%
Ethnic mix Indo-European 97%, Mestizo 2%, Amerindian 1%
Government Presidential system
Currency Argentine peso = 100 centavos
Literacy rate 98%
Calorie consumption 3155 kilocalories

ARMENIA
Southwest Asia

Page 95 F3

The smallest of the ex-Soviet republics, landlocked Armenia lies in the Lesser Caucasus mountains. It was the first country to adopt Christianity as the state religion in the 4th century AD.

Official name Republic of Armenia
Formation 1991 / 1991
Capital Yerevan
Population 3 million / 261 people per sq mile (101 people per sq km)
Total area 11,506 sq miles (29,800 sq km)
Languages Armenian*, Azeri, Russian
Religions Armenian Apostolic Church (Orthodox) 88%, Other 6%, Armenian Catholic Church 6%
Ethnic mix Armenian 98%, Other 1%, Yezidi 1%
Government Parliamentary system
Currency Dram = 100 luma
Literacy rate 99%
Calorie consumption 2809 kilocalories

AUSTRALIA
Australasia & Oceania

Page 125 B5

An island continent between the Indian and Pacific oceans, Australia was settled by Europeans from 1788, but recent immigrants are mostly Asian. Minerals underpin the economy.

Official name Commonwealth of Australia
Formation 1901 / 1901
Capital Canberra
Population 23.3 million / 8 people per sq mile (3 people per sq km)
Total area 2,967,893 sq miles (7,686,850 sq km)
Languages English*, Italian, Cantonese, Greek, Arabic, Vietnamese, Aboriginal languages
Religions Roman Catholic 26%, Nonreligious 19%, Anglican 19%, Other 23%, Other Christian 13%
Ethnic mix European 90%, Asian 7%, Aboriginal 2%, Other 1%
Government Parliamentary system
Currency Australian dollar = 100 cents
Literacy rate 99%
Calorie consumption 3265 kilocalories

AUSTRIA
Central Europe

Page 73 D7

Nestled in Central Europe, Austria was created after the Austro-Hungarian Empire was defeated in World War I. Absorbed into Hitler's Germany in 1938, it re-emerged in 1955.

Official name Republic of Austria
Formation 1918 / 1919
Capital Vienna
Population 8.5 million / 266 people per sq mile (103 people per sq km)
Total area 32,378 sq miles (83,858 sq km)
Languages German*, Croatian, Slovenian, Hungarian (Magyar)
Religions Roman Catholic 78%, Nonreligious 9%, Other 8%, Protestant 5%
Ethnic mix Austrian 93%, Croat, Slovene, and Hungarian 6%, Other 1%
Government Parliamentary system
Currency Euro = 100 cents
Literacy rate 99%
Calorie consumption 3784 kilocalories

AZERBAIJAN
Southwest Asia

Page 95 G2

On the west coast of the Caspian Sea, oil-rich Azerbaijan regained its independence from the USSR in 1991. A territorial dispute with Armenia remains unresolved.

Official name Republic of Azerbaijan
Formation 1991 / 1991
Capital Baku
Population 9.4 million / 281 people per sq mile (109 people per sq km)
Total area 33,436 sq miles (86,600 sq km)
Languages Azeri*, Russian
Religions Shi'a Muslim 68%, Sunni Muslim 26%, Russian Orthodox 3%, Armenian Apostolic Church (Orthodox) 2%, Other 1%
Ethnic mix Azeri 91%, Other 3%, Armenian 2%, Russian 2%, Lazs 2%
Government Presidential system
Currency New manat = 100 gopik
Literacy rate 99%
Calorie consumption 2952 kilocalories

BAHAMAS, THE
West Indies

Page 32 C1

Located in the western Atlantic, off the Florida coast, the Bahamas comprise some 700 islands and 2400 cays; only 30 are inhabited. Financial services and shipping support the economy.

Official name Commonwealth of the Bahamas
Formation 1973 / 1973
Capital Nassau
Population 400,000 / 103 people per sq mile (40 people per sq km)
Total area 5382 sq miles (13,940 sq km)
Languages English*, English Creole, French Creole
Religions Baptist 32%, Anglican 20%, Roman Catholic 19%, Other 17%, Methodist 6%, Church of God 6%
Ethnic mix Black African 85%, European 12%, Asian and Hispanic 3%
Government Parliamentary system
Currency Bahamian dollar = 100 cents
Literacy rate 96%
Calorie consumption 2575 kilocalories

BAHRAIN
Southwest Asia

Page 98 C4

Only three of Bahrain's 33 islands lying between the Qatar peninsula and Saudi Arabian are inhabited. The first Gulf emirate to export oil, reserves are expected to last another 10 to 15 years.

Official name Kingdom of Bahrain
Formation 1971 / 1971
Capital Manama
Population 1.3 million / 4762 people per sq mile (1841 people per sq km)
Total area 239 sq miles (620 sq km)
Languages Arabic*
Religions Muslim (mainly Shi'a) 99%, Other 1%
Ethnic mix Bahraini 63%, Asian 19%, Other Arab 10%, Iranian 8%
Government Monarchical / parliamentary system
Currency Bahraini dinar = 1000 fils
Literacy rate 95%
Calorie consumption Not available

BANGLADESH
South Asia

Page 113 G3

Low-lying Bangladesh on the Bay of Bengal suffers annual monsoon flooding. It seceded from Pakistan in 1971. Political instability and corruption are ongoing problems.

Official name People's Republic of Bangladesh
Formation 1971 / 1971
Capital Dhaka
Population 157 million / 3029 people per sq mile (1169 people per sq km)
Total area 55,598 sq miles (144,000 sq km)
Languages Bengali*, Urdu, Chakma, Marma (Magh), Garo, Khasi, Santhali, Tripuri, Mro
Religions Muslim (mainly Sunni) 88%, Hindu 11%, Other 1%
Ethnic mix Bengali 98%, Other 2%
Government Parliamentary system
Currency Taka = 100 poisha
Literacy rate 59%
Calorie consumption 2430 kilocalories

BARBADOS
West Indies

Page 33 H4

The most easterly of the Windward Islands, Barbados was under British rule from the 1620s. A sugar exporter in the 18th century, it now relies on tourism and financial services.

Official name Barbados
Formation 1966 / 1966
Capital Bridgetown
Population 300,000 / 1807 people per sq mile (698 people per sq km)
Total area 166 sq miles (430 sq km)
Languages Bajan (Barbadian English), English*
Religions Anglican 40%, Other 24%, Nonreligious 17%, Pentecostal 8%, Methodist 7%, Roman Catholic 4%
Ethnic mix Black African 92%, Other 3%, White 3%, Mixed race 2%
Government Parliamentary system
Currency Barbados dollar = 100 cents
Literacy rate 99%
Calorie consumption 3047 kilocalories

BELARUS
Eastern Europe

Page 85 B6

Landlocked in eastern Europe, forested Belarus, which means "White Russia," was reluctant to become independent of the USSR in 1991, and has been slow to reform its economy since.

Official name Republic of Belarus
Formation 1991 / 1991
Capital Minsk
Population 9.4 million / 117 people per sq mile (45 people per sq km)
Total area 80,154 sq miles (207,600 sq km)
Languages Belarussian*, Russian*
Religions Orthodox Christian 80%, Roman Catholic 14%, Other 4%, Protestant 2%
Ethnic mix Belarussian 81%, Russian 11%, Polish 4%, Ukrainian 2%, Other 2%
Government Presidential system
Currency Belarussian rouble = 100 kopeks
Literacy rate 99%
Calorie consumption 3253 kilocalories

BELGIUM
Northwest Europe

Page 65 B6

Located in Northwest Europe, Belgium has forests in the south and canals in the flat north. Its history and politics are marked by the division between its Flemish and Walloon communities.

Official name Kingdom of Belgium
Formation 1830 / 1919
Capital Brussels
Population 11.1 million / 876 people per sq mile (338 people per sq km)
Total area 11,780 sq miles (30,510 sq km)
Languages Dutch*, French*, German*
Religions Roman Catholic 88%, Other 10%, Muslim 2%
Ethnic mix Fleming 58%, Walloon 33%, Other 6%, Italian 2%, Moroccan 1%
Government Parliamentary system
Currency Euro = 100 cents
Literacy rate 99%
Calorie consumption 3793 kilocalories

BELIZE
Central America

Page 30 B1

The last Central American country to gain independence, this former British colony lies on the eastern shore of the Yucatan Peninsula. Offshore is the world's second-largest barrier reef.

Official name Belize
Formation 1981 / 1981
Capital Belmopan
Population 300,000 / 34 people per sq mile (13 people per sq km)
Total area 8867 sq miles (22,966 sq km)
Languages English Creole, Spanish, English*, Mayan, Garifuna (Carib)
Religions Roman Catholic 62%, Other 16%, Anglican 12%, Methodist 6%, Mennonite 4%
Ethnic mix Mestizo 49%, Creole 25%, Maya 11%, Garifuna 6%, Other 6%, Asian Indian 3%
Government Parliamentary system
Currency Belizean dollar = 100 cents
Literacy rate 75%
Calorie consumption 2757 kilocalories

BENIN
West Africa

Page 53 F4

Stretching north from the West African coast, this ex-French colony suffered military rule after independence but in recent decades has been a leading example of African democratization.

Official name Republic of Benin
Formation 1960 / 1960
Capital Porto-Novo
Population 10.3 million / 241 people per sq mile (93 people per sq km)
Total area 43,483 sq miles (112,620 sq km)
Languages Fon, Bariba, Yoruba, Adja, Houeda, Somba, French*
Religions Indigenous beliefs and Voodoo 50%, Christian 30%, Muslim 20%
Ethnic mix Fon 41%, Other 21%, Adja 16%, Yoruba 12%, Bariba 10%
Government Presidential system
Currency CFA franc = 100 centimes
Literacy rate 29%
Calorie consumption 2594 kilocalories

BHUTAN
South Asia

Page 113 G3

This landlocked Buddhist kingdom, perched in the eastern Himalayas between India and China, is carefully protecting its cultural identity from modernization and the outside world.

Official name Kingdom of Bhutan
Formation 1656 / 1865
Capital Thimphu
Population 800,000 / 44 people per sq mile (17 people per sq km)
Total area 18,147 sq miles (47,000 sq km)
Languages Dzongkha*, Nepali, Assamese
Religions Mahayana Buddhist 75%, Hindu 25%
Ethnic mix Drukpa 50%, Nepalese 35%, Other 15%
Government Monarchical / parliamentary system
Currency Ngultrum = 100 chetrum
Literacy rate 53%
Calorie consumption Not available

BOLIVIA
South America

Page 39 F3

Bolivia lies landlocked high in central South America. Mineral riches once made it the region's wealthiest state, but wars, coups, and poor governance have reduced it to the poorest.

Official name Plurinational State of Bolivia
Formation 1825 / 1938
Capital La Paz (administrative); Sucre (judicial)
Population 10.7 million / 26 people per sq mile (10 people per sq km)
Total area 424,162 sq miles (1,098,580 sq km)
Languages Aymara*, Quechua*, Spanish*
Religions Roman Catholic 93%, Other 7%
Ethnic mix Quechua 37%, Aymara 32%, Mixed race 13%. European 10%, Other 8%
Government Presidential system
Currency Boliviano = 100 centavos
Literacy rate 94%
Calorie consumption 2254 kilocalories

BOSNIA & HERZEGOVINA
Southeast Europe

Page 78 B3

In the mountainous western Balkans this state, born out of the bitter conflicts of Yugoslavia's collapse, has two key concerns: balancing ethnic rivalries, and integrating with Europe.

Official name Bosnia and Herzegovina
Formation 1992 / 1992
Capital Sarajevo
Population 3.8 million / 192 people per sq mile (74 people per sq km)
Total area 19,741 sq miles (51,129 sq km)
Languages Bosnian*, Serbian*, Croatian*
Religions Muslim (mainly Sunni) 40%, Orthodox Christian 31%, Roman Catholic 15%, Other 14%
Ethnic mix Bosniak 48%, Serb 34%, Croat 16%, Other 2%
Government Parliamentary system
Currency Marka = 100 pfeninga
Literacy rate 98%
Calorie consumption 3130 kilocalories

BOTSWANA
Southern Africa

Page 56 C3

Botswana, once the British protectorate of Bechuanaland, lies landlocked in Southern Africa. Diamonds provide it with a relatively prosperous economy, but the rate of HIV infection is high.

Official name Republic of Botswana
Formation 1966 / 1966
Capital Gaborone
Population 2 million / 9 people per sq mile (4 people per sq km)
Total area 231,803 sq miles (600,370 sq km)
Languages Setswana, English*, Shona, San, Khoikhoi, isiNdebele
Religions Christian (mainly Protestant) 70%, Nonreligious 20%, Traditional beliefs 6%, Other (including Muslim) 4%
Ethnic mix Tswana 79%, Kalanga 11%, Other 10%
Government Presidential system
Currency Pula = 100 thebe
Literacy rate 87%
Calorie consumption 2285 kilocalories

BRAZIL
South America

Page 40 C2

Brazil covers more than half of South America and is the site of the world's largest rain forest. It has immense natural resources and produces a third of the world's coffee.

Official name Federative Republic of Brazil
Formation 1822 / 1828
Capital Brasília
Population 200 million / 61 people per sq mile (24 people per sq km)
Total area 3,286,470 sq miles (8,511,965 sq km)
Languages Portuguese*, German, Italian, Spanish, Polish, Japanese, Amerindian languages
Religions Roman Catholic 74%, Protestant 15%, Atheist 7%, Other 3%, Afro-American Spiritist 1%
Ethnic mix White 54%, Mixed race 38%, Black 6%, Other 2%
Government Presidential system
Currency Real = 100 centavos
Literacy rate 91%
Calorie consumption 3287 kilocalories

BRUNEI
Southeast Asia

Page 116 D3

On the northwest coast of the island of Borneo, Brunei is surrounded and divided in two by the Malaysian state of Sarawak. Oil and gas revenues have brought a high standard of living.

Official name Brunei Darussalam
Formation 1984 / 1984
Capital Bandar Seri Begawan
Population 400,000 / 197 people per sq mile (76 people per sq km)
Total area 2228 sq miles (5770 sq km)
Languages Malay*, English, Chinese
Religions Muslim (mainly Sunni) 66%, Buddhist 14%, Christian 10%, Other 10%
Ethnic mix Malay 67%, Chinese 16%, Other 11%, Indigenous 6%
Government Monarchy
Currency Brunei dollar = 100 cents
Literacy rate 95%
Calorie consumption 2949 kilocalories

BULGARIA
Southeast Europe

Page 82 C2

Bulgaria is located on the western shore of the Black Sea. After the fall of its communist regime in 1990, economic and political reform were slow, but EU membership was achieved in 2007.

Official name Republic of Bulgaria
Formation 1908 / 1947
Capital Sofia
Population 7.2 million / 169 people per sq mile (65 people per sq km)
Total area 42,822 sq miles (110,910 sq km)
Languages Bulgarian*, Turkish, Romani
Religions Bulgarian Orthodox 83%, Muslim 12%, Other 4%, Roman Catholic 1%
Ethnic mix Bulgarian 84%, Turkish 9%, Roma 5%, Other 2%
Government Parliamentary system
Currency Lev = 100 stotinki
Literacy rate 98%
Calorie consumption 2877 kilocalories

BURKINA FASO
West Africa

Page 53 E4

Known as Upper Volta until 1984, Burkina Faso is landlocked in the semiarid Sahel of West Africa. It has been under military rule for most of its post-independence history.

Official name Burkina Faso
Formation 1960 / 1960
Capital Ouagadougou
Population 16.9 million / 160 people per sq mile (62 people per sq km)
Total area 105,869 sq miles (274,200 sq km)
Languages Mossi, Fulani, French*, Tuareg, Dyula, Songhai
Religions Muslim 55%, Christian 25%, Traditional beliefs 20%
Ethnic mix Mossi 48%, Other 21%, Peul 10%, Lobi 7%, Bobo 7%, Mandé 7%
Government Transitional regime
Currency CFA franc = 100 centimes
Literacy rate 29%
Calorie consumption 2655 kilocalories

BURUNDI
Central Africa

Page 51 B7

Small, landlocked Burundi lies just south of the Equator, on the Nile–Congo watershed. A decade of brutal conflict between Hutu and Tutsi from 1993 led to power-sharing in governance.

Official name Republic of Burundi
Formation 1962 / 1962
Capital Bujumbura
Population 10.2 million / 1030 people per sq mile (398 people per sq km)
Total area 10,745 sq miles (27,830 sq km)
Languages Kirundi*, French*, Kiswahili
Religions Roman Catholic 62%, Traditional beliefs 23%, Muslim 10%, Protestant 5%
Ethnic mix Hutu 85%, Tutsi 14%, Twa 1%
Government Presidential system
Currency Burundian franc = 100 centimes
Literacy rate 87%
Calorie consumption 1604 kilocalories

CAMBODIA
Southeast Asia

Page 115 D5

This ancient Southeast Asian kingdom suffered the brutal totalitarian Khmer Rouge regime in the 1970s and then a decade of Vietnamese puppet rule. Free elections were only held in 1993.

Official name Kingdom of Cambodia
Formation 1953 / 1953
Capital Phnom Penh
Population 15.1 million / 222 people per sq mile (86 people per sq km)
Total area 69,900 sq miles (181,040 sq km)
Languages Khmer*, French, Chinese, Vietnamese, Cham
Religions Buddhist 93%, Muslim 6%, Christian 1%
Ethnic mix Khmer 90%, Vietnamese 5%, Other 4%, Chinese 1%
Government Parliamentary system
Currency Riel = 100 sen
Literacy rate 74%
Calorie consumption 2411 kilocalories

CAMEROON
Central Africa

Page 54 A4

A former trading hub on the central West African coast, Cameroon was effectively a one-party state for 30 years. Elections since 1992 have brought no change in leadership.

Official name Republic of Cameroon
Formation 1960 / 1961
Capital Yaoundé
Population 22.3 million / 124 people per sq mile (48 people per sq km)
Total area 183,567 sq miles (475,400 sq km)
Languages Bamileke, Fang, Fulani, French*, English*
Religions Roman Catholic 35%, Traditional beliefs 25%, Muslim 22%, Protestant 18%
Ethnic mix Cameroon highlanders 31%, Other 21%, Equatorial Bantu 19%, Kirdi 11%, Fulani 10%, Northwestern Bantu 8%
Government Presidential system
Currency CFA franc = 100 centimes
Literacy rate 71%
Calorie consumption 2586 kilocalories

CANADA
North America

Page 15 E4

The world's second-largest country spans six time zones, extends north from its US border into the Arctic, and is rich in natural resources. Separatism is strong in French-speaking Québec.

Official name Canada
Formation 1867 / 1949
Capital Ottawa
Population 35.2 million / 10 people per sq mile (4 people per sq km)
Total area 3,855,171 sq miles (9,984,670 sq km)
Languages English*, French*, Chinese, Italian, German, Ukrainian, Portuguese, Inuktitut, Cree
Religions Roman Catholic 44%, Protestant 29%, Other and nonreligious 27%
Ethnic mix British, French, and other European 87%, Asian 9%, Amerindian, Métis, and Inuit 4%
Government Parliamentary system
Currency Canadian dollar = 100 cents
Literacy rate 99%
Calorie consumption 3419 kilocalories

CAPE VERDE
Atlantic Ocean

Page 52 A2

The mostly volcanic islands that make up Cape Verde lie off Africa's west coast. A Portuguese colony until 1975, it has been a stable democracy since its first multiparty elections in 1991.

Official name Republic of Cape Verde
Formation 1975 / 1975
Capital Praia
Population 500,000 / 321 people per sq mile (124 people per sq km)
Total area 1557 sq miles (4033 sq km)
Languages Portuguese Creole, Portuguese*
Religions Roman Catholic 97%, Other 2%, Protestant (Church of the Nazarene) 1%
Ethnic mix Mestiço 71%, African 28%, European 1%
Government Presidential / parliamentary system
Currency Escudo = 100 centavos
Literacy rate 85%
Calorie consumption 2716 kilocalories

CENTRAL AFRICAN REPUBLIC
Central Africa

Page 54 C4

A landlocked plateau dividing the Chad and Congo river basins, the CAR has been plagued by rebellions since military rule ended in 1993. The arid north is sparsely populated.

Official name Central African Republic
Formation 1960 / 1960
Capital Bangui
Population 4.6 million / 19 people per sq mile (7 people per sq km)
Total area 240,534 sq miles (622,984 sq km)
Languages Sango, Banda, Gbaya, French*
Religions Traditional beliefs 35%, Roman Catholic 25%, Protestant 25%, Muslim 15%
Ethnic mix Baya 33%, Banda 27%, Other 17%, Mandjia 13%, Sara 10%
Government Transitional regime
Currency CFA franc = 100 centimes
Literacy rate 37%
Calorie consumption 2154 kilocalories

CHAD
Central Africa

Page 54 C3

Landlocked in north Central Africa, Chad has been torn by intermittent periods of civil war since it gained independence from France in 1960. It became a net oil exporter in 2003.

Official name Republic of Chad
Formation 1960 / 1960
Capital N'Djaména
Population 12.8 million / 26 people per sq mile (10 people per sq km)
Total area 495,752 sq miles (1,284,000 sq km)
Languages French*, Sara, Arabic*, Maba
Religions Muslim 51%, Christian 35%, Animist 7%, Traditional beliefs 7%
Ethnic mix Other 30%, Sara 28%, Mayo-Kebbi 12%, Arab 12%, Ouaddai 9%, Kanem-Bornou 9%
Government Presidential system
Currency CFA franc = 100 centimes
Literacy rate 37%
Calorie consumption 2061 kilocalories

CHILE
South America

Page 42 B3

Extending in a ribbon down the Pacific coast of South America, Chile restored democracy in 1989 after a referendum rejected its military dictator. It is the world's largest copper producer.

Official name Republic of Chile
Formation 1818 / 1883
Capital Santiago
Population 17.6 million / 61 people per sq mile (24 people per sq km)
Total area 292,258 sq miles (756,950 sq km)
Languages Spanish*, Amerindian languages
Religions Roman Catholic 89%, Other and nonreligious 11%
Ethnic mix Mestizo and European 90%, Other Amerindian 9%, Mapuche 1%
Government Presidential system
Currency Chilean peso = 100 centavos
Literacy rate 99%
Calorie consumption 2989 kilocalories

CHINA
East Asia

Page 104 C4

This vast East Asian country, home to a fifth of the global population, became a communist state in 1949. It has now emerged as one of the world's major political and economic powers.

Official name People's Republic of China
Formation 960 / 1999
Capital Beijing
Population 1.39 billion / 385 people per sq mile (149 people per sq km)
Total area 3,705,386 sq miles (9,596,960 sq km)
Languages Mandarin*, Wu, Cantonese, Hsiang, Min, Hakka, Kan
Religions Nonreligious 59%, Traditional beliefs 20%, Other 13%, Buddhist 6%, Muslim 2%
Ethnic mix Han 92%, Other 4%, Zhuang 1%, Hui 1%, Manchu 1%, Miao 1%
Government One-party state
Currency Renminbi (known as yuan) = 10 jiao = 100 fen
Literacy rate 95%
Calorie consumption 3074 kilocalories

COLOMBIA
South America

Page 36 B3

Lying in northwest South America, Colombia has suffered civil war since 1964, with over three million internal refugees. It is noted for coffee, gold, emeralds, and narcotics trafficking.

Official name Republic of Colombia
Formation 1819 / 1903
Capital Bogotá
Population 48.3 million / 120 people per sq mile (47 people per sq km)
Total area 439,733 sq miles (1,138,910 sq km)
Languages Spanish*, Wayuu, Páez, and other Amerindian languages
Religions Roman Catholic 95%, Other 5%
Ethnic mix Mestizo 58%, White 20%, European–African 14%, African 4%, African–Amerindian 3%, Amerindian 1%
Government Presidential system
Currency Colombian peso = 100 centavos
Literacy rate 94%
Calorie consumption 2593 kilocalories

COMOROS
Indian Ocean

Page 57 F2

The Comoros islands lie between Mozambique and Madagascar. There have been many coups and secession attempts by the smaller islands since independence from France in 1975.

Official name Union of the Comoros
Formation 1975 / 1975
Capital Moroni
Population 700,000 / 813 people per sq mile (314 people per sq km)
Total area 838 sq miles (2170 sq km)
Languages Arabic*, Comoran*, French*
Religions Muslim (mainly Sunni) 98%, Other 1%, Roman Catholic 1%
Ethnic mix Comoran 97%, Other 3%
Government Presidential system
Currency Comoros franc = 100 centimes
Literacy rate 76%
Calorie consumption 2139 kilocalories

CONGO
Central Africa

Page 55 B5

Astride the Equator in Central Africa, this former French colony emerged from 26 years of Marxist-Leninist rule in 1990, though the Marxist-era dictator seized power again in 1997.

Official name Republic of the Congo
Formation 1960 / 1960
Capital Brazzaville
Population 4.4 million / 33 people per sq mile (13 people per sq km)
Total area 132,046 sq miles (342,000 sq km)
Languages Kongo, Teke, Lingala, French*
Religions Traditional beliefs 50%, Roman Catholic 35%, Protestant 13%, Muslim 2%
Ethnic mix Bakongo 51%, Teke 17%, Other 16%, Mbochi 11%, Mbédé 5%
Government Presidential system
Currency CFA franc = 100 centimes
Literacy rate 79%
Calorie consumption 2195 kilocalories

CONGO, DEM. REP.
Central Africa

Page 55 C6

Straddling the Equator in east Central Africa, mineral-rich Dem. Rep. Congo is Africa's second-largest country. The former Belgian colony has endured years of corrupt rule and conflict.

Official name Democratic Republic of the Congo
Formation 1960 / 1960
Capital Kinshasa
Population 67.5 million / 77 people per sq mile (30 people per sq km)
Total area 905,563 sq miles (2,345,410 sq km)
Languages Kiswahili, Tshiluba, Kikongo, Lingala, French*
Religions Roman Catholic 50%, Protestant 20%, Traditional beliefs and other 20%, Muslim 10%
Ethnic mix Other 55%, Mongo, Luba, Kongo, and Mangbetu-Azande 45%
Government Presidential system
Currency Congolese franc = 100 centimes
Literacy rate 61%
Calorie consumption 1585 kilocalories

COSTA RICA
Central America

Page 31 E4

Costa Rica is the most stable country in Central America. It abolished its army in 1948 and its neutrality in foreign affairs is long-standing, but it has very strong ties with the US.

Official name Republic of Costa Rica
Formation 1838 / 1838
Capital San José
Population 4.9 million / 249 people per sq mile (96 people per sq km)
Total area 19,730 sq miles (51,100 sq km)
Languages Spanish*, English Creole, Bribri, Cabecar
Religions Roman Catholic 71%, Evangelical 14%, Nonreligious 11%, Other 4%
Ethnic mix Mestizo and European 94%, Black 3%, Chinese 1%, Other 1%, Amerindian 1%
Government Presidential system
Currency Costa Rican colón = 100 céntimos
Literacy rate 97%
Calorie consumption 2898 kilocalories

CÔTE D'IVOIRE (IVORY COAST)
West Africa

Page 52 D4

One of the larger countries on the West African coast, this ex-French colony is the world's biggest cocoa producer. Coups and recent conflicts have destroyed its reputation for stability.

Official name Republic of Côte d'Ivoire
Formation 1960 / 1960
Capital Yamoussoukro
Population 20.3 million / 165 people per sq mile (64 people per sq km)
Total area 124,502 sq miles (322,460 sq km)
Languages Akan, French*, Krou, Voltaïque
Religions Muslim 38%, Roman Catholic 25%, Traditional beliefs 25%, Protestant 6%, Other 6%
Ethnic mix Akan 42%, Voltaïque 18%, Mandé du Nord 17%, Krou 11%, Mandé du Sud 10%, Other 2%
Government Presidential system
Currency CFA franc = 100 centimes
Literacy rate 41%
Calorie consumption 2781 kilocalories

CROATIA
Southeast Europe

Page 78 B2

Post-independence fighting afflicted this former Yugoslav republic until 1995. It is now capitalizing on its location on the eastern Adriatic coast and joined the EU in 2013.

Official name Republic of Croatia
Formation 1991 / 1991
Capital Zagreb
Population 4.3 million / 197 people per sq mile (76 people per sq km)
Total area 21,831 sq miles (56,542 sq km)
Languages Croatian*
Religions Roman Catholic 88%, Other 7%, Orthodox Christian 4%, Muslim 1%
Ethnic mix Croat 90%, Serb 5%, Other 5%
Government Parliamentary system
Currency Kuna = 100 lipa
Literacy rate 99%
Calorie consumption 3052 kilocalories

CUBA
West Indies

Page 32 C2

Cuba is the largest island in the Caribbean and the only communist country in the Americas. It was led by Fidel Castro for almost 40 years until he stepped down in 2008.

Official name Republic of Cuba
Formation 1902 / 1902
Capital Havana
Population 11.3 million / 264 people per sq mile (102 people per sq km)
Total area 42,803 sq miles (110,860 sq km)
Languages Spanish
Religions Nonreligious 49%, Roman Catholic 40%, Atheist 6%, Other 4%, Protestant 1%
Ethnic mix Mulatto (mixed race) 51%, White 37%, Black 11%, Chinese 1%
Government One-party state
Currency Cuban peso = 100 centavos
Literacy rate 99%
Calorie consumption 3277 kilocalories

CYPRUS
Southeast Europe

Page 80 C5

Cyprus lies south of Turkey in the eastern Mediterranean. Since 1974, it has been partitioned between the Turkish-occupied north and the Greek south (which joined the EU in 2004).

Official name Republic of Cyprus
Formation 1960 / 1960
Capital Nicosia
Population 1.1 million / 308 people per sq mile (119 people per sq km)
Total area 3571 sq miles (9250 sq km)
Languages Greek*, Turkish*
Religions Orthodox Christian 78%, Muslim 18%, Other 4%
Ethnic mix Greek 81%, Turkish 11%, Other 8%
Government Presidential system
Currency Euro = 100 cents (In TRNC, new Turkish lira = 100 kurus)
Literacy rate 99%
Calorie consumption 2661 kilocalories

CZECH REPUBLIC
Central Europe

Page 77 A5

Lanalocked in Central Europe, and formerly part of communist Czechoslovakia, it peacefully dissolved its federal union with Slovakia in 1993, and joined the EU in 2004.

Official name Czech Republic
Formation 1993 / 1993
Capital Prague
Population 10.7 million / 351 people per sq mile (136 people per sq km)
Total area 30,450 sq miles (78,866 sq km)
Languages Czech*, Slovak, Hungarian (Magyar)
Religions Roman Catholic 39%, Atheist 38%, Other 13%, Protestant 3%, Hussite 2%
Ethnic mix Czech 90%, Moravian 4%, Other 4%, Slovak 2%
Government Parliamentary system
Currency Czech koruna = 100 haleru
Literacy rate 99%
Calorie consumption 3292 kilocalories

DENMARK
Northern Europe

Page 63 A7

Denmark occupies the low-lying Jutland peninsula and over 400 islands. In the 1930s it set up one of the first welfare systems. Greenland and the Faroe Islands are self-governing territories.

Official name Kingdom of Denmark
Formation 950 / 1944
Capital Copenhagen
Population 5.6 million / 342 people per sq mile (132 people per sq km)
Total area 16,639 sq miles (43,094 sq km)
Languages Danish*
Religions Evangelical Lutheran 95%, Roman Catholic 3%, Muslim 2%
Ethnic mix Danish 96%, Other (including Scandinavian and Turkish) 3%, Faroese and Inuit 1%
Government Parliamentary system
Currency Danish krone = 100 øre
Literacy rate 99%
Calorie consumption 3363 kilocalories

DJIBOUTI
East Africa

Page 50 D4

Once known as French Somaliland, this city state with a desert hinterland lies on the coast of the Horn of Africa. Its economy relies on its Red Sea port, a vital trade link for landlocked Ethiopia.

Official name Republic of Djibouti
Formation 1977 / 1977
Capital Djibouti
Population 900,000 / 101 people per sq mile (39 people per sq km)
Total area 8494 sq miles (22,000 sq km)
Languages Somali, Afar, French*, Arabic*
Religions Muslim (mainly Sunni) 94%, Christian 6%
Ethnic mix Issa 60%, Afar 35%, Other 5%
Government Presidential system
Currency Djibouti franc = 100 centimes
Literacy rate 70%
Calorie consumption 2526 kilocalories

DOMINICA
West Indies

Page 33 H4

This Caribbean island, known for its lush flora and fauna, resisted European colonization until the 18th century, when it came first under French and then British rule.

Official name Commonwealth of Dominica
Formation 1978 / 1978
Capital Roseau
Population 73,286 / 253 people per sq mile (98 people per sq km)
Total area 291 sq miles (754 sq km)
Languages French Creole, English*
Religions Roman Catholic 77%, Protestant 15%, Other 8%
Ethnic mix Black 87%, Mixed race 9%, Carib 3%, Other 1%
Government Parliamentary system
Currency East Caribbean dollar = 100 cents
Literacy rate 88%
Calorie consumption 3047 kilocalories

DOMINICAN REPUBLIC
West Indies

Page 33 E2

Occupying the eastern two-thirds of the island of Hispaniola, the Dominican Republic is the Caribbean's top tourist destination and largest economy. Ties with the US are strong.

Official name Dominican Republic
Formation 1865 / 1865
Capital Santo Domingo
Population 10.4 million / 557 people per sq mile (215 people per sq km)
Total area 18,679 sq miles (48,380 sq km)
Languages Spanish*, French Creole
Religions Roman Catholic 95%, Other and nonreligious 5%
Ethnic mix Mixed race 73%, European 16%, Black African 11%
Government Presidential system
Currency Dominican Republic peso = 100 centavos
Literacy rate 91%
Calorie consumption 2597 kilocalories

EAST TIMOR
Southeast Asia

Page 116 F5

This former Portuguese colony on the island of Timor in the East Indies was invaded by Indonesia in 1975. In 1999 it voted for independence, achieved in 2002 after a turbulent transition.

Official name Democratic Republic of Timor-Leste
Formation 2002 / 2002
Capital Dili
Population 1.1 million / 195 people per sq mile (75 people per sq km)
Total area 5756 sq miles (14,874 sq km)
Languages Tetum* (Portuguese/Austronesian), Bahasa Indonesia, Portuguese*
Religions Roman Catholic 95%, Other 5%
Ethnic mix Papuan groups approx. 85%, Indonesian groups approx. 13%, Chinese 2%
Government Parliamentary system
Currency US dollar = 100 cents
Literacy rate 58%
Calorie consumption 2083 kilocalories

ECUADOR
South America

Page 38 A2

Once part of the Inca heartland on the northwest coast of South America, Ecuador is the world's leading banana producer. Its territory includes the wildlife-rich Galapagos Islands.

Official name Republic of Ecuador
Formation 1830 / 1942
Capital Quito
Population 15.7 million / 147 people per sq mile (57 people per sq km)
Total area 109,483 sq miles (283,560 sq km)
Languages Spanish*, Quechua, other Amerindian languages
Religions Roman Catholic 95%, Protestant, Jewish, and other 5%
Ethnic mix Mestizo 77%, White 11%, Amerindian 7%, Black African 5%
Government Presidential system
Currency US dollar = 100 cents
Literacy rate 93%
Calorie consumption 2477 kilocalories

EGYPT
North Africa

Page 50 B2

Egypt lies in Africa's northeast corner; the fertile Nile valley divides desert lands. Nearly 50 years of de facto military rule was interrupted in 2011 by the "Arab Spring" popular uprising.

Official name Arab Republic of Egypt
Formation 1936 / 1982
Capital Cairo
Population 82.1 million / 214 people per sq mile (82 people per sq km)
Total area 386,660 sq miles (1,001,450 sq km)
Languages Arabic*, French, English, Berber
Religions Muslim (mainly Sunni) 90%, Coptic Christian and other 9%, Other Christian 1%
Ethnic mix Egyptian 99%, Nubian, Armenian, Greek, and Berber 1%
Government Transitional regime
Currency Egyptian pound = 100 piastres
Literacy rate 74%
Calorie consumption 3557 kilocalories

EL SALVADOR
Central America

Page 30 B3

El Salvador is Central America's smallest country. Since a 12-year war between the US-backed army and left-wing guerrillas ended in 1992, crime and gang violence have been key issues.

Official name Republic of El Salvador
Formation 1841 / 1841
Capital San Salvador
Population 6.3 million / 788 people per sq mile (304 people per sq km)
Total area 8124 sq miles (21,040 sq km)
Languages Spanish*
Religions Roman Catholic 80%, Evangelical 18%, Other 2%
Ethnic mix Mestizo 90%, White 9%, Amerindian 1%
Government Presidential system
Currency Salvadorean colón = 100 centavos; US dollar = 100 cents
Literacy rate 86%
Calorie consumption 2513 kilocalories

EQUATORIAL GUINEA
Central Africa

Page 55 A5

Equatorial Guinea comprises the Rio Muni mainland in west Central Africa and five islands. Free elections were first held in 1988, but the former ruling party still dominates.

Official name Republic of Equatorial Guinea
Formation 1968 / 1968
Capital Malabo
Population 800,000 / 74 people per sq mile (29 people per sq km)
Total area 10,830 sq miles (28,051 sq km)
Languages Spanish*, Fang, Bubi, French*
Religions Roman Catholic 90%, Other 10%
Ethnic mix Fang 85%, Other 11%, Bubi 4%
Government Presidential system
Currency CFA franc = 100 centimes
Literacy rate 94%
Calorie consumption Not available

ERITREA
East Africa

Page 50 C4

Lying on the shores of the Red Sea, this former Italian colony was annexed by Ethiopia in 1952. It successfully seceded in 1993, following a 30-year war for independence.

Official name State of Eritrea
Formation 1993 / 2002
Capital Asmara
Population 6.3 million / 139 people per sq mile (54 people per sq km)
Total area 46,842 sq miles (121,320 sq km)
Languages Tigrinya*, English*, Tigre, Afar, Arabic*, Saho, Bilen, Kunama, Nara, Hadareb
Religions Christian 50%, Muslim 48%, Other 2%
Ethnic mix Tigray 50%, Tigre 31%, Other 9%, Saho 5%, Afar 5%
Government Presidential / parliamentary system
Currency Nakfa = 100 cents
Literacy rate 70%
Calorie consumption 1640 kilocalories

ESTONIA
Northeast Europe

Page 84 D2

The smallest, richest, most developed Baltic state has emphasized advanced IT and integration with Europe since renouncing the Soviet model. Joined the EU in 2004.

Official name Republic of Estonia
Formation 1991 / 1991
Capital Tallinn
Population 1.3 million / 75 people per sq mile (29 people per sq km)
Total area 17,462 sq miles (45,226 sq km)
Languages Estonian*, Russian
Religions Evangelical Lutheran 56%, Orthodox Christian 25%, Other 19%
Ethnic mix Estonian 69%, Russian 25%, Other 4%, Ukrainian 2%
Government Parliamentary system
Currency Euro = 100 cents
Literacy rate 99%
Calorie consumption 3214 kilocalories

FINLAND
Northern Europe

Page 62 D4

A low-lying country of forests and lakes, Finland joins Scandinavia to Russia. Its language is related to only two others in Europe. Finnish women were the first in Europe to get the vote, in 1906.

Official name Republic of Finland
Formation 1917 / 1947
Capital Helsinki
Population 5.4 million / 46 people per sq mile (18 people per sq km)
Total area 130,127 sq miles (337,030 sq km)
Languages Finnish*, Swedish*, Sámi
Religions Evangelical Lutheran 83%, Other 15%, Roman Catholic 1%, Orthodox Christian 1%
Ethnic mix Finnish 93%, Other (including Sámi) 7%
Government Parliamentary system
Currency Euro = 100 cents
Literacy rate 99%
Calorie consumption 3285 kilocalories

GAMBIA
West Africa

Page 52 B3

A narrow state along the Gambia River on Africa's west coast and surrounded by Senegal, Gambia was renowned for its stability until a coup in 1994; the coup leader remains in power.

Official name Republic of the Gambia
Formation 1965 / 1965
Capital Banjul
Population 1.8 million / 466 people per sq mile (180 people per sq km)
Total area 4363 sq miles (11,300 sq km)
Languages Mandinka, Fulani, Wolof Jola, Soninke, English*
Religions Sunni Muslim 90%, Christian 8%, Traditional beliefs 2%
Ethnic mix Mandinka 42%, Fulani 18%, Wolof 16%, Jola 10%, Serahuli 9%, Other 5%
Government Presidential system
Currency Dalasi = 100 butut
Literacy rate 52%
Calorie consumption 2849 kilocalories

GHANA
West Africa

Page 53 E5

Once known as the Gold Coast, Ghana was the first colony in West Africa to gain independence. In recent decades multiparty democracy has been consolidated despite economic issues.

Official name Republic of Ghana
Formation 1957 / 1957
Capital Accra
Population 25.9 million / 292 people per sq mile (113 people per sq km)
Total area 92,100 sq miles (238,540 sq km)
Languages Twi, Fanti Ewe, Ga, Adangbe, Gurma, Dagomba (Dagbani), English*
Religions Christian 69%, Muslim 16%, Traditional beliefs 9%, Other 6%
Ethnic mix Akan 49%, Mole-Dagbani 17%, Ewe 13%, Other 9%, Ga and Ga-Adangbe 8%, Guan 4%
Government Presidential system
Currency Cedi = 100 pesewas
Literacy rate 72%
Calorie consumption 3003 kilocalories

ETHIOPIA
East Africa

Page 51 C5

Ethiopia, the only African country to escape colonization, was a Marxist regime in 1974–1991. Now landlocked in the Horn of Africa, it has suffered economic, civil, and natural crises.

Official name Federal Democratic Republic of Ethiopia
Formation 1896 / 2002
Capital Addis Ababa
Population 94.1 million / 220 people per sq mile (85 people per sq km)
Total area 435,184 sq miles (1,127,127 sq km)
Languages Amharic*, Tigrinya, Galla, Sidamo, Somali, English, Arabic
Religions Orthodox Christian 40%, Muslim 40%, Traditional beliefs 15%, Other 5%
Ethnic mix Oromo 40%, Amhara 25%, Other 35%
Government Parliamentary system
Currency Birr = 100 cents
Literacy rate 39%
Calorie consumption 2105 kilocalories

FRANCE
Western Europe

Page 68 B4

Straddling Western Europe from the English Channel to the Mediterranean Sea, France was Europe's first modern republic. It is now one of the world's leading industrial powers.

Official name French Republic
Formation 987 / 1919
Capital Paris
Population 64.3 million / 303 people per sq mile (117 people per sq km)
Total area 211,208 sq miles (547,030 sq km)
Languages French*, Provençal, German, Breton, Catalan, Basque
Religions Roman Catholic 88%, Muslim 8%, Protestant 2%, Jewish 1%, Buddhist 1%
Ethnic mix French 90%, North African (mainly Algerian) 6%, German (Alsace) 2%, Other 2%
Government Presidential / parliamentary system
Currency Euro = 100 cents
Literacy rate 99%
Calorie consumption 3524 kilocalories

GEORGIA
Southwest Asia

Page 95 F2

Located in the Caucasus on the Black Sea's eastern shore, Georgia is noted for its wine. Conflict broke out after the breakup of the USSR; the northern provinces have de facto autonomy.

Official name Georgia
Formation 1991 / 1991
Capital Tbilisi
Population 4.3 million / 160 people per sq mile (62 people per sq km)
Total area 26,911 sq miles (69,700 sq km)
Languages Georgian*, Russian, Azeri, Armenian, Mingrelian, Ossetian, Abkhazian
Religions Georgian Orthodox 74%, Russian Orthodox 10%, Muslim 10%, Other 6%
Ethnic mix Georgian 84%, Armenian 6%, Azeri 6%, Russian 2%, Other 1%, Ossetian 1%
Government Presidential system
Currency Lari = 100 tetri
Literacy rate 99%
Calorie consumption 2731 kilocalories

GREECE
Southeast Europe

Page 83 A5

The southernmost Balkan nation has a mountainous mainland and over 2000 islands, engendering its seafaring tradition. High state debt has led to recent unpopular austerity measures.

Official name Hellenic Republic
Formation 1829 / 1947
Capital Athens
Population 11.1 million / 220 people per sq mile (85 people per sq km)
Total area 50,942 sq miles (131,940 sq km)
Languages Greek*, Turkish, Macedonian, Albanian
Religions Orthodox Christian 98%, Other 1%, Muslim 1%
Ethnic mix Greek 98%, Other 2%
Government Parliamentary system
Currency Euro = 100 cents
Literacy rate 97%
Calorie consumption 3433 kilocalories

FIJI
Australasia & Oceania

Page 123 E5

Fiji is a volcanic archipelago of 882 islands in the southern Pacific Ocean. Tensions between ethnic Fijians and Indo-Fijians provoked coups in 1987 and 2000. Sugar is the main export.

Official name Republic of the Fiji Islands
Formation 1970 / 1970
Capital Suva
Population 900,000 / 128 people per sq mile (49 people per sq km)
Total area 7054 sq miles (18,270 sq km)
Languages Fijian, English*, Hindi, Urdu, Tamil, Telugu
Religions Hindu 38%, Methodist 37%, Roman Catholic 9%, Muslim 8%, Other 8%
Ethnic mix Melanesian 51%, Indian 44%, Other 5%
Government Parliamentary system
Currency Fiji dollar = 100 cents
Literacy rate 94%
Calorie consumption 2930 kilocalories

GABON
Central Africa

Page 55 A5

A former French colony straddling the Equator on Central Africa's west coast, it returned to multiparty politics in 1990, after 22 years of one-party rule. The economy relies on oil revenue.

Official name Gabonese Republic
Formation 1960 / 1960
Capital Libreville
Population 1.7 million / 17 people per sq mile (7 people per sq km)
Total area 103,346 sq miles (267,667 sq km)
Languages Fang, French*, Punu, Sira, Nzebi, Mpongwe
Religions Christian (mainly Roman Catholic) 55%, Traditional beliefs 40%, Other 4%, Muslim 1%
Ethnic mix Fang 26%, Shira-punu 24%, Other 16%, Foreign residents 15%, Nzabi-duma 11%, Mbédé-Teke 8%
Government Presidential system
Currency CFA franc = 100 centimes
Literacy rate 82%
Calorie consumption 2781 kilocalories

GERMANY
Northern Europe

Page 72 B4

Germany is Europe's major economic power and a leading influence in the EU. Divided after World War II, its democratic west and communist east were re-unified in 1990.

Official name Federal Republic of Germany
Formation 1871 / 1990
Capital Berlin
Population 82.7 million / 613 people per sq mile (237 people per sq km)
Total area 137,846 sq miles (357,021 sq km)
Languages German*, Turkish
Religions Protestant 34%, Roman Catholic 33%, Other 30%, Muslim 3%
Ethnic mix German 92%, Other 3%, Other European 3%, Turkish 2%
Government Parliamentary system
Currency Euro = 100 cents
Literacy rate 99%
Calorie consumption 3539 kilocalories

GRENADA
West Indies

Page 33 G5

The most southerly Windward gained worldwide notoriety in 1983, when the US invaded to sever its growing links with Cuba. It is the world's second-biggest nutmeg producer.

Official name Grenada
Formation 1974 / 1974
Capital St. George's
Population 109,590 / 837 people per sq mile (322 people per sq km)
Total area 131 sq miles (340 sq km)
Languages English*, English Creole
Religions Roman Catholic 68%, Anglican 17%, Other 15%
Ethnic mix Black African 82%, Mulatto (mixed race) 13%, East Indian 3%, Other 2%
Government Parliamentary system
Currency East Caribbean dollar = 100 cents
Literacy rate 96%
Calorie consumption 2453 kilocalories

GUATEMALA
Central America

Page 30 A2

Once the heart of the Mayan civilization, the largest and most populous state on the Central American isthmus is consolidating its fledgling democracy after years of civil war and army rule.

Official name Republic of Guatemala
Formation 1838 / 1838
Capital Guatemala City
Population 15.5 million / 370 people per sq mile (143 people per sq km)
Total area 42,042 sq miles (108,890 sq km)
Languages Quiché, Mam, Cakchiquel, Kekchí, Spanish*
Religions Roman Catholic 65%, Protestant 33%, Other and nonreligious 2%
Ethnic mix Amerindian 60%, Mestizo 30%, Other 10%
Government Presidential system
Currency Quetzal = 100 centavos
Literacy rate 78%
Calorie consumption 2502 kilocalories

GUINEA
West Africa

Page 52 C4

A former French colony on Africa's west coast, Guinea chose a Marxist path, then came under army rule. The 2010 polls brought fresh hope, before the Ebola epidemic struck in 2014.

Official name Republic of Guinea
Formation 1958 / 1958
Capital Conakry
Population 11.7 million / 123 people per sq mile (48 people per sq km)
Total area 94,925 sq miles (245,857 sq km)
Languages Pulaar, Malinké, Soussou, French*
Religions Muslim 85%, Christian 8%, Traditional beliefs 7%
Ethnic mix Peul 40%, Malinké 30%, Soussou 20%, Other 10%
Government Presidential system
Currency Guinea franc = 100 centimes
Literacy rate 25%
Calorie consumption 2553 kilocalories

GUINEA-BISSAU
West Africa

Page 52 B4

Known as Portuguese Guinea in colonial times, Guinea-Bissau is situated on Africa's west coast. One of the world's poorest countries, it has now become a transit point for cocaine trafficking.

Official name Republic of Guinea-Bissau
Formation 1974 / 1974
Capital Bissau
Population 1.7 million / 157 people per sq mile (60 people per sq km)
Total area 13,946 sq miles (36,120 sq km)
Languages Portuguese Creole, Balante, Fulani, Malinké, Portuguese*
Religions Traditional beliefs 50%, Muslim 40%, Christian 10%
Ethnic mix Balante 30%, Fulani 20%, Other 16%, Mandyako 14%, Mandinka 13%, Papel 7%
Government Presidential system
Currency CFA franc = 100 centimes
Literacy rate 57%
Calorie consumption 2304 kilocalories

GUYANA
South America

Page 37 F3

A land of rain forest, mountains, coastal plains, and savanna, Guyana is South America's only English-speaking state. It became a republic in 1970, four years after independence from Britain.

Official name Cooperative Republic of Guyana
Formation 1966 / 1966
Capital Georgetown
Population 800,000 / 11 people per sq mile (4 people per sq km)
Total area 83,000 sq miles (214,970 sq km)
Languages English Creole, Hindi, Tamil, Amerindian languages, English*
Religions Christian 57%, Hindu 28%, Muslim 10%, Other 5%
Ethnic mix East Indian 43%, Black African 30%, Mixed race 17%, Amerindian 9%, Other 1%
Government Presidential system
Currency Guyanese dollar = 100 cents
Literacy rate 85%
Calorie consumption 2648 kilocalories

HAITI
West Indies

Page 32 D3

The western third of the Caribbean island of Hispaniola, Haiti became the world's first black republic in 1804. Natural disasters and periodic anarchy perpetuate its endemic poverty.

Official name Republic of Haiti
Formation 1804 / 1884
Capital Port-au-Prince
Population 10.3 million / 968 people per sq mile (374 people per sq km)
Total area 10,714 sq miles (27,750 sq km)
Languages French Creole*, French*
Religions Roman Catholic 55%, Protestant 28%, Other (including Voodoo) 16%, Nonreligious 1%
Ethnic mix Black African 95%, Mulatto (mixed race) and European 5%
Government Presidential system
Currency Gourde = 100 centimes
Literacy rate 49%
Calorie consumption 2105 kilocalories

HONDURAS
Central America

Page 30 C2

Straddling the Central American isthmus, Honduras returned to civilian rule in 1984, after a succession of military regimes. Crime is high and it has the world's worst murder rate.

Official name Republic of Honduras
Formation 1838 / 1838
Capital Tegucigalpa
Population 8.1 million / 187 people per sq mile (72 people per sq km)
Total area 43,278 sq miles (112,090 sq km)
Languages Spanish*, Garifuna (Carib), English Creole
Religions Roman Catholic 97%, Protestant 3%
Ethnic mix Mestizo 90%, Black African 5%, Amerindian 4%, White 1%
Government Presidential system
Currency Lempira = 100 centavos
Literacy rate 85%
Calorie consumption 2651 kilocalories

HUNGARY
Central Europe

Page 77 C6

Hungary is bordered by seven states in Central Europe. After the fall of communism in 1989, it introduced political and economic reforms and joined the EU in 2004.

Official name Republic of Hungary
Formation 1918 / 1947
Capital Budapest
Population 10 million / 280 people per sq mile (108 people per sq km)
Total area 35,919 sq miles (93,030 sq km)
Languages Hungarian* (Magyar)
Religions Roman Catholic 52%, Calvinist 16%, Other 15%, Nonreligious 14%, Lutheran 3%
Ethnic mix Magyar 90%, Roma 4%, German 3%, Serb 2%, Other 1%
Government Parliamentary system
Currency Forint = 100 fillér
Literacy rate 99%
Calorie consumption 2968 kilocalories

ICELAND
Northwest Europe

Page 61 E4

This northerly island outpost of Europe, sitting on the mid-Atlantic ridge, has stunning, sparsely inhabited volcanic terrain. Its economy crashed heavily in the 2008 global credit crunch.

Official name Republic of Iceland
Formation 1944 / 1944
Capital Reykjavik
Population 300,000 / 8 people per sq mile (3 people per sq km)
Total area 39,768 sq miles (103,000 sq km)
Languages Icelandic*
Religions Evangelical Lutheran 84%, Other (mostly Christian) 10%, Nonreligious 3%, Roman Catholic 3%
Ethnic mix Icelandic 94%, Other 5%, Danish 1%
Government Parliamentary system
Currency Icelandic króna = 100 aurar
Literacy rate 99%
Calorie consumption 3339 kilocalories

INDIA
South Asia

Page 112 D4

The Indian subcontinent, divided from the rest of Asia by the Himalayas, was once the jewel of the British empire. India is the world's largest democracy and second most populous country.

Official name Republic of India
Formation 1947 / 1947
Capital New Delhi
Population 1.25 billion / 1091 people per sq mile (421 people per sq km)
Total area 1,269,338 sq miles (3,287,590 sq km)
Languages Hindi*, English*, Urdu, Bengali, Marathi, Telugu, Tamil, Bihari, Gujarati, Kanarese
Religions Hindu 81%, Muslim 13%, Sikh 2%, Christian 2%, Buddhist 1%, Other 1%
Ethnic mix Indo-Aryan 72%, Dravidian 25%, Mongoloid and other 3%
Government Parliamentary system
Currency Indian rupee = 100 paise
Literacy rate 63%
Calorie consumption 2459 kilocalories

INDONESIA
Southeast Asia

Page 116 C4

The world's largest archipelago spans over 3100 miles (5000 km), from the Indian to the Pacific Ocean. Formerly the Dutch East Indies, it produces palm oil, rubber, spices, and natural gas.

Official name Republic of Indonesia
Formation 1949 / 1999
Capital Jakarta
Population 250 million / 360 people per sq mile (139 people per sq km)
Total area 741,096 sq miles (1,919,440 sq km)
Languages Javanese, Sundanese, Madurese, Bahasa Indonesia*, Dutch
Religions Sunni Muslim 86%, Christian 9%, Hindu 2%, Other 2%, Buddhist 1%
Ethnic mix Javanese 41%, Other 29%, Sundanese 15%, Coastal Malays 12%, Madurese 3%
Government Presidential system
Currency Rupiah = 100 sen
Literacy rate 93%
Calorie consumption 2713 kilocalories

IRAN
Southwest Asia

Page 98 C3

After the 1979 Islamist revolution led by Ayatollah Khomeini deposed the shah, this Middle Eastern country became the world's largest theocracy. It has large oil and natural gas reserves.

Official name Islamic Republic of Iran
Formation 1502 / 1990
Capital Tehran
Population 77.4 million / 123 people per sq mile (47 people per sq km)
Total area 636,293 sq miles (1,648,000 sq km)
Languages Farsi*, Azeri, Luri, Gilaki, Mazanderani, Kurdish, Turkmen, Arabic, Baluchi
Religions Shi'a Muslim 89%, Sunni Muslim 9%, Other 2%
Ethnic mix Persian 51%, Azari 24%, Other 10%, Lur and Bakhtiari 8%, Kurdish 7%
Government Islamic theocracy
Currency Iranian rial = 100 dinars
Literacy rate 84%
Calorie consumption 3058 kilocalories

IRAQ
Southwest Asia

Page 98 B3

Oil-rich Iraq is situated in the central Middle East. A US-led invasion in 2003 toppled Saddam Hussein's regime, but sectarian violence since then has caused political and social turmoil.

Official name Republic of Iraq
Formation 1932 / 1990
Capital Baghdad
Population 33.8 million / 200 people per sq mile (77 people per sq km)
Total area 168,753 sq miles (437,072 sq km)
Languages Arabic*, Kurdish*, Turkic languages, Armenian, Assyrian
Religions Shi'a Muslim 60%, Sunni Muslim 35%, Other (including Christian) 5%
Ethnic mix Arab 80%, Kurdish 15%, Turkmen 3%, Other 2%
Government Parliamentary system
Currency New Iraqi dinar = 1000 fils
Literacy rate 79%
Calorie consumption 2489 kilocalories

IRELAND
Northwest Europe

Page 67 A6

British rule ended in 1922 for 80% of the island of Ireland, which became the Irish Republic in 1949. The economy is now recovering after suffering heavily in the 2008 global financial crisis.

Official name Ireland
Formation 1922 / 1922
Capital Dublin
Population 4.6 million / 173 people per sq mile (67 people per sq km)
Total area 27,135 sq miles (70,280 sq km)
Languages English*, Irish*
Religions Roman Catholic 87%, Other and nonreligious 10%, Anglican 3%
Ethnic mix Irish 99%, Other 1%
Government Parliamentary system
Currency Euro = 100 cents
Literacy rate 99%
Calorie consumption 3591 kilocalories

JAMAICA
West Indies

Page 32 C3

Colonized by Spain and then Britain, Jamaica was the first Caribbean island to gain independence in the postwar era. Jamaican popular music culture developed reggae, ska, and dancehall.

Official name Jamaica
Formation 1962 / 1962
Capital Kingston
Population 2.8 million / 670 people per sq mile (259 people per sq km)
Total area 4243 sq miles (10,990 sq km)
Languages English Creole, English*
Religions Other and nonreligious 45%, Other Protestant 20%, Church of God 18%, Baptist 10%, Anglican 7%
Ethnic mix Black African 91%, Mulatto (mixed race) 7%, European and Chinese 1%, East Indian 1%
Government Parliamentary system
Currency Jamaican dollar = 100 cents
Literacy rate 88%
Calorie consumption 2789 kilocalories

KAZAKHSTAN
Central Asia

Page 92 B4

Second-largest of the former Soviet republics, mineral-rich Kazakhstan is Central Asia's major economic power. The former communist leader remains in charge, facing little opposition.

Official name Republic of Kazakhstan
Formation 1991 / 1991
Capital Astana
Population 16.4 million / 16 people per sq mile (6 people per sq km)
Total area 1,049,150 sq miles (2,717,300 sq km)
Languages Kazakh*, Russian, Ukrainian, German, Uzbek, Tatar, Uighur
Religions Muslim (mainly Sunni) 47%, Orthodox Christian 44%, Other 7%, Protestant 2%
Ethnic mix Kazakh 57%, Russian 27%, Other 8%, Ukrainian 3%, Uzbek 3%, German 2%
Government Presidential system
Currency Tenge = 100 tiyn
Literacy rate 99%
Calorie consumption 3107 kilocalories

KOSOVO (not fully recognized)
Southeast Europe

Page 79 D5

NATO intervention in 1999 ended ethnic cleansing by the Serbs of Kosovo's majority Albanian population, and nine years later the region unilaterally declared independence from Serbia.

Official name Republic of Kosovo
Formation 2008 / 2008
Capital Priština
Population 1.8 million / 427 people per sq mile (165 people per sq km)
Total area 4212 sq miles (10,908 sq km)
Languages Albanian*, Serbian*, Bosniak, Gorani, Roma, Turkish
Religions Muslim 92%, Orthodox Christian 4%, Roman Catholic 4%
Ethnic mix Albanian 92%, Serb 4%, Bosniak and Gorani 2%, Roma 1%, Turkish 1%
Government Parliamentary system
Currency Euro = 100 cents
Literacy rate 92%
Calorie consumption Not available

ISRAEL
Southwest Asia

Page 97 A7

In 1948 this Jewish state was carved out of Palestine on the east coast of the Mediterranean. It has gained land from its Arab neighbors, and the status of the Palestinians remains unresolved.

Official name State of Israel
Formation 1948 / 1994
Capital Jerusalem (not internationally recognized)
Population 7.7 million / 981 people per sq mile (379 people per sq km)
Total area 8019 sq miles (20,770 sq km)
Languages Hebrew*, Arabic*, Yiddish, German, Russian, Polish, Romanian, Persian
Religions Jewish 76%, Muslim (mainly Sunni) 16%, Other 4%, Druze 2%, Christian 2%
Ethnic mix Jewish 76%, Arab 20%, Other 4%
Government Parliamentary system
Currency Shekel = 100 agorot
Literacy rate 98%
Calorie consumption 3619 kilocalories

JAPAN
East Asia

Page 108 C4

Japan has four main islands and over 3000 smaller ones. Rebuilding after defeat in World War II, by 1990 it was the world's second-biggest economy. It retains its emperor as head of state.

Official name Japan
Formation 1590 / 1972
Capital Tokyo
Population 127 million / 874 people per sq mile (338 people per sq km)
Total area 145,882 sq miles (377,835 sq km)
Languages Japanese*, Korean, Chinese
Religions Shinto and Buddhist 76%, Buddhist 16%, Other (including Christian) 8%
Ethnic mix Japanese 99%, Other (mainly Korean) 1%
Government Parliamentary system
Currency Yen = 100 sen
Literacy rate 99%
Calorie consumption 2719 kilocalories

KENYA
East Africa

Page 51 C6

Straddling the Equator on Africa's east coast, Kenya has known both stable periods and internal strife since independence in 1963. Corruption is now a key political issue.

Official name Republic of Kenya
Formation 1963 / 1963
Capital Nairobi
Population 44.4 million / 203 people per sq mile (78 people per sq km)
Total area 224,961 sq miles (582,650 sq km)
Languages Kiswahili*, English*, Kikuyu, Luo, Kalenjin, Kamba
Religions Christian 80%, Muslim 10%, Traditional beliefs 9%, Other 1%
Ethnic mix Other 28%, Kikuyu 22%, Luo 14%, Luhya 14%, Kamba 11%, Kalenjin 11%
Government Presidential system
Currency Kenya shilling = 100 cents
Literacy rate 72%
Calorie consumption 2189 kilocalories

KUWAIT
Southwest Asia

Page 98 C4

Kuwait, on the Persian Gulf, was a British protectorate from 1914 to 1961. Oil-rich since the 1950s, it was annexed briefly in 1990 by Iraq but US-led intervention restored the ruling amir.

Official name State of Kuwait
Formation 1961 / 1961
Capital Kuwait City
Population 3.4 million / 494 people per sq mile (191 people per sq km)
Total area 6880 sq miles (17,820 sq km)
Languages Arabic*, English
Religions Sunni Muslim 45%, Shi'a Muslim 40%, Christian, Hindu, and other 15%
Ethnic mix Kuwaiti 45%, Other Arab 35%, South Asian 9%, Other 7%, Iranian 4%
Government Monarchy
Currency Kuwaiti dinar = 1000 fils
Literacy rate 96%
Calorie consumption 3471 kilocalories

ITALY
Southern Europe

Page 74 B3

A boot-shaped peninsula jutting into the Mediterranean, Italy is a world leader in product design, fashion, and textiles. Divisions exist between the industrial north and poorer south.

Official name Italian Republic
Formation 1861 / 1947
Capital Rome
Population 61 million / 537 people per sq mile (207 people per sq km)
Total area 116,305 sq miles (301,230 sq km)
Languages Italian*, German, French, Rhaeto-Romanic, Sardinian
Religions Roman Catholic 85%, Other and nonreligious 13%, Muslim 2%
Ethnic mix Italian 94%, Other 4%, Sardinian 2%
Government Parliamentary system
Currency Euro = 100 cents
Literacy rate 99%
Calorie consumption 3539 kilocalories

JORDAN
Southwest Asia

Page 97 B6

This Middle Eastern kingdom stretches from the east bank of the Jordan River into largely uninhabited desert. Calls for greater democratization have engendered some reforms.

Official name Hashemite Kingdom of Jordan
Formation 1946 / 1967
Capital Amman
Population 7.3 million / 213 people per sq mile (82 people per sq km)
Total area 35,637 sq miles (92,300 sq km)
Languages Arabic*
Religions Sunni Muslim 92%, Christian 6%, Other 2%
Ethnic mix Arab 98%, Circassian 1%, Armenian 1%
Government Monarchy
Currency Jordanian dinar = 1000 fils
Literacy rate 98%
Calorie consumption 3149 kilocalories

KIRIBATI
Australasia & Oceania

Page 123 F3

Part of the British colony of the Gilbert and Ellice Islands until independence in 1979, Kiribati comprises 33 islands in the mid-Pacific Ocean. Phosphate deposits on Banaba ran out in 1980.

Official name Republic of Kiribati
Formation 1979 / 1979
Capital Bairiki (Tarawa Atoll)
Population 103,248 / 377 people per sq mile (145 people per sq km)
Total area 277 sq miles (717 sq km)
Languages English*, Kiribati
Religions Roman Catholic 55%, Kiribati Protestant Church 36%, Other 9%
Ethnic mix Micronesian 99%, Other 1%
Government Presidential system
Currency Australian dollar = 100 cents
Literacy rate 99%
Calorie consumption 3022 kilocalories

KYRGYZSTAN
Central Asia

Page 101 F2

This mountainous, landlocked state in Central Asia is the most rural of the ex-Soviet republics. Popular protests ousted the long-term president in 2005 and his successor in 2010.

Official name Kyrgyz Republic
Formation 1991 / 1991
Capital Bishkek
Population 5.5 million / 72 people per sq mile (28 people per sq km)
Total area 76,641 sq miles (198,500 sq km)
Languages Kyrgyz*, Russian*, Uzbek, Tatar, Ukrainian
Religions Muslim (mainly Sunni) 70%, Orthodox Christian 30%
Ethnic mix Kyrgyz 69%, Uzbek 14%, Russian 9%, Other 6%, Uighur 1%, Dungan 1%
Government Presidential system
Currency Som = 100 tyiyn
Literacy rate 99%
Calorie consumption 2828 kilocalories

LAOS
Southeast Asia

Page 114 D4

Landlocked Laos suffered a long civil war after French rule ended, and was badly bombed by US forces engaged in Vietnam. It has been under communist rule since 1975.

Official name Lao People's Democratic Republic
Formation 1953 / 1953
Capital Vientiane
Population 6.8 million / 76 people per sq mile (29 people per sq km)
Total area 91,428 sq miles (236,800 sq km)
Languages Lao*, Mon-Khmer, Yao, Vietnamese, Chinese, French
Religions Buddhist 65%, Other (including animist) 34%, Christian 1%
Ethnic mix Lao Loum 66%, Lao Theung 30%, Other 2%, Lao Soung 2%
Government One-party state
Currency Kip = 100 at
Literacy rate 73%
Calorie consumption 2356 kilocalories

LATVIA
Northeast Europe

Page 84 C3

Situated on the low-lying eastern shores of the Baltic Sea, Latvia, like its Baltic neighbors, regained its independence at the collapse of the USSR in 1991. It retains a large Russian population.

Official name Republic of Latvia
Formation 1991 / 1991
Capital Riga
Population 2.1 million / 84 people per sq mile (33 people per sq km)
Total area 24,938 sq miles (64,589 sq km)
Languages Latvian*, Russian
Religions Other 43%, Lutheran 24%, Roman Catholic 18%, Orthodox Christian 15%
Ethnic mix Latvian 62%, Russian 27%, Other 4%, Belarussian 3%, Ukrainian 2%, Polish 2%
Government Parliamentary system
Currency Euro = 100 cents
Literacy rate 99%
Calorie consumption 3293 kilocalories

LEBANON
Southwest Asia

Page 96 A4

Lebanon is dwarfed by its two powerful neighbors, Syria and Israel. Muslims and Christians fought a 14-year civil war until agreeing to share power in 1989, however, instability continues.

Official name Republic of Lebanon
Formation 1941 / 1941
Capital Beirut
Population 4.8 million / 1215 people per sq mile (469 people per sq km)
Total area 4015 sq miles (10,400 sq km)
Languages Arabic*, French, Armenian, Assyrian
Religions Muslim 60%, Christian 39%, Other 1%
Ethnic mix Arab 95%, Armenian 4%, Other 1%
Government Parliamentary system
Currency Lebanese pound = 100 piastres
Literacy rate 90%
Calorie consumption 3181 kilocalories

LESOTHO
Southern Africa

Page 56 D5

Lesotho lies within South Africa, on whom it is economically dependent. Elections in 1993 ended military rule, but South Africa has had to intervene in politics since. AIDS is a problem.

Official name Kingdom of Lesotho
Formation 1966 / 1966
Capital Maseru
Population 2.1 million / 179 people per sq mile (69 people per sq km)
Total area 11,720 sq miles (30,355 sq km)
Languages English*, Sesotho*, isiZulu
Religions Christian 90%, Traditional beliefs 10%
Ethnic mix Sotho 99%, European and Asian 1%
Government Parliamentary system
Currency Loti = 100 lisente; South African rand = 100 cents
Literacy rate 76%
Calorie consumption 2595 kilocalories

LIBERIA
West Africa

Page 52 C5

Facing the Atlantic Ocean, Liberia is Africa's oldest republic, founded in 1847 by freed US slaves. Recovery from the 1990s' civil war has been set back by the 2014 Ebola epidemic.

Official name Republic of Liberia
Formation 1847 / 1847
Capital Monrovia
Population 4.3 million / 116 people per sq mile (45 people per sq km)
Total area 43,000 sq miles (111,370 sq km)
Languages Kpelle, Vai, Bassa, Kru, Grebo, Kissi, Gola, Loma, English*
Religions Traditional beliefs 40%, Christian 40%, Muslim 20%
Ethnic mix Indigenous tribes (12 groups) 49%, Kpellé 20%, Bassa 16%, Gio 8%, Krou 7%
Government Presidential system
Currency Liberian dollar = 100 cents
Literacy rate 43%
Calorie consumption 2251 kilocalories

LIBYA
North Africa

Page 49 F3

On the Mediterranean coast, Libya was ruled from 1969 by the idiosyncratic Col. Gaddafi. The 2011 "Arab Spring" turned to civil war, toppling his regime, but leaving Libya in anarchy.

Official name State of Libya
Formation 1951 / 1951
Capital Tripoli
Population 6.2 million / 9 people per sq mile (4 people per sq km)
Total area 679,358 sq miles (1,759,540 sq km)
Languages Arabic*, Tuareg
Religions Muslim (mainly Sunni) 97%, Other 3%
Ethnic mix Arab and Berber 97%, Other 3%
Government Transitional regime
Currency Libyan dinar = 1000 dirhams
Literacy rate 90%
Calorie consumption 3211 kilocalories

LIECHTENSTEIN
Central Europe

Page 73 B7

Tucked in the Alps between Switzerland and Austria, Liechtenstein became an independent principality of the Holy Roman Empire in 1719. Switzerland handles its foreign affairs and defense.

Official name Principality of Liechtenstein
Formation 1719 / 1719
Capital Vaduz
Population 37,000 / 597 people per sq mile (231 people per sq km)
Total area 62 sq miles (160 sq km)
Languages German*, Alemannish dialect, Italian
Religions Roman Catholic 79%, Other 13%, Protestant 8%
Ethnic mix Liechtensteiner 66%, Other 12%, Swiss 10%, Austrian 6%, German 3%, Italian 3%
Government Parliamentary system
Currency Swiss franc = 100 rappen/centimes
Literacy rate 99%
Calorie consumption Not available

LITHUANIA
Northeast Europe

Page 84 B4

A flat land of lakes, moors, and bogs, Lithuania is the largest of the three Baltic states. It has historical ties to Poland and was the first former Soviet republic to declare independence.

Official name Republic of Lithuania
Formation 1991 / 1991
Capital Vilnius
Population 3 million / 119 people per sq mile (46 people per sq km)
Total area 25,174 sq miles (65,200 sq km)
Languages Lithuanian*, Russian
Religions Roman Catholic 77%, Other 17%, Russian Orthodox 4%, Protestant 1%, Old Believers 1%
Ethnic mix Lithuanian 85%, Polish 7%, Russian 6%, Belarussian 1%, Other 1%
Government Parliamentary system
Currency Litas = 100 centu
Literacy rate 99%
Calorie consumption 3463 kilocalories

LUXEMBOURG
Northwest Europe

Page 65 D8

Part of the forested Ardennes plateau in Northwest Europe, Luxembourg is Europe's last independent duchy and one of its richest states. It is a banking center and hosts EU institutions.

Official name Grand Duchy of Luxembourg
Formation 1867 / 1867
Capital Luxembourg-Ville
Population 500,000 / 501 people per sq mile (193 people per sq km)
Total area 998 sq miles (2586 sq km)
Languages Luxembourgish*, German*, French*
Religions Roman Catholic 97%, Protestant, Orthodox Christian, and Jewish 3%
Ethnic mix Luxembourger 62%, Foreign residents 38%
Government Parliamentary system
Currency Euro = 100 cents
Literacy rate 99%
Calorie consumption 3568 kilocalories

LIECHTENSTEIN (MACEDONIA)

MACEDONIA
Southeast Europe

Page 79 D6

This ex-Yugoslav state is landlocked in the southern Balkans. Its EU candidacy is held back over Greek fears that its name implies a claim to its own northern province of Macedonia.

Official name Republic of Macedonia
Formation 1991 / 1991
Capital Skopje
Population 2.1 million / 212 people per sq mile (82 people per sq km)
Total area 9781 sq miles (25,333 sq km)
Languages Macedonian*, Albanian*, Turkish, Romani, Serbian
Religions Orthodox Christian 65%, Muslim 29%, Roman Catholic 4%, Other 2%
Ethnic mix Macedonian 64%, Albanian 25%, Turkish 4%, Roma 3%, Other 2%, Serb 2%
Government Presidential / parliamentary system
Currency Macedonian denar = 100 deni
Literacy rate 98%
Calorie consumption 2923 kilocalories

MADAGASCAR
Indian Ocean

Page 57 F4

Off Africa's southeast coast, this former French colony is the world's fourth-largest island. Free elections in 1993 ended 18 years of socialism, but power struggles have blighted politics since.

Official name Republic of Madagascar
Formation 1960 / 1960
Capital Antananarivo
Population 22.9 million / 102 people per sq mile (39 people per sq km)
Total area 226,656 sq miles (587,040 sq km)
Languages Malagasy*, French*, English*
Religions Traditional beliefs 52%, Christian (mainly Roman Catholic) 41%, Muslim 7%
Ethnic mix Other Malay 46%, Merina 26%, Betsimisaraka 15%, Betsileo 12%, Other 1%
Government Presidential / parliamentary system
Currency Ariary = 5 iraimbilanja
Literacy rate 64%
Calorie consumption 2092 kilocalories

MALAWI
Southern Africa

Page 57 E1

This landlocked former British colony lies along the Great Rift Valley and Lake Nyasa, Africa's third-largest lake. Multiparty elections in 1994 ended three decades of single-party rule.

Official name Republic of Malawi
Formation 1964 / 1964
Capital Lilongwe
Population 16.4 million / 451 people per sq mile (174 people per sq km)
Total area 45,745 sq miles (118,480 sq km)
Languages Chewa, Lomwe, Yao, Ngoni, English*
Religions Protestant 55%, Roman Catholic 20%, Muslim 20%, Traditional beliefs 5%
Ethnic mix Bantu 99%, Other 1%
Government Presidential system
Currency Malawi kwacha = 100 tambala
Literacy rate 61%
Calorie consumption 2334 kilocalories

MALAYSIA
Southeast Asia

Page 116 B3

Three separate territories, Peninsular Malaysia, and Sarawak and Sabah on Borneo, make up Malaysia. Relations between indigenous Malays and the Chinese minority dominate politics.

Official name Federation of Malaysia
Formation 1963 / 1965
Capital Kuala Lumpur; Putrajaya (administrative)
Population 29.7 million / 234 people per sq mile (90 people per sq km)
Total area 127,316 sq miles (329,750 sq km)
Languages Bahasa Malaysia*, Malay, Chinese, Tamil, English
Religions Muslim (mainly Sunni) 61%, Buddhist 19%, Christian 9%, Hindu 6%, Other 5%
Ethnic mix Malay 53%, Chinese 26%, Indigenous tribes 12%, Indian 8%, Other 1%
Government Parliamentary system
Currency Ringgit = 100 sen
Literacy rate 93%
Calorie consumption 2855 kilocalories

MALDIVES
Indian Ocean

Page 110 A4

Of this group of over 1000 small low-lying coral islands in the Indian Ocean, only 200 are inhabited. A few families dominate politics and have reversed the electoral upsets of 2008 and 2009.

Official name Republic of Maldives
Formation 1965 / 1965
Capital Male'
Population 300,000 / 2586 people per sq mile (1000 people per sq km)
Total area 116 sq miles (300 sq km)
Languages Dhivehi* (Maldivian), Sinhala, Tamil, Arabic
Religions Sunni Muslim 100%
Ethnic mix Arab–Sinhalese–Malay 100%
Government Presidential system
Currency Rufiyaa = 100 laari
Literacy rate 98%
Calorie consumption 2722 kilocalories

MALI
West Africa

Page 53 E2

Mali's power as a trans-Saharan trading empire peaked 700 years ago. Modern Mali, a one-party state until 1992, called in former colonial power France to suppress Islamist rebels in 2013.

Official name Republic of Mali
Formation 1960 / 1960
Capital Bamako
Population 15.3 million / 32 people per sq mile (13 people per sq km)
Total area 478,764 sq miles (1,240,000 sq km)
Languages Bambara, Fulani, Senufo, Soninke, French*
Religions Muslim (mainly Sunni) 90%, Traditional beliefs 6%, Christian 4%
Ethnic mix Bambara 52%, Other 14%, Fulani 11%, Saracolé 7%, Soninka 7%, Tuareg 5%, Mianka 4%
Government Presidential system
Currency CFA franc = 100 centimes
Literacy rate 34%
Calorie consumption 2833 kilocalories

MALTA
Southern Europe

Page 80 A5

The Maltese archipelago lies off Sicily. Only Malta, Kemmuna, and Gozo are inhabited. Its mid-Mediterranean location has made it a gateway for illegal migration from Africa to Europe.

Official name Republic of Malta
Formation 1964 / 1964
Capital Valletta
Population 400,000 / 3226 people per sq mile (1250 people per sq km)
Total area 122 sq miles (316 sq km)
Languages Maltese*, English*
Religions Roman Catholic 98%, Other and nonreligious 2%
Ethnic mix Maltese 96%, Other 4%
Government Parliamentary system
Currency Euro = 100 cents
Literacy rate 92%
Calorie consumption 3389 kilocalories

MARSHALL ISLANDS
Australasia & Oceania

Page 122 D1

This group of 34 atolls was under US rule as part of the UN Trust Territory of the Pacific Islands until 1986. The economy depends on US aid and rent for the US missile base on Kwajalein.

Official name Republic of the Marshall Islands
Formation 1986 / 1986
Capital Majuro
Population 69,747 / 996 people per sq mile (385 people per sq km)
Total area 70 sq miles (181 sq km)
Languages Marshallese*, English*, Japanese, German
Religions Protestant 90%, Roman Catholic 8%, Other 2%
Ethnic mix Micronesian 90%, Other 10%
Government Presidential system
Currency US dollar = 100 cents
Literacy rate 91%
Calorie consumption Not available

MAURITANIA
West Africa

Page 52 C2

Two-thirds of this former French colony is desert. The Maures oppress the black minority. Multiparty elections from 1991 returned the military leader to power until a coup in 2005.

Official name Islamic Republic of Mauritania
Formation 1960 / 1960
Capital Nouakchott
Population 3.9 million / 10 people per sq mile (4 people per sq km)
Total area 397,953 sq miles (1,030,700 sq km)
Languages Arabic*, Hassaniyah Arabic, Wolof, French
Religions Sunni Muslim 100%
Ethnic mix Maure 81%, Wolof 7%, Tukolor 5%, Other 4%, Soninka 3%
Government Presidential system
Currency Ouguiya = 5 khoums
Literacy rate 46%
Calorie consumption 2791 kilocalories

MAURITIUS
Indian Ocean

Page 57 H3

East of Madagascar in the Indian Ocean, Mauritius became a republic 24 years after independence from Britain. Its diversified economy includes tourism, financial services, and outsourcing.

Official name Republic of Mauritius
Formation 1968 / 1968
Capital Port Louis
Population 1.2 million / 1671 people per sq mile (645 people per sq km)
Total area 718 sq miles (1860 sq km)
Languages French Creole, Hindi, Urdu, Tamil, Chinese, English*, French
Religions Hindu 48%, Roman Catholic 24%, Muslim 17%, Protestant 9%, Other 2%
Ethnic mix Indo-Mauritian 68%, Creole 27%, Sino-Mauritian 3%, Franco-Mauritian 2%
Government Parliamentary system
Currency Mauritian rupee = 100 cents
Literacy rate 89%
Calorie consumption 3055 kilocalories

MEXICO
North America

Page 28 D3

Located between the US and the Central American states, Mexico was a Spanish colony for 300 years. Sprawling Mexico City is built on the site of the Aztec capital, Tenochtitlán.

Official name United Mexican States
Formation 1836 / 1848
Capital Mexico City
Population 122 million / 166 people per sq mile (64 people per sq km)
Total area 761,602 sq miles (1,972,550 sq km)
Languages Spanish*, Nahuatl, Mayan, Zapotec, Mixtec, Otomi, Totonac, Tzotzil, Tzeltal
Religions Roman Catholic 77%, Other 14%, Protestant 6%, Nonreligious 3%
Ethnic mix Mestizo 60%, Amerindian 30%, European 9%, Other 1%
Government Presidential system
Currency Mexican peso = 100 centavos
Literacy rate 94%
Calorie consumption 3024 kilocalories

MICRONESIA
Australasia & Oceania

Page 122 B1

The Federated States of Micronesia, situated in the western Pacific, comprises 607 islands and atolls grouped into four main island states. The economy relies on US aid.

Official name Federated States of Micronesia
Formation 1986 / 1986
Capital Palikir (Pohnpei Island)
Population 106,104 / 392 people per sq mile (151 people per sq km)
Total area 271 sq miles (702 sq km)
Languages Trukese, Pohnpeian, Kosraean, Yapese, English*
Religions Roman Catholic 50%, Protestant 47%, Other 3%
Ethnic mix Chuukese 49%, Pohnpeian 24%, Other 14%, Kosraean 6%, Yapese 5%, Asian 2%
Government Nonparty system
Currency US dollar = 100 cents
Literacy rate 81%
Calorie consumption Not available

MOLDOVA
Southeast Europe

Page 86 D3

The smallest and most densely populated of the ex-Soviet republics, Moldova has strong linguistic and cultural ties with Romania to the west. It exports tobacco, wine, and fruit.

Official name Republic of Moldova
Formation 1991 / 1991
Capital Chisinau
Population 3.5 million / 269 people per sq mile (104 people per sq km)
Total area 13,067 sq miles (33,843 sq km)
Languages Moldovan*, Ukrainian, Russian
Religions Orthodox Christian 93%, Other 6%, Baptist 1%
Ethnic mix Moldovan 84%, Ukrainian 7%, Gagauz 5%, Russian 2%, Bulgarian 1%, Other 1%
Government Parliamentary system
Currency Moldovan leu = 100 bani
Literacy rate 99%
Calorie consumption 2837 kilocalories

MONACO
Southern Europe

Page 69 E6

The destiny of this tiny enclave on France's Côte d'Azur was changed in 1863 when its prince opened a casino. A jet-set image and thriving service sector define its modern identity.

Official name Principality of Monaco
Formation 1861 / 1861
Capital Monaco-Ville
Population 36,136 / 48,181 people per sq mile (18,531 people per sq km)
Total area 0.75 sq miles (1.95 sq km)
Languages French*, Italian, Monégasque, English
Religions Roman Catholic 89%, Protestant 6%, Other 5%
Ethnic mix French 47%, Other 21%, Italian 16%, Monégasque 16%
Government Monarchical / parliamentary system
Currency Euro = 100 cents
Literacy rate 99%
Calorie consumption Not available

MONGOLIA
East Asia

Page 104 D2

Vast Mongolia is sparsely populated and mostly desert. Under the sway of its giant neighbors, Russia and China, it was communist from independence from China in 1924 until 1990.

Official name Mongolia
Formation 1924 / 1924
Capital Ulan Bator
Population 2.8 million / 5 people per sq mile (2 people per sq km)
Total area 604,247 sq miles (1,565,000 sq km)
Languages Khalkha Mongolian*, Kazakh, Chinese, Russian
Religions Tibetan Buddhist 50%, Nonreligious 40%, Shamanist and Christian 6%, Muslim 4%
Ethnic mix Khalkh 95%, Kazakh 4%, Other 1%
Government Presidential / parliamentary system
Currency Tugrik (tögrög) = 100 möngö
Literacy rate 98%
Calorie consumption 2463 kilocalories

MONTENEGRO
Southeast Europe

Page 79 C5

Part of the former Yugoslavia, the tiny republic of Montenegro broke away from Serbia in 2006. Its attractive coast and mountains are a big tourist draw. It hopes to join the EU soon.

Official name Montenegro
Formation 2006 / 2006
Capital Podgorica
Population 600,000 / 113 people per sq mile (43 people per sq km)
Total area 5332 sq miles (13,812 sq km)
Languages Montenegrin*, Serbian, Albanian, Bosniak, Croatian
Religions Orthodox Christian 74%, Muslim 18%, Other 4%, Roman Catholic 4%
Ethnic mix Montenegrin 43%, Serb 32%, Other 12%, Bosniak 8%, Albanian 5%
Government Parliamentary system
Currency Euro = 100 cents
Literacy rate 98%
Calorie consumption 3568 kilocalories

MOROCCO
North Africa

Page 48 C2

A former French colony in northwest Africa, Morocco has occupied the disputed territory of Western Sahara since 1975. The king has handed more power to parliament since 2011.

Official name Kingdom of Morocco
Formation 1956 / 1969
Capital Rabat
Population 33 million / 192 people per sq mile (74 people per sq km)
Total area 172,316 sq miles (446,300 sq km)
Languages Arabic*, Tamazight (Berber), French, Spanish
Religions Muslim (mainly Sunni) 99%, Other (mostly Christian) 1%
Ethnic mix Arab 70%, Berber 29%, European 1%
Government Monarchical / parliamentary system
Currency Moroccan dirham = 100 centimes
Literacy rate 67%
Calorie consumption 3334 kilocalories

MOZAMBIQUE
Southern Africa

Page 57 E3

Mozambique, on the southeast African coast, frequently suffers both floods and droughts. It was torn by civil war from 1977 to 1992 as the Marxist state fought South African-backed rebels.

Official name Republic of Mozambique
Formation 1975 / 1975
Capital Maputo
Population 25.8 million / 85 people per sq mile (33 people per sq km)
Total area 309,494 sq miles (801,590 sq km)
Languages Makua, Xitsonga, Sena, Lomwe, Portuguese*
Religions Traditional beliefs 56%, Christian 30%, Muslim 14%
Ethnic mix Makua Lomwe 47%, Tsonga 23%, Malawi 12%, Shona 11%, Yao 4%, Other 3%
Government Presidential system
Currency New metical = 100 centavos
Literacy rate 51%
Calorie consumption 2267 kilocalories

MYANMAR (BURMA)
Southeast Asia

Page 114 A3

Myanmar, on the eastern shores of the Bay of Bengal and the Andaman Sea, has suffered years of ethnic conflict and repressive military rule since independence from Britain in 1948.

Official name Republic of the Union of Myanmar
Formation 1948 / 1948
Capital Nay Pyi Taw
Population 53.3 million / 210 people per sq mile (81 people per sq km)
Total area 261,969 sq miles (678,500 sq km)
Languages Burmese* (Myanmar), Shan, Karen, Rakhine, Chin, Yangbye, Kachin, Mon
Religions Buddhist 89%, Christian 4%, Muslim 4%, Other 2%, Animist 1%
Ethnic mix Burman (Bamah) 68%, Other 12%, Shan 9%, Karen 7%, Rakhine 4%
Government Presidential system
Currency Kyat = 100 pyas
Literacy rate 93%
Calorie consumption 2528 kilocalories

NAMIBIA
Southern Africa

Page 56 B3

On Africa's southwest coast, this mineral-rich ex-German colony was governed by South Africa from 1915 to 1990. The white minority controls the economy, a legacy of apartheid.

Official name Republic of Namibia
Formation 1990 / 1994
Capital Windhoek
Population 2.3 million / 7 people per sq mile (3 people per sq km)
Total area 318,694 sq miles (825,418 sq km)
Languages Ovambo, Kavango, English*, Bergdama, German, Afrikaans
Religions Christian 90%, Traditional beliefs 10%
Ethnic mix Ovambo 50%, Other tribes 22%, Kavango 9%, Herero 7%, Damara 7%, Other 5%
Government Presidential system
Currency Namibian dollar = 100 cents; South African rand = 100 cents
Literacy rate 76%
Calorie consumption 2086 kilocalories

NAURU
Australasia & Oceania

Page 122 D3

The world's smallest republic, 2480 miles (4000 km) northeast of Australia, grew rich from its phosphate deposits, but these have almost run out and poor investment has caused financial crisis.

Official name Republic of Nauru
Formation 1968 / 1968
Capital None
Population 9434 / 1165 people per sq mile (449 people per sq km)
Total area 8.1 sq miles (21 sq km)
Languages Nauruan*, Kiribati, Chinese, Tuvaluan, English
Religions Nauruan Congregational Church 60%, Roman Catholic 35%, Other 5%
Ethnic mix Nauruan 93%, Chinese 5%, Other Pacific islanders 1%, European 1%
Government Nonparty system
Currency Australian dollar = 100 cents
Literacy rate 95%
Calorie consumption Not available

NEPAL
South Asia

Page 113 E3

Nestled in the Himalayas, Nepal had an absolute monarchy until 1990. Unstable coalitions typify politics. Abolition of the monarchy was a condition for ending the Maoist rebellion in 2008.

Official name Federal Democratic Republic of Nepal
Formation 1769 / 1769
Capital Kathmandu
Population 27.8 million / 526 people per sq mile (203 people per sq km)
Total area 54,363 sq miles (140,800 sq km)
Languages Nepali*, Maithili, Bhojpuri
Religions Hindu 81%, Buddhist 11%, Muslim 4%, Other (including Christian) 4%
Ethnic mix Other 52%, Chhetri 16%, Hill Brahman 13%, Magar 7%, Tharu 7%, Tamang 5%
Government Transitional regime
Currency Nepalese rupee = 100 paisa
Literacy rate 57%
Calorie consumption 2580 kilocalories

NETHERLANDS
Northwest Europe

Page 64 C3

Astride the delta of four major rivers in northwest Europe, the Netherlands was ruled by Spain until 1648. It has a long trading tradition, and Rotterdam remains the world's largest port.

Official name Kingdom of the Netherlands
Formation 1648 / 1839
Capital Amsterdam; The Hague (administrative)
Population 16.8 million / 1283 people per sq mile (495 people per sq km)
Total area 16,033 sq miles (41,526 sq km)
Languages Dutch*, Frisian
Religions Roman Catholic 36%, Other 34%, Protestant 27%, Muslim 3%
Ethnic mix Dutch 82%, Other 12%, Surinamese 2%, Turkish 2%, Moroccan 2%
Government Parliamentary system
Currency Euro = 100 cents
Literacy rate 99%
Calorie consumption 3147 kilocalories

NEW ZEALAND
Australasia & Oceania

Page 128 A4

This former British colony, on the Pacific Rim, has a volcanic, more populous North Island and a mountainous South Island. It was the first country to give women the vote, in 1893.

Official name New Zealand
Formation 1947 / 1947
Capital Wellington
Population 4.5 million / 43 people per sq mile (17 people per sq km)
Total area 103,737 sq miles (268,680 sq km)
Languages English*, Maori*
Religions Anglican 24%, Other 22%, Presbyterian 18%, Nonreligious 16%, Roman Catholic 15%, Methodist 5%
Ethnic mix European 75%, Maori 15%, Other 7%, Samoan 3%
Government Parliamentary system
Currency New Zealand dollar = 100 cents
Literacy rate 99%
Calorie consumption 3170 kilocalories

NICARAGUA
Central America

Page 30 D3

Nicaragua lies at the heart of Central America. Left-wing Sandinistas threw out a brutal dictator in 1978, then faced conflict with US-backed Contras. Polls have since swung back and forth.

Official name Republic of Nicaragua
Formation 1838 / 1838
Capital Managua
Population 6.1 million / 133 people per sq mile (51 people per sq km)
Total area 49,998 sq miles (129,494 sq km)
Languages Spanish*, English Creole, Miskito
Religions Roman Catholic 80%, Protestant Evangelical 17%, Other 3%
Ethnic mix Mestizo 69%, White 17%, Black 9%, Amerindian 5%
Government Presidential system
Currency Córdoba oro = 100 centavos
Literacy rate 78%
Calorie consumption 2564 kilocalories

NIGER
West Africa

Page 53 G3

Landlocked Niger is linked to the sea by the River Niger. This ex-French colony has suffered coups, military rule, civil unrest, and severe droughts. It is one of the poorest countries in the world.

Official name Republic of Niger
Formation 1960 / 1960
Capital Niamey
Population 17.8 million / 36 people per sq mile (14 people per sq km)
Total area 489,188 sq miles (1,267,000 sq km)
Languages Hausa, Djerma, Fulani, Tuareg, Teda, French*
Religions Muslim 99%, Other (including Christian) 1%
Ethnic mix Hausa 53%, Djerma and Songhai 21%, Tuareg 11%, Fulani 7%, Kanuri 6%, Other 2%
Government Presidential system
Currency CFA franc = 100 centimes
Literacy rate 16%
Calorie consumption 2546 kilocalories

NIGERIA
West Africa

Page 53 G4

Nigeria has Africa's largest population, whose religious and ethnic rivalries have brought down both civilian and military regimes in the past. Islamic extremists are one current challenge.

Official name Federal Republic of Nigeria
Formation 1960 / 1961
Capital Abuja
Population 174 million / 494 people per sq mile (191 people per sq km)
Total area 356,667 sq miles (923,768 sq km)
Languages Hausa, English*, Yoruba, Ibo
Religions Muslim 50%, Christian 40%, Traditional beliefs 10%
Ethnic mix Other 29%, Hausa 21%, Yoruba 21%, Ibo 18%, Fulani 11%
Government Presidential system
Currency Naira = 100 kobo
Literacy rate 51%
Calorie consumption 2724 kilocalories

NORTH KOREA
East Asia

Page 106 E3

The maverick communist state in Korea's northern half has been isolated from the outside world since 1948. Its shattered state-run economy leaves people short of food and power.

Official name Democratic People's Republic of Korea
Formation 1948 / 1953
Capital Pyongyang
Population 24.9 million / 536 people per sq mile (207 people per sq km)
Total area 46,540 sq miles (120,540 sq km)
Languages Korean*
Religions Atheist 100%
Ethnic mix Korean 100%
Government One-party state
Currency North Korean won = 100 chon
Literacy rate 99%
Calorie consumption 2103 kilocalories

PAKISTAN
South Asia

Page 112 B2

Once part of British India, Pakistan was created in 1947 as a Muslim state. Today, this nuclear-armed country is struggling to deal with complex domestic and international tensions.

Official name Islamic Republic of Pakistan
Formation 1947 / 1971
Capital Islamabad
Population 182 million / 612 people per sq mile (236 people per sq km)
Total area 310,401 sq miles (803,940 sq km)
Languages Punjabi, Sindhi, Pashtu, Urdu*, Baluchi, Brahui
Religions Sunni Muslim 77%, Shi'a Muslim 20%, Hindu 2%, Christian 1%
Ethnic mix Punjabi 56%, Pathan (Pashtun) 15%, Sindhi 14%, Mohajir 7%, Other 4%, Baluchi 4%
Government Parliamentary system
Currency Pakistani rupee = 100 paisa
Literacy rate 55%
Calorie consumption 2428 kilocalories

PAPUA NEW GUINEA
Australasia & Oceania

Page 122 B3

The world's most linguistically diverse country, mineral-rich PNG occupies the east of the island of New Guinea and several other island groups. It was administered by Australia before 1975.

Official name Independent State of Papua New Guinea
Formation 1975 / 1975
Capital Port Moresby
Population 7.3 million / 42 people per sq mile (16 people per sq km)
Total area 178,703 sq miles (462,840 sq km)
Languages Pidgin English, Papuan, English*, Motu, 800 (est.) native languages
Religions Protestant 60%, Roman Catholic 37%, Other 3%
Ethnic mix Melanesian and mixed race 100%
Government Parliamentary system
Currency Kina = 100 toea
Literacy rate 63%
Calorie consumption 2193 kilocalories

PHILIPPINES
Southeast Asia

Page 117 E1

This 7107-island archipelago between the South China Sea and the Pacific is subject to earthquakes and volcanic activity. After 21 years of dictatorship, democracy was restored in 1986.

Official name Republic of the Philippines
Formation 1946 / 1946
Capital Manila
Population 98.4 million / 855 people per sq mile (330 people per sq km)
Total area 115,830 sq miles (300,000 sq km)
Languages Filipino*, English*, Tagalog, Cebuano, Ilocano, Hiligaynon, many other local languages
Religions Roman Catholic 81%, Protestant 9%, Muslim 5%, Other (including Buddhist) 5%
Ethnic mix Other 34%, Tagalog 28%, Cebuano 13%, Ilocano 9%, Hiligaynon 8%, Bisaya 8%
Government Presidential system
Currency Philippine peso = 100 centavos
Literacy rate 95%
Calorie consumption 2608 kilocalories

NORWAY
Northern Europe

Page 63 A5

Lying on the rugged western coast of Scandinavia, most people live in southern, coastal areas. Oil and gas wealth has brought one of the world's best standards of living.

Official name Kingdom of Norway
Formation 1905 / 1905
Capital Oslo
Population 5 million / 42 people per sq mile (16 people per sq km)
Total area 125,181 sq miles (324,220 sq km)
Languages Norwegian* (Bokmål "book language" and Nynorsk "new Norsk"), Sámi
Religions Evangelical Lutheran 88%, Other and nonreligious 8%, Muslim 2%, Roman Catholic 1%, Pentecostal 1%
Ethnic mix Norwegian 93%, Other 6%, Sámi 1%
Government Parliamentary system
Currency Norwegian krone = 100 øre
Literacy rate 99%
Calorie consumption 3484 kilocalories

PALAU
Australasia & Oceania

Page 122 A2

This archipelago of over 200 islands, only ten of which are inhabited, lies in the western Pacific Ocean. Until 1994 it was under US administration. The economy relies on US aid and tourism.

Official name Republic of Palau
Formation 1994 / 1994
Capital Ngerulmud
Population 21,108 / 108 people per sq mile (42 people per sq km)
Total area 177 sq miles (458 sq km)
Languages Palauan*, English*, Japanese, Angaur, Tobi, Sonsorolese
Religions Christian 66%, Modekngei 34%
Ethnic mix Palauan 74%, Filipino 16%, Other 6%, Chinese and other Asian 4%
Government Nonparty system
Currency US dollar = 100 cents
Literacy rate 99%
Calorie consumption Not available

PARAGUAY
South America

Page 42 D2

South America's longest dictatorship held power in landlocked Paraguay from 1954 to 1989. Now under democratic rule, the country's economy is still largely agricultural.

Official name Republic of Paraguay
Formation 1811 / 1938
Capital Asunción
Population 6.8 million / 44 people per sq mile (17 people per sq km)
Total area 157,046 sq miles (406,750 sq km)
Languages Guaraní*, Spanish*, German
Religions Roman Catholic 90%, Protestant (including Mennonite) 10%
Ethnic mix Mestizo 91%, Other 7%, Amerindian 2%
Government Presidential system
Currency Guaraní = 100 céntimos
Literacy rate 94%
Calorie consumption 2698 kilocalories

POLAND
Northern Europe

Page 76 B3

Poland's low-lying plains extend from the Baltic Sea into the heart of Europe. It has undergone massive political and economic change since the fall of communism. It joined the EU in 2004.

Official name Republic of Poland
Formation 1918 / 1945
Capital Warsaw
Population 38.2 million / 325 people per sq mile (125 people per sq km)
Total area 120,728 sq miles (312,685 sq km)
Languages Polish*
Religions Roman Catholic 93%, Other and nonreligious 5%, Orthodox Christian 2%
Ethnic mix Polish 98%, Other 2%
Government Parliamentary system
Currency Zloty = 100 groszy
Literacy rate 99%
Calorie consumption 3485 kilocalories

OMAN
Southwest Asia

Page 99 D6

Situated on the eastern corner of the Arabian Peninsula, Oman is the least developed of the Gulf states, despite modest oil exports. The current sultan has been in power since 1970.

Official name Sultanate of Oman
Formation 1951 / 1951
Capital Muscat
Population 3.6 million / 44 people per sq mile (17 people per sq km)
Total area 82,031 sq miles (212,460 sq km)
Languages Arabic*, Baluchi, Farsi, Hindi, Punjabi
Religions Ibadi Muslim 75%, Other Muslim and Hindu 25%
Ethnic mix Arab 88%, Baluchi 4%, Indian and Pakistani 3%, Persian 3%, African 2%
Government Monarchy
Currency Omani rial = 1000 baisa
Literacy rate 87%
Calorie consumption Not available

PANAMA
Central America

Page 31 F5

The US invaded Central America's southernmost country in 1989 to oust its dictator. The Panama Canal is a vital shortcut for shipping between the Atlantic and Pacific oceans.

Official name Republic of Panama
Formation 1903 / 1903
Capital Panama City
Population 3.9 million / 133 people per sq mile (51 people per sq km)
Total area 30,193 sq miles (78,200 sq km)
Languages English Creole, Spanish*, Amerindian languages, Chibchan languages
Religions Roman Catholic 84%, Protestant 15%, Other 1%
Ethnic mix Mestizo 70%, Black 14%, White 10%, Amerindian 6%
Government Presidential system
Currency Balboa = 100 centésimos; US dollar
Literacy rate 94%
Calorie consumption 2644 kilocalories

PERU
South America

Page 38 C3

On the Pacific coast of South America, Peru was once the heart of the Inca empire, before the Spanish conquest in the 16th century. It elected its first Amerindian president in 2001.

Official name Republic of Peru
Formation 1824 / 1941
Capital Lima
Population 30.4 million / 62 people per sq mile (24 people per sq km)
Total area 496,223 sq miles (1,285,200 sq km)
Languages Spanish*, Quechua*, Aymara
Religions Roman Catholic 81%, Other 19%
Ethnic mix Amerindian 45%, Mestizo 37%, White 15%, Other 3%
Government Presidential system
Currency New sol = 100 céntimos
Literacy rate 94%
Calorie consumption 2624 kilocalories

PORTUGAL
Southwest Europe

Page 70 B3

Portugal, on the Iberian Peninsula, is the westernmost country in mainland Europe. Isolated under 44 years of dictatorship until 1974, it modernized fast after joining the EU in 1986.

Official name Republic of Portugal
Formation 1139 / 1640
Capital Lisbon
Population 10.6 million / 299 people per sq mile (115 people per sq km)
Total area 35,672 sq miles (92,391 sq km)
Languages Portuguese*
Religions Roman Catholic 92%, Protestant 4%, Nonreligious 2%, Other 2%
Ethnic mix Portuguese 98%, African and other 2%
Government Parliamentary system
Currency Euro = 100 cents
Literacy rate 94%
Calorie consumption 3456 kilocalories

QATAR
Southwest Asia

Page 98 C4

Projecting north from the Arabian Peninsula into the Persian Gulf, Qatar is mostly flat, semiarid desert. Massive reserves of oil and gas have made it one of the world's wealthiest states.

Official name State of Qatar
Formation 1971 / 1971
Capital Doha
Population 2.2 million / 518 people per sq mile (200 people per sq km)
Total area 4416 sq miles (11,437 sq km)
Languages Arabic*
Religions Muslim (mainly Sunni) 95%, Other 5%
Ethnic mix Qatari 20%, Other Arab 20%, Indian 20%, Nepalese 13%, Filipino 10%, Other 10%, Pakistani 7%
Government Monarchy
Currency Qatar riyal = 100 dirhams
Literacy rate 97%
Calorie consumption Not available

ROMANIA
Southeast Europe

Page 86 B4

Romania lies on the western shores of the Black Sea. Its communist regime was overthrown in 1989 and, despite a slow transition to a free-market economy, it joined the EU in 2007.

Official name Romania
Formation 1878 / 1947
Capital Bucharest
Population 21.7 million / 244 people per sq mile (94 people per sq km)
Total area 91,699 sq miles (237,500 sq km)
Languages Romanian*, Hungarian (Magyar), Romani, German
Religions Romanian Orthodox 87%, Protestant 5%, Roman Catholic 5%, Other 3%
Ethnic mix Romanian 89%, Magyar 7%, Roma 3%, Other 1%
Government Presidential system
Currency New Romanian leu = 100 bani
Literacy rate 99%
Calorie consumption 3363 kilocalories

RUSSIAN FEDERATION
Europe / Asia

Page 92 D4

The world's largest country, with vast mineral and energy reserves, Russia dominated the former USSR and is still a major power. It has over 150 ethnic groups, many with their own territory.

Official name Russian Federation
Formation 1480 / 1991
Capital Moscow
Population 143 million / 22 people per sq mile (8 people per sq km)
Total area 6,592,735 sq miles (17,075,200 sq km)
Languages Russian*, Tatar, Ukrainian, Chavash, various other national languages
Religions Orthodox Christian 75%, Muslim 14%, Other 11%
Ethnic mix Russian 80%, Other 12%, Tatar 4%, Ukrainian 2%, Chavash 1%, Bashkir 1%
Government Presidential / parliamentary system
Currency Russian rouble = 100 kopeks
Literacy rate 99%
Calorie consumption 3358 kilocalories

RWANDA
Central Africa

Page 51 B6

Rwanda lies just south of the Equator in Central Africa. Ethnic violence flared into genocide in 1994, when almost a million died. The main victims, the Tutsi, dominate government now.

Official name Republic of Rwanda
Formation 1962 / 1962
Capital Kigali
Population 11.8 million / 1225 people per sq mile (473 people per sq km)
Total area 10,169 sq miles (26,338 sq km)
Languages Kinyarwanda*, French*, Kiswahili, English*
Religions Christian 94%, Muslim 5%, Traditional beliefs 1%
Ethnic mix Hutu 85%, Tutsi 14%, Other (including Twa) 1%
Government Presidential system
Currency Rwanda franc = 100 centimes
Literacy rate 66%
Calorie consumption 2148 kilocalories

ST KITTS AND NEVIS
West Indies

Page 33 G3

Saint Kitts and Nevis are part of the Caribbean Leeward Islands. A former British colony, the country is a popular tourist destination. Less-developed Nevis is famed for its hot springs.

Official name Federation of Saint Christopher and Nevis
Formation 1983 / 1983
Capital Basseterre
Population 51,134 / 368 people per sq mile (142 people per sq km)
Total area 101 sq miles (261 sq km)
Languages English*, English Creole
Religions Anglican 33%, Methodist 29%, Other 22%, Moravian 9%, Roman Catholic 7%
Ethnic mix Black 95%, Mixed race 3%, White 1%, Other and Amerindian 1%
Government Parliamentary system
Currency East Caribbean dollar = 100 cents
Literacy rate 98%
Calorie consumption 2507 kilocalories

ST LUCIA
West Indies

Page 33 G4

One of the most beautiful Caribbean Windward Islands, Saint Lucia retains both French and British influences from its colonial history. Tourism and fruit production dominate the economy.

Official name Saint Lucia
Formation 1979 / 1979
Capital Castries
Population 162,781 / 690 people per sq mile (267 people per sq km)
Total area 239 sq miles (620 sq km)
Languages English*, French Creole
Religions Roman Catholic 90%, Other 10%
Ethnic mix Black 83%, Mulatto (mixed race) 13%, Asian 3%, Other 1%
Government Parliamentary system
Currency East Caribbean dollar = 100 cents
Literacy rate 95%
Calorie consumption 2629 kilocalories

ST VINCENT & THE GRENADINES
West Indies

Page 33 G4

Formerly ruled by Britain, these volcanic islands form part of the Caribbean Windward Islands. The economy relies on tourism and bananas, and it is the world's largest arrowroot producer.

Official name Saint Vincent and the Grenadines
Formation 1979 / 1979
Capital Kingstown
Population 103,220 / 788 people per sq mile (304 people per sq km)
Total area 150 sq miles (389 sq km)
Languages English*, English Creole
Religions Anglican 47%, Methodist 28%, Roman Catholic 13%, Other 12%
Ethnic mix Black 66%, Mulatto (mixed race) 19%, Other 12%, Carib 2%, Asian 1%
Government Parliamentary system
Currency East Caribbean dollar = 100 cents
Literacy rate 88%
Calorie consumption 2960 kilocalories

SAMOA
Australasia & Oceania

Page 123 F4

Samoa, in the southern Pacific, was ruled by New Zealand before 1962. Four of the nine islands are inhabited. The traditional Samoan way of life is communal and conservative.

Official name Independent State of Samoa
Formation 1962 / 1962
Capital Apia
Population 200,000 / 183 people per sq mile (71 people per sq km)
Total area 1104 sq miles (2860 sq km)
Languages Samoan*, English*
Religions Christian 99%, Other 1%
Ethnic mix Polynesian 91%, Euronesian 7%, Other 2%
Government Parliamentary system
Currency Tala = 100 sene
Literacy rate 99%
Calorie consumption 2872 kilocalories

SAN MARINO
Southern Europe

Page 74 C3

Perched on the slopes of Monte Titano in the Italian Appennino, San Marino has been a city-state since the 4th century AD, and was recognized as independent by the pope in 1631.

Official name Republic of San Marino
Formation 1631 / 1631
Capital San Marino
Population 32,448 / 1352 people per sq mile (532 people per sq km)
Total area 23.6 sq miles (61 sq km)
Languages Italian*
Religions Roman Catholic 93%, Other and nonreligious 7%
Ethnic mix Sammarinese 88%, Italian 10%, Other 2%
Government Parliamentary system
Currency Euro = 100 cents
Literacy rate 99%
Calorie consumption Not available

SAO TOME & PRINCIPE
West Africa

Page 55 A5

This ex-Portuguese colony off Africa's west coast has two main islands and smaller islets. Multiparty democracy, adopted in 1990, ended 15 years of Marxism. Cocoa is the main export.

Official name Democratic Republic of São Tomé and Príncipe
Formation 1975 / 1975
Capital São Tomé
Population 200,000 / 539 people per sq mile (208 people per sq km)
Total area 386 sq miles (1001 sq km)
Languages Portuguese Creole, Portuguese*
Religions Roman Catholic 84%, Other 16%
Ethnic mix Black 90%, Portuguese and Creole 10%
Government Presidential system
Currency Dobra = 100 céntimos
Literacy rate 70%
Calorie consumption 2676 kilocalories

SAUDI ARABIA
Southwest Asia

Page 99 B5

The desert kingdom of Saudi Arabia, rich in oil and gas, covers an area the size of Western Europe. It includes Islam's holiest cities, Medina and Mecca. Women's rights are restricted.

Official name Kingdom of Saudi Arabia
Formation 1932 / 1932
Capital Riyadh
Population 28.8 million / 35 people per sq mile (14 people per sq km)
Total area 756,981 sq miles (1,960,582 sq km)
Languages Arabic*
Religions Sunni Muslim 85%, Shi'a Muslim 15%
Ethnic mix Arab 72%, Foreign residents (mostly south and southeast Asian) 20%, Afro-Asian 8%
Government Monarchy
Currency Saudi riyal = 100 halalat
Literacy rate 94%
Calorie consumption 3122 kilocalories

SENEGAL
West Africa

Page 52 B3

This ex-French colony was ruled by one party for 40 years after independence, despite the adoption of multipartyism in 1981. Its capital, Dakar, stands on the westernmost cape of Africa.

Official name Republic of Senegal
Formation 1960 / 1960
Capital Dakar
Population 14.1 million / 190 people per sq mile (73 people per sq km)
Total area 75,749 sq miles (196,190 sq km)
Languages Wolof, Pulaar, Serer, Diola, Mandinka, Malinké, Soninké, French*
Religions Sunni Muslim 95%, Christian (mainly Roman Catholic) 4%, Traditional beliefs 1%
Ethnic mix Wolof 43%, Serer 15%, Peul 14%, Other 14%, Toucouleur 9%, Diola 5%
Government Presidential system
Currency CFA franc = 100 centimes
Literacy rate 52%
Calorie consumption 2426 kilocalories

SERBIA
Southeast Europe

Page 78 D4

Tne former Yugoslavia begar. breaking up in 1991, and Serbia has found itself the sole successor republic. It refuses to acknowledge the 2008 secession of Albanian-dominated Kosovo.

Official name Republic of Serbia
Formation 2006 / 2008
Capital Belgrade
Population 9.5 million / 318 people per sq mile (123 people per sq km)
Total area 29,905 sq miles (77,453 sq km)
Languages Serbian*, Hungarian (Magyar)
Religions Orthodox Christian 85%, Rcman Catholic 6%, Other 6%, Muslim 3%
Ethnic mix Serb 83%, Other 10%, Magyar 4%, Bcsniak 2%, Roma 1%
Government Parliamentary system
Currency Serbian dinar = 100 para
Literacy rate 98%
Calorie consumption 2724 kilocalories

SINGAPORE
Southeast Asia

Page 116 A1

A city state linked to the southern tip of the Malay Peninsula by a causeway, Singapore is one of Asia's major commercial centers. Politics has been dominated for decades by one party.

Official name Republic of Singapore
Formation 1965 / 1965
Capital Singapore
Population 5.4 million / 22,881 people per sq mile (8852 people per sq km)
Total area 250 sq miles (648 sq km)
Languages Mandarin*, Malay*, Tamil*, English*
Religions Buddhist 55%, Taoist 22%, Muslim 16%, Hindu, Christian, and Sikh 7%
Ethnic mix Chinese 74%, Malay 14%, Indian 9%, Other 3%
Government Parliamentary system
Currency Singapore dollar = 100 cents
Literacy rate 96%
Calorie consumption Not available

SOLOMON ISLANDS
Australasia & Oceania

Page 122 C3

This archipelago of around 1000 islands scattered in the southwest Pacific was formerly ruled by Britain. Most people live on six main islands. Ethnic conflict from 1998 led to devolved governance.

Official name Solomon Islands
Formation 1978 / 1978
Capital Honiara
Population 600,000 / 56 people per sq mile (21 people per sq km)
Total area 10,985 sq miles (28,450 sq km)
Languages English*, Pidgin English, Melanesian Pidgin, around 120 native languages
Religions Church of Melanesia (Anglican) 34%, Roman Catholic 19%, South Seas Evangelical Church 17%, Methodist 11%, Other 19%
Ethnic mix Melanesian 93%, Polynesian 4%, Other 3%
Government Parliamentary system
Currency Solomon Islands dollar = 100 cents
Literacy rate 77%
Calorie consumption 2473 kilocalories

SOUTH KOREA
East Asia

Page 106 E4

Allied with the US, the southern ha'f of the Korean peninsula was separcted from the communist North in 1948. It is the world's leading shipbuilder and a major force in high-tech industries.

Official name Republic of Korea
Formation 1948 / 1953
Capital Seoul; Sejong City (administrative)
Population 49.3 million / 1293 people per sq mile (499 people per sq km)
Total area 38,023 sq miles (98,480 sq km)
Languages Korean*
Religions Mahayana Buddhist 47%, Protestant 38%, Roman Catholic 11%, Confucianist 3%, Other 1%
Ethnic mix Korean 100%
Government Presidential system
Currency South Korean won = 100 chon
Literacy rate 99%
Calorie consumption 3329 kilocalories

SEYCHELLES
Indian Ocean

Page 57 G1

This ex-British colony spans 115 islands in the Indian Ocean. Multiparty polls in 1993 ended 14 years of one-party rule. Unique flora includes the world's largest seed, the coco-de-mer.

Official name Republic of Seychelles
Formation 1976 / 1976
Capital Victoria
Population 90,846 / 874 people per sq mile (336 people per sq km)
Total area 176 sq miles (455 sq km)
Languages French Creole*, English*, French*
Religions Roman Catholic 82%, Anglican 6%, Other (including Muslim) 6%, Other Christian 3%, Hindu 2%, Seventh-day Adventist 1%
Ethnic mix Creole 89%, Indian 5%, Other 4%, Chinese 2%
Government Presidential system
Currency Seychelles rupee = 100 cents
Literacy rate 92%
Calor e consumption 2426 kilocalories

SLOVAKIA
Central Europe

Page 77 C6

After 900 years of Hungarian control, Slovakia was the less-developed half of communist Czechoslovakia in the 20th century. It became independent in 1993 and joined the EU in 2004.

Official name Slovak Republic
Formation 1993 / 1993
Capital Bratislava
Population 5.5 million / 290 people per sq mile (112 people per sq km)
Total area 18,859 sq miles (48,845 sq km)
Languages Slovak*, Hungarian (Magyar), Czech
Religions Roman Catholic 69%, Other 13%, Nonreligious 13%, Greek Catholic (Uniate) 4%, Orthodox Christian 1%
Ethnic mix Slovak 86%, Magyar 10%, Roma 2%, Other 1%, Czech 1%
Government Parliamentary system
Currency Euro = 100 cents
Literacy rate 99%
Calorie consumption 2902 kilocalories

SOMALIA
East Africa

Page 51 E5

Italian and British Somaliland were united to create this semiarid state on the Horn of Africa. Anarchy since 1991 has caused mass hunger, a refugee crisis, and ineffective central authority.

Official name Federal Republic of Somalia
Formation 1960 / 1960
Capital Mogadishu
Population 10.5 million / 43 people per sq mile (17 people per sq km)
Total area 246,199 sq miles (637,657 sq km)
Languages Somali*, Arabic*, English, Ital an
Religions Sunni Muslim 99%, Christian 1%
Ethnic mix Somali 85%, Other 15%
Government Nonparty system
Currency Somali shilin = 100 senti
Literacy rate 24%
Calorie consumption 1696 kilocalories

SOUTH SUDAN
East Africa

Page 51 B5

Landlocked and little developed, this mostly Christian region seceded from the mainly Muslim north of Sudan in 2011 after years of civil war. Oil production is the economic mainstay.

Official name Republic of South Sudan
Formation 2011 / 2011
Capital Juba
Population 11.3 million / 45 people per sq mile (18 people per sq km)
Total area 248,777 sq miles (644,329 sq km)
Languages Arabic, Dinka, Nuer, Zande, Bari, Shilluk, Lotuko, English*
Religions Over 50% Christian/traditional be iefs
Ethnic mix Dinka 40%, Nuer 15%, Shilluk/Anwak 10%, Azande 10%, Arab 10%, Bari 10%, Other 5%
Government Transitional regime
Currency South Sudan Pound = 100 piastres
Literacy rate 37%
Calorie consumption Not available

SIERRA LEONE
West Africa

Page 52 C4

Founded in 1787 as a British colony for freed slaves, Sierra Leone gained independence in 1961. Recovery from civil war in the 1990s was set back in 2014 by West Africa's Ebola epidemic.

Official name Republic of Sierra Leone
Formation 1961 / 1961
Capital Freetown
Population 6.1 million / 221 people per sq mile (85 people per sq km)
Total area 27,698 sq miles (71,740 sq km)
Languages Mende, Temne, Krio, English*
Religions Muslim 60%, Christian 30%, Traditional beliefs 10%
Ethnic mix Mende 35%, Temne 32%, Other 21%, Limba 8%, Kuranko 4%
Government Presidential system
Currency Leone = 100 cents
Literacy rate 44%
Calorie consumption 2333 kilocalories

SLOVENIA
Central Europe

Page 73 D8

The northernmost of the ex-Yugoslav republics was the first to break away, with little violence, in 1991. It always had the closest links with Western Europe, and joined the EU in 2004.

Official name Republic of Slovenia
Formation 1991 / 1991
Capital Ljubljana
Population 2.1 million / 269 people per sq mile (104 people per sq km)
Total area 7820 sq miles (20,253 sq km)
Languages Slovenian*
Rel gions Roman Catholic 58%, Other 28%, Atheist 10%, Muslim 2%, Orthodox Christian 2%
Ethnic mix Slovene 83%, Other 12%, Serb 2%, Croat 2%, Bosnian 1%
Government Parliamentary system
Currency Euro = 100 cents
Literacy rate 99%
Calorie consumption 3173 kilocalories

SOUTH AFRICA
Southern Africa

Page 56 C4

Mineral-rich South Africa was settled by the Dutch and the British. Multiracial polls in 1994 ended decades of white minority rule and apartheid. AIDS, poverty, and crime are problems.

Official name Republic of South Africa
Formation 1934 / 1994
Capital Pretoria; Cape Town; Bloemfontein
Population 52.8 million / 112 people per sq mile (43 people per sq km)
Total area 471,008 sq miles (1,219,912 sq km)
Languages English*, isiZulu*, isiXhosa*, Afrikaans*, Sepedi*, Setswana*, Sesotho*, Xitsonga*, siSwati*, Tshivenda*, isiNdebele*
Religions Christian 68%, Traditional beliefs and animist 29%, Muslim 2%, Hindu 1%
Ethnic mix Black 80%, White 9%, Colored 9%, Asian 2%
Government Presidential system
Currency Rand = 100 cents
Literacy rate 94%
Calorie consumption 3007 kilocalories

SPAIN
Southwest Europe

Page 70 D2

At the gateway to the Mediterraneon, Spain became a world power once united in 1492. A vigorous regionalism now exists, with separatist movements in the Basque Country and Catalonia.

Official name Kingdom cf Spain
Formation 1492 / 1713
Capital Madrid
Population 46.9 million / 243 people per sq mile (94 people per sq km)
Total area 194,896 sq miles (504,782 sq km)
Languages Spanish*, Catalan*, Galician*, Basque*
Religions Roman Catholic 96%, Other 4%
Ethnic mix Castilian Span sh 72%, Catalan 17%, Galician 6%, Basque 2%, Other 2%, Roma 1%
Government Parliamentary system
Currency Euro = 100 cents
Literacy rate 98%
Calorie consumption 3183 kilocalories

SRI LANKA
South Asia

Page 110 D3

A former British colony, the island republic of Sri Lanka is separated from India by the narrow Palk Strait. A brutal 26-year civil war between the Sinhalese and Tamils ended in 2009.

Official name Democratic Socialist Republic of Sri Lanka
Formation 1948 / 1948
Capital Colombo; Sri Jayewardenapura Kotte
Population 21.3 million / 852 people per sq mile (329 people per sq km)
Total area 25,332 sq miles (65,610 sq km)
Languages Sinhala*, Tamil*, Sinhala-Tamil, English
Religions Buddhist 69%, Hindu 15%, Muslim 8%, Christian 8%
Ethnic mix Sinhalese 74%, Tamil 18%, Moor 7%, Other 1%
Government Presidential / parliamentary system
Currency Sri Lanka rupee = 100 cents
Literacy rate 91%
Calorie consumption 2488 kilocalories

SUDAN
East Africa

Page 50 B4

On the west coast of the Red Sea, Sudan has been ruled by a military Islamic regime since a coup in 1989. In 2011, it lost its southern third (and most of its oil reserves) after years of civil war.

Official name Republic of the Sudan
Formation 1956 / 2011
Capital Khartoum
Population 38 million / 53 people per sq mile (20 people per sq km)
Total area 718 722 sq miles (1,861,481 sq km)
Languages Arabic*, Nubian, Beja, Fur
Religions Almost 100% Muslim (mainly Sunni)
Ethnic mix Arab 60%, Other 18%, Nubian 10%, Beja 8%, Fur 3%, Zaghawa 1%
Government Presidential system
Currency New Sudanese pound = 100 piastres
Literacy rate 73%
Calorie consumption 2346 kilocalories

SURINAME
South America

Page 37 G3

This former Dutch colony on the north coast of South America has some of the world's richest bauxite reserves. Democracy was restored in 1991, after almost 11 years of military rule.

Official name Republic of Suriname
Formation 1975 / 1975
Capital Paramaribo
Population 500,000 / 8 people per sq mile (3 people per sq km)
Total area 63,039 sq miles (163,270 sq km)
Languages Sranan (creole), Dutch*, Javanese, Sarnami Hindi, Saramaccan, Chinese, Carib
Religions Hindu 27%, Protestant 25%, Roman Catholic 23%, Muslim 20%, Traditional beliefs 5%
Ethnic mix East Indian 27%, Creole 18%, Black 15%, Javanese 15%, Mixed race 13%, Other 12%
Government Presidential / parliamentary system
Currency Surinamese dollar = 100 cents
Literacy rate 95%
Calorie consumption 2727 kilocalories

SWAZILAND
Southern Africa

Page 56 D4

This tiny kingdom, ruled by Britain until 1968, depends economically on its neighbor South Africa. Its absolute monarch has banned political parties. It has the world's highest rate of HIV.

Official name Kingdom of Swaziland
Formation 1968 / 1968
Capital Mbabane
Population 1.2 million / 181 people per sq mile (70 people per sq km)
Total area 6704 sq miles (17,363 sq km)
Languages English*, siSwati*, isiZulu, Xitsonga
Religions Traditional beliefs 40%, Other 30%, Roman Catholic 20%, Muslim 10%
Ethnic mix Swazi 97%, Other 3%
Government Monarchy
Currency Lilangeni = 100 cents
Literacy rate 83%
Calorie consumption 2275 kilocalories

SWEDEN
Northern Europe

Page 62 B4

Densely forested Sweden is the largest and most populous Scandinavian country and stretches into the Arctic Circle. Its strong industrial base helps to fund its extensive welfare system.

Official name Kingdom of Sweden
Formation 1523 / 1921
Capital Stockholm
Population 9.6 million / 60 people per sq mile (23 people per sq km)
Total area 173,731 sq miles (449,964 sq km)
Languages Swedish*, Finnish, Sámi
Religions Evangelical Lutheran 75%, Other 13%, Muslim 5%, Other Protestant 5%, Roman Catholic 2%
Ethnic mix Swedish 86%, Foreign-born or first-generation immigrant 12%, Finnish & Sámi 2%
Government Parliamentary system
Currency Swedish krona = 100 öre
Literacy rate 99%
Calorie consumption 3160 kilocalories

SWITZERLAND
Central Europe

Page 73 A7

One of the world's richest countries, with a long tradition of neutrality, this mountainous nation lies at the center of Europe geographically, but outside it politically, having not joined the EU.

Official name Swiss Confederation
Formation 1291 / 1857
Capital Bern
Population 8.1 million / 528 people per sq mile (204 people per sq km)
Total area 15,942 sq miles (41,290 sq km)
Languages German*, Swiss-German, French*, Italian*, Romansch*
Religions Roman Catholic 42%, Protestant 35%, Other and nonreligious 19%, Muslim 4%
Ethnic mix German 64%, French 20%, Other 9.5%, Italian 6%, Romansch 0.5%
Government Parliamentary system
Currency Swiss franc = 100 rappen/centimes
Literacy rate 99%
Calorie consumption 3487 kilocalories

SYRIA
Southwest Asia

Page 96 B3

Syria's borders were drawn in 1941 at the end of French rule. Suppression of pro-democracy protests in 2011 erupted into civil war; in 2014 Islamist militias took control of the Euphrates Valley.

Official name Syrian Arab Republic
Formation 1941 / 1967
Capital Damascus
Population 21.9 million / 308 people per sq mile (119 people per sq km)
Total area 71,498 sq miles (184,180 sq km)
Languages Arabic*, French, Kurdish, Armenian, Circassian, Turkic languages, Assyrian, Aramaic
Religions Sunni Muslim 74%, Alawi 12%, Christian 10%, Druze 3%, Other 1%
Ethnic mix Arab 90%, Kurdish 9%, Armenian, Turkmen, and Circassian 1%
Government Presidential system
Currency Syrian pound = 100 piastres
Literacy rate 85%
Calorie consumption 3106 kilocalories

SWEDEN — (TAIWAN)

TAIWAN
East Asia

Page 107 D6

China's nationalist government fled to Taiwan in 1949 when ousted by the communists. China regards the island, 80 miles (130 km) southeast of the mainland, as a renegade province.

Official name Republic of China (ROC)
Formation 1949 / 1949
Capital Taipei
Population 23.3 million / 1871 people per sq mile (722 people per sq km)
Total area 13,892 sq miles (35,980 sq km)
Languages Amoy Chinese, Mandarin Chinese*, Hakka Chinese
Religions Buddhist, Confucianist, and Taoist 93%, Christian 5%, Other 2%
Ethnic mix Han (pre-20th-century migration) 84%, Han (20th-century migration) 14%, Aboriginal 2%
Government Presidential system
Currency Taiwan dollar = 100 cents
Literacy rate 98%
Calorie consumption 2959 kilocalories

TAJIKISTAN
Central Asia

Page 101 F3

The poorest of the ex-Soviet republics lies landlocked on the western slopes of the Pamirs. Tajiks are of Persian (Iranian) origin rather than Turkic like their Central Asian neighbors.

Official name Republic of Tajikistan
Formation 1991 / 1991
Capital Dushanbe
Population 8.2 million / 148 people per sq mile (57 people per sq km)
Total area 55,251 sq miles (143,100 sq km)
Languages Tajik*, Uzbek, Russian
Religions Sunni Muslim 95%, Shi'a Muslim 3%, Other 2%
Ethnic mix Tajik 80%, Uzbek 15%, Other 3%, Russian 1%, Kyrgyz 1%
Government Presidential system
Currency Somoni = 100 diram
Literacy rate 99%
Calorie consumption 2101 kilocalories

TANZANIA
East Africa

Page 51 B7

This East African state was formed in 1964 by the union of Tanganyika and Zanzibar. A third of its area is game reserve or national park, including Africa's highest peak, Mt. Kilimanjaro.

Official name United Republic of Tanzania
Formation 1964 / 1964
Capital Dodoma
Population 49.3 million / 144 people per sq mile (56 people per sq km)
Total area 364,898 sq miles (945,087 sq km)
Languages Kiswahili*, Sukuma, Chagga, Nyamwezi, Hehe, Makonde, Yao, Sandawe, English*
Religions Christian 63%, Muslim 35%, Other 2%
Ethnic mix Native African (over 120 tribes) 99%, European, Asian, and Arab 1%
Government Presidential system
Currency Tanzanian shilling = 100 cents
Literacy rate 68%
Calorie consumption 2167 kilocalories

THAILAND
Southeast Asia

Page 115 C5

Thailand lies at the heart of the Indochinese Peninsula. Formerly Siam, it has been an independent kingdom for most of its history. The military has frequently intervened in politics.

Official name Kingdom of Thailand
Formation 1238 / 1907
Capital Bangkok
Population 67 million / 340 people per sq mile (131 people per sq km)
Total area 198,455 sq miles (514,000 sq km)
Languages Thai*, Chinese, Malay, Khmer, Mon, Karen, Miao
Religions Buddhist 95%, Muslim 4%, Other (including Christian) 1%
Ethnic mix Thai 83%, Chinese 12%, Malay 3%, Khmer and Other 2%
Government Transitional regime
Currency Baht = 100 satang
Literacy rate 96%
Calorie consumption 2757 kilocalories

TOGO
West Africa

Page 53 F4

Togo lies sandwiched between Ghana and Benin in West Africa. Its long-term military leader, and then his son and successor, have won every election held there since 1993.

Official name Republic of Togo
Formation 1960 / 1960
Capital Lomé
Population 6.8 million / 324 people per sq mile (125 people per sq km)
Total area 21,924 sq miles (56,785 sq km)
Languages Ewe, Kabye, Gurma, French*
Religions Christian 47%, Traditional beliefs 33%, Muslim 14%, Other 6%
Ethnic mix Ewe 46%, Other African 41%, Kabye 12%, European 1%
Government Presidential system
Currency CFA franc = 100 centimes
Literacy rate 60%
Calorie consumption 2366 kilocalories

TONGA
Australasia & Oceania

Page 123 E4

Northeast of New Zealand, Tonga is a 170-island archipelago, 45 of which are inhabited. Politics is effectively controlled by the king, though limited democratic reforms are taking place.

Official name Kingdom of Tonga
Formation 1970 / 1970
Capital Nuku'alofa
Population 106,322 / 382 people per sq mile (148 people per sq km)
Total area 289 sq miles (748 sq km)
Languages English*, Tongan*
Religions Free Wesleyan 41%, Other 17%, Roman Catholic 16%, Church of Jesus Christ of Latter-day Saints 14%, Free Church of Tonga 12%
Ethnic mix Tongan 98%, Other 2%
Government Monarchy
Currency Pa'anga (Tongan dollar) = 100 seniti
Literacy rate 99%
Calorie consumption Not available

TRINIDAD AND TOBAGO
West Indies

Page 33 H5

This former British colony is the most southerly of the Windward Islands, just 9 miles (15 km) off the coast of Venezuela. Politics is mainly polarized by race. Oil and gas are exported.

Official name Republic of Trinidad and Tobago
Formation 1962 / 1962
Capital Port-of-Spain
Population 1.3 million / 656 people per sq mile (253 people per sq km)
Total area 1980 sq miles (5128 sq km)
Languages English Creole, English*, Hindi, French, Spanish
Religions Other 30%, Roman Catholic 26%, Hindu 23%, Anglican 8%, Baptist 7%, Muslim 6%
Ethnic mix East Indian 40%, Black 38%, Mixed race 20%, White and Chinese 1%, Other 1%
Government Parliamentary system
Currency Trinidad and Tobago dollar = 100 cents
Literacy rate 99%
Calorie consumption 2889 kilocalories

TUNISIA
North Africa

Page 49 E2

North Africa's smallest country, one of the more liberal yet stable Arab states, had only two post-independence rulers until the "Arab Spring" of 2011. Moderate Islamists then won power.

Official name Republic of Tunisia
Formation 1956 / 1956
Capital Tunis
Population 11 million / 183 people per sq mile (71 people per sq km)
Total area 63,169 sq miles (163,610 sq km)
Languages Arabic*, French
Religions Muslim (mainly Sunni) 98%, Christian 1%, Jewish 1%
Ethnic mix Arab and Berber 98%, European 1%, Jewish 1%
Government Transitional regime
Currency Tunisian dinar = 1000 millimes
Literacy rate 80%
Calorie consumption 3362 kilocalories

TURKEY
Asia / Europe

Page 94 B3

With land in Europe and Asia, Turkey guards the entrance to the Black Sea. The secular/Islamic divide is key to its politics. It is the only Muslim member of NATO, and hopes to join the EU.

Official name Republic of Turkey
Formation 1923 / 1939
Capital Ankara
Population 74.9 million / 252 people per sq mile (97 people per sq km)
Total area 301,382 sq miles (780,580 sq km)
Languages Turkish*, Kurdish, Arabic, Circassian, Armenian, Greek, Georgian, Ladino
Religions Muslim (mainly Sunni) 99%, Other 1%
Ethnic mix Turkish 70%, Kurdish 20%, Other 8%, Arab 2%
Government Parliamentary system
Currency Turkish lira = 100 kurus
Literacy rate 95%
Calorie consumption 3680 kilocalories

TURKMENISTAN
Central Asia

Page 100 B2

Stretching from the Caspian Sea into Central Asia's deserts, this ex-Soviet state exploits vast gas reserves. The pre-independence president built a personality cult and ruled until 2007.

Official name Turkmenistan
Formation 1991 / 1991
Capital Ashgabat
Population 5.2 million / 28 people per sq mile (11 people per sq km)
Total area 188,455 sq miles (488,100 sq km)
Languages Turkmen*, Uzbek, Russian, Kazakh, Tatar
Religions Sunni Muslim 89%, Orthodox Christian 9%, Other 2%
Ethnic mix Turkmen 85%, Other 6%, Uzbek 5%, Russian 4%
Government Presidential system
Currency New manat = 100 tenge
Literacy rate 99%
Calorie consumption 2883 kilocalories

TUVALU
Australasia & Oceania

Page 123 E3

Known as the Ellice Islands under British rule, Tuvalu is a chain of nine atolls in the Central Pacific. It has the world's smallest GNI, but made substancial earnings leasing its ".tv" internet suffix.

Official name Tuvalu
Formation 1978 / 1978
Capital Fongafale (Funafuti Atoll)
Population 10,698 / 1070 people per sq mile (411 people per sq km)
Total area 10 sq miles (26 sq km)
Languages Tuvaluan, Kiribati, English*
Religions Church of Tuvalu 97%, Other 1%, Baha'i 1%, Seventh-day Adventist 1%
Ethnic mix Polynesian 96%, Micronesian 4%
Government Nonparty system
Currency Australian dollar = 100 cents; Tuvaluan dollar = 100 cents
Literacy rate 98%
Calorie consumption Not available

UGANDA
East Africa

Page 51 B6

Landlocked Uganda faced ethnic strife under 1970s' dictator Idi Amin. From 1986, reconciliation was aided by two decades of "no-party" democracy, but insurgency continued in the north.

Official name Republic of Uganda
Formation 1962 / 1962
Capital Kampala
Population 37.6 million / 488 people per sq mile (188 people per sq km)
Total area 91,135 sq miles (236,040 sq km)
Languages Luganda, Nkole, Chiga, Lango, Acholi, Teso, Lugbara, English*
Religions Christian 85%, Muslim (mainly Sunni) 12%, Other 3%
Ethnic mix Other 50%, Baganda 17%, Banyakole 10%, Basoga 9%, Bakiga 7%, Iteso 7%
Government Parliamentary system
Currency Uganda shilling = 100 cents
Literacy rate 73%
Calorie consumption 2279 kilocalories

UKRAINE
Eastern Europe

Page 86 C2

Bordered by seven states, fertile Ukraine was the "breadbasket" of the USSR. Its political divide between pro-Russian sentiment and assertive nationalism exploded into civil war in 2014.

Official name Ukraine
Formation 1991 / 1991
Capital Kiev
Population 45.2 million / 194 people per sq mile (75 people per sq km)
Total area 223,089 sq miles (603,700 sq km)
Languages Ukrainian*, Russian, Tatar
Religions Christian (mainly Orthodox) 95%, Other 5%
Ethnic mix Ukrainian 78%, Russian 17%, Other 5%
Government Presidential system
Currency Hryvna = 100 kopiykas
Literacy rate 99%
Calorie consumption 3142 kilocalories

UNITED ARAB EMIRATES
Southwest Asia

Page 99 D5

Bordering the Persian Gulf on the north of the Arabian Peninsula, the United Arab Emirates is a federation of seven states. Wealth once relied on pearls, but oil and gas are now exported.

Official name United Arab Emirates
Formation 1971 / 1972
Capital Abu Dhabi
Population 9.3 million / 288 people per sq mile (111 people per sq km)
Total area 32,000 sq miles (82,880 sq km)
Languages Arabic*, Farsi, Indian and Pakistani languages, English
Religions Muslim (mainly Sunni) 96%, Christian, Hindu, and other 4%
Ethnic mix Asian 60%, Emirian 25%, Other Arab 12%, European 3%
Government Monarchy
Currency UAE dirham = 100 fils
Literacy rate 90%
Calorie consumption 3215 kilocalories

UNITED KINGDOM
Northwest Europe

Page 67 C5

Lying across the English Channel from France, the UK comprises England, Wales, Scotland, and Northern Ireland. Its prominent role in world affairs is a legacy of its once-vast empire.

Official name United Kingdom of Great Britain and Northern Ireland
Formation 1707 / 1922
Capital London
Population 63.1 million / 676 people per sq mile (261 people per sq km)
Total area 94,525 sq miles (244,820 sq km)
Languages English*, Welsh* (in Wales), Gaelic
Religions Anglican 45%, Other & nonreligious 39%, Roman Catholic 9%, Presbyterian 4%, Muslim 3%
Ethnic mix English 80%, Scottish 9%, West Indian, Asian, & other 5%, Welsh 3%, Northern Irish 3%
Government Parliamentary system
Currency Pound sterling = 100 pence
Literacy rate 99%
Calorie consumption 3414 kilocalories

UNITED STATES
North America

Page 13 B5

Stretching across the most temperate part of North America, and with many natural resources, the USA is the sole truly global superpower and has the world's largest economy.

Official name United States of America
Formation 1776 / 1959
Capital Washington D.C.
Population 320 million / 90 people per sq mile (35 people per sq km)
Total area 3,717,792 sq miles (9,626,091 sq km)
Languages English*, Spanish, Chinese, French, Polish, German, Tagalog, Vietnamese, Italian, Korean, Russian
Religions Protestant 52% Roman Catholic 25%, Other & nonreligious 20%, Jewish 2%, Muslim 1%
Ethnic mix White 60%, Hispanic 17%, Black American/African 14%, Asian 6%, Other 3%
Government Presidential system
Currency US dollar = 100 cents
Literacy rate 99%
Calorie consumption 3639 kilocalories

URUGUAY
South America

Page 42 D4

Uruguay, in southeastern South America, has much rich low-lying pasture land and is a major wool exporter. Military rule from 1973 to 1985 has given way to democracy.

Official name Eastern Republic of Uruguay
Formation 1828 / 1828
Capital Montevideo
Population 3.4 million / 50 people per sq mile (19 people per sq km)
Total area 68,039 sq miles (176,220 sq km)
Languages Spanish*
Religions Roman Catholic 66%, Other and nonreligious 30%, Jewish 2%, Protestant 2%
Ethnic mix White 90%, Mestizo 6%, Black 4%
Government Presidential system
Currency Uruguayan peso = 100 centésimos
Literacy rate 98%
Calorie consumption 2939 kilocalories

UZBEKISTAN
Central Asia

Page 100 D2

The most populous of the Central Asian republics lies on the ancient Silk Road between Asia and Europe. Today, its main exports are cotton and gold. Its pre-independence ruler retains power.

Official name Republic of Uzbekistan
Formation 1991 / 1991
Capital Tashkent
Population 28.9 million / 167 people per sq mile (65 people per sq km)
Total area 172,741 sq miles (447,400 sq km)
Languages Uzbek*, Russian, Tajik, Kazakh
Religions Sunni Muslim 88%, Orthodox Christian 9%, Other 3%
Ethnic mix Uzbek 80%, Other 6%, Russian 6%, Tajik 5%, Kazakh 3%
Government Presidential system
Currency Som = 100 tiyin
Literacy rate 99%
Calorie consumption 2675 kilocalories

VANUATU
Australasia & Oceania

Page 122 D4

This South Pacific archipelago of 82 islands and islets boasts the world's highest per capita density of languages. Until independence, it was under joint Anglo-French rule.

Official name Republic of Vanuatu
Formation 1980 / 1980
Capital Port Vila
Population 300,000 / 64 people per sq mile (25 people per sq km)
Total area 4710 sq miles (12,200 km)
Languages Bislama* (Melanesian pidgin), English*, French*, other indigenous languages
Religions Presbyterian 37%, Other 19%, Roman Catholic 15%, Anglican 15%, Traditional beliefs 8%, Seventh-day Adventist 6%
Ethnic mix ni-Vanuatu 94%, European 4%, Other 2%
Government Parliamentary system
Currency Vatu = 100 centimes
Literacy rate 83%
Calorie consumption 2820 kilocalories

VATICAN CITY
Southern Europe

Page 75 A8

The Vatican City, seat of the Roman Catholic Church, is a walled enclave in Rome. It is the world's smallest country. Its head, the pope, is elected for life by a college of cardinals.

Official name State of the Vatican City
Formation 1929 / 1929
Capital Vatican City
Population 839 / 4935 people per sq mile (1907 people per sq km)
Total area 0.17 sq miles (0.44 sq km)
Languages Italian*, Latin*
Religions Roman Catholic 100%
Ethnic mix Most resident lay persons are Italian
Government Papal state
Currency Euro = 100 cents
Literacy rate 99%
Calorie consumption Not available

VENEZUELA
South America

Page 36 D2

Located on the Caribbean coast of South America, Venezuela has the continent's most urbanized society, and some of the largest known oil deposits outside the Middle East.

Official name Bolivarian Republic of Venezuela
Formation 1830 / 1830
Capital Caracas
Population 30.4 million / 89 people per sq mile (34 people per sq km)
Total area 352,143 sq miles (912,050 sq km)
Languages Spanish*, Amerindian languages
Religions Roman Catholic 96%, Protestant 2%, Other 2%
Ethnic mix Mestizo 69%, White 20%, Black 9%, Amerindian 2%
Government Presidential system
Currency Bolívar fuerte = 100 céntimos
Literacy rate 96%
Calorie consumption 2880 kilocalories

VIETNAM
Southeast Asia

Page 114 D4

The eastern strip of the Indochinese Peninsula, Vietnam was partitioned in 1954, and only reunited after the communist north's victory in the devastating 1962–75 Vietnam War.

Official name Socialist Republic of Vietnam
Formation 1976 / 1976
Capital Hanoi
Population 91.7 million / 730 people per sq mile (282 people per sq km)
Total area 127,243 sq miles (329,560 sq km)
Languages Vietnamese*, Chinese, Thai, Khmer, Muong, Nung, Miao, Yao, Jarai
Religions Other 74%, Buddhist 14%, Roman Catholic 7%, Cao Dai 3%, Protestant 2%
Ethnic mix Vietnamese 86%, Other 8%, Thai 2%, Muong 2%, Tay 2%
Government One-party state
Currency Đồng = 10 hao = 100 xu
Literacy rate 94%
Calorie consumption 2703 kilocalories

YEMEN
Southwest Asia

Page 99 C7

The Arab world's only Marxist regime and a military-run republic united in 1990 to form Yemen, stretching across southern Arabia. Islamist militants and tribal insurgency threaten its stability.

Official name Republic of Yemen
Formation 1990 / 1990
Capital Sana
Population 24.4 million / 112 people per sq mile (43 people per sq km)
Total area 203,849 sq miles (527,970 sq km)
Languages Arabic*
Religions Sunni Muslim 55%, Shi'a Muslim 42%, Christian, Hindu, and Jewish 3%
Ethnic mix Arab 99%, Afro-Arab, Indian, Somali, and European 1%
Government Transitional regime
Currency Yemeni rial = 100 fils
Literacy rate 66%
Calorie consumption 2185 kilocalories

ZAMBIA
Southern Africa

Page 56 C2

Landlocked in southern Africa, copper-rich Zambia (once known as Northern Rhodesia) has seen its politics dogged by corruption both before and after the end of single-party rule in 1991.

Official name Republic of Zambia
Formation 1964 / 1964
Capital Lusaka
Population 14.5 million / 51 people per sq mile (20 people per sq km)
Total area 290,584 sq miles (752,614 sq km)
Languages Bemba, Tonga, Nyanja, Lozi, Lala-Bisa, Nsenga, English*
Religions Christian 63%, Traditional beliefs 36%, Muslim and Hindu 1%
Ethnic mix Bemba 34%, Other African 26%, Tonga 16%, Nyanja 14%, Lozi 9%, European 1%
Government Presidential system
Currency New Zambian kwacha = 100 ngwee
Literacy rate 61%
Calorie consumption 1937 kilocalories

ZIMBABWE
Southern Africa

Page 56 D3

Full independence from Britain in 1980 ended 15 years of troubled white-minority rule. Poor governance, violent land redistribution, and severe drought have destroyed the economy.

Official name Republic of Zimbabwe
Formation 1980 / 1980
Capital Harare
Population 14.1 million / 94 people per sq mile (36 people per sq km)
Total area 150,803 sq miles (390,580 sq km)
Languages Shona, isiNdebele, English*
Religions Syncretic 50%, Christian 25%, Traditional beliefs 24%, Other (including Muslim) 1%
Ethnic mix Shona 71%, Ndebele 16%, Other African 11%, White 1%, Asian 1%
Government Presidential system
Currency Zimbabwe dollar suspended in 2009; nine other currencies are legal tender
Literacy rate 84%
Calorie consumption 2210 kilocalories

Overseas Territories and Dependencies

Despite the rapid process of decolonization since the end of the Second World War, around 10 million people in more than 50 territories around the world continue to live under the protection of a parent state.

AUSTRALIA

ASHMORE & CARTIER ISLANDS
Indian Ocean
Claimed 1931
Capital not applicable
Area 2 sq miles (5 sq km)
Population None

CHRISTMAS ISLAND
Indian Ocean
Claimed 1958
Capital The Settlement
Area 52 sq miles (135 sq km)
Population 1530

COCOS ISLANDS
Indian Ocean
Claimed 1955
Capital West Island
Area 5.5 sq miles (14 sq km)
Population 596

CORAL SEA ISLANDS
Southwest Pacific
Claimed 1969
Capital None
Area Less than 1.2 sq miles (3 sq km)
Population below 10 (scientists)

HEARD & McDONALD ISLANDS
Indian Ocean
Claimed 1947
Capital not applicable
Area 161 sq miles (417 sq km)
Population None

NORFOLK ISLAND
Southwest Pacific
Claimed 1774
Capital Kingston
Area 13.3 sq miles (34 sq km)
Population 2210

DENMARK

FAROE ISLANDS
North Atlantic
Claimed 1380
Capital Tórshavn
Area 540 sq miles (1399 sq km)
Population 49,469

GREENLAND
North Atlantic
Claimed 1380
Capital Nuuk
Area 840,000 sq miles (2,175,516 sq km)
Population 56,483

FRANCE

CLIPPERTON ISLAND
East Pacific
Claimed 1935
Capital not applicable
Area 2.7 sq miles (7 sq km)
Population None

FRENCH GUIANA
South America
Claimed 1817
Capital Cayenne
Area 35,135 sq miles (90,996 sq km)
Population 250,109

FRENCH POLYNESIA
South Pacific
Claimed 1843
Capital Papeete
Area 1,608 sq miles (4165 sq km)
Population 276,831

GUADELOUPE
West Indies
Claimed 1635
Capital Basse-Terre
Area 629 sq miles (1628 sq km)
Population 405,739

MARTINIQUE
West Indies
Claimed 1635
Capital Fort-de-France
Area 425 sq miles (1100 sq km)
Population 386,486

MAYOTTE
Indian Ocean
Claimed 1843
Capital Mamoudzou
Area 144 sq miles (374 sq km)
Population 212,645

NEW CALEDONIA
Southwest Pacific
Claimed 1853
Capital Nouméa
Area 7,374 sq miles (19,103 sq km)
Population 262,000

RÉUNION
Indian Ocean
Claimed 1638
Capital Saint-Denis
Area 970 sq miles (2512 sq km)
Population 840,974

ST. PIERRE & MIQUELON
North America
Claimed 1604
Capital Saint-Pierre
Area 93 sq miles (242 sq km)
Population 5716

WALLIS & FUTUNA
South Pacific
Claimed 1842
Capital Matá'Utu
Area 106 sq miles (274 sq km)
Population 15,561

NETHERLANDS

ARUBA
West Indies
Claimed 1643
Capital Oranjestad
Area 75 sq miles (194 sq km)
Population 102,911

BONAIRE
West Indies
Claimed 1816
Capital Kralendijk
Area 113 sq miles (294 sq km)
Population 18,413

CURAÇAO
West Indies
Claimed 1815
Capital Willemstad
Area 171 sq miles (444 sq km)
Population 153,500

SABA
West Indies
Claimed 1816
Capital The Bottom
Area 5 sq miles (13 sq km)
Population 1846

SINT-EUSTATIUS
West Indies
Claimed 1784
Capital Oranjestad
Area 8 sq miles (21 sq km)
Population 4020

SINT-MAARTEN
West Indies
Claimed 1648
Capital Phillipsburg
Area 13 sq miles (34 sq km)
Population 39,689

NEW ZEALAND

COOK ISLANDS
South Pacific
Claimed 1901
Capital Avarua
Area 91 sq miles (235 sq km)
Population 13,700

NIUE
South Pacific
Claimed 1901
Capital Alofi
Area 102 sq miles (264 sq km)
Population 1190

TOKELAU
South Pacific
Claimed 1926
Capital not applicable
Area 4 sq miles (10 sq km)
Population 1337

NORWAY

BOUVET ISLAND
South Atlantic
Claimed 1928
Capital not applicable
Area 22 sq miles (58 sq km)
Population None

JAN MAYEN
North Atlantic
Claimed 1929
Capital not applicable
Area 147 sq miles (381 sq km)
Population 18 (scientists)

PETER I ISLAND
Antarctica
Claimed 1931
Capital not applicable
Area 69 sq miles (180 sq km)
Population None

SVALBARD
Arctic Ocean
Claimed 1920
Capital Longyearbyen
Area 24,289 sq miles (62,906 sq km)
Population 1872

UNITED KINGDOM

ANGUILLA
West Indies
Claimed 1650
Capital The Valley
Area 37 sq miles (96 sq km)
Population 16,086

ASCENSION ISLAND
South Atlantic
Claimed 1673
Capital Georgetown
Area 34 sq miles (88 sq km)
Population 880

BERMUDA
North Atlantic
Claimed 1612
Capital Hamilton
Area 20 sq miles (53 sq km)
Population 65,024

BRITISH INDIAN OCEAN TERRITORY
Indian Ocean
Claimed 1814
Capital Diego Garcia
Area 23 sq miles (60 sq km)
Population 4000

BRITISH VIRGIN ISLANDS
West Indies
Claimed 1672
Capital Road Town
Area 59 sq miles (153 sq km)
Population 32,680

CAYMAN ISLANDS
West Indies
Claimed 1670
Capital George Town
Area 100 sq miles (259 sq km)
Population 58,435

FALKLAND ISLANDS
South Atlantic
Claimed 1832
Capital Stanley
Area 4699 sq miles (12,173 sq km)
Population 2840

GIBRALTAR
Southwest Europe
Claimed 1713
Capital Gibraltar
Area 2.5 sq miles (6.5 sq km)
Population 29,185

GUERNSEY
Northwest Europe
Claimed 1066
Capital St Peter Port
Area 25 sq miles (65 sq km)
Population 65,849

ISLE OF MAN
Northwest Europe
Claimed 1765
Capital Douglas
Area 221 sq miles (572 sq km)
Population 85,888

JERSEY
Northwest Europe
Claimed 1066
Capital St. Helier
Area 45 sq miles (116 sq km)
Population 96,513

MONTSERRAT
West Indies
Claimed 1632
Capital Brades (de facto); Plymouth (de jure)
Area 40 sq miles (102 sq km)
Population 5215

PITCAIRN GROUP OF ISLANDS
South Pacific
Claimed 1887
Capital Adamstown
Area 18 sq miles (47 sq km)
Population 48

ST. HELENA
South Atlantic
Claimed 1673
Capital Jamestown
Area 47 sq miles (122 sq km)
Population 3800

SOUTH GEORGIA & THE SOUTH SANDWICH ISLANDS
South Atlantic
Capital not applicable
Claimed 1775
Area 1387 sq miles (3592 sq km)
Population None

TRISTAN DA CUNHA
South Atlantic
Claimed 1612
Capital Edinburgh
Area 38 sq miles (98 sq km)
Population 264

TURKS & CAICOS ISLANDS
West Indies
Claimed 1766
Capital Cockburn Town
Area 166 sq miles (430 sq km)
Population 33,098

UNITED STATES OF AMERICA

AMERICAN SAMOA
South Pacific
Claimed 1900
Capital Pago Pago
Area 75 sq miles (195 sq km)
Population 55,165

BAKER & HOWLAND ISLANDS
Central Pacific
Claimed 1856
Capital not applicable
Area 0.54 sq miles (1.4 sq km)
Population None

GUAM
West Pacific
Claimed 1898
Capital Hagåtña
Area 212 sq miles (549 sq km)
Population 165,124

JARVIS ISLAND
Central Pacific
Claimed 1856
Capital not applicable
Area 1.7 sq miles (4.5 sq km)
Population None

NORTHERN MARIANA ISLANDS
West Pacific
Claimed 1947
Capital Saipan
Area 177 sq miles (457 sq km)
Population 53,855

PALMYRA ATOLL
Central Pacific
Claimed 1898
Capital not applicable
Area 5 sq miles (12 sq km)
Population None

PUERTO RICO
West Indies
Claimed 1898
Capital San Juan
Area 3515 sq miles (9104 sq km)
Population 3.62 million

VIRGIN ISLANDS
West Indies
Claimed 1917
Capital Charlotte Amalie
Area 137 sq miles (355 sq km)
Population 104,737

WAKE ISLAND
Central Pacific
Claimed 1898
Capital not applicable
Area 2.5 sq miles (6.5 sq km)
Population 150 (US air base)

Geographical comparisons

Largest countries

Russian Federation	6,592,735 sq miles	(17,075,200 sq km)
Canada	3,855,171 sq miles	(9,984,670 sq km)
USA	3,717,792 sq miles	(9,626,091 sq km)
China	3,705,386 sq miles	(9,596,960 sq km)
Brazil	3,286,470 sq miles	(8,511,965 sq km)
Australia	2,967,893 sq miles	(7,686,850 sq km)
India	1,269,338 sq miles	(3,287,590 sq km)
Argentina	1,068,296 sq miles	(2,766,890 sq km)
Kazakhstan	1,049,150 sq miles	(2,717,300 sq km)
Algeria	919,590 sq miles	(2,381,740 sq km)

Smallest countries

Vatican City	0.17 sq miles	(0.44 sq km)
Monaco	0.75 sq miles	(1.95 sq km)
Nauru	8 sq miles	(21 sq km)
Tuvalu	10 sq miles	(26 sq km)
San Marino	24 sq miles	(61 sq km)
Liechtenstein	62 sq miles	(160 sq km)
Marshall Islands	70 sq miles	(181 sq km)
St. Kitts & Nevis	101 sq miles	(261 sq km)
Maldives	116 sq miles	(300 sq km)
Malta	122 sq miles	(316 sq km)

Largest islands

Greenland	840,000 sq miles (2,175,600 sq km)
New Guinea	312,000 sq miles (808,000 sq km)
Borneo	292,222 sq miles (757,050 sq km)
Madagascar	226,656 sq miles (587,040 sq km)
Sumatra	202,300 sq miles (524,000 sq km)
Baffin Island	183,800 sq miles (476,000 sq km)
Honshu	88,800 sq miles (230,000 sq km)
Britain	88,700 sq miles (229,800 sq km)
Victoria Island	81,900 sq miles (212,000 sq km)
Ellesmere Island	75,700 sq miles (196,000 sq km)

Richest countries

(GNI per capita, in US$)

Monaco	186,950
Liechtenstein	136,770
Norway	102,610
Switzerland	86,600
Qatar	85,550
Luxembourg	71,810
Australia	65,520
Denmark	61,160
Sweden	59,240
Singapore	54,040

Poorest countries

(GNI per capita, in US$)

Malawi	270
Burundi	280
Somalia	288
Central African Republic	320
Congo, Democratic Republic	400
Niger	410
Liberia	410
Madagascar	440
Guinea	460
Ethiopia	470

Most populous countries

China	1.386 billion
India	1.252 billion
USA	320 million
Indonesia	250 million
Brazil	200 million
Pakistan	182 million

Most populous countries *continued*

Nigeria	174 million
Bangladesh	157 million
Russian Federation	143 million
Japan	127 million

Least populous countries

Vatican City	839
Nauru	9434
Tuvalu	10,698
Palau	21,108
San Marino	32,448
Monaco	36,136
Liechtenstein	37,000
St. Kitts & Nevis	51,134
Marshall Islands	69,747
Dominica	73,286

Most densely populated countries

Monaco	48,181 people per sq mile (18,531 per sq km)
Singapore	22,881 people per sq mile (8852 per sq km)
Vatican City	4935 people per sq mile (1907 per sq km)
Bahrain	4762 people per sq mile (1841 per sq km)
Malta	3226 people per sq mile (1250 per sq km)
Bangladesh	3029 people per sq mile (1169 per sq km)
Maldives	2586 people per sq mile (1000 per sq km)
Taiwan	1871 people per sq mile (722 per sq km)
Barbados	1807 people per sq mile (698 per sq km)
Mauritius	1671 people per sq mile (645 per sq km)

Most sparsely populated countries

Mongolia	5 people per sq mile (2 per sq km)
Namibia	7 people per sq mile (3 per sq km)
Iceland	8 people per sq mile (3 per sq km)
Suriname	8 people per sq mile (3 per sq km)
Australia	8 people per sq mile (3 per sq km)
Botswana	9 people per sq mile (4 per sq km)
Libya	9 people per sq mile (4 per sq km)
Mauritania	10 people per sq mile (4 per sq km)
Canada	10 people per sq mile (4 per sq km)
Guyana	11 people per sq mile (4 per sq km)

Most widely spoken languages

1. Chinese (Mandarin)	6. Portuguese
2. Spanish	7. Bengali
3. English	8. Russian
4. Hindi	9. Japanese
5. Arabic	10. Javanese

Largest conurbations

Tokyo (Japan)	39,400,000
Guangzhou (China)	32,600,000
Shanghai (China)	29,600,000
Jakarta (Indonesia)	27,000,000
Delhi (India)	25,300,000
Seoul (South Korea)	24,200,000
Karachi (Pakistan)	23,200,000
Mumbai (India)	22,600,000
Manila (Philippines)	22,500,000
Mexico City (Mexico)	22,200,000
New York (USA)	21,800,000
São Paulo (Brazil)	21,700,000
Beijing (China)	19,900,000
Osaka (Japan)	17,800,000
Los Angeles (USA)	17,300,000
Dhaka (Bangladesh)	16,700,000
Moscow (Russian Federation)	16,700,000
Cairo (Egypt)	16,400,000

Longest rivers

Nile (Northeast Africa)	4160 miles	(6695 km)
Amazon (South America)	4049 miles	(6516 km)
Yangtze (China)	3915 miles	(6299 km)
Mississippi/Missouri (USA)	3710 miles	(5969 km)
Ob'-Irtysh (Russian Federation)	3461 miles	(5570 km)
Yellow River (China)	3395 miles	(5464 km)
Congo (Central Africa)	2900 miles	(4667 km)
Mekong (Southeast Asia)	2749 miles	(4425 km)
Lena (Russian Federation)	2734 miles	(4400 km)
Mackenzie (Canada)	2640 miles	(4250 km)
Yenisey (Russian Federation)	2541 miles	(4090 km)

Highest mountains

(Height above sea level)

Everest	29,035 ft	(8850 m)
K2	28,253 ft	(8611 m)
Kanchenjunga I	28,210 ft	(8598 m)
Makalu I	27,767 ft	(8463 m)
Cho Oyu	26,907 ft	(8201 m)
Dhaulagiri I	26,796 ft	(8167 m)
Manaslu I	26,783 ft	(8163 m)
Nanga Parbat I	26,661 ft	(8126 m)
Annapurna I	26,547 ft	(8091 m)
Gasherbrum I	26,471 ft	(8068 m)

Largest bodies of inland water

(Area & depth)

Caspian Sea	143,243 sq miles (371,000 sq km)	3215 ft (980 m)
Lake Superior	32,151 sq miles (83,270 sq km)	1289 ft (393 m)
Lake Victoria	26,560 sq miles (68,880 sq km)	328 ft (100 m)
Lake Huron	23,436 sq miles (60,700 sq km)	751 ft (229 m)
Lake Michigan	22,402 sq miles (58,020 sq km)	922 ft (281 m)
Lake Tanganyika	12,703 sq miles (32,900 sq km)	4700 ft (1435 m)
Great Bear Lake	12,274 sq miles (31,790 sq km)	1047 ft (319 m)
Lake Baikal	11,776 sq miles (30,500 sq km)	5712 ft (1741 m)
Great Slave Lake	10,981 sq miles (28,440 sq km)	459 ft (140 m)
Lake Erie	9915 sq miles (25,680 sq km)	197 ft (60 m)

Deepest ocean features

Challenger Deep, Mariana Trench (Pacific)	36,201 ft (11,034 m)
Vityaz III Depth, Tonga Trench (Pacific)	35,704 ft (10,882 m)
Vityaz Depth, Kurile-Kamchatka Trench (Pacific)	34,588 ft (10,542 m)
Cape Johnson Deep, Philippine Trench (Pacific)	34,441 ft (10,497 m)
Kermadec Trench (Pacific)	32,964 ft (10,047 m)
Ramapo Deep, Japan Trench (Pacific)	32,758 ft (9984 m)
Milwaukee Deep, Puerto Rico Trench (Atlantic)	30,185 ft (9200 m)
Argo Deep, Torres Trench (Pacific)	30,070 ft (9165 m)
Meteor Depth, South Sandwich Trench (Atlantic)	30,000 ft (9144 m)
Planet Deep, New Britain Trench (Pacific)	29,988 ft (9140 m)

Greatest waterfalls

(Mean flow of water)

Boyoma (Congo, Dem. Rep.)	600,400 cu. ft/sec (17,000 cu.m/sec)
Khône (Laos/Cambodia)	410,000 cu. ft/sec (11,600 cu.m/sec)
Niagara (USA/Canada)	195,000 cu. ft/sec (5500 cu.m/sec)
Grande (Uruguay)	160,000 cu. ft/sec (4500 cu.m/sec)
Paulo Afonso (Brazil)	100,000 cu. ft/sec (2800 cu.m/sec)
Urubupunga (Brazil)	97,000 cu. ft/sec (2750 cu.m/sec)
Iguaçu (Argentina/Brazil)	62,000 cu. ft/sec (1700 cu.m/sec)
Maribondo (Brazil)	53,000 cu. ft/sec (1500 cu.m/sec)
Victoria (Zimbabwe)	39,000 cu. ft/sec (1100 cu.m/sec)

Greatest waterfalls *continued*

Kabalega (Uganda)	42,000 cu. ft/sec (1200 cu.m/sec)
Churchill (Canada)	35,000 cu. ft/sec (1000 cu.m/sec)
Cauvery (India)	33,000 cu. ft/sec (900 cu.m/sec)

Highest waterfalls

Angel (Venezuela)	3212 ft	(979 m)
Tugela (South Africa)	3110 ft	(948 m)
Utigard (Norway)	2625 ft	(800 m)
Mongefossen (Norway)	2539 ft	(774 m)
Mtarazi (Zimbabwe)	2500 ft	(762 m)
Yosemite (USA)	2425 ft	(739 m)
Ostre Mardola Foss (Norway)	2156 ft	(657 m)
Tyssestrengane (Norway)	2119 ft	(646 m)
*Cuquenan (Venezuela)	2001 ft	(610 m)
Sutherland (New Zealand)	1903 ft	(580 m)
*Kjellfossen (Norway)	1841 ft	(561 m)

indicates that the total height is a single leap

Largest deserts

Sahara	3,450,000 sq miles (9,065,000 sq km)
Gobi	500,000 sq miles (1,295,000 sq km)
Ar Rub al Khali	289,600 sq miles (750,000 sq km)
Great Victorian	249,800 sq miles (647,000 sq km)
Sonoran	120,000 sq miles (311,000 sq km)
Kalahari	120,000 sq miles (310,800 sq km)
Garagum	115,800 sq miles (300,000 sq km)
Takla Makan	100,400 sq miles (260,000 sq km)
Namib	52,100 sq miles (135,000 sq km)
Thar	33,670 sq miles (130,000 sq km)

NB – Most of Antarctica is a polar desert, with only 2 inches (50 mm) of precipitation annually

Hottest inhabited places

Djibouti (Djibouti)	86.0°F	(30.0°C)
Timbouctou (Mali)	84.7°F	(29.3°C)
Tirunelveli (India)	84.7°F	(29.3°C)
Tuticorin (India)	84.7°F	(29.3°C)
Nellore (India)	84.5°F	(29.2°C)
Santa Marta (Colombia)	84.5°F	(29.2°C)
Aden (Yemen)	84.0°F	(29.0°C)
Madurai (India)	84.0°F	(29.0°C)
Niamey (Niger)	84.0°F	(29.0°C)

Driest inhabited places

Aswân (Egypt)	0.02 in	(0.5 mm)
Luxor (Egypt)	0.03 in	(0.7 mm)
Arica (Chile)	0.04 in	(1.1 mm)
Ica (Peru)	0.10 in	(2.3 mm)
Antofagasta (Chile)	0.20 in	(4.9 mm)
El Minya (Egypt)	0.20 in	(5.1 mm)
Asyût (Egypt)	0.20 in	(5.2 mm)
Callao (Peru)	0.50 in	(12.0 mm)
Trujillo (Peru)	0.55 in	(14.0 mm)
El Faiyûm (Egypt)	0.80 in	(19.0 mm)

Wettest inhabited places

Buenaventura (Colombia)	265 in	(6743 mm)
Monrovia (Liberia)	202 in	(5131 mm)
Pago Pago (American Samoa)	196 in	(4990 mm)
Moulmein (Myanmar)	191 in	(4852 mm)
Lae (Papua New Guinea)	183 in	(4645 mm)
Baguio (Luzon I., Philippines)	180 in	(4573 mm)
Sylhet (Bangladesh)	176 in	(4457 mm)
Padang (Sumatra, Indonesia)	166 in	(4225 mm)
Bogor (Java, Indonesia)	166 in	(4225 mm)
Conakry (Guinea)	171 in	(4341 mm)

Aa – Almere

A

Aa see Gauja
Aachen 72 A4 Dut. Aken, Fr. Aix-la-Chapelle; anc. Aquae Grani, Aquisgranum. Nordrhein-Westfalen, W Germany
Aaiún see Laâyoune
Aalborg 63 B7 var. Ålborg, Ålborg-Nørresundby; anc. Alburgum. Nordjylland, N Denmark
Aalen 73 B6 Baden-Württemberg, S Germany
Aalsmeer 64 C3 Noord-Holland, C Netherlands
Aalst 65 B6 Oost-Vlaanderen, C Belgium
Aalten 64 E4 Gelderland, E Netherlands
Aalter 65 B5 Oost-Vlaanderen, NW Belgium
Aanaarjärvi see Inarijärvi
Äänekoski 63 D5 Länsi-Suomi, W Finland
Aar see Aare
Aare 73 A7 var. Aar. river W Switzerland
Aarhus see Århus
Aarlen see Arlon
Aat see Ath
Aba 55 E5 Orientale, NE Dem. Rep. Congo
Aba 53 G5 Abia, S Nigeria
Abā as Su'ūd see Najrān
Abaco Island see Great Abaco, N Bahamas
Ābādān 98 C4 Khūzestān, SW Iran
Abadan 100 C3 prev. Bezmein, Büzmeýin, Rus. Byuzmeyin. Ahal Welaýaty, C Turkmenistan
Abai see Blue Nile
Abakan 92 D4 Respublika Khakasiya, S Russian Federation
Abancay 38 D4 Apurímac, SE Peru
Abariringa see Kanton
Abashiri 108 D2 var. Abasiri. Hokkaidō, NE Japan
Abasiri see Abashiri
Ābay Wenz see Blue Nile
Abbaia see Ābaya Hāyk'
Abbatis Villa see Abbeville
Abbazia see Opatija
Abbeville 68 C2 anc. Abbatis Villa. Somme, N France
'Abd al 'Azīz, Jabal 96 D2 mountain range NE Syria
Abéché 54 C3 var. Abécher, Abeshr. Ouaddaï, SE Chad
Abécher see Abéché
Abela see Ávila
Abellinum see Avellino
Abemama 122 D2 var. Apamama; prev. Roger Simpson Island. atoll Tungaru, W Kiribati
Abengourou 53 E5 E Côte d'Ivoire
Aberbrothock see Arbroath
Abercorn see Mbala
Aberdeen 66 D3 anc. Devana. NE Scotland, United Kingdom
Aberdeen 23 E2 South Dakota, N USA
Aberdeen 24 B2 Washington, NW USA
Abergwaun see Fishguard
Abertawe see Swansea
Aberystwyth 67 C6 W Wales, United Kingdom
Abeshr see Abéché
Abhā 99 B6 'Asīr, SW Saudi Arabia
Abidavichy 85 D7 Rus. Obidovichi. Mahilyowskaya Voblasts', E Belarus
Abidjan 53 E5 S Côte d'Ivoire
Abilene 27 F3 Texas, SW USA
Abingdon see Pinta, Isla
Abkhazia see Ap'khazet'i
Åbo see Turku
Aboisso 53 E5 SE Côte d'Ivoire
Abo, Massif d' 54 B1 mountain range NW Chad
Abomey 53 F5 S Benin
Abou-Déïa 54 C3 Salamat, SE Chad
Aboudouhour see Abū aḍ Ḍuhūr
Abou Kémal see Abū Kamāl
Abrantes 70 B3 var. Abrántes. Santarém, C Portugal
Abrashlare see Brezovo
Abrolhos Bank 34 E4 undersea bank W Atlantic Ocean
Abrova 85 B6 Rus. Obrovo. Brestskaya Voblasts', SW Belarus
Abrud 86 B4 Ger. Gross-Schlatten, Hung. Abrudbánya. Alba, SW Romania
Abrudbánya see Abrud
Abruzzese, Appennino 74 C4 mountain range C Italy
Absaroka Range 22 B2 mountain range Montana/Wyoming, NW USA
Abū aḍ Ḍuhūr 96 B3 Fr. Aboudouhour. Idlib, NW Syria
Abu Dhabi see Abū Ẓabī
Abu Hamed 50 C3 River Nile, N Sudan
Abū Ḥardān 96 E3 var. Hajîne. Dayr az Zawr, E Syria
Abuja 53 G4 country capital (Nigeria) Federal Capital District, C Nigeria
Abū Kamāl 96 E3 Fr. Abou Kémal. Dayr az Zawr, E Syria
Abula see Ávila
Abunã, Rio 40 C2 var. Río Abuná. river Bolivia/Brazil
Abut Head 129 B6 headland South Island, New Zealand
Abuye Meda 50 D4 mountain C Ethiopia
Abū Ẓabī 99 C5 var. Abū Ẓabī, Eng. Abu Dhabi. country capital (United Arab Emirates) Abū Ẓaby, C United Arab Emirates
Abū Ẓabī see Abū Ẓabī
Abyad, Al Baḥr al see White Nile
Abyla see Ávila
Abyssinia see Ethiopia
Acalayong 55 A5 SW Equatorial Guinea
Acaponeta 28 D4 Nayarit, C Mexico
Acapulco 29 E5 var. Acapulco de Juárez. Guerrero, S Mexico
Acapulco de Juárez see Acapulco
Acarai Mountains 37 F4 Sp. Serra Acaraí. mountain range Brazil/Guyana
Acaraí, Serra see Acarai Mountains
Acarigua 36 D2 Portuguesa, N Venezuela
Accra 53 E5 country capital (Ghana) SE Ghana
Achacachi 39 E4 La Paz, W Bolivia
Achara 95 F2 var. Ajaria. autonomous republic SW Georgia
Acklins Island 32 C2 island SE Bahamas
Aconcagua, Cerro 42 B4 mountain W Argentina
Açores/Açores, Arquipélago dos/Açores, Ilhas dos see Azores
A Coruña 70 B1 Cast. La Coruña, Eng. Corunna; anc. Caronium. Galicia, NW Spain
Acre 40 C2 off. Estado do Acre. state W Brazil
Açu see Assu
Acunum Acusio see Montélimar
Ada 78 D3 Vojvodina, N Serbia
Ada 27 G2 Oklahoma, C USA
Ada Bazar see Adapazarı
Adalia see Antalya
Adalia, Gulf of see Antalya Körfezi
Adama see Nazrēt
'Adan 99 B7 Eng. Aden. SW Yemen
Adana 94 D4 var. Seyhan. Adana, S Turkey
Adâncata see Horlivka
Adapazarı 94 B2 prev. Ada Bazar. Sakarya, NW Turkey
Adare, Cape 132 B4 cape Antarctica
Ad Dahna 98 C4 desert E Saudi Arabia
Ad Dakhla 48 A4 var. Dakhla. SW Western Sahara
Ad Dalanj see Dilling
Ad Damar see Ed Damer
Ad Damazīn see Ed Damazin
Ad Dāmir see Ed Damer
Ad Dammān 98 C4 var. Dammām. Ash Sharqīyah, NE Saudi Arabia
Ad Dāmūr see Damoûr
Ad Dawḥah 98 C4 Eng. Doha. country capital (Qatar) C Qatar
Aḍ Ḍiffah see Libyan Plateau
Addis Ababa see Ādīs Ābeba
Addoo Atoll see Addu Atoll
Addu Atoll 110 A5 var. Addoo Atoll, Seenu Atoll. atoll S Maldives
Adelaide 127 B6 state capital South Australia
Adelsberg see Postojna
Aden see 'Adan
Aden, Gulf of 99 C7 gulf SW Arabian Sea
Adige 74 C2 Ger. Etsch. river N Italy
Adirondack Mountains 19 F2 mountain range New York, NE USA
Ādīs Ābeba 51 C5 Eng. Addis Ababa. country capital (Ethiopia) Ādīs Ābeba, C Ethiopia
Adıyaman 95 E4 Adıyaman, SE Turkey
Adjud 86 C4 Vrancea, E Romania
Admiralty Islands 122 B3 island group N Papua New Guinea
Adra 71 E5 Andalucía, S Spain
Adrar 48 D3 C Algeria
Adrian 18 C3 Michigan, N USA
Adrianople/Adrianopolis see Edirne
Adriatico, Mare see Adriatic Sea
Adriatic Sea 81 E2 Alb. Deti Adriatik, It. Mare Adriatico, SCr. Jadransko More, Slvn. Jadransko Morje. sea N Mediterranean Sea
Adriatik, Deti see Adriatic Sea
Adycha 93 F2 river NE Russian Federation
Aegean Sea 83 C5 Gk. Aigaíon Pelagos, Aigaío Pélagos, Turk. Ege Denizi. sea NE Mediterranean Sea
Aegviidu 84 D2 Ger. Charlottenhof. Harjumaa, NW Estonia
Aegyptus see Egypt
Aelana see Al 'Aqabah
Aelok see Ailuk Atoll
Aelōnlaplap see Ailinglaplap Atoll
Aemona see Ljubljana
Aeolian Islands 75 C6 var. Isole Lipari, Eng. Aeolian Islands, Lipari Islands. island group S Italy
Aeolian Islands see Eolie, Isole
Æsernia see Isernia
Afar Depression see Danakil Desert
Afars et des Issas, Territoire Français des see Djibouti
Afghānestān, Dowlat-e Eslāmī-ye see Afghanistan
Afghanistan 100 C4 off. Islamic Republic of Afghanistan, Per. Dowlat-e Eslāmī-ye Afghānestān; prev. Republic of Afghanistan. country C Asia
Afmadow 51 D6 Jubbada Hoose, S Somalia
Africa 46 continent
Africa, Horn of 46 E4 physical region Ethiopia/Somalia
Africana Seamount 119 A6 seamount SW Indian Ocean
'Afrīn 96 B2 Ḥalab, N Syria
Afyon 94 B3 prev. Afyonkarahisar. Afyon, W Turkey
Agadès see Agadez
Agadez 53 G3 prev. Agadès. Agadez, C Niger
Agadir 48 B3 SW Morocco
Agana/Agaña see Hagåtña
Āgaro 51 C5 Oromīya, C Ethiopia
Agassiz Fracture Zone 121 G5 fracture zone S Pacific Ocean
Agatha see Agde
Agathónisi 83 D6 island Dodekánisa, Greece, Aegean Sea
Agde 69 C6 anc. Agatha. Hérault, S France
Agedabia see Ajdābiyā
Agen 69 B5 anc. Aginnum. Lot-et-Garonne, SW France
Agendicum see Sens
Aghri Dagh see Büyükağrı Dağı
Agiá 82 B4 var. Ayiá. Thessalía, C Greece
Agialoúsa see Yenierenköy
Agía Marína 83 E6 Léros, Dodekánisa, Greece, Aegean Sea
Aginnum see Agen
Ágios Efstrátios 82 D4 var. Áyios Evstrátios, Hagios Evstrátios. island E Greece
Ágios Nikólaos 83 D8 var. Áyios Nikólaos. Kríti, Greece, E Mediterranean Sea
Āgra 112 D3 Uttar Pradesh, N India
Agra and Oudh, United Provinces of see Uttar Pradesh
Agram see Zagreb
Ağrı 95 F3 var. Karaköse; prev. Karakılısse. Ağrı, NE Turkey
Agri Dagi see Büyükağrı Dağı
Agrigento 75 C7 Gk. Akragas; prev. Girgenti. Sicilia, Italy, C Mediterranean Sea
Agriovótano 83 C5 Évvoia, C Greece
Agropoli 75 D5 Campania, S Italy
Aguachica 36 B2 Cesar, N Colombia
Aguadulce 31 F5 Coclé, S Panama
Agua Prieta 28 B1 Sonora, NW Mexico
Aguascalientes 28 D4 Aguascalientes, C Mexico
Aguaytía 38 C3 Ucayali, C Peru
Aguilas 71 E4 Murcia, SE Spain
Aguililla 28 D4 Michoacán, SW Mexico
Agulhas Basin 47 D8 undersea basin SW Indian Ocean
Agulhas, Cape 56 C5 headland SW South Africa
Agulhas Plateau 45 D6 undersea plateau SW Indian Ocean
Ahaggar 53 F2 high plateau region SE Algeria
Ahlen 72 B4 Nordrhein-Westfalen, W Germany
Ahmadābād 112 C4 var. Ahmedabad. Gujarāt, W India
Ahmadnagar 112 C5 var. Ahmednagar. Mahārāshtra, W India
Ahmedabad see Ahmadābād
Ahmednagar see Ahmadnagar
Ahuachapán 30 B3 Ahuachapán, W El Salvador
Ahvāz 98 C3 var. Ahwāz; prev. Nāsiri. Khūzestān, SW Iran
Ahvenanmaa see Åland
Ahwāz see Ahvāz
Aigaíon Pelagos/Aigaío Pélagos see Aegean Sea
Aígina 83 C6 var. Aíyina, Egina. Aígina, C Greece
Aígio 83 B5 var. Egio; prev. Aíyion. Dytikí Ellás, S Greece
Aiken 21 E2 South Carolina, SE USA
Ailinglaplap Atoll 122 D2 var. Aelōnlaplap. atoll Ralik Chain, S Marshall Islands
Ailuk Atoll 122 D1 var. Aelok. atoll Ratak Chain, NE Marshall Islands
Ainaži 84 D3 Est. Heinaste, Ger. Hainasch. Limbaži, N Latvia
'Aïn Ben Tili 52 D1 Tiris Zemmour, N Mauritania
Aintab see Gaziantep
Aïoun el Atrous/Aïoun el Atroûss see 'Ayoûn el 'Atroûs
Aiquile 39 F4 Cochabamba, C Bolivia
Aïr see Aïr, Massif de l'
Air du Azbine see Aïr, Massif de l'
Aïr, Massif de l' 53 G2 var. Aïr, Air du Azbine, Asben. mountain range NC Niger
Aiud 86 B4 Ger. Strassburg, Hung. Nagyenyed; prev. Engeten. Alba, SW Romania
Aix see Aix-en-Provence
Aix-en-Provence 69 D6 var. Aix; anc. Aquae Sextiae. Bouches-du-Rhône, SE France
Aix-la-Chapelle see Aachen
Aíyina see Aígina
Aíyion see Aígio
Aizkraukle 84 C4 Aizkraukle, S Latvia
Ajaccio 69 E7 Corse, France, C Mediterranean Sea
Ajaria see Achara
Ajastan see Armenia
Aj Bogd Uul 104 D2 mountain SW Mongolia
Ajdābiyā 49 G2 var. Agedabia, Ajdābiyah. NE Libya
Ajdābiyah see Ajdābiyā
Ajjinena see El Geneina
Ajmer 112 D3 var. Ajmere. Rājasthān, N India
Ajo 26 A3 Arizona, SW USA
Akaba see Al 'Aqabah
Akamagaseki see Shimonoseki
Akasha 50 B3 Northern, N Sudan
Akchâr 52 C2 desert W Mauritania
Aken see Aachen
Akermanceaster see Bath
Akhaltsikhe 95 F2 prev. Akhalts'ikhe. SW Georgia
Akhalts'ikhe see Akhaltsikhe
Akhisar 94 A3 Manisa, W Turkey
Akhmīm 50 B2 var. Akhmîm; anc. Panopolis. C Egypt
Akhtubinsk 89 C7 Astrakhanskaya Oblast', SW Russian Federation
Akhtyrka see Okhtyrka
Akimiski Island 16 C3 island Nunavut, C Canada
Akinovka 87 F4 Zaporiz'ka Oblast', S Ukraine
Akita 108 D4 Akita, Honshū, C Japan
Akjoujt 52 C2 prev. Fort-Repoux. Inchiri, W Mauritania
Akkeshi 108 E2 Hokkaidō, NE Japan
Aklavik 14 D3 Northwest Territories, NW Canada
Akmola see Astana
Akmolinsk see Astana
Aknavásár see Târgu Ocna
Akpatok Island 17 E1 island Nunavut, E Canada
Akragas see Agrigento
Akron 18 D4 Ohio, N USA
Akrotiri see Akrotírion
Akrotírion 80 C5 var. Akrotiri. UK air base S Cyprus
Aksai Chin 102 B2 Chin. Aksayqin. disputed region China/India
Aksaray 94 C4 Aksaray, C Turkey
Aksayqin see Aksai Chin
Akşehir 94 B4 Konya, W Turkey
Aktash see Oqtosh
Aktau 92 A4 Kaz. Aqtaū; prev. Shevchenko. Mangistau, W Kazakhstan
Aktjubinsk/Aktyubinsk see Aktobe
Aktobe 92 B4 Kaz. Aqtöbe; prev. Aktjubinsk, Aktyubinsk. Aktyubinsk, NW Kazakhstan
Aktsyabrski 85 C7 Rus. Oktyabr'skiy; prev. Karpilovka. Homyel'skaya Voblasts', SE Belarus
Aktyubinsk see Aktobe
Akula 55 C5 Equateur, NW Dem. Rep. Congo
Akureyri 61 E4 Nordhurland Eystra, N Iceland
Akyab see Sittwe
Alabama 20 C2 off. State of Alabama, also known as Camellia State, Heart of Dixie, The Cotton State, Yellowhammer State. state S USA
Alabama River 20 C3 river Alabama, S USA
Alaca 94 C3 Çorum, N Turkey
Alacant see Alicante
Alagoas 41 G2 off. Estado de Alagoas. region E Brazil
Alagoas 41 G2 off. Estado de Alagoas. state E Brazil
Alais see Alès
Alajuela 31 E4 Alajuela, C Costa Rica
Alakanuk 14 C2 Alaska, USA
Al 'Alamayn 50 B1 var. El 'Alamein. N Egypt
Al 'Amārah 98 C3 var. Amara. Maysān, E Iraq
Alamo 25 D6 Nevada, W USA
Alamogordo 26 D3 New Mexico, SW USA
Alamosa 22 C5 Colorado, C USA
Åland 63 C6 var. Aland Islands, Fin. Ahvenanmaa. island group SW Finland
Aland Islands see Åland
Aland Sea see Ålands Hav
Ålands Hav 63 C6 var. Aland Sea. strait Baltic Sea/Gulf of Bothnia
Alanya 94 C4 Antalya, S Turkey
Alappuzha 110 C3 var. Alleppey. Kerala, SW India
Al 'Aqabah 97 B8 var. Akaba, Aqaba, 'Aqaba; anc. Aelana, Elath. Al 'Aqabah, SW Jordan
Al 'Arabīyah as Su'ūdīyah see Saudi Arabia
Alasca, Golfo de see Alaska, Gulf of
Alaşehir 94 A4 Manisa, W Turkey
Al 'Ashārah 96 E3 var. Ashara. Dayr az Zawr, E Syria
Alaska 14 C3 off. State of Alaska, also known as Land of the Midnight Sun, The Last Frontier, Seward's Folly; prev. Russian America. state NW USA
Alaska, Gulf of 14 C4 var. Golfo de Alasca. gulf Canada/USA
Alaska Peninsula 14 C3 peninsula Alaska, USA
Alaska Range 12 B2 mountain range Alaska, USA
Al-Asnam see Chlef
Alattio see Alta
Al Awaynāt see Al 'Uwaynāt
Alaykel'/Alay-Kuu see Kök-Art
Al 'Aynā 97 B7 Al Karak, W Jordan
Alazeya 93 G2 river NE Russian Federation
Al Bāb 96 B2 Ḥalab, N Syria
Albacete 71 E3 Castilla-La Mancha, C Spain
Al Baghdādī 98 B3 var. Khān al Baghdādī. Al Anbār, SW Iraq
Al Bāha see Al Bāḥah
Al Bāḥah 99 B5 var. Al Bāha. Al BāḤah, SW Saudi Arabia
Al Baḥrayn see Bahrain
Alba Iulia 86 B4 Ger. Weissenburg, Hung. Gyulafehérvár; prev. Bălgrad, Karlsburg, Károly-Fehérvár. Alba, W Romania
Albania 79 C7 off. Republic of Albania, Alb. Republika e Shqipqërisë, Shqipëria; prev. People's Socialist Republic of Albania. country SE Europe
Albania see Aubagne
Albany 125 B7 Western Australia
Albany 20 D3 Georgia, SE USA
Albany 19 F3 state capital New York, NE USA
Albany 24 B3 Oregon, NW USA
Albany 16 C3 river Ontario, S Canada
Alba Regia see Székesfehérvár
Al Bāridah 96 C4 var. Bāridah. Ḥimṣ, C Syria
Al Baṣrah 98 C3 Eng. Basra, hist. Busra, Bussora. Al Baṣrah, SE Iraq
Al Batrūn see Batroûn
Al Bayḍā' 49 G2 var. Beida. NE Libya
Albemarle Island see Isabela, Isla
Albemarle Sound 21 G1 inlet W Atlantic Ocean
Albergaria-a-Velha 70 B2 Aveiro, N Portugal
Albert 68 C3 Somme, N France
Alberta 15 E4 province SW Canada
Albert Edward Nyanza see Edward, Lake
Albert, Lake 51 B6 var. Albert Nyanza, Lac Mobutu Sese Seko. lake Uganda/Dem. Rep. Congo
Albert Lea 23 F3 Minnesota, N USA
Albert Nyanza see Albert, Lake
Albertville see Kalemie
Albi 69 C6 anc. Albiga. Tarn, S France
Albiga see Albi
Ålborg see Aalborg
Ålborg-Nørresundby see Aalborg
Alborz, Reshteh-ye Kūhhā-ye 98 C2 Eng. Elburz Mountains. mountain range N Iran
Albuquerque 26 D2 New Mexico, SW USA
Al Burayqah see Marsá al Burayqah
Alburgum see Aalborg
Albury 127 C7 New South Wales, SE Australia
Alcácer do Sal 70 B4 Setúbal, W Portugal
Alcalá de Henares 71 E3 Ar. Alkal'a; anc. Complutum. Madrid, C Spain
Alcamo 75 C7 Sicilia, Italy, C Mediterranean Sea
Alcañiz 71 F2 Aragón, NE Spain
Alcántara, Embalse de 70 C3 reservoir W Spain
Alcaudete 70 D4 Andalucía, S Spain
Alcázar see Ksar-el-Kebir
Alcazarquivir see Ksar-el-Kebir
Alcoi see Alcoy
Alcoy 71 F4 Cat. Alcoi. País Valenciano, E Spain
Aldabra Group 57 G2 island group SW Seychelles
Aldan 93 F3 river NE Russian Federation
al Dar al Baida see Rabat
Alderney 68 A2 island Channel Islands
Aleg 52 C3 Brakna, SW Mauritania
Aleksandriya see Oleksandriya
Aleksandropol' see Gyumri
Aleksandrovka see Oleksandrivka
Aleksandrovsk see Zaporizhzhya
Aleksin 89 B5 Tul'skaya Oblast', W Russian Federation
Aleksinac 78 E4 Serbia, SE Serbia
Alençon 68 B3 Orne, N France
Alenquer 41 E2 Pará, NE Brazil
Alep/Aleppo see Ḥalab
Alert 15 F1 Ellesmere Island, Nunavut, N Canada
Alès 69 C6 prev. Alais. Gard, S France
Aleşd 86 B3 Hung. Élesd. Bihor, SW Romania
Alessandria 74 B2 Fr. Alexandrie. Piemonte, N Italy
Ålesund 63 A5 Møre og Romsdal, S Norway
Aleutian Basin 91 G3 undersea basin Bering Sea
Aleutian Islands 14 A3 island group Alaska, USA
Aleutian Range 12 A2 mountain range Alaska, USA
Aleutian Trench 91 H3 trench S Bering Sea
Alexander Archipelago 14 D4 island group Alaska, USA
Alexander City 20 D2 Alabama, S USA
Alexander Island 132 A3 island Antarctica
Alexander Range see Kirghiz Range
Alexandra 129 B7 Otago, South Island, New Zealand
Alexándreia 82 B4 var. Alexándria. Kentrikí Makedonía, N Greece
Alexandretta see İskenderun
Alexandretta, Gulf of see İskenderun Körfezi
Alexandria 50 B1 Ar. Al Iskandarīyah. N Egypt
Alexandria 86 C5 Teleorman, S Romania
Alexandria 20 B3 Louisiana, S USA
Alexandria 23 F2 Minnesota, N USA
Alexándria see Alexándreia
Alexandrie see Alessandria
Alexandroúpoli 82 D3 var. Alexandroúpolis, Turk. Dedeagaç, Dedeagach. Anatolikí Makedonía kai Thráki, NE Greece
Alexandroúpolis see Alexandroúpoli
Al Fāshir see El Fasher
Alfatar 82 E1 Silistra, NE Bulgaria
Alfeiós 83 B6 prev. Alfiós; anc. Alpheius, Alpheus. river S Greece
Alfiós see Alfeiós
Alföld see Great Hungarian Plain
Al-Furāt see Euphrates
Alga 92 B4 Kaz. Algha. Aktyubinsk, NW Kazakhstan
Algarve 70 B4 cultural region S Portugal
Algeciras 70 C5 Andalucía, SW Spain
Algemesí 71 F3 País Valenciano, E Spain
Al-Genain see El Geneina
Alger 49 E1 var. Algiers, El Djazaïr, Al Jazair. country capital (Algeria) N Algeria
Algeria 48 C3 off. Democratic and Popular Republic of Algeria. country N Africa
Algeria, Democratic and Popular Republic of see Algeria
Algerian Basin 58 C5 var. Balearic Plain. undersea basin W Mediterranean Sea
Algha see Alga
Al Ghābah 99 E5 var. Ghaba. C Oman
Alghero 75 A5 Sardegna, Italy, C Mediterranean Sea
Al Ghurdaqah 50 C2 var. Hurghada, Ghurdaqah. E Egypt
Algiers see Alger
Al Golea see El Goléa
Algona 23 F3 Iowa, C USA
Al Hajar al Gharbī 99 D5 mountain range N Oman
Al Hamad see Syrian Desert
Al Ḥasakah 96 D2 var. Al Hasijah, El Haseke, Fr. Hassetché. Al Ḥasakah, NE Syria
Al Hasijah see Al Ḥasakah
Al Ḥillah 98 B3 var. Hilla. Bābil, C Iraq
Al Ḥisā 97 B7 Aṭ Ṭafīlah, W Jordan
Al Ḥudaydah 99 B6 Eng. Hodeida. W Yemen
Al Hufūf 98 C4 var. Hofuf. Ash Sharqīyah, NE Saudi Arabia
Aliákmon see Aliákmonas
Aliákmonas 82 B4 prev. Aliákmon; anc. Haliacmon. river N Greece
Alíartos 83 C5 Stereá Ellás, C Greece
Alicante 71 F4 Cat. Alacant, Lat. Lucentum. País Valenciano, SE Spain
Alice 27 G5 Texas, SW USA
Alice Springs 126 A4 Northern Territory, C Australia
Alifu Atoll see Ari Atoll
Aligandí 31 G4 Kuna Yala, NE Panama
Aliki see Alykí
Alima 55 B6 river C Congo
Al Imārāt al 'Arabīyah al Muttaḥidah see United Arab Emirates
Alindao 54 C4 Basse-Kotto, S Central African Republic
Aliquippa 18 D4 Pennsylvania, NE USA
Al Iskandarīyah see Alexandria
Al Ismā'īlīya 50 B1 var. Ismailia, Ismâ'ilîya. N Egypt
Alistráti 82 C3 Kentrikí Makedonía, NE Greece
Alivéri 83 C5 var. Alivérion. Évvoia, C Greece
Alivérion see Alivéri
Al Jabal al Akhḍar 49 G2 mountain range NE Libya
Al Jafr 97 B7 Ma'ān, S Jordan
Al Jaghbūb 49 H3 NE Libya
Al Jahrā' 98 C4 var. Al Jahrah, Jahra. C Kuwait
Al Jahrah see Al Jahrā'
Al Jamāhīrīyah al 'Arabīyah al Lībīyah ash Sha'bīyah al Ishtirākīy see Libya
Al Jawf 98 B4 off. Jauf. Al Jawf, NW Saudi Arabia
Al Jawlān see Golan Heights
Al Jazair see Alger
Al Jazīrah 96 E2 physical region Iraq/Syria
Al Jīzah see Gîza
Al Junaynah see El Geneina
Alkal'a see Alcalá de Henares
Al Karak 97 B7 var. El Kerak, Karak, Kerak; anc. Kir Moab, Kir of Moab. Al Karak, W Jordan
Al-Kasr al-Kebir see Ksar-el-Kebir
Al Khalīl see Hebron
Al Khārijah 50 B2 var. El Khârga. C Egypt
Al Khums 49 F2 var. Homs, Khoms, Khums. NW Libya
Alkmaar 64 C2 Noord-Holland, NW Netherlands
Al Kufrah 49 H4 SE Libya
Al Kūt 98 C3 var. Kūt al 'Amārah, Kut al Imara. Wāsiṭ, E Iraq
Al-Kuwait see Al Kuwayt
Al Kuwayt 98 C4 var. Al-Kuwait, Eng. Kuwait, Kuwait City; prev. Qurein. country capital (Kuwait) E Kuwait
Al Lādhiqīyah 96 A3 Eng. Latakia, Fr. Lattaquié; anc. Laodicea, Laodicea ad Mare. Al Lādhiqīyah, W Syria
Allahābād 113 E3 Uttar Pradesh, N India
Allanmyo see Aunglan
Allegheny Plateau 19 E3 mountain range New York/Pennsylvania, NE USA
Allenstein see Olsztyn
Allentown 19 F4 Pennsylvania, NE USA
Alleppey see Alappuzha
Alliance 22 D3 Nebraska, C USA
Al Līth 99 B5 Makkah, SW Saudi Arabia
Al Lubnān see Lebanon
Alma-Ata see Almaty
Almada 70 B4 Setúbal, W Portugal
Al Madīnah 99 A5 Eng. Medina. Al Madīnah, W Saudi Arabia
Al Mafraq 97 B6 var. Mafraq. Al Mafraq, N Jordan
Al Mahdīyah see Mahdia
Al Mahrah 99 C6 mountain range E Yemen
Al Majma'ah 98 B4 Ar Riyāḍ, C Saudi Arabia
Al Mālikīyah 96 E1 var. Malkiye. Al Ḥasakah, N Syria
Almalyk see Olmaliq
Al Mamlakah see Morocco
Al Mamlaka al Urdunīya al Hashemīyah see Jordan
Al Manāmah 98 C4 Eng. Manama. country capital (Bahrain) N Bahrain
Al Manāṣif 96 E3 mountain range E Syria
Almansa 71 F4 Castilla-La Mancha, C Spain
Al-Mariyya see Almería
Al Marj 49 G2 var. Barka, It. Barce. NE Libya
Almaty 92 C5 var. Alma-Ata. Almaty, SE Kazakhstan
Al Mawṣil 98 B2 Eng. Mosul. Nīnawá, N Iraq
Al Mayādīn 96 D3 var. Mayadin, Fr. Meyadine. Dayr az Zawr, E Syria
Al Mazra' see Al Mazra'ah
Al Mazra'ah 97 B6 var. Al Mazra', Mazra'a. Al Karak, W Jordan
Almelo 64 E3 Overijssel, E Netherlands
Almendra, Embalse de 70 C2 reservoir Castilla-León, NW Spain
Almendralejo 70 C4 Extremadura, W Spain
Almere 64 C3 var. Almere-stad. Flevoland, C Netherlands

Almere-stad – Arīhā

Almere-stad see Almere
Almería 71 E5 Ar. Al-Mariyya; anc. Unci, Lat. Portus Magnus. Andalucía, S Spain
Al'met'yevsk 89 D5 Respublika Tatarstan, W Russian Federation
Al Mīnā' see El Mina
Al Minyā 50 B2 var. El Minya, Minya. C Egypt
Almirante 31 E4 Bocas del Toro, NW Panama
Al Mudawwarah 97 B8 Ma'ān, SW Jordan
Al Mukallā 99 C6 var. Mukalla. SE Yemen
Al Obayyid see El Obeid
Alofi 123 F4 dependent territory capital (Niue) W Niue
Aloha State see Hawaii
Aloja 84 D3 Limbaži, N Latvia
Alónnisos 83 C5 island Vóreies Sporádes, Greece, Aegean Sea
Álora 70 D5 Andalucía, S Spain
Alor, Kepulauan 117 E5 island group E Indonesia
Al Oued see El Oued
Alpen see Alps
Alpena 18 D2 Michigan, N USA
Alpes see Alps
Alpha Cordillera 133 B3 var. Alpha Ridge. seamount range Arctic Ocean
Alpha Ridge see Alpha Cordillera
Alpheius see Alfeiós
Alphen see Alphen aan den Rijn
Alphen aan den Rijn 64 C3 var. Alphen. Zuid-Holland, C Netherlands
Alpheus see Alfeiós
Alpi see Alps
Alpine 27 E4 Texas, SW USA
Alps 80 C1 Fr. Alpes, Ger. Alpen, It. Alpi. mountain range C Europe
Al Qaḍārif see Gedaref
Al Qāhirah see Cairo
Al Qāmishlī 96 E1 var. Kamishli, Qamishly. Al Ḥasakah, NE Syria
Al Qaṣrayn see Kasserine
Al Qayrawān see Kairouan
Al-Qsar al-Kbir see Ksar-el-Kebir
Al Qubayyāt see Qoubaïyât
Al Quds/Al Quds ash Sharīf see Jerusalem
Alqueva, Barragem do 70 C4 reservoir Portugal/Spain
Al Qunayṭirah 97 B5 var. El Kuneitra, El Quneitra, Kuneitra, Qunaytra. Al Qunayṭirah, SW Syria
Al Quṣayr 96 B4 var. El Quseir, Quṣayr, Fr. Kousseir. Ḥimṣ, W Syria
Al Quwayrah 97 B8 var. El Quweira. Al 'Aqabah, SW Jordan
Alsace 68 E3 Ger. Elsass; anc. Alsatia. cultural region NE France
Alsatia see Alsace
Alsdorf 72 A4 Nordrhein-Westfalen, W Germany
Alt see Olt
Alta 62 D2 Fin. Alattio. Finnmark, N Norway
Altai see Altai Mountains
Altai Mountains 104 C2 var. Altai, Chin. Altay Shan, Rus. Altay. mountain range Asia/Europe
Altamaha River 21 E3 river Georgia, SE USA
Altamira 41 E2 Pará, NE Brazil
Altamura 75 E5 anc. Lupatia. Puglia, SE Italy
Altar, Desierto de 28 A1 var. Sonoran Desert. desert Mexico/USA
Altar, Desierto de see Sonoran Desert
Altay 104 C2 Xinjiang Uygur Zizhiqu, NW China
Altay 104 D2 prev. Yösönbulag. Govĭ-Altay, W Mongolia
Altay Altai Mountains, Asia/Europe
Altay Shan see Altai Mountains
Altbetsche see Bečej
Altenburg see Bucureşti, Romania
Altin Köprü 98 B3 var. Altun Kupri. At Ta'mīn, N Iraq
Altiplano 39 F4 physical region W South America
Altkanischa see Kanjiža
Alton 18 B5 Illinois, N USA
Alton 18 B4 Missouri, C USA
Altoona 19 E4 Pennsylvania, NE USA
Alto Paraná see Paraná
Altpasua see Stara Pazova
Alt-Schwanenburg see Gulbene
Altsohl see Zvolen
Altun Kupri see Altin Köprü
Altun Shan 104 C3 var. Altyn Tagh. mountain range NW China
Altus 27 F2 Oklahoma, C USA
Altyn Tagh see Altun Shan
Al Ubayyiḍ see El Obeid
Alūksne 84 D3 Ger. Marienburg. Alūksne, NE Latvia
Al 'Ulā 98 A4 Al Madīnah, NW Saudi Arabia
Al 'Umarī 97 C6 'Ammān, E Jordan
Alupka 87 F5 Respublika Krym, S Ukraine
Al Uqṣur see Luxor
Al Urdunn see Jordan
Alushta 87 F5 Respublika Krym, S Ukraine
Al 'Uwaynāt 49 F4 var. Al Awaynāt. SW Libya
Alva 27 F1 Oklahoma, C USA
Alvarado 29 F4 Veracruz-Llave, E Mexico
Alvin 27 H4 Texas, SW USA
Al Wajh 98 A4 Tabūk, NW Saudi Arabia
Alwar 112 D3 Rājasthān, N India
Al Wari'ah 98 C4 Ash Sharqīyah, N Saudi Arabia
Al Yaman see Yemen
Alykí 82 C4 var. Aliki. Thásos, N Greece
Alytus 85 B5 Pol. Olita. Alytus, S Lithuania
Alzette 65 D8 river S Luxembourg
Amadeus, Lake 125 D5 seasonal lake Northern Territory, C Australia
Amadi 51 B5 W Equatoria, S South Sudan
Amadjuak Lake 15 G3 lake Baffin Island, Nunavut, N Canada
Amakusa-nada 109 A7 gulf SW Japan
Åmål 63 B6 Västra Götaland, S Sweden
Amami-gunto 108 A3 island group SW Japan
Amami-o-shima 108 A3 island S Japan
Amantea 75 D6 Calabria, SW Italy
Amapá 41 E1 off. Estado de Amapá; prev. Território de Amapá. region NE Brazil
Amapá 41 E1 off. Estado de Amapá; prev. Território de Amapá. state NE Brazil
Amapá, Estado de see Amapá
Amapá, Território de see Amapá
Amara see Al 'Amārah
Amarapura 114 B3 Mandalay, C Myanmar (Burma)
Amarillo 27 E2 Texas, SW USA
Amay 65 C6 Liège, E Belgium
Amazon 41 E1 Sp. Amazonas. river Brazil/Peru
Amazonas see Amazon
Amazon Basin 40 D2 basin N South America
Amazon, Mouths of the 41 F1 delta NE Brazil
Ambam 55 B5 Sud, S Cameroon
Ambanja 57 G2 Antsiranana, N Madagascar
Ambarchik 93 G2 Respublika Sakha (Yakutiya), NE Russian Federation
Ambato 38 B1 Tungurahua, C Ecuador
Ambérieu-en-Bugey 69 D5 Ain, E France
Ambianum see Amiens
Amboasary 57 F4 Toliara, S Madagascar
Amboina see Ambon
Ambon 117 F4 prev. Amboina, Amboyna. Pulau Ambon, E Indonesia
Ambositra 57 G3 Fianarantsoa, SE Madagascar
Amboyna see Ambon
Ambracia see Árta
Ambre, Cap d' see Bobaomby, Tanjona
Ambrim see Ambrym
Ambriz 56 A1 Bengo, NW Angola
Ambrym 122 D4 var. Ambrim. island C Vanuatu
Amchitka Island 14 A2 island Aleutian Islands, Alaska, USA
Amdo 104 C5 Xizang Zizhiqu, W China
Ameland 54 D1 Fris. It Amelân. island Wadden eilanden, N Netherlands
Amelân, It see Ameland
America see United States of America
America-Antarctica Ridge 45 C7 undersea ridge S Atlantic Ocean
America in Miniature see Maryland
American Falls Reservoir 24 E4 reservoir Idaho, NW USA
American Samoa 123 E4 US unincorporated territory W Polynesia
Amersfoort 64 D3 Utrecht, C Netherlands
Ames 23 F3 Iowa, C USA
Amfilochía 83 A5 var. Amfilokhía. Dytikí Ellás, C Greece
Amfilokhía see Amfilochía
Amga 93 F3 river NE Russian Federation
Amherst 17 F4 Nova Scotia, SE Canada
Amherst see Kyaikkami
Amida see Diyarbakır
Amiens 68 C3 anc. Ambianum, Samarobriva. Somme, N France
Amíndaion/Amindeo see Amýntaio
Amindivi Islands 110 A2 island group Lakshadweep, India, N Indian Ocean
Amirante Islands 57 G1 var. Amirantes Group. island group C Seychelles
Amirantes Group see Amirante Islands
Amistad, Presa de la see Amistad Reservoir
Amistad Reservoir 27 F4 var. Presa de la Amistad. reservoir Mexico/USA
Amisus see Samsun
Ammaia see Portalegre
'Ammān 97 B6 anc. Philadelphia, Bibl. Rabbah Ammon, Rabbath Ammon. country capital (Jordan) 'Ammān, NW Jordan
Ammassalik 60 D4 var. Angmagssalik. Tunu, S Greenland
Ammóchostos see Gazimağusa
Ammóchostos, Kólpos see Gazimağusa Körfezi
Amnok-kang see Yalu
Amoea see Portalegre
Amoentai see Amuntai
Āmol 98 D2 var. Amul. Māzandarān, N Iran
Amorgós 83 D6 Amorgós, Kykládes, Greece, Aegean Sea
Amorgós 83 D6 island Kykládes, Greece, Aegean Sea
Amos 16 D4 Québec, SE Canada
Amourj 52 D3 Hodh ech Chargui, SE Mauritania
Amoy see Xiamen
Ampato, Nevado 39 E4 mountain S Peru
Amposta 71 F2 Cataluña, NE Spain
Amraoti see Amrāvati
Amrāvati 112 D4 prev. Amraoti. Mahārāshtra, C India
Amritsar 112 D2 Punjab, N India
Amstelveen 64 C3 Noord-Holland, C Netherlands
Amsterdam 64 C3 country capital (Netherlands) Noord-Holland, C Netherlands
Amsterdam Island 119 C6 island NE French Southern and Antarctic Lands
Am Timan 54 C3 Salamat, SE Chad
Amu Darya 100 D2 Rus. Amudar'ya, Taj. Dar"yoi Amu, Turkm. Amyderya, Uzb. Amudaryo; anc. Oxus. river C Asia
Amu-Dar'ya see Amyderya
Amudar'ya/Amudaryo/Amu, Dar"yoi see Amu Darya
Amul see Āmol
Amund Ringnes Island 15 F2 Island Nunavut, N Canada
Amundsen Basin see Fram Basin
Amundsen Plain 132 A4 abyssal plain S Pacific Ocean
Amundsen-Scott 132 B3 US research station Antarctica
Amundsen Sea 132 A4 sea S Pacific Ocean
Amuntai 116 D4 prev. Amoentai. Borneo, C Indonesia
Amur 93 G4 Chin. Heilong Jiang. river China/Russian Federation
Amvrosiyevka see Amvrosiyivka
Amvrosiyivka 87 H3 Rus. Amvrosiyevka. Donets'ka Oblast', SE Ukraine
Amyderýa 101 E3 Rus. Amu-Dar'ya. Lebap Welaýaty, NE Turkmenistan
Amyderya see Amu Darya
Amýntaio 82 B4 var. Amindeo; prev. Amíndaion. Dytikí Makedonía, N Greece
Anabar 93 E2 river NE Russian Federation
An Abhainn Mhór see Blackwater
Anaco 37 E2 Anzoátegui, NE Venezuela
Anaconda 22 B2 Montana, NW USA
Anacortes 24 B1 Washington, NW USA
Anadolu Dağları see Doğu Karadeniz Dağları
Anadyr' 93 H1 Chukotskiy Avtonomnyy Okrug, NE Russian Federation
Anadyr' 93 G1 river NE Russian Federation
Anadyr, Gulf of see Anadyrskiy Zaliv
Anadyrskiy Zaliv 93 H1 Eng. Gulf of Anadyr. gulf NE Russian Federation
Anáfi 83 D7 anc. Anaphe. island Kykládes, Greece, Aegean Sea
'Ānah see 'Annah
Anaheim 24 E2 California, W USA
Anaiza see Unayzah
Analalava 57 G2 Mahajanga, NW Madagascar
Anamur 94 C5 İçel, S Turkey
Anantapur 110 C2 Andhra Pradesh, S India
Anaphe see Anáfi
Anápolis 41 F3 Goiás, C Brazil
Anār 98 D3 Kermān, C Iran
Anatolia 94 C4 plateau C Turkey
Anatom see Aneityum
Añatuya 42 C3 Santiago del Estero, N Argentina
An Bhearú see Barrow
Anchorage 14 C3 Alaska, USA
Ancona 74 C3 Marche, C Italy
Ancud 43 B6 prev. San Carlos de Ancud. Los Lagos, S Chile
Ancyra see Ankara
Åndalsnes 63 A5 Møre og Romsdal, S Norway
Andalucía 70 D4 cultural region S Spain
Andalusia 20 C3 Alabama, S USA
Andaman Islands 102 B4 island group India, NE Indian Ocean
Andaman Sea 102 C4 sea NE Indian Ocean
Andenne 65 C6 Namur, SE Belgium
Anderlues 65 B7 Hainaut, S Belgium
Anderson 18 C4 Indiana, N USA
Andes 42 B3 mountain range W South America
Andhra Pradesh 113 E5 cultural region E India
Andijon 101 F2 Rus. Andizhan. Andijon Viloyati, E Uzbekistan
Andikíthira see Antikýthira
Andipaxi see Antípaxoi
Andípsara see Antípsara
Ándissa see Ántissa
Andizhan see Andijon
Andkhvoy 100 D3 Fāryāb, N Afghanistan
Andorra 69 A7 off. Principality of Andorra, Cat. Valls d'Andorra, Fr. Vallée d'Andorre. country SW Europe
Andorra see Andorra la Vella
Andorra la Vella 69 A8 var. Andorra, Fr. Andorre la Vielle, Sp. Andorra la Vieja. country capital (Andorra) C Andorra
Andorra la Vieja see Andorra la Vella
Andorra, Principality of see Andorra
Andorra, Valls d'/Andorra, Vallée d' see Andorra
Andorre la Vielle see Andorra la Vella
Andover 67 D7 S England, United Kingdom
Andøya 62 C2 island C Norway
Andreanof Islands 14 A3 island group Aleutian Islands, Alaska, USA
Andrews 27 E3 Texas, SW USA
Andrew Tablemount 118 A4 var. Gora Andryu. seamount W Indian Ocean
Andria 75 D5 Puglia, SE Italy
An Droichead Nua see Newbridge
Andropov see Rybinsk
Ándros 83 D6 Ándros, Kykládes, Greece, Aegean Sea
Ándros 83 C6 island Kykládes, Greece, Aegean Sea
Andros Island 32 B2 island NW Bahamas
Andros Town 32 C1 Andros Island, NW Bahamas
Andryu, Gora see Andrew Tablemount
Aneityum 122 D5 var. Anatom; prev. Kéamu. island S Vanuatu
Änewetak see Enewetak Atoll
Angara 93 E4 river C Russian Federation
Angarsk 93 E4 Irkutskaya Oblast', S Russian Federation
Ånge 63 C5 Västernorrland, C Sweden
Ángel de la Guarda, Isla 28 B2 island NW Mexico
Angeles 117 E1 off. Angeles City. Luzon, N Philippines
Angeles City see Angeles
Angel Falls 37 E3 Eng. Angel Falls. waterfall E Venezuela
Angel Falls see Ángel, Salto
Angerburg see Węgorzewo
Ångermanälven 62 C4 river N Sweden
Angermünde 72 D3 Brandenburg, NE Germany
Angers 68 B4 anc. Juliomagus. Maine-et-Loire, NW France
Anglesey 67 C5 island NW Wales, United Kingdom
Anglet 69 A6 Pyrénées-Atlantiques, SW France
Angleton 27 H4 Texas, SW USA
Anglia see England
Anglo-Egyptian Sudan see Sudan
Angmagssalik see Ammassalik
Ang Nam Ngum 114 C4 lake C Laos
Angola 56 B2 off. Republic of Angola; prev. People's Republic of Angola, Portuguese West Africa. country SW Africa
Angola Basin 47 B5 undersea basin E Atlantic Ocean
Angola, People's Republic of see Angola
Angola, Republic of see Angola
Angora see Ankara
Angostura see Ciudad Bolívar
Angostura, Presa de la 29 G5 reservoir SE Mexico
Angoulême 69 B5 anc. Iculisma. Charente, W France
Angoumois 69 B5 cultural region W France
Angra Pequena see Lüderitz
Angren 101 F2 Toshkent Viloyati, E Uzbekistan
Anguilla 33 G3 UK dependent territory E West Indies
Anguilla Cays 32 B2 islets SW Bahamas
Anhui 106 C5 var. Anhui Sheng, Anhwei, Wan. province E China
AnhuiSheng/Anhwei Wan see Anhui
Anicium see le Puy
Anina 86 A4 Ger. Steierdorf, Hung. Stájerlakanina; prev. Ştaierdorf-Anina, Steierdorf-Anina, Steyerlak-Anina. Caraş-Severin, SW Romania
Anjou 68 B4 cultural region NW France
Anjouan 57 F2 var. Nzwani, Johanna Island. island SE Comoros
Ankara 94 C3 prev. Angora; anc. Ancyra. country capital (Turkey) Ankara, C Turkey
Ankeny 23 F3 Iowa, C USA
Anklam 72 D2 Mecklenburg-Vorpommern, NE Germany
An Mhuir Cheilteach see Celtic Sea
Annaba 49 E1 prev. Bône. NE Algeria
An Nafūd 98 B4 desert NW Saudi Arabia
'Annah 98 B3 var. 'Ānah. Al Anbār, NW Iraq
An Najaf 98 B3 var. Najaf. An Najaf, S Iraq
Annamite Mountains 114 D4 Fr. Annamitique, Chaîne. mountain range C Laos
Annamitique, Chaîne see Annamite Mountains
Annapolis 19 F4 state capital Maryland, NE USA
Annapurna 113 E3 mountain C Nepal
An Nāqūrah see En Nâqoûra
Ann Arbor 18 C3 Michigan, N USA
An Nāṣirīyah 98 C3 var. Nasiriya. Dhī Qār, SE Iraq
Anneciacum see Annecy
Annecy 69 D5 anc. Anneciacum. Haute-Savoie, E France
An Nīl al Abyaḍ see White Nile
An Nīl al Azraq see Blue Nile
Anniston 20 D2 Alabama, S USA
Annotto Bay 32 B4 C Jamaica
An Ómaigh see Omagh
Anqing 106 D5 Anhui, E China
Anse La Raye 33 F1 NW Saint Lucia
Anshun 106 B6 Guizhou, S China
Ansongo 53 E3 Gao, E Mali
An Srath Bán see Strabane
Antakya 94 D4 anc. Antioch, Antiochia. Hatay, S Turkey
Antalaha 57 G2 Antsirañana, NE Madagascar
Antalya 94 B4 prev. Adalia; anc. Attaleia, Bibl. Attalia. Antalya, SW Turkey
Antalya, Gulf of 94 B4 var. Gulf of Adalia, Eng. Gulf of Antalya. gulf SW Turkey
Antalya, Gulf of see Antalya Körfezi
Antananarivo 57 G3 prev. Tananarive. country capital (Madagascar) Antananarivo, C Madagascar
Antarctica 132 B3 continent
Antarctic Peninsula 132 A2 peninsula Antarctica
Antep see Gaziantep
Antequera 70 D5 anc. Anticaria, Antiquaria. Andalucía, S Spain
Antequera see Oaxaca
Antibes 69 D6 anc. Antipolis. Alpes-Maritimes, SE France
Anticaria see Antequera
Anticosti, Île d' 17 F3 Eng. Anticosti Island. island Québec, E Canada
Anticosti Island see Anticosti, Île d'
Antigua 33 G3 island S Antigua and Barbuda, Leeward Islands
Antigua and Barbuda 33 G3 country E West Indies
Antikýthira 83 B7 var. Andikíthira. island S Greece
Anti-Lebanon 96 B4 var. Jebel esh Sharqi, Ar. Al Jabal ash Sharqī, Fr. Anti-Liban. mountain range Lebanon/Syria
Anti-Liban see Anti-Lebanon
Antioch see Antakya
Antiochia see Antakya
Antípaxoi 83 A5 var. Andipaxi. island Iónia Nísiá, Greece, C Mediterranean Sea
Antipodes Islands 120 D5 island group S New Zealand
Antipolis see Antibes
Antípsara 83 D5 var. Andípsara. island E Greece
Antiquaria see Antequera
Ántissa 83 D5 var. Ándissa. Lésvos, E Greece
An tIúr see Newry
Antivari see Bar
Antofagasta 42 B2 Antofagasta, N Chile
Antony 68 E2 Hauts-de-Seine, N France
An tSionainn see Shannon
Antsirañana 57 G2 province N Madagascar
Antsohihy 57 G2 Mahajanga, NW Madagascar
An-tung see Dandong
Antwerpen 65 C5 Eng. Antwerp, Fr. Anvers. Antwerpen, N Belgium
Anuradhapura 110 D3 North Central Province, C Sri Lanka
Anvers see Antwerpen
Anyang 106 C4 Henan, C China
A'nyêmaqên Shan 104 D4 mountain range C China
Anykščiai 84 C4 Utena, E Lithuania
Anzio 75 C5 Lazio, C Italy
Ao Krung Thep 115 C5 var. Krung Thep Mahanakhon, Eng. Bangkok. country capital (Thailand) Bangkok, C Thailand
Aomori 108 D3 Aomori, Honshū, C Japan
Aóos see Vjosës, Lumi i
Aoraki 129 B6 prev. Aorangi, Mount Cook. mountain South Island, New Zealand
Aorangi see Aoraki
Aosta 74 A1 anc. Augusta Praetoria. Valle d'Aosta, NW Italy
Aoukâr 52 D3 var. Aouker. plateau C Mauritania
Aouk, Bahr 54 C4 river Central African Republic/Chad
Aouker see Aoukâr
Aozou 54 C1 Borkou-Ennedi-Tibesti, N Chad
Apalachee Bay 20 D3 bay Florida, SE USA
Apalachicola River 20 D3 river Florida, SE USA
Apamama see Abemama
Apaporis, Río 36 C4 river Brazil/Colombia
Apatity 88 C2 Murmanskaya Oblast', NW Russian Federation
Ape 84 D3 Alūksne, NE Latvia
Apeldoorn 64 D3 Gelderland, E Netherlands
Apennines 74 E2 Eng. Apennines. mountain range Italy/San Marino
Apennines see Appennino
Āpia 123 F4 country capital (Samoa) Upolu, SE Samoa
Ap'khazet'i 95 E1 var. Abkhazia. autonomous republic NW Georgia
Apoera 37 G3 Sipaliwini, NW Suriname
Apostle Islands 18 B1 island group Wisconsin, N USA
Appalachian Mountains 13 D5 mountain range E USA
Appingedam 64 E1 Groningen, NE Netherlands
Appleton 18 B2 Wisconsin, N USA
Apulia see Puglia
Apure, Río 36 C2 river W Venezuela
Apurímac, Río 38 D3 river S Peru
Apuseni, Munții 86 A4 mountain range W Romania
Aqaba/'Aqaba see Al 'Aqabah
Aqaba, Gulf of 98 A4 var. Gulf of Elat, Ar. Khalīj al 'Aqabah; anc. Sinus Aelaniticus. gulf NE Red Sea
'Aqabah, Khalīj al see Aqaba, Gulf of
Āqchah 101 E3 var. Āqcheh. Jowzjān, N Afghanistan
Āqcheh see Āqchah
Aqmola see Astana
Aqtöbe see Aktobe
Aquae Augustae see Dax
Aquae Calidae see Bath
Aquae Flaviae see Chaves
Aquae Grani see Aachen
Aquae Sextiae see Aix-en-Provence
Aquae Solis see Bath
Aquae Tarbelicae see Dax
Aquidauana 41 E4 Mato Grosso do Sul, S Brazil
Aquila/Aquila degli Abruzzi see L'Aquila
Aquisgranum see Aachen
Aquitaine 69 B6 cultural region SW France
'Arabah, Wadi al 97 B7 Heb. Ha'Arava. dry watercourse Israel/Jordan
Arabian Basin 102 A4 undersea basin N Arabian Sea
Arabian Desert see Sahara el Sharqîya
Arabian Peninsula 99 B5 peninsula SW Asia
Arabian Sea 102 A3 sea NW Indian Ocean
Arabicus, Sinus see Red Sea
'Arabī, Khalīj al see Persian Gulf
'Arabīyah as Su'ūdīyah, Al Mamlakah al see Saudi Arabia
'Arabīyah Jumhūrīyah, Miṣr al see Egypt
Arab Republic of Egypt see Egypt
Aracaju 41 G3 state capital Sergipe, E Brazil
Araçuai 41 F3 Minas Gerais, SE Brazil
Arad 97 B7 Southern, S Israel
Arad 86 A4 Arad, W Romania
Arafura Sea 120 A3 Ind. Laut Arafuru. sea W Pacific Ocean
Arafuru, Laut see Arafura Sea
Aragón 71 E2 autonomous community E Spain
Araguaia, Río 41 E3 var. Araguaya. river C Brazil
Araguari 41 F3 Minas Gerais, SE Brazil
Araguaya see Araguaia, Río
Ara Jovis see Aranjuez
Arāk 98 C3 prev. Sultānābād. Markazī, W Iran
Arakan Yoma 114 A3 mountain range W Myanmar (Burma)
Araks/Arak's see Aras
Aral see Aral'sk, Kazakhstan
Aral Sea 100 C1 Kaz. Aral Tengizi, Rus. Aral'skoye More, Uzb. Orol Dengizi. inland sea Kazakhstan/Uzbekistan
Aral'sk 92 B4 Kaz. Aral. Kzylorda, SW Kazakhstan
Aral'skoye More/Aral Tengizi see Aral Sea
Aranda de Duero 70 D2 Castilla-León, N Spain
Arandelovac 78 D4 prev. Arandjelovac. Serbia, C Serbia
Arandjelovac see Arandelovac
Aranjuez 70 D3 anc. Ara Jovis. Madrid, C Spain
Araouane 53 E2 Tombouctou, N Mali
'Ar'ar 98 B3 Al Ḥudūd ash Shamālīyah, NW Saudi Arabia
Ararat, Mount see Büyükağrı Dağı
Aras 95 G3 Arm. Arak's, Az. Araz Nehri, Per. Rūd-e Aras, Rus. Araks; prev. Araxes. river SW Asia
Aras, Rūd-e see Aras
Arauca 36 C2 Arauca, NE Colombia
Arauca, Río 36 C2 river Colombia/Venezuela
Arausio see Orange
Araxes see Aras
Araz Nehri see Aras
Arbela see Arbīl
Arbīl 98 B2 var. Erbil, Irbil, Kurd. Hawlêr; anc. Arbela. Arbīl, N Iraq
Arbroath 66 D3 anc. Aberbrothock. E Scotland, United Kingdom
Arbuzinka see Arbuzynka
Arbuzynka 87 E3 Rus. Arbuzinka. Mykolayivs'ka Oblast', S Ukraine
Arcachon 69 B5 Gironde, SW France
Arcae Remorum see Châlons-en-Champagne
Arcata 24 A4 California, W USA
Archangel see Arkhangel'sk
Archangel Bay see Chëshskaya Guba
Archidona 70 D5 Andalucía, S Spain
Arco 74 C2 Trentino-Alto Adige, N Italy
Arctic Mid Oceanic Ridge see Nansen Cordillera
Arctic Ocean 133 B3 ocean
Arda 82 C3 var. Ardhas, Gk. Ardas. river Bulgaria/Greece
Ardabīl 98 C2 var. Ardebil. Ardabīl, NW Iran
Ardakān 98 D3 Yazd, C Iran
Ardas 82 D3 var. Ardhas, Bul. Arda. river Bulgaria/Greece
Ard aş Şawwān 97 C7 var. Ardh es Suwwān. plain S Jordan
Ardeal see Transylvania
Ardebil see Ardabīl
Ardèche 69 C5 cultural region E France
Ardennes 65 C8 physical region Belgium/France
Ardhas see Arda/Ardas
Ardh es Suwwān see Ard aş Şawwān
Ardino 82 D3 Kŭrdzhali, S Bulgaria
Ard Mhacha see Armagh
Ardmore 27 G2 Oklahoma, C USA
Arel see Arlon
Arelas/Arelate see Arles
Arendal 63 A6 Aust-Agder, S Norway
Arensburg see Kuressaare
Arenys de Mar 71 G2 Cataluña, NE Spain
Areópoli 83 B7 prev. Areópolis. Pelopónnisos, S Greece
Areópolis see Areópoli
Arequipa 39 E4 Arequipa, SE Peru
Arezzo 74 C3 anc. Arretium. Toscana, C Italy
Argalastí 83 C5 Thessalía, C Greece
Argenteuil 68 D1 Val-d'Oise, N France
Argentina 43 B5 off. Argentine Republic. country S South America
Argentina Basin see Argentine Basin
Argentine Basin 35 C7 var. Argentina Basin. undersea basin SW Atlantic Ocean
Argentine Republic see Argentina
Argentine Rise see Falkland Plateau
Argentoratum see Strasbourg
Arghandab, Darya-ye 101 E5 river SE Afghanistan
Argirocastro see Gjirokastër
Argo 50 B3 Northern, N Sudan
Argo Fracture Zone 119 C5 tectonic Feature C Indian Ocean
Árgos 83 B6 Pelopónnisos, S Greece
Argostóli 83 A5 var. Argostólion. Kefallonía, Iónia Nísiá, Greece, C Mediterranean Sea
Argostólion see Argostóli
Argun 103 E1 Chin. Ergun He, Rus. Argun'. river China/Russian Federation
Argyrokastron see Gjirokastër
Århus 63 B7 var. Aarhus. Århus, C Denmark
Aria see Herāt
Ari Atoll 110 A4 var. Alifu Atoll. atoll C Maldives
Arica 42 B1 hist. San Marcos de Arica. Tarapacá, N Chile
Aridaía 82 B3 var. Aridea, Aridhaía. Dytikí Makedonía, N Greece
Aridea see Aridaía
Aridhaía see Aridaía
Arīhā 96 B3 Eng. Jericho. Al Karak, W Jordan

China 102 C2 off. People's Republic of China,
  Chin. Chung-hua Jen-min Kung-ho-kuo,
  Zhonghua Renmin Gongheguo; prev. Chinese
  Empire. country E Asia
Chi-nan/Chinan see Jinan
Chinandega 30 C3 Chinandega,
  NW Nicaragua
China, People's Republic of see China
China, Republic of see Taiwan
Chincha Alta 38 D4 Ica, SW Peru
Chin-chiang see Quanzhou
Chin-chou/Chinchow see Jinzhou
Chindwin see Chindwinn
Chindwinn 114 B2 var. Chindwin. river
  N Myanmar (Burma)
Chinese Empire see China
Ch'ing Hai see Qinghai Hu, China
Chinghai see Qinghai
Chingola 56 D2 Copperbelt, C Zambia
Ching-Tao/Ch'ing-tao see Qingdao
Chinguetti 52 C2 var. Chinguetti. Adrar,
  C Mauritania
Chin Hills 114 A3 mountain range W Myanmar
  (Burma)
Chinhsien see Jinzhou
Chinnereth see Tiberias, Lake
Chinook Trough 91 H4 trough N Pacific Ocean
Chioggia 74 C2 anc. Fossa Claudia. Veneto,
  NE Italy
Chíos 83 D5 var. Hios, Khíos, It. Scio, Turk. Sakiz-
  Adasi. Chíos, E Greece
Chíos 83 D5 var. Khíos. island E Greece
Chipata 56 D2 prev. Fort Jameson. Eastern,
  E Zambia
Chiquián 38 C3 Ancash, W Peru
Chiquimula 30 B2 Chiquimula, SE Guatemala
Chirāla 110 D1 Andhra Pradesh, E India
Chirchik see Chirchiq
Chirchiq 101 E2 Rus. Chirchik. Toshkent Viloyati,
  E Uzbekistan
Chiriquí Gulf 31 E5 Eng. Chiriqui Gulf. gulf
  SW Panama
Chiriqui Gulf see Chiriquí, Golfo de
Chiriquí, Laguna de 31 E5 lagoon NW Panama
Chiriquí, Volcán de see Barú, Volcán
Chirripó, Cerro see Chirripó Grande, Cerro
Chirripó Grande, Cerro 30 D4 var. Cerro
  Chirripó. mountain SE Costa Rica
Chisec 30 B2 Alta Verapaz, C Guatemala
Chisholm 23 F1 Minnesota, N USA
Chisimaio/Chisimayu see Kismaayo
Chişinău 86 D4 Rus. Kishinev. country capital
  (Moldova) C Moldova
Chita 93 F4 Chitinskaya Oblast', S Russian
  Federation
Chitangwiza see Chitungwiza
Chitato 56 C1 Lunda Norte, NE Angola
Chitina 14 D3 Alaska, USA
Chitose 108 D2 var. Titose. Hokkaidō, NE Japan
Chitré 31 F5 Herrera, S Panama
Chittagong 113 G4 Ben. Chāttagām. Chittagong,
  SE Bangladesh
Chitungwiza 56 D3 prev. Chitangwiza.
  Mashonaland East, NE Zimbabwe
Chkalov see Orenburg
Chlef 48 D2 var. Ech Cheliff, Ech Chleff; prev. Al-
  Asnam, El Asnam, Orléansville. NW Algeria
Chocolate Mountains 25 D8 mountain range
  California, W USA
Chodorów see Khodoriv
Chodzież 76 C3 Wielkopolskie, C Poland
Choele Choel 43 C5 Río Negro, C Argentina
Choiseul 122 C4 var. Lauru. island NW Solomon
  Islands
Chojnice 76 C2 Ger. Konitz. Pomorskie, N Poland
Ch'ok'ē 50 C4 var. Choke Mountains. mountain
  range NW Ethiopia
Choke Mountains see Ch'ok'ē
Cholet 68 B4 Maine-et-Loire, NW France
Choluteca 30 C3 Choluteca, S Honduras
Chol uteca, Río 30 C3 river SW Honduras
Choma 56 D2 Southern, S Zambia
Chomutov 76 A4 Ger. Komotau. Ústecký Kraj,
  NW Czech Republic
Chona 91 E2 river C Russian Federation
Chon Buri 115 C5 prev. Bang Pla Soi. Chon Buri,
  S Thailand
Chone 38 A1 Manabí, W Ecuador
Ch'ŏngjin 107 E3 NE North Korea
Chongqing 107 B5 var. Ch'ung-ching, Ch'ung-
  ch'ing, Chungking, Pahsien, Tchongking,
  Yuzhou. Chongqing Shi, C China
Chongqing Shi 107 B5 province C China
Chonnacht see Connaught
Chonos, Archipiélago de los 43 A6 island
  group S Chile
Chóra 83 D7 Kyklades, Greece, Aegean Sea
Chóra Sfakíon 83 C8 var. Sfákia. Kríti, Greece,
  E Mediterranean Sea
Chorne More see Black Sea
Chornomors'ke 87 E4 Rus. Chernomorskoye.
  Respublika Krym, S Ukraine
Chorokh/Chorokhi see Çoruh Nehri
Chortkiv 86 C2 Rus. Chortkov. Ternopil's'ka
  Oblast', W Ukraine
Chortkov see Chortkiv
Chorzów 77 C5 Ger. Königshütte; prev. Królewska
  Huta. Śląskie, S Poland
Chosebuz see Cottbus
Chosen-kaikyo see Korea Strait
Chōshi 109 D5 var. Tyōsi. Chiba, Honshū,
  S Japan
Choson-minjujuŭi-inmin-kanghwaguk see
  North Korea
Choszczno 76 B3 Ger. Arnswalde. Zachodnio-
  pomorskie, NW Poland
Chota Nagpur 113 E4 plateau N India
Choûm 52 C2 Adrar, C Mauritania
Choybalsan 105 F2 prev. Byan Tumen. Dornod,
  E Mongolia
Christchurch 129 C6 Canterbury, South Island,
  New Zealand
Christiana 32 B5 C Jamaica
Christiania see Oslo
Christiansand see Kristiansand
Christianshåb see Qasigiannguit
Christiansund see Kristiansund
Christmas Island 119 D5 Australian external
  territory E Indian Ocean
Christmas Island see Kiritimati
Christmas Ridge 121 E1 undersea ridge C Pacific
  Ocean
Chuan see Sichuan

Ch'uan-chou see Quanzhou
Chubek see Moskva
Chubut, Río 43 B6 river SE Argentina
Ch'u-chiang see Shaoguan
Chudskoye Ozero see Peipus, Lake
Chugoku-sanchi 109 B6 mountain range Honshū,
  SW Japan
Chui see Chuy
Chukai see Cukai
Chukchi Plain 133 B2 abyssal plain Arctic Ocean
Chukchi Plateau 132 C2 undersea plateau Arctic
  Ocean
Chukchi Sea 12 B2 Rus. Chukotskoye More. sea
  Arctic Ocean
Chukotskoye More see Chukchi Sea
Chula Vista 25 C8 California, W USA
Chulucanas 38 B2 Piura, NW Peru
Chulym 92 D4 river C Russian Federation
Chumphon 115 C6 var. Jumporn. Chumphon,
  SW Thailand
Chuncheon 107 E4 prev. Ch'unch'ŏn, Jap.
  Shunsen. N South Korea
Ch'unch'ŏn see Chuncheon
Chung-ch'ing/Ch'ung-ching see Chongqing
Chung-hua Jen-min Kung-ho-kuo see China
Chungking see Chongqing
Chunya 93 E3 river C Russian Federation
Chuquicamata 42 B2 Antofagasta, N Chile
Chuquisaca see Sucre
Chur 73 B7 Fr. Coire, It. Coira, Rmsch. Cuera,
  Quera; anc. Curia Rhaetorum. Graubünden,
  E Switzerland
Churchill 15 G4 Manitoba, C Canada
Churchill 15 F2 river Manitoba/Saskatchewan,
  C Canada
Churchill 17 F2 river Newfoundland and
  Labrador, E Canada
Chuska Mountains 26 C1 mountain range
  Arizona/New Mexico, SW USA
Chusovoy 89 D5 Permskaya Oblast', NW Russian
  Federation
Chust see Khust
Chuuk Islands 122 B2 var. Hogoley Islands; prev.
  Truk Islands. island group Caroline Islands,
  C Micronesia
Chuy 42 E4 var. Chuí. Rocha, E Uruguay
Chyhyryn 87 E2 Rus. Chigirin. Cherkas'ka
  Oblast', N Ukraine
Ciadâr-Lunga 86 D4 var. Ceadâr-Lunga, Rus.
  Chadyr-Lunga. S Moldova
Cide 94 C2 Kastamonu, N Turkey
Ciechanów 76 D3 prev. Zichenau. Mazowieckie,
  C Poland
Ciego de Ávila 32 C2 Ciego de Ávila, C Cuba
Ciénaga 36 B1 Magdalena, N Colombia
Cienfuegos 32 B2 Cienfuegos, C Cuba
Cieza 71 E4 Murcia, SE Spain
Cihanbeyli 94 C3 Konya, C Turkey
Cikobia 123 E4 prev. Thikombia. island N Fiji
Cilacap 116 C5 prev. Tjilatjap. Jawa, C Indonesia
Cill Airne see Killarney
Cill Chainnigh see Kilkenny
Cilli see Celje
Cill Mhantáin see Wicklow
Cimpina see Câmpina
Cîmpulung see Câmpulung
Cina Selatan, Laut see South China Sea
Cincinnati 18 C4 Ohio, N USA
Ciney 65 C7 Namur, SE Belgium
Cinto, Monte 69 E7 mountain Corse, France,
  C Mediterranean Sea
Cintra see Sintra
Cipolletti 43 B5 Río Negro, C Argentina
Cirebon 116 C4 prev. Tjirebon. Jawa, S Indonesia
Cirkvenica see Crikvenica
Cirò Marina 75 E6 Calabria, S Italy
Cirquenizza see Crikvenica
Cisnădie 86 B4 Ger. Heltau, Hung. Nagydisznód.
  Sibiu, SW Romania
Citharista see la Ciotat
Citlaltépetl see Orizaba, Volcán Pico de
Citrus Heights 25 B5 California, W USA
Ciudad Acuña 28 D2 var. Villa Acuña
Ciudad Bolívar 37 E2 prev. Angostura. Bolívar,
  E Venezuela
Ciudad Camargo 28 D2 Chihuahua, N Mexico
Ciudad Cortés see Cortés
Ciudad Darío 30 D3 var. Dario. Matagalpa,
  W Nicaragua
Ciudad de Dolores Hidalgo see Dolores Hidalgo
Ciudad de Guatemala 30 B2 Eng. Guatemala City;
  prev. Santiago de los Caballeros. country capital
  (Guatemala) Guatemala, C Guatemala
Ciudad del Carmen see Carmen
Ciudad del Este 42 E2 prev. Ciudad Presidente
  Stroessner, Présidente Stroessner, Puerto
  Presidente Stroessner. Alto Paraná, SE Paraguay
Ciudad Delicias see Delicias
Ciudad de México see México
Ciudad de Panamá see Panamá
Ciudad Guayana 37 E2 prev. San Tomé de
  Guayana, Santo Tomé de Guayana. Bolívar,
  NE Venezuela
Ciudad Guzmán 29 E4 Jalisco, SW Mexico
Ciudad Hidalgo 29 G5 Chiapas, SE Mexico
Ciudad Juárez 28 C1 Chihuahua, N Mexico
Ciudad Lerdo 28 D3 Durango, C Mexico
Ciudad Madero 29 E3 var. Villa Cecilia.
  Tamaulipas, C Mexico
Ciudad Mante 29 E3 Tamaulipas, C Mexico
Ciudad Miguel Alemán 29 E2 Tamaulipas,
  C Mexico
Ciudad Obregón 28 B2 Sonora, NW Mexico
Ciudad Ojeda 36 C1 Zulia, NW Venezuela
Ciudad Porfirio Díaz see Piedras Negras
Ciudad Presidente Stroessner see Ciudad del Este
Ciudad Quesada see Quesada
Ciudad Real 70 D3 Castilla-La Mancha, C Spain
Ciudad-Rodrigo 70 C3 Castilla-León, N Spain
Ciudad Trujillo see Santo Domingo
Ciudad Valles 29 E3 San Luis Potosí, C Mexico
Ciudad Victoria 29 E3 Tamaulipas, C Mexico
Ciutadella see Ciutadella de Menorca
Ciutadella 71 H3 var. Ciutadella de Menorca.
  Menorca, Spain, W Mediterranean Sea
Ciutadella Ciutadella de Menorca see Ciutadella
Civitanova Marche 74 D3 Marche, C Italy
Civitas Altae Ripae see Brzeg
Civitas Carnutum see Chartres
Civitas Eburovicum see Évreux
Civitavecchia 74 C4 anc. Centum Cellae, Trajani
  Portus. Lazio, C Italy
Claremont 27 D1 Oklahoma, C USA
Clarence 129 C5 Canterbury, South Island,
  New Zealand

Clarence 129 C5 river South Island, New Zealand
Clarence Town 32 D2 Long Island, C Bahamas
Clarinda 23 F4 Iowa, C USA
Clarion Fracture Zone 131 E2 tectonic feature
  NE Pacific Ocean
Clarión, Isla 28 A5 island W Mexico
Clark Fork 22 A1 river Idaho/Montana, NW USA
Clark Hill Lake 21 E2 var. J.Storm Thurmond
  Reservoir. reservoir Georgia/South Carolina,
  SE USA
Clarksburg 18 D4 West Virginia, NE USA
Clarksdale 20 B2 Mississippi, S USA
Clarksville 20 C1 Tennessee, S USA
Clausentum see Southampton
Clayton 27 E1 New Mexico, SW USA
Clearwater 21 E4 Florida, SE USA
Clearwater Mountains 24 D2 mountain range
  Idaho, NW USA
Cleburne 27 G3 Texas, SW USA
Clermont 126 D4 Queensland, E Australia
Clermont-Ferrand 69 C5 Puy-de-Dôme, C France
Cleveland 18 D3 Ohio, N USA
Cleveland 20 D1 Tennessee, S USA
Clifton 26 C2 Arizona, SW USA
Clinton 20 B2 Mississippi, S USA
Clinton 27 F1 Oklahoma, C USA
Clipperton Fracture Zone 131 E3 tectonic feature
  E Pacific Ocean
Clipperton Island 13 A7 French dependency of
  French Polynesia E Pacific Ocean
Cloncurry 126 B3 Queensland, C Australia
Clonmel 67 B6 Ir. Cluain Meala. S Ireland
Cloppenburg 72 B3 Niedersachsen, NW Germany
Cloquet 23 G2 Minnesota, N USA
Cloud Peak 22 C3 mountain Wyoming, C USA
Clovis 27 E2 New Mexico, SW USA
Cluain Meala see Clonmel
Cluj see Cluj-Napoca
Cluj-Napoca 86 B3 Ger. Klausenburg, Hung.
  Kolozsvár; prev. Cluj. Cluj, NW Romania
Clyde 66 C4 river W Scotland, United Kingdom
Coari 40 D2 Amazonas, N Brazil
Coast Mountains 14 D4 Fr. Chaîne Côtière.
  mountain range Canada/USA
Coast Ranges 24 A4 mountain range W USA
Coats Island 15 G3 island Nunavut, NE Canada
Coats Land 132 B2 physical region Antarctica
Coatzacoalcos 29 G4 var. Quetzalcoalco; prev.
  Puerto México. Veracruz-Llave, E Mexico
Cobán 30 B2 Alta Verapaz, C Guatemala
Cobar 127 C6 New South Wales, SE Australia
Cobija 39 E3 Pando, NW Bolivia
Coblence/Coblenz see Koblenz
Coburg 73 C5 Bayern, SE Germany
Coca see Puerto Francisco de Orellana
Cocanada see Kākināda
Cochabamba 39 F4 hist. Oropeza. Cochabamba,
  C Bolivia
Cochin see Kochi
Cochinos, Bahía de 32 B2 Eng. Bay of Pigs. bay
  SE Cuba
Cochrane 16 C4 Ontario, S Canada
Cochrane 43 B7 Aisén, S Chile
Cocibolca see Nicaragua, Lago de
Cockburn Town 32 B2 San Salvador, E Bahamas
Cockpit Country, The 32 A4 physical region
  W Jamaica
Cocobeach 55 A5 Estuaire, NW Gabon
Coconino Plateau 26 B1 plain Arizona, SW USA
Coco, Río 31 E2 var. Río Wanki, Segoviao
  Wangki. river Honduras/Nicaragua
Cocos Basin 102 C3 undersea basin E Indian
  Ocean
Cocos Island Ridge see Cocos Ridge
Cocos Islands 119 D5 island group E Indian Ocean
Cocos Ridge 13 C8 var. Cocos Island Ridge.
  undersea ridge E Pacific Ocean
Cod, Cape 19 G3 headland Massachusetts,
  NE USA
Codfish Island 129 A8 island SW New Zealand
Codlea 86 C4 Ger. Zeiden, Hung. Feketehalom.
  Braşov, C Romania
Cody 22 C2 Wyoming, C USA
Coeur d'Alene 24 C2 Idaho, NW USA
Coevorden 64 E2 Drenthe, NE Netherlands
Coffs Harbour 127 E6 New South Wales,
  SE Australia
Cognac 69 B5 anc. Compniacum. Charente,
  W France
Cohalm see Rupea
Coiba, Isla de 31 E5 island SW Panama
Coihaique 43 B6 var. Coyhaique. Aisén,
  S Chile
Coimbatore 110 C3 Tamil Nādu, S India
Coimbra 70 B3 anc. Conimbria, Conimbriga.
  Coimbra, W Portugal
Coín 70 D5 Andalucía, S Spain
Coira/Coire see Chur
Coirib, Loch see Corrib, Lough
Colby 23 E4 Kansas, C USA
Colchester 67 E6 Connecticut, NE USA
Coleman 27 F3 Texas, SW USA
Coleraine 66 B4 Ir. Cúil Raithin. N Northern
  Ireland, United Kingdom
Colesberg 56 C5 Northern Cape, C South Africa
Colima 28 D4 Colima, S Mexico
Coll 66 B3 island W Scotland, United Kingdom
College Station 27 G3 Texas, SW USA
Collie 125 A7 Western Australia
Collipo see Leiria
Colmar 68 E4 Ger. Kolmar. Haut-Rhin, NE France
Cöln see Köln
Cologne see Köln
Colomb-Béchar see Béchar
Colombia 36 B3 off. Republic of Colombia.
  country N South America
Colombian Basin 34 A1 undersea basin
  SW Caribbean Sea
Colombia, Republic of see Colombia
Colombie-Britannique see British Columbia
Colombo 110 C4 country capital (Sri Lanka)
  Western Province, W Sri Lanka
Colón 34 B4 island SW Panama
Colón, Archipiélago de see Galápagos Islands
Colón Ridge 131 B8 undersea ridge E Pacific Ocean
Colorado 22 C4 off. State of Colorado, also known
  as Centennial State, Silver State. state C USA
Colorado City 27 F3 Texas, SW USA
Colorado Plateau 26 B1 plain SW USA
Colorado, Río 43 C5 river E Argentina
Colorado, Río see Colorado River

Colorado River 13 B5 var. Río Colorado. river
  Mexico/USA
Colorado River 27 G4 river Texas, SW USA
Colorado Springs 22 D5 Colorado, C USA
Columbia 19 E4 Maryland, NE USA
Columbia 23 G5 Missouri, C USA
Columbia 21 E2 state capital South Carolina,
  SE USA
Columbia 20 C1 Tennessee, S USA
Columbia River 24 B3 river Canada/USA
Columbia Plateau 24 C3 plateau Idaho/Oregon,
  NW USA
Columbus 20 D2 Georgia, SE USA
Columbus 18 C4 Indiana, N USA
Columbus 20 C2 Mississippi, S USA
Columbus 23 F4 Nebraska, C USA
Columbus 18 D4 state capital Ohio, N USA
Colville Channel 128 D2 channel North Island,
  New Zealand
Colville River 14 D2 river Alaska, USA
Comacchio 74 C2 var. Commachio; anc.
  Comactium. Emilia-Romagna, N Italy
Comactium see Comacchio
Comalcalco 29 G4 Tabasco, SE Mexico
Coma Pedrosa, Pic de 69 A7 mountain
  NW Andorra
Comarapa 39 F4 Santa Cruz, C Bolivia
Comayagua 30 C2 Comayagua, W Honduras
Comer See see Como, Lago di
Comilla 113 G4 Ben. Kumillā. Chittagong,
  E Bangladesh
Comino see Kemmuna
Comitán 29 G5 var. Comitán de Domínguez.
  Chiapas, SE Mexico
Comitán de Domínguez see Comitán
Commachio see Comacchio
Commissioner's Point 20 A5 headland
  W Bermuda
Communism Peak 101 F3 prev. Qullai
  Kommunizm, Kommunizm. mountain E Tajikistan
Como 74 B2 anc. Comum. Lombardia, N Italy
Comodoro Rivadavia 43 B6 Chubut, SE Argentina
Como, Lago di 74 B2 var. Lario, Eng. Lake Como,
  Ger. Comer See. lake N Italy
Como, Lake see Como, Lago di
Comores, République Fédérale Islamique des
  see Comoros
Comoros 57 F2 off. Federal Islamic Republic of the
  Comoros, Fr. République Fédérale Islamique des
  Comores. country W Indian Ocean
Comoros, Federal Islamic Republic of the see
  Comoros
Compiègne 68 C3 Oise, N France
Complutum see Alcalá de Henares
Compniacum see Cognac
Compostella see Santiago de Compostela
Comrat 86 D4 Rus. Komrat. S Moldova
Comum see Como
Conca see Cuenca
Concarneau 68 A3 Finistère, NW France
Concepción 39 G3 Santa Cruz, E Bolivia
Concepción 43 B5 Bío Bío, C Chile
Concepción 42 D2 var. Villa Concepción.
  Concepción, C Paraguay
Concepción see La Concepción
Concepción de la Vega see La Vega
Conchos, Río 26 D4 river NW Mexico
Conchos, Río 28 D2 river C Mexico
Concord 19 G3 state capital New Hampshire,
  NE USA
Concordia 42 D4 Entre Ríos, E Argentina
Concordia 23 F4 Kansas, C USA
Côn Đao see Côn Đao Son
Côn Đao Son 115 E7 var. Côn Đao, Con Son.
  island S Vietnam
Condate see Rennes, Ille-et-Vilaine, France
Condate see St-Claude, Jura, France
Condega 30 D3 Estelí, NW Nicaragua
Condivincum see Nantes
Confluentes see Koblenz
Công Hoa Xa Hôi Chu Nghia Viêt Nam see
  Vietnam
Congo 55 D5 off. Republic of the Congo, Fr.
  Moyen-Congo; prev. Middle Congo. country
  C Africa
Congo 55 C6 off. Democratic Republic of Congo;
  prev. Zaire, Belgian Congo, Congo (Kinshasa).
  country C Africa
Congo 55 C6 var. Kongo, Fr. Zaire. river C Africa
Congo Basin 55 C6 drainage basin W Dem.
  Rep. Congo
Congo/Congo (Kinshasa) see Congo (Democratic
  Republic of)
Coni see Cuneo
Conimbria/Conimbriga see Coimbra
Conjeeveram see Kānchipuram
Connacht see Connaught
Connaught 67 A5 var. Connacht, Ir. Chonnacht,
  Cúige. province W Ireland
Connecticut 19 F3 off. State of Connecticut,
  also known as Blue Law State, Constitution
  State, Land of Steady Habits, Nutmeg State.
  state NE USA
Connecticut 19 G3 river Canada/USA
Conroe 27 G3 Texas, SW USA
Consentia see Cosenza
Consolación del Sur 32 A2 Pinar del Río, W Cuba
Con Son see Côn Đao Son
Constance see Konstanz
Constance, Lake 73 B7 Ger. Bodensee. lake
  C Europe
Constanţa 86 D5 var. Küstendje, Eng. Constanza,
  Ger. Konstanza, Turk. Kistence. Constanţa,
  SE Romania
Constantia see Coutances
Constantia see Konstanz
Constantine 49 E2 var. Qacentina, Ar.
  Qoussantina. NE Algeria
Constantinople see İstanbul
Constantiola see Oltenita
Constanz see Konstanz
Constanza see Constanţa
Constitution State see Connecticut
Coo see Kos
Coober Pedy 127 A5 South Australia
Cookeville 20 D1 Tennessee, S USA
Cook Islands 123 F4 territory in free association
  with New Zealand S Pacific Ocean
Cook, Mount see Aoraki
Cook Strait 129 D5 var. Raukawa. strait
  New Zealand

Cooktown 126 D2 Queensland, NE Australia
Coolgardie 125 B6 Western Australia
Cooma 127 D7 New South Wales, SE Australia
Coomassie see Kumasi
Coon Rapids 23 F2 Minnesota, N USA
Cooper Creek 126 C4 var. Barcoo, Cooper's
  Creek. seasonal river Queensland/
  South Australia, Australia
Cooper's Creek see Cooper Creek
Coos Bay 24 A3 Oregon, NW USA
Cootamundra 127 D6 New South Wales,
  SE Australia
Copacabana 39 E4 La Paz, W Bolivia
Copenhagen see København
Copiapó 42 B3 Atacama, N Chile
Copperas Cove 27 G3 Texas, SW USA
Coppermine see Kugluktuk
Copper State see Arizona
Coquilhatville see Mbandaka
Coquimbo 42 B3 Coquimbo, N Chile
Corabia 86 B5 Olt, S Romania
Coral Harbour 15 G3 Southampton Island,
  Nunavut, NE Canada
Coral Sea 120 B3 sea SW Pacific Ocean
Coral Sea Islands 122 B4 Australian external
  territory SW Pacific Ocean
Corantijn Rivier see Courantyne River
Corcovado, Golfo 43 B6 gulf S Chile
Corcyra Nigra see Korčula
Cordele 20 D3 Georgia, SE USA
Córdoba 42 C3 Córdoba, C Argentina
Córdoba 29 F4 Veracruz-Llave, E Mexico
Córdoba 70 D4 var. Cordoba, Eng. Cordova; anc.
  Corduba. Andalucía, SW Spain
Cordova 14 C3 Alaska, USA
Cordova/Cordoba see Córdoba
Corduba see Córdoba
Corentyne Rive see Courantyne River
Corfu see Kérkyra
Coria 70 C3 Extremadura, W Spain
Corinth 20 C1 Mississippi, S USA
Corinth, Gulf of Corinthiacus Sinus see
  Korinthiakós Kólpos
Corinthus see Kórinthos
Corinto 30 C3 Chinandega, NW Nicaragua
Cork 67 A6 Ir. Corcaigh. S Ireland
Çorlu 94 A2 Tekirdağ, NW Turkey
Corner Brook 17 G3 Newfoundland,
  Newfoundland and Labrador, E Canada
Cornhusker State see Nebraska
Corn Islands 31 E3 var. Corn Islands. island
  group SE Nicaragua
Corn Islands see Maíz, Islas del
Cornwallis Island 15 F2 Island Nunavut,
  N Canada
Coro 36 C1 prev. Santa Ana de Coro. Falcón,
  NW Venezuela
Corocoro 39 F4 La Paz, W Bolivia
Coromandel 128 D2 Waikato, North Island,
  New Zealand
Coromandel Coast 110 D2 coast E India
Coromandel Peninsula 128 D2 peninsula North
  Island, New Zealand
Coronado, Bahía de 30 D5 gulf S Costa Rica
Coronel Dorrego 43 C5 Buenos Aires, E Argentina
Coronel Oviedo 42 D2 Caaguazú, SE Paraguay
Corozal 30 C1 Corozal, N Belize
Corpus Christi 27 G4 Texas, SW USA
Corrales 26 D2 New Mexico, SW USA
Corrib, Lough 67 A5 Ir. Loch Coirib. lake
  W Ireland
Corrientes 42 D3 Corrientes, NE Argentina
Corriza see Korçë
Corsica 67 F4 Eng. Corsica. island France,
  C Mediterranean Sea
Corsica see Corse
Corsicana 27 G3 Texas, SW USA
Cortegana 70 C4 Andalucía, S Spain
Cortés 31 E5 var. Ciudad Cortés. Puntarenas,
  SE Costa Rica
Cortez, Sea of see California, Golfo de
Cortina d'Ampezzo 74 C1 Veneto, NE Italy
Coruche 70 B3 Santarém, C Portugal
Çoruh Nehri 95 E3 Geor. Chorokh, Rus. Chorokhi.
  river Georgia/Turkey
Çorum 94 D3 var. Chorum. Çorum, N Turkey
Corunna see A Coruña
Corvallis 24 B3 Oregon, NW USA
Corvo 70 A5 var. Ilha do Corvo. island Azores,
  Portugal, NE Atlantic Ocean
Corvo, Ilha do see Corvo
Cos see Kos
Cosenza 75 D6 anc. Consentia. Calabria, SW Italy
Cosne-Cours-sur-Loire 68 C4 Nièvre, Bourgogne,
  C France Europe
Costa Mesa 24 D2 California, W USA North
  America
Costa Rica 31 E4 off. Republic of Costa Rica.
  country Central America
Costa Rica, Republic of see Costa Rica
Costermansville see Bukavu
Cotagaita 39 F5 Potosí, S Bolivia
Côte d'Ivoire 52 C4 off. République de la Côte
  d'Ivoire; Eng. Ivory Coast. country W Africa
Côte d'Ivoire, République de la see Côte d'Ivoire
Côte d'Or 68 C4 cultural region C France
Côte Française des Somalis see Djibouti
Côtière, Chaîne see Coast Mountains
Cotonou 53 F5 var. Kotonu. S Benin
Cotrone see Crotone
Cotswold Hills 67 D6 var. Cotswolds. hill range
  S England, United Kingdom
Cotswolds see Cotswold Hills
Cottbus 72 D4 Lus. Chóśebuz; prev. Kottbus.
  Brandenburg, E Germany
Cotton State, The see Alabama
Cotyora see Ordu
Couentrey see Coventry
Council Bluffs 23 F4 Iowa, C USA
Courantyne River 37 G3 var. Corantijn Rivier,
  Corentyne River. river Guyana/Suriname
Courland Lagoon 84 A4 Ger. Kurisches Haff,
  Rus. Kurskiy Zaliv. lagoon Lithuania/Russian
  Federation
Courtai see Kortrijk
Coutances 68 B3 anc. Constantia. Manche,
  N France
Couvin 65 C7 Namur, S Belgium
Coventry 67 D6 anc. Couentrey. C England,
  United Kingdom
Covilhã 70 C3 Castelo Branco, E Portugal
Cowan, Lake 125 B6 lake Western Australia

Niedenburg – Oldenburg in Holstein

Niedenburg *see* Nidzica
Niedere Tauern *77 A6* mountain range C Austria
Niemen *see* Neman
Nieśwież *see* Nyasvizh
Nieuw Amsterdam *37 G3* Commewijne, NE Suriname
Nieuw-Bergen *64 D4* Limburg, SE Netherlands
Nieuwegein *64 C4* Utrecht, C Netherlands
Nieuw Guinea *see* New Guinea
Nieuw Nickerie *37 G3* Nickerie, NW Suriname
Niewenstat *see* Neustadt an der Weinstrasse
Niğde *94 C4* Niğde, C Turkey
Niger *53 F3* off. Republic of Niger. country W Africa
Niger *53 F4* river W Africa
Nigeria *53 F4* off. Federal Republic of Nigeria. country W Africa
Nigeria, Federal Republic of *see* Nigeria
Niger, Mouths of the *53 F5* delta S Nigeria
Niger, Republic of *see* Niger
Nihon *see* Japan
Niigata *109 D5* Niigata, Honshū, C Japan
Niihama *109 B7* Ehime, Shikoku, SW Japan
Ni'ihau *25 A7* var. Niihau. island Hawaii, USA, C Pacific Ocean
Nii-jima *109 D6* island E Japan
Nijkerk *64 D3* Gelderland, C Netherlands
Nijlen *65 C5* Antwerpen, N Belgium
Nijmegen *64 D4* Ger. Nimwegen; anc. Noviomagus. Gelderland, SE Netherlands
Nikaria *see* Ikaría
Nikel' *88 C2* Finn. Kolosjoki. Murmanskaya Oblast', NW Russian Federation
Nikiniki *117 E5* Timor, S Indonesia
Niklasmarkt *see* Gheorgheni
Nikolainkaupunki *see* Vaasa
Nikolayev *see* Mykolayiv
Nikol'sk *see* Ussuriysk
Nikol'sk-Ussuriyskiy *see* Ussuriysk
Nikopol' *87 F3* Dnipropetrovs'ka Oblast', SE Ukraine
Nikšić *79 C5* C Montenegro
Nikumaroro *123 E3* ; prev. Gardner Island. atoll Phoenix Islands, C Kiribati
Nikunau *123 E3* var. Nukunau; prev. Byron Island. atoll Tungaru, W Kiribati
Nile *50 B2* former province NW Uganda
Nile *46 D3* Ar. Nahr an Nīl. river N Africa
Nile Delta *50 B1* delta N Egypt
Nīl, Nahr an *see* Nile
Nîmes *69 C6* anc. Nemausus, Nismes. Gard, S France
Nimwegen *see* Nijmegen
Nine Degree Channel *110 B3* channel India/ Maldives
Ninetyeast Ridge *119 D5* undersea feature E Indian Ocean
Ninety Mile Beach *128 C1* beach North Island, New Zealand
Ningbo *106 D5* var. Ning-po, Yin-hsien; prev. Ninghsien. Zhejiang, SE China
Ning-hsia *see* Ningxia
Ninghsien *see* Ningbo
Ning-po *see* Ningbo
Ningsia/Ningsia Hui/Ningsia Hui Autonomous Region *see* Ningxia
Ningxia *106 B4* off. Ningxia Huizu Zizhiqu, var. Ning-hsia, Ningsia, Eng. Ningsia Hui, Ningsia Hui Autonomous Region. autonomous region N China
Ningxia Huizu Zizhiqu *see* Ningxia
Nio *see* Íos
Niobrara River *23 E3* river Nebraska/Wyoming, C USA
Nioro *52 D3* var. Nioro du Sahel. Kayes, W Mali
Nioro du Sahel *see* Nioro
Niort *68 B4* Deux-Sèvres, W France
Nipigon *16 B4* Ontario, S Canada
Nipigon, Lake *16 B3* lake Ontario, S Canada
Nippon *see* Japan
Niš *79 E5* Eng. Nish, Ger. Nisch; anc. Naissus. Serbia, SE Serbia
Nişab *98 B4* Al Ḥudūd ash Shamālīyah, N Saudi Arabia
Nisch/Nish *see* Niš
Nisibin *see* Nusaybin
Nisiros *see* Nísyros
Nisko *76 E4* Podkrapackie, SE Poland
Nismes *see* Nîmes
Nistru *see* Dniester
Nísyros *83 E7* var. Nisiros. island Dodekánisa, Greece, Aegean Sea
Nitra *77 C6* Ger. Neutra, Hung. Nyitra. Nitriansky Kraj, SW Slovakia
Nitra *77 C6* Ger. Neutra, Hung. Nyitra. river W Slovakia
Niuatobutabu *see* Niuatoputapu
Niuatoputapu *123 E4* var. Niuatobutabu; prev. Keppel Island. island N Tonga
Niue *123 F4* self-governing territory in free association with New Zealand S Pacific Ocean
Niulakita *123 E3* var. Nurakita. atoll S Tuvalu
Niutao *123 E3* atoll NW Tuvalu
Nivernais *68 C4* cultural region C France
Nizāmābād *112 D5* Telangana, C India
Nizhnegorskiy *see* Nyzhn'ohirs'kyy
Nizhnekamsk *89 C5* Respublika Tatarstan, W Russian Federation
Nizhnevartovsk *92 D3* Khanty-Mansiyskiy Avtonomnyy Okrug-Yugra, C Russian Federation
Nizhniy Novgorod *89 C5* prev. Gor'kiy. Nizhegorodskaya Oblast', W Russian Federation
Nizhniy Odes *88 D4* Respublika Komi, NW Russian Federation
Nizhnyaya Tunguska *93 E3* Eng. Lower Tunguska. river N Russian Federation
Nizhyn *87 E1* Rus. Nezhin. Chernihivs'ka Oblast', NE Ukraine
Nizza *see* Nice
Njombe *51 C8* Iringa, S Tanzania
Nkayi *55 B6* prev. Jacob. Bouenza, S Congo
Nkongsamba *54 A4* var. N'Kongsamba. Littoral, W Cameroon
N'Kongsamba *see* Nkongsamba
Nmai Hka *114 B2* var. Me Hka. river N Myanmar (Burma)
Nobeoka *109 B7* Miyazaki, Kyūshū, SW Japan
Noboribetsu *108 D3* var. Noboribetu. Hokkaidō, NE Japan
Noboribetu *see* Noboribetsu
Nogales *28 B1* Sonora, NW Mexico
Nogales *26 B3* Arizona, SW USA
Nogal Valley *see* Dooxo Nugaaleed
Noire, Rivi`ere *see* Black River
Nokia *63 D5* Länsi-Suomi, W Finland
Nokou *54 B3* Kanem, W Chad
Nola *55 B5* Sangha-Mbaéré, SW Central African Republic
Nolinsk *89 C5* Kirovskaya Oblast', NW Russian Federation
Nongkaya *see* Nong Khai
Nong Khai *114 C4* var. Mi Chai, Nongkaya. Nong Khai, E Thailand
Nonouti *122 D2* prev. Sydenham Island. atoll Tungaru, W Kiribati
Noord-Beveland *64 B4* var. North Beveland. island SW Netherlands
Noordwijk aan Zee *64 C3* Zuid-Holland, W Netherlands
Noordzee *see* North Sea
Nora *63 C6* Örebro, C Sweden
Norak *101 E3* Rus. Nurek. W Tajikistan
Nord *61 F1* Avannaarsua, N Greenland
Nordaustlandet *61 G1* island NE Svalbard
Norden *72 A3* Niedersachsen, NW Germany
Norderstedt *72 B3* Schleswig-Holstein, N Germany
Nordfriesische Inseln *see* North Frisian Islands
Nordhausen *72 C4* Thüringen, C Germany
Nordhorn *72 A3* Niedersachsen, NW Germany
Nord, Mer du *see* North Sea
Nord-Ouest, Territoires du *see* Northwest Territories
Nordsee/Nordsjøen/Nordsøen *see* North Sea
Norfolk *23 E3* Nebraska, C USA
Norfolk *19 F5* Virginia, NE USA
Norfolk Island *120 D4* Australian external territory SW Pacific Ocean
Norfolk Ridge *120 D4* undersea feature W Pacific Ocean
Norge *see* Norway
Norias *27 G5* Texas, SW USA
Noril'sk *92 D3* Taymyrskiy (Dolgano-Nenetskiy) Avtonomnyy Okrug, N Russian Federation
Norman *27 G1* Oklahoma, C USA
Normandes, Îles *see* Channel Islands
Normandie *68 B3* Eng. Normandy. cultural region N France
Normandy *see* Normandie
Normanton *126 C3* Queensland, NE Australia
Norrköping *63 C6* Östergötland, S Sweden
Norrtälje *63 C6* Stockholm, C Sweden
Norseman *125 B6* Western Australia
Norske Havet *see* Norwegian Sea
North Albanian Alps *79 C5* Alb. Bjeshkët e Namuna, SCr. Prokletije. mountain range SE Europe
Northallerton *67 D5* N England, United Kingdom
Northam *125 A6* Western Australia
North America *12* continent
Northampton *67 D6* C England, United Kingdom
North Andaman *111 F2* island Andaman Islands, India, NE Indian Ocean
North Australian Basin *119 E5* Fr. Bassin Nord de l' Australie. undersea feature E Indian Ocean
North Bay *16 D4* Ontario, S Canada
North Beveland *see* Noord-Beveland
North Borneo *see* Sabah
North Cape *128 C1* headland North Island, New Zealand
North Cape *62 D1* Eng. North Cape. headland N Norway
North Cape *see* Nordkapp
North Carolina *21 E1* off. State of North Carolina, also known as Old North State, Tar Heel State, Turpentine State. state SE USA
North Channel *18 D2* lake channel Canada/USA
North Charleston *21 F2* South Carolina, SE USA
North Dakota *22 D2* off. State of North Dakota, also known as Flickertail State, Peace Garden State, Sioux State. state N USA
North Devon Island *see* Devon Island
North East Frontier Agency/North East Frontier Agency of Assam *see* Arunāchal Pradesh
Northeast Providence Channel *32 C1* channel N Bahamas
Northeim *72 B4* Niedersachsen, C Germany
Northern Cook Islands *123 F4* island group N Cook Islands
Northern Dvina *see* Severnaya Dvina
Northern Ireland *66 B4* var. The Six Counties. cultural region Northern Ireland, United Kingdom
Northern Mariana Islands *120 B1* US commonwealth territory W Pacific Ocean
Northern Rhodesia *see* Zambia
Northern Sporades *see* Vóreies Sporádes
Northern Territory *122 A5* territory N Australia
North European Plain *59 E3* plain N Europe
Northfield *23 F2* Minnesota, N USA
North Fiji Basin *120 D3* undersea feature N Coral Sea
North Frisian Islands *72 B2* var. Nordfriesische Inseln. island group N Germany
North Huvadhu Atoll *110 B5* var. Gaafu Alifu Atoll. atoll S Maldives
North Island *128 B2* island N New Zealand
North Korea *107 E3* off. Democratic People's Republic of Korea, Kor. Chosŏn-minjujuŭi-inmin-kanghwaguk. country E Asia
North Little Rock *20 B1* Arkansas, C USA
North Minch *see* Minch, The
North Mole *71 G4* harbour wall NW Gibraltar Europe
North Platte *23 E4* Nebraska, C USA
North Platte River *22 D4* river C USA
North Pole *133 B3* pole Arctic Ocean
North Saskatchewan *15 F5* river Alberta/ Saskatchewan, S Canada
North Sea *58 D3* Dan. Nordsøen, Dut. Noordzee, Fr. Mer du Nord, Ger. Nordsee, Nor. Nordsjøen; prev. German Ocean, Lat. Mare Germanicum. sea NW Europe
North Siberian Lowland *93 E2* var. North Siberian Plain, Eng. North Siberian Lowland. lowlands N Russian Federation
North Siberian Lowland/North Siberian Plain *see* Severo-Sibirskaya Nizmennost'
North Star State *see* Minnesota
North Taranaki Bight *128 C3* gulf North Island, New Zealand
North Uist *66 B3* island NW Scotland, United Kingdom
Northwest Atlantic Mid-Ocean Canyon *12 E4* undersea feature N Atlantic Ocean
North West Highlands *66 C3* mountain range N Scotland, United Kingdom
Northwest Pacific Basin *91 G4* undersea feature NW Pacific Ocean
Northwest Territories *15 E3* Fr. Territoires du Nord-Ouest. territory NW Canada
Northwind Plain *133 B2* undersea feature Arctic Ocean
Norton Sound *14 C2* inlet Alaska, USA
Norway *63 A5* off. Kingdom of Norway, Nor. Norge. country N Europe
Norway, Kingdom of *see* Norway
Norwegian Basin *61 F4* undersea feature NW Norwegian Sea
Norwegian Sea *61 F4* var. Norske Havet. sea NE Atlantic Ocean
Norwich *67 E6* E England, United Kingdom
Nösen *see* Bistrița
Noshiro *108 D4* var. Nosiro; prev. Noshirominato. Akita, Honshū, C Japan
Noshirominato/Nosiro *see* Noshiro
Nosivka *87 E1* Rus. Nosovka. Chernihivs'ka Oblast', NE Ukraine
Nosop *56 C4* river E Namibia
Nosovka *see* Nosivka
Noşratābād *98 E3* Sīstān va Balūchestān, E Iran
Noteć *76 C3* Ger. Netze. river NW Poland
Nóties Sporádes *see* Dodekánisa
Nottingham *67 D6* C England, United Kingdom
Nouâdhibou *52 B2* prev. Port-Étienne. Dakhlet Nouâdhibou, W Mauritania
Nouakchott *52 B2* country capital (Mauritania) Nouakchott District, SW Mauritania
Nouméa *122 C5* dependent territory capital (New Caledonia) Province Sud, S New Caledonia
Nouveau-Brunswick *see* New Brunswick
Nouvelle-Calédonie *see* New Caledonia
Nouvelle Écosse *see* Nova Scotia
Nova Civitas *see* Neustadt an der Weinstrasse
Nova Gorica *73 D8* W Slovenia
Nova Gradiška *78 C3* Ger. Neugradisk, Hung. Újgradiska. Brod-Posavina, NE Croatia
Nova Iguaçu *41 F4* Rio de Janeiro, SE Brazil
Nova Lisboa *see* Huambo
Novara *74 B2* anc. Novaria. Piemonte, NW Italy
Novaria *see* Novara
Nova Scotia *17 F4* Fr. Nouvelle Écosse. province SE Canada
Nova Scotia *13 E5* physical region SE Canada
Novaya Sibir', Ostrov *93 F1* island Novosibirskiye Ostrova, NE Russian Federation
Novaya Zemlya *88 D1* island group N Russian Federation
Novaya Zemlya Trough *see* East Novaya Zemlya Trough
Novgorod *see* Velikiy Novgorod
Novi Grad *see* Bosanski Novi
Novi Iskŭr *82 C2* Sofiya-Grad, W Bulgaria
Noviodunum *see* Nevers, Nièvre, France
Noviomagus *see* Lisieux, Calvados, France
Noviomagus *see* Nijmegen, Netherlands
Novi Pazar *79 D5* Turk. Yenipazar. Serbia, S Serbia
Novi Sad *78 D3* Ger. Neusatz, Hung. Újvidék. Vojvodina, N Serbia
Novoazovs'k *87 G4* Rus. Novoazovsk. Donets'ka Oblast', E Ukraine
Novocheboksarsk *89 C5* Chuvashskaya Respublika, W Russian Federation
Novocherkassk *89 B7* Rostovskaya Oblast', SW Russian Federation
Novodvinsk *88 C3* Arkhangel'skaya Oblast', NW Russian Federation
Novograd-Volynskiy *see* Novohrad-Volyns'kyy
Novogrudok *see* Navahrudak
Novohrad-Volyns'kyy *86 D2* Rus. Novograd-Volynskiy. Zhytomyrs'ka Oblast', N Ukraine
Novokazalinsk *see* Ayteke Bi
Novokuznetsk *92 D4* prev. Stalinsk. Kemerovskaya Oblast', S Russian Federation
Novolazarevskaya *132 C2* Russian research station Antarctica
Novo mesto *73 E8* Ger. Rudolfswert; prev. Ger. Neustadtl. SE Slovenia
Novomoskovsk *89 B5* Tul'skaya Oblast', W Russian Federation
Novomoskovs'k *87 F3* Rus. Novomoskovsk. Dnipropetrovs'ka Oblast', E Ukraine
Novopolotsk *see* Navapolatsk
Novoradomsk *see* Radomsko
Novo Redondo *see* Sumbe
Novorossiysk *89 A7* Krasnodarskiy Kray, SW Russian Federation
Novoshakhtinsk *89 B6* Rostovskaya Oblast', SW Russian Federation
Novosibirsk *92 D4* Novosibirskaya Oblast', C Russian Federation
Novosibirskiye Ostrova *93 F1* Eng. New Siberian Islands. island group N Russian Federation
Novotroitsk *89 D6* Orenburgskaya Oblast', W Russian Federation
Novotroitskoye *see* Novotroyits'ke, Ukraine
Novotroyits'ke *87 F4* Rus. Novotroitskoye. Khersons'ka Oblast', S Ukraine
Novo-Urgench *see* Urganch
Novovolyns'k *86 C1* Rus. Novovolynsk. Volyns'ka Oblast', NW Ukraine
Novy Dvor *85 B6* Rus. Novyy Dvor. Hrodzyenskaya Voblasts', W Belarus
Novyy Bug *see* Novyy Buh
Novyy Buh *87 E3* Rus. Novyy Bug. Mykolayivs'ka Oblast', S Ukraine
Novyy Dvor *see* Novy Dvor
Novyy Margilan *see* Farg'ona
Novyy Uzen' *see* Zhanaozen
Nowa Sól *76 B4* var. Nowasól, Ger. Neusalz an der Oder. Lubuskie, W Poland
Nowasól *see* Nowa Sól
Nowogard *76 B2* var. Nowógard, Ger. Naugard. Zachodnio-pomorskie, NW Poland
Nowogródek *see* Navahrudak
Nowo-Minsk *see* Mińsk Mazowiecki
Nowy Dwór Mazowiecki *76 D3* Mazowieckie, C Poland
Nowy Sącz *77 D5* Ger. Neu Sandec. Małopolskie, S Poland
Nowy Tomyśl *76 B3* var. Nowy Tomysl. Wielkopolskie, C Poland
Nowy Tomysl *see* Nowy Tomyśl
Noyon *68 C3* Oise, N France
Nsanje *57 E3* Southern, S Malawi
Nsawam *53 E5* SE Ghana
Ntomba, Lac *55 C6* var. Lac Tumba. lake NW Dem. Rep. Congo
Nubian Desert *50 B3* desert NE Sudan
Nu Chiang *see* Salween
Nu'eima *97 E7* E West Bank Asia
Nueva Caceres *see* Naga
Nueva Gerona *32 B2* Isla de la Juventud, S Cuba
Nueva Rosita *28 D2* Coahuila, NE Mexico
Nuevitas *32 C2* Camagüey, E Cuba
Nuevo, Bajo *31 G1* island NW Colombia South America
Nuevo Casas Grandes *28 C1* Chihuahua, N Mexico
Nuevo, Golfo *43 C6* gulf S Argentina
Nuevo Laredo *29 E2* Tamaulipas, NE Mexico
Nui Atoll *123 E3* atoll W Tuvalu
Nu Jiang *see* Salween
Nûk *see* Nuuk
Nukha *see* Şäki
Nuku'alofa *123 E5* country capital (Tonga) Tongatapu, S Tonga
Nukufetau Atoll *123 E3* atoll C Tuvalu
Nukulaelae Atoll *123 E3* var. Nukulailai. atoll E Tuvalu
Nukulailai *see* Nukulaelae Atoll
Nukunau *see* Nikunau
Nukunonu Atoll *123 E3* island C Tokelau
Nukus *100 C2* Qoraqalpog'iston Respublikasi, W Uzbekistan
Nullarbor Plain *125 C6* plateau South Australia/ Western Australia
Nunap Isua *60 C5* var. Uummannarsuaq, Dan. Kap Farvel, Eng. Cape Farewell. cape S Greenland
Nunavut *15 F3* territory N Canada
Nuneaton *67 D6* C England, United Kingdom
Nunivak Island *14 B2* island Alaska, USA
Nunspeet *64 D3* Gelderland, E Netherlands
Nuoro *75 A5* Sardegna, Italy, C Mediterranean Sea
Nuquí *36 A3* Chocó, W Colombia
Nurakita *see* Niulakita
Nurata *see* Nurota
Nurek *see* Norak
Nuremberg *see* Nürnberg
Nurmes *62 E4* Itä-Suomi, E Finland
Nürnberg *73 C5* Eng. Nuremberg. Bayern, S Germany
Nurota *101 E2* Rus. Nurata. Navoiy Viloyati, C Uzbekistan
Nusaybin *95 F4* var. Nisibin. Manisa, SE Turkey
Nussdorf *see* Năsăud
Nutmeg State *see* Connecticut
Nuuk *60 C4* var. Nûk, Dan. Godthaab, Godthåb. dependent territory capital (Greenland) Kitaa, SW Greenland
Nyagan' *92 C3* Khanty-Mansiyskiy Avtonomnyy Okrug-Yugra, N Russian Federation
Nyainqentanglha Shan *104 C5* mountain range W China
Nyala *50 A4* Southern Darfur, W Sudan
Nyamapanda *56 D3* Mashonaland East, NE Zimbabwe
Nyamtumbo *51 C8* Ruvuma, S Tanzania
Nyanda *see* Masvingo
Nyandoma *88 C4* Arkhangel'skaya Oblast', NW Russian Federation
Nyantakara *51 B7* Kagera, NW Tanzania
Nyasa, Lake *57 E2* var. Lake Malawi; prev. Lago Nyassa. lake E Africa
Nyasaland/Nyasaland Protectorate *see* Malawi
Nyassa, Lago *see* Nyasa, Lake
Nyasvizh *85 C6* Pol. Nieśwież, Rus. Nesvizh. Minskaya Voblasts', C Belarus
Nyaunglebin *114 B4* Bago, SW Myanmar (Burma)
Nyeri *51 C6* Central, C Kenya
Nyíregyháza *77 D6* Szabolcs-Szatmár-Bereg, NE Hungary
Nyitra *see* Nitra
Nykøbing *63 B8* Storstrøm, SE Denmark
Nyköping *63 C6* Södermanland, S Sweden
Nylstroom *see* Modimolle
Nyngan *127 D6* New South Wales, SE Australia
Nyoman *see* Neman
Nyurba *93 F3* Respublika Sakha (Yakutiya), NE Russian Federation
Nyzhn'ohirs'kyy *87 F4* Rus. Nizhnegorskiy. Respublika Krym, S Ukraine
NZ *see* New Zealand
Nzega *51 C7* Tabora, C Tanzania
Nzérékoré *52 D4* SE Guinea
Nzwani *see* Anjouan

O

Oa'hu *25 A7* var. Oahu. island Hawai'ian Islands, Hawaii, USA
Oak Harbor *24 B1* Washington, NW USA
Oakland *25 B6* California, W USA
Oamaru *129 B7* Otago, South Island, New Zealand
Oaxaca *29 F5* var. Oaxaca de Juárez; prev. Antequera. Oaxaca, SE Mexico
Oaxaca de Juárez *see* Oaxaca
Ob' *90 C2* river C Russian Federation
Obal' *85 D5* Rus. Obol'. Vitsyebskaya Voblasts', N Belarus
Oban *66 C4* W Scotland, United Kingdom
Oban *see* Halfmoon Bay
Obando *see* Puerto Inírida
Obdorsk *see* Salekhard
Óbecse *see* Bečej
Obeliai *84 C4* Panevėžys, NE Lithuania
Oberhollabrunn *see* Tulln
Ob', Gulf of *see* Obskaya Guba
Obidovichi *see* Abidavichy
Obihiro *108 D2* Hokkaidō, NE Japan
Obo *54 D4* Haut-Mbomou, E Central African Republic
Obock *50 D4* E Djibouti
Obol' *see* Obal'
Oborniki *76 C3* Wielkolpolskie, W Poland
Obrovo *see* Abrova
Obskaya Guba *92 D3* Eng. Gulf of Ob. gulf N Russian Federation
Ob' Tablemount *119 B7* undersea feature S Indian Ocean
Ocala *21 E4* Florida, SE USA
Ocaña *36 B2* Norte de Santander, N Colombia
Ocaña *70 D3* Castilla-La Mancha, C Spain
O Carballiño *70 C1* Cast. Carballiño. Galicia, NW Spain
Occidental, Cordillera *36 B2* mountain range W South America
Occidental, Cordillera *39 E4* mountain range Bolivia/Chile
Ocean Falls *14 D5* British Columbia, SW Canada
Ocean Island *see* Banaba
Oceanside *25 C8* California, W USA
Ocean State *see* Rhode Island
Ochakiv *87 E4* Rus. Ochakov. Mykolayivs'ka Oblast', S Ukraine
Ochakov *see* Ochakiv
Ochamchire *95 E2* prev. Och'amch'ire. W Georgia
Och'amch'ire *see* Ochamchire
Ocho Rios *32 B4* C Jamaica
Ochrida *see* Ohrid
Ochrida, Lake *see* Ohrid, Lake
Ocotal *30 D3* Nueva Segovia, NW Nicaragua
Ocozocuautla *29 G5* Chiapas, SE Mexico
October Revolution Island *see* Oktyabr'skoy Revolyutsii, Ostrov
Ocú *31 F5* Herrera, S Panama
Ōdate *108 D3* Akita, Honshū, C Japan
Oddur *see* Xuddur
Ödemiş *94 A4* İzmir, SW Turkey
Ödenburg *see* Sopron
Odenpäh *see* Otepää
Odense *63 B7* Fyn, C Denmark
Oder *76 B3* Cz./Pol. Odra. river C Europe
Oderhaff *see* Szczeciński, Zalew
Odesa *87 E4* Rus. Odessa. Odes'ka Oblast', SW Ukraine
Odessa *27 E3* Texas, SW USA
Odessa *see* Odesa
Odessus *see* Varna
Odienné *52 D4* NW Côte d'Ivoire
Odisha *113 F4* prev. Orissa. cultural region NE India
Ŏdŏngk *115 D6* Kâmpóng Spoe, S Cambodia
Odoorn *64 E2* Drenthe, NE Netherlands
Odra *see* Oder
Oesel *see* Saaremaa
Of *95 E2* Trabzon, NE Turkey
Ofanto *75 D5* river S Italy
Offenbach *73 B5* var. Offenbach am Main. Hessen, W Germany
Offenbach am Main *see* Offenbach
Offenburg *73 B6* Baden-Württemberg, SW Germany
Ogaadeen *see* Ogaden
Ogaden *51 D5* Som. Ogaadeen. plateau Ethiopia/ Somalia
Ōgaki *109 C6* Gifu, Honshū, SW Japan
Ogallala *22 D4* Nebraska, C USA
Ogbomosho *53 F4* var. Ogmoboso. Oyo, W Nigeria
Ogden *22 B4* Utah, W USA
Ogdensburg *19 F2* New York, NE USA
Ogmoboso *see* Ogbomosho
Ogulin *78 A3* Karlovac, NW Croatia
Ohio *18 C4* off. State of Ohio, also known as Buckeye State. state N USA
Ohio River *18 C4* river N USA
Ohlau *see* Oława
Ohri *see* Ohrid
Ohrid *79 D6* Turk. Ochrida, Ohri. SW FYR Macedonia
Ohrid, Lake *79 D6* var. Lake Ochrida, Alb. Liqeni i Ohrit, Mac. Ohridsko Ezero. lake Albania/ FYR Macedonia
Ohridsko Ezero/Ohrit, Liqeni i *see* Ohrid, Lake
Ohura *128 D3* Manawatu-Wanganui, North Island, New Zealand
Oirschot *65 C5* Noord-Brabant, S Netherlands
Oise *68 C3* river N France
Oistins *33 G2* S Barbados
Ōita *109 B7* Ōita, Kyūshū, SW Japan
Ojinaga *28 D2* Chihuahua, N Mexico
Ojos del Salado, Cerro *42 B3* mountain W Argentina
Okaihau *128 C2* Northland, North Island, New Zealand
Ókanizsa *see* Kanjiža
Okāra *112 C2* Punjab, E Pakistan
Okavanggo *see* Cubango/Okavango
Okavango *see* Cubango
Okavango Delta *56 C3* wetland N Botswana
Okayama *109 B6* Okayama, Honshū, SW Japan
Okazaki *109 C6* Aichi, Honshū, C Japan
Okeechobee, Lake *21 E4* lake Florida, SE USA
Okefenokee Swamp *21 E3* wetland Georgia, SE USA
Okhotsk *93 G3* Khabarovskiy Kray, E Russian Federation
Okhotsk, Sea of *91 F3* sea NW Pacific Ocean
Okhtyrka *87 F2* Rus. Akhtyrka. Sums'ka Oblast', NE Ukraine
Oki-guntō *see* Oki-shotō
Okinawa *108 A3* island SW Japan
Okinawa-shoto *108 A3* island group Nansei-shotō, SW Japan Asia
Oki-shoto *109 B6* var. Oki-guntō. island group SW Japan
Oklahoma *27 F2* off. State of Oklahoma, also known as The Sooner State. state C USA
Oklahoma City *27 G1* state capital Oklahoma, C USA
Okmulgee *27 G1* Oklahoma, C USA
Oko, Wadi *50 C3* river NE Sudan
Oktyabr'skiy *89 D6* Volgogradskaya Oblast', SW Russian Federation
Oktyabr'skiy *see* Aktsyabrski
Oktyabr'skoy Revolyutsii, Ostrov *93 E2* Eng. October Revolution Island. island Severnaya Zemlya, N Russian Federation
Okulovka *88 B4* var. Okulovka. Novgorodskaya Oblast', W Russian Federation
Okulovka *see* Okulovka
Okushiri-to *108 C3* var. Okusiri Tô. island NE Japan
Okusiri Tô *see* Okushiri-tō
Oláh-Toplicza *see* Toplița
Öland *63 C7* island S Sweden
Olavarría *43 D5* Buenos Aires, E Argentina
Oława *76 C4* Ger. Ohlau. Dolnośląskie, SW Poland
Olbia *75 A5* prev. Terranova Pausania. Sardegna, Italy, C Mediterranean Sea
Old Bay State/Old Colony State *see* Massachusetts
Old Dominion *see* Virginia
Oldebroek *64 D3* Gelderland, E Netherlands
Oldenburg *72 B3* Niedersachsen, NW Germany
Oldenburg *72 C2* var. Oldenburg in Holstein. Schleswig-Holstein, N Germany
Oldenburg in Holstein *see* Oldenburg

China *102 C2 off.* People's Republic of China, *Chin.* Chung-hua Jen-min Kung-ho-kuo, Zhonghua Renmin Gongheguo; *prev.* Chinese Empire. *country* E Asia
Chi-nan/Chinan *see* Jinan
Chinandega *30 C3* Chinandega, NW Nicaragua
China, People's Republic of *see* China
China, Republic of *see* Taiwan
Chincha Alta *38 D4* Ica, SW Peru
Chin-chiang *see* Quanzhou
Chin-chou/Chinchow *see* Jinzhou
Chindwin *see* Chindwinn
Chindwinn *114 B2 var.* Chindwin. *river* N Myanmar (Burma)
Chinese Empire *see* China
Ch'ing Hai *see* Qinghai Hu, China
Ch'ing-hai *see* Qinghai
Chinghai *56 D2* Copperbelt, C Zambia
Chingola *56 D2* Copperbelt, C Zambia
Ching Tao/Ch'ing tao *see* Qingdao
Chinguetti *52 C2 var.* Chinguetti. Adrar, C Mauritania
Chin Hills *114 A3 mountain range* W Myanmar (Burma)
Chinhsien *see* Jinzhou
Chinnereth *see* Tiberias, Lake
Chinook Trough *91 H4 trough* N Pacific Ocean
Chioggia *74 C2 anc.* Fossa Claudia. Veneto, NE Italy
Chíos *83 D5 var.* Hios, Khíos, *It.* Scio, *Turk.* Sakiz-Adasi. Chíos, E Greece
Chíos *83 D5 var.* Khíos. *island* E Greece
Chipata *56 D2 prev.* Fort Jameson. Eastern, E Zambia
Chiquián *38 C3* Ancash, W Peru
Chiquimula *30 C2* Chiquimula, SE Guatemala
Chirāla *110 D1* Andhra Pradesh, E India
Chirchik *see* Chirchiq
Chirchiq *101 E2 Rus.* Chirchik. Toshkent Viloyati, E Uzbekistan
Chiriqui Gulf *31 E5 Eng.* Chiriqui Gulf. *gulf* SW Panama
Chiriqui Gulf *see* Chiriquí, Golfo de
Chiriquí, Laguna de *31 E5 lagoon* NW Panama
Chiriquí, Volcán *see* Barú, Volcán
Chirripó, Cerro *see* Chirripó Grande, Cerro
Chirripó Grande, Cerro *31 E5 var.* Cerro Chirripó. *mountain* SE Costa Rica
Chisec *30 B2* Alta Verapaz, C Guatemala
Chisholm *23 F1* Minnesota, N USA
Chisimaio/Chisimayu *see* Kismaayo
Chişinău *86 D4 Rus.* Kishinev. *country capital* (Moldova) C Moldova
Chita *93 F4* Chitinskaya Oblast', S Russian Federation
Chitangwisa *see* Chitungwiza
Chitato *56 C1* Lunda Norte, NE Angola
Chitina *14 D3* Alaska, C USA
Chitose *108 D2 var.* Titose. Hokkaidō, NE Japan
Chitré *31 F5* Herrera, S Panama
Chittagong *113 G4 Ben.* Chāttagām. Chittagong, SE Bangladesh
Chitungwiza *56 D3 prev.* Chitangwisa. Mashonaland East, NE Zimbabwe
Chkalov *see* Orenburg
Chlef *48 D2 var.* Ech Cheliff, Ech Chleff; *prev.* Al-Asnam, El Asnam, Orléansville. NW Algeria
Chocolate Mountains *25 D8 mountain range* California, W USA
Chodorów *see* Khodoriv
Chodzież *76 C3* Wielkopolskie, C Poland
Choele Choel *43 C5* Río Negro, C Argentina
Choiseul *122 C3 var.* Lauru. *island* NW Solomon Islands
Chojnice *76 C2 Ger.* Konitz. Pomorskie, N Poland
Ch'ok'ē *50 C4 var.* Choke Mountains. *mountain range* NW Ethiopia
Choke Mountains *see* Ch'ok'ē
Cholet *68 B4* Maine-et-Loire, NW France
Choluteca *30 C3* Choluteca, S Honduras
Choluteca, Río *30 C3 river* SW Honduras
Choma *56 D2* Southern, S Zambia
Chomutov *76 A4 Ger.* Komotau. Ústecký Kraj, NW Czech Republic
Chona *91 E2 river* C Russian Federation
Chon Buri *115 C5 prev.* Bang Pla Soi. Chon Buri, S Thailand
Chone *38 A1* Manabí, W Ecuador
Ch'ŏngjin *107 E3* NE North Korea
Chongqing *107 B5 var.* Ch'ung-ching, Ch'ung-ch'ing, Chungking, Pahsien, Tchongking, Yuzhou. Chongqing Shi, C China
Chongqing Shi *107 B5 province* C China
Chonnacht *see* Connaught
Chonos, Archipiélago de los *43 A6 island group* S Chile
Chóra *83 D7* Kykládes, Greece, Aegean Sea
Chóra Sfakíon *83 C8 var.* Sfákia. Kríti, Greece, E Mediterranean Sea
Chorne More *see* Black Sea
Chornomors'ke *87 F4 Rus.* Chernomorskoye. Respublika Krym, S Ukraine
Chorokh/Chorokhi *see* Çoruh Nehri
Chortkiv *86 C2 Rus.* Chortkov. Ternopil's'ka Oblast', W Ukraine
Chortkov *see* Chortkiv
Chorzów *77 C5 Ger.* Königshütte; *prev.* Królewska Huta. Śląskie, S Poland
Choseburg *see* Cottbus
Chōsen-kaikyō *see* Korea Strait
Chōshi *109 D5 var.* Tyósi. Chiba, Honshu, S Japan
Chosŏn-minjujuŭi-inmin-kanghwaguk *see* North Korea
Choszczno *76 B3 Ger.* Arnswalde. Zachodnio-pomorskie, NW Poland
Chota Nagpur *113 E4 plateau* N India
Choûm *52 C2* Adrar, C Mauritania
Choybalsan *105 F2 prev.* Byan Tumen. Dornod, E Mongolia
Christchurch *129 C6* Canterbury, South Island, New Zealand
Christiana *32 B5* C Jamaica
Christiania *see* Oslo
Christiansand *see* Kristiansand
Christianshåb *see* Qasigiannguit
Christiansund *see* Kristiansund
Christmas Island *119 D5 Australian external territory* E Indian Ocean
Christmas Ridge *121 G2 undersea ridge* C Pacific Ocean
Chuan *see* Sichuan

Ch'uan-chou *see* Quanzhou
Chubek *see* Moskva
Chubut, Río *43 B6 river* SE Argentina
Ch'u-chiang *see* Shaoguan
Chudskoye Ozero *see* Peipus, Lake
Chugoku-sanchi *109 B6 mountain range* Honshū, SW Japan
Chui *see* Chuy
Chukai *see* Cukai
Chukchi Plain *133 B2 abyssal plain* Arctic Ocean
Chukchi Plateau *12 C2 undersea plateau* Arctic Ocean
Chukchi Sea *12 B2 Rus.* Chukotskoye More. *sea* Arctic Ocean
Chukotskoye More *see* Chukchi Sea
Chula Vista *25 C8* California, W USA
Chulucanas *38 B2* Piura, NW Peru
Chulym *92 D4 river* C Russian Federation
Chumphon *115 C6 var.* Chumpon. Chumphon, SW Thailand
Chumpon *see* Chumphon
Chuncheon *107 E4 prev.* Ch'unch'ŏn, *Jap.* Shunsen. N South Korea
Ch'unch'ŏn *see* Chuncheon
Ch'ung-ch'ing/Ch'ung-ching *see* Chongqing
Chungking *see* Chongqing
Chunya *93 E3 river* C Russian Federation
Chuquicamata *42 B2* Antofagasta, N Chile
Chuquisaca *see* Sucre
Chur *73 B7 Fr.* Coire, *It.* Coira, *Rmsch.* Cuera, Quera; *anc.* Curia Rhaetorum. Graubünden, E Switzerland
Churchill *15 G4* Manitoba, C Canada
Churchill *16 B2 river* Manitoba/Saskatchewan, C Canada
Churchill *17 F2 river* Newfoundland and Labrador, E Canada
Chuska Mountains *26 C1 mountain range* Arizona/New Mexico, SW USA
Chusovoy *89 D5* Permskaya Oblast', NW Russian Federation
Chust *see* Khust
Chuuk Islands *122 B2 var.* Hogoley Islands; *prev.* Truk Islands. *island group* Caroline Islands, C Micronesia
Chuy *42 B4 var.* Chuí. Rocha, E Uruguay
Chyhyryn *87 E2 Rus.* Chigirin. Cherkas'ka Oblast', N Ukraine
Ciadâr-Lunga *86 D4 var.* Ceadâr-Lunga, *Rus.* Chadyr-Lunga. S Moldova
Cide *94 C2* Kastamonu, N Turkey
Ciechanów *76 D3 prev.* Zichenau. Mazowieckie, C Poland
Ciego de Ávila *32 C2* Ciego de Ávila, C Cuba
Ciénaga *36 B1* Magdalena, N Colombia
Cienfuegos *32 B2* Cienfuegos, C Cuba
Cieza *71 E4* Murcia, SE Spain
Cihanbeyli *94 C3* Konya, C Turkey
Cikobia *123 E4 prev.* Thikombia. *island* N Fiji
Cilacap *116 C5 prev.* Tjilatjap. Jawa, C Indonesia
Cill Airne *see* Killarney
Cill Chainnigh *see* Kilkenny
Cilli *see* Celje
Cill Mhantáin *see* Wicklow
Câmpina *see* Câmpina
Câmpulung *see* Câmpulung
Cina Selatan, Laut *see* South China Sea
Cincinnati *18 C4* Ohio, N USA
Ciney *65 C7* Namur, SE Belgium
Cinto, Monte *69 E7 mountain* Corse, France, C Mediterranean Sea
Cintra *see* Sintra
Cipolletti *43 B5* Río Negro, C Argentina
Cirebon *116 C4 prev.* Tjirebon. Jawa, S Indonesia
Cirkvenica *see* Crikvenica
Cirò Marina *75 E6* Calabria, S Italy
Cirquenizza *see* Crikvenica
Cisnădie *86 B4 Ger.* Heltau, *Hung.* Nagydiszno. Sibiu, SW Romania
Citharista *see* la Ciotat
Citlaltépetl *see* Orizaba, Volcán Pico de
Citrus Heights *25 B5* California, W USA
Ciudad Acuña *see* Villa Acuña
Ciudad Bolívar *37 E2 prev.* Angostura. Bolívar, E Venezuela
Ciudad Camargo *28 D2* Chihuahua, N Mexico
Ciudad Darío *30 D3 var.* Darío. Matagalpa, W Nicaragua
Ciudad Cortés *see* Cortés
Ciudad de Dolores Hidalgo *see* Dolores Hidalgo
Ciudad de Guatemala *30 B2 Eng.* Guatemala City; *prev.* Santiago de los Caballeros. *country capital* (Guatemala) Guatemala, C Guatemala
Ciudad del Carmen *see* Carmen
Ciudad del Este *42 E2 prev.* Ciudad Presidente Stroessner, Presidente Stroessner, Puerto Presidente Stroessner. Alto Paraná, SE Paraguay
Ciudad Delicias *see* Delicias
Ciudad de México *see* México
Ciudad de Panamá *see* Panamá
Ciudad Guayana *37 E2 prev.* San Tomé de Guayana, Santo Tomé de Guayana. Bolívar, NE Venezuela
Ciudad Guzmán *28 D4* Jalisco, SW Mexico
Ciudad Hidalgo *29 G5* Chiapas, SE Mexico
Ciudad Juárez *28 C1* Chihuahua, N Mexico
Ciudad Lerdo *28 D3* Durango, C Mexico
Ciudad Madero *29 E3 var.* Villa Cecilia. Tamaulipas, C Mexico
Ciudad Mante *29 E3* Tamaulipas, C Mexico
Ciudad Miguel Alemán *29 E2* Tamaulipas, C Mexico
Ciudad Obregón *28 B2* Sonora, NW Mexico
Ciudad Ojeda *36 C1* Zulia, NW Venezuela
Ciudad Porfirio Díaz *see* Piedras Negras
Ciudad Presidente Stroessner *see* Ciudad del Este
Ciudad Quesada *see* Quesada
Ciudad Real *70 D3* Castilla-La Mancha, C Spain
Ciudad-Rodrigo *70 C3* Castilla-León, N Spain
Ciudad Trujillo *see* Santo Domingo
Ciudad Valles *29 E3* San Luis Potosí, C Mexico
Ciudad Victoria *29 E3* Tamaulipas, C Mexico
Ciutadella *71 H3 var.* Ciutadella de Menorca. Menorca, Spain, W Mediterranean Sea
Ciutadella de Menorca *see* Ciutadella
Civitanova Marche *74 D3* Marche, C Italy
Civitas Altae Ripae *see* Brzeg
Civitas Carnutum *see* Chartres
Civitas Eburovicum *see* Évreux
Civitavecchia *74 C4 anc.* Centum Cellae, Trajani Portus. Lazio, C Italy
Claremore *27 G1* Oklahoma, C USA
Clarence *129 C5* Canterbury, South Island, New Zealand

Clarence *129 C5 river* South Island, New Zealand
Clarence Town *32 D2* Long Island, C Bahamas
Clarinda *23 F4* Iowa, C USA
Clarion Fracture Zone *131 E2 tectonic feature* NE Pacific Ocean
Clarión, Isla *28 A5 island* W Mexico
Clark Fork *22 A1 river* Idaho/Montana, NW USA
Clark Hill Lake *21 E2 var.* J. Storm Thurmond Reservoir. *reservoir* Georgia/South Carolina, SE USA
Clarksburg *18 D4* West Virginia, NE USA
Clarksdale *20 B2* Mississippi, S USA
Clarksville *20 C1* Tennessee, S USA
Clausentum *see* Southampton
Clayton *27 E1* New Mexico, SW USA
Clearwater *21 E4* Florida, SE USA
Clearwater Mountains *24 D2 mountain range* Idaho, NW USA
Cleburne *27 G3* Texas, SW USA
Clermont *126 D4* Queensland, E Australia
Clermont-Ferrand *69 C5* Puy-de Dôme, C France
Cleveland *18 D3* Ohio, N USA
Cleveland *20 D1* Tennessee, S USA
Clifton *26 C2* Arizona, SW USA
Clinton *20 B2* Mississippi, S USA
Clinton *27 F1* Oklahoma, C USA
Clipperton Fracture Zone *131 E3 tectonic feature* E Pacific Ocean
Clipperton Island *13 A7 French dependency of* French Polynesia E Pacific Ocean
Cloncurry *126 B3* Queensland, C Australia
Clonmel *67 B6 Ir.* Cluain Meala. S Ireland
Cloppenburg *72 B3* Niedersachsen, NW Germany
Cloquet *23 G2* Minnesota, N USA
Cloud Peak *22 C3 mountain* Wyoming, C USA
Clovis *27 E2* New Mexico, SW USA
Cluain Meala *see* Clonmel
Cluj *see* Cluj-Napoca
Cluj-Napoca *86 B3 Ger.* Klausenburg, *Hung.* Kolozsvár; *prev.* Cluj. Cluj, NW Romania
Clutha *129 B7 river* South Island, New Zealand
Clyde *66 C4 river* W Scotland, United Kingdom
Coari *40 D2* Amazonas, N Brazil
Coast Mountains *14 D4 Fr.* Chaîne Côtière. *mountain range* Canada/USA
Coast Ranges *24 A4 mountain range* W USA
Coats Island *15 G3 island* Nunavut, NE Canada
Coats Land *132 B2 physical region* Antarctica
Coatzacoalcos *29 G4 var.* Quetzalcoalco; *prev.* Puerto México. Veracruz-Llave, E Mexico
Cobán *30 B2* Alta Verapaz, C Guatemala
Cobar *127 C6* New South Wales, SE Australia
Cobija *39 E3* Pando, NW Bolivia
Coblence/Coblenz *see* Koblenz
Coburg *73 C5* Bayern, SE Germany
Coca *see* Puerto Francisco de Orellana
Cocanada *see* Kākināda
Cochabamba *39 F4 hist.* Oropeza. Cochabamba, C Bolivia
Cochin *see* Kochi
Cochinos, Bahía de *32 B2 Eng.* Bay of Pigs. *bay* SE Cuba
Cochrane *16 C4* Ontario, S Canada
Cochrane *43 B7* Aisén, S Chile
Cocibolca, Lago de *see* Nicaragua, Lago de
Cockade State *see* Maryland
Cockburn Town *33 E2* San Salvador, E Bahamas
Cockpit Country, The *32 A4 physical region* W Jamaica
Cocobeach *55 A5* Estuaire, W Gabon
Coconino Plateau *26 B1 plain* Arizona, SW USA
Coco, Río *31 E2 var.* Río Wanki, Segovtao Wangki. *river* Honduras/Nicaragua
Cocos Basin *119 C5 undersea basin* E Indian Ocean
Cocos Island Ridge *see* Cocos Ridge
Cocos Islands *119 D5 island group* E Indian Ocean
Cocos Ridge *13 C8 var.* Cocos Island Ridge. *undersea ridge* E Pacific Ocean
Cod, Cape *19 G3 headland* Massachusetts, NE USA
Codfish Island *129 A8 island* SW New Zealand
Codlea *86 C4 Ger.* Zeiden, *Hung.* Feketehalom. Braşov, C Romania
Cody *22 C2* Wyoming, C USA
Coeur d'Alene *24 C2* Idaho, NW USA
Coevorden *64 E2* Drenthe, NE Netherlands
Coffs Harbour *127 E6* New South Wales, SE Australia
Cognac *69 B5 anc.* Compniacum. Charente, W France
Cohalm *see* Rupea
Coiba, Isla de *31 E5 island* SW Panama
Coihaique *43 B6 var.* Coyhaique. Aisén, S Chile
Coimbatore *110 C3* Tamil Nādu, S India
Coimbra *70 B3 anc.* Conimbria, Conimbriga. Coimbra, W Portugal
Coín *70 D5* Andalucía, S Spain
Coíra/Coire *see* Chur
Coirib, Loch *see* Corrib, Lough
Colby *23 E4* Kansas, C USA
Colchester *67 E6* Connecticut, NE USA
Coleman *27 F3* Texas, SW USA
Coleraine *66 B4 Ir.* Cúil Raithin. N Northern Ireland, United Kingdom
Colesberg *56 C5* Northern Cape, C South Africa
Colima *28 D4* Colima, S Mexico
Coll *66 B3 island* W Scotland, United Kingdom
College Station *27 G3* Texas, SW USA
Collie *125 A7* Western Australia
Collipo *see* Leiria
Colmar *68 E4 Ger.* Kolmar. Haut-Rhin, NE France
Cöln *see* Köln
Cologne *see* Köln
Colomb-Béchar *see* Béchar
Colombia *36 B3 off.* Republic of Colombia. *country* N South America
Colombian Basin *34 A1 undersea basin* SW Caribbean Sea
Colombia, Republic of *see* Colombia
Colombie-Britannique *see* British Columbia
Colombo *110 C4 country capital* (Sri Lanka) Western Province, W Sri Lanka
Colón *31 G4 prev.* Aspinwall. Colón, C Panama
Colón, Archipiélago de *see* Galápagos Islands
Colón Ridge *13 B8 undersea ridge* E Pacific Ocean
Colorado *22 C4 off.* State of Colorado, *also known as* Centennial State, Silver State. *state* C USA
Colorado Plateau *26 B1 plateau* W USA
Colorado, Río *43 C5 river* E Argentina
Colorado, Río *see* Colorado River

Colorado River *13 B5 var.* Río Colorado. *river* Mexico/USA
Colorado River *27 G4 river* Texas, SW USA
Colorado Springs *22 D5* Colorado, C USA
Columbia *19 E1* Maryland, NE USA
Columbia *23 G4* Missouri, C USA
Columbia *21 E2 state capital* South Carolina, SE USA
Columbia River *24 B3 river* Canada/USA
Columbia Plateau *24 C3 plateau* Idaho/Oregon, NW USA
Columbus *20 D2* Georgia, SE USA
Columbus *18 C4* Indiana, N USA
Columbus *20 C2* Mississippi, S USA
Columbus *23 F4* Nebraska, C USA
Columbus *18 D4 state capital* Ohio, N USA
Colville Channel *128 D2 channel* North Island, New Zealand
Colville River *14 D2 river* Alaska, USA
Comacchio *74 C3 var.* Commachio; *anc.* Comactium. Emilia-Romagna, N Italy
Comactium *see* Comacchio
Comalcalco *29 G4* Tabasco, SE Mexico
Coma Pedrosa, Pic de *69 A7 mountain* NW Andorra
Comarapa *39 F4* Santa Cruz, C Bolivia
Comayagua *30 C2* Comayagua, W Honduras
Comer See *see* Como, Lago di
Comilla *113 G4 Ben.* Kumillā. Chittagong, E Bangladesh
Comino *see* Kemmuna
Comitán *29 G5 var.* Comitán de Domínguez. Chiapas, SE Mexico
Comitán de Domínguez *see* Comitán
Commachio *see* Comacchio
Commissioner's Point *20 A5 headland* W Bermuda
Communism Peak *101 F3 prev.* Qullai Kommunizm. *mountain* E Tajikistan
Como *74 B2 anc.* Comum. Lombardia, N Italy
Comodoro Rivadavia *43 B6* Chubut, SE Argentina
Como, Lake *74 B2 var.* Lario, *Eng.* Lake Como, *Ger.* Comer See. *lake* N Italy
Como, Lake *see* Como, Lago di
Comores, République Fédérale Islamique des *see* Comoros
Comoros *57 F2 off.* Federal Islamic Republic of the Comoros, *Fr.* République Fédérale Islamique des Comores. *country* W Indian Ocean
Comoros, Federal Islamic Republic of the *see* Comoros
Compiègne *68 C3* Oise, N France
Complutum *see* Alcalá de Henares
Compniacum *see* Cognac
Compostella *see* Santiago de Compostela
Comrat *86 D4 Rus.* Komrat. S Moldova
Comum *see* Como
Conakry *52 C4 country capital* (Guinea) SW Guinea
Conca *see* Cuenca
Concarneau *68 A3* Finistère, NW France
Concepción *39 G3* Santa Cruz, E Bolivia
Concepción *43 B5* Bío Bío, C Chile
Concepción *42 D2 var.* Villa Concepción. Concepción, C Paraguay
Concepción *see* La Concepción
Concepción de la Vega *see* La Vega
Conchos, Río *26 D4 river* NW Mexico
Conchos, Río *28 D2 river* C Mexico
Concord *19 G3 state capital* New Hampshire, NE USA
Concordia *42 D4* Entre Ríos, E Argentina
Concordia *23 F4* Kansas, C USA
Côn Dao *see* Côn Dao Son
Condate *see* Rennes, Ille-et-Vilaine, France
Condate *see* St-Claude, Jura, France
Condega *30 D3* Estelí, NW Nicaragua
Condivincum *see* Nantes
Confluentes *see* Koblenz
Công Hoa Xa Hôi Chu Nghia Viêt Nam *see* Vietnam
Congo *55 D5 off.* Republic of the Congo, *Fr.* Moyen-Congo; *prev.* Middle Congo. *country* C Africa
Congo *55 C6 off.* Democratic Republic of Congo; *prev.* Zaire, Belgian Congo, Congo (Kinshasa). *country* C Africa
Congo *55 C6 var.* Kongo, *Fr.* Zaïre. *river* C Africa
Congo Basin *55 C6 drainage basin* W Dem. Rep. Congo
Congo/Congo (Kinshasa) *see* Congo (Democratic Republic of)
Coni *see* Cuneo
Conimbria/Conimbriga *see* Coimbra
Conjeeveram *see* Kānchipuram
Connacht *see* Connaught
Connaught *67 A5 var.* Connacht, *Ir.* Chonnacht, Cúige. *province* W Ireland
Connecticut *19 F3 off.* State of Connecticut, *also known as* Blue Law State, Constitution State, Land of Steady Habits, Nutmeg State. *state* NE USA
Connecticut *19 G3 river* Canada/USA
Conroe *27 G3* Texas, SW USA
Consentia *see* Cosenza
Consolación del Sur *32 A2* Pinar del Río, W Cuba
Con Son *see* Côn Dao Son
Constance *see* Konstanz
Constance, Lake *73 B7 Ger.* Bodensee. *lake* C Europe
Constanţa *86 D5 var.* Küstendje, *Eng.* Constanza, *Ger.* Konstanza, *Turk.* Küstence. Constanţa, SE Romania
Constantia *see* Coutances
Constantia *see* Constanţa
Constantine *49 E2 var.* Qacentina, *Ar.* Qoussantina. NE Algeria
Constantinople *see* İstanbul
Constantiola *see* Oltenita
Constanz *see* Konstanz
Constanza *see* Constanţa
Constitution State *see* Connecticut
Coober Pedy *127 A5* South Australia
Cookeville *20 D1* Tennessee, S USA
Cook Islands *123 F4 territory in free association with* New Zealand S Pacific Ocean
Cook, Mount *see* Aoraki
Cook Strait *129 D5 var.* Raukawa. *strait* New Zealand

Cooktown *126 D2* Queensland, NE Australia
Coolgardie *125 B6* Western Australia
Cooma *127 D7* New South Wales, SE Australia
Coomassie *see* Kumasi
Coon Rapids *23 F2* Minnesota, N USA
Cooper Creek *126 C4 var.* Barcoo, Cooper's Creek. *seasonal river* Queensland/ South Australia, Australia
Cooper's Creek *see* Cooper Creek
Coos Bay *24 A3* Oregon, NW USA
Cootamundra *127 D6* New South Wales, SE Australia
Copacabana *39 E4* La Paz, W Bolivia
Copenhagen *see* København
Copiapó *42 B3* Atacama, N Chile
Copperas Cove *27 G3* Texas, SW USA
Coppermine *see* Kugluktuk
Copper State *see* Arizona
Coquilhatville *see* Mbandaka
Coquimbo *42 B3* Coquimbo, N Chile
Corabia *86 B5* Olt, S Romania
Coral Harbour *15 G3* Southampton Island, Nunavut, NE Canada
Coral Sea *120 B4* Pacific Ocean
Coral Sea Islands *122 B4 Australian external territory* SW Pacific Ocean
Corantijn Rivier *see* Courantyne River
Corcovado, Golfo *43 B6 gulf* S Chile
Corcyra Nigra *see* Korčula
Cordele *20 D3* Georgia, SE USA
Córdoba *42 C3* Córdoba, C Argentina
Córdoba *29 F4* Veracruz-Llave, E Mexico
Córdoba *70 D4 var.* Cordoba, *Eng.* Cordova; *anc.* Corduba. Andalucía, SW Spain
Cordova *14 C3* Alaska, USA
Cordova/Córdoba *see* Córdoba
Corduba *see* Córdoba
Corentyne River *see* Courantyne River
Corfu *see* Kérkyra
Coria *70 C3* Extremadura, W Spain
Corinth *20 C1* Mississippi, S USA
Corinth *see* Kórinthos
Corinth, Gulf of/Corinthiacus Sinus *see* Korinthiakós Kólpos
Corinthus *see* Kórinthos
Corinto *30 C3* Chinandega, NW Nicaragua
Cork *67 A6 Ir.* Corcaigh. S Ireland
Çorlu *94 A2* Tekirdağ, NW Turkey
Corner Brook *17 G3* Newfoundland, Newfoundland and Labrador, E Canada
Cornhusker State *see* Nebraska
Corn Islands *31 E3 var.* Corn Islands. *island group* SE Nicaragua
Corn Islands *see* Maíz, Islas del
Cornwallis Island *15 F2 Island* Nunavut, N Canada
Coro *36 C1 prev.* Santa Ana de Coro. Falcón, NW Venezuela
Corocoro *39 F4* La Paz, W Bolivia
Coromandel *128 D2* Waikato, North Island, New Zealand
Coromandel Coast *110 D2 coast* E India
Coromandel Peninsula *128 D2 peninsula* North Island, New Zealand
Coronado, Bahía de *30 D5 bay* S Costa Rica
Coronel Dorrego *43 C5* Buenos Aires, E Argentina
Coronel Oviedo *42 D2* Caaguazú, SE Paraguay
Corozal *30 C1* Corozal, N Belize
Corpus Christi *27 G4* Texas, SW USA
Corrales *26 D2* New Mexico, SW USA
Corrib, Lough *67 A5 Ir.* Loch Coirib. *lake* W Ireland
Corrientes *42 D3* Corrientes, NE Argentina
Corriza *see* Korçë
Corse *69 E7 Eng.* Corsica. *island* France, C Mediterranean Sea
Corsica *see* Corse
Corsicana *27 G3* Texas, SW USA
Cortegana *70 C4* Andalucía, S Spain
Cortés *31 E5 var.* Ciudad Cortés. Puntarenas, SE Costa Rica
Cortez, Sea of *see* California, Golfo de
Cortina d'Ampezzo *74 C1* Veneto, NE Italy
Coruche *70 B3* Santarém, C Portugal
Çoruh Nehri *95 E3 Geor.* Chorokh, *Rus.* Chorokhi. *river* Georgia/Turkey
Çorum *94 D3 var.* Chorum. Çorum, N Turkey
Corunna *see* A Coruña
Corvallis *24 B3* Oregon, NW USA
Corvo *70 A5 var.* Ilha do Corvo. *island* Azores, Portugal, NE Atlantic Ocean
Corvo, Ilha do *see* Corvo
Cos *see* Kos
Cosenza *75 D6 anc.* Consentia. Calabria, SW Italy
Cosne-Cours-sur-Loire *68 C4* Nièvre, Bourgogne, C France Europe
Costa Mesa *24 D2* California, W USA North America
Costa Rica *31 E4 off.* Republic of Costa Rica. *country* Central America
Costa Rica, Republic of *see* Costa Rica
Costermansville *see* Bukavu
Cotagaita *39 F5* Potosí, S Bolivia
Côte d'Ivoire *52 D4 off.* République de la Côte d'Ivoire; *Eng.* Ivory Coast. *country* W Africa
Côte d'Ivoire, République de la *see* Côte d'Ivoire
Côte d'Or *68 D4 cultural region* C France
Côte Française des Somalis *see* Djibouti
Côtière, Chaîne *see* Coast Mountains
Cotonou *53 F5 var.* Kotonu. S Benin
Cotrone *see* Crotone
Cotswold Hills *67 D6 var.* Cotswolds, *hill range* S England, United Kingdom
Cotswolds *see* Cotswold Hills
Cottbus *72 D4 Lus.* Chośebuz; *prev.* Kottbus. Brandenburg, E Germany
Cotton State, The *see* Alabama
Cotyora *see* Ordu
Couentrey *see* Coventry
Council Bluffs *23 F3* Iowa, C USA
Courantyne River *37 G4 var.* Corantijn Rivier, Corentyne River. *river* Guyana/Suriname
Courland Lagoon *84 A4 Ger.* Kurisches Haff, *Rus.* Kurskiy Zaliv. *lagoon* Lithuania/Russian Federation
Courtrai *see* Kortrijk
Coutances *68 B3 anc.* Constantia. Manche, N France
Couvin *65 C7* Namur, S Belgium
Coventry *67 D6 anc.* Couentrey. C England, United Kingdom
Covilhã *70 C3* Castelo Branco, E Portugal
Cowan, Lake *125 B6 lake* Western Australia

Djajapura – Ellen, Mount

Djajapura see Jayapura
Djakarta see Jakarta
Djakovo see Đakovo
Djambala 55 B6 Plateaux, C Congo
Djambi see Jambi
Djambi see Hari, Batang
Djanet 49 E4 prev. Fort Charlet. SE Algeria
Djéblé see Jablah
Djelfa 48 D2 var. El Djelfa. N Algeria
Djéma 54 D4 Haut-Mbomou, E Central African Republic
Djember see Jember
Djérablous see Jarābulus
Djerba 49 F2 var. Djerba, Jazīrat Jarbah. island E Tunisia
Djerba see Jerba, Île de
Djérem 54 B4 river C Cameroon
Djevdjelija see Gevgelija
Djibouti 50 D4 var. Jibuti. country capital (Djibouti) E Djibouti
Djibouti 50 D4 off. Republic of Djibouti, var. Jibuti; prev. French Somaliland, French Territory of the Afars and Issas, Fr. Côte Française des Somalis, Territoire Français des Afars et des Issas. country E Africa
Djibouti, Republic of see Djibouti
Djokjakarta see Yogyakarta
Djourab, Erg du 54 C2 desert N Chad
Djúpivogur 61 E5 Austurland, SE Iceland
Dmitriyevsk see Makiyivka
Dnepr see Dnieper
Dneprodzerzhinsk see Romaniv
Dneprodzerzhinskoye Vodokhranilishche see Dniprodzerzhyns'ke Vodoskhovyshche
Dnepropetrovsk see Dnipropetrovs'k
Dneprorudnoye see Dniprorudne
Dnestr see Dniester
Dnieper 59 F4 Bel. Dnyapro, Rus. Dnepr, Ukr. Dnipro. river E Europe
Dnieper Lowland 87 E2 Bel. Prydnyaprowskaya Nizina, Ukr. Prydniprovs'ka Nyzovyna. lowlands Belarus/Ukraine
Dniester 59 E4 Rom. Nistru, Rus. Dnestr, Ukr. Dnister; anc. Tyras. river Moldova/Ukraine
Dnipro see Dnieper
Dniprodzerzhyns'k see Romaniv
Dniprodzerzhyns'ke Vodoskhovyshche 87 F3 Rus. Dneprodzerzhinskoye Vodokhranilishche. reservoir C Ukraine
Dnipropetrovs'k 87 F3 Rus. Dnepropetrovsk; prev. Yekaterinoslav. Dnipropetrovs'ka Oblast', E Ukraine
Dniprorudne 87 F3 Rus. Dneprorudnoye. Zaporiz'ka Oblast', SE Ukraine
Dnister see Dniester
Dnyapro see Dnieper
Doba 54 C4 Logone-Oriental, S Chad
Döbeln 72 D4 Sachsen, E Germany
Doberai Peninsula 117 G4 Dut. Vogelkop. peninsula Papua, E Indonesia
Doboj 78 C3 Republiks Srpska, N Bosnia and Herzegovina
Dobre Miasto 76 D2 Ger. Guttstadt. Warmińsko-mazurskie, NE Poland
Dobrich 82 E1 Rom. Bazargic; prev. Tolbukhin. Dobrich, NE Bulgaria
Dobrush 85 D7 Homyel'skaya Voblasts', SE Belarus
Dobryn' see Dabryn'
Dodecanese see Dodekánisa
Dodekánisa 83 D6 var. Nóties Sporádes, Eng. Dodecanese; prev. Dhodhekánisos, Dodekanisos. island group SE Greece
Dodekanisos see Dodekánisa
Dodge City 23 E5 Kansas, C USA
Dodoma 47 D5 country capital (Tanzania) Dodoma, C Tanzania
Dogana 74 E1 NE San Marino Europe
Dogo 109 B6 island Oki-shotō, SW Japan
Dogondoutchi 53 F3 Dosso, SW Niger
Dogrular see Pravda
Doğubayazıt 95 F3 Ağrı, E Turkey
Doğu Karadeniz Dağları 95 E3 var. Anadolu Dağları. mountain range NE Turkey
Doha see Ad Dawḩah
Doire see Londonderry
Dokdo see Liancourt Rocks
Dokkum 64 D1 Friesland, N Netherlands
Dokuchayevs'k 87 G3 var. Dokuchayevsk. Donets'ka Oblast', SE Ukraine
Dokuchayevsk see Dokuchayevs'k
Doldrums Fracture Zone 44 C4 fracture zone W Atlantic Ocean
Dôle 68 D4 Jura, E France
Dolina see Dolyna
Dolinskaya see Dolyns'ka
Dolisie 55 B6 prev. Loubomo. Niari, S Congo
Dolna Oryakhovitsa 82 D2 prev. Polikrayshte. Veliko Tŭrnovo, N Bulgaria
Dolni Chiflik 82 E2 prev. Rudnik. Varna, E Bulgaria
Dolomites 74 C1 var. Dolomiti, Eng. Dolomites. mountain range NE Italy
Dolomites/Dolomiti see Dolomitiche, Alpi
Dolores 42 D4 Buenos Aires, E Argentina
Dolores 30 B1 Petén, N Guatemala
Dolores 42 D4 Soriano, SW Uruguay
Dolores Hidalgo 29 E4 var. Ciudad de Dolores Hidalgo. Guanajuato, C Mexico
Dolyna 86 B2 Rus. Dolina. Ivano-Frankivs'ka Oblast', W Ukraine
Dolyns'ka 87 F3 Rus. Dolinskaya. Kirovohrads'ka Oblast', S Ukraine
Domachëvo/Domaczewo see Damachava
Dombås 63 B5 Oppland, S Norway
Domel Island see Letsôk-aw Kyun
Domesnes, Cape see Kolkasrags
Domeyko 42 B3 Atacama, N Chile
Dominica 33 H4 off. Commonwealth of Dominica. country E West Indies
Dominica Channel see Martinique Passage
Dominica, Commonwealth of see Dominica
Dominican Republic 33 E2 country C West Indies
Domokós 83 B5 var. Dhomokós. Stereá Ellás, C Greece
Don 89 B6 var. Duna, Tanais. river SW Russian Federation
Donau see Danube
Donauwörth 73 C6 Bayern, S Germany
Don Benito 70 C3 Extremadura, W Spain
Doncaster 67 D5 anc. Danum. N England, United Kingdom
Dondo 56 B1 Cuanza Norte, NW Angola
Donegal 67 B5 Ir. Dún na nGall. Donegal, NW Ireland
Donegal Bay 67 A5 Ir. Bá Dhún na nGall. bay NW Ireland
Donets 87 G2 river Russian Federation/Ukraine
Donets'k 87 G3 Rus. Donetsk; prev. Stalino. Donets'ka Oblast', E Ukraine
Dongfang 106 B7 var. Basuo. Hainan, S China
Dongguan 106 C6 Guangdong, S China
Đông Hà 114 E4 Quang Tri, C Vietnam
Dong Hai see East China Sea
Đông Hơi 114 D4 Quang Binh, C Vietnam
Dongliao see Liaoyuan
Dongola 50 B3 var. Donqola, Dunqulah. Northern, N Sudan
Dongou 55 C5 Likouala, NE Congo
Dong Rak, Phanom see Dângrêk, Chuŏr Phnum
Dongting Hu 106 C5 var. Tung-t'ing Hu. lake S China
Donostia 71 E1 País Vasco, N Spain see also San Sebastián
Donqola see Dongola
Doolow 51 D5 Sumalē, E Ethiopia
Doornik see Tournai
Door Peninsula 18 C2 peninsula Wisconsin, N USA
Dooxo Nugaaleed 51 E5 var. Nogal Valley. valley E Somalia
Dordogne 69 B5 cultural region SW France
Dordogne 69 B5 river W France
Dordrecht 64 C4 var. Dordt, Dort. Zuid-Holland, SW Netherlands
Dordt see Dordrecht
Dorohoi 86 C3 Botoşani, NE Romania
Dorotea 62 C4 Västerbotten, N Sweden
Dorpat see Tartu
Dorre Island 125 A5 island Western Australia
Dort see Dordrecht
Dortmund 72 A4 Nordrhein-Westfalen, W Germany
Dos Hermanas 70 C4 Andalucía, S Spain
Dospad Dagh see Rhodope Mountains
Dospat 82 C3 Smolyan, S Bulgaria
Dothan 20 D3 Alabama, S USA
Dotnuva 84 B4 Kaunas, C Lithuania
Douai 68 C2 prev. Douay; anc. Duacum. Nord, N France
Douala 55 A5 var. Duala. Littoral, W Cameroon
Douay see Douai
Douglas 67 C5 dependent territory capital (Isle of Man) E Isle of Man
Douglas 26 C3 Arizona, SW USA
Douglas 22 D3 Wyoming, C USA
Douma see Dūmā
Douro see Duero
Douvres see Dover
Dover 67 E7 Fr. Douvres, Lat. Dubris Portus. SE England, United Kingdom
Dover 19 F4 state capital Delaware, NE USA
Dover, Strait of 68 C2 var. Straits of Dover, Fr. Pas de Calais. strait England, United Kingdom/France
Dover, Straits of see Dover, Strait of
Dovrefjell 63 B5 plateau S Norway
Downpatrick 67 B5 Ir. Dún Pádraig. SE Northern Ireland, United Kingdom
Dozen 109 B6 island Oki-shotō, SW Japan
Drâa, Hammada du see Dra, Hamada du
Drač/Draç see Durrës
Drachten 64 D2 Friesland, N Netherlands
Drăgăşani 86 B5 Vâlcea, SW Romania
Dragoman 82 B2 Sofiya, W Bulgaria
Dra, Hamada du 48 C3 var. Hammada du Drâa, Haut Plateau du Dra. plateau W Algeria
Dra, Haut Plateau du see Dra, Hamada du
Drahichyn 85 B6 Pol. Drohiczyn Poleski, Rus. Drogichin. Brestskaya Voblasts', SW Belarus
Drakensberg 56 D5 mountain range Lesotho/ South Africa
Drake Passage 35 B8 passage Atlantic Ocean/ Pacific Ocean
Dralfa 82 D2 Tŭrgovishte, N Bulgaria
Dráma 82 C3 var. Dhráma. Anatolikí Makedonía kai Thráki, NE Greece
Dramburg see Drawsko Pomorskie
Drammen 63 B6 Buskerud, S Norway
Drau see Drava
Drava 78 C3 var. Drau, Eng. Drave, Hung. Dráva. river C Europe
Dráva/Drave see Drau/Drava
Drawsko Pomorskie 76 B3 Ger. Dramburg. Zachodnio pomorskie, NW Poland
Drépano, Akrotírio 82 C4 var. Akrotírio Dhrepanon. headland N Greece
Drepanum see Trapani
Dresden 72 D4 Sachsen, E Germany
Drin see Drinit, Lumi i
Drina 78 C3 river Bosnia and Herzegovina/Serbia
Drinit, Lumi i 79 D5 var. Drin. river NW Albania
Drinit të Zi, Lumi i see Black Drin
Drissa see Drysa
Drobeta-Turnu Severin 86 B5 prev. Turnu Severin. Mehedinţi, SW Romania
Drogheda 67 B5 Ir. Droichead Átha. NE Ireland
Drogichin see Drahichyn
Drogobych see Drohobych
Drohiczyn Poleski see Drahichyn
Drohobych 86 B2 Pol. Drohobycz, Rus. Drogobych. L'vivs'ka Oblast', NW Ukraine
Drohobycz see Drohobych
Droichead Átha see Drogheda
Drôme 69 D5 cultural region E France
Dronning Maud Land 132 B2 physical region Antarctica
Drontheim see Trondheim
Drug see Durg
Druk-yul see Bhutan
Drummondville 17 E4 Québec, SE Canada
Druskienniki see Druskininkai
Druskininkai 85 B5 Pol. Druskienniki. Alytus, S Lithuania
Dryden 16 B3 Ontario, C Canada
Drysa 85 D5 Rus. Drissa. river N Belarus
Duacum see Douai
Duala see Douala
Dubai see Dubayy
Dubăsari 86 D3 Rus. Dubossary. NE Moldova
Dubawnt 15 F4 river Nunavut, NW Canada
Dubayy 98 D4 Eng. Dubai. Dubayy, NE United Arab Emirates
Dubbo 127 D6 New South Wales, SE Australia
Dublin 67 B5 Ir. Baile Átha Cliath; anc. Eblana. country capital (Ireland) Dublin, E Ireland
Dublin 21 E2 Georgia, SE USA
Dubno 86 C2 Rivnens'ka Oblast', NW Ukraine
Dubossary see Dubăsari
Dubris Portus see Dover
Dubrovnik 79 B5 It. Ragusa. Dubrovnik-Neretva, SE Croatia
Dubuque 23 G3 Iowa, C USA
Dudelange 65 D8 var. Forge du Sud, Ger. Dudelingen. Luxembourg, S Luxembourg
Dudelingen see Dudelange
Duero 70 D2 Port. Douro. river Portugal/Spain
Duesseldorf see Düsseldorf
Duffel 65 C5 Antwerpen, C Belgium
Dugi Otok 78 A4 var. Isola Grossa, It. Isola Lunga. island W Croatia
Duinekerke see Dunkerque
Duisburg 72 A4 prev. Duisburg-Hamborn. Nordrhein-Westfalen, W Germany
Duisburg-Hamborn see Duisburg
Duiven 64 D4 Gelderland, E Netherlands
Duk Faiwil 51 B5 Jonglei, C South Sudan
Dulan 104 D4 var. Qagan Us. Qinghai, C China
Dulce, Golfo 31 E5 gulf S Costa Rica
Dulce, Golfo see Izabal, Lago de
Dülmen 72 A4 Nordrhein-Westfalen, W Germany
Dulovo 82 E1 Silistra, NE Bulgaria
Duluth 23 G2 Minnesota, N USA
Dūmā 97 B5 Fr. Douma. Dimashq, SW Syria
Dumas 27 E1 Texas, SW USA
Dumfries 66 C4 S Scotland, United Kingdom
Dumont d'Urville 132 C4 French research station Antarctica
Dumyāt 50 B1 var. Dumyât, Eng. Damietta. N Egypt
Duna see Danube, C Europe
Düna see Western Dvina
Duna see Don, Russian Federation
Dünaburg see Daugavpils
Dunaj see Wien, Austria
Dunaj see Danube, C Europe
Dunapentele see Dunaújváros
Dunărea see Danube
Dunaújváros 77 C7 prev. Dunapentele, Sztálinváros. Fejér, C Hungary
Dunav see Danube
Dunavska Ravnina 82 C2 Eng. Danubian Plain. lowlands N Bulgaria
Duncan 27 G2 Oklahoma, C USA
Dundalk 67 B5 Ir. Dún Dealgan. Louth, NE Ireland
Dún Dealgan see Dundalk
Dundee 56 D4 KwaZulu/Natal, E South Africa
Dundee 66 C4 E Scotland, United Kingdom
Dunedin 129 B7 Otago, South Island, New Zealand
Dunfermline 66 C4 C Scotland, United Kingdom
Dungu 55 E5 Orientale, NE Dem. Rep. Congo
Dungun 116 B3 var. Kuala Dungun. Terengganu, Peninsular Malaysia
Dunholme see Durham
Dunkerque 68 C2 Eng. Dunkirk, Flem. Duinekerke; prev. Dunquerque. Nord, N France
Dunkirk see Dunkerque
Dún Laoghaire 67 B6 Eng. Dunleary; prev. Kingstown. E Ireland
Dunleary see Dún Laoghaire
Dún Pádraig see Downpatrick
Dunquerque see Dunkerque
Dunqulah see Dongola
Dupnitsa 82 C2 prev. Marek, Stanke Dimitrov. Kyustendil, W Bulgaria
Duqm 99 E5 var. Daqm. E Oman
Durance 69 D6 river SE France
Durango 28 D3 var. Victoria de Durango. Durango, W Mexico
Durango 22 C5 Colorado, C USA
Durankulak 82 E1 Rom. Răcari; prev. Blatnitsa, Duranulac. Dobrich, NE Bulgaria
Durant 27 G2 Oklahoma, C USA
Duranulac see Durankulak
Durazzo see Durrës
Durban 56 D4 var. Port Natal. KwaZulu/Natal, E South Africa
Durbe 84 B3 Ger. Durben. Liepāja, W Latvia
Durben see Durbe
Durg 113 E4 prev. Drug. Chhattīsgarh, C India
Durham 67 D5 hist. Dunholme. N England, United Kingdom
Durham 21 F1 North Carolina, SE USA
Durocortorum see Reims
Durostorum see Silistra
Durovernum see Canterbury
Durrës 79 C6 var. Durrësi, Dursi, It. Durazzo, SCr. Drač, Turk. Draç. Durrës, W Albania
Durrësi see Durrës
Dursi see Durrës
Durūz, Jabal ad 97 C5 mountain SW Syria
D'Urville Island 128 C4 island C New Zealand
Dusa Mareb/Dusa Marreb see Dhuusa Marreeb
Dushanbe 101 E3 var. Dyushambe; prev. Stalinabad, Taj. Stalinobod. country capital (Tajikistan) W Tajikistan
Düsseldorf 72 A4 var. Duesseldorf. Nordrhein-Westfalen, W Germany
Dŭsti 101 E3 Rus. Dusti. SW Tajikistan
Dutch East Indies see Indonesia
Dutch Guiana see Suriname
Dutch Harbor 14 B3 Unalaska Island, Alaska, USA
Dutch New Guinea see Papua
Duzdab see Zāhedān
Dvina Bay see Chëshskaya Guba
Dvinsk see Daugavpils
Dyanev see Galkynyş
Dyersburg 20 C1 Tennessee, S USA
Dyushambe see Dushanbe
Dza Chu see Mekong
Dzaudzhikau see Vladikavkaz
Dzerzhinsk 89 C5 Nizhegorodskaya Oblast', W Russian Federation
Dzerzhinskiy see Nar'yan-Mar
Dzhalal-Abad 101 F2 Kir. Jalal-Abad. Dzhalal-Abadskaya Oblast', W Kyrgyzstan
Dzhambul see Taraz
Dzhankoy 87 F4 Respublika Krym, S Ukraine
Dzharkurgan see Jarqo'rg'on
Dzhelandy 101 F3 SE Tajikistan
Dzhergalan 101 G2 Kir. Jyrgalan. Issyk-Kul'skaya Oblast', NE Kyrgyzstan
Dzhezkazgan see Zhezkazgan
Dzhizak see Jizzax
Dzhugdzhur, Khrebet 93 G3 mountain range E Russian Federation
Dzhusaly see Zhosaly
Działdowo 76 D3 Warmińsko-Mazurskie, C Poland
Dzuunmod 105 E2 Töv, C Mongolia
Dzüün Soyonï Nuruu see Vostochnyy Sayan
Dzvina see Western Dvina

E

Eagle Pass 27 F4 Texas, SW USA
East Açores Fracture Zone see East Azores Fracture Zone
East Antarctica 132 C3 var. Greater Antarctica. physical region Antarctica
East Australian Basin see Tasman Basin
East Azores Fracture Zone 44 C3 var. East Açores Fracture Zone. tectonic feature E Atlantic Ocean
Eastbourne 67 E7 SE England, United Kingdom
East Cape 128 E3 headland North Island, New Zealand
East China Sea 103 E2 Chin. Dong Hai. sea W Pacific Ocean
Easter Fracture Zone 131 G4 tectonic feature E Pacific Ocean
Easter Island see Pascua, Isla de
Eastern Desert 46 D3 var. Aş Şaḩrā' ash Sharqīyah, Eng. Arabian Desert, Eastern Desert. desert E Egypt
Eastern Desert see Sahara el Sharqîya
Eastern Ghats 102 B3 mountain range SE India
Eastern Sayans see Vostochnyy Sayan
Eastern Sierra Madre see Madre Oriental, Sierra
East Falkland 43 D8 var. Isla Soledad. island E Falkland Islands
East Frisian Islands 72 A3 Eng. East Frisian Islands. island group NW Germany
East Frisian Islands see Ostfriesische Inseln
East Grand Forks 23 E1 Minnesota, N USA
East Indiaman Ridge 119 D6 undersea ridge E Indian Ocean
East Indies 130 A3 island group SE Asia
East Kilbride 66 C4 S Scotland, United Kingdom
East Korea Bay 107 E3 bay E North Korea
Eastleigh 67 D7 S England, United Kingdom
East London 56 D5 Afr. Oos-Londen; prev. Emonti, Port Rex. Eastern Cape, S South Africa
Eastmain 16 D3 river Québec, C Canada
East Mariana Basin 120 B1 undersea basin W Pacific Ocean
East Novaya Zemlya Trough 90 C1 var. Novaya Zemlya Trough. trough W Kara Sea
East Pacific Rise 131 F4 undersea rise E Pacific Ocean
East Pakistan see Bangladesh
East Saint Louis 18 B4 Illinois, N USA
East Scotia Basin 45 C7 undersea basin SE Scotia Sea
East Sea 108 A4 var. Sea of Japan, Rus. Yapanskoye More. Sea NW Pacific Ocean
East Siberian Sea see Vostochno-Sibirskoye More
East Timor 117 F5 var. Loro Sae; prev. Portuguese Timor, Timor Timur. country S Indonesia
Eau Claire 18 A2 Wisconsin, N USA
Eau Claire, Lac à L' see St. Clair, Lake
Eauripik Rise 120 B2 undersea rise W Pacific Ocean
Ebensee 73 D6 Oberösterreich, N Austria
Eberswalde-Finow 72 D3 Brandenburg, E Germany
Ebetsu 108 D2 var. Ebetu. Hokkaidō, NE Japan
Ebetu see Ebetsu
Eblana see Dublin
Ebolowa 55 A5 Sud, S Cameroon
Ebon Atoll 122 D2 var. Epoon. atoll Ralik Chain, S Marshall Islands
Ebora see Évora
Eboracum see York
Ebro 71 E2 river NE Spain
Eburacum see York
Ebusus see Eivissa
Ecbatana see Hamadān
Ech Cheliff/Ech Chleff see Chlef
Echo Bay 15 E3 Northwest Territories, NW Canada
Echt 65 D5 Limburg, SE Netherlands
Ecija 70 D4 anc. Astigi. Andalucía, SW Spain
Eckengraf see Viesīte
Ecuador 38 B1 off. Republic of Ecuador. country NW South America
Ecuador, Republic of see Ecuador
Ed Da'ein 50 A4 Southern Darfur, W Sudan
Ed Damazin 50 C4 var. Ad Damazīn. Blue Nile, E Sudan
Ed Damer 50 C3 var. Ad Dāmir, Ad Damar. River Nile, NE Sudan
Ed Debba 50 B3 Northern, N Sudan
Ede 64 D4 Gelderland, C Netherlands
Ede 53 F5 Osun, SW Nigeria
Edéa 55 A5 Littoral, SW Cameroon
Edessa see Şanlıurfa
Edfu see Idfū
Edgeøya 61 G2 island S Svalbard
Edgware 67 A7 Harrow, SE England, United Kingdom
Edinburg 27 G5 Texas, SW USA
Edinburgh 66 C4 national capital S Scotland, United Kingdom
Edingen see Enghien
Edirne 94 A2 Eng. Adrianople; anc. Adrianopolis, Hadrianopolis. Edirne, NW Turkey
Edmonds 24 B2 Washington, NW USA
Edmonton 15 E5 province capital Alberta, SW Canada
Edmundston 17 E4 New Brunswick, SE Canada
Edna 27 G4 Texas, SW USA
Edolo 74 B1 Lombardia, N Italy
Edremit 94 A3 Balıkesir, NW Turkey
Edward, Lake 55 E5 var. Albert Edward Nyanza, Edward Nyanza, Lac Idi Amin, Lake Rutanzige. lake Uganda/Dem. Rep. Congo
Edward Nyanza see Edward, Lake
Edwards Plateau 27 F3 plain Texas, SW USA
Edzo 31 E4 prev. Rae-Edzo. Northwest Territories, NW Canada
Eeklo 65 B5 var. Eekloo. Oost-Vlaanderen, NW Belgium
Eekloo see Eeklo
Eems see Ems
Eersel 65 C5 Noord-Brabant, S Netherlands
Eesti Vabariik see Estonia
Efate 122 D4 var. Efate, Fr. Vaté; prev. Sandwich Island. island C Vanuatu
Efate see Efate
Effingham 18 B4 Illinois, N USA
Eforie-Sud 86 D5 Constanţa, E Romania
Egadi Is. 75 B7 island group S Italy
Ege Denizi see Aegean Sea
Eger 77 D6 Ger. Erlau. Heves, NE Hungary
Eger see Cheb, Czech Republic
Egeria Fracture Zone 119 C5 tectonic feature W Indian Ocean
Éghezèe 65 C6 Namur, C Belgium
Egina see Aígina
Egio see Aígio
Egmont see Taranaki, Mount
Egmont, Cape 128 C4 headland North Island, New Zealand
Egoli see Johannesburg
Egypt 50 B2 off. Arab Republic of Egypt, Ar. Jumhūrīyah Mişr al 'Arabīyah, prev. United Arab Republic; anc. Aegyptus. country NE Africa
Eibar 71 E1 País Vasco, N Spain
Eibergen 64 E3 Gelderland, E Netherlands
Eidfjord 63 A5 Hordaland, S Norway
Eier-Berg see Suur Munamägi
Eifel 73 A5 plateau W Germany
Eiger 73 B7 mountain C Switzerland
Eigg 66 B3 island W Scotland, United Kingdom
Eight Degree Channel 110 B3 channel India/ Maldives
Eighty Mile Beach 124 B4 beach Western Australia
Eijsden 65 D6 Limburg, SE Netherlands
Eilat see Elat
Eindhoven 65 D5 Noord-Brabant, S Netherlands
Eipel see Ipel'
Éire see Ireland
Éireann, Muir see Irish Sea
Eisenhüttenstadt 72 D4 Brandenburg, E Germany
Eisenmarkt see Hunedoara
Eisenstadt 73 E6 Burgenland, E Austria
Eisleben 72 C4 Sachsen-Anhalt, C Germany
Eivissa 71 G3 var. Iviza, Cast. Ibiza; anc. Ebusus. Ibiza, Spain, W Mediterranean Sea
Ejea de los Caballeros 71 E2 Aragón, NE Spain
Ejin Qi see Dalain Hob
Ekapa see Cape Town
Ekaterinodar see Krasnodar
Ekvyvatapskiy Khrebet 93 G1 mountain range NE Russian Federation
El 'Alamein see Al 'Alamayn
El Asnam see Chlef
Elat 97 B8 var. Eilat, Elath. Southern, S Israel
Elat, Gulf of see Aqaba, Gulf of
Elath see Elat, Israel
Elath see Al 'Aqabah, Jordan
El'Atrun 50 B3 Northern Darfur, NW Sudan
Elâzığ 95 E3 var. Elâzig, Elâziz. Elâzığ, E Turkey
Elba 74 B4 island Archipelago Toscano, C Italy
Elbasan 79 D6 var. Elbasani. Elbasan, C Albania
Elbasani see Elbasan
Elbe 58 D3 Cz. Labe. river Czech Republic/ Germany
Elbert, Mount 22 C4 mountain Colorado, C USA
Elbing see Elbląg
Elbląg 76 C2 var. Elblag, Ger. Elbing. Warmińsko-Mazurskie, NE Poland
El Boulaida/El Bouláida see Blida
El'brus 89 A8 var. Gora El'brus. mountain SW Russian Federation
El'brus, Gora see El'brus
El Burgo de Osma 71 E2 Castilla-León, C Spain
Elburz Mountains see Alborz, Reshteh-ye Kūhhā-ye
El Cajon 25 C8 California, W USA
El Calafate 43 B7 var. Calafate. Santa Cruz, S Argentina
El Callao 37 E2 Bolívar, E Venezuela
El Campo 27 G4 Texas, SW USA
El Carmen de Bolívar 36 B2 Bolívar, NW Colombia
El Cayo see San Ignacio
El Centro 25 D8 California, W USA
Elche 71 F4 Cat. Elx; anc. Ilici, Lat. Illicis. País Valenciano, E Spain
Elda 71 F4 País Valenciano, E Spain
El Djazaïr see Alger
El Djelfa see Djelfa
Eldorado 42 E3 Misiones, NE Argentina
El Dorado 28 C3 Sinaloa, C Mexico
El Dorado 20 B2 Arkansas, C USA
El Dorado 23 F5 Kansas, C USA
El Dorado 37 F2 Bolívar, E Venezuela
El Dorado see California
Eldoret 51 C6 Rift Valley, W Kenya
Elektrostal' 89 B5 Moskovskaya Oblast', W Russian Federation
Elemi Triangle 51 B5 disputed region Kenya/Sudan
Elephant Butte Reservoir 26 C2 reservoir New Mexico, SW USA
Élesd see Aleşd
Eleuthera Island 32 C1 island N Bahamas
El Fasher 50 A4 var. Al Fāshir. Northern Darfur, W Sudan
El Ferrol/El Ferrol del Caudillo see Ferrol
El Gedaref see Gedaref
El Geneina 50 A4 var. Ajjinena, Al-Genain, Al Junaynah. Western Darfur, W Sudan
Elgin 66 C3 NE Scotland, United Kingdom
Elgin 18 B3 Illinois, N USA
El Gîza see Gîza
El Goléa 48 D3 var. Al Golea. C Algeria
El Hank 52 D1 cliff N Mauritania
El Haseke see Al Ḩasakah
Elimberrum see Auch
Eliocroca see Lorca
Élisabethville see Lubumbashi
Elista 89 B7 Respublika Kalmykiya, SW Russian Federation
Elizabeth 127 B6 South Australia
Elizabeth City 21 G1 North Carolina, SE USA
Elizabethtown 18 C5 Kentucky, S USA
El-Jadida 48 C2 prev. Mazagan. W Morocco
Ełk 76 E2 Ger. Lyck. Warmińsko-mazurskie, NE Poland
Elk City 27 F1 Oklahoma, C USA
El Khalil see Hebron
El Khârga see Al Khārijah
Elkhart 18 C3 Indiana, N USA
El Khartûm see Khartoum
Elk River 23 F2 Minnesota, N USA
El Kuneitra see Al Qunayţirah
Ellás see Greece
Ellef Ringnes Island 15 E1 island Nunavut, N Canada
Ellen, Mount 22 B5 mountain Utah, W USA

Ellensburg – Forchheim

Ellensburg *24 B2* Washington, NW USA
Ellesmere Island *15 F1 island* Queen Elizabeth Islands, Nunavut, N Canada
Ellesmere, Lake *129 C6 lake* South Island, New Zealand
Ellice Islands *see* Tuvalu
Elliston *127 A6* South Australia
Ellsworth Land *132 A3 physical region* Antarctica
El Mahbas *48 B3 var.* Mahbés. SW Western Sahara
El Mina *96 B4 var.* Al Mīnā'. N Lebanon
El Minya *see* Al Minyā
Elmira *19 E3* New York, NE USA
El Mreyyé *52 D2 desert* E Mauritania
Elmshorn *72 B3* Schleswig-Holstein, N Germany
El Muglad *50 B4* Western Kordofan, C Sudan
El Obeid *50 B4 var.* Al Obayyid, Al Ubayyiḍ. Northern Kordofan, C Sudan
El Ouâdi *see* El Oued
El Oued *49 E2 var.* Al Oued, El Ouâdi, El Wad. NE Algeria
Eloy *26 B2* Arizona, SW USA
El Paso *26 D3* Texas, SW USA
El Porvenir *31 G4* Kuna Yala, N Panama
El Progreso *30 C2* Yoro, NW Honduras
El Puerto de Santa María *70 C5* Andalucía, S Spain
El Qâhira *see* Cairo
El Quneitra *see* Al Qunayṭirah
El Quseir *see* Al Quṣayr
El Quweira *see* Al Quwayrah
El Rama *31 E3* Región Autónoma Atlántico Sur, SE Nicaragua
El Real *31 H5 var.* El Real de Santa María. Darién, SE Panama
El Real de Santa María *see* El Real
El Reno *27 F1* Oklahoma, C USA
El Salvador *30 B3 off.* Republica de El Salvador. *country* Central America
El Salvador, Republica de *see* El Salvador
Elsass *see* Alsace
El Sáuz *28 C2* Chihuahua, N Mexico
El Serrat *69 A7* N Andorra Europe
Elst *64 D4* Gelderland, E Netherlands
El Sueco *28 C2* Chihuahua, N Mexico
El Suweida *see* As Suwaydā'
El Suweis *see* Suez
Eltanin Fracture Zone *131 E5 tectonic feature* SE Pacific Ocean
El Tigre *37 E2* Anzoátegui, NE Venezuela
Elvas *70 C4* Portalegre, C Portugal
El Vendrell *71 G2* Cataluña, NE Spain
El Vigía *36 C2* Mérida, NW Venezuela
El Wad *see* El Oued
Elwell, Lake *22 B1 reservoir* Montana, NW USA
Elx *see* Elche
Ely *25 D5* Nevada, W USA
El Yopal *see* Yopal
Emajõgi *84 D3 Ger.* Embach. *river* SE Estonia
Emāmrūd *see* Shāhrūd
Emāmshahr *see* Shāhrūd
Emba *92 B4 Kaz.* Embi. Aktyubinsk, W Kazakhstan
Embach *see* Emajõgi
Embi *see* Emba
Emden *72 A3* Niedersachsen, NW Germany
Emerald *126 D4* Queensland, E Australia
Emerald Isle *see* Montserrat
Emesa *see* Ḥimṣ
Emmaste *84 C2* Hiiumaa, W Estonia
Emmeloord *64 D2* Flevoland, N Netherlands
Emmen *64 E2* Drenthe, NE Netherlands
Emmendingen *73 A6* Baden-Württemberg, SW Germany
Emona *see* Ljubljana
Emonti *see* East London
Emory Peak *27 E4 mountain* Texas, SW USA
Empalme *28 B2* Sonora, NW Mexico
Emperor Seamounts *91 G3 seamount range* NW Pacific Ocean
Empire State of the South *see* Georgia
Emporia *23 F5* Kansas, C USA
Empty Quarter *see* Ar Rub 'al Khālī
Ems *72 A3 Dut.* Eems. *river* NW Germany
Enareträsk *see* Inarijärvi
Encamp *69 A8* Encamp, C Andorra Europe
Encarnación *42 D3* Itapúa, S Paraguay
Encinitas *25 C8* California, W USA
Encs *77 D6* Borsod-Abaúj-Zemplén, NE Hungary
Endeavour Strait *126 C1 strait* Queensland, NE Australia
Enderbury Island *123 F3 atoll* Phoenix Islands, C Kiribati
Enderby Land *132 C2 physical region* Antarctica
Enderby Plain *132 D2 abyssal plain* S Indian Ocean
Endersdorf *see* Jędrzejów
Enewetak Atoll *122 C1 var.* Ānewetak, Eniwetok. *atoll* Ralik Chain, W Marshall Islands
Enfield *67 A7* United Kingdom
Engeten *see* Aiud
Enghien *65 B6 Dut.* Edingen. Hainaut, SW Belgium
England *67 D5 Lat.* Anglia. *cultural region* England, United Kingdom
Englewood *22 D4* Colorado, C USA
English Channel *67 D8 var.* The Channel, *Fr.* la Manche. *channel* NW Europe
Engure *84 C3* Tukums, W Latvia
Engures Ezers *84 B3 lake* NW Latvia
Enguri *95 F1 Rus.* Inguri. *river* NW Georgia
Enid *27 F1* Oklahoma, C USA
Enikale Strait *see* Kerch Strait
Eniwetok *see* Enewetak Atoll
En Nâqoûra *97 A5 var.* An Nāqūrah. SW Lebanon
En Nazira *see* Natzrat
Ennedi *54 D2 plateau* E Chad
Ennis *67 A6 Ir.* Inis. Clare, W Ireland
Ennis *27 G3* Texas, SW USA
Enniskillen *67 B5 var.* Inniskilling, *Ir.* Inis Ceithleann. SW Northern Ireland, United Kingdom
Enns *73 D6 river* C Austria
Enschede *64 E3* Overijssel, E Netherlands
Ensenada *28 A1* Baja California Norte, NW Mexico
Entebbe *51 B6* S Uganda
Entroncamento *70 B3* Santarém, C Portugal
Enugu *53 G5* Enugu, S Nigeria
Epanomí *82 B4* Kentrikí Makedonía, N Greece
Epéna *55 B5* Likouala, NE Congo
Eperies/Eperjes *see* Prešov
Epi *122 D4 var.* Épi. *island* C Vanuatu
Épi *see* Epi
Épinal *68 D4* Vosges, NE France
Epiphania *see* Ḥamāh
Epoon *see* Ebon Atoll
Epsom *67 A8* United Kingdom
Equality State *see* Wyoming
Equatorial Guinea *55 A5 off.* Equatorial Guinea, Republic of. *country* C Africa
Equatorial Guinea, Republic of *see* Equatorial Guinea
Erautini *see* Johannesburg
Erbil *see* Arbīl
Erciş *95 F3* Van, E Turkey
Erdély *see* Transylvania
Erdélyi-Havasok *see* Carpaţii Meridionalii
Erdenet *105 E2* Orhon, N Mongolia
Erdi *54 C2 plateau* NE Chad
Erdi Ma *54 D2 desert* NE Chad
Erebus, Mount *132 B4 volcano* Ross Island, Antarctica
Ereğli *94 C4* Konya, S Turkey
Erenhot *105 F2 var.* Erlian. Nei Mongol Zizhiqu, NE China
Erfurt *72 C4* Thüringen, C Germany
Ergene Çayı *see* Ergene Irmaği
Ergene Irmaği *94 A2 var.* Ergene Çayı. *river* NW Turkey
Ergun *105 F1 var.* Labudalin; *prev.* Ergun Youqi. Nei Mongol Zizhiqu, N China
Ergun He *see* Argun
Ergun Youqi *see* Ergun
Erie *18 D3* Pennsylvania, NE USA
Érié, Lac *see* Erie, Lake
Erie, Lake *18 D3 Fr.* Lac Érié. *lake* Canada/USA
Eritrea *50 C4 off.* State of Eritrea, Ērtra. *country* E Africa
Eritrea, State of *see* Eritrea
Erivan *see* Yerevan
Erlangen *73 C5* Bayern, S Germany
Erlau *see* Eger
Erlian *see* Erenhot
Ermelo *64 D3* Gelderland, C Netherlands
Ermióni *83 C6* Pelopónnisos, S Greece
Ermoúpoli *83 D6 var.* Hermoupolis; *prev.* Ermoúpolis. Sýyros, Kykládes, Greece, Aegean Sea
Ermoúpolis *see* Ermoúpoli
Ernākulam *110 C3* Kerala, SW India
Erode *110 C2* Tamil Nādu, SE India
Erquelinnes *65 B7* Hainaut, S Belgium
Er-Rachidia *48 C2 var.* Ksar al Soule. E Morocco
Er Rahad *50 B4 var.* Ar Rahad. Northern Kordofan, C Sudan
Erromango *122 D4 island* S Vanuatu
Ertis *see* Irtysh, C Asia
Ērtra *see* Eritrea
Erzerum *see* Erzurum
Erzgebirge *73 C5 Cz.* Krušné Hory, *Eng.* Ore Mountains. *mountain range* Czech Republic/Germany
Erzincan *95 E3 var.* Erzinjan. Erzincan, E Turkey
Erzinjan *see* Erzincan
Erzurum *95 E3 prev.* Erzerum. Erzurum, NE Turkey
Esbjerg *63 A7* Ribe, W Denmark
Esbo *see* Espoo
Escaldes *69 A8* Escaldes Engordany, C Andorra Europe
Escanaba *18 C2* Michigan, N USA
Escaut *see* Scheldt
Esch-sur-Alzette *65 D8* Luxembourg, S Luxembourg
Esclaves, Grand Lac des *see* Great Slave Lake
Escondido *25 C8* California, W USA
Escuinapa *28 D3 var.* Escuinapa de Hidalgo. Sinaloa, C Mexico
Escuinapa de Hidalgo *see* Escuinapa
Escuintla *30 B2* Escuintla, S Guatemala
Escuintla *29 G5* Chiapas, SE Mexico
Esenguly *100 B3 Rus.* Gasan-Kuli. Balkan Welayaty, W Turkmenistan
Eşfahān *98 C3 Eng.* Isfahan; *anc.* Aspadana. Eşfahān, C Iran
Esh Sharā *see* Ash Sharāh
Esil *see* Ishim, Kazakhstan/Russian Federation
Eskimo Point *see* Arviat
Eskişehir *94 B3 var.* Eskishehr. Eskişehir, W Turkey
Eskishehr *see* Eskişehir
Eslāmābād *98 C3 var.* Eslāmābād-e Gharb; *prev.* Harunabad, Shāhābād. Kermānshāhān, W Iran
Eslāmābād-e Gharb *see* Eslāmābād
Esmeraldas *38 A1* Esmeraldas, N Ecuador
Esna *see* Isnā
España *see* Spain
Espanola *26 D1* New Mexico, SW USA
Esperance *125 B7* Western Australia
Esperanza *28 B2* Sonora, NW Mexico
Esperanza *132 A2 Argentinian research station* Antarctica
Espinal *36 B3* Tolima, C Colombia
Espinhaço, Serra do *34 D4 mountain range* SE Brazil
Espírito Santo *41 F4 off.* Estado do Espírito Santo. *region* E Brazil
Espírito Santo *41 F4 off.* Estado do Espírito Santo. *state* E Brazil
Espírito Santo, Estado do *see* Espírito Santo
Espiritu Santo *122 C4 var.* Santo. *island* W Vanuatu
Espoo *63 D6 Swe.* Esbo. Etelä-Suomi, S Finland
Esquel *43 B6* Chubut, SW Argentina
Essaouira *48 B2 prev.* Mogador. W Morocco
Esseg *see* Osijek
Es Semara *see* Smara
Essen *65 C5* Antwerpen, N Belgium
Essen *72 A4 var.* Essen an der Ruhr. Nordrhein-Westfalen, W Germany
Essen an der Ruhr *see* Essen
Essequibo River *37 F3 river* C Guyana
Es Suweida *see* As Suwaydā'
Estacado, Llano *27 E2 plain* New Mexico/Texas, SW USA
Estados, Isla de los *43 C8 prev. Eng.* Staten Island. *island* S Argentina
Estância *41 G3* Sergipe, E Brazil
Estelí *30 D3* Esteli, NW Nicaragua
Estella *71 E1 Bas.* Lizarra. Navarra, N Spain
Estepona *70 D5* Andalucía, S Spain
Estevan *15 F5* Saskatchewan, S Canada
Estland *see* Estonia
Estonia *84 D2 off.* Republic of Estonia, *Est.* Eesti Vabariik, *Ger.* Estland, *Latv.* Igaunija; *prev.* Estonian SSR, *Rus.* Estonskaya SSR. *country* NE Europe
Estonian SSR *see* Estonia
Estonia, Republic of *see* Estonia
Estonskaya SSR *see* Estonia
Estrela, Serra da *70 C3 mountain range* C Portugal
Estremadura *see* Extremadura
Estremoz *70 C4* Évora, S Portugal
Eszék *see* Osijek
Esztergom *77 C6 Ger.* Gran; *anc.* Strigonium. Komárom-Esztergom, N Hungary
Étalle *65 D8* Luxembourg, SE Belgium
Etāwah *112 D3* Uttar Pradesh, N India
Ethiopia *51 C5 off.* Federal Democratic Republic of Ethiopia; *prev.* Abyssinia, People's Democratic Republic of Ethiopia. *country* E Africa
Ethiopia, Federal Democratic Republic of *see* Ethiopia
Ethiopian Highlands *51 C5 var.* Ethiopian Plateau. *plateau* N Ethiopia
Ethiopian Plateau *see* Ethiopian Highlands
Ethiopia, People's Democratic Republic of *see* Ethiopia
Etna, Monte *75 C7 Eng.* Mount Etna. *volcano* Sicilia, Italy, C Mediterranean Sea
Etna, Mount *see* Etna, Monte
Etosha Pan *56 B3 salt lake* N Namibia
Etoumbi *55 B5* Cuvette Ouest, NW Congo
Etsch *see* Adige
Et Tafila *see* Aṭ Ṭafīlah
Ettelbrück *65 D8* Diekirch, C Luxembourg
'Eua *123 E5 prev.* Middleburg Island. *island* Tongatapu Group, SE Tonga
Euboea *83 C5 Lat.* Euboea. *island* C Greece
Euboea *see* Évvoia
Eucla *125 D6* Western Australia
Euclid *18 D3* Ohio, N USA
Eufaula Lake *27 G1 var.* Eufaula Reservoir. *reservoir* Oklahoma, C USA
Eufaula Reservoir *see* Eufaula Lake
Eugene *24 B3* Oregon, NW USA
Eumolpias *see* Plovdiv
Eupen *65 D6* Liège, E Belgium
Euphrates *90 B4 Ar.* Al-Furāt, *Turk.* Firat Nehri. *river* SW Asia
Eureka *25 A5* California, W USA
Eureka *22 A1* Montana, NW USA
Europa Point *71 H5 headland* S Gibraltar
Europe *58 continent*
Eutin *72 C2* Schleswig-Holstein, N Germany
Euxine Sea *see* Black Sea
Evansdale *23 G3* Iowa, C USA
Evanston *18 B3* Illinois, N USA
Evanston *22 B4* Wyoming, C USA
Evansville *18 B5* Indiana, N USA
Eveleth *23 G1* Minnesota, N USA
Everard, Lake *127 A6 salt lake* South Australia
Everest, Mount *104 B5 Chin.* Qomolangma Feng, *Nep.* Sagarmāthā. *mountain* China/Nepal
Everett *24 B2* Washington, NW USA
Everglades, The *21 F5 wetland* Florida, SE USA
Evje *63 A6* Aust-Agder, S Norway
Evmolpia *see* Plovdiv
Évora *70 B4 anc.* Ebora, *Lat.* Liberalitas Julia. Évora, C Portugal
Évreux *68 C3 anc.* Civitas Eburovicum. Eure, N France
Évros *see* Maritsa
Évry *68 E2* Essonne, N France
Ewarton *32 B5* C Jamaica
Excelsior Springs *23 F4* Missouri, C USA
Exe *67 C7 river* SW England, United Kingdom
Exeter *67 C7 anc.* Isca Damnoniorum. SW England, United Kingdom
Exmoor *67 C7 moorland* SW England, United Kingdom
Exmouth *124 A4* Western Australia
Exmouth *67 C7* SW England, United Kingdom
Exmouth Gulf *124 A4 gulf* Western Australia
Exmouth Plateau *119 E5 undersea plateau* E Indian Ocean
Extremadura *70 C3 var.* Estremadura. *autonomous community* W Spain
Exuma Cays *32 C1 islets* C Bahamas
Exuma Sound *32 C1 sound* C Bahamas
Eyre Mountains *129 A7 mountain range* South Island, New Zealand
Eyre North, Lake *127 A5 salt lake* South Australia
Eyre Peninsula *127 A6 peninsula* South Australia
Eyre South, Lake *127 A5 salt lake* South Australia
Ezo *see* Hokkaidō

F

Faadhippolhu Atoll *110 B4 var.* Fadiffolu, Lhaviyani Atoll. *atoll* N Maldives
Fabens *26 D3* Texas, SW USA
Fada *54 C2* Borkou-Ennedi-Tibesti, E Chad
Fada-Ngourma *53 E4* E Burkina
Fadiffolu *see* Faadhippolhu Atoll
Faenza *74 C3 anc.* Faventia. Emilia-Romagna, N Italy
Faeroe Islands *see* Faero Islands
Færøerne *see* Faroe Islands
Faetano *74 E2* E San Marino
Făgăraş *86 C4 Ger.* Fogarasch, *Hung.* Fogaras. Braşov, C Romania
Fagibina, Lake *see* Faguibine, Lac
Fagne *65 C7 hill range* S Belgium
Faguibine, Lac *53 E3 var.* Lake Fagibina. *lake* NW Mali
Fahlun *see* Falun
Fahraj *98 E4* Kermān, SE Iran
Faial *70 A5 var.* Ilha do Faial. *island* Azores, Portugal, NE Atlantic Ocean
Faial, Ilha do *see* Faial
Faifo *see* Hôi An
Fairbanks *14 D3* Alaska, USA
Fairfield *25 B6* California, W USA
Fair Isle *66 D2 island* NE Scotland, United Kingdom
Fairlie *129 B6* Canterbury, South Island, New Zealand
Fairmont *23 F3* Minnesota, N USA
Faisalābād *112 C2 prev.* Lyallpur. Punjab, NE Pakistan
Faizābād *113 E3* Uttar Pradesh, N India
Faizabad/Faizābād *see* Feyzābād
Fakaofo Atoll *123 F3 island* SE Tokelau
Falam *114 A3* Chin State, W Myanmar (Burma)
Falconara Marittima *74 C3* Marche, C Italy
Falkenau an der Eger *see* Sokolov
Falkland Islands *43 D7 var.* Falklands, Islas Malvinas. *UK dependent territory* SW Atlantic Ocean
Falkland Plateau *35 D7 var.* Argentine Rise. *undersea feature* SW Atlantic Ocean
Falklands *see* Falkland Islands
Falknov nad Ohří *see* Sokolov
Fallbrook *25 C8* California, W USA
Falmouth *32 A4* W Jamaica
Falmouth *67 C7* SW England, United Kingdom
Falster *63 B8 island* SE Denmark
Fălticeni *86 C3 Hung.* Falticsén. Suceava, NE Romania
Falticsén *see* Fălticeni
Falun *63 C6 var.* Fahlun. Kopparberg, C Sweden
Famagusta *see* Gazimağusa
Famagusta Bay *see* Gazimağusa Körfezi
Famenne *65 C7 physical region* SE Belgium
Fang *114 C3* Chiang Mai, NW Thailand
Fanning Island *see* Tabuaeran
Fanø *74 C3 island* W Denmark
Farafangana *57 G4* Fianarantsoa, SE Madagascar
Farāh *100 D4 var.* Farah, Fararud. Farāh, W Afghanistan
Farah Rud *100 D4 river* W Afghanistan
Faranah *52 C4* Haute-Guinée, S Guinea
Fararud *see* Farāh
Farasan, Jaza'ir *99 A6 island group* SW Saudi Arabia
Farewell, Cape *128 C4 headland* South Island, New Zealand
Farewell, Cape *see* Nunap Isua
Fargo *23 F2* North Dakota, N USA
Farg'ona *101 F2 Rus.* Fergana; *prev.* Novyy Margilan. Farg'ona Viloyati, E Uzbekistan
Faribault *23 F2* Minnesota, N USA
Farīdābād *112 D3* Haryāna, N India
Farkhor *101 E3 Rus.* Parkhar. SW Tajikistan
Farmington *23 G5* Missouri, C USA
Farmington *26 C1* New Mexico, SW USA
Faro *70 B5* Faro, S Portugal
Faroe-Iceland Ridge *58 C1 undersea ridge* NW Norwegian Sea
Faroe Islands *61 E5 var.* Faero Islands, *Dan.* Færøerne, *Faer.* Føroyar. *Danish external territory* N Atlantic Ocean
Faroe-Shetland Trough *58 C2 trough* NE Atlantic Ocean
Farquhar Group *57 G2 island group* S Seychelles
Fars, Khalij-e *see* Persian Gulf
Farvel, Kap *see* Nunap Isua
Fastiv *87 E2 Rus.* Fastov. Kyyivs'ka Oblast', NW Ukraine
Fastov *see* Fastiv
Fauske *62 C3* Nordland, C Norway
Faventia *see* Faenza
Faxa Bay *see* Faxaflói
Faxaflói *60 D5 Eng.* Faxa Bay. *bay* W Iceland
Faya *54 C2 prev.* Faya-Largeau, Largeau. Borkou-Ennedi-Tibesti, N Chad
Faya-Largeau *see* Faya
Fayetteville *20 A1* Arkansas, C USA
Fayetteville *21 F1* North Carolina, SE USA
Fdérick *see* Fdérik
Fdérik *52 C2 var.* Fdérick, *Fr.* Fort Gouraud. Tiris Zemmour, NW Mauritania
Fear, Cape *21 F2 headland* Bald Head Island, North Carolina, SE USA
Fécamp *68 B3* Seine-Maritime, N France
Fédala *see* Mohammedia
Federal Capital Territory *see* Australian Capital Territory
Fehérgyarmat *77 E6* Szabolcs-Szatmár-Bereg, E Hungary
Fehértemplom *see* Bela Crkva
Fehmarn *72 C2 island* N Germany
Fehmarn Belt *72 C2 Dan.* Femern Bælt, *Ger.* Fehmarnbelt. *strait* Denmark /Germany
Fehmarnbelt Fehmarn Belt/Femer Bælt
Feijó *40 C2* Acre, W Brazil
Feilding *128 D4* Manawatu-Wanganui, North Island, New Zealand
Feira *see* Feira de Santana
Feira de Santana *41 G3 var.* Feira. Bahia, E Brazil
Feketehalom *see* Codlea
Felanitx *71 G3* Mallorca, Spain, W Mediterranean Sea
Felicitas Julia *see* Lisboa
Felidhu Atoll *110 B4 atoll* C Maldives
Felipe Carrillo Puerto *29 H4* Quintana Roo, SE Mexico
Felixstowe *67 E6* E England, United Kingdom
Fellin *see* Viljandi
Felsőbánya *see* Baia Sprie
Felsőmuzslya *see* Mužlja
Femunden *63 B5 lake* S Norway
Fénérive *see* Fenoarivo Atsinanana
Fengcheng *106 D3 var.* Feng-cheng, Fenghwangcheng. Liaoning, NE China
Feng-cheng *see* Fengcheng
Fenghwangcheng *see* Fengcheng
Fengtien *see* Shenyang, China
Fengtien *see* Liaoning, China
Fenoarivo Atsinanana *57 G3 Fr.* Fénérive. Toamasina, E Madagascar
Fens, The *67 E6 wetland* E England, United Kingdom
Feodosiya *87 F5 var.* Kefe, *It.* Kaffa; *anc.* Theodosia. Respublika Krym, S Ukraine
Ferdinand *see* Montana, Bulgaria
Ferdinandsberg *see* Oţelu Roşu
Féres *82 D3* Anatolikí Makedonía kai Thráki, NE Greece
Fergana *see* Farg'ona
Fergus Falls *23 F2* Minnesota, N USA
Ferizaj *79 D5 Serb.* Uroševac. C Kosovo
Ferkessédougou *52 D4* N Côte d'Ivoire
Fermo *74 C4 anc.* Firmum Picenum. Marche, C Italy
Fernandina, Isla *38 A5 var.* Narborough Island. *island* Galápagos Islands, Ecuador, E Pacific Ocean
Fernando de Noronha *41 H2 island* E Brazil
Fernando Po/Fernando Póo *see* Bioco, Isla de
Ferrara *74 C2 anc.* Forum Alieni. Emilia-Romagna, N Italy
Ferreñafe *38 B3* Lambayeque, W Peru
Ferro *see* Hierro
Ferrol *70 B1 var.* El Ferrol; *prev.* El Ferrol del Caudillo. Galicia, NW Spain
Fertő *see* Neusiedler See
Ferwerd *see* Ferwert
Ferwert *64 D1 Dutch.* Ferwerd. Friesland, N Netherlands
Fès *48 C2 Eng.* Fez. N Morocco
Feteşti *86 D5* Ialomiţa, SE Romania
Fethiye *94 B4* Muğla, SW Turkey
Fetlar *66 D1 island* NE Scotland, United Kingdom
Feuilles, Rivière aux *16 D2 river* Québec, E Canada
Feyzābād *101 F3 var.* Faizabad, Faizābād, Feyzābād, Fyzabad. Badakhshān, NE Afghanistan
Feyzābād *see* Feyzābād
Fez *see* Fès
Fianarantsoa *57 F3* Fianarantsoa, C Madagascar
Fianga *54 B4* Mayo-Kébbi, SW Chad
Fier *79 C6 var.* Fieri. Fier, SW Albania
Fieri *see* Fier
Figeac *69 C5* Lot, S France
Figig *see* Figuig
Figueira da Foz *70 B3* Coimbra, W Portugal
Figueres *71 G2* Cataluña, E Spain
Figuig *48 D2 var.* Figig. E Morocco
Fiji *123 E5 off.* Sovereign Democratic Republic of Fiji, *Fij.* Viti. *country* SW Pacific Ocean
Fiji, Sovereign Democratic Republic of *see* Fiji
Filadelfia *30 D4* Guanacaste, W Costa Rica
Filiaşi *86 B5* Dolj, SW Romania
Filipstad *63 B6* Värmland, C Sweden
Finale Ligure *74 A3* Liguria, NW Italy
Finchley *67 A7* United Kingdom
Findlay *18 C4* Ohio, N USA
Finike *94 B4* Antalya, SW Turkey
Finland *62 D4 off.* Republic of Finland, *Fin.* Suomen Tasavalta, Suomi. *country* N Europe
Finland, Gulf of *63 D6 Est.* Soome Laht, *Fin.* Suomenlahti, *Ger.* Finnischer Meerbusen, *Rus.* Finskiy Zaliv, *Swe.* Finska Viken. *gulf* E Baltic Sea
Finland, Republic of *see* Finland
Finnischer Meerbusen *see* Finland, Gulf of
Finnmarksvidda *62 D2 physical region* N Norway
Finska Viken/Finskiy Zaliv *see* Finland, Gulf of
Finsterwalde *72 D4* Brandenburg, E Germany
Fiordland *129 A7 physical region* South Island, New Zealand
Fiorina *74 E1* NE San Marino
Firat Nehri *see* Euphrates
Firenze *74 C3 Eng.* Florence; *anc.* Florentia. Toscana, C Italy
Firmum Picenum *see* Fermo
First State *see* Delaware
Fischbacher Alpen *73 E7 mountain range* E Austria
Fischhausen *see* Primorsk
Fish *56 B4 var.* Vis. *river* S Namibia
Fishguard *67 C6 Wel.* Abergwaun. SW Wales, United Kingdom
Fisterra, Cabo *70 B1 headland* NW Spain
Fitzroy Crossing *124 C3* Western Australia
Fitzroy River *124 C3 river* Western Australia
Fiume *see* Rijeka
Flagstaff *26 B2* Arizona, SW USA
Flanders *65 A6 Dut.* Vlaanderen, *Fr.* Flandre. *cultural region* Belgium/France
Flandre *see* Flanders
Flathead Lake *22 B1 lake* Montana, NW USA
Flat Island *106 C8 island* NE Spratly Islands
Flatts Village *20 B5 var.* The Flatts Village. C Bermuda
Flensburg *72 B2* Schleswig-Holstein, N Germany
Flessingue *see* Vlissingen
Flickertail State *see* North Dakota
Flinders Island *127 C8 island* Furneaux Group, Tasmania, SE Australia
Flinders Ranges *127 B6 mountain range* South Australia
Flinders River *126 C3 river* Queensland, NE Australia
Flin Flon *15 F5* Manitoba, C Canada
Flint *18 C3* Michigan, N USA
Flint Island *123 G4 island* Line Islands, E Kiribati
Floreana, Isla *see* Santa María, Isla
Florence *20 C1* Alabama, S USA
Florence *21 F2* South Carolina, SE USA
Florence *see* Firenze
Florencia *36 B4* Caquetá, S Colombia
Florentia *see* Firenze
Flores *30 B1* Petén, N Guatemala
Flores *117 E5 island* Nusa Tenggara, C Indonesia
Flores *70 A5 island* Azores, Portugal, NE Atlantic Ocean
Flores, Laut *see* Flores Sea
Flores Sea *116 D5 Ind.* Laut Flores. *sea* C Indonesia
Floriano *41 F2* Piauí, E Brazil
Florianópolis *41 F5 prev.* Destêrro. *state capital* Santa Catarina, S Brazil
Florida *42 D4* Florida, S Uruguay
Florida *21 E4 off.* State of Florida, *also known as* Peninsular State, Sunshine State. *state* SE USA
Florida Bay *21 E5 bay* Florida, SE USA
Florida Keys *21 E5 island group* Florida, SE USA
Florida, Straits of *32 B1 strait* Atlantic Ocean/Gulf of Mexico
Flórina *82 B4 var.* Phlórina. Dytikí Makedonía, N Greece
Florissant *23 G4* Missouri, C USA
Floúda, Akrotírio *83 D7 headland* Astypálaia, Kykládes, Greece, Aegean Sea
Flushing *see* Vlissingen
Flylân *see* Vlieland
Foča *78 C4 var.* Srbinje. SE Bosnia and Herzegovina
Focşani *86 C4* Vrancea, E Romania
Fogaras/Fogarasch *see* Făgăraş
Foggia *75 D5* Puglia, SE Italy
Fogo *52 A3 island* Ilhas de Sotavento, SW Cape Verde
Foix *69 B6* Ariège, S France
Folégandros *83 C7 island* Kykládes, Greece, Aegean Sea
Foleyet *16 C4* Ontario, S Canada
Foligno *74 C4* Umbria, C Italy
Folkestone *67 E7* SE England, United Kingdom
Fond du Lac *18 B2* Wisconsin, N USA
Fongafale *123 E3 var.* Funafuti. *country capital* (Tuvalu) Funafuti Atoll, SE Tuvalu
Fonseca, Golfo de *see* Fonseca, Gulf of
Fonseca, Gulf of *30 C3 Sp.* Golfo de Fonseca. *gulf* C Central America
Fontainebleau *68 C3* Seine-et-Marne, N France
Fontenay-le-Comte *68 B4* Vendée, NW France
Fontvieille *69 B8* SW Monaco Europe
Fonyód *77 C7* Somogy, W Hungary
Foochow *see* Fuzhou
Foochow *see* Fuzhou
Forchheim *73 C5* Bayern, SE Germany

Forel, Mont - Girin

Forel, Mont 60 D4 *mountain* SE Greenland
Forfar 66 C3 E Scotland, United Kingdom
Forge du Sud *see* Dudelange
Forlì 74 C3 *anc.* Forum Livii. Emilia-Romagna, N Italy
Formentera 71 G4 *anc.* Ophiusa, *Lat.* Frumentum. *island* Islas Baleares, Spain, W Mediterranean Sea
Formosa 42 D2 Formosa, NE Argentina
Formosa/Formo'sa *see* Taiwan
Formosa, Serra 41 E3 *mountain range* C Brazil
Formosa Strait *see* Taiwan Strait
Føroyar *see* Faroe Islands
Forrest City 20 B1 Arkansas, C USA
Fort Albany 16 C3 Ontario, C Canada
Fortaleza 39 F2 Pando, N Bolivia
Fortaleza 41 G2 *prev.* Ceará. *state capital* Ceará, NE Brazil
Fort-Archambault *see* Sarh
Fort-Bayard *see* Zhanjiang
Fort-Cappolani *see* Tidjikja
Fort Charlet *see* Djanet
Fort-Chimo *see* Kuujjuaq
Fort Collins 22 D4 Colorado, C USA
Fort-Crampel *see* Kaga Bandoro
Fort Davis 27 E3 Texas, SW USA
Fort-de-France 33 H1 *prev.* Fort-Royal. *dependent territory capital* (Martinique) W Martinique
Fort Dodge 23 F3 Iowa, C USA
Fortescue River 124 A4 *river* Western Australia
Fort-Foureau *see* Kousséri
Fort Frances 16 B4 Ontario, S Canada
Fort Good Hope 15 E3 *var.* Rádeyilikóé. Northwest Territories, NW Canada
Fort Gouraud *see* Fdérik
Forth 66 C4 *river* C Scotland, United Kingdom
Forth, Firth of 66 C4 *estuary* E Scotland, United Kingdom
Fortín General Eugenio Garay *see* General Eugenio A. Garay
Fort Jameson *see* Chipata
Fort-Lamy *see* Ndjamena
Fort Lauderdale 21 F5 Florida, SE USA
Fort Liard 15 E4 *var.* Liard. Northwest Territories, W Canada
Fort Madison 23 G4 Iowa, C USA
Fort McMurray 15 E4 Alberta, C Canada
Fort McPherson 14 D3 *var.* McPherson. Northwest Territories, NW Canada
Fort Morgan 22 D4 Colorado, C USA
Fort Myers 21 E5 Florida, SE USA
Fort Nelson 15 E4 British Columbia, W Canada
Fort Peck Lake 22 C1 *reservoir* Montana, NW USA
Fort Pierce 21 F4 Florida, SE USA
Fort Providence 15 E4 *var.* Providence. Northwest Territories, W Canada
Fort-Repoux *see* Akjoujt
Fort Rosebery *see* Mansa
Fort Rousset *see* Owando
Fort-Royal *see* Fort-de-France
Fort St. John 15 E4 British Columbia, W Canada
Fort Scott 23 F5 Kansas, C USA
Fort Severn 16 C2 Ontario, C Canada
Fort-Shevchenko 92 A4 Mangistau, W Kazakhstan
Fort-Sibut *see* Sibut
Fort Simpson 15 E4 *var.* Simpson. Northwest Territories, W Canada
Fort Smith 15 E4 Northwest Territories, W Canada
Fort Smith 20 B1 Arkansas, C USA
Fort Stockton 27 E3 Texas, SW USA
Fort-Trinquet *see* Bir Mogreïn
Fort Vermilion 15 E4 Alberta, W Canada
Fort Victoria *see* Masvingo
Fort Walton Beach 20 C3 Florida, SE USA
Fort Wayne 18 C4 Indiana, N USA
Fort William 66 C3 N Scotland, United Kingdom
Fort Worth 27 G2 Texas, SW USA
Fort Yukon 14 D3 Alaska, USA
Forum Alieni *see* Ferrara
Forum Livii *see* Forlì
Fossa Claudia *see* Chioggia
Fougamou 55 A6 Ngounié, C Gabon
Fougères 68 B3 Ille-et-Vilaine, NW France
Fou-hsin *see* Fuxin
Foulwind, Cape 129 B5 *headland* South Island, New Zealand
Foumban 54 A4 Ouest, NW Cameroon
Fou-shan *see* Fushun
Foveaux Strait 129 A8 *strait* S New Zealand
Foxe Basin 15 G3 *sea* Nunavut, N Canada
Fox Glacier 129 B6 West Coast, South Island, New Zealand
Fraga 71 F2 Aragón, NE Spain
Fram Basin 133 C3 *var.* Amundsen Basin. *undersea basin* Arctic Ocean
France 68 B4 *off.* French Republic, *It./Sp.* Francia; *prev.* Gaul, Gaule, *Lat.* Gallia. *country* W Europe
Franceville 55 B6 *var.* Massoukou, Masuku. Haut-Ogooué, E Gabon
Francfort *see* Frankfurt am Main
Franche-Comté 68 D4 *cultural region* E France
Francia *see* France
Francis Case, Lake 23 E3 *reservoir* South Dakota, N USA
Francisco Escárcega 29 G4 Campeche, SE Mexico
Francistown 56 D3 North East, NE Botswana
Franconian Jura *see* Fränkische Alb
Frankenalb *see* Fränkische Alb
Frankenstein/Frankenstein in Schlesien *see* Ząbkowice Śląskie
Frankfort 18 C5 *state capital* Kentucky, S USA
Frankfort on the Main *see* Frankfurt am Main
Frankfurt *see* Frankfurt am Main, Germany
Frankfurt *see* Słubice, Poland
Frankfurt am Main 73 B5 *var.* Frankfurt, *Fr.* Francfort; *prev. Eng.* Frankfort on the Main. Hessen, SW Germany
Frankfurt an der Oder 72 D3 Brandenburg, E Germany
Fränkische Alb 73 C6 *var.* Frankenalb, *Eng.* Franconian Jura. *mountain range* S Germany
Franklin 20 C1 Tennessee, S USA
Franklin D. Roosevelt Lake 24 C1 *reservoir* Washington, NW USA
Franz Josef Land 92 D1 *Eng.* Franz Josef Land. *island group* N Russian Federation
Franz Josef Land *see* Frantsa-Iosifa, Zemlya
Fraserburgh 66 D3 NE Scotland, United Kingdom
Fraser Island 126 E4 *var.* Great Sandy Island. *island* Queensland, E Australia
Fraunbach *see* Baia Mare
Frauenburg *see* Saldus, Latvia
Fredericksburg 19 E5 Virginia, NE USA
Fredericton 17 F4 *province capital* New Brunswick, SE Canada
Frederikshåb *see* Paamiut
Fredrikshald *see* Halden
Fredrikstad 63 B6 Østfold, S Norway
Freeport 32 C1 Grand Bahama Island, N Bahamas
Freeport 27 H4 Texas, SW USA
Free State *see* Maryland
Freetown 52 C4 *country capital* (Sierra Leone) W Sierra Leone
Freiburg *see* Freiburg im Breisgau, Germany
Freiburg im Breisgau 73 A6 *var.* Freiburg, *Fr.* Fribourg-en-Brisgau. Baden-Württemberg, SW Germany
Freiburg in Schlesien *see* Świebodzice
Fremantle 125 A6 Western Australia
Fremont 23 F4 Nebraska, C USA
French Guiana 37 H3 *var.* Guiana, Guyane. *French overseas department* N South America
French Guinea *see* Guinea
French Polynesia 121 F4 *French overseas territory* S Pacific Ocean
French Republic *see* France
French Somaliland *see* Djibouti
French Southern and Antarctic Lands 119 B7 *Fr.* Terres Australes et Antarctiques Françaises. *French overseas territory* S Indian Ocean
French Sudan *see* Mali
French Territory of the Afars and Issas *see* Djibouti
French Togoland *see* Togo
Fresnillo 28 D3 *var.* Fresnillo de González Echeverría. Zacatecas, C Mexico
Fresnillo de González Echeverría *see* Fresnillo
Fresno 25 C6 California, W USA
Frías 42 C3 Catamarca, N Argentina
Fribourg-en-Brisgau *see* Freiburg im Breisgau
Friedek-Mistek *see* Frýdek-Místek
Friedrichshafen 73 B7 Baden-Württemberg, S Germany
Friendly Islands *see* Tonga
Frisches Haff *see* Vistula Lagoon
Frobisher Bay 60 B3 *inlet* Baffin Island, Nunavut, NE Canada
Frobisher Bay *see* Iqaluit
Frohavet 62 B4 *sound* C Norway
Frome, Lake 127 B6 *salt lake* South Australia
Frontera 29 G4 Tabasco, SE Mexico
Frontignan 69 C6 Hérault, S France
Frostviken *see* Kvarnbergsvattnet
Frøya 62 A4 *island* W Norway
Frumentum *see* Formentera
Frunze *see* Bishkek
Frýdek-Místek 77 C5 *Ger.* Friedek-Mistek. Moravskoslezský Kraj, E Czech Republic
Fu-chien *see* Fujian
Fu-chou *see* Fuzhou
Fuengirola 70 D5 Andalucía, S Spain
Fuerte Olimpo 42 D2 *var.* Olimpo. Alto Paraguay, NE Paraguay
Fuerte, Río 26 C5 *river* C Mexico
Fuerteventura 48 B3 *island* Islas Canarias, Spain, NE Atlantic Ocean
Fuhkien *see* Fujian
Fu-hsin *see* Fuxin
Fuji 109 D6 *var.* Huzi. Shizuoka, Honshū, S Japan
Fujian 106 D6 *var.* Fu-chien, Fuhkien, Fukien, Min, Fujian Sheng. *province* SE China
Fujian Sheng *see* Fujian
Fuji, Mount/Fujiyama *see* Fuji-san
Fuji-san 109 C6 *var.* Fujiyama, *Eng.* Mount Fuji. *mountain* Honshū, SE Japan
Fukang 104 C2 Xinjiang Uygur Zizhiqu, W China
Fukien *see* Fujian
Fukui 109 C6 *var.* Hukui. Fukui, Honshū, SW Japan
Fukuoka 109 A7 *var.* Hukuoka, *hist.* Najima. Fukuoka, Kyūshū, SW Japan
Fukushima 108 D4 *var.* Hukusima. Fukushima, Honshū, C Japan
Fulda 73 B5 Hessen, C Germany
Funafuti *see* Fongafale
Funafuti Atoll 123 E3 *atoll* C Tuvalu
Funchal 48 A2 Madeira, Portugal, NE Atlantic Ocean
Fundy, Bay of 17 F5 *bay* Canada/USA
Fünen *see* Fyn
Fünfkirchen *see* Pécs
Furnes *see* Veurne
Fürth 73 C5 Bayern, S Germany
Furukawa 108 D4 *var.* Hurukawa, Ōsaki Miyagi, Honshū, C Japan
Fusan *see* Busan
Fushë Kosovë 79 D5 *Serb.* Kosovo Polje. C Kosovo
Fushun 106 D3 *var.* Fou-shan, Fu-shun. Liaoning, NE China
Fu-shun *see* Fushun
Fusin *see* Fuxin
Füssen 73 C7 Bayern, S Germany
Futog 78 D3 Vojvodina, NW Serbia
Futuna, Île 123 E4 *island* S Wallis and Futuna
Fuxin 106 D3 *var.* Fou-hsin, Fu-hsin, Fusin. Liaoning, NE China
Fuzhou 106 D6 *var.* Foochow, Fu-chou. *province capital* Fujian, SE China
Fyn 63 B8 *Ger.* Fünen. *island* C Denmark
FYR Macedonia/FYROM *see* Macedonia, FYR
Fyzabad *see* Feyzābād

G

Gaafu Alifu Atoll *see* North Huvadhu Atoll
Gaalkacyo 51 E5 *var.* Galka'yo, *It.* Galcaio. Mudug, C Somalia
Gabela 56 B2 Cuanza Sul, W Angola
Gaberones *see* Gaborone
Gabès 49 E2 *var.* Qābis. E Tunisia
Gabès, Golfe de 49 F2 *Ar.* Khalīj Qābis. *gulf* E Tunisia
Gabon 55 B6 *off.* Gabonese Republic. *country* C Africa
Gabonese Republic *see* Gabon
Gaborone 56 C4 *prev.* Gaberones. *country capital* (Botswana) South East, SE Botswana
Gabrovo 82 D2 Gabrovo, N Bulgaria
Gadag 110 C1 Karnātaka, W India
Gades/Gadier/Gadir/Gadire *see* Cádiz
Gadsden 20 D2 Alabama, S USA
Gaeta 75 C5 Lazio, C Italy
Gaeta, Golfo di 75 C5 *var.* Gulf of Gaeta. *gulf* C Italy
Gaeta, Gulf of *see* Gaeta, Golfo di
Gäfle *see* Gävle
Gafsa 49 E2 *var.* Qafṣah. W Tunisia
Gagnoa 52 D5 C Côte d'Ivoire
Gagra 95 E1 NW Georgia
Gaillac 69 C6 *var.* Gaillac-sur-Tarn. Tarn, S France
Gaillac-sur-Tarn *see* Gaillac
Gaillimh *see* Galway
Gaillimhe, Cuan na *see* Galway Bay
Gainesville 21 E3 Florida, SE USA
Gainesville 20 D2 Georgia, SE USA
Gainesville 27 G2 Texas, SW USA
Lake Gairdner 127 A6 *salt lake* South Australia
Gaizina Kalns *see* Gaiziņkalns
Gaiziņkalns 84 C3 *var.* Gaizina Kalns. *mountain* E Latvia
Galán, Cerro 42 B3 *mountain* NW Argentina
Galanta 77 C6 *Hung.* Galánta. Trnavský Kraj, W Slovakia
Galapagos Fracture Zone 131 E3 *tectonic feature* E Pacific Ocean
Galápagos Islands 131 F3 *var.* Islas de los Galápagos, *Sp.* Archipiélago de Colón, *Eng.* Galapagos Islands, Tortoise Islands. *island group* Ecuador, E Pacific Ocean
Galapagos Islands *see* Galápagos Islands
Galápagos, Islas de los *see* Galápagos Islands
Galapagos Rise 131 F3 *undersea rise* E Pacific Ocean
Galashiels 66 C4 SE Scotland, United Kingdom
Galați 86 D4 *Ger.* Galatz. Galați, E Romania
Galatz *see* Galați
Galcaio *see* Gaalkacyo
Galesburg 18 B3 Illinois, N USA
Galicia 70 B1 *anc.* Gallaecia. *autonomous community* NW Spain
Galicia Bank 58 B4 *undersea bank* E Atlantic Ocean
Galilee, Sea of *see* Tiberias, Lake
Galka'yo *see* Gaalkacyo
Galkynyş 100 D3 *prev. Rus.* Deynau, Dyanev, *Turkm.* Dänew. Lebap Welaýaty, NE Turkmenistan
Gallaecia *see* Galicia
Galle 110 D4 *prev.* Point de Galle. Southern Province, SW Sri Lanka
Gallego Rise 131 F3 *undersea rise* E Pacific Ocean
Gallegos *see* Río Gallegos
Gallia *see* France
Gallipoli 75 E6 Puglia, SE Italy
Gällivare 62 C3 *Lapp.* Váhtjer. Norrbotten, N Sweden
Gallup 26 C1 New Mexico, SW USA
Galtat-Zemmour 48 B3 C Western Sahara
Galveston 27 H4 Texas, SW USA
Galway 67 A5 *Ir.* Gaillimh. W Ireland
Galway Bay 67 A6 *Ir.* Cuan na Gaillimhe. *bay* W Ireland
Gámas *see* Kaamanen
Gambell 14 C2 Saint Lawrence Island, Alaska, USA
Gambia 52 B3 *off.* Republic of The Gambia, The Gambia. *country* W Africa
Gambia 52 C3 *Fr.* Gambie. *river* W Africa
Gambia, Republic of The *see* Gambia
Gambia, The *see* Gambia
Gambie *see* Gambia
Gambier, Îles 121 G4 *island group* E French Polynesia
Gamboma 55 B6 Plateaux, E Congo
Gamlakarleby *see* Kokkola
Gan 110 B5 Addu Atoll, C Maldives
Gan *see* Gansu, China
Gan *see* Jiangxi, China
Ganaane *see* Juba
Gäncä 95 G2 *Rus.* Gyandzha; *prev.* Kirovabad, Yelisavetpol. W Azerbaijan
Gand *see* Gent
Gandajika 55 D7 Kasai-Oriental, S Dem. Rep. Congo
Gander 17 G3 Newfoundland and Labrador, SE Canada
Gāndhīdhām 112 C4 Gujarāt, W India
Gandia 71 F3 *prev.* Gandía. País Valenciano, E Spain
Gandía *see* Gandia
Ganges 113 F3 *Ben.* Padma. *river* Bangladesh/India
Ganges Cone *see* Ganges Fan
Ganges Fan 118 D3 *var.* Ganges Cone. *undersea fan* N Bay of Bengal
Ganges, Mouths of the 113 G4 *delta* Bangladesh/India
Gangra *see* Çankırı
Gangtok 113 F3 *state capital* Sikkim, N India
Gansos, Lago dos *see* Goose Lake
Gansu 106 B4 *var.* Gan, Gansu Sheng, Kansu. *province* N China
Gansu Sheng *see* Gansu
Gantsevichi *see* Hantsavichy
Ganzhou 106 D6 Jiangxi, S China
Gao 53 E3 Gao, E Mali
Gaocheng *see* Litang
Gaoual 52 C4 N Guinea
Gaoxiong 106 D6 *var.* Kaohsiung, *Jap.* Takao, Takow. S Taiwan
Gap 69 D5 *anc.* Vapincum. Hautes-Alpes, SE France
Gaplaňgyr Platosy 100 C2 *Rus.* Plato Kaplangky. *ridge* Turkmenistan/Uzbekistan
Gar *see* Gar Xincun
Garabil Belentligi 100 D3 *Rus.* Vozvyshennost' Karabil'. *mountain range* S Turkmenistan
Garabogaz Aylagy 100 B2 *Rus.* Zaliv Kara-Bogaz-Gol. *bay* NW Turkmenistan
Garachiné 31 G5 Darién, SE Panama
Garagum 100 C3 *var.* Garagumy, Qara Qum, *Eng.* Black Sand Desert, Kara Kum; *prev.* Peski Karakumy. *desert* C Turkmenistan
Garagum Canal 100 D3 *var.* Kara Kum Canal, *Rus.* Karagumskiy Kanal, Karakumskiy Kanal. *canal* C Turkmenistan
Garagumy *see* Garagum
Gara Khitrino 82 D2 Shumen, NE Bulgaria
Gárassavon *see* Kaaresuvanto
Garda, Lago di 74 C2 *var.* Benaco, *Eng.* Lake Garda, *Ger.* Gardasee. *lake* NE Italy
Garda, Lake *see* Garda, Lago di
Gardasee *see* Garda, Lago di
Garden City 23 E5 Kansas, C USA
Garden State, The *see* New Jersey
Gardēz 101 E4 *prev.* Gardīz. E Afghanistan
Gardīz *see* Gardēz
Gardner Island *see* Nikumaroro
Garegegasnjárga *see* Karigasniemi
Gargždai 84 B3 Klaipėda, W Lithuania
Garissa 51 D6 Coast, E Kenya
Garland 27 G2 Texas, SW USA
Garoe *see* Garoowe
Garonne 69 B5 *anc.* Garumna. *river* S France
Garoowe 51 E5 *var.* Garoe. Nugaal, N Somalia
Garoua 54 B4 *var.* Garua. Nord, N Cameroon
Garrygala *see* Magtymguly
Garry Lake 15 F3 *lake* Nunavut, N Canada
Garsen 51 D6 Coast, S Kenya
Garua *see* Garoua
Garumna *see* Garonne
Garwolin 76 D4 Mazowieckie, E Poland
Gar Xincun 104 A4 *prev.* Gar. Xizang Zizhiqu, W China
Gary 18 B3 Indiana, N USA
Garzón 36 B4 Huila, S Colombia
Gasan-Kuli *see* Esenguly
Gascogne 69 B6 *Eng.* Gascony. *cultural region* S France
Gascony *see* Gascogne
Gascoyne River 125 A5 *river* Western Australia
Gaspé 17 F3 Québec, SE Canada
Gaspé, Péninsule de 17 E4 *var.* Péninsule de la Gaspésie. *peninsula* Québec, SE Canada
Gaspésie, Péninsule de la *see* Gaspé, Péninsule de
Gastonia 21 E1 North Carolina, SE USA
Gastoúni 83 B6 Dytikí Elláda, S Greece
Gatchina 88 B4 Leningradskaya Oblast', NW Russian Federation
Gatineau 16 D4 Québec, SE Canada
Gatooma *see* Kadoma
Gatún, Lake 31 F4 *reservoir* C Panama
Gauhāti *see* Guwāhāti
Gauja 84 D3 *Ger.* Aa. *river* Estonia/Latvia
Gaul/Gaule *see* France
Gauteng *see* Johannesburg, South Africa
Gāvbandī 98 D4 Hormozgān, S Iran
Gávdos 83 C8 *island* SE Greece
Gavere 65 B6 Oost-Vlaanderen, NW Belgium
Gävle 63 C6 *var.* Gäfle; *prev.* Gefle. Gävleborg, C Sweden
Gawler 127 B6 South Australia
Gaya 113 F3 Bihār, N India
Gaya *see* Kyjov
Gayndah 127 E5 Queensland, E Australia
Gaysin *see* Haysyn
Gaza 97 A6 *Ar.* Ghazzah, *Heb.* 'Azza. NE Gaza Strip
Gaz-Achak *see* Gazojak
Gazandzhyk/Gazanjyk *see* Bereket
Gaza Strip 97 A7 *Ar.* Qita Ghazzah. *disputed region* SW Asia
Gaziantep 94 D4 *var.* Gazi Antep; *prev.* Aintab, Antep. Gaziantep, S Turkey
Gazi Antep *see* Gaziantep
Gazimağusa 80 D5 *var.* Famagusta, *Gk.* Ammóchostos. E Cyprus
Gazimağusa Körfezi 80 C5 *var.* Famagusta Bay, *Gk.* Kólpos Ammóchostos. *bay* E Cyprus
Gazli 100 D2 Buxoro Viloyati, C Uzbekistan
Gazojak 100 D2 *Rus.* Gaz-Achak. Lebap Welaýaty, NE Turkmenistan
Gbanga 52 D5 *var.* Gbarnga. N Liberia
Gbarnga *see* Gbanga
Gdańsk 76 C2 *Fr.* Dantzig, *Ger.* Danzig. Pomorskie, N Poland
Gdan'skaya Bukhta/Gdańsk, Gulf of *see* Danzig, Gulf of
Gdańska, Zakota *see* Danzig, Gulf of
Gdingen *see* Gdynia
Gdynia 76 C2 *Ger.* Gdingen. Pomorskie, N Poland
Gedaref 50 C4 *var.* Al Qaḍārif, El Gedaref. Gedaref, E Sudan
Gediz 94 B3 Kütahya, W Turkey
Gediz Nehri 94 A3 *river* W Turkey
Geel 65 C5 *var.* Gheel. Antwerpen, N Belgium
Geelong 127 C7 Victoria, SE Australia
Ge'e'mu *see* Golmud
Gefle *see* Gävle
Geilo 63 A5 Buskerud, S Norway
Gejiu 106 B6 *var.* Kochiu. Yunnan, S China
Gëkdepe *see* Gökdepe
Gela 75 C7 *prev.* Terranova di Sicilia. Sicilia, Italy, C Mediterranean Sea
Geldermalsen 64 C4 Gelderland, C Netherlands
Geleen 65 D6 Limburg, SE Netherlands
Gelib *see* Jilib
Gellinsor 51 E5 Mudug, C Somalia
Gembloux 65 C6 Namur, Belgium
Gemena 55 C5 Equateur, NW Dem. Rep. Congo
Gem of the Mountains *see* Idaho
Gemona del Friuli 74 D2 Friuli-Venezia Giulia, NE Italy
Gem State *see* Idaho
Genalē Wenz *see* Juba
Genck *see* Genk
General Alvear 42 B4 Mendoza, W Argentina
General Carrera, Lago *see* Buenos Aires, Lago
General Eugenio A. Garay 42 C1 *var.* Fortín General Eugenio Garay; *prev.* Yrendagüé. Nueva Asunción, NW Paraguay
General José F.Uriburu *see* Zárate
General Machado *see* Camacupa
General Santos 117 F3 *off.* General Santos City. Mindanao, S Philippines
General Santos City *see* General Santos
Gênes *see* Genova
Geneva *see* Genève
Geneva, Lake 73 A7 *Fr.* Lac de Genève, Lac Léman, le Léman, *Ger.* Genfer See. *lake* France/Switzerland
Genève 73 A7 *Eng.* Geneva, *Ger.* Genf, *It.* Ginevra. Genève, SW Switzerland
Genève, Lac de *see* Geneva, Lake
Genf *see* Genève
Genfer See *see* Geneva, Lake
Genichesk *see* Heniches'k
Genk 65 D6 *var.* Genck. Limburg, NE Belgium
Gennep 64 D4 Limburg, SE Netherlands
Genoa *see* Genova
Genoa, Gulf of 74 A3 *Eng.* Gulf of Genoa. *gulf* NW Italy
Genoa, Gulf of *see* Genova, Golfo di
Genova 80 D1 *Eng.* Genoa; *anc.* Genua, *Fr.* Gênes. Liguria, NW Italy
Genovesa, Isla 38 B5 *var.* Tower Island. *island* Galápagos Islands, Ecuador, E Pacific Ocean
Gent 65 B5 *Eng.* Ghent, *Fr.* Gand. Oost-Vlaanderen, NW Belgium
Genua *see* Genova
Geok-Tepe *see* Gökdepe
George 56 C5 Western Cape, S South Africa
George 60 A4 *river* Newfoundland and Labrador/Québec, E Canada
George, Lake 21 E3 *lake* Florida, SE USA
Georgenburg *see* Jurbarkas
Georges Bank 13 D5 *undersea bank* W Atlantic Ocean
George Sound 129 A7 *sound* South Island, New Zealand
Georges River 126 D2 *river* New South Wales, E Australia
Georgetown 37 F2 *country capital* (Guyana) N Guyana
George Town 32 C2 Great Exuma Island, C Bahamas
George Town 32 B3 *var.* Georgetown. *dependent territory capital* (Cayman Islands) Grand Cayman, SW Cayman Islands
George Town 116 B3 *var.* Penang, Pinang. Pinang, Peninsular Malaysia
Georgetown 21 F2 South Carolina, SE USA
Georgetown *see* George Town
George V Land 132 C4 *physical region* Antarctica
Georgia 95 F2 *off.* Republic of Georgia, *Geor.* Sak'art'velo, *Rus.* Gruzinskaya SSR, Gruziya. *country* SW Asia
Georgia 20 D2 *off.* State of Georgia, *also known as* Empire State of the South, Peach State. *state* SE USA
Georgian Bay 18 D2 *lake bay* Ontario, S Canada
Georgia, Republic of *see* Georgia
Georgia, Strait of 24 A1 *strait* British Columbia, W Canada
Georgi Dimitrov *see* Kostenets
Georgiu-Dezh *see* Liski
Georg von Neumayer 132 A2 *German research station* Antarctica
Gera 72 C4 Thüringen, E Germany
Geráki 83 B6 Pelopónnisos, S Greece
Geraldine 129 B6 Canterbury, South Island, New Zealand
Geraldton 125 A6 Western Australia
Geral, Serra 35 D5 *mountain range* S Brazil
Gerede 94 C2 Bolu, N Turkey
Gereshk 100 D5 Helmand, SW Afghanistan
Gering 22 D3 Nebraska, C USA
German East Africa *see* Tanzania
Germanicopolis *see* Çankırı
Germanicum, Mare/German Ocean *see* North Sea
German Southwest Africa *see* Namibia
Germany 72 B4 *off.* Federal Republic of Germany, Bundesrepublik Deutschland, *Ger.* Deutschland. *country* N Europe
Germany, Federal Republic of *see* Germany
Geroliménas 83 B7 Pelopónnisos, S Greece
Gerona *see* Girona
Gerpinnes 65 C7 Hainaut, S Belgium
Gerunda *see* Girona
Gerze 94 D2 Sinop, N Turkey
Gesoriacum *see* Boulogne-sur-Mer
Gessoriacum *see* Boulogne-sur-Mer
Getafe 70 D3 Madrid, C Spain
Gevaş 95 F3 Van, SE Turkey
Gevgeli *see* Gevgelija
Gevgelija 79 E6 *var.* Đevđelija, Djevdjelija, *Turk.* Gevgeli. SE Macedonia
Ghaba *see* Al Ghābah
Ghana 53 E5 *off.* Republic of Ghana. *country* W Africa
Ghanzi 56 C3 *var.* Khanzi. Ghanzi, W Botswana
Gharandal 97 B7 Al 'Aqabah, SW Jordan
Gharbt, Jabal al *see* Liban, Jebel
Ghardaïa 48 D2 N Algeria
Gharvān *see* Gharyān
Gharyān 49 F2 *var.* Gharvān. NW Libya
Ghawdex *see* Gozo
Ghaznī 101 E4 *var.* Ghazni. Ghaznī, E Afghanistan
Ghazzah *see* Gaza
Gheel *see* Geel
Ghent *see* Gent
Gheorgheni 86 C4 *prev.* Gheorghieni, Sîn-Miclăuş, *Ger.* Niklasmarkt, *Hung.* Gyergyószentmiklós. Harghita, C Romania
Gheorghieni *see* Gheorgheni
Ghōrīān 100 D4 *prev.* Ghūrīān. Herāt, W Afghanistan
Ghūdara 101 F3 *var.* Gudara, *Rus.* Kudara. SE Tajikistan
Ghurdaqah *see* Al Ghurdaqah
Ghūrīān *see* Ghōrīān
Giamame *see* Jamaame
Giannitsá 82 B4 *var.* Yiannitsá. Kentrikí Makedonía, N Greece
Gibraltar 71 C1 *UK dependent territory* SW Europe
Gibraltar, Bay of 71 G5 *bay* Gibraltar/Spain Europe Mediterranean Sea Atlantic Ocean
Gibraltar, Détroit de/Gibraltar, Estrecho de *see* Gibraltar, Strait of
Gibraltar, Strait of 70 C5 *Fr.* Détroit de Gibraltar, *Sp.* Estrecho de Gibraltar. *strait* Atlantic Ocean/Mediterranean Sea
Gibson Desert 125 B5 *desert* Western Australia
Giedraičiai 85 C5 Utena, E Lithuania
Giessen 73 B5 Hessen, W Germany
Gifu 109 C6 *var.* Gihu. Gifu, Honshū, SW Japan
Giganta, Sierra de la 28 B3 *mountain range* NW Mexico
Gihu *see* Gifu
G'ijduvon 100 D2 *Rus.* Gizhduvon. Buxoro Viloyati, C Uzbekistan
Gijón 70 D1 *var.* Xixón. Asturias, NW Spain
Gila River 26 A2 *river* Arizona, SW USA
Gilbert Islands *see* Tungaru
Gilbert River 126 C3 *river* Queensland, NE Australia
Gilf Kebir Plateau *see* Haḍabat al Jilf al Kabīr
Gillette 22 D3 Wyoming, C USA
Gilolo *see* Halmahera, Pulau
Gilroy 25 B6 California, W USA
Gimie, Mount 33 F1 *mountain* C Saint Lucia
Gimma *see* Jīma
Ginevra *see* Genève
Gingin 125 A6 Western Australia
Giohar *see* Jawhar
Gipeswic *see* Ipswich
Girardot 36 B3 Cundinamarca, C Colombia
Giresun 95 E2 *var.* Kerasunt; *anc.* Cerasus, Pharnacia. Giresun, NE Turkey
Girgenti *see* Agrigento
Girin *see* Jilin

Girne – Gýtheio

Girne 80 C5 Gk. Kerýneia, Kyrenia. N Cyprus
Giron see Kiruna
Girona 71 G2 var. Gerona; anc. Gerunda. Cataluña, NE Spain
Gisborne 128 E3 Gisborne, North Island, New Zealand
Gissar Range 101 E3 Rus. Gissarskiy Khrebet. mountain range Tajikistan/Uzbekistan
Gissarskiy Khrebet see Gissar Range
Githio see Gýtheio
Giulianova 74 D4 Abruzzi, C Italy
Giumri see Gyumri
Giurgiu 86 C5 Giurgiu, S Romania
Gîza 50 B1 var. Al Jīzah, El Gîza, Gizeh. N Egypt
Gizhduvon see G'ijduvon
Giżycko 76 D2 Ger. Lötzen. Warmińsko-Mazurskie, NE Poland
Gjakovë 79 D5 Serb. Đakovica. W Kosovo
Gjilan 79 D5 Serb. Gnjilane. E Kosovo
Gjinokastër see Gjirokastër
Gjirokastër 79 C7 var. Gjirokastra; prev. Gjinokastër, Gk. Argyrokastron, It. Argirocastro. Gjirokastër, S Albania
Gjirokastra see Gjirokastër
Gjoa Haven 15 F3 var. Uqsuqtuuq. King William Island, Nunavut, NW Canada
Gjøvik 63 B5 Oppland, S Norway
Glace Bay 17 G4 Cape Breton Island, Nova Scotia, SE Canada
Gladstone 126 E4 Queensland, E Australia
Gláma 63 B5 var. Glommen. river S Norway
Glasgow 66 C4 S Scotland, United Kingdom
Glavinitsa 82 D1 prev. Pravda, Dogrular. Silistra, NE Bulgaria
Glavn'a Morava see Velika Morava
Glazov 89 D5 Udmurtskaya Respublika, NW Russian Federation
Gleiwitz see Gliwice
Glendale 26 B2 Arizona, SW USA
Glendive 22 D2 Montana, NW USA
Glens Falls 19 F3 New York, NE USA
Glevum see Gloucester
Glina 78 B3 var. Banijska Palanka. Sisak-Moslavina, NE Croatia
Glittertind 63 A5 mountain S Norway
Gliwice 77 C5 Ger. Gleiwitz. Śląskie, S Poland
Globe 26 B2 Arizona, SW USA
Globino see Hlobyne
Glogau see Głogów
Głogów 76 B4 Ger. Glogau, Glogow. Dolnośląskie, SW Poland
Glogow see Głogów
Glomma see Gláma
Glommen see Gláma
Gloucester 67 D6 hist. Caer Glou, Lat. Glevum. C England, United Kingdom
Głowno 76 D4 Łódź, C Poland
Glubokoye see Hlybokaye
Glukhov see Hlukhiv
Gnesen see Gniezno
Gniezno 76 C3 Ger. Gnesen. Weilkopolskie, C Poland
Gnjilane see Gjilan
Gobabis 56 B3 Omaheke, E Namibia
Gobi 104 D3 desert China/Mongolia
Gobō 109 C6 Wakayama, Honshū, SW Japan
Godāvari 102 B3 var. Godavari. river C India
Godavari see Godāvari
Godhavn see Qeqertarsuaq
Godhra 112 C4 Gujarāt, W India
Göding see Hodonín
Godoy Cruz 42 B4 Mendoza, W Argentina
Godthaab/Godthåb see Nuuk
Godwin Austen, Mount see K2
Goede Hoop, Kaap de see Good Hope, Cape of
Goeie Hoop, Kaap die see Good Hope, Cape of
Goeree 64 B4 island SW Netherlands
Goes 65 B5 Zeeland, SW Netherlands
Goettingen see Göttingen
Gogebic Range 18 B1 hill range Michigan/Wisconsin, N USA
Goiânia 41 E3 prev. Goyania. state capital Goiás, C Brazil
Goiás 41 E3 off. Estado de Goiás; prev. Goiaz, Goyaz. region C Brazil
Goiás 41 E3 off. Estado de Goiás; prev. Goiaz, Goyaz. state C Brazil
Goiás, Estado de see Goiás
Goiaz see Goiás
Goidhoo Atoll see Horsburgh Atoll
Gojōme 108 D4 Akita, Honshū, NW Japan
Gökçeada 82 D4 var. Imroz Adasi, Gk. Imbros. island NW Turkey
Gökdepe 100 C3 Rus. Gëkdepe, Geok-Tepe. Ahal Welaýaty, C Turkmenistan
Göksun 94 D4 Kahramanmaraş, C Turkey
Gol 63 A5 Buskerud, S Norway
Golan Heights 97 B5 Ar. Al Jawlān, Heb. HaGolan. mountain range SW Syria
Golaya Pristan see Hola Prystan'
Gołdap 76 E2 Ger. Goldap. Warmińsko-Mazurskie, NE Poland
Gold Coast 127 E5 cultural region Queensland, E Australia
Golden Bay 128 C4 bay South Island, New Zealand
Golden State, The see California
Goldingen see Kuldīga
Goldsboro 21 F1 North Carolina, SE USA
Goleniów 76 B3 Ger. Gollnow. Zachodnio-pomorskie, NW Poland
Gollnow see Goleniów
Golmo see Golmud
Golmud 104 D4 var. Ge'e'mu, Golmo, Chin. Ko-erh-mu. Qinghai, C China
Golovanevsk see Holovanivs'k
Golub-Dobrzyń 76 C3 Kujawski-pomorskie, C Poland
Goma 55 E6 Nord-Kivu, NE Dem. Rep. Congo
Gombi 53 H4 Adamawa, E Nigeria
Gombroon see Bandar-e 'Abbās
Gomel' see Homyel'
Gomera 48 A3 island Islas Canarias, Spain, NE Atlantic Ocean
Gómez Palacio 28 D3 Durango, C Mexico
Gonaïves 32 D3 var. Les Gonaïves. N Haiti
Gonâve, Île de la 32 D3 island C Haiti
Gondar see Gonder
Gonder 50 C4 var. Gondar. Āmara, NW Ethiopia
Gondia 113 E4 Mahārāshtra, C India
Gonggar 104 C5 var. Gyixong. Xizang Zizhiqu, W China
Gongola 53 G4 river E Nigeria
Gongtang see Damxung
Gonni/Gónnos see Gónnoi
Gónnoi 82 B4 var. Gonni, Gónnos; prev. Dereli. Thessalía, C Greece
Good Hope, Cape of 56 B5 Afr. Kaap de Goede Hoop, Kaap die Goeie Hoop. headland SW South Africa
Goodland 22 D4 Kansas, C USA
Goondiwindi 127 D5 Queensland, E Australia
Goor 64 E3 Overijssel, E Netherlands
Goose Green 43 D7 var. Prado del Ganso. East Falkland, Falkland Islands
Goose Lake 24 B4 var. Lago dos Gansos. lake California/Oregon, W USA
Gopher State see Minnesota
Göppingen 73 B6 Baden-Württemberg, SW Germany
Góra Kalwaria 92 D4 Mazowieckie, C Poland
Gorakhpur 113 E3 Uttar Pradesh, N India
Gorany see Harany
Goražde 78 C4 Federacija Bosna I Hercegovina, SE Bosnia and Herzegovina
Gorbovichi see Harbavichy
Goré 54 C4 Logone-Oriental, S Chad
Gorē 51 C5 Oromīya, C Ethiopia
Gore 129 B7 Southland, South Island, New Zealand
Gorgān 98 D2 var. Astarabad, Astrabad, Gurgan, prev. Asterābād; anc. Hyrcania. Golestān, N Iran
Gori 95 F2 C Georgia
Gorinchem 64 C4 var. Gorkum. Zuid-Holland, C Netherlands
Goris 95 G3 SE Armenia
Gorki see Horki
Gor'kiy see Nizhniy Novgorod
Gorkum see Gorinchem
Görlitz 72 D4 Sachsen, E Germany
Görlitz see Zgorzelec
Gorlovka see Horlivka
Gorna Dzhumaya see Blagoevgrad
Gornja Mužlja see Mužlja
Gornji Milanovac 78 C4 Serbia, C Serbia
Gorodets see Haradzyets
Gorodishche see Horodyshche
Gorodnya see Horodnya
Gorodok see Haradok
Gorodok/Gorodok Yagellonski see Horodok
Gorontalo 117 E4 Sulawesi, C Indonesia
Gorontalo, Teluk see Tomini, Gulf of
Gorssel 64 D3 Gelderland, E Netherlands
Goryn see Horyn'
Gorzów Wielkopolski 76 B3 Ger. Landsberg, Landsberg an der Warthe. Lubuskie, W Poland
Gosford 127 D6 New South Wales, SE Australia
Goshogawara 108 D3 var. Gosyogawara. Aomori, Honshū, C Japan
Gospić 78 A3 Lika-Senj, C Croatia
Gostivar 79 D6 W FYR Macedonia
Gosyogawara see Goshogawara
Göteborg 63 B7 Eng. Gothenburg. Västra Götaland, S Sweden
Gotel Mountains 53 G5 mountain range E Nigeria
Gotha 72 C4 Thüringen, C Germany
Gothenburg see Göteborg
Gotland 63 C7 island SE Sweden
Gotō-retto 109 A7 island group SW Japan
Gotska Sandön 84 B1 island SE Sweden
Gōtsu 109 B6 var. Gôtu. Shimane, Honshū, SW Japan
Göttingen 72 B4 var. Goettingen. Niedersachsen, C Germany
Gottschee see Kočevje
Gottwaldov see Zlín
Gôtu see Gōtsu
Gouda 64 C4 Zuid-Holland, C Netherlands
Gough Fracture Zone 45 C6 tectonic feature S Atlantic Ocean
Gough Island 47 B8 island Tristan da Cunha, S Atlantic Ocean
Gouin, Réservoir 16 D4 reservoir Québec, SE Canada
Goulburn 127 D6 New South Wales, SE Australia
Goundam 53 E3 Tombouctou, NW Mali
Gouré 53 G3 Zinder, SE Niger
Goverla, Gora see Hoverla, Hora
Governador Valadares 41 F4 Minas Gerais, SE Brazil
Govi Altayn Nuruu 105 E3 mountain range S Mongolia
Goya 42 D3 Corrientes, NE Argentina
Goyania see Goiânia
Goyaz see Goiás
Goz Beïda 54 C3 Ouaddaï, SE Chad
Gozo 75 C8 var. Ghawdex. island N Malta
Graciosa 70 A5 var. Ilha Graciosa. island Azores, Portugal, NE Atlantic Ocean
Graciosa, Ilha see Graciosa
Gradačac 78 C3 Federacija Bosna I Hercegovina, N Bosnia and Herzegovina
Gradaús, Serra dos 41 E3 mountain range C Brazil
Gradiška see Bosanska Gradiška
Grafton 127 E5 New South Wales, SE Australia
Grafton 23 E1 North Dakota, N USA
Graham Land 132 A2 physical region Antarctica
Grajewo 76 E3 Podlaskie, NE Poland
Grampian Mountains 66 C3 mountain range C Scotland, United Kingdom
Gran see Esztergom, Hungary
Granada 30 D3 Granada, SW Nicaragua
Granada 70 D5 Andalucía, S Spain
Gran Canaria 48 A3 var. Grand Canary. island Islas Canarias, Spain, NE Atlantic Ocean
Gran Chaco 42 D2 var. Chaco. lowland plain South America
Grand Bahama Island 32 B1 island N Bahamas
Grand Banks of Newfoundland 12 E4 undersea basin NW Atlantic Ocean
Grand Bassa see Buchanan
Grand Canary see Gran Canaria
Grand Canyon 26 A1 canyon Arizona, SW USA
Grand Canyon State see Arizona
Grand Cayman 32 B3 island SW Cayman Islands
Grand Duchy of Luxembourg see Luxembourg
Grande, Bahía 43 B7 bay S Argentina
Grande-Comore see Ngazidja
Grande de Chiloé, Isla see Chiloé, Isla de
Grande Prairie 15 E4 Alberta, W Canada
Grand Erg Occidental 48 D3 desert W Algeria
Grand Erg Oriental 49 E3 desert Algeria/Tunisia
Rio Grande 29 E2 var. Río Bravo, Sp. Río Bravo del Norte, Bravo del Norte. river Mexico/USA
Grande Terre 33 G3 island E West Indies
Grand Falls 17 G3 Newfoundland, Newfoundland and Labrador, SE Canada
Grand Forks 23 E1 North Dakota, N USA
Grandichi see Hrandzichy
Grand Island 23 E4 Nebraska, C USA
Grand Junction 22 C4 Colorado, C USA
Grand Paradis see Gran Paradiso
Grand Rapids 18 C3 Michigan, N USA
Grand Rapids 23 F1 Minnesota, N USA
Grand-Saint-Bernard, Col du see Great Saint Bernard Pass
Grand-Santi 37 G3 W French Guiana
Granite State see New Hampshire
Gran Lago see Nicaragua, Lago de
Gran Malvina see West Falkland
Gran Paradiso 74 A2 Fr. Grand Paradis. mountain NW Italy
Gran San Bernardo, Passo di see Great Saint Bernard Pass
Gran Santiago see Santiago
Grants 26 C2 New Mexico, SW USA
Grants Pass 24 B4 Oregon, NW USA
Granville 68 B3 Manche, N France
Gratianopolis see Grenoble
Gratz see Graz
Graudenz see Grudziądz
Graulhet 69 C6 Tarn, S France
Grave 64 D4 Noord-Brabant, SE Netherlands
Grayling 14 C2 Alaska, USA
Graz 73 E7 prev. Gratz. Steiermark, SE Austria
Great Abaco 32 C1 var. Abaco Island. island N Bahamas
Great Alfold see Great Hungarian Plain
Great Ararat see Büyükağrı Dağı
Great Australian Bight 125 D7 bight S Australia
Great Barrier Island 128 D2 island N New Zealand
Great Barrier Reef 126 D2 reef Queensland, NE Australia
Great Basin 25 C5 basin W USA
Great Bear Lake 15 E3 Fr. Grand Lac de l'Ours. lake Northwest Territories, NW Canada
Great Belt 63 B8 var. Store Bælt, Eng. Great Belt, Storebelt. channel Baltic Sea/Kattegat
Great Belt see Storebælt
Great Bend 23 E5 Kansas, C USA
Great Britain see Britain
Great Dividing Range 126 D4 mountain range NE Australia
Greater Antilles 32 D3 island group West Indies
Greater Caucasus 95 G2 mountain range Azerbaijan/Georgia/Russian Federation Asia/Europe
Greater Sunda Islands 102 D5 var. Sunda Islands. island group Indonesia
Great Exhibition Bay 128 C1 inlet North Island, New Zealand
Great Exuma Island 32 C2 island C Bahamas
Great Falls 22 B1 Montana, NW USA
Great Grimsby see Grimsby
Great Hungarian Plain 77 C7 var. Great Alfold, Plain of Hungary, Hung. Alföld. plain SE Europe
Great Inagua 32 D2 var. Inagua Islands. island S Bahamas
Great Indian Desert see Thar Desert
Great Khingan Range see Da Hinggan Ling
Great Lake see Tônlé Sap
Great Lakes 13 C5 lakes Ontario, Canada/USA
Great Lakes State see Michigan
Great Meteor Seamount see Great Meteor Tablemount
Great Meteor Tablemount 44 B3 var. Great Meteor Seamount. seamount E Atlantic Ocean
Great Nicobar 111 G3 island Nicobar Islands, India, NE Indian Ocean
Great Plain of China 103 E2 plain E China
Great Plains 23 E3 var. High Plains. plains Canada/USA
Great Rift Valley 51 C5 var. Rift Valley. depression Asia/Africa
Great Ruaha 51 C7 river S Tanzania
Great Saint Bernard Pass 74 A1 Fr. Col du Grand-Saint-Bernard, It. Passo del Gran San Bernardo. pass Italy/Switzerland
Great Salt Desert see Kavīr, Dasht-e
Great Salt Lake 22 A3 salt lake Utah, W USA
Great Salt Lake Desert 22 A4 plain Utah, W USA
Great Sand Sea 49 H3 desert Egypt/Libya
Great Sandy Desert 124 C4 desert Western Australia
Great Sandy Desert see Ar Rub 'al Khālī
Great Sandy Island see Fraser Island
Great Slave Lake 15 E4 Fr. Grand Lac des Esclaves. lake Northwest Territories, NW Canada
Great Socialist People's Libyan Arab Jamahiriya see Libya
Great Sound 20 A5 sound Bermuda, NW Atlantic Ocean
Great Victoria Desert 125 C5 desert South Australia/Western Australia
Great Wall of China 106 C4 ancient monument N China Asia
Great Yarmouth 67 E6 var. Yarmouth. E England, United Kingdom
Grebenka see Hrebinka
Gredos, Sierra de 70 D3 mountain range W Spain
Greece 83 A5 off. Hellenic Republic, Gk. Ellás; anc. Hellas. country SE Europe
Greeley 22 D4 Colorado, C USA
Green Bay 18 B2 Wisconsin, N USA
Green Bay 18 B2 lake bay Michigan/Wisconsin, N USA
Greeneville 21 E1 Tennessee, S USA
Greenland 60 D3 Dan. Grønland, Inuit Kalaallit Nunaat. Danish external territory NE North America
Greenland Sea 61 F2 sea Arctic Ocean
Green Mountains 19 G2 mountain range Vermont, NE USA
Green Mountain State see Vermont
Greenock 66 C4 W Scotland, United Kingdom
Green River 22 B3 Wyoming, C USA
Green River 18 C5 river Kentucky, C USA
Green River 22 B4 river Utah, W USA
Greensboro 21 F1 North Carolina, SE USA
Greenville 20 B2 Mississippi, S USA
Greenville 21 F1 North Carolina, SE USA
Greenville 21 E1 South Carolina, SE USA
Greenville 27 G2 Texas, SW USA
Greenwich 67 B8 United Kingdom
Greenwood 20 B2 Mississippi, S USA
Greenwood 21 E2 South Carolina, SE USA
Gregory Range 126 C3 mountain range Queensland, E Australia
Greifenberg/Greifenberg in Pommern see Gryfice
Greifswald 72 D2 Mecklenburg-Vorpommern, NE Germany
Grenada 20 C2 Mississippi, S USA
Grenada 33 G5 country SE West Indies
Grenadines, The 33 H4 island group Grenada/St Vincent and the Grenadines
Grenoble 69 D5 anc. Cularo, Gratianopolis. Isère, E France
Gresham 24 B3 Oregon, NW USA
Grevená 82 B4 Dytikí Makedonía, N Greece
Grevenmacher 65 E8 Grevenmacher, E Luxembourg
Greymouth 129 B5 West Coast, South Island, New Zealand
Grey Range 127 C5 mountain range New South Wales/Queensland, E Australia
Greytown see San Juan del Norte
Griffin 20 D2 Georgia, SE USA
Grimari 54 C4 Ouaka, C Central African Republic
Grimsby 67 E5 prev. Great Grimsby. E England, United Kingdom
Grobin see Grobiņa
Grobiņa 84 B3 Ger. Grobin. Liepāja, W Latvia
Gródek Jagielloński see Horodok
Grodno see Hrodna
Grodzisk Wielkopolski 76 B3 Wielkopolskie, C Poland
Groesbeek 64 D4 Gelderland, SE Netherlands
Grójec 76 D4 Mazowieckie, C Poland
Groningen 64 E1 Groningen, NE Netherlands
Grønland see Greenland
Groote Eylandt 126 B2 island Northern Territory, N Australia
Grootfontein 56 B3 Otjozondjupa, N Namibia
Groot Karasberge 56 B4 mountain range S Namibia
Gros Islet 33 F1 N Saint Lucia
Grossa, Isola see Dugi Otok
Grossbetschkerek see Zrenjanin
Grosse Morava see Velika Morava
Grosser Sund see Suur Väin
Grosseto 74 B4 Toscana, C Italy
Grossglockner 73 C7 mountain W Austria
Grosskanizsa see Nagykanizsa
Gross-Karol see Carei
Grosskikinda see Kikinda
Grossmichel see Michalovce
Gross-Schlatten see Abrud
Grosswardein see Oradea
Groznyy 89 B8 Chechenskaya Respublika, SW Russian Federation
Grudovo see Sredets
Grudziądz 76 C3 Ger. Graudenz. Kujawsko-pomorskie, C Poland
Grums 63 B6 Värmland, C Sweden
Grünberg/Grünberg in Schlesien see Zielona Góra
Grüneberg see Zielona Góra
Gruzinskaya SSR/Gruziya see Georgia
Gryazi 89 B6 Lipetskaya Oblast', W Russian Federation
Gryfice 76 B2 Ger. Greifenberg, Greifenberg in Pommern. Zachodnio-pomorskie, NW Poland
Guabito 31 E4 Bocas del Toro, NW Panama
Guadalajara 28 D4 Jalisco, C Mexico
Guadalajara 71 E3 Ar. Wad Al-Hajarah; anc. Arriaca. Castilla-La Mancha, C Spain
Guadalcanal 122 C3 island C Solomon Islands
Guadalquivir 70 D4 river W Spain
Guadalupe 28 D3 Zacatecas, C Mexico
Guadalupe Peak 26 D3 mountain Texas, SW USA
Guadalupe River 27 G4 river SW USA
Guadarrama, Sierra de 71 E2 mountain range C Spain
Guadeloupe 33 H3 French overseas department E West Indies
Guadiana 70 C4 river Portugal/Spain
Guadix 71 E4 Andalucía, S Spain
Guaimaca 30 C2 Francisco Morazán, C Honduras
Guajira, Península de la 36 B1 peninsula N Colombia
Gualaco 30 D2 Olancho, C Honduras
Gualán 30 B2 Zacapa, C Guatemala
Gualdicciolo 74 D1 NW San Marino
Gualeguaychú 42 D4 Entre Ríos, E Argentina
Guam 122 B1 US unincorporated territory W Pacific Ocean
Guamúchil 28 C3 Sinaloa, C Mexico
Guanabacoa 32 B2 La Habana, W Cuba
Guanajuato 29 E4 Guanajuato, C Mexico
Guanare 36 C2 Portuguesa, N Venezuela
Guanare, Río 36 D2 river W Venezuela
Guangdong 106 C6 var. Guangdong Sheng, Kuang-tung, Kwangtung, Yue. province S China
Guangdong Sheng see Guangdong
Guangju see Gwangju
Guangxi see Guangxi Zhuangzu Zizhiqu
Guangxi Zhuangzu Zizhiqu 106 C6 var. Guangxi, Gui, Kuang-hsi, Kwangsi, Eng. Kwangsi Chuang Autonomous Region. autonomous region S China
Guangyuan 106 B5 var. Kuang-yuan, Kwangyuan. Sichuan, C China
Guangzhou 106 C6 var. Kuang-chou, Kwangchow, Eng. Canton. province capital Guangdong, S China
Guantánamo 32 D3 Guantánamo, SE Cuba
Guantánamo, Bahía de 32 D3 Eng. Guantanamo Bay. US military base SE Cuba
Guantanamo Bay see Guantánamo, Bahía de
Guaporé, Rio 40 D3 var. Río Iténez. river Bolivia/Brazil
Guarda 70 C3 Guarda, N Portugal
Guarumal 31 F5 Veraguas, S Panama
Guasave 28 C3 Sinaloa, C Mexico
Guatemala 30 A2 off. Republic of Guatemala. country Central America
Guatemala Basin 13 B7 undersea basin E Pacific Ocean
Guatemala City see Ciudad de Guatemala
Guatemala, Republic of see Guatemala
Guaviare 34 B2 off. Comisaría Guaviare. province S Colombia
Guaviare, Comisaría see Guaviare
Guaviare, Río 36 D3 river E Colombia
Guayanas, Macizo de las see Guiana Highlands
Guayaquil 38 A2 var. Santiago de Guayaquil. Guayas, SW Ecuador
Guayaquil, Golfo de 38 A2 var. Gulf of Guayaquil. gulf SW Ecuador
Guayaquil, Gulf of see Guayaquil, Golfo de
Guaymas 28 B2 Sonora, NW Mexico
Gubadag 100 C2 Turkm. Tel'man; prev. Tel'mansk. Daşoguz Welaýaty, N Turkmenistan
Guben 72 D4 var. Wilhelm-Pieck-Stadt. Brandenburg, E Germany
Gudara see Ghŭdara
Gudaut'a 95 E1 NW Georgia
Guéret 68 C4 Creuse, C France
Guernsey 67 D8 British Crown Dependency Channel Islands, NW Europe
Guerrero Negro 28 A2 Baja California Sur, NW Mexico
Gui see Guangxi Zhuangzu Zizhiqu
Guiana see French Guiana
Guiana Highlands 40 D1 var. Macizo de las Guayanas. mountain range N South America
Guiba see Juba
Guidder see Guider
Guider 54 B4 var. Guidder. Nord, N Cameroon
Guidimouni 53 G3 Zinder, S Niger
Guildford 67 D7 SE England, United Kingdom
Guilin 106 C6 var. Kuei-lin, Kweilin. Guangxi Zhuangzu Zizhiqu, S China
Guimarães 70 B2 var. Guimaráes. Braga, N Portugal
Guimaráes see Guimarães
Guinea 52 C4 off. Republic of Guinea, var. Guinée; prev. French Guinea, People's Revolutionary Republic of Guinea. country W Africa
Guinea Basin 47 A5 undersea basin E Atlantic Ocean
Guinea-Bissau 52 B4 off. Republic of Guinea-Bissau, Fr. Guinée-Bissau, Port. Guiné-Bissau; prev. Portuguese Guinea. country W Africa
Guinea-Bissau, Republic of see Guinea-Bissau
Guinea, Gulf of 46 B4 Fr. Golfe de Guinée. gulf E Atlantic Ocean
Guinea, People's Revolutionary Republic of see Guinea
Guinea, Republic of see Guinea
Guiné-Bissau see Guinea-Bissau
Guinée see Guinea
Guinée-Bissau see Guinea-Bissau
Guinée, Golfe de see Guinea, Gulf of
Güiria 37 E1 Sucre, NE Venezuela
Guiyang 106 B6 var. Kuei-Yang, Kuei-yang, Kueyang, Kweiyang; prev. Kweichu. province capital Guizhou, S China
Guizhou 106 B6 Guangdong, SE China
Gujarāt 112 C4 var. Gujerat. cultural region W India
Gujerat see Gujarāt
Gujrānwāla 112 D2 Punjab, NE Pakistan
Gujrāt 112 D2 Punjab, E Pakistan
Gulbarga 110 C1 Karnātaka, C India
Gulbene 84 D3 Ger. Alt-Schwanenburg. Gulbene, NE Latvia
Gulf of Liaotung see Liaodong Wan
Gulfport 20 C3 Mississippi, S USA
Gulf, The see Persian Gulf
Gulistan see Guliston
Guliston 101 E2 Rus. Gulistan. Sirdaryo Viloyati, E Uzbekistan
Gulja see Yining
Gulkana 14 D3 Alaska, USA
Gulu 51 B6 N Uganda
Gulyantsi 82 C1 Pleven, N Bulgaria
Guma see Pishan
Gumbinnen see Gusev
Gumpolds see Humpolec
Gümülcine/Gümüljina see Komotiní
Gümüşane see Gümüşhane
Gümüşhane 95 E3 var. Gümüşane, Gumushkhane. Gümüşhane, NE Turkey
Gumushkhane see Gümüşhane
Güney Doğu Toroslar 95 E4 mountain range SE Turkey
Gunnbjørn Fjeld 60 D4 var. Gunnbjörns Bjerge. mountain C Greenland
Gunnbjörns Bjerge see Gunnbjørn Fjeld
Gunnedah 127 D6 New South Wales, SE Australia
Gunnison 22 C5 Colorado, C USA
Gurbansoltan Eje 100 C2 prev. Ylanly, Rus. Il'yaly. Daşoguz Welaýaty, N Turkmenistan
Gurbantünggüt Shamo 104 B2 desert W China
Gurgan see Gorgān
Guri, Embalse de 37 E2 reservoir E Venezuela
Gurkfeld see Krško
Gurktaler Alpen 73 D7 mountain range S Austria
Gürün 94 D3 Sivas, C Turkey
Gur'yev/Gur'yevskaya Oblast' see Atyrau
Gusau 53 G4 Zamfara, NW Nigeria
Gusev 84 B4 Ger. Gumbinnen. Kaliningradskaya Oblast', W Russian Federation
Gustavus 14 D4 Alaska, USA
Güstrow 72 C3 Mecklenburg-Vorpommern, NE Germany
Guta/Gúta see Kolárovo
Gütersloh 72 B4 Nordrhein-Westfalen, W Germany
Gutta see Kolárovo
Guttstadt see Dobre Miasto
Guwāhāti 113 G3 prev. Gauhāti. Assam, NE India
Guyana 37 F3 off. Co-operative Republic of Guyana; prev. British Guiana. country N South America
Guyana, Co-operative Republic of see Guyana
Guyane see French Guiana
Guymon 27 E1 Oklahoma, C USA
Güzelyurt Körfezi 80 C5 Gk. Kólpos Mórfu, Morphou. W Cyprus
Gvardeysk 84 A4 Ger. Tapaiu. Kaliningradskaya Oblast', W Russian Federation
Gwādar 112 A3 var. Gwadur. Baluchistān, SW Pakistan
Gwadur see Gwādar
Gwalior 112 D3 Madhya Pradesh, C India
Gwanda 56 D3 Matabeleland South, SW Zimbabwe
Gwangju 107 E4 off. Gwangju Gwang-yeoksi, prev. Kwangju, var. Guangju, Kwangchu, Jap. Kōshū. SW South Korea
Gwangju Gwang-yeoksi see Gwangju
Gwy see Wye
Gyandzha see Gäncä
Gyangzê 104 C5 Xizang Zizhiqu, W China
Gyaring Co 104 C5 lake W China
Gyêgu see Yushu
Gyergyószentmiklós see Gheorgheni
Gyixong see Gonggar
Gympie 127 E5 Queensland, E Australia
Gyomaendrőd 77 D7 Békés, SE Hungary
Gyöngyös 77 D6 Heves, NE Hungary
Győr 77 C6 Ger. Raab, Lat. Arrabona. Győr-Moson-Sopron, NW Hungary
Gýtheio 83 B6 var. Githio; prev. Ýithion. Pelopónnisos, S Greece

Gyulafehérvár – Horsburgh Atoll

Gyulafehérvár *see* Alba Iulia
Gyumri *95 F2 var.* Giumri, *Rus.* Kumayri; *prev.* Aleksandropol', Leninakan. W Armenia
Gyzyrlabat *see* Serdar

H

Haabai *see* Ha'apai Group
Haacht *65 C6* Vlaams Brabant, C Belgium
Haaksbergen *64 E3* Overijssel, E Netherlands
Ha'apai Group *123 F4 var.* Haabai. *island group* C Tonga
Haapsalu *84 D2 Ger.* Hapsal. Läänemaa, W Estonia
Ha'Arava *see* 'Arabah, Wādī al
Haarlem *64 C3 prev.* Harlem. Noord-Holland, W Netherlands
Haast *129 B6* West Coast, South Island, New Zealand
Hachijo-jima *109 D6 island* Izu-shotō, SE Japan
Hachinohe *108 D3* Aomori, Honshū, C Japan
Ḥaḍabat al Jilf al Kabīr *50 A2 var.* Gilf Kebir Plateau. *plateau* SW Egypt
Hadama *see* Nazrēt
Hadejia *53 G4* Jigawa, N Nigeria
Hadejia *53 G3 river* N Nigeria
Hadera *97 A6 var.* Khadera; *prev.* Ḥadera. Haifa, C Israel
Ḥadera *see* Hadera
Hadhdhunmathi Atoll *110 A5 atoll* S Maldives
Ha Đông *114 D3 var.* Hadong. Ha Tây, N Vietnam
Hadong *see* Ha Đông
Hadramaut *see* Ḥaḍramawt
Ḥaḍramawt *99 C6 Eng.* Hadramaut. *mountain range* S Yemen
Hadrianopolis *see* Edirne
Haerbin/Haerhpin/Ha-erh-pin *see* Harbin
Hafnia *see* Denmark
Hafnia *see* København
Hafren *see* Severn
Hafun, Ras *see* Xaafuun, Raas
Hagåtña *122 B1, var.* Agaña. *dependent territory capital* (Guam) NW Guam
Hagerstown *19 E4* Maryland, NE USA
Ha Giang *114 D3* Ha Giang, N Vietnam
Hagios Evstrátios *see* Ágios Efstrátios
HaGolan *see* Golan Heights
Hagondange *68 D3* Moselle, NE France
Haguenau *68 E3* Bas-Rhin, NE France
Haibowan *see* Wuhai
Haicheng *106 D3* Liaoning, NE China
Haidarabad *see* Hyderābād
Haifa *see* Hefa
Haifa, Bay of *see* Mifrats Hefa
Haifong *see* Hai Phong
Haikou *106 C7 var.* Hai-k'ou, Hoihow, *Fr.* Hoï-Hao. *province capital* Hainan, S China
Hai-k'ou *see* Haikou
Ḥā'il *98 B4* Ḥā'il, NW Saudi Arabia
Hailuoto *62 D4 Swe.* Karlö. *island* W Finland
Hainan *106 B7 var.* Hainan Sheng, Qiong. *province* S China
Hainan Dao *106 C7 island* S China
Hainan Sheng *see* Hainan
Hainasch *see* Ainaži
Haines *14 D4* Alaska, USA
Hainichen *72 D4* Sachsen, E Germany
Hai Phong *114 D3 var.* Haifong, Haiphong. N Vietnam
Haiphong *see* Hai Phong
Haiti *32 D3 off.* Republic of Haiti. *country* C West Indies
Haiti, Republic of *see* Haiti
Haiya *50 C3* Red Sea, NE Sudan
Hajdúhadház *77 D6* Hajdú-Bihar, E Hungary
Hajîne *see* Abū Ḥardān
Hajnówka *76 E3 Ger.* Hermhausen. Podlaskie, NE Poland
Hakodate *108 D3* Hokkaidō, NE Japan
Hal *see* Halle
Ḥalab *96 B2 Eng.* Aleppo, *Fr.* Alep; *anc.* Beroea. Ḥalab, NW Syria
Hala'ib Triangle *50 C3 region* Egypt/Sudan
Ḥalāniyāt, Juzur al *99 D6 var.* Jazā'ir Bin Ghalfān, *Eng.* Kuria Muria Islands. *island group* S Oman
Halberstadt *72 C4* Sachsen-Anhalt, C Germany
Halden *63 B6 prev.* Fredrikshald. Østfold, S Norway
Halfmoon Bay *129 A8 var.* Oban. Stewart Island, Southland, New Zealand
Haliacmon *see* Aliákmonas
Halifax *17 F4 province capital* Nova Scotia, SE Canada
Halkida *see* Chalkída
Halle *65 B6 Fr.* Hal. Vlaams Brabant, C Belgium
Halle *72 C4 var.* Halle an der Saale. Sachsen-Anhalt, C Germany
Halle an der Saale *see* Halle
Halle-Neustadt *72 C4* Sachsen-Anhalt, C Germany
Halley *132 B2 UK research station* Antarctica
Hall Islands *120 B2 island group* C Micronesia
Halls Creek *124 C3* Western Australia
Halmahera, Laut *117 F3 Eng.* Halmahera Sea; *sea* E Indonesia
Halmahera, Pulau *117 F3 prev.* Djailolo, Gilolo, Jailolo. *island* E Indonesia
Halmahera Sea *see* Halmahera, Laut
Halmstad *63 B7* Halland, S Sweden
Ha Long *114 E3 prev.* Hông Gai; *var.* Hon Gai, Hongay. Quang Ninh, N Vietnam
Hälsingborg *see* Helsingborg
Hamada *109 B6* Shimane, Honshū, SW Japan
Hamadān *98 C3 anc.* Ecbatana. Hamadān, W Iran
Ḥamāh *96 B3 var.* Hama; *anc.* Epiphania, *Bibl.* Hamath. Ḥamāh, W Syria
Hamamatsu *109 D6 var.* Hamamatu. Shizuoka, Honshū, S Japan
Hamamatu *see* Hamamatsu
Hamar *63 B5 prev.* Storhammer. Hedmark, S Norway
Hamath *see* Ḥamāh
Hamburg *72 B3* Hamburg, N Germany
Hamd, Wadi al *98 A4 dry watercourse* W Saudi Arabia
Hämeenlinna *63 D5 Swe.* Tavastehus. Etelä-Suomi, S Finland
HaMela h, Yam *see* Dead Sea
Hamersley Range *124 A4 mountain range* Western Australia
Hamhŭng *107 E3* C North Korea
Hami *104 C3 var.* Ha-mi, *Uigh.* Kumul, Qomul. Xinjiang Uygur Zizhiqu, NW China
Ha-mi *see* Hami
Hamilton *20 A5 dependent territory capital* (Bermuda) C Bermuda
Hamilton *16 D5* Ontario, S Canada
Hamilton *128 D3* Waikato, North Island, New Zealand
Hamilton *66 C4* S Scotland, United Kingdom
Hamilton *20 C2* Alabama, S USA
Hamim, Wadi al *49 G2 river* NE Libya
Hamïs Musait *see* Khamīs Mushayt
Hamm *72 B4 var.* Hamm in Westfalen. Nordrhein-Westfalen, W Germany
Ḥammāmāt, Khalīj al *see* Hammamet, Golfe de
Hammamet, Golfe de *80 D3 Ar.* Khalīj al Ḥammāmāt. *gulf* NE Tunisia
Ḥammār, Hawr al *98 C3 lake* SE Iraq
Hamm in Westfalen *see* Hamm
Hampden *129 B7* Otago, South Island, New Zealand
Hampstead *67 A7* Maryland, USA
Ḥamrun *80 B5* C Malta
Hāmūn, Daryācheh-ye *see* Şāberī, Hāmūn-e/ Sīstān, Daryācheh-ye
Hamwih *see* Southampton
Hâncești *see* Hînceşti
Hancewicze *see* Hantsavichy
Handan *106 C4 var.* Han-tan. Hebei, E China
Haneda *108 A2* (Tōkyō) Tōkyō, Honshū, S Japan
HaNegev *97 A7 Eng.* Negev. *desert* S Israel
Hanford *25 C6* California, W USA
Hangayn Nuruu *104 D2 mountain range* C Mongolia
Hang-chou/Hangchow *see* Hangzhou
Hangö *see* Hanko
Hangzhou *106 D5 var.* Hang-chou, Hangchow. *province capital* Zhejiang, SE China
Hania *see* Chaniá
Hanka, Lake *see* Khanka, Lake
Hanko *63 D6 Swe.* Hangö. Etelä-Suomi, SW Finland
Han-kou/Han-k'ou/Hankow *see* Wuhan
Hanmer Springs *129 C5* Canterbury, South Island, New Zealand
Hannibal *23 G4* Missouri, C USA
Hannover *72 B3 Eng.* Hanover. Niedersachsen, NW Germany
Hanöbukten *63 B7 bay* S Sweden
Ha Nôi *114 D3 Eng.* Hanoi, *Fr.* Hanoï. *country capital* (Vietnam) N Vietnam
Hanover *see* Hannover
Han Shui *105 E4 river* C China
Han-tan *see* Handan
Hantsavichy *85 B6 Pol.* Hancewicze, *Rus.* Gantsevichi. Brestskaya Voblasts', SW Belarus
Hanyang *see* Wuhan
Hanzhong *106 B5* Shaanxi, C China
Hāora *113 F4 prev.* Howrah. West Bengal, NE India
Haparanda *62 D4* Norrbotten, N Sweden
Hapsal *see* Haapsalu
Haradok *85 E5 Rus.* Gorodok. Vitsyebskaya Voblasts', N Belarus
Haradzyets *85 B6 Rus.* Gorodets. Brestskaya Voblasts', SW Belarus
Haramachi *108 D4* Fukushima, Honshū, E Japan
Harany *85 D5 Rus.* Gorany. Vitsyebskaya Voblasts', N Belarus
Harare *56 D3 prev.* Salisbury. *country capital* (Zimbabwe) Mashonaland East, NE Zimbabwe
Harbavichy *85 E6 Rus.* Gorbovichi. Mahilyowskaya Voblasts', E Belarus
Harbel *52 C5* W Liberia
Harbin *107 E2 var.* Haerbin, Ha-erh-pin, Kharbin; *prev.* Haerhpin, Pingkiang, Pinkiang. *province capital* Heilongjiang, NE China
Hardangerfjorden *63 A6 fjord* S Norway
Hardangervidda *63 A6 plateau* S Norway
Hardenberg *64 E3* Overijssel, E Netherlands
Harelbeke *65 A6 var.* Harlebeke. West-Vlaanderen, W Belgium
Harem *see* Ḥārim
Haren *64 E2* Groningen, NE Netherlands
Hārer *51 D5* E Ethiopia
Hargeisa *see* Hargeysa
Hargeysa *51 D5 var.* Hargeisa. Woqooyi Galbeed, NW Somalia
Hariana *see* Haryāna
Hari, Batang *116 B4 prev.* Djambi. *river* Sumatera, W Indonesia
Ḥārim *96 B2 var.* Harem. Idlib, W Syria
Harima-nada *109 B6 sea* S Japan
Harirud *101 E4 var.* Tedzhen, *Turkm.* Tejen. *river* Afghanistan/Iran
Harlan *23 F3* Iowa, C USA
Harlebeke *see* Harelbeke
Harlem *see* Haarlem
Harlingen *64 D2 Fris.* Harns. Friesland, N Netherlands
Harlingen *27 G5* Texas, SW USA
Harlow *67 E6* E England, United Kingdom
Harney Basin *24 B4 basin* Oregon, NW USA
Härnösand *63 C5 var.* Hernösand. Västernorrland, C Sweden
Harns *see* Harlingen
Harper *52 D5 var.* Cape Palmas. NE Liberia
Harricana *16 D3 river* Québec, SE Canada
Harris *66 B3 physical region* NW Scotland, United Kingdom
Harrisburg *19 E4 state capital* Pennsylvania, NE USA
Harrisonburg *19 E4* Virginia, NE USA
Harrison, Cape *17 F2 headland* Newfoundland and Labrador, E Canada
Harris Ridge *see* Lomonosov Ridge
Harrogate *67 D5* N England, United Kingdom
Hârşova *86 D5 prev.* Hîrşova. Constanţa, SE Romania
Harstad *62 C2* Troms, N Norway
Hartford *19 G3 state capital* Connecticut, NE USA
Hartlepool *67 D5* N England, United Kingdom
Harunabad *see* Eslāmābād
Har Us Gol *104 C2 lake* Hovd, W Mongolia
Har Us Nuur *104 C2 lake* NW Mongolia
Harwich *67 E6* E England, United Kingdom
Haryāna *112 D2 var.* Hariana. *cultural region* N India
Hashemite Kingdom of Jordan *see* Jordan
Hasselt *65 C6* Limburg, NE Belgium
Hassetché *see* Al Ḥasakah
Hasta Colonia/Hasta Pompeia *see* Asti
Hastings *128 E4* Hawke's Bay, North Island, New Zealand
Hastings *67 E7* SE England, United Kingdom
Hastings *23 E4* Nebraska, C USA
Haţeg *86 B4 Ger.* Wallenthal, *Hung.* Hátszeg; *prev.* Hatzeg, Hötzing. Hunedoara, SW Romania
Hátszeg *see* Haţeg
Hattem *64 D3* Gelderland, E Netherlands
Hatteras, Cape *21 G1 headland* North Carolina, SE USA
Hatteras Plain *13 D6 abyssal plain* W Atlantic Ocean
Hattiesburg *20 C3* Mississippi, S USA
Hatton Bank *see* Hatton Ridge
Hatton Ridge *58 B2 var.* Hatton Bank. *undersea ridge* N Atlantic Ocean
Hat Yai *115 C7 var.* Ban Hat Yai. Songkhla, SW Thailand
Hatzeg *see* Haţeg
Hatzfeld *see* Jimbolia
Haugesund *63 A6* Rogaland, S Norway
Haukeligrend *63 A6* Telemark, S Norway
Haukivesi *63 E5 lake* SE Finland
Hauraki Gulf *128 D2 gulf* North Island, N New Zealand
Hauroko, Lake *129 A7 lake* South Island, New Zealand
Haut Atlas *48 C2 Eng.* High Atlas. *mountain range* C Morocco
Hautes Fagnes *65 D6 Ger.* Hohes Venn. *mountain range* E Belgium
Hauts Plateaux *48 D2 plateau* Algeria/Morocco
Hauzenberg *73 D6* Bayern, SE Germany
Havana *13 D6* Illinois, N USA
Havana *see* La Habana
Havant *67 D7* S England, United Kingdom
Havelock *21 F1* North Carolina, SE USA
Havelock North *128 E4* Hawke's Bay, North Island, New Zealand
Haverfordwest *67 C6* SW Wales, United Kingdom
Havířov *77 C5* Moravskoslezský Kraj, E Czech Republic
Havre *22 C1* Montana, NW USA
Havre *see* le Havre
Havre-St-Pierre *17 F3* Québec, E Canada
Hawaii *25 A8 off.* State of Hawaii, *also known as* Aloha State, Paradise of the Pacific, *var.* Hawai'i. *state* USA, C Pacific Ocean
Hawai'i *25 B8 var.* Hawaii. *island* Hawai'ian Islands, USA, C Pacific Ocean
Hawai'ian Islands *130 D2 prev.* Sandwich Islands. *island group* Hawaii, USA
Hawaiian Ridge *130 H4 undersea ridge* N Pacific Ocean
Hawea, Lake *129 B6 lake* South Island, New Zealand
Hawera *128 D4* Taranaki, North Island, New Zealand
Hawick *66 C4* SE Scotland, United Kingdom
Hawke Bay *128 E4 bay* North Island, New Zealand
Hawkeye State *see* Iowa
Hawlēr *see* Arbīl
Hawthorne *25 C6* Nevada, W USA
Hay *127 C6* New South Wales, SE Australia
HaYarden *see* Jordan
Hayastani Hanrapetut'yun *see* Armenia
Hayes *16 B2 river* Manitoba, C Canada
Hay River *15 E4* Northwest Territories, W Canada
Hays *23 E5* Kansas, C USA
Haysyn *86 D3 Rus.* Gaysin. Vinnyts'ka Oblast', C Ukraine
Hazar *100 B2 prev. Rus.* Cheleken. Balkan Welaýaty, W Turkmenistan
Heard and McDonald Islands *119 B7 Australian external territory* S Indian Ocean
Hearst *16 C4* Ontario, S Canada
Heart of Dixie *see* Alabama
Heathrow *67 A8* (London) SE England, United Kingdom
Hebei *106 C4 var.* Hebei Sheng, Hopeh, Hopei, Ji; *prev.* Chihli. *province* E China
Hebei Sheng *see* Hebei
Hebron *97 A6 var.* Al Khalīl, El Khalil, *Heb.* Hevron; *anc.* Kiriath-Arba. S West Bank
Heemskerk *64 C3* Noord-Holland, W Netherlands
Heerde *64 D3* Gelderland, E Netherlands
Heerenveen *64 D2 Fris.* It Hearrenfean. Friesland, N Netherlands
Heerhugowaard *64 C2* Noord-Holland, NW Netherlands
Heerlen *65 D6* Limburg, SE Netherlands
Heerwegen *see* Polkowice
Hefa *97 A5 var.* Haifa, *hist.* Caiffa, Caiphas; *anc.* Sycaminum. Haifa, N Israel
Hefa, Mifraz *see* Mifrats Hefa
Hefei *106 D5 var.* Hofei, *hist.* Luchow. *province capital* Anhui, E China
Hegang *107 E2* Heilongjiang, NE China
Hei *see* Heilongjiang
Heide *72 B2* Schleswig-Holstein, N Germany
Heidelberg *73 B5* Baden-Württemberg, SW Germany
Heidenheim *see* Heidenheim an der Brenz
Heidenheim an der Brenz *73 B6 var.* Heidenheim. Baden-Württemberg, S Germany
Hei-ho *see* Nagqu
Heilbronn *73 B6* Baden-Württemberg, SW Germany
Heiligenbeil *see* Mamonovo
Heilongjiang *106 D2 var.* Hei, Heilongjiang Sheng, Hei-lung-chiang, Heilungkiang. *province* NE China
Heilong Jiang *see* Amur
Heilongjiang Sheng *see* Heilongjiang
Heiloo *64 C3* Noord-Holland, NW Netherlands
Heilsberg *see* Lidzbark Warmiński
Hei-lung-chiang/Heilungkiang *see* Heilongjiang
Heimdal *63 B5* Sør-Trøndelag, S Norway
Heinaste *see* Ainaži
Hekimhan *94 D3* Malatya, C Turkey
Helena *22 B2 state capital* Montana, NW USA
Helensville *128 D2* Auckland, North Island, New Zealand
Helgoland Bay *see* Helgoländer Bucht
Helgoländer Bucht *72 A2 var.* Helgoland Bay, Heligoland Bight. *bay* NW Germany
Heligoland Bight *see* Helgoländer Bucht
Heliopolis *see* Baalbek
Hellas *see* Greece
Hellenic Republic *see* Greece
Hellevoetsluis *64 B4* Zuid-Holland, SW Netherlands
Hellín *71 E4* Castilla-La Mancha, C Spain
Darya-ye Helmand *100 D5 var.* Rūd-e Hīrmand. *river* Afghanistan/Iran
Helmantica *see* Salamanca
Helmond *65 D5* Noord-Brabant, S Netherlands
Helsingborg *63 B7 prev.* Hälsingborg. Skåne, S Sweden
Helsingfors *see* Helsinki
Helsinki *63 D6 Swe.* Helsingfors. *country capital* (Finland) Etelä-Suomi, S Finland
Heltau *see* Cisnădie
Helvetia *see* Switzerland
Henan *106 C5 var.* Henan Sheng, Honan, Yu. *province* C China
Henderson *18 B5* Kentucky, S USA
Henderson *25 D7* Nevada, W USA
Henderson *27 H3* Texas, SW USA
Hendū Kosh *see* Hindu Kush
Hengchow *see* Hengyang
Hengduan Shan *106 A5 mountain range* SW China
Hengelo *64 E3* Overijssel, E Netherlands
Hengnan *see* Hengyang
Hengyang *106 C6 var.* Hengnan, Heng-yang; *prev.* Hengchow. Hunan, S China
Heng-yang *see* Hengyang
Heniches'k *87 F4 Rus.* Genichesk. Khersons'ka Oblast', S Ukraine
Hennebont *68 A3* Morbihan, NW France
Henrique de Carvalho *see* Saurimo
Henzada *see* Hinthada
Herakleion *see* Irákleio
Herāt *100 D4 var.* Herat; *anc.* Aria. Herāt, W Afghanistan
Heredia *31 E4* Heredia, C Costa Rica
Hereford *27 E2* Texas, SW USA
Herford *72 B4* Nordrhein-Westfalen, NW Germany
Héristal *see* Herstal
Herk-de-Stad *65 C6* Limburg, NE Belgium
Herlen Gol/Herlen He *see* Kerulen
Hermannstadt *see* Sibiu
Hermansverk *63 A5* Sogn Og Fjordane, S Norway
Ḥermhausen *see* Hajnówka
Hermiston *24 C2* Oregon, NW USA
Hermon, Mount *97 B5 Ar.* Jabal ash Shaykh. *mountain* S Syria
Hermosillo *28 B2* Sonora, NW Mexico
Hermoupolis *see* Ermoúpoli
Hernösand *see* Härnösand
Herrera del Duque *70 D3* Extremadura, W Spain
Herselt *65 C5* Antwerpen, C Belgium
Herstal *65 D6 Fr.* Héristal. Liège, E Belgium
Herzogenbusch *see* 's-Hertogenbosch
Hesse *see* Hessen
Hessen *73 B5 Eng./Fr.* Hesse. *state* C Germany
Hevron *see* Hebron
Heydebrech *see* Kędzierzyn-Koźle
Heydekrug *see* Šilutė
Heywood Islands *124 C3 island group* Western Australia
Hibbing *23 F1* Minnesota, N USA
Hibernia *see* Ireland
Hidalgo del Parral *28 C2 var.* Parral. Chihuahua, N Mexico
Hida-sanmyaku *109 C5 mountain range* Honshū, S Japan
Hierosolyma *see* Jerusalem
Hierro *48 A3 var.* Ferro. *island* Islas Canarias, Spain, NE Atlantic Ocean
High Atlas *see* Haut Atlas
High Plains *see* Great Plains
High Point *21 E1* North Carolina, SE USA
Hiiumaa *84 C2 Ger.* Dagden, *Swe.* Dagö. *island* W Estonia
Hikurangi *128 D2* Northland, North Island, New Zealand
Hildesheim *72 B4* Niedersachsen, N Germany
Hilla *see* Al Ḥillah
Hillaby, Mount *33 G1 mountain* N Barbados
Hill Bank *30 C1* Orange Walk, N Belize
Hillegom *64 C3* Zuid-Holland, W Netherlands
Hilo *25 B8* Hawaii, USA, C Pacific Ocean
Hilton Head Island *21 E2* South Carolina, SE USA
Hilversum *64 C3* Noord-Holland, C Netherlands
Himalaya/Himalaya Shan *see* Himalayas
Himalayas *113 E2 var.* Himalaya, *Chin.* Himalaya Shan. *mountain range* S Asia
Himeji *109 C6 var.* Himezi. Hyōgo, Honshū, SW Japan
Himezi *see* Himeji
Ḥimş *96 B4 var.* Homs; *anc.* Emesa. Ḥimş, C Syria
Hînceşti *86 D4 var.* Hânceşti; *prev.* Kotovsk. C Moldova
Hinchinbrook Island *126 D3 island* Queensland, NE Australia
Hinds *129 C6* Canterbury, South Island, New Zealand
Hindu Kush *101 F4 Per.* Hendū Kosh. *mountain range* Afghanistan/Pakistan
Hinesville *21 E3* Georgia, SE USA
Hinnøya *62 C3 Lapp.* Iinnasuolu. *island* C Norway
Hinson Bay *20 A5 bay* W Bermuda W Atlantic Ocean
Hinthada *114 B4 var.* Henzada. Ayeyarwady, SW Myanmar (Burma)
Hios *see* Chíos
Hirfanlı Barajı *94 C3 reservoir* C Turkey
Hīrmand, Rūd-e *see* Helmand, Daryā-ye
Hirosaki *108 D3* Aomori, Honshū, C Japan
Hiroshima *109 B6 var.* Hirosima. Hiroshima, Honshū, SW Japan
Hirschberg/Hirschberg im Riesengebirge/ Hirschberg in Schlesien *see* Jelenia Góra
Hirson *68 D3* Aisne, N France
Hîrşova *see* Hârşova
Hispalis *see* Sevilla
Hispana/Hispania *see* Spain
Hispaniola *34 B1 island* Dominion Republic/Haiti
Hitachi *109 D5 var.* Hitati. Ibaraki, Honshū, S Japan
Hitati *see* Hitachi
Hitra *62 A4 prev.* Hitteren. *island* S Norway
Hitteren *see* Hitra
Hjälmaren *63 C6 Eng.* Lake Hjalmar. *lake* C Sweden
Hjalmar, Lake *see* Hjälmaren
Hjørring *63 B7* Nordjylland, N Denmark
Hkakabo Razi *114 B1 mountain* Myanmar (Burma)/China
Hlobyne *87 F2 Rus.* Globino. Poltavs'ka Oblast', NE Ukraine
Hlukhiv *87 F1 Rus.* Glukhov. Sums'ka Oblast', NE Ukraine
Hlybokaye *85 D5 Rus.* Glubokoye. Vitsyebskaya Voblasts', N Belarus
Hoa Binh *114 D3* Hoa Binh, N Vietnam
Hoang Lien Son *114 D3 mountain range* N Vietnam
Hobart *127 C8 prev.* Hobarton, Hobart Town. *state capital* Tasmania, SE Australia
Hobarton/Hobart Town *see* Hobart
Hobbs *27 E3* New Mexico, SW USA
Hobro *63 A7* Nordjylland, N Denmark
Hô Chi Minh *115 E6 var.* Ho Chi Minh City; *prev.* Saigon. S Vietnam
Ho Chi Minh City *see* Hô Chi Minh
Hodeida *see* Al Ḥudaydah
Hódmezővásárhely *77 D7* Csongrád, SE Hungary
Hodna, Chott El *80 C4 var.* Chott el-Hodna, *Ar.* Shatt al-Hodna. *salt lake* N Algeria
Hodna, Chott el-/Hodna, Shatt al- *see* Hodna, Chott El
Hodonín *77 C5 Ger.* Göding. Jihomoravský Kraj, SE Czech Republic
Hoei *see* Huy
Hoey *see* Huy
Hof *73 C5* Bayern, SE Germany
Hofei *see* Hefei
Hōfu *109 B7* Yamaguchi, Honshū, SW Japan
Hofuf *see* Al Hufūf
Hogoley Islands *see* Chuuk Islands
Hohensalza *see* Inowrocław
Hohenstadt *see* Zábřeh
Hohes Venn *see* Hautes Fagnes
Hohe Tauern *73 C7 mountain range* W Austria
Hohhot *105 F3 var.* Huhehot, Huhohaote, *Mong.* Kukukhoto; *prev.* Kweisui, Kwesui. Nei Mongol Zizhiqu, N China
Hôi An *115 E5 prev.* Faifo. Quang Nam-Đa Năng, C Vietnam
Hoï-Hao/Hoihow *see* Haikou
Hokianga Harbour *128 C2 inlet* SE Tasman Sea
Hokitika *129 B5* West Coast, South Island, New Zealand
Hokkaido *108 C2 prev.* Ezo, Yeso, Yezo. *island* NE Japan
Hola Prystan' *87 E4 Rus.* Golaya Pristan. Khersons'ka Oblast', S Ukraine
Holbrook *26 B2* Arizona, SW USA
Holetown *33 G1 prev.* Jamestown. W Barbados
Holguín *32 C2* Holguín, SE Cuba
Hollabrunn *73 E6* Niederösterreich, NE Austria
Holland *see* Netherlands
Hollandia *see* Jayapura
Holly Springs *20 C1* Mississippi, S USA
Holman *15 E3* Victoria Island, Northwest Territories, N Canada
Holmsund *62 D4* Västerbotten, N Sweden
Holon *97 A6 var.* Kholon; *prev.* Ḥolon. Tel Aviv, C Israel
Ḥolon *see* Holon
Holovanivs'k *87 E3 Rus.* Golovanevsk. Kirovohrads'ka Oblast', C Ukraine
Holstebro *63 A7* Ringkøbing, W Denmark
Holsteinborg/Holsteinsborg/Holstenborg/ Holstensborg *see* Sisimiut
Holyhead *67 C5 Wel.* Caer Gybi. NW Wales, United Kingdom
Hombori *53 E3* Mopti, S Mali
Homs *see* Al Khums, Libya
Homs *see* Ḥimş
Homyel' *85 D7 Rus.* Gomel'. Homyel'skaya Voblasts', SE Belarus
Honan *see* Luoyang, China
Honan *see* Henan, China
Hondo *27 F4* Texas, SW USA
Hondo *see* Honshū
Honduras *30 C2 off.* Republic of Honduras. *country* Central America
Honduras, Golfo de *see* Honduras, Gulf of
Honduras, Gulf of *30 C2 Sp.* Golfo de Honduras. *gulf* W Caribbean Sea
Honduras, Republic of *see* Honduras
Hønefoss *63 B6* Buskerud, S Norway
Honey Lake *25 B5 lake* California, W USA
Hon Gai *see* Ha Long
Hongay *see* Ha Long
Hông Gai *see* Ha Long
Hông Hà, Sông *see* Red River
Hong Kong *106 A1* Hong Kong, S China
Hong Kong Island *106 B2 island* S China Asia
Honiara *122 C3 country capital* (Solomon Islands) Guadalcanal, C Solomon Islands
Honjō *108 D4 var.* Honzyô, Yurihonjō. Akita, Honshū, C Japan
Honolulu *25 A8 state capital* O'ahu, Hawaii, USA, C Pacific Ocean
Honshu *109 E5 var.* Hondo, Honsyû. *island* SW Japan
Honsyû *see* Honshū
Honte *see* Westerschelde
Honzyô *see* Honjō
Hoogeveen *64 E2* Drenthe, NE Netherlands
Hoogezand-Sappemeer *64 E2* Groningen, NE Netherlands
Hoorn *64 C2* Noord-Holland, NW Netherlands
Hoosier State *see* Indiana
Hopa *95 E2* Artvin, NE Turkey
Hope *14 C3* British Columbia, SW Canada
Hopedale *17 F2* Newfoundland and Labrador, NE Canada
Hopeh/Hopei *see* Hebei
Hopkinsville *18 B5* Kentucky, S USA
Horasan *95 F3* Erzurum, NE Turkey
Horizon Deep *130 D4 trench* W Pacific Ocean
Horki *85 E6 Rus.* Gorki. Mahilyowskaya Voblasts', E Belarus
Horlivka *87 G3 Rom.* Adâncata, *Rus.* Gorlovka. Donets'ka Oblast', E Ukraine
Hormoz, Tangeh-ye *see* Hormuz, Strait of
Hormuz, Strait of *98 D4 var.* Strait of Ormuz, *Per.* Tangeh-ye Hormoz. *strait* Iran/Oman
Cape Horn *43 C8 Eng.* Cape Horn. *headland* S Chile
Horn, Cape *see* Hornos, Cabo de
Hornsby *126 E1* New South Wales, SE Australia
Horodnya *87 E1 Rus.* Gorodnya. Chernihivs'ka Oblast', NE Ukraine
Horodok *86 B2 Pol.* Gródek Jagielloński, *Rus.* Gorodok, Gorodok Yagellonski. L'vivs'ka Oblast', NW Ukraine
Horodyshche *87 E2 Rus.* Gorodishche. Cherkas'ka Oblast', C Ukraine
Horoshiri-dake *108 D2 var.* Horosiri Dake. *mountain* Hokkaidō, N Japan
Horosiri Dake *see* Horoshiri-dake
Horsburgh Atoll *110 A4 var.* Goidhoo Atoll. *atoll* N Maldives

Jablah – Kapsukas

Jablah *96 A3 var.* Jeble, *Fr.* Djéblé. Al Lādhiqīyah, W Syria
Jaca *71 F1* Aragón, NE Spain
Jacaltenango *30 A2* Huehuetenango, W Guatemala
Jackson *20 B2 state capital* Mississippi, S USA
Jackson *23 H5* Missouri, C USA
Jackson *20 C1* Tennessee, S USA
Jackson Head *129 A6 headland* South Island, New Zealand
Jacksonville *21 E3* Florida, SE USA
Jacksonville *18 B4* Illinois, N USA
Jacksonville *21 F1* North Carolina, SE USA
Jacksonville *27 G3* Texas, SW USA
Jacmel *32 D3 var.* Jaquemel. S Haiti
Jacob *see* Nkayi
Jacobābād *112 B3* Sind, SE Pakistan
Jadotville *see* Likasi
Jadransko More/Jadransko Morje *see* Adriatic Sea
Jaén *38 B2* Cajamarca, N Peru
Jaén *70 D4* Andalucía, SW Spain
Jaffna *110 D3* Northern Province, N Sri Lanka
Jagannath *see* Puri
Jagdalpur *113 E5* Chhattīsgarh, C India
Jagdaqi *105 G1* Nei Mongol Zizhiqu, N China
Jagodina *78 D4 prev.* Svetozarevo. Serbia, C Serbia
Jahra *see* Al Jahrā'
Jailolo *see* Halmahera, Pulau
Jaipur *112 D3 prev.* Jeypore. *state capital* Rājasthān, N India
Jaisalmer *112 C3* Rājasthān, NW India
Jajce *78 B3* Federacija Bosna I Hercegovina, W Bosnia and Herzegovina
Jakarta *116 C5 prev.* Djakarta, *Dut.* Batavia. *country capital* (Indonesia) Jawa, C Indonesia
Jakobstad *62 D4 Fin.* Pietarsaari. Länsi-Suomi, W Finland
Jakobstadt *see* Jēkabpils
Jalālābād *101 F4 var.* Jalalabad, Jelalabad. Nangarhār, E Afghanistan
Jalal-Abad *see* Dzhalal-Abad, Dzhalal-Abadskaya Oblast', Kyrgyzstan
Jalandhar *112 D2 prev.* Jullundur. Punjab, N India
Jalapa *30 D3* Nueva Segovia, NW Nicaragua
Jalpa *28 D4* Zacatecas, C Mexico
Jālū *49 G3 var.* Jūlā. NE Libya
Jaluit Atoll *122 D2 var.* Jālwōj. *atoll* Ralik Chain, S Marshall Islands
Jālwōj *see* Jaluit Atoll
Jamaame *51 D6 It.* Giamame; *prev.* Margherita. Jubbada Hoose, S Somalia
Jamaica *32 A4 country* W West Indies
Jamaica *34 A1 island* W West Indies
Jamaica Channel *32 D3 channel* Haiti/Jamaica
Jamālpur *113 F3* Bihār, NE India
Jambi *116 B4 var.* Telanaipura; *prev.* Djambi. Sumatera, W Indonesia
Jamdena *see* Yamdena, Pulau
James Bay *16 C3 bay* Ontario/Québec, E Canada
James River *23 E2 river* North Dakota/South Dakota, N USA
James River *19 E5 river* Virginia, NE USA
Jamestown *19 E3* New York, NE USA
Jamestown *23 E2* North Dakota, N USA
Jamestown *see* Holetown
Jammu *112 D2 prev.* Jummoo. *state capital* Jammu and Kashmir, NW India
Jammu and Kashmīr *112 D1 disputed region* India/Pakistan
Jāmnagar *112 C4 prev.* Navanagar. Gujarāt, W India
Jamshedpur *113 F4* Jhārkhand, NE India
Jamuna *see* Brahmaputra
Janaúba *41 F3* Minas Gerais, SE Brazil
Janesville *18 B3* Wisconsin, N USA
Janina *see* Ioánnina
Janischken *see* Joniškis
Jankovac *see* Jánoshalma
Jan Mayen *61 F4 Norwegian dependency* N Atlantic Ocean
Jánoshalma *77 C7 SCr.* Jankovac. Bács-Kiskun, S Hungary
Janów *see* Ivanava, Belarus
Janow/Janów *see* Jonava, Lithuania
Janów Poleski *see* Ivanava
Japan *108 C4 var.* Nippon, *Jap.* Nihon. *country* E Asia
Japan, Sea of *108 A4 var.* East Sea, *Rus.* Yapanskoye More. *sea* NW Pacific Ocean
Japan Trench *103 F1 trench* NW Pacific Ocean
Japen *see* Yapen, Pulau
Japiim *40 C2 var.* Máncio Lima. Acre, W Brazil
Japurá, Rio *40 C2 var.* Río Caquetá, Yapurá. *river* Brazil/Colombia
Japurá, Rio *see* Caquetá, Río
Jaqué *31 G5* Darién, SE Panama
Jaquemel *see* Jacmel
Jarablos *see* Jarābulus
Jarābulus *96 C2 var.* Jarablos, Jerablus, *Fr.* Djérablous. Ḩalab, N Syria
Jarbah, Jazīrat *see* Jerba, Île de
Jardines de la Reina, Archipiélago de los *32 B2 island group* C Cuba
Jarīd, Shaṭṭ al *see* Jerid, Chott el
Jarocin *76 C4* Wielkopolskie, C Poland
Jarosłau *see* Jarosław
Jarosław *77 E5 Ger.* Jaroslau, *Rus.* Yaroslav. Podkarpackie, SE Poland
Jarqo'rg'on *101 E3 Rus.* Dzharkurgan. Surkhondaryo Viloyati, S Uzbekistan
Jarvis Island *123 G2 US unincorporated territory* C Pacific Ocean
Jasło *77 D5* Podkarpackie, SE Poland
Jastrzębie-Zdrój *77 C5* Śląskie, S Poland
Jataí *41 E3* Goiás, C Brazil
Jativa *see* Xàtiva
Jauf *see* Al Jawf
Jaunpiebalga *84 D3* Gulbene, NE Latvia
Jaunpur *113 E3* Uttar Pradesh, N India
Java *130 A3* South Dakota, N USA
Javalambre *71 E3 mountain* E Spain
Java Sea *116 D4 Ind.* Laut Jawa. *sea* W Indonesia
Java Trench *102 D5 var.* Sunda Trench. *trench* E Indian Ocean
Jawa, Laut *see* Java Sea
Jawhar *51 D6 var.* Jowhar, *It.* Giohar. Shabeellaha Dhexe, S Somalia
Jaworów *see* Yavoriv
Jaya, Puncak *117 G4 prev.* Puntjak Carstensz, Puntjak Sukarno. *mountain* Papua, E Indonesia
Jayapura *117 H4 var.* Djajapura, *Dut.* Hollandia; *prev.* Kotabaru, Sukarnapura. Papua, E Indonesia
Jay Dairen *see* Dalian
Jayhawker State *see* Kansas
Jaz Murian, Hamun-e *98 E4 lake* SE Iran
Jebba *53 F4* Kwara, W Nigeria
Jebel, Bahr el *see* White Nile
Jeble *see* Jablah
Jedda *see* Jiddah
Jędrzejów *76 D4 Ger.* Endersdorf. Świętokrzyskie, C Poland
Jefferson City *23 G5 state capital* Missouri, C USA
Jega *53 F4* Kebbi, NW Nigeria
Jehol *see* Chengde
Jeju-do *107 E4 Jap.* Saishū; *prev.* Cheju-do, Quelpart. *island* S South Korea
Jeju Strait *107 E4 var.* Jeju-haehyŏp; *prev.* Cheju-Strait. *strait* S South Korea
Jeju-haehyŏp *see* Jeju Strait
Jēkabpils *84 D4 Ger.* Jakobstadt. Jēkabpils, S Latvia
Jelalabad *see* Jalālābād
Jelenia Góra *76 B4 Ger.* Hirschberg, Hirschberg im Riesengebirge, Hirschberg im Riesengebirge, Hirschberg in Schlesien. Dolnośląskie, SW Poland
Jelgava *84 C3 Ger.* Mitau. Jelgava, C Latvia
Jemappes *65 B6* Hainaut, S Belgium
Jember *116 D5 prev.* Djember. Jawa, C Indonesia
Jena *72 C4* Thüringen, C Germany
Jengish Chokusu *see* Tomür Feng
Jenin *97 A6* N West Bank
Jerablus *see* Jarābulus
Jerada *48 D2* NE Morocco
Jérémie *32 D3* SW Haiti
Jerez *see* Jeréz de la Frontera, Spain
Jerez de la Frontera *70 C5 var.* Jerez; *prev.* Xeres. Andalucía, SW Spain
Jerez de los Caballeros *70 C4* Extremadura, W Spain
Jericho *see* Arīḩā
Jerid, Chott el *49 E2 var.* Shaṭṭ al Jarīd. *salt lake* SW Tunisia
Jersey *67 D8 British Crown Dependency* Channel Islands, NW Europe
Jerusalem *81 H4 Ar.* Al Quds, Al Quds ash Sharīf, *Heb.* Yerushalayim; *anc.* Hierosolyma. *country capital* (Israel) Jerusalem, NE Israel
Jesenice *73 D7 Ger.* Assling. NW Slovenia
Jesselton *see* Kota Kinabalu
Jessore *113 G4* Khulna, W Bangladesh
Jesús María *42 C3* Córdoba, C Argentina
Jeypore *see* Jaipur, Rājasthān, India
Jhānsi *112 D3* Uttar Pradesh, N India
Jhārkhand *113 F4 cultural region* NE India
Jhelum *112 C2* Punjab, NE Pakistan
Ji *see* Hebei, China
Ji *see* Jilin, China
Jiangmen *106 C6* Guangdong, S China
Jiangsu *106 D4 var.* Chiang-su, Jiangsu Sheng, Kiangsu, Su. *province* E China
Jiangsu *see* Nanjing
Jiangsu Sheng *see* Jiangsu
Jiangxi *106 C6 var.* Chiang-hsi, Gan, Jiangxi Sheng, Kiangsi. *province* S China
Jiangxi Sheng *see* Jiangxi
Jiaxing *106 D5* Zhejiang, SE China
Jiayi *106 D6 prev.* Chiai; *var.* Chia-i, Chiayi, Kiayi, Jiayi, *Jap.* Kagi. C Taiwan
Jibuti *see* Djibouti
Jiddah *99 A5 Eng.* Jedda. Makkah, W Saudi Arabia
Jih-k'a-tse *see* Xigazê
Jihlava *77 B5 Ger.* Iglau, *Pol.* Igława. Vysocina, S Czech Republic
Jilib *51 D6 It.* Gelib. Jubbada Dhexe, S Somalia
Jilin *106 E3 var.* Chi-lin, Girin, Kirin; *prev.* Yungki, Yunki. Jilin, NE China
Jilin *106 E3 var.* Chi-lin, Girin, Ji, Jilin Sheng, Kirin. *province* NE China
Jilin Sheng *see* Jilin
Jilong *106 D6 prev.* Chilung; *var.* Keelung, *Jap.* Kirun, Kirun'; *prev. Sp.* Santissima Trinidad. N Taiwan
Jima *51 C5 var.* Jimma, *It.* Gimma. Oromīya, C Ethiopia
Jimbolia *86 A4 Ger.* Hatzfeld, *Hung.* Zsombolya. Timiș, W Romania
Jiménez *28 D2* Chihuahua, N Mexico
Jimma *see* Jīma
Jimsar *104 C3* Xinjiang Uygur Zizhiqu, NW China
Jin *see* Shanxi
Jin *see* Tianjin Shi
Jinan *106 C4 var.* Chinan, Chi-nan, Tsinan. *province capital* Shandong, E China
Jingdezhen *106 C5* Jiangxi, S China
Jinghong *106 A6 var.* Yunjinghong. Yunnan, SW China
Jinhua *106 D5* Zhejiang, SE China
Jining *105 F3* Shandong, E China
Jinja *51 C6* S Uganda
Jinotega *30 D3* Jinotega, NW Nicaragua
Jinotepe *30 D3* Carazo, SW Nicaragua
Jinsen *see* Incheon
Jinzhong *106 C4 var.* Yuci. Shanxi, C China
Jinzhou *106 D3 var.* Chin-chou, Chinchow; *prev.* Chinhsien. Liaoning, NE China
Jirgalanta *see* Hovd
Jisr ash Shadadi *see* Ash Shadādah
Jiu *86 B5 Ger.* Schil, Schyl, *Hung.* Zsil, Zsily. *river* S Romania
Jiujiang *106 C5* Jiangxi, S China
Jixi *107 E2* Heilongjiang, NE China
Jīzān *99 B6 var.* Qīzān. Jīzān, SW Saudi Arabia
Jizzax *101 E2 Rus.* Dzhizak. Jizzax Viloyati, C Uzbekistan
João Belo *see* Xai-Xai
João Pessoa *41 G2 prev.* Paraíba. *state capital* Paraíba, E Brazil
Joazeiro *see* Juazeiro
Job'urg *see* Johannesburg
Jo-ch'iang *see* Ruoqiang
Jodhpur *112 C3* Rājasthān, NW India
Joensuu *63 E5* Itä-Suomi, SE Finland
Jōetsu *109 C5 var.* Zyôetu. Niigata, Honshū, C Japan
Jogjakarta *see* Yogyakarta
Johannesburg *56 D4 var.* Egoli, Erautini, Gauteng, *abbrev.* Job'urg. Gauteng, NE South Africa
Johannisburg *see* Pisz
John Day River *24 C3 river* Oregon, NW USA
John o'Groats *66 C2* N Scotland, United Kingdom
Johnston Atoll *121 E1 US unincorporated territory* C Pacific Ocean
Johor Baharu *see* Johor Bahru
Johor Bahru *116 B3 var.* Johor Baharu, Johore Bahru. Johor, Peninsular Malaysia
Johore Bahru *see* Johor Bahru
Johore Strait *116 A1 strait* Johor, Peninsular Malaysia, Malaysia/Singapore Asia Andaman Sea/ South China Sea
Joinvile *see* Joinville
Joinville *41 E4 var.* Joinvile. Santa Catarina, S Brazil
Jokkmokk *62 C3 Lapp.* Dálvvadis. Norrbotten, N Sweden
Jokyakarta *see* Yogyakarta
Joliet *18 B3* Illinois, N USA
Jonava *84 B4 Ger.* Janow, *Pol.* Janów. Kaunas, C Lithuania
Jonesboro *20 B1* Arkansas, C USA
Joniškis *84 C3 Ger.* Janischken. Šiaulai, N Lithuania
Jönköping *63 B7* Jönköping, S Sweden
Jonquière *17 E4* Québec, SE Canada
Joplin *23 F5* Missouri, C USA
Jordan *97 B6 off.* Hashemite Kingdom of Jordan, *Ar.* Al Mamlaka al Urdunīya al Hashemīyah, Al Urdunn; *prev.* Transjordan. *country* SW Asia
Jordan *97 B5 Ar.* Urdunn, *Heb.* HaYarden. *river* SW Asia
Jorhāt *113 H3* Assam, NE India
Jos *53 G4* Plateau, C Nigeria
Joseph Bonaparte Gulf *124 D2 gulf* N Australia
Jos Plateau *53 G4 plateau* C Nigeria
Jotunheimen *63 A5 mountain range* S Norway
Joûnié *96 A4 var.* Junīyah. W Lebanon
Joure *64 D2 Fris.* De Jouwer. Friesland, N Netherlands
Joutseno *63 E5* Etelä-Suomi, SE Finland
Jowhar *see* Jawhar
J.Storm Thurmond Reservoir *see* Clark Hill Lake
Juan Aldama *28 D3* Zacatecas, C Mexico
Juan de Fuca, Strait of *24 A1 strait* Canada/USA
Juan Fernández, Islas *35 A6 Eng.* Juan Fernandez Islands. *island group* W Chile
Juan Fernandez Islands *see* Juan Fernández, Islas
Juazeiro *41 G2 prev.* Joazeiro. Bahia, E Brazil
Juazeiro do Norte *41 G2* Ceará, E Brazil
Juba *51 B5 var.* Jūbā. *country capital* (South Sudan) Bahr el Gabel, S South Sudan
Juba *51 D6 Amh.* Genalē Wenz, *It.* Guiba, *Som.* Ganaane, Webi Jubba. *river* Ethiopia/Somalia
Jubba, Webi *see* Juba
Jubbulpore *see* Jabalpur
Júcar *71 E3 var.* Jucar. *river* C Spain
Juchitán *29 F5 var.* Juchitán de Zaragosa. Oaxaca, SE Mexico
Juchitán de Zaragosa *see* Juchitán
Judayyidat Hāmir *98 B3* Al Anbār, S Iraq
Judenburg *73 D7* Steiermark, C Austria
Jugoslavija *see* Serbia
Juigalpa *30 D3* Chontales, S Nicaragua
Juiz de Fora *41 F4* Minas Gerais, SE Brazil
Jujuy *see* San Salvador de Jujuy
Jūlā *see* Jālū, Libya
Julia Beterrae *see* Béziers
Juliaca *39 E4* Puno, SE Peru
Juliana Top *37 G3 mountain* C Suriname
Julianehåb *see* Qaqortoq
Julio Briga *see* Bragança
Juliobriga *see* Logroño
Juliomagus *see* Angers
Jullundur *see* Jalandhar
Jumilla *71 E4* Murcia, SE Spain
Jummoo *see* Jammu
Jumna *see* Yamuna
Jumporn *see* Chumphon
Junction City *23 F4* Kansas, C USA
Juneau *14 D4 state capital* Alaska, USA
Junín *42 C4* Buenos Aires, E Argentina
Junīyah *see* Joûnié
Junkseylon *see* Phuket
Jur *51 B5 river* C Sudan
Jura *68 D4 cultural region* E France
Jura *73 A7 var.* Jura Mountains. *mountain range* France/Switzerland
Jura *66 B4 island* SW Scotland, United Kingdom
Jura Mountains *see* Jura
Jurbarkas *84 B4 Ger.* Georgenburg, Jurburg. Tauragė, W Lithuania
Jurburg *see* Jurbarkas
Jūrmala *84 C3* Rīga, C Latvia
Juruá, Rio *40 C2 var.* Río Yuruá. *river* Brazil/Peru
Juruena, Rio *40 D3 river* W Brazil
Jutiapa *30 B2* Jutiapa, S Guatemala
Juticalpa *30 D2* Olancho, C Honduras
Jutland *63 A7 Den.* Jylland. *peninsula* W Denmark
Juvavum *see* Salzburg
Juventud, Isla de la *32 A2 var.* Isla de Pinos, *Eng.* Isle of Youth; *prev.* The Isle of the Pines. *island* W Cuba
Južna Morava *79 E5 Ger.* Südliche Morava. *river* SE Serbia
Jwaneng *56 C4* Southern, S Botswana
Jylland *see* Jutland
Jyrgalan *see* Dzhergalan
Jyväskylä *63 D5* Länsi-Suomi, C Finland

K

K2 *104 A4 Chin.* Qogir Feng, *Eng.* Mount Godwin Austen. *mountain* China/Pakistan
Kaafu Atoll *see* Male' Atoll
Kaaimanston *37 G3* Sipaliwini, N Suriname
Kaakhka *see* Kaka
Kaala *see* Caála
Kaamanen *62 D2 Lapp.* Gámas. Lappi, N Finland
Kaapstad *see* Cape Town
Kaaresuvanto *62 C3 Lapp.* Gárassavon. Lappi, N Finland
Kabale *51 B6* SW Uganda
Kabinda *55 D7* Kasai-Oriental, SE Dem. Rep. Congo
Kabinda *see* Cabinda
Kābol *see* Kābul
Kabompo *56 C2 river* W Zambia
Kābul *101 E4 prev.* Kābol. *country capital* (Afghanistan) Kābul, E Afghanistan
Kabul *101 E4 var.* Daryā-ye Kābul. *river* Afghanistan/Pakistan
Kābul, Daryā-ye *see* Kabul
Kabwe *56 D2* Central, C Zambia
Kachchh, Gulf of *112 B4 var.* Gulf of Cutch, Gulf of Kutch. *gulf* W India
Kachchh, Rann of *112 B4 var.* Rann of Kachh, Rann of Kutch. *salt marsh* India/Pakistan
Kachh, Rann of *see* Kachchh, Rann of
Kadan Kyun *115 B5 prev.* King Island. *island* Myeik Archipelago, S Myanmar (Burma)
Kadavu *123 E4 prev.* Kandavu. *island* S Fiji
Kadoma *56 D3 prev.* Gatooma. Mashonaland West, C Zimbabwe
Kadugli *50 B4* Southern Kordofan, S Sudan
Kaduna *53 G4* Kaduna, C Nigeria
Kadzhi-Say *101 G2 Kir.* Kajisay. Issyk-Kul'skaya Oblast', NE Kyrgyzstan
Kaédi *52 C3* Gorgol, S Mauritania
Kaffa *see* Feodosiya
Kafue *56 D2* Lusaka, SE Zambia
Kafue *56 C2 river* C Zambia
Kaga Bandoro *54 C4 prev.* Fort-Crampel. Nana-Grébizi, C Central African Republic
Kagan *see* Kogon
Kāgheṭ *52 D1 var.* Karet. *physical region* N Mauritania
Kagi *see* Jiayi
Kagoshima *109 B8 var.* Kagosima. Kagoshima, Kyūshū, SW Japan
Kagoshima-wan *109 A8 bay* SW Japan
Kagosima *see* Kagoshima
Kagul *see* Cahul
Darya-ye Kahmard *101 E4 prev.* Darya-i-surkhab. *river* NE Afghanistan
Kahramanmaraş *94 D4 var.* Kahraman Maraş, Maraş, Marash. Kahramanmaraş, S Turkey
Kaiapoi *129 C6* Canterbury, South Island, New Zealand
Kaifeng *106 C4* Henan, C China
Kai, Kepulauan *117 F4 prev.* Kei Islands. *island group* Maluku, SE Indonesia
Kaikohe *128 C2* Northland, North Island, New Zealand
Kaikoura *129 C5* Canterbury, South Island, New Zealand
Kaikoura Peninsula *129 C5 peninsula* South Island, New Zealand
Kainji Lake *see* Kainji Reservoir
Kainji Reservoir *53 F4 var.* Kainji Lake. *reservoir* W Nigeria
Kaipara Harbour *128 C2 harbour* North Island, New Zealand
Kairouan *49 E2 var.* Al Qayrawān. E Tunisia
Kaisaria *see* Kayseri
Kaiserslautern *73 A5* Rheinland-Pfalz, SW Germany
Kaišiadorys *85 B5* Kaunas, S Lithuania
Kaitaia *128 C2* Northland, North Island, New Zealand
Kajaani *62 E4 Swe.* Kajana. Oulu, C Finland
Kajan *see* Kayan, Sungai
Kajana *see* Kajaani
Kajisay *see* Kadzhi-Say
Kaka *100 C2 Rus.* Kaakhka. Ahal Welaýaty, S Turkmenistan
Kake *14 D4* Kupreanof Island, Alaska, USA
Kakhovka *87 F4* Khersons'ka Oblast', S Ukraine
Kakhovs'ke Vodoskhovyshche *87 F4 Rus.* Kakhovskoye Vodokhranilishche. *reservoir* SE Ukraine
Kakhovskoye Vodokhranilishche *see* Kakhovs'ke Vodoskhovyshche
Kākināda *110 D1 prev.* Cocanada. Andhra Pradesh, E India
Kakshaal-Too, Khrebet *see* Kokshaal-Tau
Kaktovik *14 D2* Alaska, USA
Kalaallit Nunaat *see* Greenland
Kalahari Desert *56 B4 desert* Southern Africa
Kalaikhum *see* Qal'aikhum
Kalámai *see* Kalámata
Kalamariá *82 B4* Kentrikí Makedonía, N Greece
Kalamás *82 A4 var.* Thiamis; *prev.* Thýamis. *river* W Greece
Kalámata *83 B6 prev.* Kalámai. Pelopónnisos, S Greece
Kalamazoo *18 C3* Michigan, N USA
Kalambaka *see* Kalampáka
Kálamos *83 C5* Attikí, C Greece
Kalampáka *82 B4 var.* Kalambaka. Thessalía, C Greece
Kalanchak *87 F4* Khersons'ka Oblast', S Ukraine
Kalarash *see* Călărași
Kalasin *114 D4 var.* Muang Kalasin. Kalasin, E Thailand
Kālat *112 B2 var.* Kelat, Khelat. Baluchistān, SW Pakistan
Kalāt *see* Qalāt
Kalbarri *125 A5* Western Australia
Kalecik *94 C3* Ankara, N Turkey
Kalemie *55 E6 prev.* Albertville. Katanga, SE Dem. Rep. Congo
Kale Sultanie *see* Çanakkale
Kalgan *see* Zhangjiakou
Kalgoorlie *125 B6* Western Australia
Kalima *55 D6* Maniema, E Dem. Rep. Congo
Kalimantan *116 D4 Eng.* Indonesian Borneo. *geopolitical region* Borneo, C Indonesia
Kalinin *see* Tver'
Kaliningrad *84 A4* Kaliningradskaya Oblast', W Russian Federation
Kaliningrad *see* Kaliningradskaya Oblast'
Kaliningradskaya Oblast' *84 B4 var.* Kaliningrad. *province and enclave* W Russian Federation
Kalinkavichy *85 C7 Rus.* Kalinkovichi. Homyel'skaya Voblasts', SE Belarus
Kalinkovichi *see* Kalinkavichy
Kalisch/Kalish *see* Kalisz
Kalispell *22 B1* Montana, NW USA
Kalisz *76 C4 Ger.* Kalisch, *Rus.* Kalish; *anc.* Calisia. Wielkopolskie, C Poland
Kalix *62 D4* Norrbotten, N Sweden
Kalixälven *62 D3 river* N Sweden
Kallaste *84 E3 Ger.* Krasnogor. Tartumaa, SE Estonia
Kallavesi *63 E5 lake* SE Finland
Kalloní *83 D5* Lésvos, E Greece
Kalmar *63 C7 var.* Calmar. Kalmar, S Sweden
Kalmthout *65 C5* Antwerpen, N Belgium
Kalpáki *82 A4* Ípeiros, W Greece
Kalpeni Island *110 B3 island* Lakshadweep, India, N Indian Ocean
Kaltdorf *see* Pruszków
Kaluga *89 B5* Kaluzhskaya Oblast', W Russian Federation
Kalush *86 C2 Pol.* Kałusz. Ivano-Frankivs'ka Oblast', W Ukraine
Kałusz *see* Kalush
Kalutara *110 D4* Western Province, SW Sri Lanka
Kalvarija *85 B5 Pol.* Kalwaria. Marijampolė, S Lithuania
Kalwaria *see* Kalvarija
Kalyān *112 C5* Mahārāshtra, W India
Kálymnos *83 D6 var.* Kálimnos. *island* Dodekánisa, Greece, Aegean Sea
Kama *88 D4 river* NW Russian Federation
Kamarang *37 F3* W Guyana
Kambryk *see* Cambrai
Kamchatka *see* Kamchatka, Poluostrov
Kamchatka, Poluostrov *93 G3 Eng.* Kamchatka. *peninsula* E Russian Federation
Kamenets-Podol'skiy *see* Kam"yanets'-Podil's'kyy
Kamenka Dneprovskaya *see* Kam"yanka-Dniprovs'ka
Kamenskoye *see* Romaniv
Kamensk-Shakhtinskiy *89 B6* Rostovskaya Oblast', SW Russian Federation
Kamina *55 D7* Katanga, S Dem. Rep. Congo
Kamishli *see* Al Qāmishlī
Kamloops *15 E5* British Columbia, SW Canada
Kammu Seamount *130 C2 guyot* N Pacific Ocean
Kampala *51 B6 country capital* (Uganda) S Uganda
Kâmpóng Cham *115 D6 prev.* Kompong Cham. Kâmpóng Cham, C Cambodia
Kâmpóng Chhnăng *115 D6 prev.* Kompong. Kâmpóng Chhnăng, C Cambodia
Kâmpóng Saôm *see* Sihanoukville
Kâmpóng Spoe *115 D6 prev.* Kompong Speu. Kâmpóng Spœ, S Cambodia
Kâmpóng Thum *115 D5 prev.* Trâpeăng Vêng. Kâmpóng Thum, C Cambodia
Kâmpóng Trâbêk *115 D5 prev.* Phumĭ Kâmpóng Trâbêk, Phum Kompong Trabek. Kâmpóng Thum, C Cambodia
Kâmpôt *115 D6* Kâmpôt, SW Cambodia
Kampuchea *see* Cambodia
Kampuchea, Democratic *see* Cambodia
Kampuchea, People's Democratic Republic of *see* Cambodia
Kam"yanets'-Podil's'kyy *86 C3 Rus.* Kamenets-Podol'skiy. Khmel'nyts'ka Oblast', W Ukraine
Kam"yanka-Dniprovs'ka *87 F3 Rus.* Kamenka Dneprovskaya. Zaporiz'ka Oblast', SE Ukraine
Kamyshin *89 B6* Volgogradskaya Oblast', SW Russian Federation
Kanaky *see* New Caledonia
Kananga *55 D6 prev.* Luluabourg. Kasai-Occidental, S Dem. Rep. Congo
Kanara *see* Karnātaka
Kanash *89 C5* Chuvashskaya Respublika, W Russian Federation
Kanazawa *109 C5* Ishikawa, Honshū, SW Japan
Kanbe *114 B4* Yangon, SW Myanmar (Burma)
Kānchīpuram *110 C2 prev.* Conjeeveram. Tamil Nādu, SE India
Kandahār *101 E5 Per.* Qandahār. Kandahār, S Afghanistan
Kandalakša *see* Kandalaksha
Kandalaksha *88 B2 var.* Kandalakša, *Fin.* Kantalahti. Murmanskaya Oblast', NW Russian Federation
Kandangan *116 D4* Borneo, C Indonesia
Kandau *see* Kandava
Kandava *84 C3 Ger.* Kandau. Tukums, W Latvia
Kandavu *see* Kadavu
Kandi *53 F4* N Benin
Kandy *110 D3* Central Province, C Sri Lanka
Kane Fracture Zone *44 B4 fracture zone* NW Atlantic Ocean
Kāne'ohe *25 A8 var.* Kaneohe. O'ahu, Hawaii, USA, C Pacific Ocean
Kanestron, Akrotírio *see* Palioúri, Akrotírio
Kanëv *see* Kaniv
Kanevskoye Vodokhranilishche *see* Kanivs'ke Vodoskhovyshche
Kangān *see* Bandar-e Kangān
Kangaroo Island *127 A7 island* South Australia
Kangertittivaq *61 E4 Dan.* Scoresby Sund. *fjord* E Greenland
Kangikajik *61 E4 var.* Kap Brewster. *headland* E Greenland
Kaniv *87 E2 Rus.* Kanëv. Cherkas'ka Oblast', C Ukraine
Kanivs'ke Vodoskhovyshche *87 E2 Rus.* Kanevskoye Vodokhranilishche. *reservoir* C Ukraine
Kanjiža *78 D2 Ger.* Altkanischa, *Hung.* Magyarkanizsa, Ókanizsa; *prev.* Stara Kanjiža. Vojvodina, N Serbia
Kankaanpää *63 D5* Länsi-Suomi, SW Finland
Kankakee *18 B3* Illinois, N USA
Kankan *52 D4* E Guinea
Kannur *110 B2 var.* Cannanore. Kerala, SW India
Kano *53 G4* Kano, N Nigeria
Kānpur *113 E3 Eng.* Cawnpore. Uttar Pradesh, N India
Kansas *23 F5 off.* State of Kansas, *also known as* Jayhawker State, Sunflower State. *state* C USA
Kansas City *23 F4* Kansas, C USA
Kansas City *23 F4* Missouri, C USA
Kansas River *23 F5 river* Kansas, C USA
Kansk *93 E4* Krasnoyarskiy Kray, S Russian Federation
Kansu *see* Gansu
Kantalahti *see* Kandalaksha
Kántanos *83 C7* Kríti, Greece, E Mediterranean Sea
Kantemirovka *89 B6* Voronezhskaya Oblast', W Russian Federation
Kantipur *see* Kathmandu
Kanton *123 F3 var.* Abariringa, Canton Island; *prev.* Mary Island. *atoll* Phoenix Islands, C Kiribati
Kanye *56 C4* Southern, SE Botswana
Kaohsiung *see* Gaoxiong
Kaolack *52 B3 var.* Kaolak. W Senegal
Kaolak *see* Kaolack
Kaolan *see* Lanzhou
Kaoma *56 C2* Western, W Zambia
Kapelle *65 B5* Zeeland, SW Netherlands
Kapellen *65 C5* Antwerpen, N Belgium
Kapka, Massif du *54 C2 mountain range* E Chad
Kaplangky, Plato *see* Gaplaňgyr Platosy
Kapoeas *see* Kapuas, Sungai
Kapoeta *51 C5* E Equatoria, SE South Sudan
Kaposvár *77 C7* Somogy, SW Hungary
Kappeln *72 B2* Schleswig-Holstein, N Germany
Kaproncza *see* Koprivnica
Kapstad *see* Cape Town
Kapsukas *see* Marijampolė

Kirovo-Chepetsk – Kumul

Kirovo-Chepetsk 89 D5 Kirovskaya Oblast', NW Russian Federation
Kirovohrad 87 E3 Rus. Kirovograd; prev. Kirovo, Yelizavetgrad, Zinov'yevsk. Kirovohrads'ka Oblast', C Ukraine
Kirovo/Kirovograd see Kirovohrad
Kirthar Range 112 B3 mountain range S Pakistan
Kiruna 62 C3 Lapp. Giron. Norrbotten, N Sweden
Kirun/Kirun' see Jilong
Kisalföld see Little Alföld
Kisangani 55 D5 prev. Stanleyville. Orientale, NE Dem. Rep. Congo
Kishinev see Chişinău
Kislovodsk 89 B7 Stavropol'skiy Kray, SW Russian Federation
Kismaayo 51 D6 var. Chisimayu, Kismayu, It. Chisimaio. Jubbada Hoose, S Somalia
Kismayu see Kismaayo
Kíssamos 83 C7 prev. Kastélli. Kríti, Greece, E Mediterranean Sea
Kissidougou 52 C4 Guinée-Forestière, S Guinea
Kissimmee, Lake 21 E4 lake Florida, SE USA
Kistna see Krishna
Kisumu 51 C6 prev. Port Florence. Nyanza, W Kenya
Kisvárda 77 E6 Ger. Kleinwardein. Szabolcs-Szatmár-Bereg, E Hungary
Kita 52 D3 Kayes, W Mali
Kitab see Kitob
Kitakyūshū 109 A7 var. Kitakyûsyû. Fukuoka, Kyūshū, SW Japan
Kitakyûsyû see Kitakyūshū
Kitami 108 D2 Hokkaidō, NE Japan
Kitchener 16 C5 Ontario, S Canada
Kíthnos see Kýthnos
Kitimat 14 D4 British Columbia, SW Canada
Kitinen 62 D3 river N Finland
Kitob 101 E3 Rus. Kitab. Qashqadaryo Viloyati, S Uzbekistan
Kitwe 56 D2 var. Kitwe-Nkana. Copperbelt, C Zambia
Kitwe-Nkana see Kitwe
Kitzbüheler Alpen 73 C7 mountain range W Austria
Kivalina 14 C2 Alaska, USA
Kivalo 62 D3 ridge C Finland
Kivertsi 86 C1 Pol. Kiwerce, Rus. Kivertsy. Volyns'ka Oblast', NW Ukraine
Kivertsy see Kivertsi
Kivu, Lac see Kivu, Lake
Kivu, Lake 55 E6 Fr. Lac Kivu. lake Rwanda/Dem. Rep. Congo
Kiwerce see Kivertsi
Kiyev see Kyyiv
Kiyevskoye Vodokhranilishche see Kyyivs'ke Vodoskhovyshche
Kızıl Irmak 94 C3 river C Turkey
Kizil Kum see Kyzyl Kum
Kizyl-Arvat see Serdar
Kjølen see Kölen
Kladno 77 A5 Středočeský, NW Czech Republic
Klagenfurt 73 D7 Slvn. Celovec. Kärnten, S Austria
Klaipėda 84 B3 Ger. Memel. Klaipeda, NW Lithuania
Klamath Falls 24 B4 Oregon, NW USA
Klamath Mountains 24 A4 mountain range California/Oregon, W USA
Klang 116 B3 var. Kelang; prev. Port Swettenham. Selangor, Peninsular Malaysia
Klarälven 63 B6 river Norway/Sweden
Klatovy 77 A5 Ger. Klattau. Plzeňský Kraj, W Czech Republic
Klattau see Klatovy
Klausenburg see Cluj-Napoca
Klazienaveen 64 E2 Drenthe, NE Netherlands
Kleines Ungarisches Tiefland see Little Alföld
Klein Karas 56 B4 Karas, S Namibia
Kleinwardein see Kisvárda
Kleisoúra 83 A5 Ípeiros, W Greece
Klerksdorp 56 D4 North-West, N South Africa
Klimavichy 85 E7 Rus. Klimovichi. Mahilyowskaya Voblasts', E Belarus
Klimovichi see Klimavichy
Klintsy 89 A5 Bryanskaya Oblast', W Russian Federation
Klisura 82 C2 Plovdiv, C Bulgaria
Ključ 78 B3 Federacija Bosna I Hercegovina, NW Bosnia and Herzegovina
Kłobuck 76 C4 Śląskie, S Poland
Klosters 73 B7 Graubünden, SE Switzerland
Kluang see Keluang
Kluczbork 76 C4 Ger. Kreuzburg, Kreuzburg in Oberschlesien. Opolskie, S Poland
Klyuchevskaya Sopka, Vulkan 93 H3 volcano E Russian Federation
Knin 78 B4 Šibenik-Knin, S Croatia
Knjaževac 78 E4 Serbia, E Serbia
Knokke-Heist 65 A5 West-Vlaanderen, NW Belgium
Knoxville 20 D1 Tennessee, S USA
Knud Rasmussen Land 60 D1 physical region N Greenland
Kobdo see Hovd
Kōbe 109 C6 Hyōgo, Honshū, SW Japan
København 63 B7 Eng. Copenhagen; anc. Hafnia. country capital (Denmark) Sjælland, København, E Denmark
Kobenni 52 D3 Hodh el Gharbi, S Mauritania
Koblenz 73 A5 prev. Coblenz, Fr. Coblence; anc. Confluentes. Rheinland-Pfalz, W Germany
Kobrin see Kobryn
Kobryn 85 A6 Rus. Kobrin. Brestskaya Voblasts', SW Belarus
Kobuleti 95 F2 prev. K'obulet'i. W Georgia
K'obulet'i see Kobuleti
Kočani 79 E6 NE FYR Macedonia
Kočevje 73 D8 Ger. Gottschee. S Slovenia
Koch Bihār 113 G3 West Bengal, NE India
Kochchi see Kochi
Kochi 110 C3 var. Cochin, Kochchi. Kerela, SW India
Kōchi 109 B7 var. Kôti. Kōchi, Shikoku, SW Japan
Kochiu see Gejiu
Kodiak 14 C3 Kodiak Island, Alaska, USA
Kodiak Island 14 C3 island Alaska, USA
Koedoes see Kudus
Koeln see Köln
Koepang see Kupang
Ko-erh-mu see Golmud
Koetai see Mahakam, Sungai
Koetaradja see Bandaaceh
Kōfu 109 D5 var. Kôhu. Yamanashi, Honshū, S Japan
Kogarah 126 E2 New South Wales, E Australia
Kogon 100 D2 Rus. Kagan. Buxoro Viloyati, C Uzbekistan
Kőhalom see Rupea
Kohīma 113 H3 state capital Nāgāland, E India
Koh I Noh see Büyükağrı Dağı
Kohtla-Järve 84 E2 Ida-Virumaa, NE Estonia
Kôhu see Kōfu
Kokand see Qo'qon
Kokchetav see Kokshetau
Kokkola 62 D4 Swe. Karleby; prev. Swe. Gamlakarleby. Länsi-Suomi, W Finland
Koko 53 F4 Kebbi, W Nigeria
Kokomo 18 C4 Indiana, N USA
Koko Nor see Qinghai, China
Koko Nor see Qinghai Hu, China
Kokrines 14 C2 Alaska, USA
Kokshaal-Tau 101 G2 Rus. Khrebet Kakshaal-Too. mountain range China/Kyrgyzstan
Kokshetau 92 C4 Kaz. Kökshetaū; prev. Kokchetav. Kokshetau, N Kazakhstan
Kökshetaū see Kokshetau
Koksijde 65 A5 West-Vlaanderen, W Belgium
Koksoak 16 D2 river Québec, E Canada
Kokstad 56 D5 KwaZulu/Natal, E South Africa
Kolaka 117 E4 Sulawesi, C Indonesia
K'o-la-ma-i see Karamay
Kola Peninsula see Kol'skiy Poluostrov
Kolari 62 D3 Lappi, NW Finland
Kolárovo 77 C6 Ger. Gutta; prev. Guta, Hung. Gúta. Nitriansky Kraj, SW Slovakia
Kolberg see Kołobrzeg
Kolda 52 C3 S Senegal
Kolding 63 A7 Vejle, C Denmark
Kölen 59 E1 Nor. Kjølen. mountain range Norway/Sweden
Kolguyev, Ostrov 88 C2 island NW Russian Federation
Kolhāpur 110 B1 Mahārāshtra, SW India
Kolhumadulu 110 A5 var. Thaa Atoll. atoll S Maldives
Kolín 77 B5 Ger. Kolin. Střední Čechy, C Czech Republic
Kolka 84 C2 Talsi, NW Latvia
Kolkasrags 84 C2 prev. Eng. Cape Domesnes. headland NW Latvia
Kolkata 113 G4 prev. Calcutta. West Bengal, N India
Kollam 110 C3 var. Quilon. Kerala, SW India
Kolmar see Colmar
Köln 72 A4 var. Koeln, Eng./Fr. Cologne, prev. Cöln; anc. Colonia Agrippina, Oppidum Ubiorum. Nordrhein-Westfalen, W Germany
Koło 76 C3 Wielkopolskie, C Poland
Kołobrzeg 76 B2 Ger. Kolberg. Zachodnio-pomorskie, NW Poland
Kolokani 52 D3 Koulikoro, W Mali
Kolomea see Kolomyya
Kolomna 89 B5 Moskovskaya Oblast', W Russian Federation
Kolomyya 86 C3 Ger. Kolomea. Ivano-Frankivs'ka Oblast', W Ukraine
Kolosjoki see Nikel'
Kolozsvár see Cluj-Napoca
Kolpa 78 A2 Ger. Kulpa, SCr. Kupa. river Croatia/Slovenia
Kolpino 88 B4 Leningradskaya Oblast', NW Russian Federation
Kólpos Mórfu see Güzelyurt Körfezi
Kol'skiy Poluostrov 88 C2 Eng. Kola Peninsula. peninsula NW Russian Federation
Kolwezi 55 D7 Katanga, S Dem. Rep. Congo
Kolyma 93 G2 river NE Russian Federation
Komatsu 109 C5 var. Komatu. Ishikawa, Honshū, SW Japan
Komatu see Komatsu
Kommunizm, Qullai see Ismoili Somoní, Qullai
Komoé 53 E4 var. Komoé Fleuve. river E Côte d'Ivoire
Komoé Fleuve see Komoé
Komotau see Chomutov
Komotiní 82 D3 var. Gümüljina, Turk. Gümülcine. Anatolikí Makedonía kai Thráki, NE Greece
Kompong see Kâmpóng Chhnăng
Kompong Cham see Kâmpóng Cham
Kompong Som see Sihanoukville
Kompong Speu see Kâmpóng Spoe
Komrat see Comrat
Komsomolets, Ostrov 93 E1 island Severnaya Zemlya, N Russian Federation
Komsomol'sk-na-Amure 93 G4 Khabarovskiy Kray, SE Russian Federation
Kondolovo 82 E3 Burgas, E Bulgaria
Kondopoga 88 B3 Respublika Kareliya, NW Russian Federation
Kondoz see Kunduz
Köneürgenç 100 C2 var. Köneürgench, Rus. Këneurgench; prev. Kunya-Urgench. Daşoguz Welaýaty, N Turkmenistan
Kong Christian IX Land 60 D4 Eng. King Christian IX Land. physical region SE Greenland
Kong Frederik IX Land 60 C3 physical region SW Greenland
Kong Frederik VIII Land 61 E2 Eng. King Frederik VIII Land. physical region NE Greenland
Kong Frederik VI Kyst 60 C4 Eng. King Frederik VI Coast. physical region SE Greenland
Kong Karls Land 61 G2 Eng. King Charles Islands. island group SE Svalbard
Kongo see Congo (river)
Kongolo 55 D6 Katanga, E Dem. Rep. Congo
Kongor 51 B5 Jonglei, E South Sudan
Kong Oscar Fjord 61 E3 fjord E Greenland
Kongsberg 63 B6 Buskerud, S Norway
Kông, Tônle 115 E5 var. Xê Kong. river Cambodia/Laos
Kong, Xê see Kông, Tônle
Königgrätz see Hradec Králové
Königshütte see Chorzów
Konin 76 C3 Ger. Kuhnau. Weilkopolskie, C Poland
Koninkrijk der Nederlanden see Netherlands
Konispol 79 C7 var. Konispoli. Vlorë, S Albania
Konispoli see Konispol
Kónitsa 82 A4 Ípeiros, W Greece
Konitz see Chojnice
Konjic 78 C4 Federacija Bosna I Hercegovina, S Bosnia and Herzegovina
Konosha 88 C4 Arkhangel'skaya Oblast', NW Russian Federation
Konotop 87 F1 Sums'ka Oblast', NE Ukraine
Konstantinovka see Kostyantynivka
Konstanz 73 B7 var. Constanz, Eng. Constance, hist. Kostnitz; anc. Constantia. Baden-Württemberg, S Germany
Konstanza see Constanţa
Konya 94 C4 var. Konieh, prev. Konia; anc. Iconium. Konya, C Turkey
Kopaonik 79 D5 mountain range S Serbia
Kopar see Koper
Koper 73 D8 It. Capodistria; prev. Kopar. SW Slovenia
Köpetdag Gershi 100 C3 mountain range Iran/Turkmenistan
Köpetdag Gershi/Kopetdag, Khrebet see Koppeh Dāgh
Koppeh Dagh 98 D2 Rus. Khrebet Kopetdag, Turkm. Köpetdag Gershi. mountain range Iran/Turkmenistan
Kopreinitz see Koprivnica
Koprivnica 78 B2 Ger. Kopreinitz, Hung. Kaproncza. Koprivnica-Križevci, N Croatia
Köprülü see Veles
Koptsevichi see Kaptsevichy
Kopyl' see Kapyl'
Korat see Nakhon Ratchasima
Korat Plateau 114 D4 plateau E Thailand
Korba 113 E4 Chhattīsgarh, C India
Korça see Korçë
Korçë 79 D6 var. Korça, Gk. Korytsa, It. Corriza; prev. Koritsa. Korçë, SE Albania
Korčula 78 B4 It. Curzola; anc. Corcyra Nigra. island S Croatia
Korea Bay 105 G3 bay China/North Korea
Korea, Democratic People's Republic of see North Korea
Korea, Republic of see South Korea
Korea Strait 109 A7 Jap. Chōsen-kaikyō, Kor. Taehan-haehyŏp. channel Japan/South Korea
Korhogo 52 D4 N Côte d'Ivoire
Korinthos 83 B6 anc. Corinthus Eng. Corinth. Pelopónnisos, S Greece
Korinthiakós Kólpos 83 B5 Eng. Gulf of Corinth; anc. Corinthiacus Sinus. gulf C Greece
Koritsa see Korçë
Kōriyama 109 D5 Fukushima, Honshū, C Japan
Korla 104 C3 Chin. K'u-erh-lo. Xinjiang Uygur Zizhiqu, NW China
Körmend 77 B7 Vas, W Hungary
Koróni 83 B6 Pelopónnisos, S Greece
Koror 122 A2 (Palau) Oreor, N Palau
Kőrös see Križevci
Korosten' 86 D1 Zhytomyrs'ka Oblast', NW Ukraine
Koro Toro 54 C2 Borkou-Ennedi-Tibesti, N Chad
Korsovka see Kārsava
Kortrijk 65 A6 Fr. Courtrai. West-Vlaanderen, W Belgium
Koryak Range 93 H2 var. Koryakskiy Khrebet, Eng. Koryak Range. mountain range NE Russian Federation
Koryak Range see Koryakskoye Nagor'ye
Koryakskiy Khrebet see Koryakskoye Nagor'ye
Koryazhma 88 C4 Arkhangel'skaya Oblast', NW Russian Federation
Korytsa see Korçë
Kos 83 E6 Kos, Dodekánisa, Greece, Aegean Sea
Kos 83 E6 It. Coo; anc. Cos. island Dodekánisa, Greece, Aegean Sea
Ko-saki 109 A7 headland Nagasaki, Tsushima, SW Japan
Kościan 76 B4 Ger. Kosten. Wielkopolskie, C Poland
Kościerzyna 76 C2 Pomorskie, NW Poland
Kosciusko, Mount see Kosciuszko, Mount
Kosciuszko, Mount 127 C7 prev. Mount Kosciusko. mountain New South Wales, SE Australia
K'o-shih see Kashi
Koshikijima-retto 109 A8 var. Kosikizima Rettô. island group SW Japan
Kōshū see Gwangju
Košice 77 D6 Ger. Kaschau, Hung. Kassa. Košický Kraj, E Slovakia
Kosikizima Rettô see Koshikijima-rettō
Köslin see Koszalin
Koson 101 E3 Rus. Kasan. Qashqadaryo Viloyati, S Uzbekistan
Kosovo 79 D5 prev. Autonomous Province of Kosovo and Metohija. country SE Europe
Kosovo and Metohija, Autonomous Province of see Kosovo
Kosovo Polje see Fushë Kosovë
Kosovska Mitrovica see Mitrovicë
Kosrae 122 C2 prev. Kusaie. island Caroline Islands, E Micronesia
Kossou, Lac de 52 D5 lake C Côte d'Ivoire
Kostanay 92 C4 var. Kustanay, Kaz. Qostanay. Kostanay, N Kazakhstan
Kosten see Kościan
Kostenets 82 C2 prev. Georgi Dimitrov. Sofiya, W Bulgaria
Kostnitz see Konstanz
Kostroma 88 B4 Kostromskaya Oblast', NW Russian Federation
Kostyantynivka 87 G3 Rus. Konstantinovka. Donets'ka Oblast', SE Ukraine
Kostyukovichi see Kastsyukovichy
Kostyukovka see Kastsyukowka
Koszalin 76 B2 Ger. Köslin. Zachodnio-pomorskie, NW Poland
Kota 112 D3 prev. Kotah. Rājasthān, N India
Kota Baharu see Kota Bharu
Kota Bahru see Kota Bharu
Kotabaru see Jayapura
Kota Bharu 116 B3 var. Kota Baharu, Kota Bahru. Kelantan, Peninsular Malaysia
Kotaboemi see Kotabumi
Kotabumi 116 B4 prev. Kotaboemi. Sumatera, W Indonesia
Kotah see Kota
Kota Kinabalu 116 D3 prev. Jesselton. Sabah, East Malaysia
Kotel'nyy, Ostrov 93 E2 island Novosibirskiye Ostrova, N Russian Federation
Kotka 63 E5 Etelä-Suomi, S Finland
Kotlas 88 C4 Arkhangel'skaya Oblast', NW Russian Federation
Kotonu see Cotonou
Kotor 79 C5 It. Cattaro. SW Montenegro
Kotovs'k 86 D3 Rus. Kotovsk. Odes'ka Oblast', SW Ukraine
Kotovsk see Hînceşti
Kottbus see Cottbus
Kotto 54 D4 river Central African Republic/Dem. Rep. Congo
Kotuy 93 E2 river N Russian Federation
Koudougou 53 E4 C Burkina
Koulamoutou 55 B6 Ogooué-Lolo, C Gabon
Koulikoro 52 D3 Koulikoro, SW Mali
Koumra 54 C4 Moyen-Chari, S Chad
Kourou 37 H3 N French Guiana
Kousseir see Al Quşayr
Kousséri 54 B3 prev. Fort-Foureau. Extrême-Nord, NE Cameroon
Koutiala 52 D4 Sikasso, S Mali
Kouvola 63 E5 Etelä-Suomi, S Finland
Kovel' 86 C1 Pol. Kowel. Volyns'ka Oblast', NW Ukraine
Kovno see Kaunas
Koweit see Kuwait
Kowel see Kovel'
Kowloon 106 A2 Hong Kong, S China
Kowno see Kaunas
Kozáni 82 B4 Dytikí Makedonía, N Greece
Kozara 78 B3 mountain range NW Bosnia and Herzegovina
Kozarska Dubica see Bosanska Dubica
Kozhikode 110 C2 var. Calicut. Kerala, SW India
Kozu-shima 109 D6 island E Japan
Kozyatyn 86 D2 Rus. Kazatin. Vinnyts'ka Oblast', C Ukraine
Kpalimé 53 E5 var. Palimé. SW Togo
Krâchéh 115 D6 prev. Kratie. Krâchéh, E Cambodia
Kragujevac 78 D4 Serbia, C Serbia
Krainburg see Kranj
Kra, Isthmus of 115 B6 isthmus Malaysia/Thailand
Krakau see Kraków
Kraków 77 D5 Eng. Cracow, Ger. Krakau; anc. Cracovia. Małopolskie, S Poland
Krâlănh 115 D5 Siĕmréab, NW Cambodia
Kralendijk 33 E5 dependent territory capital (Bonaire) Lesser Antilles, S Caribbean Sea
Kraljevo 78 D4 prev. Rankovićevo. Serbia, C Serbia
Kramators'k 87 G3 Rus. Kramatorsk. Donets'ka Oblast', SE Ukraine
Kramatorsk see Kramators'k
Kramfors 63 C5 Västernorrland, C Sweden
Kranéa see Kraniá
Kraniá 82 B4 var. Kranéa. Dytikí Makedonía, N Greece
Kranj 73 D7 Ger. Krainburg. NW Slovenia
Kranz see Zelenogradsk
Krāslava 84 D4 Krāslava, SE Latvia
Krasnaye 85 C5 Rus. Krasnoye. Minskaya Voblasts', C Belarus
Krasnoarmeysk 89 C6 Saratovskaya Oblast', W Russian Federation
Krasnodar 89 A7 prev. Ekaterinodar, Yekaterinodar. Krasnodarskiy Kray, SW Russian Federation
Krasnodon 87 H3 Luhans'ka Oblast', E Ukraine
Krasnogor see Kallaste
Krasnogvardeyskoye see Krasnohvardiys'ke
Krasnohvardiys'ke 87 F4 Rus. Krasnogvardeyskoye. Respublika Krym, S Ukraine
Krasnokamensk 93 F4 Chitinskaya Oblast', S Russian Federation
Krasnokamsk 89 D5 Permskaya Oblast', W Russian Federation
Krasnoperekops'k 87 F4 Rus. Krasnoperekopsk. Respublika Krym, S Ukraine
Krasnoperekopsk see Krasnoperekops'k
Krasnostav see Krasnystaw
Krasnovodsk see Türkmenbaşy
Krasnovodskiy Zaliv see Türkmenbasy Aylagy
Krasnowodsk Aylagy see Türkmenbasy Aylagy
Krasnoyarsk 92 D4 Krasnoyarskiy Kray, S Russian Federation
Krasnoye see Krasnaye
Krasnystaw 76 E4 Rus. Krasnostav. Lubelskie, SE Poland
Krasnyy Kut 89 C6 Saratovskaya Oblast', W Russian Federation
Krasnyy Luch 87 H3 prev. Krindachevka. Luhans'ka Oblast', E Ukraine
Kratie see Krâchéh
Krâvanh, Chuŏr Phnum 115 C6 Eng. Cardamom Mountains, Fr. Chaîne des Cardamomes. mountain range W Cambodia
Krefeld 72 A4 Nordrhein-Westfalen, W Germany
Kreisstadt see Krosno Odrzańskie
Kremenchug see Kremenchuk
Kremenchugskoye Vodokhranilishche/Kremenchuk Reservoir see Kremenchuts'ke Vodoskhovyshche
Kremenchuk 87 F2 Rus. Kremenchug. Poltavs'ka Oblast', NE Ukraine
Kremenchuk Reservoir 87 F2 Eng. Kremenchuk Reservoir, Rus. Kremenchugskoye Vodokhranilishche. reservoir C Ukraine
Kremenets' 86 C2 Pol. Krzemieniec, Rus. Kremenets. Ternopil's'ka Oblast', W Ukraine
Kremennaya see Kreminna
Kreminna 87 G2 Rus. Kremennaya. Luhans'ka Oblast', E Ukraine
Kresena see Kresna
Kresna 82 C3 var. Kresena. Blagoevgrad, SW Bulgaria
Kretikon Delagos see Kritikó Pélagos
Kretinga 84 B3 Ger. Krottingen. Klaipėda, NW Lithuania
Kreutz see Cristuru Secuiesc
Kreuz see Križevci, Croatia
Kreuz see Risti, Estonia
Kreuzburg/Kreuzburg in Oberschlesien see Kluczbork
Krichëv see Krychaw
Krievija see Russian Federation
Krindachevka see Krasnyy Luch
Krishna 110 C1 prev. Kistna. river C India
Krishnagiri 110 C2 Tamil Nādu, SE India
Kristiania see Oslo
Kristiansand 63 A6 var. Christiansand. Vest-Agder, S Norway
Kristianstad 63 B7 Skåne, S Sweden
Kristiansund 62 A4 var. Christiansund. Møre og Romsdal, S Norway
Kríti 83 C7 Eng. Crete. island Greece, Aegean Sea
Kritikó Pélagos 83 D7 var. Kretikon Delagos, Eng. Sea of Crete; anc. Mare Creticum. sea Greece, Aegean Sea
Krivoy Rog see Kryvyy Rih
Križevci 78 B2 Ger. Kreuz, Hung. Kőrös. Varaždin, NE Croatia
Krk 78 A3 It. Veglia; anc. Curieta. island NW Croatia
Kroatien see Croatia
Krolevets' 87 F1 Rus. Krolevets. Sums'ka Oblast', NE Ukraine
Krolevets see Krolevets'
Królewska Huta see Chorzów
Kronach 73 C5 Bayern, E Germany
Kronstadt see Braşov
Kroonstad 56 D4 Free State, C South Africa
Kropotkin 89 A7 Krasnodarskiy Kray, SW Russian Federation
Krosno 77 D5 Ger. Krossen. Podkarpackie, SE Poland
Krosno Odrzańskie 76 B3 Ger. Crossen, Kreisstadt. Lubuskie, W Poland
Krossen see Krosno
Krottingen see Kretinga
Krško 73 E8 Ger. Gurkfeld; prev. Videm-Krško. E Slovenia
Krugloye see Kruhlaye
Kruhlaye 85 D6 Rus. Krugloye. Mahilyowskaya Voblasts', E Belarus
Kruja see Krujë
Krujë 79 C6 var. Kruja, It. Croia. Durrës, C Albania
Krummau see Český Krumlov
Krung Thep, Ao 115 C5 var. Bight of Bangkok. bay S Thailand
Krung Thep Mahanakhon see Ao Krung Thep
Krupki 85 D6 Minskaya Voblasts', C Belarus
Krušné Hory see Erzgebirge
Krychaw 85 E7 Rus. Krichëv. Mahilyowskaya Voblasts', E Belarus
Kryms'ki Hory 87 F5 mountain range S Ukraine
Kryms'kyy Pivostriv 87 F5 Eng. Crimea. peninsula S Ukraine
Krynica 77 D5 Ger. Tannenhof. Małopolskie, S Poland
Kryve Ozero 87 E3 Odes'ka Oblast', SW Ukraine
Kryvyy Rih 87 F3 Rus. Krivoy Rog. Dnipropetrovs'ka Oblast', SE Ukraine
Krzemieniec see Kremenets'
Ksar al Kabir see Ksar-el-Kebir
Ksar al Soule see Er-Rachidia
Ksar-el-Kebir 48 C2 var. Alcázar, Ksar al Kabir, Ksar-el-Kébir, Ar. Al-Kasr al-Kebir, Al-Qsar al-Kbir, Sp. Alcazarquivir. NW Morocco
Ksar-el-Kébir see Ksar-el-Kebir
Kuala Dungun see Dungun
Kuala Lumpur 116 B3 country capital (Malaysia) Kuala Lumpur, Peninsular Malaysia
Kuala Terengganu 116 B3 var. Kuala Trengganu. Terengganu, Peninsular Malaysia
Kualatungkal 116 B4 Sumatera, W Indonesia
Kuang-chou see Guangzhou
Kuang-hsi see Guangxi Zhuangzu Zizhiqu
Kuang-tung see Guangdong
Kuang-yuan see Guangyuan
Kuantan 116 B3 Pahang, Peninsular Malaysia
Kuba see Quba
Kuban' 87 G5 var. Hypanis. river SW Russian Federation
Kubango see Cubango/Okavango
Kuching 116 C3 prev. Sarawak. Sarawak, East Malaysia
Kūchnay Darwāshān 100 D5 prev. Kūchnay Darweyshān. Helmand, S Afghanistan
Kūchnay Darweyshān see Kūchnay Darwāshān
Kuçova see Kuçovë
Kuçovë 79 C6 var. Kuçova; prev. Qyteti Stalin. Berat, C Albania
Kudara see Ghŭdara
Kudus 116 C5 prev. Koedoes. Jawa, C Indonesia
Kuei-lin see Guilin
Kuei-Yang/Kuei-yang see Guiyang
K'u-erh-lo see Korla
Kueyang see Guiyang
Kugaaruk 15 G3 prev. Pelly Bay. Nunavut, N Canada
Kugluktuk 31 E3 var. Qurlurtuuq; prev. Coppermine. Nunavut, NW Canada
Kuhmo 62 E4 Oulu, E Finland
Kuhnau see Konin
Kühnö see Kihnu
Kuibyshev see Kuybyshevskoye Vodokhranilishche
Kuito 56 B2 Port. Silva Porto. Bié, C Angola
Kuji 108 D3 var. Kuzi. Iwate, Honshū, C Japan
Kukës 79 D5 var. Kukësi. Kukës, NE Albania
Kukësi see Kukës
Kukong see Shaoguan
Kukukhoto see Hohhot
Kula Kangri 113 G3 var. Kulhakangri. mountain Bhutan/China
Kuldīga 84 B3 Ger. Goldingen. Kuldīga, W Latvia
Kuldja see Yining
Kulhakangri see Kula Kangri
Kullorsuaq 60 D2 var. Kuvdlorssuak. Kitaa, C Greenland
Kulm see Chełmno
Kulmsee see Chełmża
Kŭlob 101 F3 Rus. Kulyab. SW Tajikistan
Kulpa see Kolpa
Kulu 94 C3 Konya, W Turkey
Kulunda Steppe 92 C4 Kaz. Qulyndy Zhazyghy, Rus. Kulundinskaya Ravnina. grassland Kazakhstan/Russian Federation
Kulundinskaya Ravnina see Kulunda Steppe
Kulyab see Kŭlob
Kum see Qom
Kuma 89 B7 river SW Russian Federation
Kumamoto 109 A7 Kumamoto, Kyūshū, SW Japan
Kumanova see Kumanovo
Kumanovo 79 E5 Turk. Kumanova. N Macedonia
Kumasi 53 E5 prev. Coomassie. C Ghana
Kumayri see Gyumri
Kumba 55 A5 Sud-Ouest, W Cameroon
Kumertau 89 D6 Respublika Bashkortostan, W Russian Federation
Kumillā see Comilla
Kumo 53 G4 Gombe, E Nigeria
Kumon Range 114 B2 mountain range N Myanmar (Burma)
Kumul see Hami

Kunashiri – Lesnoy

Kunashiri see Kunashir, Ostrov
Kunashir, Ostrov 108 E1 var. Kunashiri. island Kuril'skiye Ostrova, SE Russian Federation
Kunda 84 E2 Lääne-Virumaa, NE Estonia
Kunduz 101 E3 prev. Kondoz. NE Afghanistan
Kunene 47 C6 var. Kunene. river Angola/Namibia
Kunene see Cunene
Kungsbacka 63 B7 Halland, S Sweden
Kungur 89 D5 Permskaya Oblast', NW Russian Federation
Kunlun Mountains see Kunlun Shan
Kunlun Shan 104 B4 Eng. Kunlun Mountains. mountain range NW China
Kunming 106 B6 var. K'un-ming; prev. Yunnan. province capital Yunnan, SW China
K'un-ming see Kunming
Kununurra 124 D3 Western Australia
Kunya-Urgench see Köneürgenç
Kuopio 63 E5 Itä-Suomi, C Finland
Kupa see Kolpa
Kupang 117 E5 prev. Koepang. Timor, C Indonesia
Kup"yans'k 87 G2 Rus. Kupyansk. Kharkivs'ka Oblast', E Ukraine
Kupyansk see Kup"yans'k
Kür see Kura
Kura 95 H3 Az. Kür, Geor. Mtkvari, Turk. Kura Nehri. river SW Asia
Kura Nehri see Kura
Kurashiki 109 B6 var. Kurasiki. Okayama, Honshū, SW Japan
Kurasiki see Kurashiki
Kurdistan 95 F4 cultural region SW Asia
Kŭrdzhali 82 D3 var. Kirdzhali. Kŭrdzhali, S Bulgaria
Kure 109 B7 Hiroshima, Honshū, SW Japan
Küre Dağları 94 C2 mountain range N Turkey
Kuressaare 84 C2 Ger. Arensburg; prev. Kingissepp. Saaremaa, W Estonia
Kureyka 90 D2 river N Russian Federation
Kurgan-Tyube see Qŭrghonteppa
Kuria Muria Islands see Ḩalāniyāt, Juzur al
Kuril'skiye Ostrova 93 H4 Eng. Kuril Islands. island group SE Russian Federation
Kuril Islands see Kuril'skiye Ostrova
Kuril-Kamchatka Depression see Kuril Trench
Kuril Trench 91 F3 var. Kuril-Kamchatka Depression. trench NW Pacific Ocean
Kuril'sk 108 E1 Jap. Shana. Kuril'skiye Ostrova, Sakhalinskaya Oblats', SE Russian Federation
Ku-ring-gai 126 E1 New South Wales, E Australia
Kurisches Haff see Courland Lagoon
Kurkund see Kilingi-Nõmme
Kurnool 110 C1 var. Karnul. Andhra Pradesh, S India
Kursk 89 A6 Kurskaya Oblast', W Russian Federation
Kurskiy Zaliv see Courland Lagoon
Kuršumlija 79 D5 Serbia, S Serbia
Kurtbunar see Tervel
Kurtitsch/Kürtös see Curtici
Kuruktag 104 C3 mountain range NW China
Kurume 109 A7 Fukuoka, Kyūshū, SW Japan
Kurupukari 37 F3 C Guyana
Kusaie see Kosrae
Kushiro 108 D2 var. Kusiro. Hokkaidō, NE Japan
Kushka see Serhetabat
Kusiro see Kushiro
Kuskokwim Mountains 14 C3 mountain range Alaska, USA
Kustanay see Kostanay
Küstence/Küstendje see Constanța
Kütahya 94 B3 prev. Kutaia. Kütahya, W Turkey
Kutai see Mahakam, Sungai
Kutaisi 95 F2 prev. K'ut'aisi 95 F2 W Georgia W Georgia
K'ut'aisi see Kutaisi
Kūt al 'Amārah see Al Kūt
Kut al Imara see Al Kūt
Kutaradja/Kutaraja see Bandaaceh
Kutch, Gulf of see Kachchh, Gulf of
Kutch, Rann of see Kachchh, Rann of
Kutina 78 B3 Sisak-Moslavina, NE Croatia
Kutno 76 C3 Łódzkie, C Poland
Kuujjuaq 17 E2 prev. Fort-Chimo. Québec, E Canada
Kuusamo 62 E3 Oulu, E Finland
Kuvango see Cubango
Kuvdlorssuak see Kullorsuaq
Kuwait 98 C4 off. State of Kuwait, var. Dawlat al Kuwait, Koweit, Kuweit. country SW Asia
Kuwait see Al Kuwayt
Kuwait City see Al Kuwayt
Kuwait, Dawlat al see Kuwait
Kuwait, State of see Kuwait
Kuwajleen see Kwajalein Atoll
Kuwayt 98 C3 Maysān, E Iraq
Kuweit see Kuwait
Kuybyshev see Samara
Kuybyshev Reservoir see Kuybyshevskoye Vodokhranilishche
Kuybyshevskoye Vodokhranilishche 89 C5 var. Kuibyshev, Eng. Kuybyshev Reservoir. reservoir W Russian Federation
Kuytun 104 B2 Xinjiang Uygur Zizhiqu, NW China
Kuzi see Kuji
Kuznetsk 89 B6 Penzenskaya Oblast', W Russian Federation
Kuźnica 76 E2 Białystok, NE Poland Europe
Kvaløya 62 C2 island N Norway
Kvarnbergsvattnet 62 B4 var. Frostviken. lake N Sweden
Kvarner 78 A3 var. Carnaro, It. Quarnero. gulf W Croatia
Kvitøya 61 G1 island NE Svalbard
Kwajalein Atoll 122 C1 var. Kuwajleen. atoll Ralik Chain, C Marshall Islands
Kwando see Cuando
Kwangchow see Guangzhou
Kwangchu see Gwangju
Kwangju see Gwangju
Kwango 55 C7 Port. Cuango. river Angola/Dem. Rep. Congo
Kwangsi/Kwangsi Chuang Autonomous Region see Guangxi Zhuangzu Zizhiqu
Kwangtung see Guangdong
Kwangyuan see Guangyuan
Kwanza see Cuanza
Kweichu see Guiyang
Kweilin see Guilin
Kweisui see Hohhot
Kweiyang see Guiyang
Kwekwe 56 D3 prev. Que Que. Midlands, C Zimbabwe
Kwesui see Hohhot
Kwidzyń 76 C2 Ger. Marienwerder. Pomorskie, N Poland
Kwigillingok 14 C3 Alaska, USA
Kwilu 55 C6 river W Dem. Rep. Congo
Kwito see Cuito
Kyabé 54 C4 Moyen-Chari, S Chad
Kyaikkami 115 B5 prev. Amherst. Mon State, S Myanmar (Burma)
Kyaiklat 114 B4 Ayeyarwady, SW Myanmar (Burma)
Kyaikto 114 B4 Mon State, S Myanmar (Burma)
Kyakhta 93 E5 Respublika Buryatiya, S Russian Federation
Kyaukse 114 B3 Mandalay, C Myanmar (Burma)
Kyjov 77 C5 Ger. Gaya. Jihomoravský Kraj, SE Czech Republic
Kykládes 83 D6 var. Kikládhes, Eng. Cyclades. island group SE Greece
Kými 83 C5 prev. Kími. Évvoia, C Greece
Kyŏngsŏng see Seoul
Kyōto 109 C6 Kyōto, Honshū, SW Japan
Kyparissía 83 B6 var. Kiparissía. Pelopónnisos, S Greece
Kypros see Cyprus
Kyrá Panagiá 83 C5 island Vóreies Sporádes, Greece, Aegean Sea
Kyrenia see Girne
Kyrgyz Republic see Kyrgyzstan
Kyrgyzstan 101 F2 off. Kyrgyz Republic, var. Kirghizia; prev. Kirgizskaya SSR, Kirghiz SSR, Republic of Kyrgyzstan. country C Asia
Kyrgyzstan, Republic of see Kyrgyzstan
Kythira 83 C7 var. Kíthira, It. Cerigo, Lat. Cythera. island S Greece
Kýthnos 83 C6 Kńythnos, Kykládes, Greece, Aegean Sea
Kythnos 83 C6 var. Kíthnos, Thermiá, It. Termia; anc. Cythnos. island Kykládes, Greece, Aegean Sea
Kythréa see Değirmenlik
Kyushu 109 B7 var. Kyûsyû. island SW Japan
Kyushu-Palau Ridge 103 F3 var. Kyusyu-Palau Ridge. undersea ridge W Pacific Ocean
Kyustendil 82 B2 anc. Pautalia. Kyustendil, W Bulgaria
Kyûsyû see Kyūshū
Kyusyu-Palau Ridge see Kyushu-Palau Ridge
Kyyiv 87 E2 Eng. Kiev, Rus. Kiyev. country capital (Ukraine) Kyyivs'ka Oblast', N Ukraine
Kyyivs'ke Vodoskhovyshche 87 E1 Eng. Kiev Reservoir, Rus. Kiyevskoye Vodokhranilishche. reservoir N Ukraine
Kyzyl 92 D4 Respublika Tyva, C Russian Federation
Kyzyl Kum 100 D2 var. Kizil Kum, Qizil Qum, Uzb. Qizilqum. desert Kazakhstan/Uzbekistan
Kyzylrabot see Qizilrabot
Kyzyl-Suu 101 G2 prev. Pokrovka. Issyk-Kul'skaya Oblast', NE Kyrgyzstan
Kzylorda 92 B5 var. Kzyl-Orda, Qizil Orda, Qyzylorda; prev. Perovsk. Kyzylorda, S Kazakhstan
Kzyl-Orda see Kzylorda

L

Laaland see Lolland
La Algaba 70 C4 Andalucía, S Spain
Laarne 65 B5 Oost-Vlaanderen, NW Belgium
La Asunción 37 E1 Nueva Esparta, NE Venezuela
Laatokka see Ladozhskoye, Ozero
Laâyoune 48 B3 var. Aaiún. country capital (Western Sahara) NW Western Sahara
La Banda Oriental see Uruguay
la Baule-Escoublac 68 A4 Loire-Atlantique, NW France
Labé 52 C4 NW Guinea
Labe see Elbe
Laborca see Laborec
Laborec 77 E5 Hung. Laborca. river E Slovakia
Labrador 17 F2 cultural region Newfoundland and Labrador, SW Canada
Labrador Basin 12 E3 var. Labrador Sea Basin. undersea basin Labrador Sea
Labrador Sea 60 A4 sea NW Atlantic Ocean
Labrador Sea Basin see Labrador Basin
Labudalin see Ergun
Labutta 115 A5 Ayeyarwady, SW Myanmar (Burma)
Laç 79 C6 var. Laci. Lezhë, C Albania
La Calera 42 B4 Valparaíso, C Chile
La Carolina 70 D4 Andalucía, S Spain
Laccadive Islands 110 A3 Eng. Laccadive Islands. island group India, N Indian Ocean
Laccadive Islands/Laccadive Minicoy and Amindivi Islands, the see Lakshadweep
La Ceiba 30 D2 Atlántida, N Honduras
Lachanás 82 B3 Kentrikí Makedonía, N Greece
La Chaux-de-Fonds 73 A7 Neuchâtel, W Switzerland
Lachlan River 127 C6 river New South Wales, SE Australia
Laci see Laç
la Ciotat 69 D6 anc. Citharista. Bouches-du-Rhône, SE France
Lacobriga see Lagos
La Concepción 31 E5 var. Concepción. Chiriquí, W Panama
La Concepción 36 C1 Zulia, NW Venezuela
La Condamine 69 C8 W Monaco
Laconia 19 G2 New Hampshire, NE USA
La Crosse 18 A2 Wisconsin, N USA
La Cruz 30 D4 Guanacaste, NW Costa Rica
Ladoga, Lake see Ladozhskoye, Ozero
Ladozhskoye, Ozero 88 B3 Eng. Lake Ladoga, Fin. Laatokka. lake NW Russian Federation
Ladysmith 18 B2 Wisconsin, N USA
Lae 122 B3 Morobe, W Papua New Guinea
La Esperanza 30 C2 Intibucá, SW Honduras
Lafayette 18 C4 Indiana, N USA
Lafayette 20 B3 Louisiana, S USA
La Fé 32 A2 Pinar del Río, W Cuba
Lafia 53 G4 Nassarawa, C Nigeria
la Flèche 68 B4 Sarthe, NW France
Lagdo, Lac de 54 B4 lake N Cameroon
Laghouat 48 D2 N Algeria
Lagos 53 F5 Lagos, SW Nigeria
Lagos 70 B5 anc. Lacobriga. Faro, S Portugal
Lagos de Moreno 29 E4 Jalisco, SW Mexico
Lagouira 48 A4 SW Western Sahara
La Grande 24 C3 Oregon, NW USA
La Guaira 44 B4 Distrito Federal, N Venezuela
Lagunas 42 B1 Tarapacá, N Chile
Lagunillas 39 G4 Santa Cruz, SE Bolivia
La Habana 32 B2 var. Havana. country capital (Cuba) Ciudad de La Habana, W Cuba
Lahat 116 B4 Sumatera, W Indonesia
La Haye see 's-Gravenhage
Laholm 63 B7 Halland, S Sweden
Lahore 112 D2 Punjab, NE Pakistan
Lahr 73 A6 Baden-Württemberg, S Germany
Lahti 63 D5 Swe. Lahtis. Etelä-Suomi, S Finland
Lahtis see Lahti
Laï 54 B4 prev. Behagle, De Behagle. Tandjilé, S Chad
Laibach see Ljubljana
Lai Châu 114 D3 Lai Châu, N Vietnam
Laila see Laylā
La Junta 22 D5 Colorado, C USA
Lake Charles 20 A3 Louisiana, S USA
Lake City 21 E3 Florida, SE USA
Lake District 67 C5 physical region NW England, United Kingdom
Lake Havasu City 26 A2 Arizona, SW USA
Lake Jackson 27 H4 Texas, SW USA
Lakeland 21 E4 Florida, SE USA
Lakeside 25 C8 California, W USA
Lake State see Michigan
Lakewood 22 D4 Colorado, C USA
Lakhnau see Lucknow
Lakonikós Kólpos 83 B7 gulf S Greece
Lakselv 62 D2 Lapp. Leavdnja. Finnmark, N Norway
la Laon see Laon
Lalibela 50 C4 Āmara, Ethiopia
La Libertad 30 B1 Petén, N Guatemala
La Ligua 42 B4 Valparaíso, C Chile
Lalín 70 C1 Galicia, NW Spain
Lalitpur 113 F3 Central, C Nepal
La Louvière 65 B6 Hainaut, S Belgium
la Maddalena 74 A4 Sardegna, Italy, C Mediterranean Sea
la Manche see English Channel
Lamar 22 D5 Colorado, C USA
La Marmora, Punta 75 A5 mountain Sardegna, Italy, C Mediterranean Sea
La Massana 69 A8 La Massana, W Andorra Europe
Lambaréné 55 A6 Moyen-Ogooué, W Gabon
Lamego 70 C2 Viseu, N Portugal
Lamesa 27 E3 Texas, SW USA
Lamezia Terme 75 D6 Calabria, SE Italy
Lamía 83 B5 Stereá Ellás, C Greece
Lamoni 23 F4 Iowa, C USA
Lampang 114 C4 var. Muang Lampang. Lampang, NW Thailand
Lámpeia 83 B6 Dytikí Ellás, S Greece
Lanbi Kyun 115 B6 prev. Sullivan Island. island Myeik Archipelago, S Myanmar (Burma)
Lancang Jiang see Mekong
Lancaster 67 D5 NW England, United Kingdom
Lancaster 25 C7 California, W USA
Lancaster 19 F4 Pennsylvania, NE USA
Lancaster Sound 15 F2 sound Nunavut, N Canada
Lan-chou/Lan-chow/Lanchow see Lanzhou
Landao see Lantau Island
Landen 65 C6 Vlaams Brabant, C Belgium
Lander 22 C3 Wyoming, C USA
Landerneau 68 A3 Finistère, NW France
Landes 69 B5 cultural region SW France
Land of Enchantment see New Mexico
The Land of Opportunity see Arkansas
Land of Steady Habits see Connecticut
Land of the Midnight Sun see Alaska
Landsberg see Gorzów Wielkopolski, Lubuskie, Poland
Landsberg an der Warthe see Gorzów Wielkopolski
Land's End 67 B8 headland SW England, United Kingdom
Landshut 73 C6 Bayern, SE Germany
Langar 101 E2 Rus. Lyangar. Navoiy Viloyati, C Uzbekistan
Langfang 106 D4 Hebei, E China
Langkawi, Pulau 115 B7 island Peninsular Malaysia
Langres 68 D4 Haute-Marne, N France
Langsa 116 A3 Sumatera, W Indonesia
Lang Shan 105 E3 mountain range N China
Lang Sơn 114 D3 var. Langson. Lang Sơn, N Vietnam
Langson see Lang Sơn
Lang Suan 115 B6 Chumphon, SW Thailand
Languedoc 69 C6 cultural region S France
Länkäran 95 H3 Rus. Lenkoran'. S Azerbaijan
Lansing 18 C3 state capital Michigan, N USA
Lanta, Ko 115 B7 island S Thailand
Lantau Island 106 A2 Cant. Tai Yue Shan, Chin. Landao. island Hong Kong, S China
Lan-ts'ang Chiang see Mekong
Lantung, Gulf of see Liaodong Wan
Lanzarote 48 B3 island Islas Canarias, Spain, NE Atlantic Ocean
Lanzhou 106 B4 var. Lan-chou, Lanchow, Lan-chow; prev. Kaolan. province capital Gansu, C China
Lao Cai 114 D3 Lao Cai, N Vietnam
Laodicea/Laodicea ad Mare see Al Lādhiqīyah
Laoet see Laut, Pulau
Laojunmiao 106 A3 prev. Yumen. Gansu, N China
Laon 68 D3 var. la Laon; anc. Laudunum. Aisne, N France
Lao People's Democratic Republic see Laos
La Orchila, Isla 36 D1 island N Venezuela
La Oroya 38 C3 Junín, C Peru
Laos 114 D4 off. Lao People's Democratic Republic. country SE Asia
La Palma 31 G5 Darién, SE Panama
La Palma 48 A3 island Islas Canarias, Spain, NE Atlantic Ocean
La Paz 39 F4 var. La Paz de Ayacucho. country capital (Bolivia-seat of government) La Paz, W Bolivia
La Paz 28 B3 Baja California Sur, NW Mexico
La Paz, Bahía de 28 B3 bay NW Mexico
La Paz de Ayacucho see La Paz
La Pérouse Strait 108 D1 Jap. Sōya-kaikyō, Rus. Proliv Laperuza. strait Japan/Russian Federation
Laperuza, Proliv see La Pérouse Strait
Lápithos see Lapta
Lapland 62 D3 Fin. Lappi, Swe. Lappland. cultural region N Europe
La Plata 42 D4 Buenos Aires, E Argentina
La Plata see Sucre
La Pola 70 D1 var. Pola de Lena. Asturias, N Spain
Lappeenranta 63 E5 Swe. Villmanstrand. Etelä-Suomi, SE Finland
Lappi/Lappland see Lapland
Lappo see Lapua
Lapta 80 C5 Gk. Lápithos. NW Cyprus
Laptev Sea see Laptevykh, More
Laptevykh, More 93 E2 Eng. Laptev Sea. sea Arctic Ocean
Lapua 63 D5 Swe. Lappo. Länsi-Suomi, W Finland
Lapurdum see Bayonne
Łapy 76 E3 Podlaskie, NE Poland
La Quiaca 42 C2 Jujuy, N Argentina
L'Aquila 74 C4 var. Aquila, Aquila degli Abruzzi. Abruzzo, C Italy
Laracha 70 B1 Galicia, NW Spain
Laramie 22 C4 Wyoming, C USA
Laramie Mountains 22 C3 mountain range Wyoming, C USA
Laredo 71 E1 Cantabria, N Spain
Laredo 27 F5 Texas, SW USA
La Réunion see Réunion
Largeau see Faya
Largo 21 E4 Florida, SE USA
Largo, Cayo 32 B2 island W Cuba
Lario see Como, Lago di
La Rioja 42 C3 La Rioja, NW Argentina
La Rioja 71 E2 autonomous community N Spain
Lárisa 82 B4 var. Larissa. Thessalía, C Greece
Larissa see Lárisa
Lärkāna 112 B3 var. Larkhana. Sind, SE Pakistan
Larkhana see Lärkāna
Larnaca see Lárnaka
Lárnaka 80 C5 var. Larnaca, Larnax. SE Cyprus
Larnax see Lárnaka
la Rochelle 68 B4 anc. Rupella. Charente-Maritime, W France
la Roche-sur-Yon 68 B4 prev. Bourbon Vendée, Napoléon-Vendée. Vendée, NW France
La Roda 71 E3 Castilla-La Mancha, C Spain
La Romana 33 E3 E Dominican Republic
Larvotto 69 C8 N Monaco Europe
La-sa see Lhasa
Las Cabezas de San Juan 70 C5 Andalucía, S Spain
Las Cruces 26 D3 New Mexico, SW USA
La See d'Urgel see La Seu d'Urgell
La Serena 42 B3 Coquimbo, C Chile
La Seu d'Urgell 71 G1 prev. La See d'Urgel, Seo de Urgel. Cataluña, NE Spain
la Seyne-sur-Mer 69 D6 Var, SE France
Lashio 114 B3 Shan State, E Myanmar (Burma)
Lashkar Gāh 100 D5 var. Lash-Kar-Gar'. Helmand, S Afghanistan
Lash-Kar-Gar' see Lashkar Gāh
La Sila 75 D6 mountain range SW Italy
La Sirena 30 D3 Región Autónoma Atlántico Sur, E Nicaragua
Łask 76 C4 Łódzkie, C Poland
Las Lomitas 42 D2 Formosa, N Argentina
La Solana 71 E4 Castilla-La Mancha, C Spain
Las Palmas 48 A3 var. Las Palmas de Gran Canaria. Gran Canaria, Islas Canarias, Spain, NE Atlantic Ocean
Las Palmas de Gran Canaria see Las Palmas
La Spezia 74 B3 Liguria, NW Italy
Lassa see Lhasa
Las Tablas 31 F5 Los Santos, S Panama
Last Frontier, The see Alaska
Las Tunas 32 C2 var. Victoria de las Tunas. Las Tunas, E Cuba
La Suisse see Switzerland
Las Vegas 25 D7 Nevada, W USA
Latacunga 38 B1 Cotopaxi, C Ecuador
Latakia see Al Lādhiqīyah
la Teste 69 B5 Gironde, SW France
Latina 75 C5 prev. Littoria. Lazio, C Italy
La Tortuga, Isla 37 E1 var. Isla Tortuga. island N Venezuela
La Tuque 17 E4 Québec, SE Canada
Latvia 84 C3 off. Republic of Latvia, Ger. Lettland, Latv. Latvija, Latvijas Republika; prev. Latvian SSR, Rus. Latviyskaya SSR. country NE Europe
Latvian SSR/Latvija/Latvijas Republika/Latviyskaya SSR see Latvia
Latvia, Republic of see Latvia
Laudunum see Laon
Laudus see St-Lô
Lauenburg/Lauenburg in Pommern see Lębork
Lau Group 123 E4 island group E Fiji
Lauis see Lugano
Launceston 127 C8 Tasmania, SE Australia
La Unión 30 C2 Olancho, C Honduras
La Unión 71 F4 Murcia, SE Spain
Laurel 20 C3 Mississippi, S USA
Laurel 22 C2 Montana, NW USA
Laurentian Highlands see Laurentian Mountains
Laurentian Mountains 17 E3 var. Laurentian Highlands, Fr. Les Laurentides. plateau Newfoundland and Labrador/Québec, Canada
Laurentides, Les see Laurentian Mountains
Lauria 75 D6 Basilicata, S Italy
Laurinburg 21 F1 North Carolina, SE USA
Lauru see Choiseul
Lausanne 73 A7 It. Losanna. Vaud, SW Switzerland
Laut, Pulau 116 D4 prev. Laoet. island Borneo, C Indonesia
Laval 16 D4 Québec, SE Canada
Laval 68 B3 Mayenne, NW France
La Vall d'Uxó 71 F3 var. Vall D'Uxó. País Valenciano, E Spain
La Vega 33 E3 var. Concepción de la Vega. C Dominican Republic
La Vila Joíosa see Villajoyosa
Lávrio 83 C6 prev. Lávrion. Attikí, C Greece
Lávrion see Lávrio
Lawrence 19 G3 Massachusetts, NE USA
Lawrenceburg 20 C1 Tennessee, S USA
Lawton 27 F2 Oklahoma, C USA
La Yarada 39 E4 Tacna, SW Peru
Laylā 99 C5 var. Laila. Ar Riyāḍ, C Saudi Arabia
Lazarev Sea 132 B1 sea Antarctica
Lázaro Cárdenas 29 E5 Michoacán, SW Mexico
Leal see Lihula
Leamhcán see Lucan
Leamington 16 C5 Ontario, S Canada
Leavdnja see Lakselv
Lebak 117 E3 Mindanao, S Philippines
Lebanese Republic see Lebanon
Lebanon 23 G5 Missouri, C USA
Lebanon 19 G2 New Hampshire, NE USA
Lebanon 24 B3 Oregon, NW USA
Lebanon 96 A4 off. Lebanese Republic, Ar. Al Lubnān, Fr. Liban. country SW Asia
Lebanon, Mount see Liban, Jebel
Lebap 100 D2 Lebapskiy Velayat, NE Turkmenistan
Lebedin see Lebedyn
Lebedyn 87 F2 Rus. Lebedin. Sums'ka Oblast', NE Ukraine
Lębork 76 C2 var. Lębórk, Ger. Lauenburg, Lauenburg in Pommern. Pomorskie, N Poland
Lebrija 70 C5 Andalucía, S Spain
Lebu 43 A5 Bío Bío, C Chile
le Cannet 69 D6 Alpes-Maritimes, SE France
Le Cap see Cap-Haïtien
Lecce 75 E6 Puglia, SE Italy
Lechainá 83 B6 var. Lehena, Lekhainá. Dytikí Ellás, S Greece
Ledo Salinarius see Lons-le-Saunier
Leduc 15 E5 Alberta, SW Canada
Leech Lake 23 F2 lake Minnesota, N USA
Leeds 67 D5 N England, United Kingdom
Leek 64 E2 Groningen, NE Netherlands
Leer 72 A3 Niedersachsen, NW Germany
Leeuwarden 64 D1 Fris. Ljouwert. Friesland, N Netherlands
Leeuwin, Cape 120 A5 headland Western Australia
Leeward Islands 33 G3 island group E West Indies
Leeward Islands see Sotavento, Ilhas de
Lefkáda 83 A5 prev. Levkás. Lefkáda, Iónia Nisiá, Greece, C Mediterranean Sea
Lefkáda 83 A5 It. Santa Maura, prev. Levkás; anc. Leucas. island Iónia Nisiá, Greece, C Mediterranean Sea
Lefká Óri 83 C7 mountain range Kríti, Greece, E Mediterranean Sea
Lefkímmi 83 A5 var. Levkímmi. Kérkyra, Iónia Nisiá, Greece, C Mediterranean Sea
Lefkosía/Lefkoşa see Nicosia
Legaceaster see Chester
Legaspi see Legazpi City
Legazpi City 117 E2 var. Legaspi. C Philippines
Leghorn see Livorno
Legnica 76 B4 Ger. Liegnitz. Dolnośląskie, SW Poland
le Havre 68 B3 Eng. Havre; prev. le Havre-de-Grâce. Seine-Maritime, N France
le Havre-de-Grâce see le Havre
Lehena see Lechainá
Leicester 67 D6 Lat. Batae Coritanorum. C England, United Kingdom
Leiden 64 B3 prev. Leyden; anc. Lugdunum Batavorum. Zuid-Holland, W Netherlands
Leie 68 D2 Fr. Lys. river Belgium/France
Leinster 67 B6 Ir. Cúige Laighean. cultural region E Ireland
Leipsic see Leipzig
Leipsoí 83 E6 island Dodekánisa, Greece, Aegean Sea
Leipzig 72 C4 Pol. Lipsk, hist. Leipsic; anc. Lipsia. Sachsen, E Germany
Leiria 70 B3 anc. Collipo. Leiria, C Portugal
Leirvik 63 A6 Hordaland, S Norway
Lek 64 C4 river SW Netherlands
Lekhainá see Lechainá
Lekhchevo see Boychinovtsi
Leksand 63 C5 Dalarna, C Sweden
Lel'chitsy see Lyel'chytsy
le Léman see Geneva, Lake
Lelystad 64 D3 Flevoland, C Netherlands
Léman, Lac see Geneva, Lake
le Mans 68 B3 Sarthe, NW France
Lemberg see L'viv
Lemesós 80 C5 var. Limassol. SW Cyprus
Lemhi Range 24 D3 mountain range Idaho, C USA North America
Lemnos see Límnos
Lemovices see Limoges
Lena 93 F3 river NE Russian Federation
Lena Tablemount 119 B7 seamount S Indian Ocean
Len Dao 106 C8 island S Spratly Islands
Lengshuitan see Yongzhou
Leninabad see Khujand
Leninakan see Gyumri
Lenine 87 G5 Rus. Lenino. Respublika Krym, S Ukraine
Leningor see Ridder
Leningrad see Sankt-Peterburg
Leningradskaya 132 B4 Russian research station Antarctica
Lenino see Lenine, Ukraine
Leninobod see Khujand
Leninogorsk see Ridder
Leninpol' 101 F2 Talasskaya Oblast', NW Kyrgyzstan
Lenin-Turkmenski see Türkmenabat
Lenkoran' see Länkäran
Lenti 77 B7 Zala, SW Hungary
Lentia see Linz
Leoben 73 E7 Steiermark, C Austria
León 29 E4 var. León de los Aldamas. Guanajuato, C Mexico
León 30 C3 León, NW Nicaragua
León 70 D1 Castilla-León, NW Spain
León de los Aldamas see León
Leonídi see Leonídio
Leonídio 83 B6 var. Leonídi. Pelopónnisos, S Greece
Léopold II, Lac see Mai-Ndombe, Lac
Léopoldville see Kinshasa
Lepe 70 C4 Andalucía, S Spain
Lepel' see Lyepyel'
le Portel 68 C2 Pas-de-Calais, N France
Le Puglie see Puglia
le Puy 69 C5 prev. le Puy-en-Velay, hist. Anicium, Podium Anicensis. Haute-Loire, C France
le Puy-en-Velay see le Puy
Léré 54 B4 Mayo-Kébbi, SW Chad
Lérida see Lleida
Lerma 70 D2 Castilla-León, N Spain
Leros 83 D6 island Dodekánisa, Greece, Aegean Sea
Lernayin Gharabakh see Nagorno-Karabakh
Lerwick 66 D1 NE Scotland, United Kingdom
Lesbos see Lésvos
Les Cayes see Cayes
Les Gonaïves see Gonaïves
Leshan 106 B5 Sichuan, C China
les Herbiers 68 B4 Vendée, NW France
Lesh/Leshi see Lezhë
Lesina see Hvar
Leskovac 79 E5 Serbia, SE Serbia
Lesnoy 92 C3 Sverdlovskaya Oblast', C Russian Federation

Luzern – Markounda

Luzern *73 B7 Fr.* Lucerne, *It.* Lucerna. Luzern, C Switzerland
Luzon *117 E1 island* N Philippines
Luzon Strait *103 E3 strait* Philippines/Taiwan
L'viv *86 B2 Ger.* Lemberg, *Pol.* Lwów, *Rus.* L'vov. L'vivs'ka Oblast', W Ukraine
L'vov *see* L'viv
Lwena *see* Luena
Lwów *see* L'viv
Lyakhavichy *85 B6 Rus.* Lyakhovichi. Brestskaya Voblasts', SW Belarus
Lyakhovichi *see* Lyakhavichy
Lyallpur *see* Faisalābād
Lyangar *see* Langar
Lyck *see* Ełk
Lycksele *62 C4* Västerbotten, N Sweden
Lycopolis *see* Asyūṭ
Lyel'chytsy *85 C7 Rus.* Lel'chitsy. Homyel'skaya Voblasts', SE Belarus
Lyepyel' *85 D5 Rus.* Lepel'. Vitsyebskaya Voblasts', N Belarus
Lyme Bay *67 C7 bay* S England, United Kingdom
Lynchburg *19 E5* Virginia, NE USA
Lynn *see* King's Lynn
Lynn Lake *15 F4* Manitoba, C Canada
Lynn Regis *see* King's Lynn
Lyon *69 D5 Eng.* Lyons; *anc.* Lugdunum. Rhône, E France
Lyons *see* Lyon
Lyozna *85 E6 Rus.* Liozno. Vitsyebskaya Voblasts', NE Belarus
Lypovets' *86 D2 Rus.* Lipovets. Vinnyts'ka Oblast', C Ukraine
Lys *see* Leie
Lysychans'k *87 H3 Rus.* Lisichansk. Luhans'ka Oblast', E Ukraine
Lyttelton *129 C6* South Island, New Zealand
Lyublin *see* Lublin
Lyubotin *see* Lyubotyn
Lyubotyn *87 G2 Rus.* Lyubotin. Kharkivs'ka Oblast', E Ukraine
Lyulyakovo *82 E2 prev.* Keremitlik. Burgas, E Bulgaria
Lyusina *85 B6 Rus.* Lyusino. Brestskaya Voblasts', SW Belarus
Lyusino *see* Lyusina

M

Maale *see* Male'
Ma'ān *97 B7* Ma'ān, SW Jordan
Maardu *84 D2 Ger.* Maart. Harjumaa, NW Estonia
Ma'aret-en-Nu'man *see* Ma'arrat an Nu'mān
Ma'arrat an Nu'mān *96 B3 var.* Ma'aret-en-Nu'man, *Fr.* Maarret enn Naamâne. Idlib, NW Syria
Maarret enn Naamâne *see* Ma'arrat an Nu'mān
Maart *see* Maardu
Maas *see* Meuse
Maaseik *65 D5 prev.* Maeseyck. Limburg, NE Belgium
Maastricht *65 D6 var.* Maestricht; *anc.* Traiectum ad Mosam, Traiectum Tungorum. Limburg, SE Netherlands
Macao *107 C6 Port.* Macau. Guangdong, SE China
Macapá *41 E1 state capital* Amapá, N Brazil
Macarsca *see* Makarska
Macassar *see* Makassar
Macău *see* Makó, Hungary
Macau *see* Macao
MacCluer Gulf *see* Berau, Teluk
Macdonnell Ranges *124 D4 mountain range* Northern Territory, C Australia
Macedonia *see* Macedonia, FYR
Macedonia, FYR *79 D6 off.* the Former Yugoslav Republic of Macedonia, *var.* Macedonia, *Mac.* Makedonija, *abbrev.* FYR Macedonia, FYROM. *country* SE Europe
Macedonia, the Former Yugoslav Republic of *see* Macedonia, FYR
Maceió *41 G3 state capital* Alagoas, E Brazil
Machachi *38 B1* Pichincha, C Ecuador
Machala *38 B2* El Oro, SW Ecuador
Machanga *57 E3* Sofala, E Mozambique
Machilīpatnam *110 D1 var.* Bandar Masulipatnam. Andhra Pradesh, E India
Machiques *36 C2* Zulia, NW Venezuela
Macías Nguema Biyogo *see* Bioco, Isla de
Măcin *86 D5* Tulcea, SE Romania
Mackay *126 D4* Queensland, NE Australia
Mackay, Lake *124 C4 salt lake* Northern Territory/ Western Australia
Mackenzie *15 E3 river* Northwest Territories, NW Canada
Mackenzie Bay *132 D3 bay* Antarctica
Mackenzie Mountains *14 D3 mountain range* Northwest Territories, NW Canada
Macleod, Lake *124 A4 lake* Western Australia
Macomb *18 A4* Illinois, N USA
Macomer *75 A5* Sardegna, Italy, C Mediterranean Sea
Mâcon *69 D5 anc.* Matisco, Matisco Ædourum. Saône-et-Loire, C France
Macon *20 D2* Georgia, SE USA
Macon *23 G4* Missouri, C USA
Macquarie Ridge *132 C5 undersea ridge* SW Pacific Ocean
Macuspana *29 G4* Tabasco, SE Mexico
Ma'dabā *97 B6 var.* Mādabā, Madeba; *anc.* Medeba. Ma'dabā, NW Jordan
Mādabā *see* Ma'dabā
Madagascar *57 F3 off.* Democratic Republic of Madagascar, *Malg.* Madagasikara; *prev.* Malagasy Republic. *country* W Indian Ocean
Madagascar *57 F3 island* W Indian Ocean
Madagascar Basin *47 E7 undersea basin* W Indian Ocean
Madagascar, Democratic Republic of *see* Madagascar
Madagascar Plateau *47 E7 var.* Madagascar Ridge, Madagascar Rise, *Rus.* Madagaskarskiy Khrebet. *undersea plateau* W Indian Ocean
Madagascar Rise/Madagascar Ridge *see* Madagascar Plateau
Madagasikara *see* Madagascar
Madagaskarskiy Khrebet *see* Madagascar Plateau
Madang *122 B3* Madang, N Papua New Guinea
Madanīyīn *see* Médenine
Mađarska *see* Hungary
Made *64 C4* Noord-Brabant, S Netherlands
Madeba *see* Ma'dabā
Madeira *48 A2 var.* Ilha de Madeira. *island* Madeira, Portugal, NE Atlantic Ocean
Madeira, Ilha de *see* Madeira
Madeira Plain *44 C3 abyssal plain* E Atlantic Ocean
Madeira, Rio *40 D2 var.* Río Madera. *river* Bolivia/Brazil
Madeleine, Îles de la *17 F4 Eng.* Magdalen Islands. *island group* Québec, E Canada
Madera *25 B6* California, W USA
Madera, Río *see* Madeira, Rio
Madhya Pradesh *113 E4 prev.* Central Provinces and Berar. *cultural region* C India
Madīnat ath Thawrah *96 C2 var.* Ath Thawrah. Ar Raqqah, N Syria
Madioen *see* Madiun
Madison *23 F3* South Dakota, N USA
Madison *18 B3 state capital* Wisconsin, N USA
Madiun *116 D5 prev.* Madioen. Jawa, C Indonesia
Madoera *see* Madura, Pulau
Madona *84 D4 Ger.* Modohn. Madona, E Latvia
Madras *see* Chennai
Madras *see* Tamil Nādu
Madre de Dios, Río *39 E3 river* Bolivia/Peru
Madre del Sur, Sierra *29 E5 mountain range* S Mexico
Madre, Laguna *29 F3 lagoon* NE Mexico
Madre, Laguna *27 G5 lagoon* Texas, SW USA
Madre Occidental, Sierra *28 C3 var.* Western Sierra Madre. *mountain range* C Mexico
Madre Oriental, Sierra *29 E3 var.* Eastern Sierra Madre. *mountain range* C Mexico
Madre, Sierra *30 B2 var.* Sierra de Soconusco. *mountain range* Guatemala/Mexico
Madrid *70 D3 country capital* (Spain) Madrid, C Spain
Madura *see* Madurai
Madurai *110 C3 prev.* Madura, Mathurai. Tamil Nādu, S India
Madura, Pulau *116 D5 prev.* Madoera. *island* C Indonesia
Maebashi *109 D5 var.* Maebasi, Mayebashi. Gunma, Honshū, S Japan
Maebasi *see* Maebashi
Mae Nam Khong *see* Mekong
Mae Nam Nan *114 C4 river* NW Thailand
Mae Nam Yom *114 C4 river* W Thailand
Maeseyck *see* Maaseik
Maestricht *see* Maastricht
Maéwo *122 D4 prev.* Aurora. *island* C Vanuatu
Mafia *51 D7 island* E Tanzania
Mafraq/Muḥāfaẓat al Mafraq *see* Al Mafraq
Magadan *93 G3* Magadanskaya Oblast', E Russian Federation
Magallanes *see* Punta Arenas
Magallanes, Estrecho de *see* Magellan, Strait of
Magangué *36 B2* Bolívar, N Colombia
Magdalena *39 F3* Beni, N Bolivia
Magdalena *28 B1* Sonora, NW Mexico
Magdalena, Isla *28 B3 island* NW Mexico
Magdalena, Río *36 B2 river* C Colombia
Magdalen Islands *see* Madeleine, Îles de la
Magdeburg *72 C4* Sachsen-Anhalt, C Germany
Magelang *116 C5* Jawa, C Indonesia
Magellan, Strait of *43 B8 Sp.* Estrecho de Magallanes. *strait* Argentina/Chile
Magerøy *see* Magerøya
Magerøya *62 D1 var.* Magerøy, *Lapp.* Máhkarávju. *island* N Norway
Maggiore, Lago *see* Maggiore, Lake
Maggiore, Lake *74 B1 It.* Lago Maggiore. *lake* Italy/Switzerland
Maglaj *78 C3* Federacija Bosna I Hercegovina, N Bosnia and Herzegovina
Maglie *75 E6* Puglia, SE Italy
Magna *22 B4* Utah, W USA
Magnesia *see* Manisa
Magnitogorsk *92 B4* Chelyabinskaya Oblast', C Russian Federation
Magnolia State *see* Mississippi
Magta' Lahjar *52 C3 var.* Magta Lahjar, Magta' Lahjar, Magtá Lahjar. Brakna, SW Mauritania
Magtymguly *100 C3 prev.* Garrygala; *Rus.* Kara-gala. W Turkmenistan
Magway *114 A3 var.* Magwe. Magway, W Myanmar (Burma)
Magyar-Becse *see* Bečej
Magyarkanizsa *see* Kanjiža
Magyarország *see* Hungary
Mahajanga *57 F2 var.* Majunga. Mahajanga, NW Madagascar
Mahakam, Sungai *116 D4 var.* Koetai, Kutai. *river* Borneo, C Indonesia
Mahalapye *56 D3 var.* Mahalatswe. Central, SE Botswana
Mahalatswe *see* Mahalapye
Māhān *98 D3* Kermān, E Iran
Mahanādi *113 F4 river* E India
Mahārāshtra *112 D5 cultural region* W India
Mahbés *see* El Mahbas
Mahbūbnagar *112 D5* Telangana, C India
Mahdia *49 F2 var.* Al Mahdīyah, Mehdia. NE Tunisia
Mahé *57 H1 island* Inner Islands, NE Seychelles
Mahia Peninsula *128 E4 peninsula* North Island, New Zealand
Mahilyow *85 D6 Rus.* Mogilëv. Mahilyowskaya Voblasts', E Belarus
Máhkarávju *see* Magerøya
Mahmūd-e 'Erāqī *see* Maḥmūd-e Rāqī
Maḥmūd-e Rāqī *101 E4 var.* Mahmūd-e 'Erāqī. Kāpīsā, NE Afghanistan
Mahón *see* Maó
Mähren *see* Moravia
Mährisch-Weisskirchen *see* Hranice
Maicao *36 C1* La Guajira, N Colombia
Mai Ceu/Mai Chio *see* Maych'ew
Maidān Shahr *101 E4 prev.* Meydān Shahr. Vardak, E Afghanistan
Maidstone *67 E7* SE England, United Kingdom
Maiduguri *53 H4* Borno, NE Nigeria
Mailand *see* Milano
Maimanah *100 D3 var.* Meymaneh, Maymana. Fāryāb, NW Afghanistan
Main *73 B5 river* C Germany
Mai-Ndombe, Lac *55 C6 prev.* Lac Léopold II. *lake* W Dem. Rep. Congo
Maine *19 G2 off.* State of Maine, *also known as* Lumber State, Pine Tree State. *state* NE USA
Maine *68 B3 cultural region* NW France
Maine, Gulf of *19 H2 gulf* NE USA
Mainland *66 C2 island* N Scotland, United Kingdom
Mainland *66 D1 island* NE Scotland, United Kingdom
Mainz *73 B5 Fr.* Mayence. Rheinland-Pfalz, SW Germany
Maio *52 A3 var.* Mayo. *island* Ilhas de Sotavento, SE Cape Verde
Maisur *see* Mysore, India
Maisur *see* Karnātaka, India
Maizhokunggar *104 C5* Xizang Zizhiqu, W China
Majorca *see* Mallorca
Mājro *see* Majuro Atoll
Majunga *see* Mahajanga
Majuro Atoll *122 D2 var.* Mājro. *atoll* Ratak Chain, SE Marshall Islands
Makale *see* Mek'elē
Makarov Basin *133 B3 undersea basin* Arctic Ocean
Makarska *78 B4 It.* Macarsca. Split-Dalmacija, SE Croatia
Makasar *see* Makassar
Makasar, Selat *see* Makassar Straits
Makassar *117 E4 var.* Macassar, Makasar; *prev.* Ujungpandang. Sulawesi, C Indonesia
Makassar Straits *116 D4 Ind.* Makasar Selat. *strait* C Indonesia
Makay *57 F3 var.* Massif du Makay. *mountain range* SW Madagascar
Makay, Massif du *see* Makay
Makedonija *see* Macedonia, FYR
Makeni *52 C4* C Sierra Leone
Makeyevka *see* Makiyivka
Makhachkala *92 A4 prev.* Petrovsk-Port. Respublika Dagestan, SW Russian Federation
Makin *122 D2 prev.* Pitt Island. *atoll* Tungaru, W Kiribati
Makira *see* San Cristobal
Makiyivka *87 G3 Rus.* Makeyevka; *prev.* Dmitriyevsk. Donets'ka Oblast', E Ukraine
Makkah *99 A5 Eng.* Mecca. Makkah, W Saudi Arabia
Makkovik *17 F2* Newfoundland and Labrador, NE Canada
Makó *77 D7 Rom.* Macău. Csongrád, SE Hungary
Makoua *55 B5* Cuvette, C Congo
Makran Coast *98 E4 coastal region* SE Iran
Makrany *85 A6 Rus.* Mokrany. Brestskaya Voblasts', SW Belarus
Mākū *98 B2* Āẕarbāyjān-e Gharbī, NW Iran
Makurdi *53 G4* Benue, C Nigeria
Mala *see* Malaita, Solomon Islands
Malabār Coast *110 B3 coast* SW India
Malabo *55 A5 prev.* Santa Isabel. *country capital* (Equatorial Guinea) Isla de Bioco, NW Equatorial Guinea
Malaca *see* Málaga
Malacca, Strait of *116 B3 Ind.* Selat Malaka. *strait* Indonesia/Malaysia
Malacka *see* Malacky
Malacky *77 C6 Hung.* Malacka. Bratislavský Kraj, W Slovakia
Maladzyechna *85 C5 Pol.* Molodeczno, *Rus.* Molodechno. Minskaya Voblasts', C Belarus
Málaga *70 D5 anc.* Malaca. Andalucía, S Spain
Malagarasi River *51 B7 river* W Tanzania Africa
Malagasy Republic *see* Madagascar
Malaita *122 C3 var.* Mala. *island* N Solomon Islands
Malakal *51 B5* Upper Nile, NE South Sudan
Malakula *see* Malekula
Malang *116 D5* Jawa, C Indonesia
Malange *see* Malanje
Malanje *56 B1 var.* Malange. Malanje, NW Angola
Mälaren *63 C6 lake* C Sweden
Malatya *95 E4 anc.* Melitene. Malatya, SE Turkey
Mala Vyska *87 E3 Rus.* Malaya Viska. Kirovohrads'ka Oblast', S Ukraine
Malawi *57 E1 off.* Republic of Malaŵi; *prev.* Nyasaland, Nyasaland Protectorate. *country* S Africa
Malawi, Lake *see* Nyasa, Lake
Malaŵi, Republic of *see* Malawi
Malaya Viska *see* Mala Vyska
Malay Peninsula *102 D4 peninsula* Malaysia/ Thailand
Malaysia *116 B3 off.* Malaysia, *var.* Federation of Malaysia; *prev.* the separate territories of Federation of Malaya, Sarawak and Sabah (North Borneo) and Singapore. *country* SE Asia
Malaysia, Federation of *see* Malaysia
Malbork *76 C2 Ger.* Marienburg, Marienburg in Westpreussen. Pomorskie, N Poland
Malchin *72 C3* Mecklenburg-Vorpommern, N Germany
Malden *23 H5* Missouri, C USA
Malden Island *123 G3 prev.* Independence Island. *atoll* E Kiribati
Maldives *110 A4 off.* Maldivian Divehi, Republic of Maldives. *country* N Indian Ocean
Maldives, Republic of *see* Maldives
Maldivian Divehi *see* Maldives
Male' *110 B4 Div.* Maale. *country capital* (Maldives) Male' Atoll, C Maldives
Male' Atoll *110 B4 var.* Kaafu Atoll. *atoll* C Maldives
Malekula *122 D4 var.* Malakula; *prev.* Mallicolo. *island* W Vanuatu
Malesína *83 C5* Stereá Ellás, E Greece
Malheur Lake *24 C3 lake* Oregon, NW USA
Mali *53 E3 off.* Republic of Mali, *Fr.* République du Mali; *prev.* French Sudan, Sudanese Republic. *country* W Africa
Malik, Wadi al *see* Milk, Wadi el
Mali Kyun *115 B5 var.* Tavoy Island. *island* Myeik Archipelago, S Myanmar (Burma)
Malin *see* Malyn
Malindi *51 D7* Coast, SE Kenya
Malines *see* Mechelen
Mali, Republic of *see* Mali
Mali, République du *see* Mali
Malkiye *see* Al Mālikīyah
Malko Tŭrnovo *82 E3* Burgas, E Bulgaria
Mallaig *66 B3* N Scotland, United Kingdom
Mallawī *50 B2 var.* Mallawi. C Egypt
Mallawi *see* Mallawī
Mallicolo *see* Malekula
Mallorca *71 G3 Eng.* Majorca; *anc.* Baleares Major. *island* Islas Baleares, Spain, W Mediterranean Sea
Malmberget *62 C3 Lapp.* Malmivaara. Norrbotten, N Sweden
Malmédy *65 D6* Liège, E Belgium
Malmivaara *see* Malmberget
Malmö *63 B7* Skåne, S Sweden
Maloelap *see* Maloelap Atoll
Maloelap Atoll *122 D1 var.* Maloelap. *atoll* E Marshall Islands
Małopolska, Wyżyna *76 D4 plateau* S Poland
Malozemel'skaya Tundra *88 D3 physical region* NW Russian Federation
Malta *84 D4* Rēzekne, SE Latvia
Malta *22 C1* Montana, NW USA
Malta *75 C8 off.* Republic of Malta. *country* C Mediterranean Sea
Malta *75 C8 island* Malta, C Mediterranean Sea
Malta, Canale di *see* Malta Channel
Malta Channel *75 C8 It.* Canale di Malta. *strait* Italy/Malta
Malta, Republic of *see* Malta
Maluku *117 F4 Dut.* Molukken, *Eng.* Moluccas; *prev.* Spice Islands. *island group* E Indonesia
Maluku, Laut *see* Molucca Sea
Malung *63 B6* Dalarna, C Sweden
Malventum *see* Benevento
Malvina, Isla Gran *see* West Falkland
Malvinas, Islas *see* Falkland Islands
Malyn *86 D2 Rus.* Malin. Zhytomyrs'ka Oblast', N Ukraine
Malyy Kavkaz *see* Lesser Caucasus
Mamberamo, Sungai *117 H4 river* Papua, E Indonesia
Mambij *see* Manbij
Mamonovo *84 A4 Ger.* Heiligenbeil. Kaliningradskaya Oblast', W Russian Federation
Mamoré, Rio *39 F3 river* Bolivia/Brazil
Mamou *52 C4* W Guinea
Mamoudzou *57 F2 dependent territory capital* (Mayotte) C Mayotte
Mamuno *56 C3* Ghanzi, W Botswana
Manacor *71 G3* Mallorca, Spain, W Mediterranean Sea
Manado *117 F3 prev.* Menado. Sulawesi, C Indonesia
Managua *30 D3 country capital* (Nicaragua) Managua, W Nicaragua
Managua, Lake *30 C3 var.* Xolotlán. *lake* W Nicaragua
Manakara *57 G4* Fianarantsoa, SE Madagascar
Manama *see* Al Manāmah
Mananjary *57 G3* Fianarantsoa, SE Madagascar
Manáos *see* Manaus
Manapouri, Lake *129 A7 lake* South Island, New Zealand
Manar *see* Mannar
Manas, Gora *101 E2 mountain* Kyrgyzstan/ Uzbekistan
Manaus *40 D2 prev.* Manáos. *state capital* Amazonas, NW Brazil
Manavgat *94 B4* Antalya, SW Turkey
Manbij *96 C2 var.* Mambij, *Fr.* Membidj. Ḥalab, N Syria
Manchester *67 D5 Lat.* Mancunium. NW England, United Kingdom
Manchester *19 G3* New Hampshire, NE USA
Man-chou-li *see* Manzhouli
Manchurian Plain *103 E1 plain* NE China
Máncio Lima *see* Japiim
Mancunium *see* Manchester
Mand *see* Mand, Rūd-e
Mandalay *114 B3* Mandalay, C Myanmar (Burma)
Mandan *23 E2* North Dakota, N USA
Mandeville *32 B5* C Jamaica
Mándra *83 C6* Attikí, C Greece
Rud-e Mand *98 D4 var.* Mand. *river* S Iran
Mandurah *125 A6* Western Australia
Manduria *75 E5* Puglia, SE Italy
Mandya *110 C2* Karnātaka, C India
Manfredonia *75 D5* Puglia, SE Italy
Mangai *55 C6* Bandundu, W Dem. Rep. Congo
Mangaia *123 G5 island group* S Cook Islands
Mangalia *86 D5 anc.* Callatis. Constanţa, SE Romania
Mangalmé *54 C3* Guéra, SE Chad
Mangalore *110 B2* Karnātaka, W India
Mangaung *see* Bloemfontein
Mango *see* Sansanné-Mango, Togo
Mangoky *57 F3 river* W Madagascar
Manhattan *23 F4* Kansas, C USA
Manicouagan, Réservoir *16 D3 lake* Québec, E Canada
Manihiki *123 G4 atoll* N Cook Islands
Manihiki Plateau *121 E3 undersea plateau* C Pacific Ocean
Maniitsoq *60 C3 var.* Manîtsoq, *Dan.* Sukkertoppen. Kitaa, S Greenland
Manila *117 E1 off.* City of Manila. *country capital* (Philippines) Luzon, N Philippines
Manila, City of *see* Manila
Manisa *94 A3 var.* Manissa, *prev.* Saruhan; *anc.* Magnesia. Manisa, W Turkey
Manissa *see* Manisa
Manitoba *15 F5 province* S Canada
Manitoba, Lake *15 F5 lake* Manitoba, S Canada
Manitoulin Island *16 C4 island* Ontario, S Canada
Manîtsoq *see* Maniitsoq
Manizales *36 B3* Caldas, W Colombia
Manjimup *125 A7* Western Australia
Mankato *23 F3* Minnesota, N USA
Manlleu *71 G2* Cataluña, NE Spain
Manly *126 E1* Iowa, C USA
Manmād *112 C5* Mahārāshtra, W India
Mannar *110 C3 var.* Manar. Northern Province, NW Sri Lanka
Mannar, Gulf of *110 C3 gulf* India/Sri Lanka
Mannheim *73 B5* Baden-Württemberg, SW Germany
Manokwari *117 G4* New Guinea, E Indonesia
Manono *55 E7* Shaba, SE Dem. Rep. Congo
Manosque *69 D6* Alpes-de-Haute-Provence, SE France
Manra *123 F3 prev.* Sydney Island. *atoll* Phoenix Islands, C Kiribati
Mansa *56 D2 prev.* Fort Rosebery. Luapula, N Zambia
Mansel Island *15 G3 island* Nunavut, NE Canada
Mansfield *18 D4* Ohio, N USA
Manta *38 A2* Manabí, W Ecuador
Manteca *25 B6* California, W USA
Mantoue *see* Mantova
Mantova *74 B2 Eng.* Mantua, *Fr.* Mantoue. Lombardia, NW Italy
Mantua *see* Mantova
Manuae *123 G4 island* S Cook Islands
Manukau *see* Manurewa
Manurewa *128 D3 var.* Manukau. Auckland, North Island, New Zealand
Manzanares *71 E3* Castilla-La Mancha, C Spain
Manzanillo *32 C3* Granma, E Cuba
Manzanillo *28 D4* Colima, SW Mexico
Manzhouli *105 F1 var.* Man-chou-li. Nei Mongol Zizhiqu, N China
Mao *54 B3* Kanem, W Chad
Maó *71 H3 Cast.* Mahón, *Eng.* Port Mahon; *anc.* Portus Magonis. Menorca, Spain, W Mediterranean Sea
Maoke, Pegunungan *117 H4 Dut.* Sneeuw-gebergte, *Eng.* Snow Mountains. *mountain range* Papua, E Indonesia
Maoming *106 C6* Guangdong, S China
Mapmaker Seamounts *103 H2 seamount range* N Pacific Ocean
Maputo *56 D4 prev.* Lourenço Marques. *country capital* (Mozambique) Maputo, S Mozambique
Marabá *41 F2* Pará, NE Brazil
Maracaibo *36 C1* Zulia, NW Venezuela
Maracaibo, Gulf of *see* Venezuela, Golfo de
Maracaibo, Lago de *36 C2 var.* Lake Maracaibo. *inlet* NW Venezuela
Maracaibo, Lake *see* Maracaibo, Lago de
Maracay *36 D2* Aragua, N Venezuela
Marada *see* Marādah
Marādah *49 G3 var.* Marada. N Libya
Maradi *53 G3* Maradi, S Niger
Maragha *see* Marāgheh
Marāgheh *98 C2 var.* Maragha. Āẕarbāyjān-e Khāvarī, NW Iran
Marajó, Baía de *41 F1 bay* N Brazil
Marajó, Ilha de *41 E1 island* N Brazil
Marakesh *see* Marrakech
Maramba *see* Livingstone
Maranhão *41 F2 off.* Estado do Maranhão. *state* E Brazil
Maranhão *41 F2 off.* Estado do Maranhão. *region* E Brazil
Maranhão, Estado do *see* Maranhão
Marañón, Río *38 B2 river* N Peru
Marathon *16 C4* Ontario, S Canada
Marathón *see* Marathónas
Marathónas *83 C5 prev.* Marathón. Attikí, C Greece
Mărăză *95 H2 Rus.* Maraza. E Azerbaijan
Maraza *see* Mărăză
Marbella *70 D5* Andalucía, S Spain
Marble Bar *124 B4* Western Australia
Marburg *see* Marburg an der Lahn, Germany
Marburg *see* Maribor, Slovenia
Marburg an der Lahn *72 B4 hist.* Marburg. Hessen, W Germany
March *see* Morava
Marche *74 C3 Eng.* Marches. *region* C Italy
Marche *69 C5 cultural region* C France
Marche-en-Famenne *65 C7* Luxembourg, SE Belgium
Marchena, Isla *38 B5 var.* Bindloe Island. *island* Galápagos Islands, Ecuador, E Pacific Ocean
Marches *see* Marche
Mar Chiquita, Laguna *42 C3 lake* C Argentina
Marcounda *see* Markounda
Mardān *112 C1* North-West Frontier Province, N Pakistan
Mar del Plata *43 D5* Buenos Aires, E Argentina
Mardin *95 E4* Mardin, SE Turkey
Maré *122 D5 island* Îles Loyauté, E New Caledonia
Marea Neagră *see* Black Sea
Mareeba *126 D3* Queensland, NE Australia
Marek *see* Dupnitsa
Marganets *see* Marhanets'
Margarita, Isla de *37 E1 island* N Venezuela
Margate *67 E7 prev.* Mergate. SE England, United Kingdom
Margherita *see* Jamaame
Margherita, Lake *51 C5 Eng.* Lake Margherita, *It.* Abbaia. *lake* SW Ethiopia
Margherita, Lake *see* Ābaya Hāyk'
Marghita *86 B3 Hung.* Margitta. Bihor, NW Romania
Margitta *see* Marghita
Marhanets' *87 F3 Rus.* Marganets. Dnipropetrovs'ka Oblast', E Ukraine
María Cleofas, Isla *28 C4 island* C Mexico
Maria Island *127 C8 island* Tasmania, SE Australia
María Madre, Isla *28 C4 island* C Mexico
María Magdalena, Isla *28 C4 island* C Mexico
Mariana Trench *103 G4 trench* W Pacific Ocean
Mariánské Lázně *77 A5 Ger.* Marienbad. Karlovarský Kraj, W Czech Republic
Marías, Islas *28 C4 island group* C Mexico
Maria-Theresiopel *see* Subotica
Maribor *73 E7 Ger.* Marburg. NE Slovenia
Marica *see* Maritsa
Maridi *51 B5* W Equatoria, S South Sudan
Marie Byrd Land *132 A3 physical region* Antarctica
Marie-Galante *33 G4 var.* Ceyre to the Caribs. *island* SE Guadeloupe
Marienbad *see* Mariánské Lázně
Marienburg *see* Alūksne, Latvia
Marienburg *see* Malbork, Poland
Marienburg in Westpreussen *see* Malbork
Marienhausen *see* Viļaka
Mariental *56 B4* Hardap, SW Namibia
Marienwerder *see* Kwidzyń
Mariestad *63 B6* Västra Götaland, S Sweden
Marietta *20 D2* Georgia, SE USA
Marijampolė *84 B4 prev.* Kapsukas. Marijampolė, S Lithuania
Marília *41 E4* São Paulo, S Brazil
Marín *70 B1* Galicia, NW Spain
Mar"ina Gorka *see* Mar"ina Horka
Mar"ina Horka *85 C6 Rus.* Mar'ina Gorka. Minskaya Voblasts', C Belarus
Maringá *41 E4* Paraná, S Brazil
Marion *23 G3* Iowa, C USA
Marion *18 D4* Ohio, N USA
Marion, Lake *21 E2 reservoir* South Carolina, SE USA
Mariscal Estigarribia *42 D2* Boquerón, NW Paraguay
Maritsa *82 D3 var.* Marica, *Gk.* Évros, *Turk.* Meriç; *anc.* Hebrus. *river* SW Europe
Maritzburg *see* Pietermaritzburg
Mariupol' *87 G4 prev.* Zhdanov. Donets'ka Oblast', SE Ukraine
Marka *51 D6 var.* Merca. Shabeellaha Hoose, S Somalia
Markham, Mount *132 B4 mountain* Antarctica
Markounda *54 C4 var.* Marcounda. Ouham, NW Central African Republic

Oldenzaal – Pará

Oldenzaal 64 E3 Overijssel, E Netherlands
Old Harbour 32 B5 C Jamaica
Old Line State see Maryland
Old North State see North Carolina
Olëkma 93 F4 river C Russian Federation
Olëkminsk 93 F3 Respublika Sakha (Yakutiya), NE Russian Federation
Oleksandrivka 87 E3 Rus. Aleksandrovka. Kirovohrads'ka Oblast', C Ukraine
Oleksandriya 87 F3 Rus. Aleksandriya. Kirovohrads'ka Oblast', C Ukraine
Olenegorsk 88 C2 Murmanskaya Oblast', NW Russian Federation
Olenëk 93 E3 Respublika Sakha (Yakutiya), NE Russian Federation
Olenëk 93 E3 river NE Russian Federation
Oléron, Île d' 69 A5 island W France
Olevs'k 86 D1 Rus. Olevsk. Zhytomyrs'ka Oblast', N Ukraine
Olevsk see Olevs'k
Ölgiy 104 C2 Bayan-Ölgiy, W Mongolia
Olhão 70 B5 Faro, S Portugal
Olifa 56 B3 Kunene, NW Namibia
Ólimbos see Ólympos
Olimpo see Fuerte Olimpo
Olisipo see Lisboa
Olita see Alytus
Oliva 71 F4 País Valenciano, E Spain
Olivet 68 C4 Loiret, C France
Olmaliq 101 E2 Rus. Almalyk. Toshkent Viloyati, E Uzbekistan
Olmütz see Olomouc
Olomouc 77 C5 Ger. Olmütz, Pol. Ołomuniec. Olomoucký Kraj, E Czech Republic
Ołomuniec see Olomouc
Olonets 88 B3 Respublika Kareliya, NW Russian Federation
Olovyannaya 93 F4 Chitinskaya Oblast', S Russian Federation
Olpe 72 B4 Nordrhein-Westfalen, W Germany
Olshanka see Vil'shanka
Olsnitz see Murska Sobota
Olsztyn 76 D2 Ger. Allenstein. Warmińsko-Mazurskie, N Poland
Olt 86 B5 var. Oltul, Ger. Alt. river S Romania
Olteniţa 86 C5 prev. Eng. Oltenitsa; anc. Constantiola. Călăraşi, SE Romania
Oltenitsa see Olteniţa
Oltul see Olt
Olvera 70 D5 Andalucía, S Spain
Ol'viopol' see Pervomays'k
Olympia 24 B2 state capital Washington, NW USA
Olympic Mountains 24 A2 mountain range Washington, NW USA
Ólympos, Mount 82 B4 var. Ólimbos, Eng. Mount Olympus. mountain N Greece
Omagh 67 B5 Ir. An Ómaigh. W Northern Ireland, United Kingdom
Omaha 23 F4 Nebraska, C USA
Oman 99 D6 off. Sultanate of Oman, Ar. Salṭanat 'Umān; prev. Muscat and Oman. country SW Asia
Oman, Gulf of 98 E4 Ar. Khalīj 'Umān. gulf N Arabian Sea
Oman, Sultanate of see Oman
Omboué 55 A6 Ogooué-Maritime, W Gabon
Omdurman 50 B4 var. Umm Durmān. Khartoum, C Sudan
Ometepe, Isla de 30 D4 island S Nicaragua
Ommen 64 E3 Overijssel, E Netherlands
Omsk 92 C4 Omskaya Oblast', C Russian Federation
Ōmuta 109 A7 Fukuoka, Kyūshū, SW Japan
Onda 71 F3 País Valenciano, E Spain
Ondjiva see N'Giva
Öndörhaan 105 E2 var. Undur Khan; prev. Tsetsen Khan. Hentiy, E Mongolia
Onega 88 C3 Arkhangel'skaya Oblast', NW Russian Federation
Onega 88 B4 river NW Russian Federation
Onega, Lake see Onezhskoye Ozero
Onex 73 A7 Genève, SW Switzerland
Onezhskoye Ozero 88 B4 Eng. Lake Onega. lake NW Russian Federation
Ongole 110 D1 Andhra Pradesh, E India
Onitsha 53 G5 Anambra, S Nigeria
Onon Gol 105 E2 river N Mongolia
Onslow 124 A4 Western Australia
Onslow Bay 21 F1 bay North Carolina, E USA
Ontario 16 B3 province S Canada
Ontario, Lake 19 E3 lake Canada/USA
Onteniente see Ontinyent
Ontinyent 71 F4 var. Onteniente. País Valenciano, E Spain
Ontong Java Rise 103 H4 undersea feature W Pacific Ocean
Onuba see Huelva
Oodeypore see Udaipur
Oos-Londen see East London
Oostakker 65 B5 Oost-Vlaanderen, NW Belgium
Oostburg 65 B5 Zeeland, SW Netherlands
Oostende 65 A5 Eng. Ostend, Fr. Ostende. West-Vlaanderen, NW Belgium
Oosterbeek 64 D4 Gelderland, SE Netherlands
Oosterhout 64 C4 Noord-Brabant, S Netherlands
Opatija 78 A2 It. Abbazia. Primorje-Gorski Kotar, NW Croatia
Opava 77 C5 Ger. Troppau. Moravskoslezský Kraj, E Czech Republic
Opazova see Stara Pazova
Opelika 20 D2 Alabama, S USA
Opelousas 20 B3 Louisiana, S USA
Ophiusa see Formentera
Opmeer 64 C2 Noord-Holland, NW Netherlands
Opochka 88 A4 Pskovskaya Oblast', W Russian Federation
Opole 76 C4 Ger. Oppeln. Opolskie, S Poland
Oporto see Porto
Opotiki 128 E3 Bay of Plenty, North Island, New Zealand
Oppeln see Opole
Oppidum Ubiorum see Köln
Oqtosh 101 E2 Rus. Aktash. Samarqand Viloyati, C Uzbekistan
Oradea 86 B3 prev. Oradea Mare, Ger. Grosswardein, Hung. Nagyvárad. Bihor, NW Romania
Oradea Mare see Oradea
Orahovac see Rahovec
Oral see Ural'sk
Oran 48 D2 var. Ouahran, Wahran. NW Algeria
Orange 127 D6 New South Wales, SE Australia
Orange 69 D6 anc. Arausio. Vaucluse, SE France
Orangeburg 21 E2 South Carolina, SE USA
Orange Cone see Orange Fan
Orange Fan 47 C7 var. Orange Cone. undersea feature SW Indian Ocean
Orange Mouth/Orangemund see Oranjemund
Orange River 56 B4 Afr. Oranjerivier. river S Africa
Orange Walk 30 C1 Orange Walk, N Belize
Oranienburg 72 D3 Brandenburg, NE Germany
Oranjemund 56 B4 var. Orangemund; prev. Orange Mouth. Karas, SW Namibia
Oranjerivier see Orange River
Oranjestad 33 E5 dependent territory capital (Aruba) Lesser Antilles, S Caribbean Sea
Orany see Varėna
Oraşul Stalin see Braşov
Oravicabánya see Oraviţa
Oraviţa 86 A4 Ger. Orawitza, Hung. Oravicabánya. Caraş-Severin, SW Romania
Orawitza see Oraviţa
Orbetello 74 B4 Toscana, C Italy
Orcadas 132 A1 Argentinian research station South Orkney Islands, Antarctica
Orchard Homes 22 B1 Montana, NW USA
Ordino 69 A8 Ordino, NW Andorra Europe
Ordos Desert see Mu Us Shadi
Ordu 94 D2 anc. Cotyora. Ordu, N Turkey
Ordzhonikidze 87 F3 Dnipropetrovs'ka Oblast', E Ukraine
Ordzhonikidze see Vladikavkaz, Russian Federation
Ordzhonikidze see Yenakiyeve, Ukraine
Orealla 37 G3 E Guyana
Örebro 63 C6 Örebro, C Sweden
Oregon 24 B3 off. State of Oregon, also known as Beaver State, Sunset State, Valentine State, Webfoot State. state NW USA
Oregon City 24 B3 Oregon, NW USA
Oregon, State of see Oregon
Orekhov see Orikhiv
Orël 89 B5 Orlovskaya Oblast', W Russian Federation
Orem 22 B4 Utah, W USA
Ore Mountains see Erzgebirge/Krušné Hory
Orenburg 89 D6 prev. Chkalov. Orenburgskaya Oblast', W Russian Federation
Orense see Ourense
Orestiáda 82 D3 prev. Orestiás. Anatolikí Makedonía kai Thráki, NE Greece
Orestiás see Orestiáda
Organ Peak 26 D3 mountain New Mexico, SW USA
Orgeyev see Orhei
Orhei 86 D3 var. Orheiu, Rus. Orgeyev. N Moldova
Orheiu see Orhei
Oriental, Cordillera 38 D3 mountain range Bolivia/Peru
Oriental, Cordillera 36 B3 mountain range C Colombia
Orihuela 71 F4 País Valenciano, E Spain
Orikhiv 87 G3 Rus. Orekhov. Zaporiz'ka Oblast', SE Ukraine
Orinoco, Río 37 E2 river Colombia/Venezuela
Orissa see Odisha
Orissaar see Orissaare
Orissaare 84 C2 Ger. Orissaar. Saaremaa, W Estonia
Oristano 75 A5 Sardegna, Italy, C Mediterranean Sea
Orito 36 A4 Putumayo, SW Colombia
Orizaba, Volcán Pico de 13 C7 var. Citlaltépetl. mountain S Mexico
Orkney see Orkney Islands
Orkney Islands 66 C2 var. Orkney, Orkneys. island group N Scotland, United Kingdom
Orkneys see Orkney Islands
Orlando 21 E4 Florida, SE USA
Orléanais 68 C4 cultural region C France
Orléans 68 C4 anc. Aurelianum. Loiret, C France
Orléansville see Chlef
Orly 68 E2 (Paris) Essonne, N France
Orlya 85 B6 Hrodzyenskaya Voblasts', W Belarus
Ormsö see Vormsi
Ormuz, Strait of see Hormuz, Strait of
Örnsköldsvik 63 C5 Västernorrland, C Sweden
Orolaunum see Arlon
Orol Dengizi see Aral Sea
Oromocto 17 F4 New Brunswick, SE Canada
Orona 123 F3 prev. Hull Island. atoll Phoenix Islands, C Kiribati
Oropeza see Cochabamba
Orosirá Rodhópis see Rhodope Mountains
Orpington 67 B8 United Kingdom
Orschowa see Orşova
Orsha 85 E6 Vitsyebskaya Voblasts', NE Belarus
Orsk 92 B4 Orenburgskaya Oblast', W Russian Federation
Orşova 86 A4 Ger. Orschowa, Hung. Orsova. Mehedinţi, SW Romania
Ortelsburg see Szczytno
Orthez 69 B6 Pyrénées-Atlantiques, SW France
Ortona 74 D4 Abruzzo, C Italy
Oruba see Aruba
Orūmīyeh, Daryācheh-ye 99 C2 var. Matianus, Sha Hi, Urumi Yeh, Eng. Lake Urmia; prev. Daryācheh-ye Reẓā'īyeh. lake NW Iran
Oruro 39 F4 Oruro, W Bolivia
Oryokko see Yalu
Oss 64 D4 Noord-Brabant, S Netherlands
Ōsaka 109 C6 hist. Naniwa. Ōsaka, Honshū, SW Japan
Ōsaki see Furukawa
Osa, Península de 31 E5 peninsula S Costa Rica
Osborn Plateau 119 D5 undersea feature E Indian Ocean
Osca see Huesca
Ösel see Saaremaa
Osh 101 F2 Oshskaya Oblast', SW Kyrgyzstan
Oshawa 16 D5 Ontario, SE Canada
Oshikango 56 B3 Ohangwena, N Namibia
O-shima 109 D6 island S Japan
Oshkosh 18 B2 Wisconsin, N USA
Oshmyany see Ashmyany
Osiek see Osijek
Osijek 78 C3 prev. Osiek, Osjek, Ger. Esseg, Hung. Eszék. Osijek-Baranja, E Croatia
Osipenko see Berdyans'k
Osipovichi see Asipovichy
Osjek see Osijek
Oskaloosa 23 G4 Iowa, C USA
Oskarshamn 63 C7 Kalmar, S Sweden
Öskemen see Ust'-Kamenogorsk
Oskol 87 G2 Rus. Oskil. river Russian Federation/Ukraine
Oskil see Oskol
Oslo 63 B6 prev. Christiania, Kristiania. country capital (Norway) Oslo, S Norway
Osmaniye 94 D4 Osmaniye, S Turkey
Osnabrück 72 A3 Niedersachsen, NW Germany
Osogov Mountains 82 B3 var. Osogovske Planine, Osogovski Planina, Mac. Osogovski Planini. mountain range Bulgaria/FYR Macedonia
Osogovske Planine/Osogovski Planina/Osogovski Planini see Osogov Mountains
Oşorhei see Târgu Mureş
Osorno 43 B5 Los Lagos, C Chile
Ossa, Serra d' 70 C4 mountain range SE Portugal
Ossora 93 H2 Koryakskiy Avtonomnyy Okrug, E Russian Federation
Ostee see Baltic Sea
Ostend/Ostende see Oostende
Oster 87 E1 Chernihivs'ka Oblast', N Ukraine
Östermyra see Seinäjoki
Osterode/Osterode in Ostpreussen see Ostróda
Österreich see Austria
Östersund 63 C5 Jämtland, C Sweden
Ostia Aterni see Pescara
Ostiglia 74 C2 Lombardia, N Italy
Ostrava 77 C5 Moravskoslezský Kraj, E Czech Republic
Ostróda 76 D3 Ger. Osterode, Osterode in Ostpreussen. Warmińsko-Mazurskie, NE Poland
Ostrołęka 76 D3 Ger. Wiesenhof, Rus. Ostrolenka. Mazowieckie, C Poland
Ostrolenka see Ostrołęka
Ostrov 88 A4 Latv. Austrava. Pskovskaya Oblast', W Russian Federation
Ostrovets see Ostrowiec Świętokrzyski
Ostrovnoy 88 C2 Murmanskaya Oblast', NW Russian Federation
Ostrów see Ostrów Wielkopolski
Ostrowiec see Ostrowiec Świętokrzyski
Ostrowiec Świętokrzyski 76 D4 var. Ostrowiec, Rus. Ostrovets. Świętokrzyskie, C Poland
Ostrów Mazowiecka 76 D3 var. Ostrów Mazowiecki. Mazowieckie, NE Poland
Ostrów Mazowiecki see Ostrów Mazowiecka
Ostrowo see Ostrów Wielkopolski
Ostrów Wielkopolski 76 C4 var. Ostrów, Ger. Ostrowo. Wielkopolskie, C Poland
Ostyako-Voguls'k see Khanty-Mansiysk
Osum see Osumit, Lumi i
Ōsumi-shotō 109 A8 island group Kagoshima, Nansei-shotō, SW Japan Asia East China Sea Pacific Ocean
Osumit, Lumi i 79 D7 var. Osum. river SE Albania
Osuna 70 D4 Andalucía, S Spain
Oswego 19 F2 New York, NE USA
Otago Peninsula 129 B7 peninsula South Island, New Zealand
Otaki 128 D4 Wellington, North Island, New Zealand
Otaru 108 C2 Hokkaidō, NE Japan
Otavalo 38 B1 Imbabura, N Ecuador
Otavi 56 B3 Otjozondjupa, N Namibia
Oţelu Roşu 86 B4 Ger. Ferdinandsberg, Hung. Nándorhgy. Caras-Severin, SW Romania
Otepää 84 D3 Ger. Odenpäh. Valgamaa, SE Estonia
Oti 53 E4 river N Togo
Otira 129 C6 West Coast, South Island, New Zealand
Otjiwarongo 56 B3 Otjozondjupa, N Namibia
Otorohanga 128 D3 Waikato, North Island, New Zealand
Otranto, Canale d' see Otranto, Strait of
Otranto, Strait of 79 C6 It. Canale d'Otranto. strait Albania/Italy
Otrokovice 77 C5 Ger. Otrokowitz. Zlínský Kraj, E Czech Republic
Otrokowitz see Otrokovice
Ōtsu 109 C6 var. Ôtu. Shiga, Honshū, SW Japan
Ottawa 16 D5 country capital (Canada) Ontario, SE Canada
Ottawa 18 B3 Illinois, N USA
Ottawa 23 F5 Kansas, C USA
Ottawa 19 E2 Fr. Outaouais. river Ontario/Québec, SE Canada
Ottawa Islands 16 C1 island group Nunavut, C Canada
Ottignies 65 C6 Wallon Brabant, C Belgium
Ottumwa 23 G4 Iowa, C USA
Ôtu see Ōtsu
Ouachita Mountains 20 A1 mountain range Arkansas/Oklahoma, C USA
Ouachita River 20 B2 river Arkansas/Louisiana, C USA
Ouagadougou 53 E4 var. Wagadugu. country capital (Burkina) C Burkina
Ouahigouya 53 E3 NW Burkina
Ouahran see Oran
Oualâta 52 D3 var. Oualata. Hodh ech Chargui, SE Mauritania
Ouanary 37 H3 E French Guiana
Ouanda Djallé 54 D4 Vakaga, NE Central African Republic
Ouarâne 52 D2 desert C Mauritania
Ouargla 49 E2 var. Wargla. NE Algeria
Ouarzazate 48 C3 S Morocco
Oubangui 55 C5 Fr. Oubangui. river C Africa
Oubangui see Ubangi
Oubangui-Chari see Central African Republic
Oubangui-Chari, Territoire de l' see Central African Republic
Oudjda see Oujda
Ouessant, Île d' 68 A3 Eng. Ushant. island NW France
Ouésso 55 B5 Sangha, NW Congo
Oujda 48 D2 Ar. Oudjda, Ujda. NE Morocco
Oujeft 52 C2 Adrar, C Mauritania
Oulu 62 D4 Swe. Uleåborg. Oulu, C Finland
Oulujärvi 62 D4 Swe. Uleträsk. lake C Finland
Oulujoki 62 D4 Swe. Uleälv. river C Finland
Ounasjoki 62 D3 river N Finland
Ounianga Kébir 54 C2 Borkou-Ennedi-Tibesti, N Chad
Oup see Auob
Oupeye 65 D6 Liège, E Belgium
Our 65 D6 river NW Europe
Ourense 70 C1 Cast. Orense, Lat. Aurium. Galicia, NW Spain
Ourique 70 B4 Beja, S Portugal
Ours, Grand Lac de l' see Great Bear Lake
Ourthe 65 D7 river E Belgium
Ouse 67 D5 river N England, United Kingdom
Outaouais see Ottawa
Outer Hebrides 66 B3 var. Western Isles. island group NW Scotland, United Kingdom
Outer Islands 57 G1 island group SW Seychelles Africa W Indian Ocean
Outes 70 B1 Galicia, NW Spain
Ouvéa 122 D5 island Îles Loyauté, NE New Caledonia
Ouyen 127 C6 Victoria, SE Australia
Ovalle 42 B3 Coquimbo, N Chile
Ovar 70 B2 Aveiro, N Portugal
Overflakkee 64 B4 island SW Netherlands
Overijse 65 C6 Vlaams Brabant, C Belgium
Oviedo 70 C1 anc. Asturias. Asturias, NW Spain
Ovilava see Wels
Ovruch 86 D1 Zhytomyrs'ka Oblast', N Ukraine
Owando 55 B5 prev. Fort Rousset. Cuvette, C Congo
Owase 109 C6 Mie, Honshū, SW Japan
Owatonna 23 F3 Minnesota, N USA
Owen Fracture Zone 118 B4 tectonic feature W Arabian Sea
Owen, Mount 129 C5 mountain South Island, New Zealand
Owensboro 18 B5 Kentucky, S USA
Owen Stanley Range 122 B3 mountain range S Papua New Guinea
Owerri 53 G5 Imo, S Nigeria
Owo 53 F5 Ondo, SW Nigeria
Owyhee River 24 C4 river Idaho/Oregon, NW USA
Oxford 129 C6 Canterbury, South Island, New Zealand
Oxford 67 D6 Lat. Oxonia. S England, United Kingdom
Oxkutzcab 29 H4 Yucatán, SE Mexico
Oxnard 25 B7 California, W USA
Oxonia see Oxford
Oxus see Amu Darya
Oyama 109 D5 Tochigi, Honshū, S Japan
Oyem 55 B5 Woleu-Ntem, N Gabon
Oyo 55 B6 Cuvette, C Congo
Oyo 53 F4 Oyo, W Nigeria
Ozark 20 D3 Alabama, S USA
Ozark Plateau 23 G5 plain Arkansas/Missouri, C USA
Ozarks, Lake of the 23 F5 reservoir Missouri, C USA
Ozbourn Seamount 130 D4 undersea feature W Pacific Ocean
Ózd 77 D6 Borsod-Abaúj-Zemplén, NE Hungary
Ozieri 75 A5 Sardegna, Italy, C Mediterranean Sea

P

Paamiut 60 B4 var. Pâmiut, Dan. Frederikshåb. S Greenland
Pa-an see Hpa-an
Pabianice 76 C4 Łodzkie, C Poland
Pabna 113 G4 Rajshahi, W Bangladesh
Pacaraima, Sierra/Pacaraim, Serra see Pakaraima Mountains
Pachuca 29 E4 var. Pachuca de Soto. Hidalgo, C Mexico
Pachuca de Soto see Pachuca
Pacific-Antarctic Ridge 132 B5 undersea feature S Pacific Ocean
Pacific Ocean 130 D3 ocean
Padalung see Phatthalung
Padang 116 B4 Sumatera, W Indonesia
Paderborn 72 B4 Nordrhein-Westfalen, NW Germany
Padma see Brahmaputra
Padma see Ganges
Padova 74 C2 Eng. Padua; anc. Patavium. Veneto, NE Italy
Padre Island 27 G5 island Texas, SW USA
Padua see Padova
Paducah 18 B5 Kentucky, S USA
Paeroa 128 D3 Waikato, North Island, New Zealand
Páfos 80 C5 var. Paphos. W Cyprus
Pag 78 A3 It. Pago. island Zadar, C Croatia
Page 26 B1 Arizona, SW USA
Pago see Pag
Pago Pago 123 F4 dependent territory capital (American Samoa) Tutuila, W American Samoa
Pahiatua 128 D4 Manawatu-Wanganui, North Island, New Zealand
Pahsien see Chongqing
Paide 84 D2 Ger. Weissenstein. Järvamaa, N Estonia
Paihia 128 D2 Northland, North Island, New Zealand
Päijänne 63 D5 lake S Finland
Paine, Cerro 43 A7 mountain S Chile
Painted Desert 26 B1 desert Arizona, SW USA
Paisance see Piacenza
Paisley 66 C4 W Scotland, United Kingdom
País Valenciano 71 F3 var. Valencia, Cat. València; anc. Valentia. autonomous community NE Spain
País Vasco 71 E1 cultural region N Spain
Paita 38 B3 Piura, NW Peru
Pakanbaru see Pekanbaru
Pakaraima Mountains 37 E3 var. Serra Pacaraim, Sierra Pacaraima. mountain range N South America
Pakistan 112 A2 off. Islamic Republic of Pakistan, var. Islami Jamhuriya e Pakistan. country S Asia
Pakistan, Islamic Republic of see Pakistan
Pakistan, Islami Jamhuriya e see Pakistan
Paknam see Samut Prakan
Pakokku 114 A3 Magway, C Myanmar (Burma)
Pak Phanang 115 C7 var. Ban Pak Phanang. Nakhon Si Thammarat, SW Thailand
Pakruojis 84 C4 Šiaulai, N Lithuania
Paks 77 C7 Tolna, S Hungary
Paksé see Pakxé
Pakxé 115 D5 var. Paksé. Champasak, S Laos
Palafrugell 71 G2 Cataluña, NE Spain
Palagruža 79 B5 It. Pelagosa. island SW Croatia
Palaiá Epídavros 83 C6 Pelopónnisos, S Greece
Palaiseau 68 D2 Essonne, N France
Palamós 71 G2 Cataluña, NE Spain
Palamuse 84 E2 Ger. Sankt-Bartholomäi. Jõgevamaa, E Estonia
Palanka see Bačka Palanka
Pālanpur 112 C4 Gujarāt, W India
Palantia see Palencia
Palapye 56 D3 Central, SE Botswana
Palau 122 A2 var. Belau. country W Pacific Ocean
Palawan 117 E2 island W Philippines
Palawan Passage 116 D2 passage W Philippines
Paldiski 84 D2 prev. Baltiski, Eng. Baltic Port, Ger. Baltischport. Harjumaa, NW Estonia
Palembang 116 B4 Sumatera, W Indonesia
Palencia 70 D2 anc. Palantia, Pallantia. Castilla-León, NW Spain
Palerme see Palermo
Palermo 75 C7 Fr. Palerme; anc. Panhormus, Panormus. Sicilia, Italy, C Mediterranean Sea
Pāli 112 C3 Rājasthān, N India
Palikir 122 C2 country capital (Micronesia) Pohnpei, E Micronesia
Palimé see Kpalimé
Palioúri, Akrotírio 82 C4 var. Akrotírio Kanestron. headland N Greece
Palk Strait 110 C3 strait India/Sri Lanka
Pallantia see Palencia
Palliser, Cape 129 D5 headland North Island, New Zealand
Palma 71 G3 var. Palma de Mallorca. Mallorca, Spain, W Mediterranean Sea
Palma del Río 70 D4 Andalucía, S Spain
Palma de Mallorca see Palma
Palmar Sur 31 E5 Puntarenas, SE Costa Rica
Palma Soriano 32 C3 Santiago de Cuba, E Cuba
Palm Beach 126 E1 New South Wales, E Australia
Palmer 132 A2 US research station Antarctica
Palmer Land 132 A3 physical region Antarctica
Palmerston 123 F4 island S Cook Islands
Palmerston see Darwin
Palmerston North 128 D4 Manawatu-Wanganui, North Island, New Zealand
Palmetto State, The see South Carolina
Palmi 75 D7 Calabria, SW Italy
Palmira 36 B3 Valle del Cauca, W Colombia
Palm Springs 25 D7 California, W USA
Palmyra see Tudmur
Palmyra Atoll 123 G2 US privately owned unincorporated territory C Pacific Ocean
Palo Alto 25 B6 California, W USA
Paloe see Denpasar, Bali, C Indonesia
Paloe see Palu
Palu 117 E4 prev. Paloe. Sulawesi, C Indonesia
Pamiers 69 B6 Ariège, S France
Pamir 101 F3 var. Daryā-ye Pāmīr, Taj. Dar"yoi Pomir. river Afghanistan/Tajikistan
Pāmīr, Daryā-ye see Pamir
Pamir/Pāmīr, Daryā-ye see Pamirs
Pamirs 101 F3 Pash. Daryā-ye Pāmīr, Rus. Pamir. mountain range C Asia
Pâmiut see Paamiut
Pamlico Sound 21 G1 sound North Carolina, SE USA
Pampa 27 E1 Texas, SW USA
Pampa Aullagas, Lago see Poopó, Lago
Pampas 42 C4 plain C Argentina
Pampeluna see Pamplona
Pamplona 36 C2 Norte de Santander, N Colombia
Pamplona 71 E1 Basq. Iruña, prev. Pampeluna; anc. Pompaelo. Navarra, N Spain
Panaji 110 B1 var. Pangim, Panjim, New Goa. state capital Goa, W India
Panamá 31 G4 var. Ciudad de Panama, Eng. Panama City. country capital (Panama) Panamá, C Panama
Panama 31 G5 off. Republic of Panama. country Central America
Panama Basin 13 C8 undersea feature E Pacific Ocean
Panama Canal 31 F4 canal E Panama
Panama City 20 D3 Florida, SE USA
Panama City see Panamá
Panamá, Golfo de 31 G5 var. Gulf of Panama. gulf S Panama
Panama, Gulf of see Panamá, Golfo de
Panama, Isthmus of see Panama, Istmo de
Panama, Istmo de 31 G4 Eng. Isthmus of Panama; prev. Isthmus of Darien. isthmus E Panama
Panama, Republic of see Panama
Panay Island 117 E2 island C Philippines
Pančevo 78 D3 Ger. Pantschowa, Hung. Pancsova. Vojvodina, N Serbia
Pancsova see Pančevo
Paneas see Bāniyās
Panevėžys 84 C4 Panevėžys, C Lithuania
Pangim see Panaji
Pangkalpinang 116 C4 Pulau Bangka, W Indonesia
Pang-Nga see Phang-Nga
Panhormus see Palermo
Panjim see Panaji
Panopolis see Akhmīm
Pánormos 83 C7 Kríti, Greece, E Mediterranean Sea
Panormus see Palermo
Pantanal 41 E3 var. Pantanalmato Grossense. swamp SW Brazil
Pantanalmato-Grossense see Pantanal
Pantelleria, Isola di 75 B7 island SW Italy
Pantschowa see Pančevo
Pánuco 29 E3 Veracruz-Llave, E Mexico
Pao-chi/Paoki see Baoji
Paola 80 B5 E Malta
Pao-shan see Baoshan
Pao-t'ou/Paotow see Baotou
Papagayo, Golfo de 30 C4 gulf NW Costa Rica
Papakura 128 D3 Auckland, North Island, New Zealand
Papantla 29 F4 var. Papantla de Olarte. Veracruz-Llave, E Mexico
Papantla de Olarte see Papantla
Papeete 123 H4 dependent territory capital (French Polynesia) Tahiti, W French Polynesia
Paphos see Páfos
Papilė 84 B3 Šiaulai, NW Lithuania
Papillion 23 F4 Nebraska, C USA
Papua 117 H4 var. Irian Barat, West Irian, West New Guinea, West Papua; prev. Dutch New Guinea, Irian Jaya, Netherlands New Guinea. province E Indonesia
Papua and New Guinea, Territory of see Papua New Guinea
Papua, Gulf of 122 B3 gulf S Papua New Guinea
Papua New Guinea 122 B3 off. Independent State of Papua New Guinea; prev. Territory of Papua and New Guinea. country NW Melanesia
Papua New Guinea, Independent State of see Papua New Guinea
Papuk 78 C3 mountain range NE Croatia
Pará 41 E2 off. Estado do Pará. state NE Brazil

Q

Qeshm Island – Romaniv

Qeshm Island/Qeshm, Jazīreh-ye see Qeshm
Qilian Shan 104 D3 var. Kilien Mountains. mountain range N China
Qimusseriarsuaq 60 C2 Dan. Melville Bugt, Eng. Melville Bay. bay NW Greenland
Qinā 50 B2 var. Qena; anc. Caene, Caenepolis. E Egypt
Qing see Qinghai
Qingdao 106 D4 var. Ching-Tao, Ch'ing-tao, Tsingtao, Tsintao, Ger. Tsingtau. Shandong, E China
Qinghai 104 C4 var. Chinghai, Koko Nor, Qing, Qinghai Sheng, Tsinghai. province C China
Qinghai Hu 104 D4 var. Ch'ing Hai, Tsing Hai, Mong. Koko Nor. lake C China
Qinghai Sheng see Qinghai
Qingzang Gaoyuan 104 B4 var. Xizang Gaoyuan, Eng. Plateau of Tibet. plateau W China
Qinhuangdao 106 D3 Hebei, E China
Qinzhou 106 B6 Guangxi Zhuangzu Zizhiqu, S China
Qiong see Hainan
Qiqihar 106 D2 var. Ch'i-ch'i-ha-erh, Tsitsihar; prev. Lungkiang. Heilongjiang, NE China
Qira 104 B4 Xinjiang Uygur Zizhiqu, NW China
Qita Ghazzah see Gaza Strip
Qitai 104 C3 Xinjiang Uygur Zizhiqu, NW China
Qīzān see Jīzān
Qizil Orda see Kzylorda
Qizil Qum/Qizilqum see Kyzyl Kum
Qizilrabot 101 G3 Rus. Kyzylrabot. SE Tajikistan
Qogir Feng see K2
Qom 98 C3 var. Kum, Qum. Qom, N Iran
Qomolangma Feng see Everest, Mount
Qomul see Hami
Qo'qon 101 F2 var. Khokand, Rus. Kokand. Farg'ona Viloyati, E Uzbekistan
Qorveh 98 C3 var. Qerveh, Qurveh. Kordestān, W Iran
Qostanay/Qostanay Oblysy see Kostanay
Qoubaïyât 96 B4 var. Al Qubayyāt. N Lebanon
Qoussantina see Constantine
Quang Ngai 115 E5 var. Quangngai, Quang Nghia. Quang Ngai, C Vietnam
Quangngai see Quang Ngai
Quang Nghia see Quang Ngai
Quan Long see Ca Mau
Quanzhou 106 D6 var. Ch'uan-chou, Tsinkiang; prev. Chin-chiang. Fujian, SE China
Quanzhou 106 C6 Guangxi Zhuangzu Zizhiqu, S China
Qu'Appelle 15 F5 river Saskatchewan, S Canada
Quarles, Pegunungan 117 E4 mountain range Sulawesi, C Indonesia
Quarnero see Kvarner
Quartu Sant' Elena 75 A6 Sardegna, Italy, C Mediterranean Sea
Quba 95 H2 Rus. Kuba. N Azerbaijan
Qubba see Ba'qūbah
Québec 17 E4 var. Quebec. province capital Québec, SE Canada
Québec 16 D3 var. Quebec. province SE Canada
Queen Charlotte Islands 14 C5 Fr. Îles de la Reine-Charlotte. island group British Columbia, SW Canada
Queen Charlotte Sound 14 C5 sea area British Columbia, W Canada
Queen Elizabeth Islands 15 E1 Fr. Îles de la Reine-Élisabeth. island group Nunavut, N Canada
Queensland 126 B4 state N Australia
Queenstown 129 B7 Otago, South Island, New Zealand
Queenstown 56 D5 Eastern Cape, S South Africa
Quelimane 57 E3 var. Kilimane, Kilmain, Quilimane. Zambézia, NE Mozambique
Quelpart see Jeju-do
Quepos 31 E4 Puntarenas, S Costa Rica
Que Que see Kwekwe
Quera see Chur
Querétaro 29 E4 Querétaro de Arteaga, C Mexico
Quesada 31 E4 var. Ciudad Quesada, San Carlos. Alajuela, N Costa Rica
Quetta 112 B2 Baluchistān, SW Pakistan
Quetzalcoalco see Coatzacoalcos
Quezaltenango 30 A2 var. Quetzaltenango. Quezaltenango, W Guatemala
Quibdó 36 A3 Chocó, W Colombia
Quilimane see Quelimane
Quillabamba 38 D3 Cusco, C Peru
Quilon see Kollam
Quimper 68 A3 anc. Quimper Corentin. Finistère, NW France
Quimper Corentin see Quimper
Quimperlé 68 A3 Finistère, NW France
Quincy 18 A4 Illinois, N USA
Qui Nhon/Quinhon see Quy Nhơn
Quissico 57 E4 Inhambane, S Mozambique
Quito 38 B1 country capital (Ecuador) Pichincha, N Ecuador
Qulyndy Zhazyghy see Kulunda Steppe
Qum see Qom
Qurein see Al Kuwayt
Qŭrghonteppa 101 E3 Rus. Kurgan-Tyube. SW Tajikistan
Qurlurtuuq see Kugluktuk
Qurveh see Qorveh
Quşayr see Al Quşayr
Quxar see Lhazê
Quy Nhơn 115 E5 var. Quinhon, Qui Nhon. Binh Đinh, C Vietnam
Qyteti Stalin see Kuçovë
Qyzylorda see Kzylorda

R

Raab 78 B1 Hung. Rába. river Austria/Hungary
Raab see Rába
Raab see Győr
Raahe 62 D4 Swe. Brahestad. Oulu, W Finland
Raalte 64 D3 Overijssel, E Netherlands
Raamsdonksveer 64 C4 Noord-Brabant, S Netherlands
Raasiku 84 D2 Ger. Rasik. Harjumaa, NW Estonia
Rába 77 B7 Ger. Raab. river Austria/Hungary
Rába see Raab
Rabat 48 C2 var. al Dar al Baida. country capital (Morocco) NW Morocco
Rabat 80 B5 W Malta
Rabat see Victoria
Rabbah Ammon/Rabbath Ammon see 'Ammān
Rabinal 30 B2 Baja Verapaz, C Guatemala
Rabka 77 D5 Małopolskie, S Poland
Râbniţa see Rîbniţa
Rabyanah Ramlat 49 G4 var. Rebiana Sand Sea, Şahrā' Rabyānah. desert SE Libya
Rabyānah, Şahrā' see Rabyānah, Ramlat
Răcari see Durankulak
Race, Cape 17 H3 headland Newfoundland, Newfoundland and Labrador, E Canada
Rach Gia 115 D6 Kiên Giang, S Vietnam
Rach Gia, Vinh 115 D6 bay S Vietnam
Racine 18 B3 Wisconsin, N USA
Rácz-Becse see Bečej
Rădăuţi 86 C3 Ger. Radautz, Hung. Rádóc. Suceava, N Romania
Radautz see Rădăuţi
Rádeyilikóé see Fort Good Hope
Rádóc see Rădăuţi
Radom 76 D4 Mazowieckie, C Poland
Radomsko 76 D4 Rus. Novoradomsk. Łódzkie, C Poland
Radomyshl' 86 D2 Zhytomyrs'ka Oblast', N Ukraine
Radoviš 79 E6 prev. Radovište. E Macedonia
Radovište see Radoviš
Radviliškis 84 B4 Šiaulai, N Lithuania
Radzyń Podlaski 76 E4 Lubelskie, E Poland
Rae-Edzo see Edzo
Raetihi 128 D4 Manawatu-Wanganui, North Island, New Zealand
Rafa see Rafah
Rafaela 42 C3 Santa Fe, E Argentina
Rafah 97 A7 var. Rafa, Rafaḥ, Heb. Rafiaḥ, Raphiah. SW Gaza Strip
Rafḩah 98 B4 Al Ḩudūd ash Shamālīyah, N Saudi Arabia
Rafiaḥ see Rafah
Raga 51 A5 W Bahr el Ghazal, W South Sudan
Ragged Island Range 32 C2 island group S Bahamas
Ragnit see Neman
Ragusa 75 C7 Sicilia, Italy, C Mediterranean Sea
Ragusa see Dubrovnik
Rahachow 85 D7 Rus. Rogachëv. Homyel'skaya Voblasts', SE Belarus
Rahaeng see Tak
Rahaţ, Ḩarrat 99 B5 lava flow W Saudi Arabia
Rahīmyār Khān 112 C3 Punjab, SE Pakistan
Rahovec 79 D5 Serb. Orahovac. W Kosovo
Raiatea 123 G4 island Îles Sous le Vent, W French Polynesia
Rāichūr 110 C1 Karnātaka, C India
Raidestos see Tekirdağ
Rainier, Mount 12 A4 volcano Washington, NW USA
Rainy Lake 16 A4 lake Canada/USA
Raipur 113 E4 Chhattīsgarh, C India
Rājahmundry 113 E5 Andhra Pradesh, E India
Rajang see Rajang, Batang
Rajang, Batang 116 D3 var. Rajang. river East Malaysia
Rājapālaiyam 110 C3 Tamil Nādu, SE India
Rājasthān 112 C3 cultural region NW India
Rājkot 112 C4 Gujarāt, W India
Rāj Nāndgaon 113 E4 Chhattīsgarh, C India
Rajshahi 113 G3 prev. Rampur Boalia. Rajshahi, W Bangladesh
Rakahanga 123 F3 atoll N Cook Islands
Rakaia 129 B6 river South Island, New Zealand
Rakka see Ar Raqqah
Rakke 84 E2 Lääne-Virumaa, NE Estonia
Rakvere 84 E2 Ger. Wesenberg. Lääne-Virumaa, N Estonia
Raleigh 21 F1 state capital North Carolina, SE USA
Ralik Chain 122 D1 island group Ralik Chain, W Marshall Islands
Ramadi see Ar Ramādī
Râmnicul-Sărat see Râmnicu Sărat
Râmnicu Sărat 86 C4 prev. Râmnicul-Sărat, Rîmnicu-Sărat. Buzău, E Romania
Râmnicu Vâlcea 86 B4 prev. Rîmnicu Vîlcea. Vâlcea, C Romania
Rampur Boalia see Rajshahi
Ramree Island 114 A4 island W Myanmar (Burma)
Ramtha see Ar Ramthā
Rancagua 42 B4 Libertador, C Chile
Rānchi 113 F4 Jhārkhand, N India
Randers 63 B7 Århus, C Denmark
Ráneš see Ringvassøya
Rangiora 129 C6 Canterbury, South Island, New Zealand
Rangitikei 128 D4 river North Island, New Zealand
Rangoon see Yangon
Rangpur 113 G3 Rajshahi, N Bangladesh
Rankin Inlet 15 G3 Nunavut, C Canada
Rankovićevo see Kraljevo
Ranong 115 B6 Ranong, SW Thailand
Rapa Nui see Pascua, Isla de
Raphiah see Rafah
Rapid City 22 D3 South Dakota, N USA
Rāpina 84 E3 Ger. Rappin. Põlvamaa, SE Estonia
Rapla 84 D2 Ger. Rappel. Raplamaa, NW Estonia
Rappel see Rapla
Rappin see Räpina
Rarotonga 123 G5 island S Cook Islands, C Pacific Ocean
Ras al 'Ain see Ra's al 'Ayn
Ra's al 'Ayn 96 D1 var. Ras al'Ain. Al Ḩasakah, N Syria
Ra's an Naqb 97 B7 Ma'ān, S Jordan
Raseiniai 84 B4 Kaunas, C Lithuania
Rasht 98 C2 var. Resht. Gīlān, NW Iran
Rasik see Raasiku
Râşnov 86 C4 prev. Rişno, Rozsnyó, Hung. Barcarozsnyó. Braşov, C Romania
Rastenburg see Kętrzyn
Ratak Chain 122 D1 island group Ratak Chain, E Marshall Islands
Ratän 63 C5 Jämtland, C Sweden
Rat Buri see Ratchaburi
Ratchaburi 115 C5 var. Rat Buri. Ratchaburi, W Thailand
Ratisbon/Ratisbona/Ratisbonne see Regensburg
Rat Islands 14 A2 island group Aleutian Islands, Alaska, USA
Ratlām 112 D4 prev. Rutlam. Madhya Pradesh, C India
Ratnapura 110 D4 Sabaragamuwa Province, S Sri Lanka
Raton 26 D1 New Mexico, SW USA
Rättvik 63 C5 Dalarna, C Sweden
Raudhatain see Ar Rawḑatayn
Raufarhöfn 61 E4 Nordhurland Eystra, NE Iceland
Raukawa see Cook Strait
Raukumara Range 128 E3 mountain range North Island, New Zealand
Rāulakela see Rāurkela
Rauma 63 D5 Swe. Raumo. Länsi-Suomi, SW Finland
Raumo see Rauma
Rāurkela 113 F4 var. Rāulakela, Rourkela. Odisha, E India
Ravenna 74 C3 Emilia-Romagna, N Italy
Ravi 112 C2 river India/Pakistan
Rāwalpindi 112 C1 Punjab, NE Pakistan
Rawa Mazowiecka 76 D4 Łódzkie, C Poland
Rawicz 76 C4 Ger. Rawitsch. Wielkopolskie, C Poland
Rawitsch see Rawicz
Rawlins 22 C3 Wyoming, C USA
Rawson 43 C6 Chubut, SE Argentina
Rayak 96 B4 var. Rayaq, Riyāq. E Lebanon
Rayaq see Rayak
Rayong 115 C5 Rayong, S Thailand
Razazah, Buhayrat ar 98 B3 var. Baḩr al Milḩ. lake C Iraq
Razdolnoye see Rozdol'ne
Razelm, Lacul see Razim, Lacul
Razgrad 82 D2 Razgrad, N Bulgaria
Razim, Lacul 86 D5 prev. Lacul Razelm. lagoon NW Black Sea
Reading 67 D7 S England, United Kingdom
Reading 19 F4 Pennsylvania, NE USA
Realicó 42 C4 La Pampa, C Argentina
Reăng Kesei 115 D5 Bātdâmbâng, W Cambodia
Greater Antarctica see East Antarctica
Rebecca, Lake 125 C6 lake Western Australia
Rebiana Sand Sea see Rabyānah, Ramlat
Rebun-to 108 C2 island NE Japan
Rechitsa see Rechytsa
Rechytsa 85 D7 Rus. Rechitsa. Brestskaya Voblasts', SW Belarus
Recife 41 G2 prev. Pernambuco. state capital Pernambuco, E Brazil
Recklinghausen 72 A4 Nordrhein-Westfalen, W Germany
Recogne 65 C7 Luxembourg, SE Belgium
Reconquista 42 D3 Santa Fe, C Argentina
Red Deer 15 E5 Alberta, SW Canada
Redding 25 B5 California, W USA
Redon 68 B4 Ille-et-Vilaine, NW France
Red River 23 E1 river Canada/USA
Red River 114 C2 var. Yuan, Chin. Yuan Jiang, Vtn. Sông Hông Hà. river China/Vietnam
Red River 13 C6 river S USA
Red River 20 B3 river Louisiana, S USA
Red Sea 50 C3 var. Sinus Arabicus. sea Africa/Asia
Red Wing 23 G2 Minnesota, N USA
Reefton 129 C5 West Coast, South Island, New Zealand
Reese River 25 C5 river Nevada, W USA
Refahiye 95 E3 Erzincan, C Turkey
Regensburg 73 C6 Eng. Ratisbon, Fr. Ratisbonne, hist. Ratisbona; anc. Castra Regina, Reginum. Bayern, SE Germany
Regenstauf 73 C6 Bayern, SE Germany
Rēgestān 100 D5 prev. Rīgestān, var. Registan. desert region S Afghanistan
Reggane 48 D3 C Algeria
Reggio see Reggio nell'Emilia
Reggio Calabria see Reggio di Calabria
Reggio di Calabria 75 D7 var. Reggio Calabria, Gk. Rhegion; anc. Regium, Rhegium. Calabria, SW Italy
Reggio Emilia see Reggio nell'Emilia
Reggio nell'Emilia 74 B2 var. Reggio Emilia, abbrev. Reggio; anc. Regium Lepidum. Emilia-Romagna, N Italy
Reghin 86 C4 Ger. Sächsisch-Reen, Hung. Szászrégen; prev. Reghinul Săsesc, Ger. Sächsisch-Regen. Mureş, C Romania
Reghinul Săsesc see Reghin
Regina 15 F5 province capital Saskatchewan, S Canada
Reginum see Regensburg
Registan see Rēgestān
Regium see Reggio di Calabria
Regium Lepidum see Reggio nell'Emilia
Rehoboth 56 B3 Hardap, C Namibia
Rehovot 97 A6; prev. Reḩovot. Central, C Israel
Reḩovot see Rehovot
Reichenau see Bogatynia, Poland
Reichenberg see Liberec
Reid 125 D6 Western Australia
Reikjavik see Reykjavík
Ré, Île de 68 A4 island W France
Reims 68 D3 Eng. Rheims; anc. Durocortorum, Remi. Marne, N France
Reindeer Lake 15 F4 lake Manitoba/Saskatchewan, C Canada
Reine-Charlotte, Îles de la see Queen Charlotte Islands
Reine-Élisabeth, Îles de la see Queen Elizabeth Islands
Reinga, Cape 128 C1 headland North Island, New Zealand
Reinosa 70 D1 Cantabria, N Spain
Reka see Rijeka
Rekhovot see Rehovot
Reliance 15 F4 Northwest Territories, C Canada
Remi see Reims
Rendina see Rentína
Rendsburg 72 B2 Schleswig-Holstein, N Germany
Rengat 116 B4 Sumatera, W Indonesia
Reni 86 D4 Odes'ka Oblast', SW Ukraine
Rennell 122 C4 var. Mu Nggava. island S Solomon Islands
Rennes 68 B3 Bret. Roazon; anc. Condate. Ille-et-Vilaine, NW France
Reno 25 C5 Nevada, W USA
Renqiu 106 C4 Hebei, E China
Rentína 83 B5 var. Rendina. Thessalía, C Greece
Reps see Rupea
Repulse Bay 15 G3 Northwest Territories, N Canada
Reschitza see Reşiţa
Resht see Rasht
Resicabánya see Reşiţa
Resistencia 42 D3 Chaco, NE Argentina
Reşiţa 86 A4 Ger. Reschitza, Hung. Resicabánya. Caraş-Severin, W Romania
Resolute 15 F2 Inuit Qausuittuq. Cornwallis Island, Nunavut, N Canada
Resolution Island 17 E1 island Nunavut, NE Canada
Resolution Island 129 A7 island SW New Zealand
Réunion 57 H4 off. La Réunion. French overseas department W Indian Ocean
Réunion 119 B5 island W Indian Ocean
Reus 71 F2 Cataluña, E Spain
Reutlingen 73 B6 Baden-Württemberg, S Germany
Reuver 65 D5 Limburg, SE Netherlands
Reval/Revel see Tallinn
Revillagigedo Island 28 B5 island Alexander Archipelago, Alaska, USA
Rexburg 24 E3 Idaho, NW USA
Reyes 39 F3 Beni, NW Bolivia
Rey, Isla del 31 G5 island Archipiélago de las Perlas, SE Panama
Reykjanes Basin 60 C5 var. Irminger Basin. undersea basin N Atlantic Ocean
Reykjanes Ridge 58 A1 undersea ridge N Atlantic Ocean
Reykjavík 61 E5 var. Reikjavik. country capital (Iceland) Höfudhborgarsvaedhi, W Iceland
Reynosa 29 E2 Tamaulipas, C Mexico
Reẓā'īyeh, Daryācheh-ye see Orūmīyeh, Daryācheh-ye
Rezé 68 A4 Loire-Atlantique, NW France
Rēzekne 84 D4 Ger. Rositten; prev. Rus. Rezhitsa. Rēzekne, SE Latvia
Rezhitsa see Rēzekne
Rezovo 82 E3 Turk. Rezve. Burgas, E Bulgaria
Rezve see Rezovo
Rhaedestus see Tekirdağ
Rhegion/Rhegium see Reggio di Calabria
Rheims see Reims
Rhein see Rhine
Rheine 72 A3 var. Rheine in Westfalen. Nordrhein-Westfalen, NW Germany
Rheine in Westfalen see Rheine
Rheinisches Schiefergebirge 73 A5 var. Rhine State Uplands, Eng. Rhenish Slate Mountains. mountain range W Germany
Rhenish Slate Mountains see Rheinisches Schiefergebirge
Rhin see Rhine
Rhine 58 D4 Dut. Rijn, Fr. Rhin, Ger. Rhein. river W Europe
Rhinelander 18 B2 Wisconsin, N USA
Rhine State Uplands see Rheinisches Schiefergebirge
Rho 74 B2 Lombardia, N Italy
Rhode Island 19 G3 off. State of Rhode Island and Providence Plantations, also known as Little Rhody, Ocean State. state NE USA
Rhodes 83 E7 var. Ródhos, Eng. Rhodes, It. Rodi; anc. Rhodos. island Dodekánisa, Greece, Aegean Sea
Rhodes see Ródos
Rhodesia see Zimbabwe
Rhodope Mountains 82 C3 var. Rodhópi Óri, Bul. Rhodope Planina, Rodopi, Gk. Orosirá Rodhópis, Turk. Dospad Dagh. mountain range Bulgaria/Greece
Rhodope Planina see Rhodope Mountains
Rhône 58 C4 river France/Switzerland
Rhum 66 B3 var. Rum. island W Scotland, United Kingdom
Ribble 67 D5 river NW England, United Kingdom
Ribeira see Santa Uxía de Ribeira
Ribeirão Preto 41 F4 São Paulo, S Brazil
Riberalta 39 F2 Beni, N Bolivia
Rîbniţa 86 D3 var. Râbniţa, Rus. Rybnitsa. NE Moldova
Rice Lake 18 A2 Wisconsin, N USA
Richard Toll 52 B3 N Senegal
Richfield 22 B4 Utah, W USA
Richland 24 C2 Washington, NW USA
Richmond 129 C5 Tasman, South Island, New Zealand
Richmond 18 C5 Kentucky, S USA
Richmond 19 E5 state capital Virginia, NE USA
Richmond Range 129 C5 mountain range South Island, New Zealand
Ricobayo, Embalse de 70 C2 reservoir NW Spain
Ricomagus see Riom
Ridder 92 D4 Kaz. Leningor, prev. Leninogorsk. Vostochnyy Kazakhstan, E Kazakhstan
Ridgecrest 25 C7 California, W USA
Ried see Ried im Innkreis
Ried im Innkreis 73 D6 var. Ried. Oberösterreich, NW Austria
Riemst 65 D6 Limburg, NE Belgium
Riesa 72 D4 Sachsen, E Germany
Rift Valley see Great Rift Valley
Riga 84 C3 Eng. Riga. country capital (Latvia) Riga, C Latvia
Rigaer Bucht see Riga, Gulf of
Riga, Gulf of 84 C3 Est. Liivi Laht, Ger. Rigaer Bucht, Latv. Rīgas Jūras Līcis, Rus. Rizhskiy Zaliv; prev. Est. Riia Laht. gulf Estonia/Latvia
Rīgas Jūras Līcis see Riga, Gulf of
Rīgestān see Rēgestān
Riia Laht see Riga, Gulf of
Riihimäki 63 D5 Etelä-Suomi, S Finland
Rijeka 78 A2 Ger. Sankt Veit am Flaum, It. Fiume, Slvn. Reka; anc. Tarsatica. Primorje-Gorski Kotar, NW Croatia
Rijn see Rhine
Rijssel see Lille
Rijssen 64 E3 Overijssel, E Netherlands
Rimah, Wadi ar 98 B4 var. Wādī ar Rummah. dry watercourse C Saudi Arabia
Rimini 74 C3 anc. Ariminum. Emilia-Romagna, N Italy
Rîmnicu-Sărat see Râmnicu Sărat
Rîmnicu Vîlcea see Râmnicu Vâlcea
Rimouski 17 E4 Québec, SE Canada
Ringebu 63 B5 Oppland, S Norway
Ringen see Rõngu
Ringkøbing Fjord 63 A7 fjord W Denmark
Ringvassøya 62 C2 Lapp. Ráneš. island N Norway
Rio see Rio de Janeiro
Riobamba 38 B1 Chimborazo, C Ecuador
Rio Branco 34 B3 state capital Acre, W Brazil
Rio Branco, Território de see Roraima
Río Bravo 29 E2 Tamaulipas, C Mexico
Río Cuarto 42 C4 Córdoba, C Argentina
Rio de Janeiro 41 F4 var. Rio. state capital Rio de Janeiro, SE Brazil
Río Gallegos 43 B7 var. Gallegos, Puerto Gallegos. Santa Cruz, S Argentina
Rio Grande 41 E5 var. São Pedro do Rio Grande do Sul. Rio Grande do Sul, S Brazil
Río Grande 28 D3 Zacatecas, C Mexico
Rio Grande do Norte 41 G2 off. Estado do Rio Grande do Norte. state E Brazil
Rio Grande do Norte 41 G2 off. Estado do Rio Grande do Norte. region E Brazil
Rio Grande do Norte, Estado do see Rio Grande do Norte
Rio Grande do Sul 41 E5 off. Estado do Rio Grande do Sul. region S Brazil
Rio Grande do Sul 41 E5 off. Estado do Rio Grande do Sul. state S Brazil
Rio Grande do Sul, Estado do see Rio Grande do Sul
Rio Grande Plateau see Rio Grande Rise
Rio Grande Rise 35 E6 var. Rio Grande Plateau. undersea plateau SW Atlantic Ocean
Ríohacha 36 B1 La Guajira, N Colombia
Río Lagartos 29 H3 Yucatán, SE Mexico
Riom 69 C5 anc. Ricomagus. Puy-de-Dôme, C France
Río Verde 29 E4 var. Rioverde. San Luis Potosí, C Mexico
Rioverde see Río Verde
Ripoll 71 G2 Cataluña, NE Spain
Rishiri-to 108 C2 var. Risiri Tô. island NE Japan
Risiri Tô see Rishiri-tō
Rişno see Râşnov
Risti 84 D2 Ger. Kreuz. Läänemaa, W Estonia
Rivas 30 D4 Rivas, SW Nicaragua
Rivera 42 D3 Rivera, NE Uruguay
River Falls 18 A2 Wisconsin, N USA
Riverside 25 C7 California, W USA
Riverton 129 A7 Southland, South Island, New Zealand
Riverton 22 C3 Wyoming, C USA
Rivière-du-Loup 17 E4 Québec, SE Canada
Rivne 86 C2 Pol. Równe, Rus. Rovno. Rivnens'ka Oblast', NW Ukraine
Rivoli 74 A2 Piemonte, NW Italy
Riyadh/Riyāḑ, Minţaqat ar see Ar Riyāḑ
Riyāq see Rayak
Rize 95 E2 Rize, NE Turkey
Rizhao 106 D4 Shandong, E China
Rizhskiy Zaliv see Riga, Gulf of
Rkîz 52 C3 Trarza, W Mauritania
Road Town 33 F3 dependent territory capital (British Virgin Islands) Tortola, C British Virgin Islands
Roanne 69 C5 anc. Rodunma. Loire, E France
Roanoke 19 E5 Virginia, NE USA
Roanoke River 21 F1 river North Carolina/Virginia, SE USA
Roatán 30 C2 var. Coxen Hole, Coxin Hole. Islas de la Bahía, N Honduras
Roat Kampuchea see Cambodia
Roazon see Rennes
Robbie Ridge 121 E3 undersea ridge W Pacific Ocean
Robert Williams see Caála
Robinson Range 125 B5 mountain range Western Australia
Robson, Mount 15 E5 mountain British Columbia, SW Canada
Robstown 27 G4 Texas, SW USA
Roca Partida, Isla 28 B5 island W Mexico
Rocas, Atol das 41 G2 island E Brazil
Rochefort 65 C7 Namur, SE Belgium
Rochefort 68 B4 var. Rochefort sur Mer. Charente-Maritime, W France
Rochefort sur Mer see Rochefort
Rochester 23 G3 Minnesota, N USA
Rochester 19 G2 New Hampshire, NE USA
Rocheuses, Montagnes/Rockies see Rocky Mountains
Rockall Bank 58 B2 undersea bank N Atlantic Ocean
Rockall Trough 58 B2 trough N Atlantic Ocean
Rockdale 126 E2 Texas, SW USA
Rockford 18 B3 Illinois, N USA
Rockhampton 126 D4 Queensland, E Australia
Rock Hill 21 E1 South Carolina, SE USA
Rockingham 125 A6 Western Australia
Rock Island 18 B3 Illinois, N USA
Rock Sound 32 C1 Eleuthera Island, C Bahamas
Rock Springs 22 C3 Wyoming, C USA
Rockstone 37 F3 C Guyana
Rocky Mount 21 F1 North Carolina, SE USA
Rocky Mountains 12 B4 var. Rockies, Fr. Montagnes Rocheuses. mountain range Canada/USA
Roden 64 E2 Drenthe, NE Netherlands
Rodez 69 C5 anc. Segodunum. Aveyron, S France
Rodhópi Óri see Rhodope Mountains
Ródhos/Rodi see Ródos
Rodopi see Rhodope Mountains
Rodosto see Tekirdağ
Rodunma see Roanne
Roermond 65 D5 Limburg, SE Netherlands
Roeselare 65 A6 Fr. Roulers; prev. Rousselaere. West-Vlaanderen, W Belgium
Rogachëv see Rahachow
Rogatica 78 C4 Republika Srpska, SE Bosnia and Herzegovina
Rogers 20 A1 Arkansas, C USA
Roger Simpson Island see Abemama
Roi Ed see Roi Et
Roi Et 115 D5 var. Muang Roi Et, Roi Ed. Roi Et, E Thailand
Roja 84 C2 Talsi, NW Latvia
Rokiškis 84 C4 Panevėžys, NE Lithuania
Rokycany 77 A5 Ger. Rokytzan. Plzeňský Kraj, W Czech Republic
Rokytzan see Rokycany
Rôlas, Ilha das 54 E2 island S Sao Tome and Principe, Africa, E Atlantic Ocean
Rolla 23 G5 Missouri, C USA
Röm see Rømø
Roma 74 C4 Eng. Rome. country capital (Italy) Lazio, C Italy
Roma 127 D5 Queensland, E Australia
Roman 82 C2 Vratsa, NW Bulgaria
Roman 86 C4 Hung. Románvásár. Neamţ, NE Romania
Romania 86 B4 Bul. Rumŭniya, Ger. Rumänien, Hung. Románia, Rom. România, SCr. Rumunjska, Ukr. Rumuniya, prev. Republica Socialistă România, Roumania, Rumania, Socialist Republic of Romania, prev.Rom. Romînia. country SE Europe
România, Republica Socialistă see Romania
Romania, Socialist Republic of see Romania
Romaniv 87 F3 Rus. Dzerzhinsk, prev. Dniprodzerzhyns'k, prev. Kamenskoye. Dnipropetrovs'ka Oblast', E Ukraine

Románvásár – San Cristóbal de Las Casas

Románvásár see Roman
Rome 20 D2 Georgia, SE USA
Rome see Roma
Romînia see Romania
Romny 87 F2 Sums'ka Oblast', NE Ukraine
Rømø 63 A7 Ger. Röm. island SW Denmark
Roncador, Serra do 34 D4 mountain range C Brazil
Ronda 70 D5 Andalucía, S Spain
Rondônia 40 D3 off. Estado de Rondônia; prev. Território de Rondônia. state W Brazil
Rondônia 40 D3 off. Estado de Rondônia; prev. Território de Rondônia. region W Brazil
Rondônia, Estado de see Rondônia
Rondônia, Território de see Rondônia
Rondonópolis 41 E3 Mato Grosso, W Brazil
Rongelap Atoll 122 D1 var. Rönlap. atoll Ralik Chain, NW Marshall Islands
Rõngu 84 D3 Ger. Ringen. Tartumaa, SE Estonia
Rönlap see Rongelap Atoll
Rønne 63 B8 Bornholm, E Denmark
Ronne Ice Shelf 132 A3 ice shelf Antarctica
Roosendaal 65 C5 Noord-Brabant, S Netherlands
Roosevelt Island 132 B4 island Antarctica
Roraima 40 D1 off. Estado de Roraima; prev. Território de Rio Branco, Território de Roraima. region N Brazil
Roraima 40 D1 off. Estado de Roraima; prev. Território de Rio Branco, Território de Roraima. state N Brazil
Roraima, Estado de see Roraima
Roraima, Mount 37 E3 mountain N South America
Roraima, Território de see Roraima
Røros 63 B5 Sør-Trøndelag, S Norway
Ross 129 B6 West Coast, South Island, New Zealand
Rosa, Lake 32 D2 lake Great Inagua, S Bahamas
Rosario 42 D4 Santa Fe, C Argentina
Rosario 42 D2 San Pedro, C Paraguay
Rosario see Rosarito
Rosarito 28 A1 var. Rosario. Baja California Norte, NW Mexico
Roscianum see Rossano
Roscommon 18 C2 Michigan, N USA
Roseau 33 G4 prev. Charlotte Town. country capital (Dominica) SW Dominica
Roseburg 24 B4 Oregon, NW USA
Rosenau see Rožňava
Rosenberg 27 G4 Texas, SW USA
Rosenberg see Ružomberok, Slovakia
Rosengarten 72 B3 Niedersachsen, N Germany
Rosenheim 73 C6 Bayern, S Germany
Rosia 71 H5 W Gibraltar Europe
Rosia Bay 71 H5 bay SW Gibraltar Europe W Mediterranean Sea Atlantic Ocean
Roșiori de Vede 86 B5 Teleorman, S Romania
Rositten see Rēzekne
Roslavl' 89 A5 Smolenskaya Oblast', W Russian Federation
Rosmalen 64 C4 Noord-Brabant, S Netherlands
Rossano 75 E6 anc. Roscianum. Calabria, SW Italy
Ross Ice Shelf 132 B4 ice shelf Antarctica
Rossiyskaya Federatsiya see Russian Federation
Rosso 52 B3 Trarza, SW Mauritania
Rossosh' 89 B6 Voronezhskaya Oblast', W Russian Federation
Ross Sea 132 B4 sea Antarctica
Rostak see Ar Rustāq
Rostock 72 C2 Mecklenburg-Vorpommern, NE Germany
Rostov see Rostov-na-Donu
Rostov-na-Donu 89 B7 var. Rostov, Eng. Rostov-on-Don. Rostovskaya Oblast', SW Russian Federation
Rostov-on-Don see Rostov-na-Donu
Roswell 26 D2 New Mexico, SW USA
Rota 122 B1 island S Northern Mariana Islands
Rotcher Island see Tamana
Rothera 132 A2 UK research station Antarctica
Rotomagus see Rouen
Rotorua 128 D3 Bay of Plenty, North Island, New Zealand
Rotorua, Lake 128 D3 lake North Island, New Zealand
Rotterdam 64 C4 Zuid-Holland, SW Netherlands
Rottweil 73 B6 Baden-Württemberg, S Germany
Rotuma 123 E4 island NW Fiji Oceania S Pacific Ocean
Roubaix 68 C2 Nord, N France
Rouen 68 C3 anc. Rotomagus. Seine-Maritime, N France
Roulers see Roeselare
Roumania see Romania
Round Rock 27 G3 Texas, SW USA
Rourkela see Rāurkela
Rousselaere see Roeselare
Roussillon 69 C6 cultural region S France
Rouyn-Noranda 16 D4 Québec, SE Canada
Rovaniemi 62 D3 Lappi, N Finland
Rovigno see Rovinj
Rovigo 74 C2 Veneto, NE Italy
Rovinj 78 A3 It. Rovigno. Istra, NW Croatia
Rovno see Rivne
Rovuma, Rio 57 F2 var. Ruvuma. river Mozambique/Tanzania
Rovuma, Rio see Ruvuma
Równe see Rivne
Roxas City 117 E2 Panay Island, C Philippines
Royale, Isle 18 B1 island Michigan, N USA
Royan 69 B5 Charente-Maritime, W France
Rozdol'ne 87 F4 Rus. Razdolnoye. Respublika Krym, S Ukraine
Rožňava 77 D6 Ger. Rosenau, Hung. Rozsnyó. Košický Kraj, E Slovakia
Rózsahegy see Ružomberok
Rozsnyó see Râșnov, Romania
Rozsnyó see Rožňava, Slovakia
Ruanda see Rwanda
Ruapehu, Mount 128 D4 volcano North Island, New Zealand
Ruapuke Island 129 B8 island SW New Zealand
Ruatoria 128 E3 Gisborne, North Island, New Zealand
Ruawai 128 D2 Northland, North Island, New Zealand
Rubezhnoye see Rubizhne
Rubizhne 87 H3 Rus. Rubezhnoye. Luhans'ka Oblast', E Ukraine
Ruby Mountains 25 D5 mountain range Nevada, W USA
Rucava 84 B3 Liepāja, SW Latvia
Rudensk see Rudzyensk
Rudiškės 85 B5 Vilnius, S Lithuania
Rudnik see Dolni Chiflik
Rudny see Rudnyy
Rudnyy 92 C4 var. Rudny. Kostanay, N Kazakhstan
Rudolf, Lake see Turkana, Lake
Rudolfswert see Novo mesto
Rudzyensk 85 C6 Rus. Rudensk. Minskaya Voblasts', C Belarus
Rufiji 51 C7 river E Tanzania
Rufino 42 C4 Santa Fe, C Argentina
Rugāji 84 D4 Balvi, E Latvia
Rügen 72 D2 headland NE Germany
Ruggell 72 E1 N Liechtenstein Europe
Ruhja see Rūjiena
Ruhnu 84 C2 var. Ruhnu Saar, Swe. Runö. island SW Estonia
Ruhnu Saar see Ruhnu
Rujen see Rūjiena
Rūjiena 84 D3 Est. Ruhja, Ger. Rujen. Valmiera, N Latvia
Rukwa, Lake 51 B7 lake SE Tanzania
Rum see Rhum
Ruma 78 D3 Vojvodina, N Serbia
Rumadiya see Ar Ramādī
Rumania/Rumänien see Romania
Rumbek 51 B5 El Buhayrat, C South Sudan
Rum Cay 32 D2 island C Bahamas
Rumia 76 C2 Pomorskie, N Poland
Rummah, Wādī ar see Rimah, Wādī ar
Rummelsburg in Pommern see Miastko
Rumuniya/Rumŭniya/Rumunjska see Romania
Runanga 129 B5 West Coast, South Island, New Zealand
Rundu 56 C3 var. Runtu. Okavango, NE Namibia
Runö see Ruhnu
Runtu see Rundu
Ruoqiang 104 C3 var. Jo-ch'iang, Uigh. Charkhlik, Charkhliq, Qarkilik. Xinjiang Uygur Zizhiqu, NW China
Rupea 86 C4 Ger. Reps, Hung. Kőhalom; prev. Cohalm. Brașov, C Romania
Rupel 65 B5 river N Belgium
Rupella see la Rochelle
Rupert, Rivière de 16 D3 river Québec, C Canada
Rusaddir see Melilla
Ruschuk/Rusçuk see Ruse
Ruse 82 D1 var. Ruschuk, Rustchuk, Turk. Rusçuk. Ruse, N Bulgaria
Russadir see Melilla
Russellville 20 A1 Arkansas, C USA
Russia see Russian Federation
Russian America see Alaska
Russian Federation 90 D2 off. Russian Federation, var. Russia, Latv. Krievija, Rus. Rossiyskaya Federatsiya. country Asia/Europe
Rustaq see Ar Rustāq
Rustavi 95 G2 prev. Rust'avi. SE Georgia
Rust'avi see Rustavi
Rustchuk see Ruse
Ruston 20 B2 Louisiana, S USA
Rutanzige, Lake see Edward, Lake
Rutba see Ar Ruṭbah
Rutlam see Ratlām
Rutland 19 F2 Vermont, NE USA
Rutog 104 A4 var. Rutög, Rutok. Xizang Zizhiqu, W China
Rutok see Rutog
Ruvuma see Rovuma, Rio
Ruwenzori 55 E5 mountain range Dem. Rep. Congo/Uganda
Ruzhany 85 B6 Brestskaya Voblasts', SW Belarus
Ružomberok 77 C5 Ger. Rosenberg, Hung. Rózsahegy. Žilinský Kraj, N Slovakia
Rwanda 51 B6 off. Rwandese Republic; prev. Ruanda. country C Africa
Rwandese Republic see Rwanda
Ryazan' 89 B5 Ryazanskaya Oblast', W Russian Federation
Rybach'ye see Balykchy
Rybinsk 88 B4 prev. Andropov. Yaroslavskaya Oblast', W Russian Federation
Rybnik 77 C5 Śląskie, S Poland
Rybnitsa see Rîbnița
Ryde 126 E1 United Kingdom
Ryki 76 D4 Lubelskie, E Poland
Rykovo see Yenakiyeve
Rypin 76 C3 Kujawsko-pomorskie, C Poland
Ryssel see Lille
Rysy 77 C5 mountain S Poland
Ryukyu Islands see Nansei-shotō
Ryukyu Trench 103 F3 var. Nansei Syotō Trench. trench S East China Sea
Rzeszów 77 E5 Podkarpackie, SE Poland
Rzhev 88 B4 Tverskaya Oblast', W Russian Federation

S

Saale 72 C4 river C Germany
Saalfeld 73 C5 var. Saalfeld an der Saale. Thüringen, C Germany
Saalfeld an der Saale see Saalfeld
Saarbrücken 73 A6 Fr. Sarrebruck. Saarland, SW Germany
Sääre 84 C2 var. Sjar. Saaremaa, W Estonia
Saare see Saaremaa
Saaremaa 84 C2 Ger. Oesel, Ösel; prev. Saare. island W Estonia
Saariselkä 62 D2 Lapp. Suoločielgi. Lappi, N Finland
Sab' Ābār 96 C4 var. Sab'a Biyar, Sa'b Bi'ār. Ḩimş, C Syria
Sab'a Biyar see Sab' Ābār
Šabac 78 D3 Serbia, W Serbia
Sabadell 71 G2 Cataluña, E Spain
Sabah 116 D3 prev. British North Borneo, North Borneo. state East Malaysia
Sabanalarga 36 B1 Atlántico, N Colombia
Sabaneta 36 C1 Falcón, N Venezuela
Sabaria see Szombathely
Sab'atayn, Ramlat as 99 C6 desert C Yemen
Sabaya 39 F4 Oruro, S Bolivia
Sa'b Bi'ār see Sab' Ābār
Saberi, Hamun-e 100 C5 var. Daryācheh-ye Hāmun, Daryācheh-ye Sīstān. lake Afghanistan/Iran
Sabhā 49 F3 C Libya
Sabi see Save
Sabinas 29 E2 Coahuila, NE Mexico
Sabinas Hidalgo 29 E2 Nuevo León, NE Mexico
Sabine River 27 H3 river Louisiana/Texas, SW USA
Sabkha see As Sabkhah
Sable, Cape 21 E5 headland Florida, SE USA
Sable Island 17 G4 island Nova Scotia, SE Canada
Ṣabyā 99 B6 Jīzān, SW Saudi Arabia
Sabzawar see Sabzevār
Sabzevār 98 D2 var. Sabzawar. Khorāsān-Razavī, NE Iran
Sachsen 72 D4 Eng. Saxony, Fr. Saxe. state E Germany
Sachs Harbour 15 E2 var. Ikaahuk. Banks Island, Northwest Territories, N Canada
Sächsisch-Reen/Sächsisch-Regen see Reghin
Sacramento 25 B5 state capital California, W USA
Sacramento Mountains 26 D2 mountain range New Mexico, SW USA
Sacramento River 25 B5 river California, W USA
Sacramento Valley 25 B5 valley California, W USA
Sá da Bandeira see Lubango
Ṣa'dah 99 B6 NW Yemen
Sado 109 C5 var. Sadoga-shima. island C Japan
Sadoga-shima see Sado
Saena Julia see Siena
Safad see Tsefat
Ṣafāqis see Sfax
Ṣafāshahr 98 D3 var. Deh Bīd. Fārs, C Iran
Safed see Tsefat
Säffle 63 B6 Värmland, C Sweden
Safford 26 C3 Arizona, SW USA
Safi 48 B2 W Morocco
Selseleh-ye Safīd Kuh 100 D4 Eng. Paropamisus Range. mountain range W Afghanistan
Sagaing 114 B3 Sagaing, C Myanmar (Burma)
Sagami-nada 109 D6 inlet SW Japan
Sagan see Żagań
Sāgar 112 D4 prev. Saugor. Madhya Pradesh, C India
Sagarmāthā see Everest, Mount
Sagebrush State see Nevada
Saghez see Saqqez
Saginaw 18 C3 Michigan, N USA
Saginaw Bay 18 D2 lake bay Michigan, N USA
Sagua la Grande 32 B2 Villa Clara, C Cuba
Sagunto 71 F3 Cat. Sagunt, Ar. Murviedro; anc. Saguntum. País Valenciano, E Spain
Sagunt/Saguntum see Sagunto
Sahara 46 B3 desert Libya/Algeria
Sahara el Gharbîya see Ṣaḩrā' al Gharbīyah
Saharan Atlas see Atlas Saharien
Sahel 52 D3 physical region C Africa
Sāḩilīyah, Jibāl as 96 B3 mountain range NW Syria
Sāhīwāl 112 C2 prev. Montgomery. Punjab, E Pakistan
Ṣaḩrā' al Gharbīyah 50 B2 var. Sahara el Gharbîya, Eng. Western Desert. desert C Egypt
Saïda 97 A5 var. Ṣaydā, Sayida; anc. Sidon. W Lebanon
Sa'īdābād see Sīrjān
Saidpur 113 G3 var. Syedpur. Rajshahi, NW Bangladesh
Saidu Sharif 112 C1 var. Mingora, Mongora. North-West Frontier Province, N Pakistan
Saigon see Hô Chi Minh
Saimaa 63 E5 lake SE Finland
St Albans 67 E6 anc. Verulamium. E England, United Kingdom
Saint Albans 18 D5 West Virginia, NE USA
St Andrews 66 C4 E Scotland, United Kingdom
Saint Anna Trough see Svyataya Anna Trough
St. Ann's Bay 32 B4 C Jamaica
St. Anthony 17 G3 Newfoundland and Labrador, SE Canada
Saint Augustine 21 E3 Florida, SE USA
St Austell 67 C7 SW England, United Kingdom
St.Botolph's Town see Boston
St-Brieuc 68 A3 Côtes d'Armor, NW France
St. Catharines 16 D5 Ontario, S Canada
St-Chamond 69 D5 Loire, E France
Saint Christopher and Nevis, Federation of see Saint Kitts and Nevis
Saint Christopher-Nevis see Saint Kitts and Nevis
Saint Clair, Lake 18 D3 var. Lac à L'Eau Claire. lake Canada/USA
St-Claude 69 D5 anc. Condate. Jura, E France
Saint Cloud 23 F2 Minnesota, N USA
Saint Croix 33 F3 island S Virgin Islands (US)
Saint Croix River 18 A2 river Minnesota/Wisconsin, N USA
St David's Island 20 B5 island E Bermuda
St-Denis 57 G4 dependent territory capital (Réunion) NW Réunion
St-Dié 68 E4 Vosges, NE France
St-Egrève 69 D5 Isère, E France
Sainte Marie, Cap see Vohimena, Tanjona
Saintes 69 B5 anc. Mediolanum. Charente-Maritime, W France
St-Étienne 69 D5 Loire, E France
St-Flour 69 C5 Cantal, C France
St-Gall/Saint Gall/St. Gallen see Sankt Gallen
St-Gaudens 69 B6 Haute-Garonne, S France
Saint George 127 D5 Queensland, E Australia
St George 20 B4 N Bermuda
Saint George 22 A5 Utah, W USA
St. George's 33 G5 country capital (Grenada) SW Grenada
St-Georges 17 E4 Québec, SE Canada
St-Georges 37 H3 E French Guiana
Saint George's Channel 67 B6 channel Ireland/Wales, United Kingdom
St George's Island 20 B4 island E Bermuda
Saint Helena 47 B6 UK dependent territory C Atlantic Ocean
St Helier 67 D8 dependent territory capital (Jersey) S Jersey, Channel Islands
St.Iago de la Vega see Spanish Town
Saint Ignace 18 C2 Michigan, N USA
St-Jean, Lac 17 E4 lake Québec, SE Canada
Saint Joe River 24 D2 river Idaho, NW USA North America
St. John 17 F4 New Brunswick, SE Canada
Saint-John see Saint John
Saint John 19 H1 Fr. Saint-John. river Canada/USA
St John's 33 G3 country capital (Antigua and Barbuda) Antigua, Antigua and Barbuda
St. John's 17 H3 province capital Newfoundland and Labrador, E Canada
Saint Joseph 23 F4 Missouri, C USA
St Julian's see San Ġiljan
St Kilda 66 A3 island NW Scotland, United Kingdom
Saint Kitts and Nevis 33 F3 off. Federation of Saint Christopher and Nevis, var. Saint Christopher-Nevis. country E West Indies
St-Laurent see St-Laurent-du-Maroni
St-Laurent-du-Maroni 37 H3 var. St-Laurent. NW French Guiana
St-Laurent, Fleuve see St. Lawrence
St. Lawrence 17 E4 Fr. Fleuve St-Laurent. river Canada/USA
St. Lawrence, Gulf of 17 F3 gulf NW Atlantic Ocean
Saint Lawrence Island 14 B2 island Alaska, USA
St-Lô 68 B3 anc. Briovera, Laudus. Manche, N France
St-Louis 68 E4 Haut-Rhin, NE France
Saint Louis 52 B3 NW Senegal
Saint Louis 23 G4 Missouri, C USA
Saint Lucia 33 E1 country SE West Indies
Saint Lucia Channel 33 H4 channel Martinique/Saint Lucia
St-Malo 68 B3 Ille-et-Vilaine, NW France
St-Malo, Golfe de 68 A3 gulf NW France
Saint Martin see Sint Maarten
St.Matthew's Island see Zadetkyi Kyun
St.Matthias Group 122 B3 island group NE Papua New Guinea
St. Moritz 73 B7 Ger. Sankt Moritz, Rmsch. San Murezzan. Graubünden, SE Switzerland
St-Nazaire 68 A4 Loire-Atlantique, NW France
Saint Nicholas see São Nicolau
Saint-Nicolas see Sint-Niklaas
St-Omer 68 C2 Pas-de-Calais, N France
Saint Paul 23 F2 state capital Minnesota, N USA
St-Paul, Île 119 C6 var. St.Paul Island. island Île St-Paul, NE French Southern and Antarctic Lands Antarctica Indian Ocea
St.Paul Island see St-Paul, Île
St Peter Port 67 D8 dependent territory capital (Guernsey) C Guernsey, Channel Islands
Saint Petersburg 21 E4 Florida, SE USA
Saint Petersburg see Sankt-Peterburg
St-Pierre and Miquelon 17 G4 Fr. Îles St-Pierre et Miquelon. French territorial collectivity NE North America
St-Quentin 68 C3 Aisne, N France
Saint Thomas see São Tomé, Sao Tome and Principe
Saint Thomas see Charlotte Amalie, Virgin Islands (US)
Saint Ubes see Setúbal
Saint Vincent 33 G4 island N Saint Vincent and the Grenadines
Saint Vincent see São Vicente
Saint Vincent and the Grenadines 33 H4 country SE West Indies
Saint Vincent, Cape see São Vicente, Cabo de
Saint Vincent Passage 33 H4 passage Saint Lucia/Saint Vincent and the Grenadines
Saint Yves see Setúbal
Saipan 120 B1 island/country capital (Northern Mariana Islands) S Northern Mariana Islands
Saishū see Jeju-do
Sajama, Nevado 39 F4 mountain W Bolivia
Sajószentpéter 77 D6 Borsod-Abaúj-Zemplén, NE Hungary
Sakākah 98 B4 Al Jawf, NW Saudi Arabia
Sakakawea, Lake 22 D1 reservoir North Dakota, N USA
Sak'art'velo see Georgia
Sakata 108 D4 Yamagata, Honshū, C Japan
Sakhalin 93 G4 var. Sakhalin. island SE Russian Federation
Sakhalin see Sakhalin, Ostrov
Sakhon Nakhon see Sakon Nakhon
Şäki 95 G2 Rus. Sheki; prev. Nukha. NW Azerbaijan
Saki see Saky
Sakishima-shoto 108 A3 var. Sakisima Syotô. island group SW Japan
Sakisima Syotô see Sakishima-shotō
Sakiz see Saqqez
Sakiz-Adasi see Chíos
Sakon Nakhon 114 D4 var. Muang Sakon Nakhon, Sakhon Nakhon. Sakon Nakhon, E Thailand
Saky 87 F5 Rus. Saki. Respublika Krym, S Ukraine
Sal 52 A3 island Ilhas de Barlavento, NE Cape Verde
Sala 63 C6 Västmanland, C Sweden
Salacgrīva 84 C3 Est. Salatsi. Limbaži, N Latvia
Sala Consilina 75 D5 Campania, S Italy
Salado, Río 40 D5 river E Argentina
Salado, Río 42 C3 river C Argentina
Şalālah 99 D6 SW Oman
Salamá 30 B2 Baja Verapaz, C Guatemala
Salamanca 42 B4 Coquimbo, C Chile
Salamanca 70 D2 anc. Helmantica, Salmantica. Castilla-León, NW Spain
Salamīyah 96 B3 var. As Salamīyah. Ḩamāh, W Syria
Salang see Phuket
Salantai 84 B3 Klaipėda, NW Lithuania
Salatsi see Salacgrīva
Salavan 115 D5 var. Saravan, Saravane. Salavan, S Laos
Salavat 89 D6 Respublika Bashkortostan, W Russian Federation
Sala y Gomez 131 F4 island Chile, E Pacific Ocean
Sala y Gomez Fracture Zone see Sala y Gomez Ridge
Sala y Gomez Ridge 131 G4 var. Sala y Gomez Fracture Zone. fracture zone SE Pacific Ocean
Salazar see N'Dalatando
Šalčininkai 85 C5 Vilnius, SE Lithuania
Salduba see Zaragoza
Saldus 84 B3 Ger. Frauenburg. Saldus, W Latvia
Sale 127 C7 Victoria, SE Australia
Salé 48 C2 NW Morocco
Salekhard 92 D3 prev. Obdorsk. Yamalo-Nenetskiy Avtonomnyy Okrug, N Russian Federation
Salem 110 C2 Tamil Nādu, SE India
Salem 24 B3 state capital Oregon, NW USA
Salerno 75 D5 anc. Salernum. Campania, S Italy
Salerno, Gulf of 75 C5 Eng. Gulf of Salerno. gulf S Italy
Salerno, Gulf of see Salerno, Golfo di
Salernum see Salerno
Salihorsk 85 C7 Rus. Soligorsk. Minskaya Voblasts', S Belarus
Salima 57 E2 Central, C Malawi
Salina 23 E5 Kansas, C USA
Salina Cruz 29 F5 Oaxaca, SE Mexico
Salinas 38 A2 Guayas, W Ecuador
Salinas 25 B6 California, W USA
Salisbury 67 D7 var. New Sarum. S England, United Kingdom
Salisbury see Harare
Sállan see Sørøya
Sallyana see Şalyān
Salmantica see Salamanca
Salmon River 24 D3 river Idaho, NW USA
Salmon River Mountains 24 D3 mountain range Idaho, NW USA
Salo 63 D6 Länsi-Suomi, SW Finland
Salon-de-Provence 69 D6 Bouches-du-Rhône, SE France
Salonica/Salonika see Thessaloníki
Salonta 86 A3 Hung. Nagyszalonta. Bihor, W Romania
Sal'sk 89 B7 Rostovskaya Oblast', SW Russian Federation
Salt see As Salṭ
Salta 42 C2 Salta, NW Argentina
Saltash 67 C7 SW England, United Kingdom
Saltillo 29 E3 Coahuila, NE Mexico
Salt Lake City 22 B4 state capital Utah, W USA
Salto 42 D4 Salto, N Uruguay
Salton Sea 25 D8 lake California, W USA
Salvador 41 G3 prev. São Salvador. state capital Bahia, E Brazil
Salween 102 C2 Bur. Thanlwin, Chin. Nu Chiang, Nu Jiang. river SE Asia
Şalyān 113 E3 var. Sallyana. Mid Western, W Nepal
Salzburg 73 D6 anc. Juvavum. Salzburg, N Austria
Salzgitter 72 C4 prev. Watenstedt-Salzgitter. Niedersachsen, C Germany
Salzwedel 72 C3 Sachsen-Anhalt, N Germany
Šamac see Bosanski Šamac
Samakhixai see Attapu
Samalayuca 28 C1 Chihuahua, N Mexico
Samar 117 F2 island C Philippines
Samara 92 B3 prev. Kuybyshev. Samarskaya Oblast', W Russian Federation
Samarang see Semarang
Samarinda 116 D4 Borneo, C Indonesia
Samarkand see Samarqand
Samarkandski/Samarkandskoye see Temirtau
Samarobriva see Amiens
Samarqand 101 E2 Rus. Samarkand. Samarqand Viloyati, C Uzbekistan
Samawa see As Samāwah
Sambalpur 113 F4 Odisha, E India
Sambava 57 G2 Antsiranana, NE Madagascar
Sambir 86 B2 Rus. Sambor. L'vivs'ka Oblast', NW Ukraine
Sambor see Sambir
Sambre 68 D2 river Belgium/France
Samfya 56 D2 Luapula, N Zambia
Saminatal 72 E2 valley Austria/Liechtenstein Europe
Samnān see Semnān
Sam Neua see Xam Nua
Samoa 123 E4 off. Independent State of Western Samoa, var. Sāmoa; prev. Western Samoa. country W Polynesia
Sāmoa see Samoa
Samoa Basin 121 E3 undersea basin W Pacific Ocean
Samobor 78 A2 Zagreb, N Croatia
Sámos 83 E6 prev. Limín Vathéos. Sámos, Dodekánisa, Greece, Aegean Sea
Sámos 83 D6 island Dodekánisa, Greece, Aegean Sea
Samothrace see Samothráki
Samothráki 82 D4 Samothráki, NE Greece
Samothraki 82 C4 anc. Samothrace. island NE Greece
Sampit 116 C4 Borneo, C Indonesia
Sâmraông 115 D5 prev. Phumĭ Sâmraông, Phum Samrong. Siĕmréab, NW Cambodia
Samsun 94 D2 anc. Amisus. Samsun, N Turkey
Samtredia 95 F2 W Georgia
Samui, Ko 115 C6 island SW Thailand
Samut Prakan 115 C5 var. Muang Samut Prakan, Paknam. Samut Prakan, C Thailand
San 52 D3 Ségou, C Mali
San 77 E5 river SE Poland
Ṣan'ā' 99 B6 Eng. Sana. country capital (Yemen) W Yemen
Sana 78 B3 river NW Bosnia and Herzegovina
Sanae 132 B2 South African research station Antarctica
Sanaga 55 B5 river C Cameroon
San Ambrosio, Isla 35 A5 Eng. San Ambrosio Island. island W Chile
San Ambrosio Island see San Ambrosio, Isla
Sanandaj 98 C3 prev. Sinneh. Kordestān, W Iran
San Andrés, Isla de 31 F3 island NW Colombia, Caribbean Sea
San Andrés Tuxtla 29 F4 var. Tuxtla. Veracruz-Llave, E Mexico
San Angelo 27 F3 Texas, SW USA
San Antonio 30 B2 Toledo, S Belize
San Antonio 42 B4 Valparaíso, C Chile
San Antonio 27 F4 Texas, SW USA
San Antonio Oeste 43 C5 Río Negro, E Argentina
San Antonio River 27 G4 river Texas, SW USA
Sanāw 99 C6 var. Sanaw. NE Yemen
San Benedicto, Isla 28 B4 island W Mexico
San Benito 30 B1 Petén, N Guatemala
San Benito 27 G5 Texas, SW USA
San Bernardino 25 C7 California, W USA
San Blas 28 C3 Sinaloa, C Mexico
San Blas, Cape 20 D3 headland Florida, SE USA
San Blas, Cordillera de 31 G4 mountain range NE Panama
San Carlos 30 D4 Río San Juan, S Nicaragua
San Carlos 26 B2 Arizona, SW USA
San Carlos see Quesada, Costa Rica
San Carlos de Ancud see Ancud
San Carlos de Bariloche 43 B5 Río Negro, SW Argentina
San Carlos del Zulia 36 C2 Zulia, W Venezuela
San Clemente Island 25 B8 island Channel Islands, California, W USA
San Cristóbal 36 C2 Táchira, W Venezuela
San Cristobal 122 C4 var. Makira. island SE Solomon Islands
San Cristóbal see San Cristóbal de Las Casas
San Cristóbal de Las Casas 29 G5 var. San Cristóbal. Chiapas, SE Mexico

Semendria – Slavyansk

Semendria see Smederevo
Semey 92 D4 prev. Semipalatinsk. Vostochnyy Kazakhstan, E Kazakhstan
Semezhevo see Syemyezhava
Seminole 27 E3 Texas, SW USA
Seminole, Lake 20 D3 reservoir Florida/Georgia, SE USA
Semipalatinsk see Semey
Semnān 98 D3 var. Samnān. Semnān, N Iran
Semois 65 C8 river SE Belgium
Sendai 108 D4 Miyagi, Honshū, C Japan
Sendai-wan 108 D4 bay E Japan
Senec 77 C6 Ger. Wartberg, Hung. Szenc; prev. Szempcz. Bratislavský Kraj, W Slovakia
Senegal 52 B3 off. Republic of Senegal, Fr. Sénégal. country W Africa
Senegal 52 C3 Fr. Sénégal. river W Africa
Senegal, Republic of see Senegal
Senftenberg 72 D4 Brandenburg, E Germany
Senia see Senj
Senica 77 C6 Ger. Senitz, Hung. Szenice. Trnavský Kraj, W Slovakia
Seniça see Sjenica
Senitz see Senica
Senj 78 A3 Ger. Zengg, It. Segna; anc. Senia. Lika-Senj, NW Croatia
Senja 62 C2 prev. Senjen. island N Norway
Senjen see Senja
Senkaku-shoto 108 A3 island group SW Japan
Senlis 68 C3 Oise, N France
Sennar 50 C4 var. Sannār. Sinnar, C Sudan
Senones see Sens
Sens 68 C3 anc. Agendicum, Senones. Yonne, C France
Sensburg see Mrągowo
Sên, Stœng 115 D5 river C Cambodia
Senta 78 D3 Hung. Zenta. Vojvodina, N Serbia
Seo de Urgel see La See d'Urgel
Seoul 107 E4 off. Seoul Teukbyeolsi, prev. Sŏul, Jap. Keijō; prev. Kyŏngsŏng. country capital (South Korea) NW South Korea
Seoul Teukbyeolsi see Seoul
Şepşi-Sângeorz/Sepsiszentgyörgy see Sfântu Gheorghe
Sept-Îles 17 E3 Québec, SE Canada
Seraing 65 D6 Liège, E Belgium
Serakhs see Sarahs
Seram, Laut 117 F4 Eng. Ceram Sea. sea E Indonesia
Pulau Seram 117 F4 var. Serang, Eng. Ceram. island Maluku, E Indonesia
Serang 116 C5 Jawa, C Indonesia
Serang see Seram, Pulau
Serasan, Selat 116 C3 strait Indonesia/Malaysia
Serbia 78 D4 off. Federal Republic of Serbia; prev. Yugoslavia, SCr. Jugoslavija. country SE Europe
Serbia, Federal Republic of see Serbia
Sercq see Sark
Serdar 100 C2 prev. Rus. Gyzyrlabat, Kizyl-Arvat. Balkan Welaýaty, W Turkmenistan
Serdica see Sofiya
Serdobol' see Sortavala
Serenje 56 D2 Central, E Zambia
Seres see Sérres
Seret/Sereth see Siret
Serhetabat 100 D4 prev. Rus. Gushgy, Kushka. Mary Welaýaty, S Turkmenistan
Sérifos 83 C6 anc. Seriphos. island Kykládes, Greece, Aegean Sea
Seriphos see Sérifos
Serov 92 C3 Sverdlovskaya Oblast', C Russian Federation
Serowe 56 D3 Central, SE Botswana
Serpa Pinto see Menongue
Serpent's Mouth, The 37 F2 Sp. Boca de la Serpiente. strait Trinidad and Tobago/Venezuela
Serpiente, Boca de la see Serpent's Mouth, The
Serpukhov 89 B5 Moskovskaya Oblast', W Russian Federation
Sérrai see Sérres
Serrana, Cayo de 31 F2 island group NW Colombia South America
Serranilla, Cayo de 31 F2 island group NW Colombia South America Caribbean Sea
Serravalle 74 E1 N San Marino
Sérres 82 C3 var. Seres; prev. Sérrai. Kentrikí Makedonía, NE Greece
Sesdlets see Siedlce
Sesto San Giovanni 74 B2 Lombardia, N Italy
Sesvete 78 B2 Zagreb, N Croatia
Setabis see Xàtiva
Sète 69 C6 prev. Cette. Hérault, S France
Setesdal 63 A6 valley S Norway
Sétif 49 E2 var. Stif. N Algeria
Setté Cama 55 A6 Ogooué-Maritime, SW Gabon
Setúbal 70 B4 Eng. Saint Ubes, Saint Yves. Setúbal, W Portugal
Setúbal, Baía de 70 B4 bay W Portugal
Seul, Lac 16 B3 lake Ontario, S Canada
Sevan 95 G2 C Armenia
Sevana Lich 95 G3 Eng. Lake Sevan, Rus. Ozero Sevan. lake E Armenia
Sevan, Lake/Sevan, Ozero see Sevana Lich
Sevastopol' 87 F5 Eng. Sebastopol. Respublika Krym, S Ukraine
Severn 16 B2 river Ontario, S Canada
Severn 67 D6 Wel. Hafren. river England/Wales, United Kingdom
Severnaya Dvina 88 C4 var. Northern Dvina. river NW Russian Federation
Severnaya Zemlya 93 E2 var. Nicholas II Land. island group N Russian Federation
Severnyy 88 E3 Respublika Komi, NW Russian Federation
Severodonetsk see Syeverodonets'k
Severodvinsk 88 C3 prev. Molotov, Sudostroy. Arkhangel'skaya Oblast', NW Russian Federation
Severomorsk 88 C2 Murmanskaya Oblast', NW Russian Federation
Severskt 92 D4 Tomskaya Oblast', C Russian Federation
Sevier Lake 22 A4 lake Utah, W USA
Sevilla 70 C4 Eng. Seville; anc. Hispalis. Andalucía, SW Spain
Seville see Sevilla
Sevlievo 82 D2 Gabrovo, N Bulgaria
Sevluš/Sevlyush see Vynohradiv
Seward's Folly see Alaska
Seychelles 57 G1 off. Republic of Seychelles. country W Indian Ocean
Seychelles, Republic of see Seychelles
Seyðisfjörður 61 E5 Austurland, E Iceland
Seýdi 100 D2 Rus. Seydi; prev. Neftezavodsk. Lebap Welaýaty, E Turkmenistan
Seyhan see Adana
Sfákia see Chóra Sfakíon
Sfântu Gheorghe 86 C4 Ger. Sankt-Georgen, Hung. Sepsiszentgyőrgy; prev. Şepşi-Sângeorz, Sfîntu Gheorghe. Covasna, C Romania
Sfax 49 F2 Ar. Şafāqis. E Tunisia
Sfîntu Gheorghe see Sfântu Gheorghe
's-Gravenhage 64 B4 var. Den Haag, Eng. The Hague, Fr. La Haye. country capital (Netherlands-seat of government) Zuid-Holland, W Netherlands
's-Gravenzande 64 B4 Zuid-Holland, W Netherlands
Shaan/Shaanxi Sheng see Shaanxi
Shaanxi 106 B5 var. Shaan, Shaanxi Sheng, Shan-hsi, Shenshi, Shensi. province C China
Shabani see Zvishavane
Shabeelle, Webi see Shebeli
Shache 104 A3 var. Yarkant. Xinjiang Uygur Zizhiqu, NW China
Shacheng see Huailai
Shackleton Ice Shelf 132 D3 ice shelf Antarctica
Shaddādī see Ash Shadādah
Shāhābād see Eslāmābād
Sha Hi see Orūmīyeh, Daryācheh-ye
Shahjahanabad see Delhi
Shahr-e Kord 98 C3 var. Shahr Kord. Chahār Maḩall va Bakhtīārī, C Iran
Shahr Kord see Shahr-e Kord
Shāhrūd 98 D2 prev. Emāmrūd, Emāmshahr. Semnān, N Iran
Shalkar 92 B4 var. Chelkar. Aktyubinsk, W Kazakhstan
Shām, Bādiyat ash see Syrian Desert
Shana see Kuril'sk
Shandī see Shendi
Shandong 106 D4 var. Lu, Shandong Sheng, Shantung. province E China
Shandong Sheng see Shandong
Shanghai 106 D5 var. Shang-hai. Shanghai Shi, E China
Shangrao 106 D5 Jiangxi, S China
Shan-hsi see Shaanxi, China
Shan-hsi see Shanxi, China
Shannon 67 A6 Ir. An tSionainn. river W Ireland
Shan Plateau 114 B3 plateau E Myanmar (Burma)
Shansi see Shanxi
Shantar Islands see Shantarskiye Ostrova
Shantarskiye Ostrova 93 G3 Eng. Shantar Islands. island group E Russian Federation
Shantou 106 D6 var. Shan-t'ou, Swatow. Guangdong, S China
Shan-t'ou see Shantou
Shantung see Shandong
Shanxi 106 C4 var. Jin, Shan-hsi, Shansi, Shanxi Sheng. province C China
Shan Xian see Sanmenxia
Shanxi Sheng see Shanxi
Shaoguan 106 C6 var. Shao-kuan, Cant. Kukong; prev. Ch'u-chiang. Guangdong, S China
Shao-kuan see Shaoguan
Shaqrā' 98 B4 Ar Riyāḑ, C Saudi Arabia
Shaqrā see Shuqrah
Shar 92 D5 var. Charsk. Vostochnyy Kazakhstan, E Kazakhstan
Shari 108 D2 Hokkaidō, NE Japan
Shari see Chari
Sharjah see Ash Shāriqah
Shark Bay 125 A5 bay Western Australia
Sharqī, Al Jabal ash/Sharqi, Jebel esh see Anti-Lebanon
Shashe 56 D3 var. Shashi. river Botswana/Zimbabwe
Shashi see Shashe
Shatskiy Rise 103 G1 undersea rise N Pacific Ocean
Shawnee 27 G1 Oklahoma, C USA
Shaykh, Jabal ash see Hermon, Mount
Shchadryn 85 D7 Rus. Shchedrin. Homyel'skaya Voblasts', SE Belarus
Shchedrin see Shchadryn
Shcheglovsk see Kemerovo
Shchëkino 89 B5 Tul'skaya Oblast', W Russian Federation
Shchors 87 E1 Chernihivs'ka Oblast', N Ukraine
Shchuchin see Shchuchyn
Shchuchinsk 92 C4 prev. Shchuchye. Akmola, N Kazakhstan
Shchuchye see Shchuchinsk
Shchuchyn 85 B5 Pol. Szczuczyn Nowogródzki, Rus. Shchuchin. Hrodzyenskaya Voblasts', W Belarus
Shebekino 89 A6 Belgorodskaya Oblast', W Russian Federation
Shebelë Wenz, Wabë see Shebeli
Shebeli 51 D5 Amh. Wabē Shebelē Wenz, It. Scebeli, Som. Webi Shabeelle. river Ethiopia/Somalia
Sheberghān see Shibirghān
Sheboygan 18 B2 Wisconsin, N USA
Shebshi Mountains 54 A4 var. Schebschi Mountains. mountain range E Nigeria
Shechem see Nablus
Shedadi see Ash Shadādah
Sheffield 67 D5 N England, United Kingdom
Shekhem see Nablus
Sheki see Şäki
Shelby 22 B1 Montana, NW USA
Sheldon 23 F3 Iowa, C USA
Shelekhov Gulf see Shelikhova, Zaliv
Shelikhova, Zaliv 93 G2 Eng. Shelekhov Gulf. gulf E Russian Federation
Shendi 50 C4 var. Shandī. River Nile, NE Sudan
Shengking see Liaoning
Shenking see Liaoning
Shenshi/Shensi see Shaanxi
Shenyang 106 D3 Chin. Shen-yang, Eng. Moukden, Mukden; prev. Fengtien. province capital Liaoning, NE China
Shen-yang see Shenyang
Shepetivka 86 D2 Rus. Shepetovka. Khmel'nyts'ka Oblast', NW Ukraine
Shepetovka see Shepetivka
Shepparton 127 C7 Victoria, SE Australia
Sherbrooke 17 E4 Québec, SE Canada
Shereik 50 C3 River Nile, N Sudan
Sheridan 22 C2 Wyoming, C USA
Sherman 27 G2 Texas, SW USA
's-Hertogenbosch 64 C4 Fr. Bois-le-Duc, Ger. Herzogenbusch. Noord-Brabant, S Netherlands
Shetland Islands 66 D1 island group NE Scotland, United Kingdom
Shevchenko see Aktau
Shibergān/Shiberghan see Shibirghān
Shibirghān 101 E3 var. Sheberghān, Shiberghan, Shiberghān. Jowzjān, N Afghanistan
Shibetsu 108 D2 var. Sibetu. Hokkaidō, NE Japan
Shibh Jazirat Sīnā' see Sinai
Shibushi-wan 109 B8 bay SW Japan
Shigatse see Xigazê
Shih-chia-chuang/Shihmen see Shijiazhuang
Shihezi 104 C2 Xinjiang Uygur Zizhiqu, NW China
Shiichi see Shyichy
Shijiazhuang 106 C4 var. Shih-chia-chuang; prev. Shihmen. province capital Hebei, E China
Shikārpur 112 B3 Sind, S Pakistan
Shikoku 109 C7 var. Sikoku. island SW Japan
Shikoku Basin 103 F2 var. Sikoku Basin. undersea basin N Philippine Sea
Shikotan, Ostrov 108 E2 Jap. Shikotan-tō. island NE Russian Federation
Shikotan-tō see Shikotan, Ostrov
Shilabo 51 D5 Sumalē, E Ethiopia
Shiliguri 113 F3 prev. Siliguri. West Bengal, NE India
Shilka 93 F4 river S Russian Federation
Shillong 113 G3 state capital Meghālaya, NE India
Shimanto see Nakamura
Shimbir Berris see Shimbiris
Shimbiris 50 E4 var. Shimbir Berris. mountain N Somalia
Shimoga 110 C2 Karnātaka, W India
Shimonoseki 109 A7 var. Simonoseki, hist. Akamagaseki, Bakan. Yamaguchi, Honshū, SW Japan
Shinano-gawa 109 C5 var. Sinano Gawa. river Honshū, C Japan
Shīndand 100 D4 prev. Shīndand. Herāt, W Afghanistan
Shindand see Shīndand
Shingū 109 C6 var. Singû. Wakayama, Honshū, SW Japan
Shinjō 108 D4 var. Sinzyô. Yamagata, Honshū, C Japan
Shinyanga 51 C7 Shinyanga, NW Tanzania
Shiprock 26 C1 New Mexico, SW USA
Shirāz 98 D4 var. Shīrāz. Fārs, S Iran
Shishchitsy see Shyshchytsy
Shivpuri 112 D3 Madhya Pradesh, C India
Shizugawa 108 D4 Miyagi, Honshū, NE Japan
Shizuoka 109 D6 var. Sizuoka. Shizuoka, Honshū, S Japan
Shklov see Shklow
Shklow 85 D6 Rus. Shklov. Mahilyowskaya Voblasts', E Belarus
Shkodër 79 C5 var. Shkodra, It. Scutari, SCr. Skadar. Shkodër, NW Albania
Shkodra see Shkodër
Shkodrës, Liqeni i see Scutari, Lake
Shkumbinit, Lumi i 79 C6 var. Shkumbi, Shkumbin. river C Albania
Shkumbi/Shkumbin see Shkumbinit, Lumi i
Sholāpur see Solāpur
Shostka 87 F1 Sums'ka Oblast', NE Ukraine
Show Low 26 B2 Arizona, SW USA
Show Me State see Missouri
Shpola 87 E3 Cherkas'ka Oblast', N Ukraine
Shqipëria/Shqipërisë, Republika e see Albania
Shreveport 20 A2 Louisiana, S USA
Shrewsbury 67 D6 hist. Scrobesbyrig'. W England, United Kingdom
Shu 92 C5 Kaz. Shū. Zhambyl, SE Kazakhstan
Shuang-liao see Liaoyuan
Shū, Kazakhstan see Shu
Shumagin Islands 14 B3 island group Alaska, USA
Shumen 82 D2 Shumen, NE Bulgaria
Shumilina 85 E5 Rus. Shumilino. Vitsyebskaya Voblasts', NE Belarus
Shumilino see Shumilina
Shunsen see Chuncheon
Shuqrah 99 B7 var. Shaqrā. SW Yemen
Shwebo 114 B3 Sagaing, C Myanmar (Burma)
Shyichy 85 C7 Rus. Shiichi. Homyel'skaya Voblasts', SE Belarus
Shymkent 92 B5 prev. Chimkent. Yuzhnyy Kazakhstan, S Kazakhstan
Shyshchytsy 85 C6 Rus. Shishchitsy. Minskaya Voblasts', C Belarus
Siam see Thailand
Siam, Gulf of see Thailand, Gulf of
Sian see Xi'an
Siang see Brahmaputra
Siangtan see Xiangtan
Šiauliai 84 B4 Ger. Schaulen. Šiauliai, N Lithuania
Siazan' see Siyäzän
Sibay 89 D6 Respublika Bashkortostan, W Russian Federation
Šibenik 78 B4 It. Sebenico. Šibenik-Knin, S Croatia
Siberia see Sibir'
Siberoet see Siberut, Pulau
Siberut, Pulau 116 A4 prev. Siberoet. island Kepulauan Mentawai, W Indonesia
Sibi 112 B2 Baluchistān, SW Pakistan
Sibir' 93 E3 var. Siberia. physical region NE Russian Federation
Sibiti 55 B6 Lékoumou, S Congo
Sibiu 86 B4 Ger. Hermannstadt, Hung. Nagyszeben. Sibiu, C Romania
Sibolga 116 B3 Sumatera, W Indonesia
Sibu 116 D3 Sarawak, East Malaysia
Sibut 54 C4 prev. Fort-Sibut. Kemo, S Central African Republic
Sibuyan Sea 117 E2 sea W Pacific Ocean
Sichon 115 C6 var. Ban Sichon, Si Chon. Nakhon Si Thammarat, SW Thailand
Si Chon see Sichon
Sichuan 106 B5 var. Chuan, Sichuan Sheng, Ssu-ch'uan, Szechuan, Szechwan. province C China
Sichuan Pendi 106 B5 basin C China
Sichuan Sheng see Sichuan
Sicilian Channel see Sicily, Strait of
Sicily 75 C7 Eng. Sicily; anc. Trinacria. island Italy, C Mediterranean Sea
Sicily, Strait of 75 B7 var. Sicilian Channel. strait C Mediterranean Sea
Sicuani 39 E4 Cusco, S Peru
Sidári 82 A4 Kérkyra, Iónia Nisiá, Greece, C Mediterranean Sea
Sidas 116 C4 Borneo, C Indonesia
Siderno 75 D7 Calabria, SW Italy
Sidhirókastron see Sidirókastro
Sîdî Barrâni 50 A1 NW Egypt
Sidi Bel Abbès 48 D2 var. Sidi bel Abbès, Sidi-Bel-Abbès. NW Algeria
Sidirókastro 82 C3 prev. Sidhirókastron. Kentrikí Makedonía, NE Greece
Sidley, Mount 132 B4 mountain Antarctica
Sidney 22 D1 Montana, NW USA
Sidney 22 D4 Nebraska, C USA
Sidney 18 C4 Ohio, N USA
Sidon see Saïda
Sidra see Surt
Sidra/Sidra, Gulf of see Surt, Khalīj, N Libya
Siebenbürgen see Transylvania
Siedlce 76 E3 Ger. Sedlez, Rus. Sesdlets. Mazowieckie, C Poland
Siegen 72 B4 Nordrhein-Westfalen, W Germany
Siemiatycze 76 E3 Podlaskie, NE Poland
Siena 74 B3 Fr. Sienne; anc. Saena Julia. Toscana, C Italy
Sienne see Siena
Sieradz 76 C4 Sieradz, C Poland
Sierpc 76 D3 Mazowieckie, C Poland
Sierra Leone 52 C4 off. Republic of Sierra Leone. country W Africa
Sierra Leone Basin 44 C4 undersea basin E Atlantic Ocean
Sierra Leone, Republic of see Sierra Leone
Sierra Leone Ridge see Sierra Leone Rise
Sierra Leone Rise 44 C4 var. Sierra Leone Ridge, Sierra Leone Schwelle. undersea rise E Atlantic Ocean
Sierra Leone Schwelle see Sierra Leone Rise
Sierra Vista 26 B3 Arizona, SW USA
Sífnos 83 C6 anc. Siphnos. island Kykládes, Greece, Aegean Sea
Sigli 116 A3 Sumatera, W Indonesia
Siglufjörður 61 E4 Nordhurland Vestra, N Iceland
Signal Peak 26 A2 mountain Arizona, SW USA
Signan see Xi'an
Signy 132 A2 UK research station South Orkney Islands, Antarctica
Siguatepeque 30 C2 Comayagua, W Honduras
Siguiri 52 D4 NE Guinea
Sihanoukville 115 D6 var. Kâmpóng Saôm; prev. Kompong Som. Kâmpóng Saôm, SW Cambodia
Siilinjärvi 62 E4 Itä-Suomi, C Finland
Siirt 95 F4 var. Sert; anc. Tigranocerta. Siirt, SE Turkey
Sikandarabad see Secunderābād
Sikasso 52 D4 Sikasso, S Mali
Sikeston 23 H5 Missouri, C USA
Sikhote-Alin', Khrebet 93 G4 mountain range SE Russian Federation
Siking see Xi'an
Siklós 77 C7 Baranya, SW Hungary
Sikoku see Shikoku
Sikoku Basin see Shikoku Basin
Šilalė 84 B4 Tauragė, W Lithuania
Silchar 113 G3 Assam, NE India
Silesia 76 B4 physical region SW Poland
Silifke 94 C4 anc. Seleucia. İçel, S Turkey
Siliguri see Shiliguri
Siling Co 104 C5 lake W China
Silinhot see Xilinhot
Silistra 82 E1 var. Silistria; anc. Durostorum. Silistra, NE Bulgaria
Silistria see Silistra
Sillamäe 84 E2 Ger. Sillamäggi. Ida-Virumaa, NE Estonia
Sillamäggi see Sillamäe
Sillein see Žilina
Šilutė 84 B4 Ger. Heydekrug. Klaipėda, W Lithuania
Silvan 95 E4 Dıyarbakır, SE Turkey
Silva Porto see Kuito
Silver State see Colorado
Silver State see Nevada
Simanichy 85 C7 Rus. Simonichi. Homyel'skaya Voblasts', SE Belarus
Simav 94 B3 Kütahya, W Turkey
Simav Çayı 94 A3 river NW Turkey
Simbirsk see Ul'yanovsk
Simeto 75 C7 river Sicilia, Italy, C Mediterranean Sea
Simeulue, Pulau 116 A3 island NW Indonesia
Simferopol' 87 F5 Respublika Krym, S Ukraine
Simitla 82 C3 Blagoevgrad, SW Bulgaria
Şimlăul Silvaniei/Şimleul Silvaniei see Şimleu Silvaniei
Şimleu Silvaniei 86 B3 Hung. Szilágysomlyó; prev. Şimlăul Silvaniei, Şimleul Silvaniei. Sălaj, NW Romania
Simonichi see Simanichy
Simonoseki see Shimonoseki
Simpelveld 65 D6 Limburg, SE Netherlands
Simplon Pass 73 B8 pass S Switzerland
Simpson see Fort Simpson
Simpson Desert 126 B4 desert Northern Territory/South Australia
Sinai 50 C2 var. Sinai Peninsula, Ar. Shibh Jazirat Sīnā', Sīnā. physical region NE Egypt
Sinaia 86 C4 Prahova, SE Romania
Sinano Gawa see Shinano-gawa
Sīnā/Sinai Peninsula see Sinai
Sincelejo 36 B2 Sucre, NW Colombia
Sind 112 B3 var. Sindh. province SE Pakistan
Sindelfingen 73 B6 Baden-Württemberg, SW Germany
Sindh see Sind
Sindi 84 D2 Ger. Zintenhof. Pärnumaa, SW Estonia
Sines 70 B4 Setúbal, S Portugal
Singan see Xi'an
Singapore 116 B3 country capital (Singapore) S Singapore
Singapore 116 A1 off. Republic of Singapore. country SE Asia
Singapore, Republic of see Singapore
Singen 73 B6 Baden-Württemberg, S Germany
Singida 51 C7 Singida, C Tanzania
Singkang 117 E4 Sulawesi, C Indonesia
Singkawang 116 C3 Borneo, C Indonesia
Singora see Songkhla
Singû see Shingū
Sining see Xining
Siniscola 75 A5 Sardegna, Italy, C Mediterranean Sea
Sinj 78 B4 Split-Dalmacija, SE Croatia
Sinkiang/Sinkiang Uighur Autonomous Region see Xinjiang Uygur Zizhiqu
Sinnamarie see Sinnamary
Sinnamary 37 H3 var. Sinnamarie. N French Guiana
Sinneh see Sanandaj
Sînnicolau Mare see Sânnicolau Mare
Sinoe, Lacul see Sinoie, Lacul
Sinoie, Lacul 86 D5 prev. Lacul Sinoe. lagoon SE Romania
Sinop 94 D2 anc. Sinope. Sinop, N Turkey
Sinope see Sinop
Sinsheim 73 B6 Baden-Württemberg, SW Germany
Sint Maarten 33 G3 Eng. Saint Martin. island Lesser Antilles
Sint-Michielsgestel 64 C4 Noord-Brabant, S Netherlands
Sîn-Miclăuş see Gheorgheni
Sint-Niklaas 65 B5 Fr. Saint-Nicolas. Oost-Vlaanderen, N Belgium
Sint-Pieters-Leeuw 65 B6 Vlaams Brabant, C Belgium
Sintra 70 B3 prev. Cintra. Lisboa, W Portugal
Sinujiif 51 E5 Nugaal, NE Somalia
Sinus Aelaniticus see Aqaba, Gulf of
Sinus Gallicus see Lion, Golfe du
Sinyang see Xinyang
Sinzyô see Shinjō
Sion 73 A7 Ger. Sitten; anc. Sedunum. Valais, SW Switzerland
Sioux City 23 F3 Iowa, C USA
Sioux Falls 23 F3 South Dakota, N USA
Sioux State see North Dakota
Siphnos see Sífnos
Siping 106 D3 var. Ssu-p'ing, Szeping; prev. Ssu-p'ing-chieh. Jilin, NE China
Siple, Mount 132 A4 mountain Siple Island, Antarctica
Siquirres 31 E4 Limón, E Costa Rica
Siracusa 75 D7 Eng. Syracuse. Sicilia, Italy, C Mediterranean Sea
Sir Edward Pellew Group 126 B2 island group Northern Territory, NE Australia
Siret 86 C3 var. Siretul, Ger. Sereth, Rus. Seret. river Romania/Ukraine
Siretul see Siret
Siria see Syria
Sirikit Reservoir 114 C4 lake N Thailand
Sīrjān 98 D4 prev. Sa'īdābād. Kermān, S Iran
Sirna see Sýrna
Şırnak 95 F4 Şırnak, SE Turkey
Síros see Sýros
Sirte see Surt
Sirti, Gulf of see Surt, Khalīj
Sisak 78 B3 var. Siscia, Ger. Sissek, Hung. Sziszek; anc. Segestica. Sisak-Moslavina, C Croatia
Siscia see Sisak
Sisimiut 60 C3 var. Holsteinborg, Holsteinsborg, Holstenborg, Holstensborg. Kitaa, S Greenland
Sissek see Sisak
Sīstān, Daryācheh-ye see Şāberī, Hāmūn-e
Sitaş Cristuru see Cristuru Secuiesc
Siteía 83 D8 var. Sitía. Kríti, Greece, E Mediterranean Sea
Sitges 71 G2 Cataluña, NE Spain
Sitía see Siteía
Sittang see Sittoung
Sittard 65 D5 Limburg, SE Netherlands
Sitten see Sion
Sittoung 114 B4 var. Sittang. river S Myanmar (Burma)
Sittwe 114 A3 var. Akyab. Rakhine State, W Myanmar (Burma)
Siuna 30 D3 Región Autónoma Atlántico Norte, NE Nicaragua
Siut see Asyūţ
Sivas 94 D3 anc. Sebastia, Sebaste. Sivas, C Turkey
Siverek 95 E4 Şanlıurfa, S Turkey
Siwa see Sīwah
Sīwah 50 A2 var. Siwa. NW Egypt
Six Counties, The see Northern Ireland
Six-Fours-les-Plages 69 D6 Var, SE France
Siyäzän 95 H2 Rus. Siazan'. NE Azerbaijan
Sjar see Sääre
Sjenica 79 D5 Turk. Seniça. Serbia, SW Serbia
Skadar see Shkodër
Skadarsko Jezero see Scutari, Lake
Skagerak see Skagerrak
Skagerrak 63 A6 var. Skagerak. channel N Europe
Skagit River 24 B1 river Washington, NW USA
Skalka 62 C3 lake N Sweden
Skarżysko-Kamienna 76 D4 Świętokrzyskie, C Poland
Skaudvilė 84 B4 Tauragė, SW Lithuania
Skegness 67 E6 E England, United Kingdom
Skellefteå 62 D4 Västerbotten, N Sweden
Skellefteälven 62 C4 river N Sweden
Ski 63 B6 Akershus, S Norway
Skíathos 83 C5 Skíathos, Vóreies Sporádes, Greece, Aegean Sea
Skidal' 85 B5 Rus. Skidel'. Hrodzyenskaya Voblasts', W Belarus
Skidel' see Skidal'
Skiermûntseach see Schiermonnikoog
Skierniewice 76 D3 Łódzkie, C Poland
Skiftet 84 C1 strait Finland Atlantic Ocean Baltic Sea Gulf of Bothnia/Gulf of Finland
Skíros see Skýros
Skópelos 83 C5 Skópelos, Vóreies Sporádes, Greece, Aegean Sea
Skopje 79 D6 var. Üsküb, Turk. Üsküp, prev. Skoplje; anc. Scupi. country capital (FYR Macedonia) N FYR Macedonia
Skoplje see Skopje
Skovorodino 93 F4 Amurskaya Oblast', SE Russian Federation
Skudnesfjorden 63 A6 fjord S Norway
Skuodas 84 B3 Ger. Schoden, Pol. Szkudy. Klaipėda, NW Lithuania
Skye, Isle of 66 B3 island NW Scotland, United Kingdom
Skylge see Terschelling
Skýros 83 C5 var. Skíros. Skýros, Vóreies Sporádes, Greece, Aegean Sea
Skýros 83 C5 var. Skíros; anc. Scyros. island Vóreies Sporádes, Greece, Aegean Sea
Slagelse 63 B7 Vestsjælland, E Denmark
Slatina 78 C3 Hung. Szlatina; prev. Podravska Slatina. Virovitica-Podravina, NE Croatia
Slatina 86 B5 Olt, S Romania
Slavgorod see Slawharad
Slavonski Brod 78 C3 Ger. Brod, Hung. Bród; prev. Brod, Brod na Savi. Brod-Posavina, NE Croatia
Slavuta 86 C2 Khmel'nyts'ka Oblast', NW Ukraine
Slavyansk see Slov"yans'k

Sulu Sea – Tehuantepec, Gulf of

Sulu Sea *117 E2 var.* Laut Sulu. *sea* SW Philippines
Sulyukta *101 E2 Kir.* Sülüktü. Batkenskaya Oblast', SW Kyrgyzstan
Sumatera *115 B8 Eng.* Sumatra. *island* W Indonesia
Sumatra *see* Sumatera
Šumava *see* Bohemian Forest
Sumba, Pulau *117 E5 Eng.* Sandalwood Island; *prev.* Soemba. *island* Nusa Tenggara, C Indonesia
Sumba, Selat *117 E5 strait* Nusa Tenggara, S Indonesia
Sumbawanga *51 B7* Rukwa, W Tanzania
Sumbe *56 B2 var.* N'Gunza, *Port.* Novo Redondo. Cuanza Sul, W Angola
Sumeih *51 B5* Southern Darfur, S Sudan
Sumgait *see* Sumqayıt, Azerbaijan
Summer Lake *24 B4 lake* Oregon, NW USA
Summit *71 H5* Alaska, USA
Sumqayıt *95 H2 Rus.* Sumgait. E Azerbaijan
Sumy *87 F2* Sums'ka Oblast', NE Ukraine
Sunbury *127 C7* Victoria, SE Australia
Sunda Islands *see* Greater Sunda Islands
Sunda, Selat *116 B5 strait* Jawa/Sumatera, SW Indonesia
Sunda Trench *see* Java Trench
Sunderland *66 D4 var.* Wearmouth. NE England, United Kingdom
Sundsvall *63 C5* Västernorrland, C Sweden
Sunflower State *see* Kansas
Sungaipenuh *116 B4 prev.* Soengaipenoeh. Sumatera, W Indonesia
Sunnyvale *25 A6* California, W USA
Sunset State *see* Oregon
Sunshine State *see* Florida
Sunshine State *see* New Mexico
Sunshine State *see* South Dakota
Suntar *93 F3* Respublika Sakha (Yakutiya), NE Russian Federation
Sunyani *53 E5* W Ghana
Suoločielgi *see* Saariselkä
Suomenlahti *see* Finland, Gulf of
Suomen Tasavalta/Suomi *see* Finland
Suomussalmi *62 E4* Oulu, E Finland
Suŏng *115 D6* Kâmpóng Cham, C Cambodia
Suoyarvi *88 B3* Respublika Kareliya, NW Russian Federation
Supe *38 C3* Lima, W Peru
Supérieur, Lac *see* Superior, Lake
Superior *18 A1* Wisconsin, N USA
Superior, Lake *18 B1 Fr.* Lac Supérieur. *lake* Canada/USA
Suqrah *see* Şawqirah
Suquṭrā *99 C7 var.* Sokotra, *Eng.* Socotra. *island* SE Yemen
Şūr *99 E5* NE Oman
Şūr *see* Soûr
Surabaya *see* Surabaya
Surabaya *116 D5 prev.* Surabaja, Soerabaja. Jawa, C Indonesia
Surakarta *116 C5 Eng.* Solo; *prev.* Soerakarta. Jawa, S Indonesia
Šurany *77 C6 Hung.* Nagysurány. Nitriansky Kraj, SW Slovakia
Sūrat *112 C4* Gujarāt, W India
Suratdhani *see* Surat Thani
Surat Thani *115 C6 var.* Suratdhani. Surat Thani, SW Thailand
Surazh *85 E5* Vitsyebskaya Voblasts', NE Belarus
Surdulica *79 E5* Serbia, SE Serbia
Sûre *65 D7 var.* Sauer. *river* W Europe
Surendranagar *112 C4* Gujarāt, W India
Surfers Paradise *127 E5* Queensland, E Australia
Surgut *92 D3* Khanty-Mansiyskiy Avtonomnyy Okrug-Yugra, C Russian Federation
Surin *115 D5* Surin, E Thailand
Surinam *see* Suriname
Suriname *37 G3 off.* Republic of Suriname, *var.* Surinam; *prev.* Dutch Guiana, Netherlands Guiana. *country* N South America
Suriname, Republic of *see* Suriname
Sūrīya/Sūrīyah, Al-Jumhūrīyah al-'Arabīyah as- *see* Syria
Surkhab, Darya-i- *see* Kahmard, Daryā-ye
Surkhob *101 F3 river* C Tajikistan
Surt *49 G2 var.* Sidra, Sirte. N Libya
Surt, Khalīj *49 F2 Eng.* Gulf of Sidra. Gulf of Sirti, Sidra. *gulf* N Libya
Surtsey *61 E5 island* S Iceland
Suruga-wan *109 D6 bay* SE Japan
Susa *74 A2* Piemonte, NE Italy
Sūsah *see* Sousse
Susanville *25 B5* California, W USA
Susitna *14 C3* Alaska, USA
Susteren *65 D5* Limburg, SE Netherlands
Susuman *93 G3* Magadanskaya Oblast', E Russian Federation
Sutlej *112 C2 river* India/Pakistan
Suur Munamägi *84 D3 var.* Munamägi, *Ger.* Eier-Berg. *mountain* SE Estonia
Suur Väin *84 C2 Ger.* Grosser Sund. *strait* W Estonia
Suva *123 E4 country capital* (Fiji) Viti Levu, W Fiji
Suvalkai/Suvalki *see* Suwałki
Suvorovo *82 E2 prev.* Vetrino. Varna, E Bulgaria
Suwałki *76 E2 Lith.* Suvalkai, *Rus.* Suvalki. Podlaskie, NE Poland
Şuwār *see* Aş Şuwār
Suways, Qanāt as *see* Suez Canal
Suweida *see* As Suwaydā'
Suzhou *106 D5 var.* Soochow, Su-chou, Suchow; *prev.* Wuhsien. Jiangsu, E China
Svalbard *61 E1 Norwegian dependency* Arctic Ocean
Svartisen *62 C3 glacier* C Norway
Svay Riěng *115 D6* Svay Riěng, S Cambodia
Sveg *63 B5* Jämtland, C Sweden
Svenstavik *63 C5* Jämtland, C Sweden
Sverdlovsk *see* Yekaterinburg
Sverige *see* Sweden
Sveti Vrach *see* Sandanski
Svetlogorsk *see* Svyetlahorsk
Svetlograd *89 B7* Stavropol'skiy Kray, SW Russian Federation
Svetlovodsk *see* Svitlovods'k
Svetozarevo *see* Jagodina
Svilengrad *82 D3 prev.* Mustafa-Pasha. Khaskovo, S Bulgaria
Svitlovods'k *87 F3 Rus.* Svetlovodsk. Kirovohrads'ka Oblast', C Ukraine
Svizzera *see* Switzerland
Svobodnyy *93 G4* Amurskaya Oblast', SE Russian Federation
Svyataya Anna Trough *133 C4 var.* Saint Anna Trough. *trough* N Kara Sea
Svyetlahorsk *85 D7 Rus.* Svetlogorsk. Homyel'skaya Voblasts', SE Belarus
Swabian Jura *see* Schwäbische Alb
Swakopmund *56 B3* Erongo, W Namibia
Swan Islands *31 E1 island group* NE Honduras North America
Swansea *67 C7 Wel.* Abertawe. S Wales, United Kingdom
Swarzędz *76 C3* Poznań, W Poland
Swatow *see* Shantou
Swaziland *56 D4 off.* Kingdom of Swaziland. *country* S Africa
Swaziland, Kingdom of *see* Swaziland
Sweden *62 B4 off.* Kingdom of Sweden, *Swe.* Sverige. *country* N Europe
Sweden, Kingdom of *see* Sweden
Sweetwater *27 F3* Texas, SW USA
Świdnica *76 B4 Ger.* Schweidnitz. Wałbrzych, SW Poland
Świdwin *76 B2 Ger.* Schivelbein. Zachodnio-pomorskie, NW Poland
Świebodzice *76 B4 Ger.* Freiburg in Schlesien, Swiebodzice. Wałbrzych, SW Poland
Świebodzin *76 B3 Ger.* Schwiebus. Lubuskie, W Poland
Świecie *76 C3 Ger.* Schwertberg. Kujawsko-pomorskie, C Poland
Swindon *67 D7* S England, United Kingdom
Swinemünde *see* Świnoujście
Świnoujście *76 B2 Ger.* Swinemünde. Zachodnio-pomorskie, NW Poland
Swiss Confederation *see* Switzerland
Switzerland *73 A7 off.* Swiss Confederation, *Fr.* La Suisse, *Ger.* Schweiz, *It.* Svizzera; *anc.* Helvetia. *country* C Europe
Sycaminum *see* Hefa
Sydenham Island *see* Nonouti
Sydney *126 D1 state capital* New South Wales, SE Australia
Sydney *17 G4* Cape Breton Island, Nova Scotia, SE Canada
Sydney Island *see* Manra
Syedpur *see* Saidpur
Syemyezhava *85 C6 Rus.* Semezhevo. Minskaya Voblasts', C Belarus
Syene *see* Aswān
Syeverodonets'k *87 H3 Rus.* Severodonetsk. Luhans'ka Oblast', E Ukraine
Syktyvkar *88 D4 prev.* Ust'-Sysol'sk. Respublika Komi, NW Russian Federation
Sylhet *113 G3* Sylhet, NE Bangladesh
Synel'nykove *87 G3* Dnipropetrovs'ka Oblast', E Ukraine
Syowa *132 C2 Japanese research station* Antarctica
Syracuse *19 E3* New York, NE USA
Syracuse *see* Siracusa
Syrdar'ya *92 B4* Sirdaryo Viloyati, E Uzbekistan
Syria *96 B3 off.* Syrian Arab Republic, *var.* Siria, Syrie, *Ar.* Al-Jumhūrīyah al-'Arabīyah as-Sūrīyah, Sūrīya. *country* SW Asia
Syrian Arab Republic *see* Syria
Syrian Desert *97 D5 Ar.* Al Hamad, Bādiyat ash Shām. *desert* SW Asia
Syrie *see* Syria
Sýrna *83 E7 var.* Sirna. *island* Kykládes, Greece, Aegean Sea
Sýros *83 C6 var.* Siros. *island* Kykládes, Greece, Aegean Sea
Syulemeshlii *see* Sredets
Syvash, Zaliv *see* Syvash, Zatoka
Syvash, Zatoka *87 F4 Rus.* Zaliv Syvash. *inlet* S Ukraine
Syzran' *89 C6* Samarskaya Oblast', W Russian Federation
Szabadka *see* Subotica
Szamotuły *76 B3* Poznań, W Poland
Szászrégen *see* Reghin
Szatmárrnémeti *see* Satu Mare
Száva *see* Sava
Szczecin *76 B3 Eng./Ger.* Stettin. Zachodnio-pomorskie, NW Poland
Szczecinek *76 B2 Ger.* Neustettin. Zachodnio-pomorskie, NW Poland
Szczeciński, Zalew *76 A2 var.* Stettiner Haff, *Ger.* Oderhaff. *bay* Germany/Poland
Szczuczyn Nowogródzki *see* Shchuchyn
Szczytno *76 D3 Ger.* Ortelsburg. Warmińsko-Mazurskie, NE Poland
Szechuan/Szechwan *see* Sichuan
Szeged *77 D7 Ger.* Szegedin, *Rom.* Seghedin. Csongrád, SE Hungary
Szegedin *see* Szeged
Székelykeresztúr *see* Cristuru Secuiesc
Székesfehérvár *77 C6 Ger.* Stuhlweissenberg; *anc.* Alba Regia. Fejér, W Hungary
Szeklerburg *see* Miercurea-Ciuc
Szekler Neumarkt *see* Târgu Secuiesc
Szekszárd *77 C7* Tolna, S Hungary
Szempcz/Szenc *see* Senec
Szenice *see* Senica
Szenttamás *see* Srbobran
Szeping *see* Siping
Szilágysomlyó *see* Şimleu Silvaniei
Szinna *see* Snina
Sziszek *see* Sisak
Szitás-Keresztúr *see* Cristuru Secuiesc
Szkudy *see* Skuodas
Szlatina *see* Slatina
Szlovákia *see* Slovakia
Szolnok *77 D6* Jász-Nagykun-Szolnok, C Hungary
Szombathely *77 B6 Ger.* Steinamanger; *anc.* Sabaria, Savaria. Vas, W Hungary
Szprotawa *76 B4 Ger.* Sprottau. Lubuskie, W Poland
Sztálinváros *see* Dunaújváros
Szucsava *see* Suceava

T

Tabariya, Bahrat *see* Tiberias, Lake
Table Rock Lake *27 G1 reservoir* Arkansas/ Missouri, C USA
Tábor *77 B5* Jihočeský Kraj, S Czech Republic
Tabora *51 B7* Tabora, W Tanzania
Tabrīz *98 C2 var.* Tebriz; *anc.* Tauris. Āžarbāyjān-e Sharqī, NW Iran
Tabuaeran *123 G2 prev.* Fanning Island. *atoll* Line Islands, E Kiribati
Tabūk *98 A4* Tabūk, NW Saudi Arabia
Täby *63 C6* Stockholm, C Sweden
Tachau *see* Tachov
Tachov *77 A5 Ger.* Tachau. Plveňský Kraj, W Czech Republic
Tacloban *117 F2 off.* Tacloban City. Leyte, C Philippines
Tacloban City *see* Tacloban
Tacna *39 E4* Tacna, SE Peru
Tacoma *24 B2* Washington, NW USA
Tacuarembó *42 D4 prev.* San Fructuoso. Tacuarembó, C Uruguay
Tademait, Plateau du *48 D3 plateau* C Algeria
Tadmor/Tadmur *see* Tudmur
Tādpatri *110 C2* Andhra Pradesh, E India
Tadzhikistan *see* Tajikistan
Taegu *see* Daegu
Taehan-haehyŏp *see* Korea Strait
Taehan Min'guk *see* South Korea
Taejŏn *see* Daejeon
Tafassâsset, Ténéré du *53 G2 desert* N Niger
Tafila/Ṭafīlah, Muḥāfaẓat at *see* Aṭ Ṭafīlah
Taganrog *89 A7* Rostovskaya Oblast', SW Russian Federation
Taganrog, Gulf of *87 G4 Rus.* Taganrogskiy Zaliv, *Ukr.* Tahanroz'ka Zatoka. *gulf* Russian Federation/Ukraine
Taganrogskiy Zaliv *see* Taganrog, Gulf of
Taguatinga *41 F3* Tocantins, C Brazil
Tagus *70 C3 Port.* Rio Tejo, *Sp.* Río Tajo. *river* Portugal/Spain
Tagus Plain *58 A4 abyssal plain* E Atlantic Ocean
Tahanroz'ka Zatoka *see* Taganrog, Gulf of
Tahat *49 E4 mountain* SE Algeria
Tahiti *123 H4 island* Îles du Vent, W French Polynesia
Tahiti, Archipel de *see* Société, Archipel de la
Tahlequah *27 G1* Oklahoma, C USA
Tahoe, Lake *25 B5 lake* California/Nevada, W USA
Tahoua *53 F3* Tahoua, W Niger
Taibei *106 D6 var.* T'aipei; *Jap.* Taihoku; *prev.* Daihoku. *country capital* (Taiwan) N Taiwan
Taichū *see* Taizhong
T'aichung *see* Tiazhong
Taiden *see* Daejeon
Taieri *129 B7 river* South Island, New Zealand
Taihape *128 D4* Manawatu-Wanganui, North Island, New Zealand
Taihoku *see* Taibei
Taikyū *see* Daegu
Tailem Bend *127 B7* South Australia
T'ainan *see* Tainan
Tainan *106 D6 prev.* T'ainan, Dainan. S Taiwan
Taipei *see* Taibei
Taiping *116 B3* Perak, Peninsular Malaysia
Taiwan *106 D6 off.* Republic of China, *var.* Formosa, Formo'sa. *country* E Asia
Taiwan *see* Tiazhong
T'aiwan Haihsia/Taiwan Haixia *see* Taiwan Strait
Taiwan Strait *106 D6 var.* Formosa Strait, *Chin.* T'aiwan Haihsia, Taiwan Haixia. *strait* China/ Taiwan
Taiyuan *106 C4 var.* T'ai-yuan, T'ai-yüan; *prev.* Yangku. *province capital* Shanxi, C China
T'ai-yuan/T'ai-yüan *see* Taiyuan
Taizhong *106 D6 Jap.* Taichū; *prev.* T'aichung, Taiwan. C Taiwan
Ta'izz *99 B7* SW Yemen
Tajikistan *101 E3 off.* Republic of Tajikistan, *Rus.* Tadzhikistan, *Taj.* Jumhurii Tojikiston; *prev.* Tajik S.S.R. *country* C Asia
Tajikistan, Republic of *see* Tajikistan
Tajik S.S.R *see* Tajikistan
Tajo, Río *see* Tagus
Tak *114 C4 var.* Rahaeng. Tak, W Thailand
Takao *see* Gaoxiong
Takaoka *109 C5* Toyama, Honshū, SW Japan
Takapuna *128 D2* Auckland, North Island, New Zealand
Takeshima *see* Liancourt Rocks
Takhiatash *see* Taxiatosh
Takhtakupyr *see* Taxtako'pir
Takikawa *108 D2* Hokkaidō, NE Japan
Takla Makan Desert *see* Taklimakan Shamo
Taklimakan Shamo *104 B3 Eng.* Takla Makan Desert. *desert* NW China
Takow *see* Gaoxiong
Takutea *123 G4 island* S Cook Islands
Talabriga *see* Aveiro, Portugal
Talabriga *see* Talavera de la Reina, Spain
Talachyn *85 D6 Rus.* Tolochin. Vitsyebskaya Voblasts', NE Belarus
Talamanca, Cordillera de *31 E5 mountain range* S Costa Rica
Talara *38 B2* Piura, NW Peru
Talas *101 F2* Talasskaya Oblast', NW Kyrgyzstan
Talaud, Kepulauan *117 F3 island group* E Indonesia
Talavera de la Reina *70 D3 anc.* Caesarobriga, Talabriga. Castilla-La Mancha, C Spain
Talca *42 B4* Maule, C Chile
Talcahuano *43 B5* Bío Bío, C Chile
Taldykorgan *92 C5 Kaz.* Taldyqorghan; *prev.* Taldy-Kurgan. Taldykorgan, SE Kazakhstan
Taldy-Kurgan/Taldyqorghan *see* Taldykorgan
Ta-lien *see* Dalian
Taliq-an *see* Tāloqān
Tal'ka *85 C6* Minskaya Voblasts', C Belarus
Talkhof *see* Puurmani
Tallahassee *20 D3 prev.* Muskogean. *state capital* Florida, SE USA
Tall al Abyaḍ *see* At Tall al Abyaḍ
Tallin *see* Tallinn
Tallinn *84 D2 Ger.* Reval, *Rus.* Tallin; *prev.* Revel. *country capital* (Estonia) Harjumaa, NW Estonia
Tall Kalakh *96 B4 var.* Tell Kalakh. Ḥimṣ, C Syria
Tallulah *20 B2* Louisiana, S USA
Talnakh *92 D3* Taymyrskiy (Dolgano-Nenetskiy) Avtonomnyy Okrug, N Russian Federation
Tal'ne *87 E3 Rus.* Tal'noye. Cherkas'ka Oblast', C Ukraine
Tal'noye *see* Tal'ne
Taloga *27 F1* Oklahoma, C USA
Tāloqān *101 E3 var.* Taliq-an. Takhār, NE Afghanistan
Talsen *see* Talsi
Talsi *84 C3 Ger.* Talsen. Talsi, NW Latvia
Taltal *42 B2* Antofagasta, N Chile
Talvik *62 D2* Finnmark, N Norway
Tamabo, Banjaran *116 D3 mountain range* East Malaysia
Tamale *53 E4* C Ghana
Tamana *123 E3 prev.* Rotcher Island. *atoll* Tungaru, W Kiribati
Tamanrasset *49 E4 var.* Tamenghest. S Algeria
Tamar *67 C7 river* SW England, United Kingdom
Tamar *see* Tudmur
Tamatave *see* Toamasina
Tamazunchale *29 E4* San Luis Potosí, C Mexico
Tambacounda *52 C3* SE Senegal
Tambov *89 B6* Tambovskaya Oblast', W Russian Federation
Tambura *51 B5* W Equatoria, SW South Sudan
Tamchaket *see* Tâmchekkeṭ
Tâmchekkeṭ *52 C3 var.* Tamchaket. Hodh el Gharbi, S Mauritania
Tamenghest *see* Tamanrasset
Tamil Nādu *110 C3 prev.* Madras. *cultural region* SE India
Tam Ky *115 E5* Quang Nam-Đa Năng, C Vietnam
Tammerfors *see* Tampere
Tampa *21 E4* Florida, SE USA
Tampa Bay *21 E4 bay* Florida, SE USA
Tampere *63 D5 Swe.* Tammerfors. Länsi-Suomi, W Finland
Tampico *29 E3* Tamaulipas, C Mexico
Tamworth *127 D6* New South Wales, SE Australia
Tanabe *109 C7* Wakayama, Honshū, SW Japan
Tana Bru *62 D2* Finnmark, N Norway
T'ana Hāyk' *50 C4 var.* Lake Tana. *lake* NW Ethiopia
Tanais *see* Don
Tana, Lake *see* T'ana Hāyk'
Tanami Desert *124 D3 desert* Northern Territory, N Australia
Tananarive *see* Antananarivo
Ţăndărei *86 D5* Ialomiţa, SE Romania
Tandil *43 D5* Buenos Aires, E Argentina
Tandjoengkarang *see* Bandar Lampung
Tanega-shima *109 B8 island* Nansei-shotō, SW Japan
Tanen Taunggyi *see* Tane Range
Tane Range *114 B4 Bur.* Tanen Taunggyi. *mountain range* W Thailand
Tanezrouft *48 D4 desert* Algeria/Mali
Ţanf, Jabal aţ *96 D4 mountain* SE Syria
Tanga *51 C7* Tanga, E Tanzania
Tanganyika and Zanzibar *see* Tanzania
Tanganyika, Lake *51 B7 lake* E Africa
Tanger *48 C2 var.* Tangiers, Tangier, *Fr./Ger.* Tangerk, *Sp.* Tánger; *anc.* Tingis. NW Morocco
Tangerk *see* Tanger
Tanggula Shan *104 C4 mountain* W China
Tangier *see* Tanger
Tangiers *see* Tanger
Tangra Yumco *104 B5 var.* Tangro Tso. *lake* W China
Tangro Tso *see* Tangra Yumco
Tangshan *106 D3 var.* T'ang-shan. Hebei, E China
T'ang-shan *see* Tangshan
Tanimbar, Kepulauan *117 F5 island group* Maluku, E Indonesia
Tanintharyi *115 B6 prev.* Tenasserim. S Myanmar (Burma)
Tanjungkarang/Tanjungkarang-Telukbetung *see* Bandar Lampung
Tanna *122 D4 island* S Vanuatu
Tannenhof *see* Krynica
Tan-Tan *48 B3* SW Morocco
Tan-tung *see* Dandong
Tanzania *51 C7 off.* United Republic of Tanzania, *Swa.* Jamhuri ya Muungano wa Tanzania; *prev.* German East Africa, Tanganyika and Zanzibar. *country* E Africa
Tanzania, Jamhuri ya Muungano wa *see* Tanzania
Tanzania, United Republic of *see* Tanzania
Taoudenit *see* Taoudenni
Taoudenni *53 E2 var.* Taoudenit. Tombouctou, N Mali
Tapa *84 E2 Ger.* Taps. Lääne-Virumaa, NE Estonia
Tapachula *29 G5* Chiapas, SE Mexico
Tapaiu *see* Gvardeysk
Tapajós, Rio *41 E2 var.* Tapajóz. *river* NW Brazil
Tapajóz *see* Tapajós, Rio
Taps *see* Tapa
Ţarābulus *49 F2 var.* Ţarābulus al Gharb, *Eng.* Tripoli. *country capital* (Libya) NW Libya
Ţarābulus al Gharb *see* Ţarābulus
Ţarābulus/Ţarābulus ash Shām *see* Tripoli
Taraclia *86 D4 Rus.* Tarakilya. S Moldova
Tarakilya *see* Taraclia
Taranaki, Mount *128 C4 var.* Egmont. *volcano* North Island, New Zealand
Tarancón *71 E3* Castilla-La Mancha, C Spain
Taranto *75 E5 var.* Tarentum. Puglia, SE Italy
Taranto, Gulf of *75 E6 Eng.* Gulf of Taranto. *gulf* S Italy
Taranto, Gulf of *see* Taranto, Golfo di
Tarapoto *38 C2* San Martín, N Peru
Tarare *69 D5* Rhône, E France
Tarascon *69 D6* Bouches-du-Rhône, SE France
Tarawa *122 D2 atoll* Tungaru, W Kiribati
Taraz *92 C5 prev.* Aulie Ata, Auliye-Ata, Dzhambul, Zhambyl. Zhambyl, S Kazakhstan
Tarazona *71 E2* Aragón, NE Spain
Tarbes *69 B6 anc.* Bigorra. Hautes-Pyrénées, S France
Tarcoola *127 A6* South Australia
Taree *127 D6* New South Wales, SE Australia
Tarentum *see* Taranto
Târgovişte *86 C5 prev.* Tîrgovişte. Dâmboviţa, S Romania
Târgu Jiu *86 B4 prev.* Tîrgu Jiu. Gorj, W Romania
Târgul-Neamţ *see* Târgu-Neamţ
Târgul-Săcuiesc *see* Târgu Secuiesc
Târgu Mureş *86 B4 prev.* Oşorhei, Tîrgu Mures, *Ger.* Neumarkt, *Hung.* Marosvásárhely. Mureş, C Romania
Târgu-Neamţ *86 C3 var.* Târgul-Neamţ; *prev.* Tîrgu-Neamţ. Neamţ, NE Romania
Târgu Ocna *86 C4 Hung.* Aknavásár; *prev.* Tîrgu Ocna. Bacău, E Romania
Târgu Secuiesc *86 C4 Ger.* Neumarkt, Szekler Neumarkt, *Hung.* Kezdivásárhely; *prev.* Chezdi-Oşorheiu, Târgul-Săcuiesc, Tîrgu Secuiesc. Covasna, E Romania
Tar Heel State *see* North Carolina
Tarija *39 G5* Tarija, S Bolivia
Tarīm *99 C6* C Yemen
Tarim Basin *see* Tarim Pendi
Tarim Pendi *102 C2 Eng.* Tarim Basin. *basin* NW China
Tarim He *104 B3 river* NW China
Tarma *38 C3* Junín, C Peru
Tarn *69 C6 cultural region* S France
Tarn *69 C6 river* S France
Tarnobrzeg *76 D4* Podkarpackie, SE Poland
Tarnopol *see* Ternopil'
Tarnów *77 D5* Małopolskie, S Poland
Tarraco *see* Tarragona
Tarragona *71 G2 anc.* Tarraco. Cataluña, E Spain
Tarrasa *see* Terrassa
Tàrrega *71 F2 var.* Tarrega. Cataluña, NE Spain
Tarsatica *see* Rijeka
Tarsus *94 C4* İçel, S Turkey
Tartous/Tartouss *see* Ţarţūs
Tartu *84 D3 Ger.* Dorpat; *prev. Rus.* Yurev, Yury'ev. Tartumaa, SE Estonia
Ţarţūs *96 A3 off.* Muḥāfaẓat Ţarţūs, *var.* Tartous, Tartus. *governorate* W Syria
Ţarţūs, Muḥāfaẓat *see* Ţarţūs
Ta Ru Tao, Ko *115 B7 island* S Thailand Asia
Tarvisio *74 D2* Friuli-Venezia Giulia, NE Italy
Tarvisium *see* Treviso
Tashauz *see* Daşoguz
Tashi Chho Dzong *see* Thimphu
Tashkent *see* Toshkent
Tash-Kömür *see* Tash-Kumyr
Tash-Kumyr *101 F2 Kir.* Tash-Kömür. Dzhalal-Abadskaya Oblast', W Kyrgyzstan
Tashqurghan *see* Khulm
Tasikmalaja *see* Tasikmalaya
Tasikmalaya *116 C5 prev.* Tasikmalaja. Jawa, C Indonesia
Tasman Basin *120 C5 var.* East Australian Basin. *undersea basin* S Tasman Sea
Tasman Bay *129 C5 inlet* South Island, New Zealand
Tasmania *127 B8 prev.* Van Diemen's Land. *state* SE Australia
Tasmania *130 B4 island* SE Australia
Tasman Plateau *120 C5 var.* South Tasmania Plateau. *undersea plateau* SW Tasman Sea
Tasman Sea *120 C5 sea* SW Pacific Ocean
Tassili-n-Ajjer *49 E4 plateau* E Algeria
Tatabánya *77 C6* Komárom Esztergom, NW Hungary
Tatar Pazardzhik *see* Pazardzhik
Tathlīth *99 B5* 'Asīr, S Saudi Arabia
Tatra Mountains *77 D5 Ger.* Tatra, *Hung.* Tátra, *Pol./Slvk.* Tatry. *mountain range* Poland/Slovakia
Tatra/Tátra *see* Tatra Mountains
Tatry *see* Tatra Mountains
Ta-t'ung/Tatung *see* Datong
Tatvan *95 F3* Bitlis, SE Turkey
Ta'ū *123 F4 var.* Tau. *island* Manua Islands, E American Samoa
Taukum, Peski *101 G1 desert* SE Kazakhstan
Taumarunui *128 D4* Manawatu-Wanganui, North Island, New Zealand
Taungdwingyi *114 B3* Magway, C Myanmar (Burma)
Taunggyi *114 B3* Shan State, C Myanmar (Burma)
Taungoo *114 B4* Bago, C Myanmar (Burma)
Taunton *67 C7* SW England, United Kingdom
Taupo *128 D3* Waikato, North Island, New Zealand
Taupo, Lake *128 D3 lake* North Island, New Zealand
Tauragė *84 B4 Ger.* Tauroggen. Tauragė, SW Lithuania
Tauranga *128 D3* Bay of Plenty, North Island, New Zealand
Tauris *see* Tabrīz
Tauroggen *see* Tauragė
Taurus Mountains *see* Toros Dağları
Tavas *94 B4* Denizli, SW Turkey
Tavastehus *see* Hämeenlinna
Tavira *70 C5* Faro, S Portugal
Tavoy *see* Dawei
Tavoy Island *see* Mali Kyun
Ta Waewae Bay *129 A7 bay* South Island, New Zealand
Tawakoni, Lake *27 G2 reservoir* Texas, SW USA
Tawau *116 D3* Sabah, East Malaysia
Ţawkar *see* Tokar
Tawzar *see* Tozeur
Taxco *29 E4 var.* Taxco de Alarcón. Guerrero, S Mexico
Taxco de Alarcón *see* Taxco
Taxiatosh *100 C2 Rus.* Takhiatash. Qoraqalpog'iston Respublikasi, W Uzbekistan
Taxtako'pir *100 D1 Rus.* Takhtakupyr. Qoraqalpog'iston Respublikasi, NW Uzbekistan
Tay *66 C3 river* C Scotland, United Kingdom
Taylor *27 G3* Texas, SW USA
Taymā' *98 A4* Tabūk, NW Saudi Arabia
Taymyr, Ozero *93 E2 lake* N Russian Federation
Taymyr, Poluostrov *93 E2 peninsula* N Russian Federation
Taz *92 D3 river* N Russian Federation
Tbilisi *95 G2 var.* T'bilisi, *Eng.* Tiflis. *country capital* (Georgia) SE Georgia
T'bilisi *see* **Tbilisi**
Tchad *see* Chad
Tchad, Lac *see* Chad, Lake
Tchien *see* Zwedru
Tchongking *see* Chongqing
Tczew *76 C2 Ger.* Dirschau. Pomorskie, N Poland
Te Anau *129 A7* Southland, South Island, New Zealand
Te Anau, Lake *129 A7 lake* South Island, New Zealand
Teapa *29 G4* Tabasco, SE Mexico
Teate *see* Chieti
Tebingtinggi *116 B3* Sumatera, N Indonesia
Tebriz *see* Tabrīz
Techirghiol *86 D5* Constanţa, SE Romania
Tecomán *28 D4* Colima, SW Mexico
Tecpan *29 E5 var.* Tecpan de Galeana. Guerrero, S Mexico
Tecpan de Galeana *see* Tecpan
Tecuci *86 C4* Galaţi, E Romania
Tedzhen *see* Harīrūd/Tejen
Tedzhen *see* Tejen
Tees *67 D5 river* N England, United Kingdom
Tefé *40 D2* Amazonas, N Brazil
Tegal *116 C4* Jawa, C Indonesia
Tegelen *65 D5* Limburg, SE Netherlands
Tegucigalpa *30 C3 country capital* (Honduras) Francisco Morazán, SW Honduras
Teheran *see* Tehrān
Tehrān *98 C3 var.* Teheran. *country capital* (Iran) Tehrān, N Iran
Tehuacán *29 F4* Puebla, S Mexico
Tehuantepec *29 F5 var.* Santo Domingo Tehuantepec. Oaxaca, SE Mexico
Tehuantepec, Golfo de *29 F5 var.* Gulf of Tehuantepec. *gulf* S Mexico
Tehuantepec, Gulf of *see* Tehuantepec, Golfo de

Tehuantepec, Isthmus of – Trbovlje

Tehuantepec, Isthmus of *see* Tehuantepec, Istmo de
Tehuantepec, Istmo de *29 F5 var.* Isthmus of Tehuantepec. *isthmus* SE Mexico
Tejen *100 C3 Rus.* Tedzhen. Ahal Welaýaty, S Turkmenistan
Tejen *see* Harīrūd
Tejo, Rio *see* Tagus
Te Kao *128 C1* Northland, North Island, New Zealand
Tekax *29 H4 var.* Tekax de Álvaro Obregón. Yucatán, SE Mexico
Tekax de Álvaro Obregón *see* Tekax
Tekeli *92 C5* Almaty, SE Kazakhstan
Tekirdağ *94 A2 It.* Rodosto; *anc.* Bisanthe, Raidestos, Rhaedestus. Tekirdağ, NW Turkey
Te Kuiti *128 D3* Waikato, North Island, New Zealand
Tela *30 C2* Atlántida, NW Honduras
Telanaipura *see* Jambi
Telangana *112 D5 cultural region* SE India
Tel Aviv-Jaffa *see* Tel Aviv-Yafo
Tel Aviv-Yafo *97 A6 var.* Tel Aviv-Jaffa. Tel Aviv, C Israel
Teles Pirés *see* São Manuel, Rio
Telish *82 C2 prev.* Azizie. Pleven, N Bulgaria
Tell Abiad/Tell Abyad *see* At Tall al Abyaḍ
Tell Kalakh *see* Tall Kalakh
Tell Shedadi *see* Ash Shadādah
Tel'man/Tel'mansk *see* Gubadag
Teloekbetoeng *see* Bandar Lampung
Telo Martius *see* Toulon
Telschen *see* Telšiai
Telšiai *84 B3 Ger.* Telschen. Telšiai, NW Lithuania
Telukbetung *see* Bandar Lampung
Temerin *78 D3* Vojvodina, N Serbia
Temeschburg/Temeschwar *see* Timişoara
Temesvár/Temeswar *see* Timişoara
Temirtau *92 C4 prev.* Samarkandski, Samarkandskoye. Karagandy, C Kazakhstan
Tempio Pausania *75 A5* Sardegna, Italy, C Mediterranean Sea
Temple *27 G3* Texas, SW USA
Temuco *43 B5* Araucanía, C Chile
Temuka *129 B6* Canterbury, South Island, New Zealand
Tenasserim *see* Tanintharyi
Ténenkou *52 D3* Mopti, C Mali
Ténéré *53 G3 physical region* C Niger
Tenerife *48 A3 island* Islas Canarias, Spain, NE Atlantic Ocean
Tengger Shamo *105 E3 desert* N China
Tengréla *52 D4 var.* Tingréla. N Côte d'Ivoire
Tenkodogo *53 E4* S Burkina
Tennant Creek *126 A3* Northern Territory, C Australia
Tennessee *20 C1 off.* State of Tennessee, *also known as* The Volunteer State. *state* SE USA
Tennessee River *20 C1 river* S USA
Tenos *see* Tínos
Tepelena *see* Tepelenë
Tepelenë *79 C7 var.* Tepelena, *It.* Tepeleni. Gjirokastër, S Albania
Tepeleni *see* Tepelenë
Tepic *28 D4* Nayarit, C Mexico
Teplice *76 A4 Ger.* Teplitz; *prev.* Teplice-Šanov, Teplitz-Schönau. Ústecký Kraj, NW Czech Republic
Teplice-Šanov/Teplitz/Teplitz-Schönau *see* Teplice
Tequila *28 D4* Jalisco, SW Mexico
Teraina *123 G2 prev.* Washington Island. *atoll* Line Islands, E Kiribati
Teramo *74 C4 anc.* Interamna. Abruzzi, C Italy
Tercan *95 E3* Erzincan, NE Turkey
Terceira *70 A5 var.* Ilha Terceira. *island* Azores, Portugal, NE Atlantic Ocean
Terceira, Ilha *see* Terceira
Terekhovka *see* Tsyerakhowka
Teresina *41 F2 var.* Therezina. *state capital* Piauí, NE Brazil
Termez *see* Termiz
Termia *see* Kýthnos
Términos, Laguna de *29 G4 lagoon* SE Mexico
Termiz *101 E3 Rus.* Termez. Surkhondaryo Viloyati, S Uzbekistan
Termoli *74 D4* Molise, C Italy
Terneuzen *65 B5 var.* Neuzen. Zeeland, SW Netherlands
Terni *74 C4 anc.* Interamna Nahars. Umbria, C Italy
Ternopil' *86 C2 Pol.* Tarnopol, *Rus.* Ternopol'. Ternopil's'ka Oblast', W Ukraine
Ternopol' *see* Ternopil'
Terracina *75 C5* Lazio, C Italy
Terranova di Sicilia *see* Gela
Terranova Pausania *see* Olbia
Terrassa *71 G2 Cast.* Tarrasa. Cataluña, E Spain
Terre Adélie *132 C4 physical region* Antarctica
Terre Haute *18 B4* Indiana, N USA
Terre Neuve *see* Newfoundland and Labrador
Terschelling *64 C1 Fris.* Skylge. *island* Waddeneilanden, N Netherlands
Teruel *71 F3 anc.* Turba. Aragón, E Spain
Tervel *82 E1 prev.* Kurtbunar, *Rom.* Curtbunar. Dobrich, NE Bulgaria
Tervueren *see* Tervuren
Tervuren *65 C6 var.* Tervueren. Vlaams Brabant, C Belgium
Teseney *50 C4 var.* Tessenei. W Eritrea
Tessalit *53 E2* Kidal, NE Mali
Tessaoua *53 G3* Maradi, S Niger
Tessenderlo *65 C5* Limburg, NE Belgium
Tessenei *see* Teseney
Testigos, Islas los *37 E1 island group* N Venezuela
Tete *57 E2* Tete, NW Mozambique
Teterow *72 C3* Mecklenburg-Vorpommern, NE Germany
Tétouan *48 C2 var.* Tetouan, Tetuán. N Morocco
Tetovo *79 D5* Razgrad, N Bulgaria
Tetschen *see* Děčín
Tetuán *see* Tétouan
Teverya *see* Tverya
Te Waewae Bay *129 A7 bay* South Island, New Zealand
Texarkana *20 A2* Arkansas, C USA
Texarkana *27 H2* Texas, SW USA
Texas *27 F3 off.* State of Texas, *also known as* Lone Star State. *state* S USA
Texas City *27 H4* Texas, SW USA
Texel *64 C2 island* Waddeneilanden, NW Netherlands
Texoma, Lake *27 G2 reservoir* Oklahoma/ Texas, C USA
Teziutlán *29 F4* Puebla, S Mexico
Thaa Atoll *see* Kolhumadulu
Thai, Ao *see* Thailand, Gulf of
Thai Binh *114 D3* Thai Binh, N Vietnam
Thailand *115 C5 off.* Kingdom of Thailand, *Th.* Prathet Thai; *prev.* Siam. *country* SE Asia
Thailand, Gulf of *115 C6 var.* Gulf of Siam, *Th.* Ao Thai, *Vtn.* Vinh Thai Lan. *gulf* SE Asia
Thailand, Kingdom of *see* Thailand
Thai Lan, Vinh *see* Thailand, Gulf of
Thai Nguyên *114 D3* Bắc Thai, N Vietnam
Thakhèk *114 D4 var.* Muang Khammouan. Khammouan, C Laos
Thamarid *see* Thamarīt
Thamarīt *99 D6 var.* Thamarid, Thumrayt. SW Oman
Thames *128 D3* Waikato, North Island, New Zealand
Thames *67 B8 river* S England, United Kingdom
Thandwe *114 A4 var.* Sandoway. Rakhine State, W Myanmar (Burma)
Thanh Hoa *114 D3* Thanh Hoa, N Vietnam
Thanintari Taungdan *see* Bilauktaung Range
Thanlwin *see* Salween
Thar Desert *112 C3 var.* Great Indian Desert, Indian Desert. *desert* India/Pakistan
Tharthar, Buhayrat ath *98 B3 lake* C Iraq
Thásos *82 C4* Thásos, E Greece
Thásos *82 C4 island* E Greece
Thaton *114 B4* Mon State, S Myanmar (Burma)
Thayetmyo *114 A4* Magway, C Myanmar (Burma)
The Crane *33 H2 var.* Crane. S Barbados
The Dalles *24 B3* Oregon, NW USA
The Flatts Village *see* Flatts Village
The Hague *see* 's-Gravenhage
Theodosia *see* Feodosiya
The Pas *15 F5* Manitoba, C Canada
Therezina *see* Teresina
Thérma *83 D6* Ikaría, Dodekánisa, Greece, Aegean Sea
Thermaic Gulf/Thermaicus Sinus *see* Thermaïkós Kólpos
Thermaïkós Kólpos *82 B4 Eng.* Thermaic Gulf; *anc.* Thermaicus Sinus. *gulf* N Greece
Thermiá *see* Kýthnos
Thérmo *83 B5* Dytikí Ellás, C Greece
The Rock *71 H4* New South Wales, SE Australia
The Sooner State *see* Oklahoma
Thessaloníki *82 C3 Eng.* Salonica, Salonika, *SCr.* Solun, *Turk.* Selânik. Kentrikí Makedonía, N Greece
The Valley *33 G3 dependent territory capital* (Anguilla) E Anguilla
The Village *27 G1* Oklahoma, C USA
The Volunteer State *see* Tennessee
Thiamis *see* Kalamás
Thian Shan *see* Tien Shan
Thibet *see* Xizang Zizhiqu
Thief River Falls *23 F1* Minnesota, N USA
Thienen *see* Tienen
Thiers *69 C5* Puy-de-Dôme, C France
Thiès *52 B3* W Senegal
Thikombia *see* Cikobia
Thimbu *see* Thimphu
Thimphu *113 G3 var.* Thimbu; *prev.* Tashi Chho Dzong. *country capital* (Bhutan) W Bhutan
Thionville *68 D3 Ger.* Diedenhofen. Moselle, NE France
Thíra *83 D7 var.* Santorini. Kykládes, Greece, Aegean Sea
Thiruvanantapuram *110 C3 var.* Trivandrum, Tiruvantapuram. *state capital* Kerala, SW India
Thitu Island *106 C8 island* NW Spratly Islands
Tholen *64 B4 island* SW Netherlands
Thomasville *20 D3* Georgia, SE USA
Thompson *15 F4* Manitoba, C Canada
Thonon-les-Bains *69 D5* Haute-Savoie, E France
Thorenburg *see* Turda
Thorlákshöfn *61 E5* Sudhurland, SW Iceland
Thorn *see* Toruń
Thornton Island *see* Millennium Island
Thorshavn *see* Tórshavn
Thospitis *see* Van Gölü
Thouars *68 B4* Deux-Sèvres, W France
Thoune *see* Thun
Thracian Sea *82 D4 Gk.* Thrakikó Pélagos; *anc.* Thracium Mare. *sea* Greece/Turkey
Thracium Mare/Thrakikó Pélagos *see* Thracian Sea
Three Gorges Reservoir *107 C5 reservoir* C China
Three Kings Islands *128 C1 island group* N New Zealand
Thrissur *110 C3 var.* Trichūr. Kerala, SW India
Thuin *65 B7* Hainaut, S Belgium
Thule *see* Qaanaaq
Thumrayt *see* Thamarīt
Thun *73 A7 Fr.* Thoune. Bern, W Switzerland
Thunder Bay *16 B4* Ontario, S Canada
Thuner See *73 A7 lake* C Switzerland
Thung Song *115 C7 var.* Cha Mai. Nakhon Si Thammarat, SW Thailand
Thurso *66 C2* N Scotland, United Kingdom
Thýamis *see* Kalamás
Tianjin *106 D4 var.* Tientsin. Tianjin Shi, E China
Tianjin *see* Tianjin Shi
Tianjin Shi *106 D4 var.* Jin, Tianjin, T'ien-ching, Tientsin. *municipality* E China
Tian Shan *see* Tien Shan
Tianshui *106 B4* Gansu, C China
Tiba *see* Chiba
Tiber *74 C4 Eng.* Tiber. *river* C Italy
Tiber *see* Tevere, Italy
Tiber *see* Tivoli, Italy
Tiberias *see* Tverya
Tiberias, Lake *97 B5 var.* Chinnereth, Sea of Bahr Tabariya, Sea of Galilee, *Ar.* Bahrat Tabariya, *Heb.* Yam Kinneret. *lake* N Israel
Tibesti *54 C2 var.* Tibesti Massif, *Ar.* Tibistī. *mountain range* N Africa
Tibesti Massif *see* Tibesti
Tibet *see* Xizang Zizhiqu
Tibetan Autonomous Region *see* Xizang Zizhiqu
Tibet, Plateau of *see* Qingzang Gaoyuan
Tibistī *see* Tibesti
Tibnī *see* At Tibnī
Tiburón, Isla *28 B2 var.* Isla del Tiburón. *island* NW Mexico
Tiburón, Isla del *see* Tiburón, Isla
Tichau *see* Tychy
Tîchît *52 D2 var.* Tichitt. Tagant, C Mauritania
Tichitt *see* Tîchît
Ticinum *see* Pavia
Ticul *29 H3* Yucatán, SE Mexico
Tidjikdja *see* Tidjikja
Tidjikja *52 C2 var.* Tidjikdja; *prev.* Fort-Cappolani. Tagant, C Mauritania
T'ien-ching *see* Tianjin Shi
Tienen *65 C6 var.* Thienen, *Fr.* Tirlemont. Vlaams Brabant, C Belgium
Tiên Giang, Sông *see* Mekong
Tien Shan *104 B3 Chin.* Thian Shan, Tian Shan, T'ien Shan, *Rus.* Tyan'-Shan'. *mountain range* C Asia
Tientsin *see* Tianjin
Tierp *63 C6* Uppsala, C Sweden
Tierra del Fuego *43 B8 island* Argentina/Chile
Tiflis *see* T'bilisi
Tifton *20 D3* Georgia, SE USA
Tifu *117 F4* Pulau Buru, E Indonesia
Tighina *86 D4 Rus.* Bendery; *prev.* Bender. E Moldova
Tigranocerta *see* Siirt
Tigris *98 B2 Ar.* Dijlah, *Turk.* Dicle. *river* Iraq/ Turkey
Tiguentourine *49 E3* E Algeria
Ti-hua/Tihwa *see* Ürümqi
Tijuana *28 A1* Baja California Norte, NW Mexico
Tikhoretsk *89 A7* Krasnodarskiy Kray, SW Russian Federation
Tikhvin *88 B4* Leningradskaya Oblast', NW Russian Federation
Tiki Basin *121 G3 undersea basin* S Pacific Ocean
Tikinsso *52 C4 river* C Guinea
Tiksi *93 F2* Respublika Sakha (Yakutiya), NE Russian Federation
Tilburg *64 C4* Noord-Brabant, S Netherlands
Tilimsen *see* Tlemcen
Tilio Martius *see* Toulon
Tillabéri *53 F3 var.* Tillabéry. Tillabéri, W Niger
Tillabéry *see* Tillabéri
Tílos *83 E7 island* Dodekánisa, Greece, Aegean Sea
Timan Ridge *see* Timanskiy Kryazh
Timanskiy Kryazh *88 D3 Eng.* Timan Ridge. *ridge* NW Russian Federation
Timaru *129 B6* Canterbury, South Island, New Zealand
Timbaki/Timbákion *see* Tympáki
Timbedgha *52 D3 var.* Timbédra. Hodh ech Chargui, SE Mauritania
Timbédra *see* Timbedgha
Timbuktu *see* Tombouctou
Timiş *86 A4 county* SW Romania
Timişoara *86 A4 Ger.* Temeschwar, Temeswar, *Hung.* Temesvár; *prev.* Temeschburg. Timiş, W Romania
Timmins *16 C4* Ontario, S Canada
Timor *103 F5 island* Nusa Tenggara, C Indonesia
Timor Sea *103 F5 sea* E Indian Ocean
Timor Timur *see* East Timor
Timor Trench *see* Timor Trough
Timor Trough *103 F5 var.* Timor Trench. *trough* NE Timor Sea
Timrå *63 C5* Västernorrland, C Sweden
Tindouf *48 C3* W Algeria
Tineo *70 C1* Asturias, N Spain
Tingis *see* Tanger
Tingo María *38 C3* Huánuco, C Peru
Tingréla *see* Tengréla
Tinhosa Grande *54 E2 island* N Sao Tome and Principe, Africa, E Atlantic Ocean
Tinhosa Pequena *54 E1 island* N Sao Tome and Principe, Africa, E Atlantic Ocean
Tinian *122 B1 island* S Northern Mariana Islands
Tínos *83 D6* Tínos, Kykládes, Greece, Aegean Sea
Tínos *83 D6 anc.* Tenos. *island* Kykládes, Greece, Aegean Sea
Tip *79 E6* Papua, E Indonesia
Tipitapa *30 D3* Managua, W Nicaragua
Tip Top Mountain *16 C4 mountain* Ontario, S Canada
Tirana *see* Tiranë
Tiranë *79 C6 var.* Tirana. *country capital* (Albania) Tiranë, C Albania
Tiraspol *86 D4 Rus.* Tiraspol'. E Moldova
Tiraspol' *see* Tiraspol
Tiree *66 B3 island* W Scotland, United Kingdom
Tîrgovişte *see* Târgovişte
Tîrgu Jiu *see* Targu Jiu
Tîrgu Mures *see* Târgu Mureş
Tîrgu-Neamţ *see* Târgu-Neamţ
Tîrgu Ocna *see* Târgu Ocna
Tîrgu Secuiesc *see* Târgu Secuiesc
Tirlemont *see* Tienen
Tirnavos *see* Týrnavos
Tirnovo *see* Veliko Tŭrnovo
Tirol *73 C7 off.* Land Tirol, *var.* Tyrol, *It.* Tirolo. *state* W Austria
Tirol, Land *see* Tirol
Tirolo *see* Tirol
Tirreno, Mare *see* Tyrrhenian Sea
Tiruchchirāppalli *110 C3 prev.* Trichinopoly. Tamil Nādu, SE India
Tiruppattūr *110 C2* Tamil Nādu, SE India
Tiruvantapuram *see* Thiruvanathapuram
Tisa *see* Tisza
Tisza *81 F1 Ger.* Theiss, *Rom./Slvn./SCr.* Tisa, *Rus.* Tissa, *Ukr.* Tysa. *river* SE Europe
Tiszakécske *77 D7* Bács-Kiskun, C Hungary
Titano, Monte *74 E1 mountain* C San Marino
Titicaca, Lake *39 E4 lake* Bolivia/Peru
Titograd *see* Podgorica
Titose *see* Chitose
Titova Mitrovica *see* Mitrovicë
Titovo Užice *see* Užice
Titu *86 C5* Dâmboviţa, S Romania
Titule *55 D5* Orientale, N Dem. Rep. Congo
Tiverton *67 C7* SW England, United Kingdom
Tivoli *74 C4 anc.* Tiber. Lazio, C Italy
Tizimín *29 H3* Yucatán, SE Mexico
Tizi Ouzou *49 E1 var.* Tizi-Ouzou. N Algeria
Tizi-Ouzou *see* Tizi Ouzou
Tiznit *48 B3* SW Morocco
Tjilatjap *see* Cilacap
Tjirebon *see* Cirebon
Tlaquepaque *28 D4* Jalisco, C Mexico
Tlascala *see* Tlaxcala
Tlaxcala *29 F4 var.* Tlascala, Tlaxcala de Xicohténcatl. Tlaxcala, C Mexico
Tlaxcala de Xicohténcatl *see* Tlaxcala
Tlemcen *48 D2 var.* Tilimsen, Tlemsen. NW Algeria
Tlemsen *see* Tlemcen
Toamasina *57 G3 var.* Tamatave. Toamasina, E Madagascar
Toba, Danau *116 B3 lake* Sumatera, W Indonesia
Tobago *33 H5 island* NE Trinidad and Tobago
Toba Kakar Range *112 B2 mountain range* NW Pakistan
Tobol *92 C4 Kaz.* Tobyl. *river* Kazakhstan/Russian Federation
Tobol'sk *92 C3* Tyumenskaya Oblast', C Russian Federation
Tobruch/Tobruk *see* Ṭubruq
Tobyl *see* Tobol
Tocantins *41 E3 off.* Estado do Tocantins. *state* C Brazil
Tocantins *41 E3 off.* Estado do Tocantins. *region* C Brazil
Tocantins, Estado do *see* Tocantins
Tocantins, Rio *41 F2 river* N Brazil
Tocoa *30 D2* Colón, N Honduras
Tocopilla *42 B2* Antofagasta, N Chile
Todi *74 C4* Umbria, C Italy
Todos os Santos, Baía de *41 G3 bay* E Brazil
Toetoes Bay *129 B8 bay* South Island, New Zealand
Tofua *123 E4 island* Ha'apai Group, C Tonga
Togo *53 E4 off.* Togolese Republic; *prev.* French Togoland. *country* W Africa
Togolese Republic *see* Togo
Tojikiston, Jumhurii *see* Tajikistan
Tokanui *129 B7* Southland, South Island, New Zealand
Tokar *50 C3 var.* Ṭawkar. Red Sea, NE Sudan
Tokat *94 D3* Tokat, N Turkey
Tokelau *123 E3 NZ overseas territory* W Polynesia
Tőketerebes *see* Trebišov
Tokio *see* Tōkyō
Tokmak *101 G2 Kir.* Tokmok. Chuyskaya Oblast', N Kyrgyzstan
Tokmak *87 G4 var.* Velykyy Tokmak. Zaporiz'ka Oblast', SE Ukraine
Tokmok *see* Tokmak
Tokoroa *128 D3* Waikato, North Island, New Zealand
Tokounou *52 C4* C Guinea
Tokushima *109 C6 var.* Tokusima. Tokushima, Shikoku, SW Japan
Tōkyō *108 A1 var.* Tokio. *country capital* (Japan) Tōkyō, Honshū, S Japan
Tōkyō-wan *108 A2 bay* S Japan
Tolbukhin *see* Dobrich
Toledo *70 D3 anc.* Toletum. Castilla-La Mancha, C Spain
Toledo *18 D3* Ohio, N USA
Toledo Bend Reservoir *27 G3 reservoir* Louisiana/ Texas, SW USA
Toletum *see* Toledo
Toliara *57 F4 var.* Toliary; *prev.* Tuléar. Toliara, SW Madagascar
Toliary *see* Toliara
Tolmein *see* Tolmin
Tolmin *73 D7 Ger.* Tolmein, *It.* Tolmino. W Slovenia
Tolmino *see* Tolmin
Tolna *77 C7 Ger.* Tolnau. Tolna, S Hungary
Tolnau *see* Tolna
Tolochin *see* Talachyn
Tolosa *71 E1* País Vasco, N Spain
Tolosa *see* Toulouse
Toluca *29 E4 var.* Toluca de Lerdo. México, S Mexico
Toluca de Lerdo *see* Toluca
Tol'yatti *89 C6 prev.* Stavropol'. Samarskaya Oblast', W Russian Federation
Tomah *18 B2* Wisconsin, N USA
Tomakomai *108 D2* Hokkaidō, NE Japan
Tomar *70 B3* Santarém, W Portugal
Tomaschow *see* Tomaszów Mazowiecki
Tomaschow *see* Tomaszów Lubelski
Tomaszów *see* Tomaszów Mazowiecki
Tomaszów Lubelski *76 E4 Ger.* Tomaschow. Lubelskie, E Poland
Tomaszów Mazowiecka *see* Tomaszów Mazowiecki
Tomaszów Mazowiecki *76 D4 var.* Tomaszów Mazowiecka; *prev.* Tomaszów, *Ger.* Tomaschow. Łódzkie, C Poland
Tombigbee River *20 C3 river* Alabama/ Mississippi, S USA
Tombouctou *53 E3 Eng.* Timbuktu. Tombouctou, N Mali
Tombua *56 A2 Port.* Porto Alexandre. Namibe, SW Angola
Tomelloso *71 E3* Castilla-La Mancha, C Spain
Tomini, Gulf of *see* Teluk Tomini
Tomini, Teluk *117 E4 Eng.* Gulf of Tomini; *prev.* Teluk Gorontalo. *bay* Sulawesi, C Indonesia
Tomsk *92 D4* Tomskaya Oblast', C Russian Federation
Tomür Feng *104 B3 pre.* Pik Pobedy; *Kyrg.* Jengish Chokusu. *mountain* China/Kyrgyzstan
Tonezh *see* Tonyezh
Tonga *123 E4 off.* Kingdom of Tonga, *var.* Friendly Islands. *country* SW Pacific Ocean
Tonga, Kingdom of *see* Tonga
Tongatapu *123 E5 island* Tongatapu Group, S Tonga
Tongatapu Group *123 E5 island group* S Tonga
Tonga Trench *121 E3 trench* S Pacific Ocean
Tongchuan *106 C4* Shaanxi, C China
Tongeren *65 D6 Fr.* Tongres. Limburg, NE Belgium
Tongking, Gulf of *see* Tonkin, Gulf of
Tongliao *105 G2* Nei Mongol Zizhiqu, N China
Tongres *see* Tongeren
Tongshan *see* Xuzhou, Jiangsu, China
Tongtian He *104 C4 river* C China
Tonj *51 B5* Warab, C South Sudan
Tonkin, Gulf of *106 B7 var.* Tongking, Gulf of, *Chin.* Beibu Wan, *Vtn.* Vinh Bắc Bộ. *gulf* China/ Vietnam
Tônlé Sap *115 D5 Eng.* Great Lake. *lake* W Cambodia
Tonopah *25 C6* Nevada, W USA
Tonyezh *85 C7 Rus.* Tonezh. Homyel'skaya Voblasts', SE Belarus
Tooele *22 B4* Utah, W USA
Toowoomba *127 E5* Queensland, E Australia
Topeka *23 F4 state capital* Kansas, C USA
Toplicza *see* Topliţa
Topliţa *86 C3 Ger.* Töplitz, *Hung.* Maroshevíz; *prev.* Topliţa Română, *Hung.* Oláh-Toplicza, Toplicza. Harghita, C Romania
Topliţa Română/Töplitz *see* Topliţa
Topoľčany *77 C6 Hung.* Nagytapolcsány. Nitriansky Kraj, W Slovakia
Topolovgrad *82 D3 prev.* Kavakli. Khaskovo, S Bulgaria
Topolya *see* Bačka Topola
Top Springs Roadhouse *124 E3* Northern Territory, N Australia
Torda *see* Turda
Torez *87 H3* Donets'ka Oblast', SE Ukraine
Torgau *72 D4* Sachsen, E Germany
Torhout *65 A5* West-Vlaanderen, W Belgium
Torino *74 A2 Eng.* Turin. Piemonte, NW Italy
Tornacum *see* Tournai
Torneå *see* Tornio
Torneträsk *62 C3 lake* N Sweden
Tornio *62 D4 Swe.* Torneå. Lappi, NW Finland
Tornionjoki *62 D3 river* Finland/Sweden
Toro *70 D2* Castilla-León, N Spain
Toronto *16 D5 province capital* Ontario, S Canada
Toros Dağları *94 C4 Eng.* Taurus Mountains. *mountain range* S Turkey
Torquay *67 C7* SW England, United Kingdom
Torrance *24 D2* California, W USA
Torre, Alto da *70 B3 mountain* C Portugal
Torre del Greco *75 D5* Campania, S Italy
Torrejón de Ardoz *71 E3* Madrid, C Spain
Torrelavega *70 D1* Cantabria, N Spain
Torrens, Lake *127 A6 salt lake* South Australia
Torrent *71 F3 Cas.* Torrente, *var.* Torrent de l'Horta. País Valenciano, E Spain
Torrent de l'Horta/Torrente *see* Torrent
Torreón *28 D3* Coahuila, NE Mexico
Torres Strait *126 C1 strait* Australia/Papua New Guinea
Torres Vedras *70 B3* Lisboa, C Portugal
Torrington *22 D3* Wyoming, C USA
Tórshavn *61 F5 Dan.* Thorshavn. *Dependent territory capital* Faroe Islands
To'rtkok'l *100 D2 var.* Türtkül, *Rus.* Turtkul'; *prev.* Petroaleksandrovsk. Qoraqalpog'iston Respublikasi, W Uzbekistan
Tortoise Islands *see* Galápagos Islands
Tortosa *71 F2 anc.* Dertosa. Cataluña, E Spain
Tortue, Montagne *37 H3 mountain range* C French Guiana
Tortuga, Isla *see* La Tortuga, Isla
Toruń *76 C3 Ger.* Thorn. Toruń, Kujawsko-pomorskie, C Poland
Tõrva *84 D3 Ger.* Törwa. Valgamaa, S Estonia
Törwa *see* Tõrva
Torzhok *88 B4* Tverskaya Oblast', W Russian Federation
Tosa-wan *109 B7 bay* SW Japan
Toscana *74 B3 Eng.* Tuscany. *region* C Italy
Toscano, Archipelago *74 B4 Eng.* Tuscan Archipelago. *island group* C Italy
Toshkent *101 E2 Eng./Rus.* Tashkent. *country capital* (Uzbekistan) Toshkent Viloyati, E Uzbekistan
Totana *71 E4* Murcia, SE Spain
Tot'ma *see* Sukhona
Totness *37 G3* Coronie, N Suriname
Tottori *109 B6* Tottori, Honshū, SW Japan
Touâjîl *52 C2* Tiris Zemmour, N Mauritania
Touggourt *49 E2* NE Algeria
Toukoto *52 C3* Kayes, W Mali
Toul *68 D3* Meurthe-et-Moselle, NE France
Toulon *69 D6 anc.* Telo Martius, Tilio Martius. Var, SE France
Toulouse *69 B6 anc.* Tolosa. Haute-Garonne, S France
Toungoo *see* Taungoo
Touraine *68 B4 cultural region* C France
Tourane *see* Đà Nẵng
Tourcoing *68 C2* Nord, N France
Tournai *65 A6 var.* Tournay, *Dut.* Doornik; *anc.* Tornacum. Hainaut, SW Belgium
Tournay *see* Tournai
Tours *68 B4 anc.* Caesarodunum, Turoni. Indre-et-Loire, C France
Tovarkovskiy *89 B5* Tul'skaya Oblast', W Russian Federation
Tower Island *see* Genovesa, Isla
Townsville *126 D3* Queensland, NE Australia
Towoeti Meer *see* Towuti, Danau
Towraghoudi *100 D4* Herāt, NW Afghanistan
Towson *19 F4* Maryland, NE USA
Towuti, Danau *117 E4 Dut.* Towoeti Meer. *lake* Sulawesi, C Indonesia
Toyama *109 C5* Toyama, Honshū, SW Japan
Toyama-wan *109 B5 bay* W Japan
Toyohara *see* Yuzhno-Sakhalinsk
Toyota *109 C6* Aichi, Honshū, SW Japan
Tozeur *49 E2 var.* Tawzar. W Tunisia
Trâblous *see* Tripoli
Trabzon *95 E2 Eng.* Trebizond; *anc.* Trapezus. Trabzon, NE Turkey
Traiectum ad Mosam/Traiectum Tungorum *see* Maastricht
Traiskirchen *73 E6* Niederösterreich, NE Austria
Trajani Portus *see* Civitavecchia
Trajectum ad Rhenum *see* Utrecht
Trakai *85 C5 Ger.* Traken, *Pol.* Troki. Vilnius, SE Lithuania
Traken *see* Trakai
Tralee *67 A6 Ir.* Trá Lí. SW Ireland
Trá Lí *see* Tralee
Tralles Aydin *see* Aydın
Trang *115 C7* Trang, S Thailand
Transantarctic Mountains *132 B3 mountain range* Antarctica
Transilvania *see* Transylvania
Transilvaniei, Alpi *see* Carpaţii Meridionalii
Transjordan *see* Jordan
Transnistria *86 D3 cultural region* NE Moldova
Transsylvanische Alpen/Transylvanian Alps *see* Carpaţii Meridionalii
Transylvania *86 B4 Eng.* Ardeal, Transilvania, *Ger.* Siebenbürgen, *Hung.* Erdély. *cultural region* NW Romania
Trapani *75 B7 anc.* Drepanum. Sicilia, Italy, C Mediterranean Sea
Trâpeăng Vêng *see* Kâmpóng Thum
Trapezus *see* Trabzon
Traralgon *127 C7* Victoria, SE Australia
Trasimenischersee *see* Trasimeno, Lago
Trasimeno, Lago *74 C4 Eng.* Lake of Perugia, *Ger.* Trasimenischersee. *lake* C Italy
Traù *see* Trogir
Traverse City *18 C2* Michigan, N USA
Tra Vinh *115 D6 var.* Phu Vinh. Tra Vinh, S Vietnam
Travis, Lake *27 F3 reservoir* Texas, SW USA
Travnik *78 C4* Federacija Bosna I Hercegovina, C Bosnia and Herzegovina
Trbovlje *73 E7 Ger.* Trifail. C Slovenia

Treasure State - Uulu

Treasure State see Montana
Třebíč 77 B5 Ger. Trebitsch. Vysočina, C Czech Republic
Trebinje 79 C5 Republika Srpska, S Bosnia and Herzegovina
Trebišov 77 D6 Hung. Tőketerebes. Košický Kraj, E Slovakia
Trebitsch see Třebíč
Trebnitz see Trzebnica
Tree Planters State see Nebraska
Trélazé 68 B4 Maine-et-Loire, NW France
Trelew 43 C6 Chubut, SE Argentina
Tremelo 65 C5 Vlaams Brabant, C Belgium
Trenčín 77 C5 Ger. Trentschin, Hung. Trencsén. Trenčiansky Kraj, W Slovakia
Trencsén see Trenčín
Trengganu, Kuala see Kuala Terengganu
Trenque Lauquen 42 C4 Buenos Aires, E Argentina
Trent see Trento
Trento 74 C2 Eng. Trent, Ger. Trient; anc. Tridentum. Trentino-Alto Adige, N Italy
Trenton 19 F4 state capital New Jersey, NE USA
Trentschin see Trenčín
Tres Arroyos 43 D5 Buenos Aires, E Argentina
Treskavica 78 C4 mountain range SE Bosnia and Herzegovina
Tres Tabernae see Saverne
Treves/Trèves see Trier
Treviso 74 C2 anc. Tarvisium. Veneto, NE Italy
Trichinopoly see Tiruchchirāppalli
Trichūr see Thrissur
Tridentum/Trient see Trento
Trier 73 A5 Eng. Treves, Fr. Trèves; anc. Augusta Treverorum. Rheinland-Pfalz, SW Germany
Triesen 72 E2 SW Liechtenstein Europe
Triesenberg 72 E2 SW Liechtenstein
Trieste 74 D2 Slvn. Trst. Friuli-Venezia Giulia, NE Italy
Trifail see Trbovlje
Tríkala 82 B4 prev. Trikkala. Thessalía, C Greece
Trikkala see Tríkala
Trimontium see Plovdiv
Trinacria see Sicilia
Trincomalee 110 D3 var. Trinkomali. Eastern Province, NE Sri Lanka
Trindade, Ilha da 45 C5 island Brazil, W Atlantic Ocean
Trinidad 39 F3 Beni, N Bolivia
Trinidad 42 D4 Flores, S Uruguay
Trinidad 22 D5 Colorado, C USA
Trinidad 33 H5 island C Trinidad and Tobago
Trinidad and Tobago 33 H5 off. Republic of Trinidad and Tobago. country SE West Indies
Trinidad and Tobago, Republic of see Trinidad and Tobago
Trinité, Montagnes de la 37 H3 mountain range C French Guiana
Trinity River 27 G3 river Texas, SW USA
Trinkomali see Trincomalee
Trípoli 83 B6 prev. Trípolis. Pelopónnisos, S Greece
Tripoli 96 B4 var. Tarābulus, Ṭarābulus ash Shām, Trâblous; anc. Tripolis. N Lebanon
Tripoli see Ṭarābulus
Trípolis see Trípoli, Greece
Tripolis see Tripoli, Lebanon
Tristan da Cunha 47 B7 UK dependent territory SE Atlantic Ocean
Triton Island 106 B7 island S Paracel Islands
Trivandrum see Thiruvananthapuram
Trnava 77 C6 Ger. Tyrnau, Hung. Nagyszombat. Trnavský Kraj, W Slovakia
Trnovo see Veliko Tŭrnovo
Trogir 78 B4 It. Traù. Split-Dalmacija, S Croatia
Troglav 78 B4 mountain Bosnia and Herzegovina/Croatia
Trois-Rivières 17 E4 Québec, SE Canada
Troki see Trakai
Trollhättan 63 B6 Västra Götaland, S Sweden
Tromsø 62 C2 Fin. Tromssa. Troms, N Norway
Tromssa see Tromsø
Trondheim 62 B4 Ger. Drontheim; prev. Nidaros, Trondhjem. Sør-Trøndelag, S Norway
Trondheimsfjorden 62 B4 fjord S Norway
Trondhjem see Trondheim
Troódos 80 C5 var. Troodos Mountains. mountain range C Cyprus
Troodos Mountains see Troódos
Troppau see Opava
Troy 20 D3 Alabama, S USA
Troy 19 F3 New York, NE USA
Troyan 82 C2 Lovech, N Bulgaria
Troyes 68 D3 anc. Augustobona Tricassium. Aube, N France
Trst see Trieste
Trstenik 78 E4 Serbia, C Serbia
Trucial States see United Arab Emirates
Trujillo 30 D2 Colón, NE Honduras
Trujillo 38 B3 La Libertad, NW Peru
Trujillo 70 C3 Extremadura, W Spain
Truk Islands see Chuuk Islands
Trŭn 82 B2 Pernik, W Bulgaria
Truro 17 F4 Nova Scotia, SE Canada
Truro 67 C7 SW England, United Kingdom
Trzcianka 76 B3 Ger. Schönlanke. Pila, Wielkopolskie, C Poland
Trzebnica 76 C4 Ger. Trebnitz. Dolnośląskie, SW Poland
Tsalka 95 F2 S Georgia Asia
Tsamkong see Zhanjiang
Tsangpo see Brahmaputra
Tsarevo 82 E2 prev. Michurin. Burgas, E Bulgaria
Tsarigrad see İstanbul
Tsaritsyn see Volgograd
Tschakathurn see Čakovec
Tschaslau see Čáslav
Tschenstochau see Częstochowa
Tsefat 97 B5 var. Safed, Ar. Safad; prev. Zefat. Northern, N Israel
Tselinograd see Astana
Tsetsen Khan see Öndörhaan
Tsetserleg 104 D2 Arhangay, C Mongolia
Tshela 55 B6 Bas-Congo, W Dem. Rep. Congo
Tshikapa 55 C7 Kasai-Occidental, SW Dem. Rep. Congo
Tshuapa 55 D6 river C Dem. Rep. Congo
Tsinan see Jinan
Tsing Hai see Qinghai Hu, China
Tsinghai see Qinghai, China
Tsingtao/Tsingtau see Qingdao
Tsinkiang see Quanzhou
Tsintao see Qingdao
Tsitsihar see Qiqihar
Tsu 109 C6 var. Tu. Mie, Honshū, SW Japan
Tsugaru-kaikyo 108 C3 strait N Japan
Tsumeb 56 B3 Otjikoto, N Namibia
Tsuruga 109 C6 var. Turuga. Fukui, Honshū, SW Japan
Tsuruoka 108 D4 var. Turuoka. Yamagata, Honshū, C Japan
Tsushima 109 A7 var. Tsushima-tō, Tusima. island group SW Japan
Tsushima-tō see Tsushima
Tsyerakhowka 85 D8 Rus. Terekhovka. Homyel'skaya Voblasts', SE Belarus
Tsyurupinsk see Tsyurupyns'k
Tsyurupyns'k 87 E4 Rus. Tsyurupinsk. Khersons'ka Oblast', S Ukraine
Tu see Tsu
Tuamotu, Archipel des see Tuamotu, Îles
Tuamotu Fracture Zone 121 H3 fracture zone E Pacific Ocean
Tuamotu, Îles 123 H4 var. Archipel des Tuamotu, Dangerous Archipelago, Tuamotu Islands. island group N French Polynesia
Tuamotu Islands see Tuamotu, Îles
Tuapi 31 E2 Región Autónoma Atlántico Norte, NE Nicaragua
Tuapse 89 A7 Krasnodarskiy Kray, SW Russian Federation
Tuba City 26 B1 Arizona, SW USA
Tubbergen 64 E3 Overijssel, E Netherlands
Tubeke see Tubize
Tubize 65 B6 Dut. Tubeke. Walloon Brabant, C Belgium
Tubmanburg 52 C5 NW Liberia
Ṭubruq 49 H2 Eng. Tobruk, It. Tobruch. NE Libya
Tubuai, Îles/Tubuai Islands see Australes, Îles
Tucker's Town 20 B5 E Bermuda
Tuckum see Tukums
Tucson 26 B3 Arizona, SW USA
Tucumán see San Miguel de Tucumán
Tucumcari 27 E2 New Mexico, SW USA
Tucupita 37 E2 Delta Amacuro, NE Venezuela
Tucuruí, Represa de 41 F2 reservoir NE Brazil
Tudela 71 E2 Basq. Tutera; anc. Tutela. Navarra, N Spain
Tudmur 96 C3 var. Tadmur, Tamar, Gk. Palmyra, Bibl. Tadmor. Ḥimṣ, C Syria
Tuguegarao 117 E1 Luzon, N Philippines
Tuktoyaktuk 15 E3 Northwest Territories, NW Canada
Tukums 84 C3 Ger. Tuckum. Tukums, W Latvia
Tula 89 B5 Tul'skaya Oblast', W Russian Federation
Tulancingo 29 E4 Hidalgo, C Mexico
Tulare Lake Bed 25 C7 salt flat California, W USA
Tulcán 38 B1 Carchi, N Ecuador
Tulcea 86 D5 Tulcea, E Romania
Tul'chin see Tul'chyn
Tul'chyn 86 D3 Rus. Tul'chin. Vinnyts'ka Oblast', C Ukraine
Tuléar see Toliara
Tulia 27 E2 Texas, SW USA
Tūlkarm 97 D7 West Bank, Israel
Tulle 69 C5 anc. Tutela. Corrèze, C France
Tulln 73 E6 var. Oberhollabrunn. Niederösterreich, NE Austria
Tully 126 D3 Queensland, NE Australia
Tulsa 27 G1 Oklahoma, C USA
Tuluá 36 B3 Valle del Cauca, W Colombia
Tulun 93 E4 Irkutskaya Oblast', S Russian Federation
Tumaco 36 A4 Nariño, SW Colombia
Tumba, Lac see Ntomba, Lac
Tumbes 38 A2 Tumbes, NW Peru
Tumkūr 110 C2 Karnātaka, W India
Tumuc-Humac Mountains 41 E1 var. Serra Tumucumaque. mountain range N South America
Tumucumaque, Serra see Tumuc-Humac Mountains
Tunca Nehri see Tundzha
Tunduru 51 C8 Ruvuma, S Tanzania
Tundzha 82 D3 Turk. Tunca Nehri. river Bulgaria/Turkey
Tungabhadra Reservoir 110 C2 lake S India
Tungaru 123 E2 prev. Gilbert Islands. island group W Kiribati
T'ung-shan see Xuzhou
Tungsten 14 D4 Northwest Territories, W Canada
Tung-t'ing Hu see Dongting Hu
Tunis 49 E1 var. Tūnis. country capital (Tunisia) NE Tunisia
Tunis, Golfe de 80 D3 Ar. Khalīj Tūnis. gulf NE Tunisia
Tunisia 49 F2 off. Tunisian Republic, Ar. Al Jumhūrīyah at Tūnisīyah, Fr. République Tunisienne. country N Africa
Tunisian Republic see Tunisia
Tunisienne, République see Tunisia
Tūnisīyah, Al Jumhūrīyah at see Tunisia
Tūnis, Khalīj see Tunis, Golfe de
Tunja 36 B3 Boyacá, C Colombia
Tuong Buong see Tương Đương
Tương Đương 114 D4 var. Tuong Buong. Nghệ An, N Vietnam
Tüp see Tyup
Tupelo 20 C2 Mississippi, S USA
Tupiza 39 G5 Potosí, S Bolivia
Turabah 99 B5 Makkah, W Saudi Arabia
Turangi 128 D4 Waikato, North Island, New Zealand
Turan Lowland 100 C2 var. Turan Plain, Kaz. Turan Oypaty, Rus. Turanskaya Nizmennost', Turk. Turan Pesligi, Uzb. Turan Pasttekisligi. plain C Asia
Turan Oypaty/Turan Pesligi/Turan Plain/Turanskaya Nizmennost' see Turan Lowland
Turan Pasttekisligi see Turan Lowland
Ṭurayf 98 A3 Al Ḥudūd ash Shamālīyah, NW Saudi Arabia
Turba see Teruel
Turbat 112 A3 Baluchistān, SW Pakistan
Turčianský Svätý Martin see Martin
Turda 86 B4 Ger. Thorenburg, Hung. Torda. Cluj, NW Romania
Turek 76 C3 Wielkopolskie, C Poland
Turfan see Turpan
Turin see Torino
Turkana, Lake 51 C6 var. Lake Rudolf. lake N Kenya
Turkestan see Turkistan
Turkey 94 B3 off. Republic of Turkey, Turk. Türkiye Cumhuriyeti. country SW Asia
Turkey, Republic of see Turkey
Turkish Republic of Northern Cyprus 80 D5 disputed territory Cyprus
Turkistan 92 B5 prev. Turkestan. Yuzhnyy Kazakhstan, S Kazakhstan
Türkiye Cumhuriyeti see Turkey
Türkmenabat 100 D3 prev. Rus. Chardzhev, Chardzhou, Chardzhui, Lenin-Turkmenski, Turkm. Chärjew. Lebap Welaýaty, E Turkmenistan
Türkmen Aylagy 100 B2 Rus. Turkmenskiy Zaliv. lake gulf W Turkmenistan
Turkmenbashi see Türkmenbaşy
Türkmenbaşy 100 B2 Rus. Turkmenbashi; prev. Krasnovodsk. Balkan Welaýaty, W Turkmenistan
Türkmenbasy Aylagy 100 A2 prev. Rus. Krasnovodskiy Zaliv, Turkm. Krasnowodsk Aylagy. lake Gulf W Turkmenistan
Turkmenistan 100 B2 ; prev. Turkmenskaya Soviet Socialist Republic. country C Asia
Turkmenskaya Soviet Socialist Republic see Turkmenistan
Turkmenskiy Zaliv see Türkmen Aylagy
Turks and Caicos Islands 33 E2 UK dependent territory N West Indies
Turku 63 D6 Swe. Åbo. Länsi-Suomi, SW Finland
Turlock 25 B6 California, W USA
Turnagain, Cape 128 D4 headland North Island, New Zealand
Turnau see Turnov
Turnhout 65 C5 Antwerpen, N Belgium
Turnov 76 B4 Ger. Turnau. Liberecký Kraj, N Czech Republic
Tŭrnovo see Veliko Tŭrnovo
Turnu Măgurele 86 B5 var. Turnu-Măgurele. Teleorman, S Romania
Turnu Severin see Drobeta-Turnu Severin
Turócszentmárton see Martin
Turoni see Tours
Turpan 104 C3 var. Turfan. Xinjiang Uygur Zizhiqu, NW China
Turpan Depression see Turpan Pendi
Turpan Pendi 104 C3 Eng. Turpan Depression. depression NW China
Turpentine State see North Carolina
Türtkül/Turtkul' see To'rtko'l
Turuga see Tsuruga
Turuoka see Tsuruoka
Tuscaloosa 20 C2 Alabama, S USA
Tuscan Archipelago see Toscano, Archipelago
Tuscany see Toscana
Tusima see Tsushima
Tutela see Tulle, France
Tutela see Tudela, Spain
Tutera see Tudela
Tuticorin 110 C3 Tamil Nādu, SE India
Tutrakan 82 D1 Silistra, NE Bulgaria
Tutuila 123 F4 island W American Samoa
Tuvalu 123 E3 prev. Ellice Islands. country SW Pacific Ocean
Tuwayq, Jabal 99 C5 mountain range C Saudi Arabia
Tuxpan 28 D4 Jalisco, C Mexico
Tuxpán 29 F4 var. Tuxpán de Rodríguez Cano. Veracruz-Llave, E Mexico
Tuxpán de Rodríguez Cano see Tuxpán
Tuxtepec 29 F4 var. San Juan Bautista Tuxtepec. Oaxaca, S Mexico
Tuxtla 29 G5 var. Tuxtla Gutiérrez. Chiapas, SE Mexico
Tuxtla see San Andrés Tuxtla
Tuxtla Gutiérrez see Tuxtla
Tuy Hoa 115 E5 Phu Yên, S Vietnam
Tuz, Lake 94 C3 lake C Turkey
Tver' 88 B4 prev. Kalinin. Tverskaya Oblast', W Russian Federation
Tverya 97 B5 var. Tiberias; prev. Teverya. Northern, N Israel
Twin Falls 24 D4 Idaho, NW USA
Tyan'-Shan' see Tien Shan
Tychy 77 D5 Ger. Tichau. Śląskie, S Poland
Tyler 27 G3 Texas, SW USA
Tylos see Bahrain
Tympáki 83 C8 var. Timbaki; prev. Timbákion. Kríti, Greece, E Mediterranean Sea
Tynda 93 F4 Amurskaya Oblast', SE Russian Federation
Tyne 66 D4 river N England, United Kingdom
Tyôsi see Chōshi
Tyras see Dniester
Tyre see Soûr
Tyrnau see Trnava
Týrnavos 82 B4 var. Tírnavos. Thessalía, C Greece
Tyrol see Tirol
Tyros see Bahrain
Tyrrhenian Sea 75 B6 It. Mare Tirreno. sea N Mediterranean Sea
Tyumen' 92 C3 Tyumenskaya Oblast', C Russian Federation
Tyup 101 G2 Kir. Tüp. Issyk-Kul'skaya Oblast', NE Kyrgyzstan
Tywyn 67 C6 W Wales, United Kingdom
Tzekung see Zigong
Tziá 83 C6 prev. Kéa, Kéos; anc. Ceos. island Kykládes, Greece, Aegean Sea

U

Uaco Cungo 56 B1 C Angola
UAE see United Arab Emirates
Uanle Uen see Wanlaweyn
Uaupés, Rio see Vaupés, Río
Ubangi-Shari see Central African Republic
Ube 109 B7 Yamaguchi, Honshū, SW Japan
Úbeda 71 E4 Andalucía, S Spain
Uberaba 41 F4 Minas Gerais, SE Brazil
Uberlândia 41 F4 Minas Gerais, SE Brazil
Ubol Rajadhani/Ubol Ratchathani see Ubon Ratchathani
Ubon Ratchathani 115 D5 var. Muang Ubon, Ubol Rajadhani, Ubol Ratchathani, Udon Ratchathani. Ubon Ratchathani, E Thailand
Ubrique 70 D5 Andalucía, S Spain
Ubsu-Nur, Ozero see Uvs Nuur
Ucayali, Río 38 D3 river C Peru
Uchiura-wan 108 D3 bay NW Pacific Ocean
Uchkuduk see Uchquduq
Uchquduq 100 D2 Rus. Uchkuduk. Navoiy Viloyati, N Uzbekistan
Uchtagan Gumy/Uchtagan, Peski see Uçtagan Gumy
Uçtagan Gumy 100 C2 var. Uchtagan Gumy, Rus. Peski Uchtagan. desert NW Turkmenistan
Udaipur 112 C3 prev. Oodeypore. Rājasthān, N India
Uddevalla 63 B6 Västra Götaland, S Sweden
Udine 74 D2 anc. Utina. Friuli-Venezia Giulia, NE Italy
Udintsev Fracture Zone 132 A5 tectonic feature S Pacific Ocean
Udipi see Udupi
Udon Ratchathani see Ubon Ratchathani
Udon Thani 114 C4 var. Ban Mak Khaeng, Udorndhani. Udon Thani, N Thailand
Udorndhani see Udon Thani
Udupi 110 B2 var. Udipi. Karnātaka, SW India
Uele 55 D5 var. Welle. river NE Dem. Rep. Congo
Uelzen 72 C3 Niedersachsen, N Germany
Ufa 89 D6 Respublika Bashkortostan, W Russian Federation
Ugāle 84 C2 Ventspils, NW Latvia
Uganda 51 B6 off. Republic of Uganda. country E Africa
Uganda, Republic of see Uganda
Uhorshchyna see Hungary
Uhuru Peak see Kilimanjaro
Uíge 56 B1 Port. Carmona, Vila Marechal Carmona. Uíge, NW Angola
Uinta Mountains 22 B4 mountain range Utah, W USA
Uitenhage 56 C5 Eastern Cape, S South Africa
Uithoorn 64 C3 Noord-Holland, C Netherlands
Ujda see Oujda
Ujelang Atoll 122 C1 var. Wujlān. atoll Ralik Chain, W Marshall Islands
Újgradiska see Nova Gradiška
Újmoldova see Moldova Noua
Ujungpandang see Makassar
Ujung Salang see Phuket
Újvidék see Novi Sad
UK see United Kingdom
Ukhta 92 C3 Respublika Komi, NW Russian Federation
Ukiah 25 B5 California, W USA
Ukmergė 84 C4 Pol. Wiłkomierz. Vilnius, C Lithuania
Ukraine 86 C2 off. Ukraine, Rus. Ukraina, Ukr. Ukrayina; prev. Ukrainian Soviet Socialist Republic, Ukrainskay S.S.R. country SE Europe
Ukraine see Ukraine
Ukrainian Soviet Socialist Republic see Ukraine
Ukrainskay S.S.R/Ukrayina see Ukraine
Ulaanbaatar 105 E2 Eng. Ulan Bator; prev. Urga. country capital (Mongolia) Töv, C Mongolia
Ulaangom 104 C2 Uvs, NW Mongolia
Ulan Bator see Ulaanbaatar
Ulanhad see Chifeng
Ulan-Ude 93 E4 prev. Verkhneudinsk. Respublika Buryatiya, S Russian Federation
Uleälv see Oulujoki
Uleträsk see Oulujärvi
Ulft 64 E4 Gelderland, E Netherlands
Ullapool 66 C3 N Scotland, United Kingdom
Ulm 73 B6 Baden-Württemberg, S Germany
Ulsan 107 E4 Jap. Urusan. SE South Korea
Ulster 67 B5 province Northern Ireland, United Kingdom/Ireland
Ulungur Hu 104 B2 lake NW China
Uluru 125 D5 var. Ayers Rock. monolith Northern Territory, C Australia
Ulyanivka 87 E3 Rus. Ul'yanovka. Kirovohrads'ka Oblast', C Ukraine
Ul'yanovka see Ulyanivka
Ul'yanovsk 89 C5 prev. Simbirsk. Ul'yanovskaya Oblast', W Russian Federation
Umán 29 H3 Yucatán, SE Mexico
Uman' 87 E3 Rus. Uman. Cherkas'ka Oblast', C Ukraine
Uman see Uman'
Umanak/Umanaq see Uummannaq
'Umān, Khalīj see Oman, Gulf of
'Umān, Salṭanat see Oman
Umbrian-Machigian Mountains see Umbro-Marchigiano, Appennino
Umbro-Marchigiano, Appennino 74 C3 Eng. Umbrian-Machigian Mountains. mountain range C Italy
Umeå 62 C4 Västerbotten, N Sweden
Umeälven 62 C4 river N Sweden
Umiat 14 D2 Alaska, USA
Umm Buru 50 A4 Western Darfur, W Sudan
Umm Durmān see Omdurman
Umm Ruwaba 50 C4 var. Umm Ruwābah, Um Ruwāba. Northern Kordofan, C Sudan
Umm Ruwābah see Umm Ruwaba
Umnak Island 14 A3 island Aleutian Islands, Alaska, USA
Um Ruwāba see Umm Ruwaba
Umtali see Mutare
Umtata see Mthatha
Una 78 B3 river Bosnia and Herzegovina/Croatia
Unac 78 B3 river W Bosnia and Herzegovina
Unalaska Island 14 A3 island Aleutian Islands, Alaska, USA
'Unayzah 98 B4 var. Anaiza. Al Qaşīm, C Saudi Arabia
Unci see Almería
Uncía 39 F4 Potosí, C Bolivia
Uncompahgre Peak 22 B5 mountain Colorado, C USA
Undur Khan see Öndörhaan
Ungaria see Hungary
Ungarisches Erzgebirge see Slovenské rudohorie
Ungarn see Hungary
Ungava Bay 17 E1 bay Québec, E Canada
Ungava Peninsula see Ungava, Péninsule d'
Ungava, Péninsule d' 16 D1 Eng. Ungava Peninsula. peninsula Québec, SE Canada
Ungeny see Ungheni
Ungheni 86 D3 Rus. Ungeny. W Moldova
Unguja see Zanzibar
Üngüz Angyrsyndaky Garagum 100 C2 Rus. Zaunguzskiye Garagumy. desert N Turkmenistan
Ungvár see Uzhhorod
Unimak Island 14 B3 island Aleutian Islands, Alaska, USA
Union 21 E1 South Carolina, SE USA
Union City 20 C1 Tennessee, S USA
Union of Myanmar see Myanmar
United Arab Emirates 99 C5 Ar. Al Imārāt al 'Arabīyah al Muttaḥidah, abbrev. UAE; prev. Trucial States. country SW Asia
United Arab Republic see Egypt
United Kingdom 67 B5 off. United Kingdom of Great Britain and Northern Ireland, abbrev. UK. country NW Europe
United Kingdom of Great Britain and Northern Ireland see United Kingdom
United Mexican States see Mexico
United Provinces see Uttar Pradesh
United States of America 13 B5 off. United States of America, var. America, The States, abbrev. U.S., USA. country North America
Unst 66 D1 island NE Scotland, United Kingdom
Ünye 94 D2 Ordu, W Turkey
Upala 30 D4 Alajuela, NW Costa Rica
Upata 37 E2 Bolívar, E Venezuela
Upemba, Lac 55 D7 lake SE Dem. Rep. Congo
Upernavik 60 C2 var. Upernivik. Kitaa, C Greenland
Upernivik see Upernavik
Upington 56 C4 Northern Cape, W South Africa
'Upolu 123 F4 island SE Samoa
Upper Klamath Lake 24 A4 lake Oregon, NW USA
Upper Lough Erne 67 A5 lake SW Northern Ireland, United Kingdom
Upper Red Lake 23 F1 lake Minnesota, N USA
Upper Volta see Burkina
Uppsala 63 C6 Uppsala, C Sweden
Uqsuqtuuq see Gjoa Haven
Ural 90 B3 Kaz. Zhayyk. river Kazakhstan/Russian Federation
Ural Mountains see Ural'skiye Gory
Ural'sk 92 B3 Kaz. Oral. Zapadnyy Kazakhstan, NW Kazakhstan
Ural'skiye Gory 92 C3 var. Ural'skiy Khrebet, Eng. Ural Mountains. mountain range Kazakhstan/Russian Federation
Ural'skiy Khrebet see Ural'skiye Gory
Uraricoera 40 D1 Roraima, N Brazil
Ura-Tyube see Üroteppa
Urbandale 23 F3 Iowa, C USA
Urdunn see Jordan
Uren' 89 C5 Nizhegorodskaya Oblast', W Russian Federation
Urga see Ulaanbaatar
Urganch 100 D2 Rus. Urgench; prev. Novo-Urgench. Xorazm Viloyati, W Uzbekistan
Urgench see Urganch
Urgut 101 E3 Samarqand Viloyati, C Uzbekistan
Urmia, Lake see Orūmīyeh, Daryācheh-ye
Uroševac see Ferizaj
Üroteppa 101 E2 Rus. Ura-Tyube. NW Tajikistan
Uruapan 29 E4 var. Uruapan del Progreso. Michoacán, SW Mexico
Uruapan del Progreso see Uruapan
Uruguai, Rio see Uruguay
Uruguay 42 D4 off. Oriental Republic of Uruguay; prev. La Banda Oriental. country E South America
Uruguay 42 D3 var. Rio Uruguai, Río Uruguay. river E South America
Uruguay, Oriental Republic of see Uruguay
Uruguay, Río see Uruguay
Urumchi see Ürümqi
Urumi Yeh see Orūmīyeh, Daryācheh-ye
Ürümqi 104 C3 var. Tihwa, Urumchi, Urumqi, Urumtsi, Wu-lu-k'o-mu-shi, Wu-lu-mu-ch'i; prev. Ti-hua. Xinjiang Uygur Zizhiqu, NW China
Urumtsi see Ürümqi
Urundi see Burundi
Urup, Ostrov 93 H4 island Kuril'skiye Ostrova, SE Russian Federation
Urusan see Ulsan
Urziceni 86 C5 Ialomiţa, SE Romania
Usa 88 E3 river NW Russian Federation
Uşak 94 B3 prev. Ushak. Uşak, W Turkey
Ushak see Uşak
Ushant see Ouessant, Île d'
Ushuaia 43 B8 Tierra del Fuego, S Argentina
Usinsk 88 E3 Respublika Komi, NW Russian Federation
Üsküb/Üsküp see Skopje
Usmas Ezers 84 B3 lake NW Latvia
Usol'ye-Sibirskoye 93 E4 Irkutskaya Oblast', C Russian Federation
Ussel 69 C5 Corrèze, C France
Ussuriysk 93 G5 prev. Nikol'sk, Nikol'sk-Ussuriyskiy, Voroshilov. Primorskiy Kray, SE Russian Federation
Ustica 75 B6 island S Italy
Ust'-Ilimsk 93 E4 Irkutskaya Oblast', C Russian Federation
Ústí nad Labem 76 A4 Ger. Aussig. Ústecký Kraj, NW Czech Republic
Ustinov see Izhevsk
Ustka 76 C2 Ger. Stolpmünde. Pomorskie, N Poland
Ust'-Kamchatsk 93 H2 Kamchatskaya Oblast', E Russian Federation
Ust'-Kamenogorsk 92 D5 Kaz. Öskemen. Vostochnyy Kazakhstan, E Kazakhstan
Ust'-Kut 93 E4 Irkutskaya Oblast', C Russian Federation
Ust'-Olenëk 93 E3 Respublika Sakha (Yakutiya), NE Russian Federation
Ustrzyki Dolne 77 E5 Podkarpackie, SE Poland
Ust'-Sysol'sk see Syktyvkar
Ust Urt see Ustyurt Plateau
Ustyurt Plateau 100 B1 var. Ust Urt, Uzb. Ustyurt Platosi. plateau Kazakhstan/Uzbekistan
Ustyurt Platosi see Ustyurt Plateau
Usulután 30 C3 Usulután, SE El Salvador
Usumacinta, Río 30 B1 river Guatemala/Mexico
Usumbura see Bujumbura
U.S./USA see United States of America
Utah 22 B4 off. State of Utah, also known as Beehive State, Mormon State. state W USA
Utah Lake 22 B4 lake Utah, W USA
Utena 84 C4 Utena, E Lithuania
Utica 19 F3 New York, NE USA
Utina see Udine
Utrecht 64 C4 Lat. Trajectum ad Rhenum. Utrecht, C Netherlands
Utsunomiya 109 D5 var. Utunomiya. Tochigi, Honshū, S Japan
Uttarakhand 113 E2 cultural region N India
Uttar Pradesh 113 E3 prev. United Provinces, United Provinces of Agra and Oudh. cultural region N India
Utunomiya see Utsunomiya
Uulu 84 D2 Pärnumaa, SW Estonia

Uummannaq – Vyerkhnyadzvinsk

Uummannaq 60 C3 var. Umanak, Umanaq. Kitaa, C Greenland
Uummannarsuaq see Nunap Isua
Uvalde 27 F4 Texas, SW USA
Uvaravichy 85 D7 Rus. Uvarovichi. Homyel'skaya Voblasts', SE Belarus
Uvarovichi see Uvaravichy
Uvea, Île 123 E4 island N Wallis and Futuna
Uvs Nuur 104 C1 var. Ozero Ubsu-Nur. lake Mongolia/Russian Federation
'Uwaynāt, Jabal al 66 A3 var. Jebel Uweinat. mountain Libya/Sudan
Uweinat, Jebel see 'Uwaynāt, Jabal al
Uyo 53 G5 Akwa Ibom, S Nigeria
Uyuni 39 F5 Potosí, W Bolivia
Uzbekistan 100 D2 off. Republic of Uzbekistan. country C Asia
Uzbekistan, Republic of see Uzbekistan
Uzhgorod see Uzhhorod
Uzhhorod 86 B2 Rus. Uzhgorod; prev. Ungvár. Zakarpats'ka Oblast', W Ukraine
Užice 78 D4 prev. Titovo Užice. Serbia, W Serbia

V

Vaal 56 D4 river C South Africa
Vaals 65 D6 Limburg, SE Netherlands
Vaasa 63 D5 Swe. Vasa; prev. Nikolainkaupunki. Länsi-Suomi, W Finland
Vaassen 64 D3 Gelderland, E Netherlands
Vác 77 C6 Ger. Waitzen. Pest, N Hungary
Vadodara 112 C4 prev. Baroda. Gujarāt, W India
Vaduz 72 E2 country capital (Liechtenstein) W Liechtenstein
Vág see Váh
Vágbeszterce see Považská Bystrica
Váh 77 C5 Ger. Waag, Hung. Vág. river W Slovakia
Váhtjer see Gällivare
Väinameri 84 C2 prev. Muhu Väin, Ger. Moon-Sund. sea E Baltic Sea
Vajdahunyad see Hunedoara
Valachia see Wallachia
Valday 88 B4 Novgorodskaya Oblast', W Russian Federation
Valdecañas, Embalse de 70 D3 reservoir W Spain
Valdepeñas 71 E4 Castilla-La Mancha, C Spain
Valdez 14 C3 Alaska, USA
Valdia see Weldiya
Valdivia 43 B5 Los Lagos, C Chile
Val-d'Or 16 D4 Québec, SE Canada
Valdosta 21 E3 Georgia, SE USA
Valence 69 D5 anc. Valentia, Valentia Julia, Ventia. Drôme, E France
Valencia 71 F3 País Valenciano, E Spain
Valencia 24 D1 California, USA
Valencia 36 D1 Carabobo, N Venezuela
Valencia, Gulf of 71 F3 var. Gulf of Valencia. gulf E Spain
Valencia, Gulf of see Valencia, Golfo de
Valencia/València see País Valenciano
Valenciennes 68 D2 Nord, N France
Valentia see Valence, France
Valentia see País Valenciano
Valentia Julia see Valence
Valentine State see Oregon
Valera 36 C2 Trujillo, NW Venezuela
Valetta see Valletta
Valga 84 D3 Ger. Walk, Latv. Valka. Valgamaa, S Estonia
Valira 69 A8 river Andorra/Spain Europe
Valjevo 78 C4 Serbia, W Serbia
Valjok see Válljohka
Valka 84 D3 Ger. Walk. Valka, N Latvia
Valka see Valga
Valkenswaard 65 D5 Noord-Brabant, S Netherlands
Valladolid 29 H3 Yucatán, SE Mexico
Valladolid 70 D2 Castilla-León, NW Spain
Vall D'Uxó see La Vall d'Uixó
Valle de La Pascua 36 D2 Guárico, N Venezuela
Valledupar 36 B1 Cesar, N Colombia
Vallejo 25 B6 California, W USA
Vallenar 42 B3 Atacama, N Chile
Valletta 75 C8 prev. Valetta. country capital (Malta) E Malta
Valley City 23 E2 North Dakota, N USA
Válljohka 62 D2 var. Valjok. Finnmark, N Norway
Valls 71 G2 Cataluña, NE Spain
Valmiera 84 D3 Est. Volmari, Ger. Wolmar. Valmiera, N Latvia
Valona see Vlorë
Valozhyn 85 C5 Pol. Wołożyn, Rus. Volozhin. Minskaya Voblasts', C Belarus
Valparaíso 42 B4 Valparaíso, C Chile
Valparaiso 18 C3 Indiana, N USA
Valverde del Camino 70 C4 Andalucía, S Spain
Van 95 F3 Van, E Turkey
Vanadzor 95 F2 prev. Kirovakan. N Armenia
Vancouver 14 D5 British Columbia, SW Canada
Vancouver 24 B3 Washington, NW USA
Vancouver Island 14 D5 island British Columbia, SW Canada
Vanda see Vantaa
Van Diemen Gulf 124 D2 gulf Northern Territory, N Australia
Van Diemen's Land see Tasmania
Vaner, Lake see Vänern
Vänern 63 B6 Eng. Lake Vaner; prev. Lake Vener. lake S Sweden
Vangaindrano 57 G4 Fianarantsoa, SE Madagascar
Van Gölü 95 F3 Eng. Lake Van; anc. Thospitis. salt lake E Turkey
Van Horn 26 D3 Texas, SW USA
Van, Lake see Van Gölü
Vannes 68 A3 anc. Dariorigum. Morbihan, NW France
Vantaa 63 D6 Swe. Vanda. Etelä-Suomi, S Finland
Vanua Levu 123 E4 island N Fiji
Vanuatu 122 C4 off. Republic of Vanuatu; prev. New Hebrides. country SW Pacific Ocean
Vanuatu, Republic of see Vanuatu
Van Wert 18 C4 Ohio, N USA
Vapincum see Gap
Varakļāni 84 D4 Madona, C Latvia
Vārānasi 113 E3 prev. Banaras, Benares, hist. Kasi. Uttar Pradesh, N India
Varangerfjorden 62 E2 Lapp. Várjjatvuotna. fjord N Norway
Varangerhalvøya 62 D2 Lapp. Várnjárga. peninsula N Norway
Varannó see Vranov nad Topl'ou
Varasd see Varaždin
Varaždin 78 B2 Ger. Warasdin, Hung. Varasd. Varaždin, N Croatia
Varberg 63 B7 Halland, S Sweden
Vardar 79 E6 Gk. Axiós. river FYR Macedonia/Greece
Varde 63 A7 Ribe, W Denmark
Vareia see Logroño
Varėna 85 B5 Pol. Orany. Alytus, S Lithuania
Varese 74 B2 Lombardia, N Italy
Vârful Moldoveanu 86 B4 var. Moldoveanul; prev. Vîrful Moldoveanu. mountain C Romania
Várjjatvuotna see Varangerfjorden
Varkaus 63 E5 Itä-Suomi, C Finland
Varna 82 E2 prev. Stalin; anc. Odessus. Varna, E Bulgaria
Varnenski Zaliv 82 E2 prev. Stalinski Zaliv. bay E Bulgaria
Várnjárga see Varangerhalvøya
Varshava see Warszawa
Vasa see Vaasa
Vasilikí 83 A5 Lefkáda, Iónia Nisiá, Greece, C Mediterranean Sea
Vasilishki 85 B5 Pol. Wasiliszki. Hrodzyenskaya Voblasts', W Belarus
Vasil'kov see Vasyl'kiv
Vaslui 86 D4 Vaslui, C Romania
Västerås 63 C6 Västmanland, C Sweden
Vasyl'kiv 87 E2 var. Vasil'kov. Kyyivs'ka Oblast', N Ukraine
Vaté see Efate
Vatican City 75 A7 off. Vatican City. country S Europe
Vatnajökull 61 E5 glacier SE Iceland
Vatter, Lake see Vättern
Vättern 63 B6 Eng. Lake Vatter; prev. Lake Vetter. lake S Sweden
Vaughn 26 D2 New Mexico, SW USA
Vaupés, Río 36 C4 var. Rio Uaupés. river Brazil/Colombia
Vava'u Group 123 E4 island group N Tonga
Vavuniya 110 D3 Northern Province, N Sri Lanka
Vawkavysk 85 B6 Pol. Wołkowysk, Rus. Volkovysk. Hrodzyenskaya Voblasts', W Belarus
Växjö 63 C7 var. Vexiö. Kronoberg, S Sweden
Vaygach, Ostrov 88 E2 island NW Russian Federation
Veendam 64 E2 Groningen, NE Netherlands
Veenendaal 64 D4 Utrecht, C Netherlands
Vega 62 B4 island C Norway
Veglia see Krk
Veisiejai 85 B5 Alytus, S Lithuania
Vejer de la Frontera 70 C5 Andalucía, S Spain
Veldhoven 65 D5 Noord-Brabant, S Netherlands
Velebit 78 A3 mountain range C Croatia
Velenje 73 E7 Ger. Wöllan. N Slovenia
Veles 79 E6 Turk. Köprülü. C FYR Macedonia
Velho see Porto Velho
Velika Kikinda see Kikinda
Velika Morava 78 D4 var. Glavn'a Morava, Morava, Ger. Grosse Morava. river C Serbia
Velikaya 91 G2 river NE Russian Federation
Veliki Bečkerek see Zrenjanin
Velikiye Luki 88 A4 Pskovskaya Oblast', W Russian Federation
Velikiy Novgorod 88 B4 prev. Novgorod. Novgorodskaya Oblast', W Russian Federation
Veliko Tŭrnovo 82 D2 prev. Tirnovo, Trnovo, Tŭrnovo. Veliko Tŭrnovo, N Bulgaria
Velingrad 82 C3 Pazardzhik, C Bulgaria
Vel'ký Krtíš 77 D6 Banskobystrický Kraj, C Slovakia
Vellore 110 C2 Tamil Nādu, SE India
Velobriga see Viana do Castelo
Velsen see Velsen-Noord
Velsen-Noord 64 C3 var. Velsen. Noord-Holland, W Netherlands
Vel'sk 88 C4 var. Velsk. Arkhangel'skaya Oblast', NW Russian Federation
Velvendos see Velvéntos
Velvéntos 82 B4 var. Velvendós. C Greece
Velykyy Tokmak see Tokmak
Vendôme 68 C4 Loir-et-Cher, C France
Venedig see Venezia
Vener, Lake see Vänern
Venetia see Venezia
Venezia 74 C2 Eng. Venice, Fr. Venise, Ger. Venedig; anc. Venetia. Veneto, NE Italy
Venezia, Golfo di see Venice, Gulf of
Venezuela 36 D2 off. Republic of Venezuela; prev. Estados Unidos de Venezuela, United States of Venezuela. country N South America
Venezuela, Estados Unidos de see Venezuela
Venezuela, Gulf of 36 C1 Eng. Gulf of Maracaibo, Gulf of Venezuela. gulf NW Venezuela
Venezuela, Gulf of see Venezuela, Golfo de
Venezuelan Basin 34 B1 undersea basin E Caribbean Sea
Venezuela, Republic of see Venezuela
Venezuela, United States of see Venezuela
Venice 20 C4 Louisiana, S USA
Venice see Venezia
Venice, Gulf of 74 C2 It. Golfo di Venezia, Slvn. Beneški Zaliv. gulf N Adriatic Sea
Venise see Venezia
Venlo 65 D5 prev. Venloo. Limburg, SE Netherlands
Venloo see Venlo
Venta 84 B3 Ger. Windau. river Latvia/Lithuania
Venta Belgarum see Winchester
Ventia see Valence
Ventimiglia 74 A3 Liguria, NW Italy
Ventspils 84 B2 Ger. Windau. Ventspils, NW Latvia
Vera 42 D3 Santa Fe, C Argentina
Veracruz 29 F4 var. Veracruz Llave. Veracruz-Llave, E Mexico
Veracruz Llave see Veracruz
Vercellae see Vercelli
Vercelli 74 A2 anc. Vercellae. Piemonte, NW Italy
Verdal see Verdalsøra
Verdalsøra 62 B4 var. Verdal. Nord-Trøndelag, C Norway
Verde, Cabo see Cape Verde
Verde, Costa 70 D1 coastal region N Spain
Verden 72 B3 Niedersachsen, NW Germany
Veria see Véroia
Verkhnedvinsk see Vyerkhnyadzvinsk
Verkhneudinsk see Ulan-Ude
Verkhoyanskiy Khrebet 93 F3 mountain range NE Russian Federation
Vermillion 23 F3 South Dakota, N USA
Vermont 19 F2 off. State of Vermont, also known as Green Mountain State. state NE USA
Vernal 22 B4 Utah, W USA
Vernon 27 F2 Texas, SW USA
Verőcze see Virovitica
Véroia 82 B4 var. Veria, Vérroia, Turk. Karaferiye. Kentrikí Makedonía, N Greece
Verona 74 C2 Veneto, NE Italy
Vérroia see Véroia
Versailles 68 D1 Yvelines, N France
Versecz see Vršac
Verulamium see St Albans
Verviers 65 D6 Liège, E Belgium
Vesdre 65 D6 river E Belgium
Veselinovo 82 D2 Shumen, NE Bulgaria
Vesontio see Besançon
Vesoul 68 D4 anc. Vesulium, Vesulum. Haute-Saône, E France
Vesterålen 62 B2 island group N Norway
Vestfjorden 62 C3 fjord C Norway
Vestmannaeyjar 61 E5 Sudhurland, S Iceland
Vesulium/Vesulum see Vesoul
Vesuna see Périgueux
Vesuvio 75 D5 Eng. Vesuvius. volcano S Italy
Vesuvius see Vesuvio
Veszprém 77 C7 Ger. Veszprim. Veszprém, W Hungary
Veszprim see Veszprém
Vetrino see Suvorovo
Vetrino see Vyetryna
Vetter, Lake see Vättern
Veurne 65 A5 var. Furnes. West-Vlaanderen, W Belgium
Vexiö see Växjö
Viacha 39 F4 La Paz, W Bolivia
Viana de Castelo see Viana do Castelo
Viana do Castelo 70 B2 var. Viana de Castelo; anc. Velobriga. Viana do Castelo, NW Portugal
Vianen 64 C4 Utrecht, C Netherlands
Viangchan 114 C4 Eng./Fr. Vientiane. country capital (Laos) C Laos
Viangphoukha 114 C3 var. Vieng Pou Kha. Louang Namtha, N Laos
Viareggio 74 B3 Toscana, C Italy
Viborg 63 A7 Viborg, NW Denmark
Vic 71 G2 var. Vich; anc. Ausa, Vicus Ausonensis. Cataluña, NE Spain
Vicentia see Vicenza
Vicenza 74 C2 anc. Vicentia. Veneto, NE Italy
Vich see Vic
Vichy 69 C5 Allier, C France
Vicksburg 20 B2 Mississippi, S USA
Victoria 57 H1 country capital (Seychelles) Mahé, SW Seychelles
Victoria 14 D5 province capital Vancouver Island, British Columbia, SW Canada
Victoria 80 A5 var. Rabat. Gozo, NW Malta
Victoria 27 G4 Texas, SW USA
Victoria 127 C7 state SE Australia
Victoria see Masvingo, Zimbabwe
Victoria Bank see Vitória Seamount
Victoria de Durango see Durango
Victoria de las Tunas see Las Tunas
Victoria Falls 56 C3 Matabeleland North, W Zimbabwe
Victoria Falls 56 C2 waterfall Zambia/Zimbabwe
Victoria Falls see Iguaçu, Saltos do
Victoria Island 15 F3 island Northwest Territories/Nunavut, NW Canada
Victoria, Lake 51 B6 var. Victoria Nyanza. lake E Africa
Victoria Land 132 C4 physical region Antarctica
Victoria Nyanza see Victoria, Lake
Victoria River 124 D3 river Northern Territory, N Australia
Victorville 25 C7 California, W USA
Vicus Ausonensis see Vic
Vicus Elbii see Viterbo
Vidalia 21 E2 Georgia, SE USA
Videm-Krško see Krško
Vídeň see Wien
Vidin 82 B1 anc. Bononia. Vidin, NW Bulgaria
Vidzy 85 C5 Vitsyebskaya Voblasts', NW Belarus
Viedma 43 C5 Río Negro, E Argentina
Vieja, Sierra 26 D3 mountain range Texas, SW USA
Vieng Pou Kha see Viangphoukha
Vienna see Wien, Austria
Vienna see Vienne, France
Vienne 69 D5 anc. Vienna. Isère, E France
Vienne 68 B4 river W France
Vientiane see Viangchan
Vientos, Paso de los see Windward Passage
Vierzon 68 C4 Cher, C France
Viesīte 84 C4 Ger. Eckengraf. Jēkabpils, S Latvia
Vietnam 114 D4 off. Socialist Republic of Vietnam, Vtn. Công Hoa Xa Hôi Chu Nghia Viêt Nam. country SE Asia
Vietnam, Socialist Republic of see Vietnam
Vietri see Viêt Tri
Viêt Tri 114 D3 var. Vietri. Vinh Phu, N Vietnam
Vieux Fort 33 F2 S Saint Lucia
Vigo 70 B2 Galicia, NW Spain
Viipuri see Vyborg
Vijayawāda 110 D1 prev. Bezwada. Andhra Pradesh, SE India
Vila see Port-Vila
Vila Artur de Paiva see Cubango
Vila da Ponte see Cubango
Vila de João Belo see Xai-Xai
Vila de Mocímboa da Praia see Mocímboa da Praia
Vila do Conde 70 B2 Porto, NW Portugal
Vila do Zumbo 56 D2 prev. Vila do Zumbu, Zumbo. Tete, NW Mozambique
Vila do Zumbu see Vila do Zumbo
Vilafranca del Penedès 71 G2 var. Villafranca del Panadés. Cataluña, NE Spain
Vila General Machado see Camacupa
Vila Henrique de Carvalho see Saurimo
Viļaka 84 D4 Ger. Marienhausen. Balvi, NE Latvia
Vilalba 70 C1 Galicia, NW Spain
Vila Marechal Carmona see Uíge
Vila Nova de Gaia 70 B2 Porto, NW Portugal
Vila Nova de Portimão see Portimão
Vila Pereira de Eça see N'Giva
Vila Real 70 C2 var. Vila Rial. Vila Real, N Portugal
Vila Rial see Vila Real
Vila Robert Williams see Caála
Vila Salazar see N'Dalatando
Vila Serpa Pinto see Menongue
Vileyka see Vilyeyka
Vilhelmina 62 C4 Västerbotten, N Sweden
Vilhena 40 D3 Rondônia, W Brazil
Vília 83 C5 Attikí, C Greece
Viliya 85 C5 Lith. Neris. river W Belarus
Viliya see Neris
Viljandi 84 D2 Ger. Fellin. Viljandimaa, S Estonia
Vilkaviškis 84 B4 Pol. Wyłkowyszki. Marijampolė, SW Lithuania
Villa Acuña 28 D2 var. Ciudad Acuña. Coahuila, NE Mexico
Villa Bella 39 F2 Beni, N Bolivia
Villacarrillo 71 E4 Andalucía, S Spain
Villa Cecilia see Ciudad Madero
Villach 73 D7 Slvn. Beljak. Kärnten, S Austria
Villacidro 75 A5 Sardegna, Italy, C Mediterranean Sea
Villa Concepción see Concepción
Villa del Pilar see Pilar
Villafranca de los Barros 70 C4 Extremadura, W Spain
Villafranca del Panadés see Vilafranca del Penedès
Villahermosa 29 G4 prev. San Juan Bautista. Tabasco, SE Mexico
Villajoyosa 71 F4 Cat. La Vila Joíosa. País Valenciano, E Spain
Villa María 42 C4 Córdoba, C Argentina
Villa Martín 39 F5 Potosí, SW Bolivia
Villa Mercedes 42 C4 San Juan, Argentina
Villanueva 28 D3 Zacatecas, C Mexico
Villanueva de la Serena 70 C3 Extremadura, W Spain
Villanueva de los Infantes 71 E4 Castilla-La Mancha, C Spain
Villarrica 42 D2 Guairá, SE Paraguay
Villavicencio 36 B3 Meta, C Colombia
Villaviciosa 70 D1 Asturias, N Spain
Villazón 39 G5 Potosí, S Bolivia
Villena 71 F4 País Valenciano, E Spain
Villeurbanne 69 D5 Rhône, E France
Villingen-Schwenningen 73 B6 Baden-Württemberg, S Germany
Villmanstrand see Lappeenranta
Vilna see Vilnius
Vilnius 85 C5 Pol. Wilno, Ger. Wilna; prev. Rus. Vilna. country capital (Lithuania) Vilnius, SE Lithuania
Vil'shanka 87 E3 Rus. Olshanka. Kirovohrads'ka Oblast', C Ukraine
Vilvoorde 65 C6 Fr. Vilvorde. Vlaams Brabant, C Belgium
Vilvorde see Vilvoorde
Vilyeyka 85 C5 Pol. Wilejka, Rus. Vileyka. Minskaya Voblasts', NW Belarus
Vilyuy 93 F3 river NE Russian Federation
Viña del Mar 42 B4 Valparaíso, C Chile
Vinaròs 71 F3 País Valenciano, E Spain
Vincennes 18 B4 Indiana, N USA
Vindhya Mountains see Vindhya Range
Vindhya Range 112 D4 var. Vindhya Mountains. mountain range N India
Vindobona see Wien
Vineland 19 F4 New Jersey, NE USA
Vinh 114 D4 Nghê An, N Vietnam
Vinh Loi see Bac Liêu
Vinishte 82 C2 Montana, NW Bulgaria
Vinita 27 G1 Oklahoma, C USA
Vinkovci 78 C3 Ger. Winkowitz, Hung. Vinkovcze. Vukovar-Srijem, E Croatia
Vinkovcze see Vinkovci
Vinnitsa see Vinnytsya
Vinnytsya 86 D2 Rus. Vinnitsa. Vinnyts'ka Oblast', C Ukraine
Vinogradov see Vynohradiv
Vinson Massif 132 A3 mountain Antarctica
Viranşehir 95 E4 Şanlıurfa, SE Turkey
Virful Moldoveanu see Vârful Moldoveanu
Virginia 23 G1 Minnesota, N USA
Virginia 19 E5 off. Commonwealth of Virginia, also known as Mother of Presidents, Mother of States, Old Dominion. state NE USA
Virginia Beach 19 F5 Virginia, NE USA
Virgin Islands see British Virgin Islands
Virgin Islands (US) 33 F3 var. Virgin Islands of the United States; prev. Danish West Indies. US unincorporated territory E West Indies
Virgin Islands of the United States see Virgin Islands (US)
Virôchey 115 E5 Rôtânôkiri, NE Cambodia
Virovitica 78 C2 Ger. Virovititz, Hung. Verőcze; prev. Ger. Werowitz. Virovitica-Podravina, NE Croatia
Virovititz see Virovitica
Virton 65 D8 Luxembourg, SE Belgium
Virtsu 84 D2 Ger. Werder. Läänemaa, W Estonia
Vis 78 B4 It. Lissa; anc. Issa. island S Croatia
Vis see Fish
Visaginas 84 C4 prev. Sniečkus. Utena, E Lithuania
Visākhapatnam 113 E5 var. Vishakhapatnam. Andhra Pradesh, SE India
Visalia 25 C6 California, W USA
Visby 63 C7 Ger. Wisby. Gotland, SE Sweden
Viscount Melville Sound 15 F2 prev. Melville Sound. sound Northwest Territories, N Canada
Visé 65 D6 Liège, E Belgium
Viseu 70 C2 prev. Vizeu. Viseu, N Portugal
Vishakhapatnam see Visākhapatnam
Vislinskiy Zaliv see Vistula Lagoon
Visoko 78 C4 Federacija Bosna I Hercegovina, C Bosnia and Herzegovina
Visttasjohka 62 D3 river N Sweden
Vistula 76 C2 Eng. Vistula, Ger. Weichsel. river C Poland
Vistula see Wisła
Vistula Lagoon 76 C2 Ger. Frisches Haff, Pol. Zalew Wiślany, Rus. Vislinskiy Zaliv. lagoon Poland/Russian Federation
Vitebsk see Vitsyebsk
Viterbo 74 C4 anc. Vicus Elbii. Lazio, C Italy
Viti see Fiji
Viti Levu 123 E4 island W Fiji
Vitim 93 F4 river C Russian Federation
Vitória 41 F4 state capital Espírito Santo, SE Brazil
Vitoria see Vitoria-Gasteiz
Vitoria Bank see Vitória Seamount
Vitória da Conquista 41 F3 Bahia, E Brazil
Vitoria-Gasteiz 71 E1 var. Vitoria, Eng. Vittoria. País Vasco, N Spain
Vitória Seamount 45 B5 var. Victoria Bank, Vitoria Bank. seamount C Atlantic Ocean
Vitré 68 B3 Ille-et-Vilaine, NW France
Vitsyebsk 85 E5 Rus. Vitebsk. Vitsyebskaya Voblasts', NE Belarus
Vittoria 75 C7 Sicilia, Italy, C Mediterranean Sea
Vittoria see Vitoria-Gasteiz
Vizcaya, Golfo de see Biscay, Bay of
Vizianagaram 113 E5 var. Vizianagram. Andhra Pradesh, E India
Vizianagram see Vizianagaram
Vjosës, Lumi i 79 C7 var. Vijosa, Vijosë, Gk. Aóos. river Albania/Greece
Vlaanderen see Flanders
Vlaardingen 64 B4 Zuid-Holland, SW Netherlands
Vladikavkaz 89 B8 prev. Dzaudzhikau, Ordzhonikidze. Respublika Severnaya Osetiya, SW Russian Federation
Vladimir 89 B5 Vladimirskaya Oblast', W Russian Federation
Vladimirovka see Yuzhno-Sakhalinsk
Vladimir-Volynskiy see Volodymyr-Volyns'kyy
Vladivostok 93 G5 Primorskiy Kray, SE Russian Federation
Vlagtwedde 64 E2 Groningen, NE Netherlands
Vlasotince 79 E5 Serbia, SE Serbia
Vlieland 64 C1 Fris. Flylân. island Waddeneilanden, N Netherlands
Vlijmen 64 C4 Noord-Brabant, S Netherlands
Vlissingen 65 B5 Eng. Flushing, Fr. Flessingue. Zeeland, SW Netherlands
Vlodava see Włodawa
Vlonë/Vlora see Vlorë
Vlorë 79 C7 prev. Vlonë, It. Valona, Vlora. Vlorë, SW Albania
Vlotslavsk see Włocławek
Vöcklabruck 73 D6 Oberösterreich, NW Austria
Vogelkop see Doberai, Jazirah
Vohimena, Tanjona 57 F4 Fr. Cap Sainte Marie. headland S Madagascar
Voiron 69 D5 Isère, E France
Vojvodina 78 D3 Ger. Wojwodina. Vojvodina, N Serbia
Volga 89 B7 river NW Russian Federation
Volga Uplands see Privolzhskaya Vozvyshennost'
Volgodonsk 89 B7 Rostovskaya Oblast', SW Russian Federation
Volgograd 89 B7 prev. Stalingrad, Tsaritsyn. Volgogradskaya Oblast', SW Russian Federation
Volkhov 88 B4 Leningradskaya Oblast', NW Russian Federation
Volkovysk see Vawkavysk
Volmari see Valmiera
Volnovakha 87 G3 Donets'ka Oblast', SE Ukraine
Volodymyr-Volyns'kyy 86 C1 Pol. Włodzimierz, Rus. Vladimir-Volynskiy. Volyns'ka Oblast', NW Ukraine
Vologda 88 B4 Vologodskaya Oblast', W Russian Federation
Vólos 83 B5 Thessalía, C Greece
Volozhin see Valozhyn
Vol'sk 89 C6 Saratovskaya Oblast', W Russian Federation
Volta 53 E5 river SE Ghana
Volta Blanche see White Volta
Volta, Lake 53 E5 reservoir SE Ghana
Volta Noire see Black Volta
Volturno 75 D5 river S Italy
Volunteer Island see Starbuck Island
Volzhskiy 89 B6 Volgogradskaya Oblast', SW Russian Federation
Võnnu 84 E3 Ger. Wendau. Tartumaa, SE Estonia
Voorst 64 D3 Gelderland, E Netherlands
Voranava 85 C5 Pol. Werenów, Rus. Voronovo. Hrodzyenskaya Voblasts', W Belarus
Vorderrhein 73 B7 river SE Switzerland
Vóreies Sporádes 83 C5 var. Vóreioi Sporádes, Vórioi Sporádhes, Eng. Northern Sporades. island group E Greece
Vóreioi Sporádes see Vóreies Sporádes
Vórioi Sporádhes see Vóreies Sporádes
Vorkuta 92 C2 Respublika Komi, NW Russian Federation
Vormsi 84 C2 var. Vormsi Saar, Ger. Worms, Swed. Ormsö. island W Estonia
Vormsi Saar see Vormsi
Voronezh 89 B6 Voronezhskaya Oblast', W Russian Federation
Voronovo see Voranava
Voroshilov see Ussuriysk
Voroshilovgrad see Luhans'k, Ukraine
Voroshilovsk see Stavropol', Russian Federation
Võru 84 D3 Ger. Werro. Võrumaa, SE Estonia
Vosges 68 E4 mountain range NE France
Vostochno-Sibirskoye More 93 F1 Eng. East Siberian Sea. sea Arctic Ocean
Vostochnyy Sayan 93 E4 Mong. Dzüün Soyonï Nuruu, Eng. Eastern Sayans. mountain range Mongolia/Russian Federation
Vostock Island see Vostok Island
Vostok 132 C3 Russian research station Antarctica
Vostok Island 123 G3 var. Vostock Island; prev. Stavers Island. island Line Islands, SE Kiribati
Voznesens'k 87 E3 Rus. Voznesensk. Mykolayivs'ka Oblast', S Ukraine
Vranje 79 E5 Serbia, SE Serbia
Vranov see Vranov nad Topl'ou
Vranov nad Topl'ou 77 D5 var. Vranov, Hung. Varannó. Prešovský Kraj, E Slovakia
Vratsa 82 C2 Vratsa, NW Bulgaria
Vrbas 78 C3 Vojvodina, NW Serbia
Vrbas 78 C3 river N Bosnia and Herzegovina
Vršac 78 E3 Ger. Werschetz, Hung. Versecz. Vojvodina, NE Serbia
Vsetín 77 C5 Ger. Wsetin. Zlínský Kraj, E Czech Republic
Vučitrn see Vushtrri
Vukovar 78 C3 Hung. Vukovár. Vukovar-Srijem, E Croatia
Vulcano, Isola 75 C7 island Isole Eolie, S Italy
Vung Tau 115 E6 prev. Fr. Cap Saint Jacques, Cap Saint-Jacques. Ba Ria-Vung Tau, S Vietnam
Vushtrri 79 D5 Serb. Vučitrn. N Kosovo
Vyatka 89 C5 river NW Russian Federation
Vyatka see Kirov
Vyborg 88 B3 Fin. Viipuri. Leningradskaya Oblast', NW Russian Federation
Vyerkhnyadzvinsk 85 D5 Rus. Verkhnedvinsk. Vitsyebskaya Voblasts', N Belarus

Yalpuh, Ozero 86 *D4 Rus.* Ozero Yalpug. *lake* SW Ukraine
Yalta 87 *F5* Respublika Krym, S Ukraine
Yalu 103 *E2 Chin.* Yalu Jiang, *Jap.* Oryokko, *Kor.* Amnok-kang. *river* China/North Korea
Yalu Jiang *see* Yalu
Yamaguchi 109 *B7 var.* Yamaguti. Yamaguchi, Honshū, SW Japan
Yamal, Poluostrov 92 *D2 peninsula* N Russian Federation
Yamaniyah, Al Jumhūriyah al *see* Yemen
Yambio 51 *B5 var.* Yambiyo. Western Equatoria, S South Sudan
Yambiyo *see* Yambio
Yambol 82 *D2 Turk.* Yanboli. Yambol, E Bulgaria
Yamdena, Pulau 117 *G5 prev.* Jamdena. *island* Kepulauan Tanimbar, E Indonesia
Yamoussoukro 52 *D5 country capital* (Côte d'Ivoire) C Côte d'Ivoire
Yamuna 112 *D3 prev.* Jumna. *river* N India
Yana 93 *F2 river* NE Russian Federation
Yanboli *see* Yambol
Yanbu 'al Baḥr 99 *A5* Al Madīnah, W Saudi Arabia
Yangambi 55 *D5* Orientale, N Dem. Rep. Congo
Yangchow *see* Yangzhou
Yangiyo'l 101 *E2 Rus.* Yangiyul'. Toshkent Viloyati, E Uzbekistan
Yangiyul' *see* Yangiyo'l
Yangku *see* Taiyuan
Yangon 114 *B4 Eng.* Rangoon. Yangon, S Myanmar (Burma)
Yangtze *see* Chang Jiang
Yangtze Kiang *see* Chang Jiang
Yangzhou 106 *D5 var.* Yangchow. Jiangsu, E China
Yankton 23 *E3* South Dakota, N USA
Yannina *see* Ioánnina
Yanskiy Zaliv 91 *F2 bay* N Russian Federation
Yantai 106 *D4 var.* Yan-t'ai; *prev.* Chefoo, Chih-fu. Shandong, E China
Yaoundé 55 *B5 var.* Yaunde. *country capital* (Cameroon) Centre, S Cameroon
Yap 122 *A1 island* Caroline Islands, W Micronesia
Yapanskoye More East Sea/Japan, Sea of
Yapen, Pulau 117 *G4 prev.* Japen. *island* E Indonesia
Yap Trench 120 *B2 var.* Yap Trough. *undersea feature* SE Philippine Sea
Yap Trough *see* Yap Trench
Yapura *see* Caquetá, Río, Brazil/Colombia
Yapurá *see* Japurá, Rio, Brazil/Colombia
Yaqui, Río 28 *C2 river* NW Mexico
Yaransk 89 *C5* Kirovskaya Oblast', NW Russian Federation
Yarega 88 *D4* Respublika Komi, NW Russian Federation
Yarkant *see* Shache
Yarlung Zangbo Jiang *see* Brahmaputra
Yarmouth 17 *F5* Nova Scotia, SE Canada
Yarmouth *see* Great Yarmouth
Yaroslav *see* Jarosław
Yaroslavl' 88 *B4* Yaroslavskaya Oblast', W Russian Federation
Yarumal 36 *B2* Antioquia, NW Colombia
Yasyel'da 85 *B7 river* SW Brestskaya Voblasts', SW Belarus Europe
Yatsushiro 109 *A7 var.* Yatusiro. Kumamoto, Kyūshū, SW Japan
Yatusiro *see* Yatsushiro
Yaunde *see* Yaoundé
Yavari *see* Javari, Rio
Río Yavari 40 *C2 var.* Yavari. *river* Brazil/Peru
Yaviza 31 *H5* Darién, SE Panama
Yavoriv 86 *B2 Pol.* Jaworów, *Rus.* Yavorov. L'vivs'ka Oblast', NW Ukraine
Yavorov *see* Yavoriv
Yazd 98 *D3 var.* Yezd. Yazd, C Iran
Yazoo City 20 *B2* Mississippi, S USA
Yding Skovhøj 63 *A7 hill* C Denmark
Ydra 83 *C6 var.* Idhra. *island* Ydra, S Greece
Ye 115 *B5* Mon State, S Myanmar (Burma)
Yecheng 104 *A3 var.* Kargilik. Xinjiang Uygur Zizhiqu, NW China
Yefremov 89 *B5* Tul'skaya Oblast', W Russian Federation
Yekaterinburg 92 *C3 prev.* Sverdlovsk. Sverdlovskaya Oblast', C Russian Federation
Yekaterinodar *see* Krasnodar
Yekaterinoslav *see* Dnipropetrovs'k
Yelets 89 *B5* Lipetskaya Oblast', W Russian Federation
Yelisavetgrad *see* Kirovohrad
Yelizovo *see* Yalizava
Yell 66 *D1 island* NE Scotland, United Kingdom
Yellowhammer State *see* Alabama
Yellowknife 15 *E4 territory capital* Northwest Territories, W Canada
Yellow River *see* Huang He
Yellow Sea 106 *D4 Chin.* Huang Hai, *Kor.* Hwang-Hae. *sea* E Asia
Yellowstone River 22 *C2 river* Montana/Wyoming, NW USA
Yel'sk 85 *C7* Homyel'skaya Voblasts', SE Belarus
Yelwa 53 *F4* Kebbi, W Nigeria
Yemen 99 *C6 off.* Republic of Yemen, *Ar.* Al Jumhurīyah al Yamaniyah, Al Yaman. *country* SW Asia
Yemen, Republic of *see* Yemen

Yemva 88 *D4 prev.* Zheleznodorozhnyy. Respublika Komi, NW Russian Federation
Yenakiyeve 87 *G3 Rus.* Yenakiyevo; *prev.* Ordzhonikidze, Rykovo. Donets'ka Oblast', E Ukraine
Yenakiyevo *see* Yenakiyeve
Yenangyaung 114 *A3* Magway, W Myanmar (Burma)
Yendi 53 *E4* NE Ghana
Yengisar 104 *A3* Xinjiang Uygur Zizhiqu, NW China
Yenierenköy 80 *D4 var.* Yialousa, *Gk.* Agialoúsa. NE Cyprus
Yenipazar *see* Novi Pazar
Yenisey 92 *D3 river* Mongolia/Russian Federation
Yenping *see* Nanping
Yeovil 67 *D7* SW England, United Kingdom
Yeppoon 126 *D4* Queensland, E Australia
Yerevan 95 *F3 Eng.* Erivan. *country capital* (Armenia) C Armenia
Yeriho *see* Jericho
Yerushalayim *see* Jerusalem
Yeso *see* Hokkaidō
Yeu, Île d' 68 *A4 island* NW France
Yevlakh *see* Yevlax
Yevlax 95 *G2 Rus.* Yevlakh. C Azerbaijan
Yevpatoriya 87 *F5* Respublika Krym, S Ukraine
Yeya 87 *H4 river* SW Russian Federation
Yezerishche *see* Yezyaryshcha
Yezo *see* Hokkaidō
Yezyaryshcha 85 *E5 Rus.* Yezerishche. Vitsyebskaya Voblasts', NE Belarus
Yialousa *see* Yenierenköy
Yiannitsá *see* Giannitsá
Yichang 106 *C5* Hubei, C China
Yıldızeli 94 *D3* Sivas, N Turkey
Yinchuan 106 *B4 var.* Yinch'uan, Yin-ch'uan, Yinchwan. *province capital* Ningxia, N China
Yinch'uan *see* Yinchuan
Yinchwan *see* Yinchuan
Yindu He *see* Indus
Yin-hsien *see* Ningbo
Yining 104 *B2 var.* I-ning, *Uigh.* Gulja, Kuldja. Xinjiang Uygur Zizhiqu, NW China
Yin-tu Ho *see* Indus
Yisrael/Yisra'el *see* Israel
Yíthion *see* Gýtheio
Yogyakarta 116 *C5 prev.* Djokjakarta, Jogjakarta, Jokyakarta. Jawa, C Indonesia
Yokohama 109 *D5* Aomori, Honshū, C Japan
Yokohama 108 *A2* Kanagawa, Honshū, S Japan
Yokote 108 *D4* Akita, Honshū, C Japan
Yola 53 *H4* Adamawa, E Nigeria
Yonago 109 *B6* Tottori, Honshū, SW Japan
Yong'an 106 *D4 var.* Yongan. Fujian, SE China
Yongzhou 107 *C6 var.* Lengshuitan. Hunan, S China
Yonkers 19 *F3* New York, NE USA
Yonne 68 *C4 river* C France
Yopal 36 *C3 var.* El Yopal. Casanare, C Colombia
York 67 *D5 anc.* Eboracum, Eburacum. N England, United Kingdom
York 23 *E4* Nebraska, C USA
York, Cape 126 *C1 headland* Queensland, NE Australia
York, Kap *see* Innaanganeq
Yorkton 15 *F5* Saskatchewan, S Canada
Yoro 30 *C2* Yoro, C Honduras
Yoshkar-Ola 89 *C5* Respublika Mariy El, W Russian Federation
Yösönbulag *see* Altay
Youngstown 18 *D4* Ohio, N USA
Youth, Isle of *see* Juventud, Isla de la
Ypres *see* Ieper
Yreka 24 *B4* California, W USA
Yrendagüé *see* General Eugenio A. Garay
Yssel *see* IJssel
Yssyk-Köl *see* Issyk-Kul', Ozero
Yssyk-Köl *see* Balykchy
Yu *see* Henan
Yuan see Red River
Yuan Jiang *see* Red River
Yuba City 25 *B5* California, W USA
Yucatán, Canal de *see* Yucatan Channel
Yucatan Channel 29 *H3 Sp.* Canal de Yucatán. *channel* Cuba/Mexico
Yucatan Peninsula *see* Yucatán, Península de
Yucatán, Península de 13 *C7 Eng.* Yucatan Peninsula. *peninsula* Guatemala/Mexico
Yuci *see* Guangdong
Yue *see* Guangdong
Yue Shan, Tai *see* Lantau Island
Yueyang 106 *C5* Hunan, S China
Yugoslavia *see* Serbia
Yukhavichy 85 *D5 Rus.* Yukhovichi. Vitsyebskaya Voblasts', N Belarus
Yukhovichi *see* Yukhavichy
Yukon River 14 *C2 river* Canada/USA
Yukon Territory 14 *D3 var.* Yukon, *Fr.* Territoire du Yukon. *territory* NW Canada
Yukon, Territoire du *see* Yukon Territory
Yulin 106 *C6* Guangxi Zhuangzu Zizhiqu, S China
Yuma 26 *A2* Arizona, SW USA
Yun *see* Yunnan
Yungki *see* Jilin
Yung-ning *see* Nanning
Yunjinghong *see* Jinghong
Yunki *see* Jilin
Yunnan 106 *A6 var.* Yun, Yunnan Sheng, Yünnan, Yun-nan. *province* SW China

Yunnan *see* Kunming
Yunnan Sheng *see* Yunnan
Yünnan/Yun-nan *see* Yunnan
Yurev *see* Tartu
Yurihonjō *see* Honjō
Yuruá, Rio *see* Juruá, Rio
Yury'ev *see* Tartu
Yushu 104 *D4 var.* Gyêgu. Qinghai, C China
Yuty 42 *D3* Caazapá, S Paraguay
Yuzhno-Sakhalinsk 93 *H4 Jap.* Toyohara; *prev.* Vladimirovka. Ostrov Sakhalin, Sakhalinskaya Oblast', SE Russian Federation
Yuzhnyy Bug *see* Pivdennyy Buh
Yuzhou *see* Chongqing
Ylanly *see* Gurbansoltan Eje

Z

Zaandam *see* Zaanstad
Zaanstad 64 *C3 prev.* Zaandam. Noord-Holland, C Netherlands
Zabaykal'sk 93 *F5* Chitinskaya Oblast', S Russian Federation
Zabern *see* Saverne
Zabid 99 *B7* W Yemen
Żabinka *see* Zhabinka
Ząbkowice *see* Ząbkowice Śląskie
Ząbkowice Śląskie 76 *B4 var.* Ząbkowice, *Ger.* Frankenstein, Frankenstein in Schlesien. Dolnośląskie, SW Poland
Zábřeh 77 *C5 Ger.* Hohenstadt. Olomoucký Kraj, E Czech Republic
Zacapa 30 *B2* Zacapa, E Guatemala
Zacatecas 28 *D3* Zacatecas, C Mexico
Zacatepec 29 *E4* Morelos, S Mexico
Zacháro 83 *B6 var.* Zaharo, Zakháro. Dytikí Elláda, S Greece
Zadar 78 *A3 It.* Zara; *anc.* Iader. Zadar, SW Croatia
Zadetkyi Kyun 115 *B6 var.* St.Matthew's Island. *island* Myeik Archipelago, S Myanmar (Burma)
Zafra 70 *C4* Extremadura, W Spain
Żagań 76 *B4 var.* Zagań, Żegań, *Ger.* Sagan. Lubuskie, W Poland
Zagazig *see* Az Zaqāziq
Zágráb *see* Zagreb
Zagreb 78 *B2 Ger.* Agram, *Hung.* Zágráb. *country capital* (Croatia) Zagreb, N Croatia
Zagros Mountains 98 *C3 Eng.* Zagros Mountains. *mountain range* W Iran
Zagros Mountains *see* Zāgros, Kūhhā-ye
Zaharo *see* Zacháro
Zāhedān 98 *E4 var.* Zahidan; *prev.* Duzdab. Sīstān va Balūchestān, SE Iran
Zahidan *see* Zāhedān
Zaḥlah *see* Zahlé
Zahlé 96 *B4 var.* Zaḥlah. C Lebanon
Záhony 77 *E6* Szabolcs-Szatmár-Bereg, NE Hungary
Zaire *see* Congo (river)
Zaire *see* Congo (Democratic Republic of)
Zaječar 78 *E4* Serbia, E Serbia
Zakataly *see* Zaqatala
Zakháro *see* Zacháro
Zakhidnyy Buh/Zakhodni Buh *see* Bug
Zākhō 98 *B2 var.* Zākhū. Dahūk, N Iraq
Zākhū *see* Zākhō
Zakopane 77 *D5* Małopolskie, S Poland
Zákynthos 83 *A6 var.* Zákinthos, *It.* Zante. *island* Iónia Nísoi, Greece, C Mediterranean Sea
Zalaegerszeg 77 *B7* Zala, W Hungary
Zalău 86 *B3 Ger.* Waltenberg, *Hung.* Zilah; *prev. Ger.* Zillenmarkt. Sălaj, NW Romania
Zalim 99 *B5* Makkah, W Saudi Arabia
Zambesi/Zambeze *see* Zambezi
Zambezi 56 *C2* North Western, W Zambia
Zambezi 56 *D2 var.* Zambesi, *Port.* Zambeze. *river* S Africa
Zambia 56 *C2 off.* Republic of Zambia; *prev.* Northern Rhodesia. *country* S Africa
Zambia, Republic of *see* Zambia
Zamboanga 117 *E3 off.* Zamboanga City. Mindanao, S Philippines
Zamboanga City *see* Zamboanga
Zambrów 76 *E3* Łomża, E Poland
Zamora 70 *D2* Castilla-León, NW Spain
Zamora de Hidalgo 28 *D4* Michoacán, SW Mexico
Zamość 76 *E4 Rus.* Zamoste. Lubelskie, E Poland
Zamoste *see* Zamość
Zancle *see* Messina
Zanda 104 *A4* Xizang Zizhiqu, W China
Zanesville 18 *D4* Ohio, N USA
Zanjan 98 *C2 var.* Zenjan, Zinjan. Zanjān, NW Iran
Zante *see* Zákynthos
Zanthus 125 *C6* Western Australia, S Australia Oceania
Zanzibar 51 *D7* Zanzibar, E Tanzania
Zanzibar 51 *C7 Swa.* Unguja. *island* E Tanzania
Zaozhuang 106 *D4* Shandong, E China
Zapadna Morava 78 *D4 Ger.* Westliche Morava. *river* C Serbia
Zapadnaya Dvina 88 *A4* Tverskaya Oblast', W Russian Federation
Zapadnaya Dvina *see* Western Dvina
Zapadno-Sibirskaya Ravnina 92 *C3 Eng.* West Siberian Plain. *plain* C Russian Federation
Zapadnyy Bug *see* Bug
Zapadnyy Sayan 92 *D4 Eng.* Western Sayans. *mountain range* S Russian Federation

Zapala 43 *B5* Neuquén, W Argentina
Zapiola Ridge 45 *B6 undersea feature* SW Atlantic Ocean
Zapolyarnyy 88 *C2* Murmanskaya Oblast', NW Russian Federation
Zaporizhzhya 87 *F3 Rus.* Zaporozh'ye; *prev.* Aleksandrovsk. Zaporiz'ka Oblast', SE Ukraine
Zaporozh'ye *see* Zaporizhzhya
Zaqatala 95 *G2 Rus.* Zakataly. NW Azerbaijan
Zara 94 *D3* Sivas, C Turkey
Zara *see* Zadar
Zarafshan *see* Zarafshon
Zarafshon 100 *D2 Rus.* Zarafshan. Navoiy Viloyati, N Uzbekistan
Zarafshon *see* Zeravshan
Zaragoza 71 *F2 Eng.* Saragossa; *anc.* Caesaraugusta, Salduba. Aragón, NE Spain
Zarand 98 *D3* Kermān, C Iran
Zaranj 100 *D5* Nīmrūz, SW Afghanistan
Zarasai 84 *C4* Utena, E Lithuania
Zárate 42 *D4 prev.* General José F.Uriburu. Buenos Aires, E Argentina
Zarautz 71 *E1 var.* Zarauz. Pais Vasco, N Spain
Zarauz *see* Zarautz
Zaria 53 *G4* Kaduna, C Nigeria
Zarqa' *see* Az Zarqā'
Żary 76 *B4 Ger.* Sorau. Lubuskie, W Poland
Zasyadko *see* Zhdanov
Żatec 76 *A4 Ger.* Saaz. Ústecký Kraj, NW Czech Republic
Zaunguzskiye Garagumy *see* Uly-Zungguz Garagumy
Zavertse *see* Zawiercie
Zawia *see* Az Zāwiyah
Zawiercie 76 *D4 Rus.* Zavertse. Śląskie, S Poland
Zaysan, Lake *see* Zaysan Köli
Zaysan Köli 92 *C5 Kaz.* Zaysan; *prev.* Ozero Zaysan. *lake* E Kazakhstan
Zduńska Wola 76 *C4* Łódzkie, C Poland
Zealand *see* Sjælland
Zeebrugge 65 *A5* West-Vlaanderen, NW Belgium
Zeeland 64 *B4* Noord-Brabant, S Netherlands

Zelenogradsk 84 *A4 Ger.* Cranz, Kranz. Kaliningradskaya Oblast', W Russian Federation
Zelle *see* Celle
Zel'va 85 *B6 Pol.* Zelwa. Hrodzyenskaya Voblasts', W Belarus
Zelwa *see* Zel'va
Zelzate 65 *B5 var.* Selzaete. Oost-Vlaanderen, NW Belgium
Žemaičiu Aukštumas 84 *B4 physical region* W Lithuania
Zemst 65 *C5* Vlaams Brabant, C Belgium
Zemun 78 *D3* Serbia, N Serbia
Zengg *see* Senj
Zenica 78 *C4* Federacija Bosna I Hercegovina, C Bosnia and Herzegovina
Zenta *see* Senta
Zeravshan 101 *E3 Taj./Uzb.* Zarafshon. *river* Tajikistan/Uzbekistan
Zevenaar 64 *D4* Gelderland, SE Netherlands
Zevenbergen 64 *C4* Noord-Brabant, S Netherlands
Zeya 91 *E3 river* SE Russian Federation
Zgierz 76 *C4 Ger.* Neuhof, *Rus.* Zgerzh. Łódź, C Poland
Zgorzelec 76 *B4 Ger.* Görlitz. Dolnośląskie, SW Poland
Zhambyl *see* Taraz
Zhanaozen 92 *A4 Kaz.* Zhangaözen; *prev.* Novyy Uzen'. Mangistau, W Kazakhstan
Zhangaözen *see* Zhanaozen
Zhangazaly *see* Ayteke Bi
Zhang-chia-k'ou *see* Zhangjiakou
Zhangdian *see* Zibo
Zhangjiakou 105 *C3 var.* Changkiakow, Zhang-chia-k'ou, *Eng.* Kalgan; *prev.* Wanchuan. Hebei, E China
Zhangzhou 106 *D6* Fujian, SE China
Zhanjiang 106 *C7 var.* Chanchiang, Chan-chiang, *Cant.* Tsamkong, *Fr.* Fort-Bayard. Guangdong, S China
Zhaoqing 106 *C6* Guangdong, S China
Zhdanov *see* Mariupol'
Zhe *see* Zhejiang
Zhejiang 106 *D5 var.* Che-chiang, Chekiang, Zhe, Zhejiang Sheng. *province* SE China
Zhejiang Sheng *see* Zhejiang
Zheleznodorozhnyy 84 *A4* Kaliningradskaya Oblast', W Russian Federation
Zheleznodorozhnyy *see* Yemva
Zheleznogorsk 89 *A5* Kurskaya Oblast', W Russian Federation
Zhêltyye Vody *see* Zhovti Vody
Zhengzhou 106 *C4 var.* Ch'eng-chou, Chengchow; *prev.* Chenghsien. *province capital* Henan, C China
Zhezkazgan 92 *C4 Kaz.* Zhezqazghan; *prev.* Dzhezkazgan, Karagandy, C Kazakhstan
Zhezqazghan *see* Zhezkazgan
Zhidachov *see* Zhydachiv
Zhitkovichi *see* Zhytkavichy
Zhitomir *see* Zhytomyr
Zhlobin 85 *D7* Homyel'skaya Voblasts', SE Belarus
Zhmerinka *see* Zhmerynka
Zhmerynka 86 *D2 Rus.* Zhmerinka. Vinnyts'ka Oblast', C Ukraine
Zhodino *see* Zhodzina
Zhodzina 85 *D6 Rus.* Zhodino. Minskaya Voblasts', C Belarus
Zholkev/Zholkva *see* Zhovkva
Zhonghua Renmin Gongheguo *see* China
Zhosaly 92 *B4 prev.* Dzhusaly. Kzylorda, SW Kazakhstan
Zhovkva 86 *B2 Pol.* Żółkiew, *Rus.* Zholkev, Zholkva; *prev.* Nesterov. L'vivs'ka Oblast', NW Ukraine
Zhovti Vody 87 *F3 Rus.* Zhëltyye Vody. Dnipropetrovs'ka Oblast', E Ukraine
Zhovtnevoye 87 *E4 Rus.* Zhovtnevoye. Mykolayivs'ka Oblast', S Ukraine
Zhovtnevoye *see* Zhovtneve
Zhydachiv 86 *B2 Pol.* Żydaczów, *Rus.* Zhidachov. L'vivs'ka Oblast', NW Ukraine
Zhytkavichy 85 *C7* Homyel'skaya Voblasts', SE Belarus
Zhytomyr 86 *D2 Rus.* Zhitomir. Zhytomyrs'ka Oblast', NW Ukraine

Zibo 106 *D4 var.* Zhangdian. Shandong, E China
Zichenau *see* Ciechanów
Zielona Góra 76 *B4 Ger.* Grünberg, Grünberg in Schlesien, Grünberg. Lubuskie, W Poland
Zierikzee 64 *B4* Zeeland, SW Netherlands
Zigong 106 *B5 var.* Tzekung. Sichuan, C China
Ziguinchor 52 *B3* SW Senegal
Zilah *see* Zalău
Žilina 77 *C5 Ger.* Sillein, *Hung.* Zsolna. Žilinský Kraj, N Slovakia
Zillenmarkt *see* Zalău
Zimbabwe 56 *D3 off.* Republic of Zimbabwe; *prev.* Rhodesia. *country* S Africa
Zimbabwe, Republic of *see* Zimbabwe
Zimnicea 86 *C5* Teleorman, S Romania
Zimovniki 89 *B7* Rostovskaya Oblast', SW Russian Federation
Zinder 53 *G3* Zinder, S Niger
Zinov'yevsk *see* Kirovohrad
Zintenhof *see* Sindi
Zipaquirá 36 *B3* Cundinamarca, C Colombia
Zittau 72 *D4* Sachsen, E Germany
Zlatni Pyasŭtsi 82 *E2* Dobrich, NE Bulgaria
Zlín 77 *C5 prev.* Gottwaldov. Zlínský Kraj, E Czech Republic
Złoczów *see* Zolochev
Złotów 76 *C3* Wielkopolskie, C Poland
Znamenka *see* Znam"yanka
Znam"yanka 87 *F3 Rus.* Znamenka. Kirovohrads'ka Oblast', C Ukraine
Żnin 76 *C3* Kujawsko-pomorskie, C Poland
Zoetermeer 64 *C4* Zuid-Holland, W Netherlands
Żółkiew *see* Zhovkva
Zolochev 85 *D2 Pol.* Złoczów, *Rus.* Zolochiv. L'vivs'ka Oblast', W Ukraine
Zolochiv 87 *G2 Rus.* Zolochev. Kharkivs'ka Oblast', E Ukraine
Zolochiv *see* Zolochev
Zolote 87 *H3 Rus.* Zolotoye. Luhans'ka Oblast', E Ukraine
Zolotonosha 87 *E2* Cherkas'ka Oblast', C Ukraine
Zolotoye *see* Zolote
Zólyom *see* Zvolen
Zomba 57 *E2* Southern, S Malawi
Zombor *see* Sombor
Zongo 55 *C5* Equateur, N Dem. Rep. Congo
Zonguldak 94 *C2* Zonguldak, NW Turkey
Zonhoven 65 *D6* Limburg, NE Belgium
Zoppot *see* Sopot
Żory 77 *C5 var.* Zory, *Ger.* Sohrau. Śląskie, S Poland
Zouar 54 *C2* Borkou-Ennedi-Tibesti, N Chad
Zouérat 52 *C2 var.* Zouérate, Zouîrât. Tiris Zemmour, N Mauritania
Zouîrât *see* Zouérat
Zrenjanin 78 *D3 prev.* Petrovgrad, Veliki Bečkerek, *Ger.* Grossbetschkerek, *Hung.* Nagybecskerek. Vojvodina, N Serbia
Zsil/Zsily *see* Jiu
Zsolna *see* Žilina
Zsombolya *see* Jimbolia
Zsupanya *see* Županja
Zubov Seamount 45 *D5 undersea feature* E Atlantic Ocean
Zueila *see* Zawīlah
Zug 73 *B7 Fr.* Zoug. Zug, C Switzerland
Zugspitze 73 *C7 mountain* S Germany
Zuid-Beveland 65 *B5 var.* South Beveland. *island* SW Netherlands
Zuider Zee *see* IJsselmeer
Zuidhorn 64 *E1* Groningen, NE Netherlands
Zuidlaren 64 *D3* Drenthe, NE Netherlands
Zula 50 *C4* E Eritrea
Züllichau *see* Sulechów
Zumbo *see* Vila do Zumbo
Zundert 65 *C5* Noord-Brabant, S Netherlands
Zunyi 106 *B5* Guizhou, S China
Županja 78 *C3 Hung.* Zsupanya. Vukovar-Srijem, E Croatia
Zürich 73 *B7 Eng./Fr.* Zurich, *It.* Zurigo. Zürich, N Switzerland
Zurich, Lake *see* Zürichsee
Zürichsee 73 *B7 Eng.* Lake Zurich. *lake* NE Switzerland
Zurigo *see* Zürich
Zutphen 64 *D3* Gelderland, E Netherlands
Zuwārah 49 *F2* NW Libya
Zuwaylah *see* Zawīlah
Zuyevka 89 *D5* Kirovskaya Oblast', NW Russian Federation
Zvenigorodka *see* Zvenyhorodka
Zvenyhorodka 87 *E2 Rus.* Zvenigorodka. Cherkas'ka Oblast', C Ukraine
Zvishavane 56 *D3 prev.* Shabani. Matabeleland South, S Zimbabwe
Zvolen 77 *C6 Ger.* Altsohl, *Hung.* Zólyom. Banskobystrický Kraj, C Slovakia
Zvornik 78 *C4* E Bosnia and Herzegovina
Zwedru 52 *D5 var.* Tchien. E Liberia
Zwettl 73 *E6* Wien, NE Austria
Zwevegem 65 *A6* West-Vlaanderen, W Belgium
Zwickau 73 *C5* Sachsen, E Germany
Zwolle 64 *D3* Overijssel, E Netherlands
Żydaczów *see* Zhydachiv
Żyōetu *see* Jōetsu
Żyrardów 76 *E3* Mazowieckie, C Poland
Zyryanovsk 92 *D5* Vostochnyy Kazakhstan, E Kazakhstan